Just Taxes

At the outbreak of the First World War, taxation was about 10 per cent of GNP; by 1979, taxes had risen to almost half of the total national income, and contributed to the rise of Margaret Thatcher. Martin Daunton continues the story he began in *Trusting Leviathan*, and offers a unique analysis of the politics of acceptance of huge tax rises after the First World War and asks why it did not provoke the same levels of discontent in Britain as it did on the continent. He also questions why acceptance gave way to hostility at the end of the period. Daunton views taxes as central to debates over the role of equality or of incentives as the driving force for equity or efficiency. He provides a detailed discussion of their potential in providing revenue for the state, and their use in shaping the social structure and influencing economic growth. *Just Taxes* places taxation in its proper place, at the centre of modern British history.

MARTIN DAUNTON is a fellow of Churchill College and professor of economic history at the University of Cambridge. He is the author of *Trusting Leviathan: The Politics of Taxation in Britain, 1799–1914* (2001), *Progress and Poverty: An Economic and Social History of Britain, 1700–1850* (1995), and editor of Volume III of *The Cambridge Urban History of Britain* (2000).

THE WINSTON TOUCH.

Chancellor of the Exchequer. "MY POOR BEAST, I'M AFRAID YOU HAVE A VERY GRIEVOUS BURDEN TO BEAR."

British Ass. "YES; CAN'T YOU DO SOMETHING SPECTACULAR ABOUT IT?"

Just Taxes

The Politics of Taxation in Britain, 1914–1979

Martin Daunton

University of Cambridge

CAMBRIDGE
UNIVERSITY PRESS

CAMBRIDGE UNIVERSITY PRESS
Cambridge, New York, Melbourne, Madrid, Cape Town, Singapore, São Paulo

Cambridge University Press
The Edinburgh Building, Cambridge CB2 8RU, UK

Published in the United States of America by Cambridge University Press, New York

www.cambridge.org
Information on this title: www.cambridge.org/9780521814003

First published 2002
This digitally printed version 2007

A catalogue record for this publication is available from the British Library

ISBN 978-0-521-81400-3 hardback
ISBN 978-0-521-03979-6 paperback

It must be recognized that taxation is no longer simply a matter of raising the revenue required with the minimum disturbance to private and public interests. The social and economic effects of taxation are so great and the possibility of the deliberate use of taxation to achieve social and economic ends so important that it is no longer possible to deal with taxation purely, or in some instances even primarily, in a fiscal sense. But once this is conceded, the resulting stresses and strains as between fiscal considerations on the one hand and economic and social considerations on the other are likely far to outweigh in importance any of the conflicts of interest of bygone days.

> PRO, T171/427, 'Enquiry into the taxation of income: review of the field' (first draft, February 1950), A. Cockfield, Director of Statistics and Intelligence, Inland Revenue

The real trouble comes in the effect of taxation on enterprise and the supply of capital . . . [I]f you have to raise a given sum and the sum is a high proportion of the national income, no manipulation of the system will do you much good. Nevertheless, there is undoubtedly a conflict between the objective of social equality and that of industrial efficiency.

> PRO, T171/427, Robert Hall to Edwin Plowden, 'Taxation enquiry', 18 May 1950

Contents

List of figures   *page* ix
List of tables   x
Preface   xiii
List of abbreviations   xvi

1   The taxing state: an introduction   1

2   'The limits of our taxable capacity': war finance,
    1914–1918   36

3   'This hideous war memorial': debt and taxation,
    1918–1925   60

4   'Adjusting the particular turns of the different
    screws': reforming the income tax, 1920–1929   103

5   'The great conflict of modern politics': redistribution,
    depression and appeasement, 1929–1939   142

6   'The exigency of war': taxation and the Second
    World War, 1939–1945   176

7   'The mortal blows of taxation': Labour and
    reconstruction, 1945–1951   194

8   'A most injurious disincentive in our economic
    system': Conservatives and taxation, 1951–1964   229

9   'Modern and dynamic economic policy': Labour
    and taxation, 1951–1970   279

10 Rethinking taxation policy: from an opportunity
    state to an enterprise society, 1964–1979   302

11 'Highly defensible ramparts': the politics of local
    taxation   339

12   Conclusion   360

     Appendix: chancellors of the Exchequer and prime ministers,
        1908–1983   370
     Bibliography   372
     Index   391

Figures

1.1 Total public expenditure as a percentage of GDP at
current market prices, 1900–1993   *page* 2

1.2 Standard rate of income tax, 1900–1980   14

1.3 Taxes on income and capital (including national
insurance contributions) and taxes on expenditure as
a percentage of central government receipts, 1900–1951   15

1.4 Structure of central government revenue: net receipts
due to the Exchequer, 1913/14 to 1978/9   16

2.1 Debt charge as a percentage of gross expenditure of
central government, 1900–1951   58

4.1 Effective rate of tax on earned income of married
couples with three children, before and after the
Royal Commission on the Income Tax   104

4.2 Direct and indirect taxation as a percentage of earned
income, married men with three children, 1903/4,
1913/14 and 1918/19   120

4.3 Incidence of national taxation (direct and indirect),
married men with three children, 1918/19, 1923/4
and 1925/6   121

5.1 Incidence of national taxation (direct and indirect),
married men with three children, 1937/8 and 1941/2   168

8.1 Percentage of money income (£2,000) and equivalent
real income (1947/8 prices) paid in income tax and
surtax, married men with two children, 1913/14 to
1956/7   276

Tables

1.1 Total public expenditure as a percentage of GDP at
current market prices, 1900–1993   *page* 3

2.1 Government income, 1914/15 to 1918/19   40

2.2 Individuals with total income above the exemption
limit for income tax, United Kingdom/Great Britain
and Northern Ireland, 1913 to 1937/8   42

2.3 Direct and indirect taxes, 1913/14 to 1929/30   46

2.4 Structure of central government revenue: net receipts
due to the Exchequer, 1913/14 and 1919/20   46

2.5 Income tax allowances and rate, 1913/14 and 1918/19   47

3.1 Debt charges as a percentage of total gross income of
government, 1913/14 to 1930/1   62

4.1 Income tax paid on wholly earned income, 1918 and
1920   117

4.2 Structure of income tax, 1920/1   138

4.3 Structure of central government revenue: net receipts
due to the Exchequer, 1928/9   140

5.1 Direct and indirect taxes as a percentage of national
revenue, 1913/14 to 1931/2   175

5.2 Structure of central government revenue: net receipts
due to the Exchequer, 1938/9   175

6.1 Individuals with income above the exemption limit for
income tax, United Kingdom, 1937/8 to 1947/8   180

6.2 Structure of central government revenue: net receipts
due to the Exchequer, 1945/6   187

7.1 Income and profits tax, 1939–1950   195

7.2 Structure of central government revenue: net receipts
     due to the Exchequer, 1950/1   195

8.1 Sources of finance for the NHS, 1950/1 to 1974/5   265

8.2 Percentage of money and equivalent real income
     (1947/8 prices) paid in income tax and surtax,
     married men with two children, 1938/9, 1945/6,
     1950/1 and 1956/7   278

8.3 Structure of central government revenue: net receipts
     due to the Exchequer, 1962/3   278

10.1 Taxation as a percentage of GNP and composition of
     tax revenues in the United Kingdom, France and
     Germany, 1962   305

10.2 Income tax, married couple with two children,
     1955/6, 1965/6 and 1979/80   311

10.3 Structure of income tax, United Kingdom, France,
     Germany and USA, c. 1976   337

10.4 Structure of central government revenue: net receipts
     due to the Exchequer, 1969/70, 1978/9 and 1988/9   338

Preface

Although this book is self-contained, it may also be read as a continuation of my previous study of the politics of taxation, *Trusting Leviathan: The Politics of Taxation in Britain, 1799–1914*, published by Cambridge University Press in 2001. The concern of the earlier book was the process of containment of the British state, as government revenues fell from a peak of 23 per cent of GNP in the Napoleonic wars to about 10 per cent in the later nineteenth century. It explained containment, and also the emergence of legitimacy and acceptance. After the Napoleonic wars, taxes were central to political controversy, at the centre of disputes over the incidence of taxes and the distribution of benefits. The success of politicians in early and mid-Victorian Britain, and especially of Peel and Gladstone, was to remove taxation from the centre of disputes and to make it appear 'normal', a symbol of British liberty and stability. Although problems reappeared around 1900 with the costs of the Boer war and social reform, Britain entered the First World War with a fiscal system that appeared more flexible and less contentious than in most other major nation-states. The subject of the present book is the massive displacement caused by the First World War, when the level of taxation returned to the peak of the Napoleonic wars – and stayed there.

The previous book provides the basis for the present study, but I hope that this volume will appeal to a different audience. The study of the 'long nineteenth century' will have most interest for historians; the present book should appeal not only to historians but to anyone concerned with current debates over fiscal policy and the wider role of the state. Taxation is – or should be – at the centre of political debate beyond a mere refusal to have a serious discussion over its virtues and vices, its form and level which marked most of the 1990s. Politicians in earlier decades of the twentieth century were not so reticent, and perhaps their successors would now prefer not to be reminded of past nostrums. The present book also turns to a different set of concepts in order to organise the argument. The central concept in the study of the 'long nineteenth century' was 'trust': how did politicians create a sense of trust in the state and in fellow taxpayers?

One way of achieving this was through the construction of a sense of disinterestedness and balance, an exclusion of taxes (as far as possible) from conflict between social groups or sectoral interests. This entailed a subtle shift over time in the definition of 'ability to pay' in order to create a general sense that the system was equitable. In the period covered by this book, the tax system was more often associated with divisions over normative definitions of society. To put the issue in a stark way for the moment, should taxes be used to create equality, whether for ethical reasons or in pursuit of a particular form of economic growth? Or should taxes be used to encourage incentives and initiative? How should the balance between economic efficiency and social justice be struck? Although the divide is clear between 'old Labour' and Mrs Thatcher, there were many intermediate positions which are discussed in the course of the book – and which might offer some historical background to current debates over the same issue.

One continuity between the two books does need to be mentioned in this preface. Both were written as a result of the same financial and intellectual support. The Nuffield Foundation generously awarded me a Social Science Research Fellowship which gave me a year to collect the material from archives around the country. I am grateful to the archivists and librarians who gave me assistance, especially at the Public Record Office, Modern Record Centre at the University of Warwick, Labour Party Archive at Manchester and the Conservative Party Archive at the Bodleian Library. The process of writing was assisted by an additional term of sabbatical leave funded by the Humanities Research Board (now the Arts and Humanities Research Board). Of course, writing was also slowed down by involvement in the tasks of quality control and research assessment which dominate academic life in Britain. I hope I have maintained sufficient optimism and objectivity to see this obsession with audit as a historically interesting theme in the changing structure of the state and definitions of accountability. I would again thank John Morrill and David Cannadine for suggesting a short book on taxation, and for their understanding as it evolved into two large books. Andrew MacLennan and Heather McCallum at Longmans, and Richard Fisher, Elizabeth Howard and Sophie Read at Cambridge University Press, dealt with the migration from one publisher to another with understanding and care. I would also thank colleagues at Cambridge for providing a challenging intellectual environment, and in particular Peter Clarke, Adam Tooze and Simon Szreter. I am grateful to Rodney Lowe for his helpful comments, especially on an early draft on the 1950s and 1960s, and for many discussions since the time we spent at the Australian National University, where Patrick Troy provided both stimulation and sociability.

I have gained much from the work of George Peden on the Treasury and Richard Whiting on the Labour party and taxation. Their recent books covered some of the same material, and I hope that our different interests and approaches will produce a richer account of British economic and social policy in the twentieth century. Peter Mandler's comments on this volume were, again, of great help. I am grateful, as before, to Linda Randall for her careful and meticulous copy-editing, and to Auriol Griffith-Jones for her splendid indexing. John van Wyhe produced the bibliography with efficiency and an eye for detail. And the two books have produced a debt to Claire which I cannot start to redeem.

Abbreviations

CPA	Conservative Party Archive
CRD	Conservative Research Department
DNB	*Dictionary of National Biography*
EEC	European Economic Community
EPD	excess profits duty
FBI	Federation of British Industries
GDP	gross domestic product
GNP	gross national product
ILP	Independent Labour party
LCC	London County Council
LPA	Labour Party Archive
LRC	Labour Representation Committee
LSE	London School of Economics
MRC	Modern Record Centre
NDC	national defence contribution
NEDC	National Economic Development Council
NHS	National Health Service
NIB	National Investment Board
PAYE	Pay As You Earn
PRO	Public Record Office
SDF	Social Democratic Federation
SET	selective employment tax
TUC	Trades Union Congress
VAT	value added tax
WEWNC	War Emergency Workers' National Committee

1   The taxing state: an introduction

> One of the clearest contrasts between Conservative and Socialist policy
> is in the field of taxation. Conservatives believe that high taxation dis-
> courages enterprise and initiative, and so tends to impoverish the whole
> nation... By contrast, Socialist policy contains little mention of tax re-
> duction and indeed most Socialists welcome high taxation as a means
> of achieving their aim of universal equality.
>
> Conservative party, *The Campaign Guide 1959: The Unique Political
> Reference Book* (London, 1959), p. 19

In 1979, the Conservatives returned to power and Margaret Thatcher[*]
became prime minister. Their success in the general election has many ex-
planations, but one important theme was the widespread sentiment that
taxes were too high and the public sector too large and unaccountable.
The Thatcher government embarked on a campaign to roll back the
state, through privatisation and the sale of council houses; it achieved
less success in reducing the overall level of fiscal extraction in order to
encourage enterprise and initiative. Taxes were 45.9 per cent of gross
domestic product (GDP) in 1979, rising to 49.9 per cent in 1984; the
figure dropped to 41.4 per cent in 1989, but returned to 46.8 per cent in
1993[1] (see table 1.1 and figure 1.1). Despite the difficulties in *reducing*
taxation as a whole, the *structure* of taxation was changed in pursuit of
Mrs Thatcher's vision of a dynamic society based on enterprise and incentives. The tax system was remade, with a marked decline in the higher
levels of income tax, a shift from direct to indirect taxes and the introduction of tax breaks on personal savings and private welfare provision.

---

[1] R. Middleton, *Government versus the Market: The Growth of the Public Sector, Economic
Management and British Economic Performance, c1890–1979* (Cheltenham, 1996), p. 91,
and *The British Economy since 1945: Engaging with the Debate* (Basingstoke, 2000), p. 77.
[*] Margaret Hilda Thatcher née Roberts (b. 1925) was born in Grantham, where her father
was a grocer and local politician. She was educated at Oxford, and was called to the
bar in 1954, specialising in tax law. She became an MP in 1959, serving as secretary
of state for education and science 1970–4; in opposition, she shadowed the chancellor
before becoming leader in 1975 and prime minister from 1979 to 1990. (K. M. Robbins
(ed.), *The Blackwell Biographical Dictionary of British Political Life in the Twentieth Century*
(Oxford, 1990), pp. 394–8.)

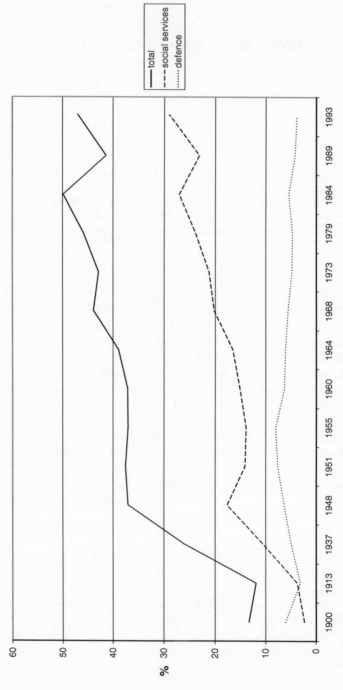

Figure 1.1 Total public expenditure as a percentage of GDP at current market prices, 1900–1993
Source: R. Middleton, *The British Economy since 1945: Engaging with the Debate* (Basingstoke, 2000), p. 77.

Table 1.1 *Total public expenditure as a percentage of GDP at current market prices, 1900–1993*

	Total	Social services	Defence
1900	13.3	2.3	6.0
1913	11.9	3.7	3.1
1937	26.0	10.5	4.9
1948	37.0	17.6	6.3
1951	37.5	14.1	7.6
1955	37.0	13.9	8.0
1960	37.1	15.1	6.3
1964	38.9	16.5	6.1
1968	43.9	20.2	5.6
1973	42.9	21.2	4.8
1979	45.9	23.9	4.7
1984	49.9	27.1	5.4
1989	41.4	23.1	4.2
1993	46.8	28.8	3.8

Source: R. Middleton, *The British Economy since 1945: Engaging with the Debate* (Basingstoke, 2000), p. 77.

Of course, the Thatcher government had its critics who feared that its policies created socially divisive inequality, and a growing sense of exclusion. Indeed, reform of the tax system contributed to the downfall of Mrs Thatcher when she attempted to overhaul local government finance with the abolition of the property rate and the introduction of the community charge or 'poll tax'. This was an attempt to create fiscal responsibility by electors and councillors in local government. Instead of each household paying a property rate on the value of the house, regardless of income and the number of wage-earners, each resident would pay a charge – and hence create a greater sensitivity to spending on local services. This proved a step too far, leading to a breakdown in compliance and contributing to the fall of Mrs Thatcher. Even so, the rating system was reformed for the first time since the abortive attempt to introduce a land tax by Lloyd George* before the First World War.[2] Meanwhile, the Labour party came to realise that the mere mention of taxes was best

[2] For Lloyd George and the land question, see A. Offer, *Property and Politics, 1870–1914: Landownership, Law, Ideology and Urban Development in England* (Cambridge, 1981), and on Mrs Thatcher and the community charge or poll tax, D. Butler, A. Adonis and T. Travers, *Failure in British Government: The Politics of the Poll Tax* (Oxford, 1994).

* David Lloyd George (1863–1945) was born in Manchester, the son of a teacher who died in 1864; he was brought up by his mother and uncle, a shoemaker in Caernarfonshire. He became a solicitor in 1884 and was a Liberal MP from 1890 to 1945. He became president of the Board of Trade 1905–8, chancellor of the Exchequer 1908–15, minister

avoided. Its defeat in the election of 1992 may be explained, at least in part, by the proposed budget for a Labour government, which allowed the Conservatives to portray the party as committed to policies of 'tax and spend'.[3] The result was a disinclination to engage in serious debate over the tax system, a fear of the political consequences of giving the impression of wishing to raise taxes.

What has been the outcome? Many British electors appear to want increased spending on education and health, and are in favour of specific forms of government expenditure. At the same time, they oppose government spending in general. In 1970, 92 per cent of respondents to an opinion poll wanted higher or stable spending on pensions and social services – yet 65 per cent wanted taxes to be cut in preference to welfare spending.[4] One response by the Labour government of 1997 was the so-called 'stealth taxes' and a continued reliance on indirect taxes which produce large yields. In 2000, the 'tax revolt' against high prices of fuel suggested that the fiscal system had reached some sort of *impasse*. The Thatcher government had de-legitimised high levels of income tax; now, indirect taxes were leading to resistance. How politicians will respond to this difficult situation, reconciling the need for more spending with hostility to taxes, is a topic for the future – and Gordon Brown's budget of 2002 might indicate a change. The debates should be informed by an understanding of the history of the British fiscal system since the First World War.

One aim of this book is to understand the background to the Thatcher reforms of the fiscal system, and to assess why taxation attracted widespread opprobrium both for its *level* and, perhaps more so, its *form*. These concerns were not simply on the right, from Conservative advocates of free markets and private enterprise. Leading economists on the progressive left were also critical of the fiscal system, especially in the report of the committee on direct taxation chaired by James Meade* and in the

of munitions 1915–16 and prime minister from 1916 to 1922. (*Dictionary of National Biography (DNB), 1941–50*, ed. L. G. Legg and E. T. Williams (London, 1959), pp. 515–29; Robbins (ed.), *Biographical Dictionary*, pp. 270–4.)

[3] On the 1992 election, see D. Butler and D. Kavanagh, *The British General Election of 1992* (Basingstoke, 1999), especially pp. 252, 255–6, 268; and I. Crewe and B. Grosschalk (eds.), *Political Communications: The General Election Campaign of 1992* (Cambridge, 1994), especially pp. 188–9.

[4] For opinion poll data, see R. Lowe, *The Welfare State in Britain since 1945* (2nd edn, Basingstoke and London, 1999), p. 97, citing P. Taylor-Gooby, *Public Opinion, Ideology and State Welfare* (London, 1985), chapter 2.

* James Edward Meade (1907–94) was educated at Oxford, and was fellow of Hertford College from 1930 to 1937; he moved to the Economic Section of the League of Nations in Geneva from 1938 to 1940. He joined the Economic Section of the Cabinet Office in 1940, and was director in 1946–7. He then returned to academic life, as professor of commerce at the London School of Economics (LSE) to 1957 and professor of political economy at Cambridge to 1968. He served as chairman of the Institute for Fiscal Studies

major study of the British tax system of the late 1970s by John Kay and
Mervyn King. These studies suggested that the British fiscal system was
incoherent, a mass of conflicting and incompatible principles. 'No one
would design such a system on purpose and nobody did. Only a historical explanation of how it came about can be offered as a justification.
That is not a justification, but a demonstration of how seemingly individually rational decisions can have absurd effects in aggregate.'[5] What
they did not explain was *why* this situation had arisen: to economists in
search of consistency, it was the product of irrationality. The aim here
is to understand how the British tax system took on the shape it did,
through a careful analysis of the politics of the fiscal system. This will
involve much more than a simple attempt to understand the roots of the
malaise of 1979; it will entail an understanding of the changing political, economic and social context of taxation over the period. In many
ways, the tax system of 1979 was a palimpsest produced by different
ideologies and electoral calculations, changing economic structures and
circumstances, as well as military and strategic imperatives. An analysis of
taxation should form a strand in the history of twentieth-century Britain,
for without it we cannot appreciate the ability of the state to secure revenue for warfare and welfare, or of political parties to create electoral
coalitions.

The chronological end point of this book is provided by a desire to
understand the origins of Mrs Thatcher's reform of the tax system. The
starting point is 1914, when the level of extraction was about to double
under the pressure of the First World War – and to stay there until it
was again displaced by the Second World War. It would be helpful to
summarise the main features of the fiscal constitution at the outbreak of
the war, which explain the acceptance of the tax system by 1914 and the
relative ease with which a much higher level of extraction was sustained
after the war. They also formed the main elements in the carefully articulated and firmly held orthodoxy of the Treasury against which innovation
would be judged well into the twentieth century.[6] Above all, the aim of this
fiscal constitution was to remove disputes over taxation from the heart of
British politics by creating a sense of balance and fairness, a feeling that
taxes and spending did not fall more heavily on one group at the expense
of another. The vocabulary of social description was based less on class
terms of labour versus capital or rich versus poor, than moral categories

from 1975 to 1977. He won the Nobel Prize for economics in 1977. (*Who Was Who*,
vol. IX: *1991–5* (London, 1996).)

[5] J. A. Kay and M. A. King, *The British Tax System* (Oxford, 1978), pp. 1, 238–41, 246;
Institute for Fiscal Studies, *The Structure and Reform of Direct Taxation: Report of a
Committee Chaired by Professor J. E. Meade* (London, 1978).

[6] See M. J. Daunton, *Trusting Leviathan: The Politics of Taxation in Britain, 1799–1914*
(Cambridge, 2001).

of idle versus active wealth, waste versus prudence, spontaneous versus industrious incomes, dissipation versus healthy consumption.

The sense of equity and balance also entailed creating an image of politicians as men of probity and trustworthiness, of moral rectitude and fiscal prudence.[7] This applied not only to ministers but also to the Commons, which should inspect and monitor public spending, subjecting the executive to constant scrutiny. The task of monitoring spending and ensuring that revenue was applied only to the intended purposes rested on a carefully devised set of accounting procedures. Revenue should not be hypothecated, that is ear-marked for particular purposes; all sources of revenue should be paid into a single, consolidated fund. The danger of hypothecation was that spending would always rise to the maximum permissible level of the specified revenue; allocation of a set amount of money from a central fund gave more control. This implied a ban on *virement*, the movement of surplus funds from one budget head to another which would also keep spending up to the highest possible level. Rather, parliament would allocate annual 'votes' of money to each service, and any surplus left under any head would be used to reduce the national debt. It followed that great stress was placed on reducing the national debt. In the early nineteenth century, many radical and Tory critics saw the debt as a danger, imposing a burden on production to benefit idle *rentiers* and a monied elite, subverting the social order. By the late nineteenth century, the debt was almost a source of pride and patriotism as the nation's 'war chest'. Confidence in the integrity and probity of the state meant that loans could easily be secured on favourable terms in times of emergency and national danger.

The administration of taxes should, as far as possible, rest on co-operation with taxpayers, even at the expense of a degree of evasion or avoidance. As far as possible, the income tax was collected 'at source', so that banks paid interest to depositors and farmers rent to landlords net of tax, handing the balance to the tax authorities. Where deduction at source was not possible in the case of income from the profits of trade, taxpayers were incorporated into the administration of the tax system as assessors, collectors and commissioners. Any threat to this pattern was denounced as 'inquisitorial' and 'despotic'. In practice, the relationship between taxpayers and the tax authorities was increasingly mediated by professional advisers, and in particular by accountants who negotiated with the tax officials. When decisions were contested and taken to court

---

[7] P. Harling and P. Mandler, 'From "fiscal-military" state to laissez-faire state, 1760–1850', *Journal of British Studies* 32 (1993), 44–70; P. Langford, 'Politics and manners from Sir Robert Walpole to Sir Robert Peel', *Proceedings of the British Academy* 94, *1996 Lectures and Memoirs* (Oxford, 1997), pp. 118–23.

for a ruling on law, the outcome was a highly specific and fragmented body of case law rather than carefully articulated general rules over issues such as the treatment of depreciation or the definition of tax-exempt charities. However, the tax code was careful to exclude tax breaks to particular trades or interests with the dangers of special pleading and favouritism which would undermine trust in the tax system and the state. Any tax concessions were cast in general terms such as tax relief to life insurance premiums in 1853 or for dependent children in 1909. These concessions could be justified on grounds of high principle, of allowing risk-takers to provide their dependants with security, and to support family responsibilities. Members of Parliament could not seek favours for their constituents or particular trades, for the budget was presented to the Commons in a fully developed form and was passed as a matter of confidence in the government.

Care was taken to create a link between taxation and the franchise in order to ensure that potential beneficiaries did not have the power to vote for higher spending which would benefit them and fall on other taxpayers. Until 1867, there was a close connection between the franchise and payment of income tax, for the property qualification for the vote and the income tax threshold were closely aligned. The second and third reform acts weakened the link but did not entirely remove it. Many skilled working men were still wary of government expenditure, stressing their independence of state welfare and the need for self-sufficiency; and many unskilled men did not have the vote until the fourth reform act of 1918. Attitudes were changing in the 1890s and 1900s, with the Trades Union Congress (TUC) and Labour party pressing for a more active, redistributive form of taxation and government action, but the link between the franchise and taxation was not fully severed until after the First World War.[8]

Although the political culture of free trade was dominant by 1860, indirect taxes remained of great importance – on condition that the duties were designed to produce revenue and not to provide protection of home producers or any distortion in the allocation of resources. As a result, customs and excise duties were imposed on a narrow range of goods. Further, most of these commodities were defined as non-essentials or even as harmful narcotics; the payment of indirect taxes was therefore seen as voluntary. The campaign for imperial preference, which would

[8] P. Thane, 'The working class and state "welfare" in Britain, 1880–1914', *Historical Journal* 27 (1984), 877–90; H. C. G. Matthew, R. I. McKibbin and J. A. Kay, 'The franchise factor in the rise of Labour', *English Historical Review* 91 (1976), 733–52; A. E. P. Duffy, 'New unionism in Britain, 1889–90: a reappraisal', *Economic History Review* 2nd ser. 14 (1961), 306–19.

provide protection for British producers as well as a source of revenue, was defeated by the Liberal victory of 1906, and the trend to a higher proportion of direct taxes was confirmed by the subsequent reform of the income tax and the demands of the First World War.

The overall level of taxation as a percentage of the GDP fell up to the close of the nineteenth century. Spending was controlled by these accounting practices, by the identity between voting and paying income tax and by the narrow range of indirect taxes. Further, pressure for spending was limited by four factors. First, economic growth from the 1840s meant an increase in revenue and the possibility of tax concessions. Secondly, part of the cost of defence and imperial expansion was passed from the metropole to the empire. Thirdly, the costs of military spending were relatively modest, for Britain was not involved in any major war and the nature of military strategy and technology meant that there was no need for a massive standing army or navy with continuing investment in research and development. The national debt incurred in past wars was reduced, and there was little or no need to issue new loans except to a modest extent in the Crimean war. Finally, demands for civilian spending were as yet muted, and a large part of spending was undertaken by local authorities rather than the central government. The result of these factors was, in the words of Michael Mann, tax concessions on a world historical scale – and not least in Britain.[9] By the end of the nineteenth century, government spending – local and central – was down to about 9 per cent of gross national product (GNP).

The underlying assumption was that taxes should not alter the shape of society and that they should follow the principle of proportionality, that is extracting more or less the same proportion of total income from everyone. Different taxes might be used to ensure that the system as a whole was balanced. Hence death duties should fall more heavily on personal property than on real property which was also liable to the local rates. Care should be taken not to graduate the income tax and provide the opportunity for socialistic attacks on the rich. It was essential that everyone pay some taxes to make them politically responsible and to contribute to society.

The overall result of the Victorian or Gladstonian fiscal constitution was to create a sense of trust and legitimacy in taxes and the state. But from the 1890s, various cracks started to appear in the edifice, leading to a debate on the future shape of the fiscal system up to the First World War. An extension of the franchise and a gradual change in the assumptions of the organised working class created pressures for change. After the wave

[9] M. Mann, *The Sources of Social Power*, vol. II: *The Rise of Classes and Nation States, 1750–1914* (Cambridge, 1993).

of so-called 'new unionism' around 1890, and the growing influence of unskilled unions within the TUC, attitudes moved in favour of a more active redistributive role for the state and taxation.[10] In part, this represented the successful containment of the state, the purging of interest and the creation of trust and legitimacy. Although the rhetoric may be seen as a means of justifying the *status quo* and containing radical challenge by presenting an image of fairness and disinterestedness, it was more than a mere imposition of a hegemonic discourse. The constraints went both ways, for politicians could not expose their rhetoric as a mere sham; to some extent they had to observe it and to *act* in a disinterested way. And it meant that organised workers in unions and the fledging Labour party could hope to work through the state and a fiscal system they perceived as fair or, at least, capable of reform by parliamentary action. From 1906, and especially 1910 when the Liberal government was more dependent on their support in the Commons, Labour MPs inserted a new, more redistributive note into fiscal debates.

The point may be extended to a more general pressure for 'civilian' spending. This is not the place to repeat the history of welfare spending and the emergence of social policy at the heart of 'high politics'.[11] We might note, however, that the existing institutional form of the British state and of civil society gave a greater role to central government taxation than in many other countries.[12] In the United States, for example, the involvement of the central state in welfare spending on civil war pensions led to suspicion of 'patronage democracy', the use of benefits to obtain votes and to benefit sectional interests. Welfare spending by the federal state meant favouritism and waste rather than efficiency.[13] Further, the emergence of large-scale firms and hostility to trade unions in the United States were associated with the growth of strong internal management hierarchies and, in some cases, the provision of welfare by employers. By comparison with Britain, trade union and friendly society welfare schemes were weak. In Britain, spending by the central state did not cause such concern on the part of many employers and unions. Although employers were divided, with some opposition to state welfare on the grounds that it would increase costs, others actively campaigned for state provision. Many industrial concerns were small, with weak internal management hierarchies and simply lacked the capacity to provide welfare.

[10] Duffy, 'New unionism'.
[11] J. Harris, 'The transition to high politics in English social policy, 1889–1914', in M. Bentley and J. Stevenson (eds.), *High and Low Politics in Modern Britain* (Oxford, 1983), pp. 58–79.
[12] M. J. Daunton, 'Payment and participation: welfare and state formation in Britain, 1900–51', *Past and Present* 150 (1996), 169–216.
[13] T. Skocpol, *Protecting Soldiers and Mothers: The Political Origins of Social Policy in the United States* (Cambridge, Mass., 1992).

Even if they opposed state action, as in the Lancashire cotton industry, their case was weakened by the absence of any alternative provision by employers.[14]

Capacity *did* exist in two places. One was local government, through the poor law, school boards and municipalities. Local expenditure increased more rapidly than central government spending in the later nineteenth century: the annual average real rate of growth in central government spending was 1.5 per cent between 1850 and 1890, compared with 2.9 per cent in local spending.[15] It was preferred by many politicians as a means of delegating responsibility to the localities. This would displace any conflicts and controversy from the central government, and would rely on responsible action by local elites who were accountable to ratepayers. Problems were emerging by 1900, for the local rate base was inflexible and regressive, and was creating tensions with implications for national politics.[16] One trend after 1906 was a move from local to central government initiatives, for central taxes were more buoyant and spending was more easily controlled by the Treasury. The situation in other countries was different. In Germany, for example, the localities and states had access to more revenue from local income taxes than did the Reich. Although local authorities in Britain continued to provide many welfare services, the central government also turned to a second group of institutions. Unions and friendly societies were given a major role as 'approved societies' in administering national insurance with a (modest) state contribution. This incorporation of self-help institutions into the state soon led to pressure from Labour to go a stage further. The problem with contributory insurance schemes was that they were regressive, with a flat-rate contribution and limited redistribution from rich to poor. Rather than pressing for a continuation of nominally democratic self-help provision, Labour realised that the state used its small contribution to control approved societies, and instead argued for tax-funded state welfare. By comparison, German workers were more likely to fear state involvement given the anti-union inspiration of Bismarck's insurance scheme.[17]

At the same time, pressure for military spending increased. Of course, civilian and military spending were related, for one prerequisite of a strong

---

[14] R. Hay, 'Employers and social policy in Britain: the evolution of welfare legislation, 1905–14', *Social History* 4 (1977), 435–55; H. F. Gospel, *Markets, Firms and the Management of Labour in Modern Britain* (Cambridge, 1992).

[15] Middleton, *Government versus the Market*, table 3.1, p. 90.

[16] J. Bulpitt, *Territory and Power in the United Kingdom: An Interpretation* (Manchester, 1983).

[17] Daunton, 'Payment and participation', 177–9; E. P. Hennock, *British Social Reform and German Precedents: The Case of Social Insurance, 1880–1914* (Oxford, 1987).

military state was a fit British population or 'imperial race'.[18] Welfare spending was therefore needed to create healthy towns and fit bodies. In addition, the nature of military strategy and technology started to change, most especially with the naval race. The outbreak of war in South Africa, with popular support for imperialism and a more powerful military presence in the formulation of policy, placed new strains on the existing tax system. The change in policy and in technology also entailed a close link between science and war, marking a move from the belief that science should contribute to peace and a new awareness that it provided the basis for a 'warfare' state. At the same time, the politics of empire were starting to change, making it more difficult to pass costs to the periphery, and especially India, where consent was more problematical.[19]

Tariff reform and imperial preference offered one response to the mounting pressure on the fiscal constitution. The policy was advocated as a way of raising more revenue from import duties, as well as solving social problems through steady employment at high wages in a protected market, and binding colonies and metropole in economic interdependence.[20] Liberals (and Labour) needed to find an alternative fiscal strategy of free trade, with the implication that the solution was to reform the income tax and create a more progressive fiscal regime. This electoral calculation was linked with a major change in what may be termed the political culture of taxation, a shift away from proportionality to taxation by ability. At one end of the spectrum, this implied a sweeping redistribution of income and wealth and a drive for equality. In the opinion of many members of the Labour party, free trade was desirable on condition that it was linked with a prosperous domestic economy based on high wages, rather than with an impoverished workforce incapable of buying goods and instead producing cheap goods for export markets.[21] A commitment to free trade could therefore have a radical, redistributive edge. It might also imply an attack on 'socially created wealth', whether an increase in the value of land or industrial profits created by the exertions of society as a whole.

---

[18] There is a large literature, starting with B. Semmel, *Imperialism and Social Reform: English Social-Imperial Thought, 1895–1914* (London, 1960).

[19] H. C. G. Matthew, *The Liberal Imperialists: The Ideas and Politics of a Post-Gladstonian Elite* (Oxford, 1973); D. Edgerton, *England and the Aeroplane: An Essay on a Militant and Technological Nation* (Basingstoke, 1991); F. Turner, *Contesting Cultural Authority: Essays in Victorian Intellectual Life* (Cambridge, 1993), chapter 8; C. Dewey, 'The end of the imperialism of free trade: the eclipse of the Lancashire lobby and the concession of fiscal autonomy to India', in C. Dewey and A. G. Hopkins (eds.), *The Imperial Impact: Studies in the Economic History of Africa and India* (London, 1978), pp. 35–67.

[20] E. H. H. Green, 'Radical conservatism: the electoral genesis of tariff reform', *Historical Journal* 28 (1985), 677–92.

[21] F. Trentmann, 'Wealth versus welfare: the British left between free trade and national political economy before the First World War', *Historical Research* 70 (1997), 70–98.

But it was not necessary to move in these potentially radical or socialist directions, which might alienate property owners and the middle class from the Liberals. A degree of redistribution could be justified on other, more conservative or prudential, grounds. Officials at the Treasury and Inland Revenue came to realise that the only way to extract more revenue would be through a degree of progression. The existing income tax was based on a single rate, with degression for smaller incomes through abatements – a tax-free allowance. As a result, modest middle-class incomes just above the abatement threshold paid a high marginal rate, and any increase in the standard rate would hit them. The only way to raise more revenue from the income tax without alienating a large part of the electorate was through an additional surtax on larger incomes, and even a *reduction* in modest middle-class incomes with family responsibilities. Such a change in policy towards a graduated, progressive income tax was justified by leading figures in neo-classical economics. The 'context of refutation' had changed, so that the onus rested on opponents of redistribution to indicate that it would harm freedom and efficiency.[22]

The present book starts at this point, after the Liberal reforms of the tax system and the introduction of differentiation, graduation and children's allowances. The First World War put this fiscal system under huge strains, on a scale unknown since the Napoleonic wars. But in many ways the British state was better placed to respond to the challenges of war than other European states. The success of the British state in creating a high level of consent and legitimacy, and in reforming the tax system by 1914, meant that the British state entered the war with a more effective fiscal system than most other combatants. In Germany, a national income tax was only introduced in 1913, and in France in 1914 without producing much revenue. At the end of the war, taxation in most European countries was a source of considerable difficulty, not least because of the issue of how to pay the national debt.[23] Indeed, in the opinion of Joseph Schumpeter, the economist and finance minister of Austria at the end of

---

[22] See the discussion in Daunton, *Trusting Leviathan*, chs. 6 and 11. For the views of the leading neo-classical economist, Alfred Marshall, see J. K. Whitaker (ed.), *The Correspondence of Alfred Marshall, Economist*, vol. III: *Towards the Close, 1903–1924* (Cambridge, 1996), pp. 231–4; and A. C. Pigou (ed.), *Memorials of Alfred Marshall* (London, 1925), pp. 443–4. The notion of the 'context of refutation' is from S. Collini, *Liberalism and Sociology: L. T. Hobhouse and Political Argument in England, 1880–1914* (Cambridge, 1979), p. 9.

[23] N. Ferguson, 'Public finance and national security: the domestic origins of the First World War revisited', *Past and Present* 142 (1994), 141–68; J. M. Hobson, 'The military-extraction gap and the wary Titan: the fiscal-sociology of British defence policy, 1870–1913', *Journal of European Economic History* 22 (1993), 461–506; C. Maier, *Recasting Bourgeois Europe: Stabilization in France, Germany and Italy after World War I* (Princeton, 1975).

the war, the outcome was a 'crisis of the tax state'.[24] In Britain, the level of fiscal extraction did not drop after the First World War – and neither was there a serious loss of consent or legitimacy. What stands out is the weakness of such a crisis, or more accurately its successful resolution. This contrasts with the serious tensions in Britain after the Napoleonic wars and in other European countries after the First World War – and the outcome had significant long-term consequences. The explanation is to be found, in part, in the very success of the process of stabilisation in the nineteenth century, the way that taxation and the state were accepted as 'fair' and 'neutral'. Politicians and officials prided themselves on their ability to maintain financial stability and political legitimacy in comparison with their counterparts in Europe, and the British fiscal constitution was held up as a source of national pride and achievement. This may be read as a culmination of the Victorian or Gladstonian fiscal constitution of balance, neutrality and fairness. The rhetoric constrained politicians – and it could also free the left to make use of taxation and the state.

The consequences were significant. In the medium term, an increase in the level of taxation permitted higher levels of spending on welfare, which in turn helped to moderate the economic and social impact of the world depression of the early 1930s. The successful resolution of the problem of the 'floating debt' after the First World War contributed to financial stability in Britain – a point deserving of more attention than it usually receives compared with the intense controversy over the gold standard.[25] The ability to keep central government taxes at a high level also affected the form of the state and of welfare, contributing to the shift from local to central funding and initiatives, and to the growth of tax-funded compared with contributory welfare.[26] And the need to maintain consent to taxation should be inserted into debates over appeasement in the 1930s. When taxation was already so high, could more money be found for rearmament?[27] The possibility of resistance from taxpayers might be counter-productive, merely suggesting that Britain lacked the capacity or willingness for war.

In the longer term, the consequences start to become more problematic. The Second World War marked a further displacement in fiscal

---

[24] J. Schumpeter, 'The crisis of the tax state', in A. Peacock, R. Turvey, W. F. Stolper and E. Henderson (eds.), *International Economic Papers IV* (London and New York, 1954), pp. 5–38.

[25] See S. Solomou, *Themes in Macroeconomic History: The UK Economy, 1919–1939* (Cambridge, 1996).

[26] Daunton, 'Payment and participation'; for another view, on the Treasury desire to shift to contributions, see J. Macnicol, *The Politics of Retirement in Britain, 1878–1948* (Cambridge, 1998).

[27] See G. C. Peden, *British Rearmament and the Treasury, 1932–39* (Edinburgh, 1979).

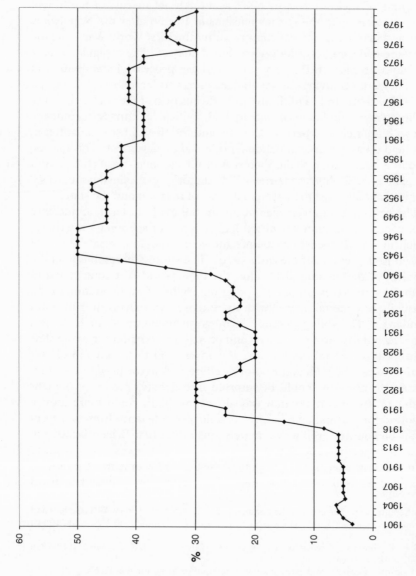

Figure 1.2 Standard rate of income tax, 1900–1980 (percentage)
Source: B. R. Mitchell, *British Historical Statistics* (Cambridge, 1988), p. 645.

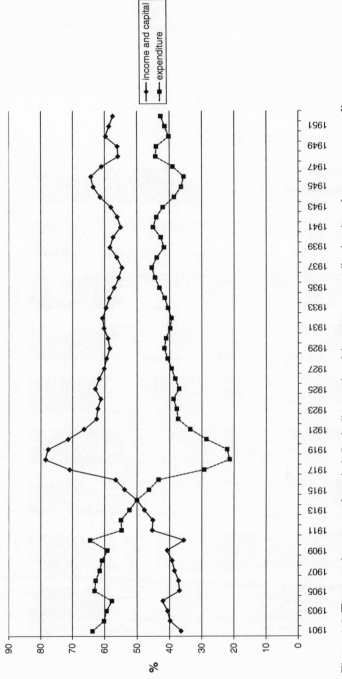

Figure 1.3 Taxes on income and capital (including national insurance contributions) and taxes on expenditure as a percentage of central government receipts, 1900–1951
Source: London and Cambridge Economic Service, *The British Economy: Key Statistics, 1900–70* (London, 1971), p. 112.

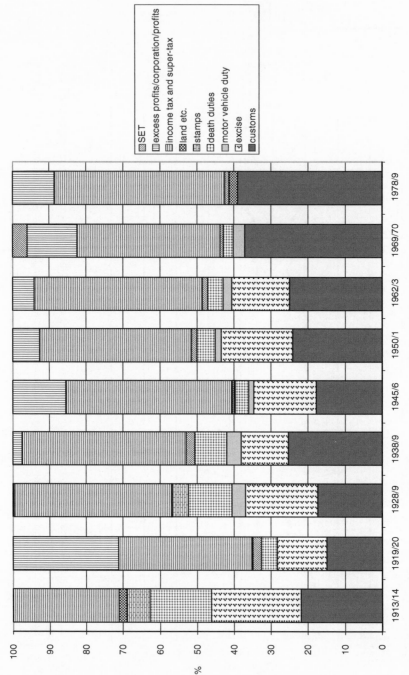

Figure 1.4 Structure of central government revenue: net receipts due to the Exchequer, 1913/14 to 1978/9
Sources: see sources for tables 2.4, 4.3, 5.2, 6.2, 7.2, 8.3 and 10.4.

extraction and a further shift to tax-funded welfare. Levels of taxation were now affecting the distribution of income and leading to a decrease in inequality. Could the result be a loss of incentive and lower levels of growth? Many historians suggest that a consensus emerged during the Second World War, leading to an acceptance of Keynesianism and the welfare state, underwritten by high levels of spending and taxation. However, it is not clear that consensus *was* so powerful.[28] Attitudes to the impact of taxation on incentives and the desirability of equality were highly contested and stood at the heart of British politics from the late 1950s. The appearance of consensus might well arise from the constraints of economic and political circumstances rather than from any ideological convergence. It was one thing to propose competing solutions; it was another thing to act, escaping from short-term management of immediate problems to articulate (and implement) a new strategy. The appearance of consensus in the 1950s might arise, as Rodney Lowe has suggested, from evading rather than addressing problems, whether from a lack of nerve by politicians, or the weaknesses in the machinery of government.[29] The adversarial nature of the two-party system meant that during the period of alternating governments of the 1960s and 1970s policy was incoherent rather than consensual. As a result, the fiscal system which once seemed a source of stability and national pride now seemed a source of inflexibility and a cause of low growth compared with other countries. The British

[28] For consensus, see R. T. Mackenzie, *British Political Parties* (London, 1965), who argues for convergence in practice, despite differences of rhetoric. D. Kavanagh and P. Morris, *Consensus Politics from Attlee to Thatcher* (Oxford, 1989), and D. Kavanagh, *Thatcherism and British Politics: The End of Consensus?* (Oxford, 1987), argue for consensus in the period from 1945 to the 1970s, based on a mixed economy, full employment, the role of unions, the welfare state and foreign and defence policy, which continued beside an adversarial party system until consensus broke down in the 1970s. For a different view of adversarial politics at the expense of consensus, see S. E. Finer, 'Adversary politics and electoral reform', in S. E. Finer (ed.), *Adversary Politics and Electoral Reform* (London, 1975), pp. 3–32, who argues that the divide between two parties gave power to the right and left wings at the expense of the centre ground, so that minor swings in the vote between parties exaggerated shifts in policy. For a more complex view of the connection between adversarial politics and consensus, see A. M. Gamble and S. A. Walkland, *The British Party System and Economic Policy, 1945–83: Studies in Adversary Politics* (Oxford, 1984). They reject the view that adversarial politics simply destroyed continuity of policy; rather, consensus was achieved by excluding major areas from debate at the expense of a ritualised party conflict on a few issues. In their opinion, the failure arose in areas which were *not* in dispute, such as the cross-party agreement that the tax base was too narrow, as well as in areas of bitter dispute. For a more sceptical view of the entire idea of consensus, see B. Pimlott, 'The myth of consensus', in L. M. Smith (ed.), *The Making of Britain: Echoes of Greatness* (London, 1988) pp. 129–41. For an overview of the debate, see D. Kavanagh, 'The postwar consensus', *Twentieth Century British History* 3 (1992), 175–90. These issues are picked up in later chapters.

[29] R. Lowe, 'Resignation at the Treasury: the Social Services Committee and the failure to reform the welfare state', *Journal of Social Policy* 18 (1989), 524.

fiscal constitution was widely criticised for its failings, and officials and politicians looked to other countries for solutions.

The present study is mainly concerned with the formulation of tax policy, and the analysis is consequently heavily dependent on the records of central government, supplemented by discussions within political parties and 'peak' organisations of labour and capital. It views the tax system through the eyes of officials and politicians, how they interpreted public attitudes to taxation and the likely outcome for tax yields and elections. The justification of this approach is in part a matter of priorities, a need to establish the main lines of tax policy over the period. But it also reflects the distinctive nature of tax policy which was shaped by civil servants and between civil servants and politicians to a much greater extent than in the nineteenth century. A major concern of this study is the character of the British state – which is not to say that ideas or non-governmental forces are ignored. The question is: how far did they influence the shaping of policy by the state? What is the relationship between the institutions of the state, and its permeability to ideas and to forces outside the government?[30]

Taxes in Britain were determined in conditions of secrecy, with a strong emphasis on the exclusion of interest groups. The obvious contrast is with the United States, where the president cannot impose a budget on Congress: it is amended in detail on the floor of the House and Senate. During this process, politicians offer support in return for amendments to protect various local or sectional interests, with the result that the tax system is a mass of exemptions and anomalies. Defeat of the budget does not lead to the fall of the government and an election, given fixed terms and the division of responsibilities between legislature and executive. Failure to pass the budget might paralyse the federal executive, but Senators and Representatives are more interested in fighting for the particular needs of their constituents in order to secure campaign funds and re-election. In Britain, the situation is very different. The annual budget is drawn up in conditions of secrecy by the leading officials of the Treasury and revenue departments, in consultation with the chancellor of the Exchequer and his junior ministers. British officials have immense authority compared with their American counterparts who lack such a high level of continuity,

---

[30] For an explanation of a similar approach to the American fiscal system, stressing an interplay between institutions and ideas or knowledge, see W. E. Brownlee, 'Reflections on the history of taxation', in W. E. Brownlee (ed.), *Funding the Modern American State, 1941–1995: The Rise and Fall of the Era of Easy Finance* (Cambridge, 1996), pp. 3–36, which is aligned with two volumes on the comparative development of the modern state: M. O. Furner and B. Supple (eds.), *The State and Economic Knowledge: The American and British Experience* (Cambridge, 1990), and M. J. Lacey and M. O. Furner (eds.), *The State and Social Investigation in Britain and the United States* (Cambridge, 1993).

both in terms of personal career and identity with a departmental ethos which went back to the creation of the Gladstonian fiscal constitution.[31] British officials could, almost instinctively, block any novel scheme proposed by a chancellor by noting that it contravened the treatment of the national debt laid down in 1829 which had made Britain so prosperous and the cynosure of other nations. It took a brave and well-informed (or an obstinate and ill-informed) chancellor to overrule such advice and to challenge British traditions. Most chancellors held office for a relatively short time and lacked real expertise, so that officials were often dominant. A few exceptional chancellors did overrule the Treasury, insisting that tradition was not sacrosanct, that circumstances could change and that the past was contingent rather than immutable. Winston Churchill[*] as chancellor between 1924 and 1929 had the time, force of character and politically astute vision to shape the fiscal constitution. Hugh Dalton,[†] Labour's chancellor after the Second World War, was unusual in having academic expertise in finance, and his knowledge gave him independence of the Treasury. But such men were exceptional.

Officials and ministers might receive deputations or written submissions from the Federation (later Confederation) of British Industries

---

[31] S. Steinmo, 'Political institutions and tax policy in the United States, Sweden and Britain', *World Politics* 41 (1988–9), 329–72; T. Skocpol, 'Bringing the state back in: strategies of analysis in current research', in P. B. Evans, D. Rueschmeyer and T. Skocpol (eds.), *Bringing the State Back In* (Cambridge, 1985), pp. 1–16; M. O. Furner and B. Supple, 'Ideas, institutions, and state in the United States and Britain: an introduction', in Furner and Supple (eds.), *The State and Economic Knowledge*, pp. 3–39.

[*] Winston Leonard Spencer Churchill (1874–1965) was educated at Harrow and Sandhurst, joining the army and also working as a war correspondent. He became a Unionist MP in 1900, moving to the Liberals in 1904 in opposition to tariff reform. He became parliamentary under-secretary of the colonies in 1906; he was president of the Board of Trade 1908–10, home secretary 1910–11 and first lord of the Admiralty 1911–15. In 1915 he became chancellor of the Duchy of Lancaster, but resigned to join the army. He returned to office as minister of munitions in 1917–18, secretary of war and air in 1918–21 and colonial secretary in 1921–2. He was out of the Commons from 1922 until 1924, when he returned as a Conservative until 1964. He was chancellor of the Exchequer 1924–9, and split from the party over the India bill in 1931. He was prime minister 1940–5 and 1951–5. (*DNB, 1961–70*, ed. E. T. Williams and C. S. Nicholls (Oxford, 1981), pp. 193–216; Robbins (ed.), *Biographical Dictionary*, pp. 98–102.)

[†] Edward Hugh John Neale Dalton (1887–1962) was the son of the chaplain to Prince George (later George V); educated at Eton and King's College, Cambridge. He was called to the bar in 1914 and served in the war; he joined the economics department of the LSE after the war and was reader between 1920 and 1936. His *Principles of Public Finance* appeared in 1923 and attempted to draw a distinction between academic neutrality and partisan argument; his other main publication was on equality of incomes. He was a Labour MP between 1924 and 1931 and 1935 and 1959. In the war-time coalition, he was minister of economic warfare 1940–2 and president of the Board of Trade 1942–5; in the postwar Labour government, he was chancellor of the Exchequer 1945–7, chancellor of the Duchy of Lancaster 1948–50 and minister of town and country planning 1950–1. (*DNB, 1961–70*, ed. Williams and Nicholls, pp. 266–9.)

(FBI), the TUC and other associations, but there was not a dialogue. These associations expressed their views and concerns, and would at most receive bland general assurances or statements of principle. The officials and ministers would not share their concerns or hint at any proposals for change in the tax system. Indeed, even the Cabinet often did not discover the main lines of the budget until shortly before it was presented to the House of Commons, when it was usually too late to make any significant changes. The spending departments made their submissions of expenditure and were largely excluded from discussion of how the money should be raised. When the budget was presented to the Commons, there was little room for adjustment. Support of the budget was a matter of 'confidence', and defeat would result in an election. This did happen on a number of occasions in the nineteenth century; it did not happen once after 1914. Party discipline and self-interest meant that few MPs on the government benches would vote against the budget, unlike in the United States where the House or Senate might be controlled by a different party from that of the president. Consequently, there were few opportunities in the British fiscal system for 'log rolling' and tax breaks or exemptions for particular groups; for that matter, neither was there much chance of serious discussion of new proposals.[32]

Such a view suggests that the British state – and especially officials in the Treasury and revenue departments – had considerable autonomy, with a firmly entrenched administrative ethos which was relatively impervious to outside influences. But it might be objected that this account misses the emergence of a more 'corporatist' polity since 1945. Interests were often expressed by organised institutions from the First World War and even more so from the Second World War, culminating in the creation of the National Economic Development Council (NEDC) and the Prices and Incomes Board. On this view, government officials bargained with fellow bureaucrats in large representative institutions, whether the leaders of the National Union of Teachers in education or the British Medical Association in health. As Manzer put it, 'stable relationships usually develop among the interests clustering about a decision-making centre', and the role of the government was largely confined to technical details or marginal adjustments. The outcome, in Mancur Olson's account, was a rigid, inflexible system of 'distributional coalitions' which were difficult to shift. Furthermore, competing administrations were tempted to offer more spending to particular interest groups in a 'bidding war', seeking to purchase support so that spending spiralled upwards and forced the

---

[32] Steinmo, 'Political institutions and tax policy', and *Taxation and Democracy: Swedish, British, and American Approaches to Financing the Modern State* (New Haven, 1993).

government to devise economic policies to produce more resources – in turn needing the consent of interest groups to its policies. Hence inflationary pressure as a result of full employment in the 1950s and 1960s made the government anxious to secure the consent of the TUC to restrain wages – and the need for union support limited the Conservative government's ability to give tax breaks to profits and high incomes. On this account, the problem was not 'log rolling' on the floor of the Congress as in the United States, but a process of corporatist brokering of deals.[33]

Some historians would argue that the greatest power was held by finance, by the interests of the City of London expressed through the common culture and social background of Treasury officials and City bankers.[34] The position adopted here is more cautious, placing the Bank and the City within a complex balancing of interests, and arguing for mutual suspicion between the City and the Treasury. Alongside the City, the two most powerful bodies were the FBI and the TUC. They expressed real, material concerns with a direct impact on the economy, such as the taxation of business profits, the definition of depreciation or the level of thresholds for different bands of income tax which affected profitability, investments and earnings. These bodies had to articulate a language to hold together potentially divisive groups, and they had to define whose interests they represented. The TUC, for example, defined 'labour' as the male breadwinner for most of the period, neglecting the demand of women for family allowances or of the unemployed or retired

---

[33] For accounts of corporatism, see S. Beer, *Modern British Politics: Parties and Pressure Groups in the Collectivist Age* (London, 1982), and *Britain Against Itself: The Political Contradictions of Collectivism* (London, 1982): he argues for the existence of corporatism, but in a form which failed to deliver agreements as a result of all parties relying on consultation and voluntary agreement (see *Britain Against Itself*, pp. 64–6). See also K. Middlemass, *Politics in Industrial Society: The British Experience since 1911* (London, 1979), and *Power, Competition and the State*, vol. I: *Britain in Search of Balance, 1940–61* (Basingstoke, 1986), who interprets British history through 'corporate bias' – the tendency of industrial associations, unions and financial institutions to make reciprocal arrangements with each other and the government, whilst avoiding overt conflict (see *Power, Competition and the State*, pp. 1, 344–7). The idea of 'distributional coalitions' acting as a barrier to changes in policy is developed in M. Olson, *The Logic of Collective Action: Public Goods and the Theory of Groups* (Cambridge, Mass., 1965), and *The Rise and Decline of Nations: Economic Growth, Stagflation and Social Rigidities* (New Haven and London, 1982). There are many discussions of corporatism and its consequences: see, for example, A. Cawson, *Corporatism and Welfare* (London, 1982); T. Smith, *The Politics of the Corporate Economy* (Oxford, 1979); J. T. Winkler, 'The corporate economy: theory and administration', in R. Scase (ed.), *Industrial Society: Class, Cleavage and Control* (London, 1977), pp. 43–58. For case studies of policy formation, see R. A. Manzer, *Teachers and Politics: The Role of the National Union of Teachers in the Making of National Educational Policy in England and Wales since 1944* (Manchester, 1970), p. 1; H. Eckstein, *Pressure Group Politics: The Case of the British Medical Association* (London, 1960).

[34] Above all, P. J. Cain and A. G. Hopkins, *British Imperialism: Innovation and Expansion, 1688–1914* (London, 1993).

for higher benefits.[35] Similarly, the FBI (and its successor, the Confederation of British Industry) represented mainly larger concerns and public companies, and was less attuned to the needs of small firms or family partnerships which were more likely to be represented by the Association of British Chambers of Commerce.

The corporatist interpretation has its shortcomings. Interest groups did matter, but usually through the perception of high-ranking officials and senior politicians of what was reasonable or convincing. The definition of what was 'reasonable' or 'convincing' differed between Conservative and Labour politicians; it would be plausible for the Conservatives to be more sympathetic to the FBI or Labour to the TUC. The result was therefore a lack of continuity as administrations alternated, rather than corporate stasis or stability. Politicians and officials had a shrewd awareness of what different associations and interests wanted, yet policy was not formulated through direct negotiation with them and was not dependent on their active participation in policy debates. Treasury officials had a long-established assumption of the 'neutrality' of the fiscal system and the needs of the state for revenue which made them anxious not to succumb to interest group pressure. Independence from interest groups was crucial to the legitimacy of the tax system. Politicians and officials did not merely broker deals between interest groups, for they had their own perception of state needs. Interests were forced to express their concerns through parties and parliament, unlike in some other European countries where corporatism was a response to the failure of these institutions after the First World War.[36] In any case, the peak organisations in Britain were often incapable of enforcing agreements, and the government was conscious that they did not represent all workers or businessmen.[37]

Politicians and officials did not simply respond to or adjudicate between the claims of industry, labour or finance; they were concerned for the autonomous needs of the state. At the end of the First World War,

---

[35] S. Pedersen, *Family, Dependence, and the Origins of the Welfare State: Britain and France, 1914–45* (Cambridge, 1993); Macnicol, *Politics of Retirement in Britain*.

[36] On corporatist solutions in other European countries after the First World War, see Maier, *Recasting Bourgeois Europe*; and on the failure of corporatism in Britain, J. Turner, 'The politics of "organised business" in the First World War', in J. Turner (ed.), *Businessmen and Politics: Studies of Business Activity in British Politics, 1900–45* (London, 1984), pp. 48–9, and C. J. Nottingham, 'Recasting bourgeois Britain? The British state in the years which followed the First World War', *International Review of Social History* 31 (1976), 244–7.

[37] See, for example, D. Marsh and W. Grant, 'Tripartism: reality or myth?' *Government and Opposition* 12 (1977), 194–211, on the failure of either the CBI or TUC to provide pillars of a tripartite agreement with the state; and D. K. Stout, 'Incomes policy and the costs of the adversarial system', in S. E. Finer (ed.), *Adversary Politics and Electoral Reform* (London, 1975), pp. 117–40, on the failure of the TUC to deliver agreement on incomes policy.

politicians and officials did not accept the claims of the FBI, TUC or City to represent the national interest, and neither did they simply seek to strike a balance between these interests. In addition, they had to respond to the existence of disaffected lower-middle-class taxpayers who attacked 'waste' and resented the erosion of their social status by the gains of workers and 'profiteers' during the war. The huge transfer of tax revenues to *rentiers* holding national debt created a volatile situation at a time of shifting political allegiances, and any perception that either industry or organised labour was securing preferential treatment would be dangerous. Industry could easily be identified with war profiteers, exploiting the lower middle class, workers and the 'public'. Similarly, organised labour could be attacked as selfish or even treacherous, gaining at the expense of unorganised groups such as pensioners living on fixed incomes. These debates entailed a contest over another identity: the divide between earned and unearned incomes, active and passive wealth. *A priori*, there is no reason why income from investments should pay a higher rate of tax: it did not in the nineteenth century and does not now. Indeed, it may even be argued that income from investments should pay a *lower* rate of tax, or that savings from income should be set against tax liability, in order to encourage investment in economic growth, self-sufficiency and 'popular capitalism'. Higher taxation of income from investments was introduced in 1907 on the grounds that it was 'unearned' by active exertion, imposing a parasitical drain of rents and interest payments on enterprising members of society. The issue was how this identity would be articulated, for it might set some members of the middle class against others, by drawing a distinction between different forms of property. On the other hand, *all* property owners might be identified as a common interest against the threat of socialism; and it might prove difficult to portray *rentiers* as harmful parasites when they included widows and the retired. These identities were constructed and contested in postwar political rhetoric, in a discourse over the meanings of waste and production, active and passive wealth. Definitions of identity were malleable, and politicians attempted to construct and shape self-perceptions at the end of the war, just as much as they responded to existing material interests. Indeed, politicians might need to claim independence from the FBI or TUC or City in order to show that they had not succumbed to interests and could be trusted to represent the 'public' – a term they tried to define for their own political purposes. Although 'real' material concerns were important, politicians and parties did not merely respond to pre-existing interests, but attempted to define and shape identities through their language and rhetoric.[38]

---

[38] For one analysis of this process, see R. McKibbin, *The Ideologies of Class: Social Relations in Britain, 1880–1950* (Oxford, 1990).

What was involved was not merely a cynical calculation of electoral advantage, for both politicians and (even more so) their officials were concerned with the need to preserve the government's revenue and financial stability. Although opposition politicians might see the attraction of condoning or even encouraging resistance to taxes, the strategy was short-sighted and likely to be regretted when they returned to office and faced the task of extracting revenue with the minimum of friction. The point was apparent to senior politicians at the end of the First World War, if not to their more populist colleagues and the popular press. It was most obvious to career civil servants who stressed the need for caution. Of course, their caution could spill over into conservatism and resistance to change in new circumstances; they could define the *status quo* as somehow 'natural' rather than the result of historical contingencies. Nevertheless, these officials did resist special pleading by organised interests. The claims of the FBI, TUC or City were filtered through the sceptical, worldly wise and impressively self-assured minds of Treasury officials. Hence at the end of the First World War Treasury officials were able to argue that industry alone could pay higher taxes – not necessarily the outcome to be expected. Senior Cabinet ministers shared this concern for the extraction of revenue with a minimum of controversy. Both officials and ministers were also concerned with financial stability. If interest on the national debt could not be paid after the war, there might be a serious loss of confidence in the finances of the British government, as in Germany.[39] British politicians and officials were not in any simple way following the dictates of the City in their concern for financial solvency; rather, they were anxious to retain independence from the City. State or national needs might therefore prevent a straightforward acceptance of the claims of any 'selfish' interest.

By the late 1950s, serious problems were starting to emerge. Some senior figures in the Treasury felt that the fiscal system needed overhaul and that it was harming the performance of the economy, but they were hampered by the structure of government which made a thorough review of fiscal policy difficult. Although politicians shared their concerns, they were usually reluctant to act – in part for the compelling reason that change in the tax system would entail losers as well as winners, and was difficult to justify on electoral grounds. There was also concern that any adjustment in fiscal policy might alienate an organised interest with serious consequences for the management of the economy. Thus a cut in

[39] T. Balderston, 'War finance and inflation in Britain and Germany, 1914–18', *Economic History Review* 2nd ser. 42 (1989), 222–44; N. Ferguson, *Paper and Iron: Hamburg Business and German Politics in the Era of Inflation, 1897–1927* (Cambridge, 1995); Maier, *Recasting Bourgeois Europe.*

the profits tax or in higher levels of income tax designed to provide an incentive to enterprise might lead the TUC to abandon wage restraint with the danger of inflation, higher labour costs and a further loss of competitiveness in export markets. Perhaps it was best to leave well alone, even if the result were harmful for economic growth.

The concern for balance in the fiscal system had its failings as well as its undoubted virtues. One outcome could be incoherence – a seemingly paradoxical result of the officials' insisting on the need for continuity. By stressing the need for stability and secrecy, Treasury officials might well displace discussion of fiscal policy into other venues, and chancellors might come into office with their own nostrum and their own independent advisers, bringing ideas from outside the government machinery – such as James Callaghan* in 1964 who was heavily influenced by Nicholas Kaldor.† The selective employment tax – a payroll tax on service employment – was devised outside the Treasury and without consultation with employers or unions. Such changes were implemented as a result of the 'elective dictatorship' of strong party discipline, without much discussion within the machinery of government or resistance from the government's benches in the Commons. The next administration could then introduce its own changes with different motivations and assumptions, so that the tax system became a palimpsest written in different languages. Indeed, the adversarial nature of party politics meant that the opposition attacked the government's proposals, even when they were themselves considering similar policies. Despite the continuity of officials and their

* James Callaghan (b. 1912) was born in Portsmouth, where his father, who died when Callaghan was still young, was in the navy. He joined the Inland Revenue in 1929, and was active in the Association of Tax Officers. He became a Labour MP in 1945, and served as parliamentary secretary to the minister of transport in 1947, and parliamentary and financial secretary to the Admiralty in 1950. In 1964, he became chancellor of the Exchequer, moving to the Home Office in 1967 after the devaluation of the pound. In 1974, he became foreign secretary and prime minister from 1976 to 1979. (Robbins (ed.), *Biographical Dictionary*, pp. 78–81.)

† Nicholas Kaldor (1908–86) was born in Budapest where was father was legal adviser to the German legation. He was educated in Budapest, at the University of Berlin and the LSE. He joined the staff of the LSE in 1932, resigning in 1947 to become director of the research and planning division of the Economic Commission for Europe in Geneva. In 1949 he became fellow of King's College and a lecturer in economics at Cambridge; he was promoted to professor in 1966 and retired in 1975. During the war, he worked on Beveridge's reports on social insurance and full employment; after the war, he was an adviser to the French *commissariat general du Plan* as well as other international consultancies. In 1951, he was appointed a member of the Royal Commission on the Taxation of Profits and Income. He gave tax advice to developing countries, and served as special adviser to the chancellor of the Exchequer in 1964–8 and 1974–6, and to the minister of health and social security in 1969. He became a life peer in 1974 and used his position to attack monetarism and the economic policies of Thatcher. (*DNB, 1986–90*, ed. C. S. Nicholls (Oxford, 1996), pp. 240–1; Robbins (ed.), *Biographical Dictionary*, pp. 238–9.)

stress on stability, their non-political character and need to serve successive administrations meant that their role was often negative, defending the *status quo* by showing why change was impossible or undesirable, rather than arguing for systematic and consistent reform which offered a better guarantee of stability. Although some officials at the Treasury did see the problems, they had little chance of reshaping the fiscal system; rather, there was a series of lurches as chancellors periodically broke with the *status quo* and introduced inconsistent change. The outcome was, paradoxically, a lack of coherence and consensus despite the deep-seated continuity of the civil service.

Most of these debates and calculations took place within the government and civil service, with some rethinking of policy within party research departments or 'think-tanks' during opposition. This study reflects the character of fiscal politics, the way that ideas and the feelings of the British public were *interpreted* by politicians and civil servants. The issue addressed here is how they thought the public might react, how they might vote at the next election, rather than what the public *did* think and how the electors *did* react. Ideally, this analysis of the state's assessment of its citizens should be complemented by a study of the taxpayers' attitudes to the state, of their resistance or compliance. We should also bear in mind that interests are not entirely 'essential' pre-existing identities represented by associations of various kinds; interests and identities are constructed discursively through the political process, and not least by debates over taxation. As David Cannadine has pointed out, British politicians had particular visions of society and 'have conceived of their task to be that of imposing their visions *of* the people *on* the people'[40] – and taxation is surely one important site. Obviously, the rhetoric of taxation should be set within a wider analysis of the social and political vision of parties, showing how it mingled with other rhetorics, how parties tried to construct social and political identities and how the electors reacted. The present study cannot hope to undertake that larger task, and concentrates on the construction of fiscal policy, on the actual shape of taxes. It only considers the rhetoric of taxation as it was used by politicians in their own deliberations of what was feasible. Similarly, the approach to ideas starts from the politicians and officials, assessing how they did (or did not) utilise ideas, rather than from a survey of ideas about taxation and related debates over equality, incentives or growth in the writings of economists and political philosophers, and in the pamphlets of policy groups. The concern is the extent to which the British state was permeable to new ideas, which are approached through the traces left in the official record,

[40] D. Cannadine, *Class in Britain* (London and New Haven, 1998), p. xi.

and in terms of the political structures and processes which shaped their impact on policy.

Changes in the fiscal system were influenced by shifts in the social and economic structure as well as by ideas or the form of the state. Peter Lindert has pointed to the significance of 'social affinity', the extent to which the median voter is close to or well below the median income. He argues that where the median voter is close to the median income, there is less electoral support for redistributive taxation than where the median voter is well below the median income and stands to gain.[41] Of course, changes in the franchise are important here. After 1832, voters were drawn from relatively affluent property owners so that the median voter was well *above* the median income and was unlikely to support redistributive taxation. After 1918, adult men and some women had the vote and the median voter was well *below* the median income. The danger, it seemed to many anxious Conservatives, was that redistributive taxation would now have greater appeal. However, changes in occupational structure meant that the danger receded, especially from the 1950s. The shift from manual to white-collar work and the rise of a professional or managerial middle class affected both income distribution and *perceptions* of social affinity. A clerical worker might earn no more than a skilled manual worker; the point is with whom he or she identifies – a large topic far beyond the scope of this study of taxation. Certainly, the sense of identity and material self-interest were affected by inflation and the level of tax thresholds. As prices and incomes rose, more people became liable to income tax or moved into higher bands, potentially creating a sense of grievance. Higher real incomes might also change attitudes to state-funded, standard welfare benefits. After the Second World War, many middle-class families agreed that tax-funded welfare was desirable, for they paid for health care, education and pensions in the past and could now benefit from state provision. The result was a sentiment of social solidarity or affinity, from which the poor benefited.[42] However, this sentiment might not persist if state provision were seen as inadequate and unaccountable, as was the case in the 1970s when prosperous middle-class families started to shift to private schemes offering greater flexibility in meeting their own particular needs. Further, attitudes to taxation were affected by the changing demographic profile of the population. In the later twentieth century, the British population aged and the elderly might

[41] P. H. Lindert, 'The rise of social spending, 1880–1930', *Explorations in Economic History* 31 (1994), 1–37, and 'What limits social spending?', *Explorations in Economic History* 33 (1996), 1–34.

[42] P. Baldwin, *The Politics of Social Solidarity: Class Bases of the European Welfare States, 1875–1975* (Cambridge, 1990).

seek generous social provision, driving up costs and imposing taxes on younger, economically active members of the workforce.[43]

Although changes in economic and demographic structures were important constraints on politicians, they did not determine policy. Political cultures and the construction of identities are important, for the sense of affinity is a cultural or social phenomenon, and one that politicians could seek to manipulate. This point was clear at the end of the First World War: Labour attempted to unite the working class and salaried or productive middle class against *rentiers* and owners of 'passive' property; the coalition government countered this strategy by defining all property owners against the selfish claims of workers. Politicians might also *fail* to respond to changes in the economic and social structure and in social attitudes. Arguably, the Labour party's rhetoric in the 1970s did not adjust to the decline in the manual working class and the emergence of a more affluent consumers' society. We also need to consider whether various interests or identities were able to make their voices heard. Although the elderly formed a larger proportion of the population and of the electorate, this does not mean that they influenced policy to the same extent as organised workers in trade unions who might well form a declining share of the electorate.[44] The impact of the economic and social structure was always mediated through political processes.

The research strategy and methodology adopted in this book therefore starts from the state and the political process, and is concerned with the way political culture, ideas and economic and social structures entered into the formulation of policy and changes in the fiscal system. Above all, this study of fiscal policy provides a way into the form of the British state. This involves more than an analysis of the relationship between officials and politicians, and their perception of the concerns of interest groups and taxpayers, important though these points are for an understanding of the state. Success in extracting revenue is also crucial for the *capacity* of the state, for without resources it simply cannot act. Further, the precise *source* of taxation – whether tax revenues came from local or central revenues, or from taxation of companies or private incomes – helps to shape the state. Thus the poor law was heavily dependent on local property taxes, with the potential danger (at least in the eyes of the Treasury) that spending could fall into the hands of 'irresponsible'

---

[43] This leads to what Niall Ferguson calls 'generation games': see *The Cash Nexus: Money and Power in the Modern World, 1700–2000* (London, 2001), pp. 214–21.

[44] For the organisation of pensioners in the interwar period, see Macnicol, *Politics of Retirement in Britain*, pp. 167, 174–5, 185, 311–22, on the National Conference on Old Age Pensions, the National Spinsters' Association and the National Federation of Old Age Pensions Associations.

local interests. Central government taxes were more buoyant and in more 'responsible' hands with closer Treasury control. The budget of 1929 marked a clear shift towards more centralised spending. The outcome was a heavy reliance on a progressive income tax as the main source for welfare spending. This might in turn be called into question. Might it blunt incentives? Might it allow employers to use labour less efficiently, in the knowledge that welfare costs were passed to the general taxpayer? Might a shift to employers' contributions or a 'payroll tax' make them more sensitive to labour costs, encouraging improved productivity and permitting a reduction in the highest levels of income tax in order to offer incentives? The British state in the 1960s was characterised less by its level of taxation or welfare spending than by the sources of taxation, and these issues were discussed with a new urgency as concern mounted about the poor growth record of the British economy.

This brings us to perceptions of the economic impact of the fiscal system. One of the crucial themes in the debate over 'modernisation' in the 1960s was the relationship between taxation and growth. After the Second World War, the Conservatives might feel that high taxes blunted incentives and growth, and that a degree of inequality might be essential for an efficient economy from which all would benefit. Labour politicians tended to disagree, stressing the use of taxation to create equality and to remove profit as the driving force for economic growth. In other words, debates over taxation offer a way into the larger question of the normative assumptions about society and human motivation. These assumptions provide a connecting thread throughout the book: should the tax system offer incentives to the pursuit of individual income as a means of stimulating growth, productivity and the welfare of the greatest number of the people? Or should the fiscal system be used in pursuit of equality as the means of creating an ethical society based on social justice? The tax system involved a contest over the extent to which incentives or equality, in what proportions and how defined, should provide the rationale for the organisation of Britain's economic and social system. This balance between equality and incentives shaped the fiscal system of the twentieth century to a much greater extent than in the nineteenth century.

A central theme in debates over taxation in the twentieth century is the definition of distributive justice. The issue was not new,[45] but was discussed with greater urgency at a time of much higher and more redistributive taxes from the First World War. Economists and political

[45] See Daunton, *Trusting Leviathan*.

philosophers debated the issue with considerable sophistication and frequent disagreement, from A. C. Pigou[*] to F. A. Hayek[†] and John Rawls – and politicians were aware of their work. Indeed, one of the leading Labour chancellors – Hugh Dalton – was himself an academic who contributed to the debates. But the impact of these economic ideas was always highly contingent upon political circumstances, economic realities and political processes. Politicians in the Conservative party took the need for incentives as axiomatic, yet in the 1950s somewhat fatalistically accepted a level of taxation which many felt to be harmful. Change in the tax regime simply seemed too difficult, posing a threat to the established method of economic management: a cut in higher tax rates or profit taxes would alienate the unions, leading to wage demands and inflation. Only in the 1980s was Mrs Thatcher willing to break out of this strait-jacket. By contrast, many in the Labour party were doubtful about the role of incentives and the free market as the basis of a just society. Consensus was more a myth than reality in postwar British politics, or at most the product of circumstances rather than ideological convergence.

The nature of distributive justice has been debated by philosophers such as Rawls, on an abstract level. Rawls places the individual behind a 'veil of ignorance', where he does not know his place in society – and to guard against the possibility of being the worst-off member of society, he will therefore wish to ensure that the position of the worst-off will not be intolerable. This suggests a high level of equality, up to the point that the loss of incentives will harm growth and make everyone worse off.[46] By contrast, historians are more inclined to ask how particular people at precise moments and in highly specific circumstances attempt to define their rights and obligations. Such is the task of this study of taxation, which considers how definitions of distributive justice changed over the period in one particular area of policy, and how the trade-off between incentives and equality was negotiated. Detailed discussion in the remainder of this book considers the texture and complexities of

[46] J. Rawls, *A Theory of Justice* (Oxford, 1972).

[*] Arthur Cecil Pigou (1887–1959) was educated at Harrow and King's College, Cambridge, where he read history and moral sciences. He became a fellow of King's in 1902 and professor of economics in 1908–43. (*DNB, 1951–60*, ed. E. T. Wilson and H. M. Palmer (London, 1971), pp. 814–17.)

[†] Friedrich August von Hayek (1899–1992) was born in Vienna and educated at the University of Vienna. From 1931 to 1950 he was professor of economics at the LSE, when he moved to Chicago and, in 1969, to Freiburg. He won the Nobel prize for economics in 1974. His *Road to Serfdom* (1944) had most popular impact and was used by Churchill in the 1945 election, to warn against the dangers of planning; it also appealed to Thatcher. He opposed Keynesianism and government intervention in the economy; he is often seen as the father of monetarism. (*Who Was Who*, vol. IX, p. 242; D. Crystal (ed.), *The Cambridge Biographical Encyclopaedia* (2nd edn, Cambridge, 1998), p. 430.)

these debates, how they changed over time and were influenced by the economic and social structure, by political and electoral calculation and by ideological or intellectual developments.

It would be useful to note a few of the main points of contention which run through the story. One was the definition, and desirability, of equality. Until the 1980s, this was a central *trope* in the rhetoric of Labour, whether on ethical grounds, a belief that equality was a prerequisite for a socialist commonwealth, or a claim that it was desirable for economic efficiency.[47] Large incomes and fortunes might be seen as 'socially created' wealth – less a reward to risk-taking and talent than a Rent secured by monopolists. This wealth might not increase the welfare of other members of society, and might be redistributed through taxes to the benefit of the less well-off. But taxation by itself might also be criticised as inadequate, and some Labour politicians stressed the efficacy of public ownership as a means of acquiring socially produced wealth for the community. Such an approach could be criticised – and not only on the right – for leading to an inflexible, highly bureaucratic and centralised economic system. Indeed, some members of the Labour party saw the need to preserve a degree of competition and dynamic initiative, so that public ownership should be confined to a narrow range of industries and the remainder left to free enterprise. Taxation would then ensure that excess profits were removed and inherited wealth strictly limited.

Alongside a concern for equality, politicians debated the desirability of planning which had implications for the use of the market as an allocative device. Economic liberals assumed that the market would create liberty and efficiency. Others disagreed. At one extreme, the 'gosplanners' in the Labour party wished to replace the market; many stopped short of this extreme position, but nevertheless felt that competition resulted in waste and inefficiency.[48] Others took a less jaundiced view of the market. In the 1920s, for example, the Independent Labour party (ILP) felt that a more equal distribution of income would allow consumers to purchase with discrimination, expressing their own identities and at the same time creating a productive system which would allow workers some expression of their character.[49] This vision faded and there was a greater emphasis on economies of scale and productive rationalism. Although this might imply public ownership, it was compatible with

---

[47] Different approaches to equality within the Labour party are explained in N. Ellison, *Egalitarian Thought and Labour Politics: Retreating Visions* (London, 1994).

[48] The phrase gosplanners was used by James Meade to describe some Labour politicians: see J. Tomlinson, 'Planning: debate and policy in the 1940s', *Twentieth Century British History* 3 (1992), 151–74.

[49] See N. Thompson, 'Hobson and the Fabians: two roads to socialism in the 1920s', *History of Political Economy* 26 (1994), 203–20.

private enterprise run by a technical, managerial elite concerned for long-run growth and development. Economists on the right, and especially Hayek, argued that planners would be unable to allocate resources in an efficient way without price signals. The point was admitted by some economists on the social democratic left, such as Meade, who accepted that much industry should remain in private hands, with the use of prices to allocate goods and any surplus removed by taxes.[50] Indeed, taxes might be used to shape behaviour within the capital market, both to prevent the emergence of socially created wealth and to allocate resources in a more efficient way. Some members of the Labour party wished to leave the allocation of capital to planners or nationalised industries. Others were willing to leave large parts of the economy in private hands, on condition that investment was not controlled by 'speculators' and financiers with the prospect of socially created wealth leading to large fortunes and 'luxury' consumption. Rather, decisions should be left to managers of large-scale concerns, who would have access to retained profits paying a lower level of tax than distributions to shareholders. Keynes argued in the 1920s that large-scale businesses, with their separation of ownership from control, gave power to career managers who acted more like public bodies, pursuing long-term strategies rather than the maximum profit for shareholders.[51] In the 1950s and 1960s, J. K. Galbraith presented a more pessimistic conclusion of the shift of industry from individuals to large corporations, which could shape tastes, control costs, devise new goods and so manipulate consumers who would lose their freedom and prefer private to public consumption.[52] But the corporations could also be viewed in a positive light, as rational and efficient, responding more effectively to price signals and new technology than their smaller competitors. Labour was more inclined to encourage growth through large corporations with an efficient use of retained profits, a strategy pursued after the Second World War and continued – somewhat fatalistically – by the Conservatives until 1958.

Whether the outcome was productive efficiency was a moot point. It might lead, as Edward Heath* remarked, to the survival of the fattest and

---

[50] Tomlinson, 'Planning'; see also J. E. Meade, *Efficiency, Equality and the Ownership of Property* (London, 1964), which continues his earlier concern with the role of prices both to allocate goods in the most efficient way, and to deal with the distribution of rewards between individuals.

[51] J. M. Keynes, 'The end of laissez-faire', reprinted in his *Essays in Persuasion* (London, 1931), pp. 314–15.

[52] J. K. Galbraith, *The Affluent Society* (London, 1958), and *The New Industrial State* (London, 1967).

* Edward Heath (b. 1916) is the son of a carpenter and builder, educated at Oxford where he was opposed to appeasement; he served in the army in the Second World War and

not the fittest by allocating resources to existing concerns in established lines of business rather than to new ventures.[53] The fundamental question by the 1950s was whether the tax system was blocking incentive and change, and harming the worst-off or average members of society. The issue arose not in the highly abstract Rawlsian social contract behind a veil of ignorance, but in election campaigns involving the impact of taxes on individuals whose position in society was known. Voters were not asking whether payment of taxes and provision of welfare services would benefit the worst-off. They were not concerned by the prospect of falling into the ranks of the desperately poor, who could be defined as victims of their own fecklessness, undeserving of support from more responsible members of society. Attitudes would depend on a variety of circumstances. As we have noted, the distribution of income in itself affected the political response, depending on whether the income of the median voter was below or above the average. The economic climate would also have an impact. Economic insecurity – or the memory of insecurity in the recent past – might create a greater level of support for transfer payments to guard against risk; economic security and prosperity might lead to a preference for individual provision of welfare through private health care or pensions. In other words, individuals defined their risk pool and the limits of transfer of resources in different ways. A state health care system would offer all members of society the same basic level of provision. For the worst-off members of society, the result was better than they could otherwise hope to afford. However, better-off members of society might prefer to support a private insurance scheme which excluded certain categories of claimant, and secured a higher level of provision for themselves. Much the same applied to state versus private pension schemes.

---

then spent a period in the civil service and as a journalist before becoming a Conservative MP in 1950. He served in the whips' office from 1951 to 1959, becoming minister of labour 1959–60, lord privy seal 1960–3 (as chief negotiator of entry into the European Economic Community (EEC)) and president of the Board of Trade 1963–4, where he abolished resale price maintenance. He became leader in 1965, undertaking a thorough review of policy; he fought the election of 1970 on a free market programme. As prime minister from 1970 to 1974, he adopted a statutory incomes policy and intervention in industry, which he had earlier opposed. He succeeded in joining the EEC in 1973, but lost two elections in 1974 when he attempted to defeat the unions. In 1975, he was replaced as leader by Thatcher who adopted many of Heath's economic policies, with the huge exception of her animosity to the continued development of the Common Market into the European Union. (Crystal (ed.), *Cambridge Biographical Encyclopaedia*, p. 432; Robbins (ed.), *Biographical Dictionary*, pp. 194–8.)

[53] See K. Arrow, *The Limits of Organization* (New York, 1974), chapter 3, 'The agenda of organization'. Arrow feared that firms might be locked into a particular 'code' or agenda which was necessary to aid communication in a large organisation, but which might also prevent the acquisition of new information not easily fitted into the code. On Heath, see below, p. 319.

As more people moved into better-paid jobs with greater security, they might reject state provision – at the expense of the worst-off members of society.[54]

The impact of systems of welfare provision on efficiency and incentives was central to political debates. As a Liberal in the government of 1906, and as chancellor in the Conservative government of 1924–9, Winston Churchill argued that social policy should encourage competition by providing a 'safety net' so that disaster did not ensue in the event of failure. The alternative, he feared, was a socialist attack on the capitalist social system. He attacked inherited wealth and wished to release active enterprise. During his administration of 1951–5, many Conservatives feared that high taxes were now destroying incentives and funding a welfare system which damaged self-sufficiency and responsibility. Perhaps the tax system should be redesigned to remove impediments to economic growth. This concern was part of a wider debate from the late 1950s about the need to 'modernise' the economy. The fundamental question was how this should be achieved, if indeed it could be without upsetting the established balance of interests and forces. Conservatives might, as a matter of principle, favour incentives to encourage efficiency and believe that the market would allocate resources efficiently. However, at this stage few Conservatives proposed a radical change to escape the existing pattern of high taxes, loss of incentive and low growth. There was a widespread sense that an attempt to increase incentives by reducing the upper levels of income tax or cutting profits tax would create a serious political problem, making the Conservatives appear as a rich man's party and alienating the unions. At a time of full employment, organised workers might simply demand higher wages so leading to cost-push inflation and a further loss of competitiveness in export markets. One response was to create an *opportunity* state, without excluding anyone. Welfare costs might be moved from direct taxes to employers, to encourage them to use labour more efficiently, and high taxes on income and profits could be reduced by introducing indirect taxes. However, welfare benefits should be offered to the poor who would suffer from higher indirect taxes, at least until the higher rates of economic growth started to become apparent. This integrative package of reforms failed in the early 1970s, and when the Conservatives returned to power in 1979 it was replaced by a different approach – an *enterprise* state would be created by offering incentives, widening the income distribution, creating an active capital market and encouraging personal equity and welfare schemes, without offering benefits to those who were excluded from the new world. Such a

---

[54] For these issues, see P. Johnson, 'Risk, redistribution and social welfare in Britain from the poor law to Beveridge', in M. J. Daunton (ed.), *Charity, Self Interest and Welfare in the English Past* (London, 1996), pp. 225–48; and Baldwin, *Politics of Social Solidarity*.

strategy was feasible when the ability of workers to demand higher wages was eroded by unemployment and a change in bargaining rights, with rigid monetary controls over inflation.

The book ends with the major changes to the fiscal system of the Thatcher governments, but the issues have not disappeared. The studies of the late 1970s, with their complaints about an incoherent fiscal system, remain as relevant now as when they were first published. The protests against fuel duty in September 2000 suggested that the move to indirect taxes has its limits – yet there has been little serious debate over how the tax system might be restructured. The Conservative opposition seized on popular resentment against fuel duties in order to propose cuts in taxes, yet at the same time many electors wished to spend more on health and education. The Labour government hesitated to justify high levels of fuel duty as an environmental tax, or to suggest a reform of the tax system as a whole. One possible response to the decline of support for spending, and the growth of hostility to taxing, is hypothecation, so that voters will support particular taxes for specific purposes – a way of increasing spending, which was exactly why Gladstone had been so hostile to the idea.[55] At the same time, there is some pressure for tax harmonisation within Europe – a potentially explosive issue. Fiscal politics are likely to be high on the agenda – and it is hoped that a historical account of how the present system evolved will help to inform the debate.

[55] Charles Kennedy to the Liberal Democrat conference in September 2000.

2   'The limits of our taxable capacity':
     war finance, 1914–1918

The main question whether resort should be had to loans or to taxes . . .
[is] to be considered with an eye partly to the present and partly to the
future. Statesmen, if they are worth the name, will measure the internal
as well as the external dangers to the society which they control. A
prolonged war may result in social chaos, ruin, and revolution at home.
Indeed, wars are frequently ended because the governments concerned
relinquish their desire to fight on for conquest or prestige through fear
that their own subjects, unable to endure more misery and want, will
rise up in revolt against them. There is a limit to human endurance and
to the economic misery which a state can inflict on its people.

F. W. Hirst, *The Political Economy of War* (London and Toronto, 1915),
p. 150

Hirst's dire prophecies were soon realised in Russia, where revolution
broke out within two years of his warning. In most other combatant nations, the problems were greatest *after* the war when the burdens of debt,
war pensions and reconstruction – and in the case of Germany, reparations – led to immense difficulties. In some ways, Britain was better
prepared in 1914 to deal with the burdens of war than other European
powers. The national debt had fallen over the previous century, and there
was confidence in the security of loans. Despite the costs of the Boer war,
the British national debt fell by 5 per cent between 1887 and 1913; in
France, it rose by 39 per cent and in Germany by 153 per cent. In 1913,
national debts were 27.6 per cent of net national product in Britain, compared with 86.5 per cent in France and 44.4 per cent in Germany. The
cost of debt service was low in Britain, and loans were readily obtained on
easy terms through the London capital market. This was reflected in the
difference in the yield on bonds in July 1914. The yield on French bonds
was about 0.6 per cent higher than on British bonds, and on German
bonds about 0.7 per cent higher, reflecting the market's assessment of
the fiscal policy and financial stability of the three countries.[1]

[1] N. Ferguson, *The Pity of War* (London, 1998), pp. 126–35.

The British income tax had a long history, and prewar reforms allowed chancellors to raise larger sums of money through a progressive tax regime. By contrast, the income tax in Germany was initially introduced by individual states who were jealous of their revenues and hostile to a Reich income tax. The Reich financed military spending from indirect taxes on imports and domestic consumption, allowing the Social Democratic party to seize on the regressive tax system as an issue. The Social Democratic party won the election in 1912 and formed an alliance with other parties to introduce a Reich income tax and to support increased military spending. But the new Reich income tax of 1913 led to state fears of loss of power, and it proved difficult to increase spending to any large extent. Although the situation in France was not complicated by tensions between central and regional government within a federal system, reform still proved difficult. In France, the proportion of revenue from direct taxes fell over the nineteenth century. These direct taxes were imposed on particular external signs of wealth and income; they were stereotyped and did not tap the growth of the economy in an effective way. However, it proved difficult to introduce a modern income tax, which was defeated in 1896, 1907 and 1911 by a combination of fear of socialist redistribution, self-interest to preserve existing low levels of direct taxes and hostility to the state. The measure finally passed in July 1914, and only came into effect in January 1916, so that France entered the war with an unreformed tax system.[2]

Before the First World War, Germany was militarily and industrially strong, but financially weak so that its defence spending was at the cost of serious political and social tensions. Britain was financially more powerful, able to raise loans on better terms, and with a reformed fiscal system. Of course, the Liberal tax reforms led to bitter political conflict, with constitutional crisis in 1909/10 over the taxes on land and problems in passing the budget in 1914.[3] The Conservatives had their own solution to the fiscal difficulties – tariff reform. But the disputes were less intense than in most European countries: the existence of a national income tax was never in dispute, and the crucial reforms to the income tax were generally accepted within the Treasury on pragmatic grounds. Britain's prewar

[2] Ferguson, *Pity of War*, chapter 5, and 'Public finance and national security'; Hobson, 'Military-extraction gap'; J. von Kruedener, 'The Franckenstein paradox in the intergovernmental relations of imperial Germany', in P.-C. Witt (ed.), *Wealth and Taxation in Central Europe: The History and Sociology of Public Finance* (Leamington Spa, 1987), pp. 111–23.

[3] B. K. Murray, *The People's Budget, 1909/10: Lloyd George and Liberal Politics* (Oxford, 1980); B. B. Gilbert, 'David Lloyd George: the reform of British land-holding and the budget of 1914', *Historical Journal* 21 (1978), 117–41.

financial superiority was not so apparent during the war when British taxation policy was 'scarcely less inadequate than the German'. After the war, a German economist – Robert Knauss – estimated that Britain met 20 per cent of its additional war expenditure from taxes compared with 6 per cent in Germany. Balderston believes that the discrepancy is overstated. On his revised estimates, tax revenues were 26.2 per cent of *total* government expenditure in the United Kingdom and 16.7 per cent in Germany (Reich and states). What stands out is a comparable reliance on loans – with the crucial difference that the domestic capital market was less able to absorb loans in Germany than in Britain, so creating greater inflationary pressure. The explanation for the divergence was in part that Britain was able to borrow abroad, and in part the greater ability of the London money market to absorb floating debt which was to be crucial in the postwar period.[4] Certainly, Britain's heavy reliance on loans during the First World War stands in stark contrast to its experience in earlier wars, as ministers and officials were well aware.

At the outbreak of the war, the Treasury presented Lloyd George with a series of memoranda on the finance of earlier wars which showed that 'the traditional policy of Great Britain has been to defray war expenditure as far as possible by increased taxation'. As R. G. Hawtrey* pointed out in 1917, taxation covered 47.1 per cent of the total cost of war with France between 1793 and 1815, rising to 86.6 per cent by 1815. In the Crimean war, taxes accounted for 52.6 per cent of expenditure.[5] During the First World War, the government relied on loans to a much greater extent than in either the wars with France or in the Crimea. This was apparent from the first war budget of Lloyd George in 1914. Although he increased taxes, a large deficit remained to be covered by borrowing and he was subsequently criticised for his caution and over-dependence on loans. How is this initial, and continuing, departure from Treasury precedent and principle to be understood?

[4] Balderston, 'War finance and inflation', 222–44; the estimate is from R. Knauss, *Die deutsche, englische und französische Kriegsfinanzierung* (Berlin and Leipzig, 1923), pp. 175–6.

[5] The earlier memorandum of 1900 was reissued: Public Record Office (PRO), T171/106 (and also T172/954), 'The financing of naval and military operations, 1793–1886', J. Bradbury, 12 Feb. 1900; T171/149, 'Pitt's war taxation', R. G. Hawtrey, 23 Sept. 1917; Knauss, *Kriegsfinanzierung*, pp. 175–6. On the earlier debates, see Daunton, *Trusting Leviathan*, p. 124.

* Ralph George Hawtrey (1879–1975) was educated at Eton and Trinity College, Cambridge, where he was elected an Apostle. He entered the civil service in 1903 and moved to the Treasury in 1904. He was appointed director of financial enquiries in 1919, the nearest the Treasury had to an economist, and remained until 1947. He was visiting professor of economics at Harvard in 1928–9, and from 1947 to 1952 was professor of international economics at the Royal Institute of International Affairs. (*DNB, 1971–80*, ed. R. Blake and C. S. Nicholls (Oxford, 1986), pp. 391–2.)

Partly, it reflected political circumstances at the outbreak of the war. In his last peace-time budget in 1914, Lloyd George planned a radical attack on land and large fortunes which he was forced to abandon by his more cautious colleagues.[6] Even so, he had a (merited) reputation for his creative use of the fiscal system in pursuit of political ideology. Not only the Conservatives but also some Liberals were uneasy about his reliability as a finance minister. His modest proposals (to later critics) were therefore attacked by the leader of the Conservative party, Andrew Bonar Law,* for going too far in raising taxes and courting 'bitter controversy'. In Bonar Law's view, 'the one important consideration was the easiest way which the large amount of money can be raised. The public I should think is not prepared for such heavy taxation as will be necessary and in my opinion the fact that such taxation is to be levied will seriously interfere with the floating of loans.'[7]

In 1915, Lloyd George continued on the same lines, opting for a policy of 'wait and see' until the summer campaign was over. He emphasised the constraints on financial policy. Any attempt to push taxes to higher levels seemed dangerous, for financial confidence was weak and should not be jeopardised. Inflationary pressure caused by borrowing was not a major concern, for he assumed that it could be kept under control by the automatic operations of the gold standard. In his view, the greater danger was *deflation*, a fear that seems curious in view of the inflationary pressure which was so obvious as the war proceeded. But the expectation in 1914 and early 1915 was that the war would disrupt trade, with mounting unemployment and falling working-class incomes. One result would be a fall in the yield of indirect taxes, which might be made good by introducing an income tax on small incomes – a proposal ruled out by administrative difficulties.[8] In other words, the sense of the fragility of

[6] Gilbert, 'David Lloyd George', 138–9.

[7] House of Lords Record Office, Bonar Law Papers, BL37/4/28, Bonar Law to Asquith, 16 Nov. 1914.

[8] PRO, T171/97, Nathan to Hamilton, 3 Aug. and 9 Sept. 1914, D. Shackleton, National Health Insurance Commission to C. F. G. Masterman, 3 Nov. 1914, 'Criticisms on a proposed scheme of raising an income tax from those who at present are exempt, by methods similar to or in association with the raising of the income on the national insurance fund', C. F. G. Masterman, 3 Nov. 1914; T170/12, Lord St Aldwyn's memorandum on Sir M. Nathan's income tax proposals; T170/12, copies of notes sent to the chancellor of the Exchequer: possible increases of existing duties, L. N. G. 21 Aug. 1914; T171/114, 'Income tax: proposals for lowering the limit of liability', 30 Apr. 1915; G. C. Peden, *The Treasury and Public Policy, 1906–1959* (Oxford, 2000), chapter 3.

* Andrew Bonar Law (1858–1923) was born in Canada, the son of a Presbyterian minister; he was brought up in Glasgow, where he entered business as a banker and iron merchant. He entered parliament in 1900 and became leader of the opposition in 1911. He strongly opposed Irish home rule. In 1915, he became secretary of state for the colonies in the coalition government; in 1916, he was invited to form an administration by George V,

Table 2.1 *Government income, 1914/15 to 1918/19*
(percentage of net receipts)

	Tax	Other receipts[a]	Borrowing
1914/15	29.7	5.8	64.5
1915/16	19.3	3.1	77.6
1916/17	23.3	2.7	74.0
1917/18	22.8	3.5	73.7
1918/19	30.5	4.1	65.4

[a] Post Office, contribution from India and other colonies.
Source: J. C. Stamp, *Taxation during the War* (London, 1932), appendix IV, p. 249.

the economy at the start of the war made Lloyd George cautious about any tax increase which might provide a 'shock' and exacerbate any downturn. At this stage, there was no suggestion that taxes should be increased to remove excess spending power from the economy in order to contain inflation and transfer resources to the government. The aim was 'business as usual'.

In any case, the costs of the war were expected to be modest. Britain entered the war with a 'limited liability' strategy dominated by three considerations. First, France and Russia would bear the brunt of the land war, with Britain providing sufficient money and munitions to prevent collapse. The British navy would meanwhile blockade Germany in order to destroy its economy. Secondly, the government feared economic collapse as a result of disruption to the financial system, with the possibility that discontented workers might force the government to make peace. Thirdly, the war was expected to be short. It followed that mobilisation could be confined to a small sector of the economy, which should be disrupted as little as possible to prevent collapse before victory was secured. Lloyd George's initial war budget reflected these assumptions. They were soon proved to be mistaken, for the blockade did not destroy the German economy and the British government was obliged to raise a large continental army.[9] The war become a very different affair, with major implications for fiscal policy.

but did not obtain support from Asquith or Lloyd George. He became chancellor of the Exchequer and leader of the Commons in Lloyd George's government. He was replaced as chancellor at the start of 1919, but continued as lord privy seal and leader of the Commons. He resigned in 1921 as a result of ill-health, but became Conservative prime minister in 1922–3 on the fall of the coalition. (*DNB, 1922–30*, ed. J. R. H. Weaver (London, 1937), pp. 483–92; Robbins (ed.), *Biographical Dictionary*, pp. 255–8.)

[9] D. W. French, *British Economic and Strategic Planning, 1905–15* (London, 1982), pp. 51, 74, 83, 85, 98, 119.

Lloyd George came to realise the need for full-scale mobilisation for war. In his new role as minister of munitions, he advocated the creation of a large army in the hope of victory in 1916, even at the cost of national bankruptcy. However, he was succeeded as chancellor of the Exchequer by Reginald McKenna,* who took the opposite side in the debate over strategic policy which divided the Cabinet. McKenna opposed the creation of a conscript army, favouring a 'long-haul war policy' as in the Napoleonic wars, based upon Britain's providing money and munitions as the 'economic powerhouse' of the allies.[10] His financial policy was therefore designed to constrain Lloyd George's ambitions. Above all, he attempted in his budget of September 1915 to produce a package of measures which would minimise tension and hostility from taxpayers.

The rate of income tax was increased and the exemption limit reduced from £160 to £130 with a cut in abatements. At a time of inflation and rising wages, a much larger proportion of the population became liable for income tax (see table 2.2). However, the impact of these changes was mitigated for married men with children by an increase in children's allowances; the bulk of the additional tax fell on single men and childless couples. Indirect taxes were raised, and Liberal tenets of free trade were breached with the imposition of duties on imported motor cars and films in order to save foreign currency and to reduce the consumption of luxuries. But the greatest novelty of the budget was an excess profits duty (EPD) of 50 per cent on profits above a prewar standard, which McKenna hoped would reduce social tensions by signalling an attack on profiteering. The fiscal impact of the budget was modest, for taxation was expected to rise from 17.0 per cent to 21.6 per cent of expenditure which was still well below the level of the Napoleonic wars. Subsequent increases in taxes covered only a small part of the mounting cost of the war, and war-time chancellors have been castigated by later historians for 'the half-heartedness with which they tackled the budgetary problem'.[11]

McKenna's fiscal policy rested on a new principle of war finance that informed policy for the rest of the war – the concept of the 'normal year'.

[10] D. W. French, *British Strategy and War Aims, 1914–16* (London, 1986), pp. 120–1, 244–9; D. W. French, *The Strategy of the Lloyd George Coalition* (Oxford, 1995), pp. 3–5.

[11] E. V. Morgan, *Studies in Financial Policy, 1914–25* (London, 1952), pp. 94–5: also French, *British Strategy*, p. 122, for McKenna's aim. On the budget, PRO, CAB37/134/14, 'War taxation', R. McKenna, 10 Sept. 1915.

* Reginald McKenna (1863–1943) was born in London, the son of a civil servant. He was educated at Trinity Hall, Cambridge, and was called to the bar in 1887. He was a Liberal MP from 1895 to 1918, serving as financial secretary to the Treasury 1905–7, president of the Board of Education 1907–8, first lord of the Admiralty 1908–11, home secretary 1911–15 and chancellor of the Exchequer 1915–16. From 1917 he was a director, and from 1919 to 1943, chairman of the Midland Bank. (*DNB, 1941–50*, ed. Legg and Williams, pp. 551–5.)

Table 2.2 *Individuals with total income above the
exemption limit for income tax, United Kingdom/Great
Britain and Northern Ireland, 1913 to 1937/8 (000)*

	Entirely relieved	Chargeable	Total
1913	70	1,130	1,200
1917/18	1,520	2,956	4,476
1919/20	3,900	3,900	7,800
1922/3	2,700	2,375	5,075
1930/1	2,900	2,200	5,100
1937/8	6,000	3,700	9,700

Source: PP 1921 xiv, *64th Report of the Commissioners of Inland Revenue
for the year ended 31 March 1921*, p. 114; PP 1929–30 xv, *72nd Report
of the Commissioners of Inland Revenue for the year ended 1928/29*, p. 74;
PP 1938–9 xii, *82nd Report of the Commissioners of Inland Revenue for
the year ended 31 March 1939*, p. 57.

It was, in the opinion of E. V. Morgan, 'one of the strangest principles
ever laid down in the history of public finance', and it certainly marked
a departure from earlier policies.[12] McKenna argued that the revenue
raised by permanent taxes (that is, excluding temporary measures such
as the EPD) should cover interest on loans and sinking fund payments,
plus ordinary peace-time expenditure based on the level at the start of
the war. McKenna therefore departed from Gladstonian fiscal orthodoxy
that expenditure should as far as possible be met out of taxes, for the
concept of the normal year assumed that the war would be largely financed from loans. The contribution of taxation to the current costs of
the war would be limited to exceptional taxes and especially the EPD.[13]
McKenna's policy merely postponed the day of fiscal reckoning, but it
did have a clear rationale. On the one hand, the concept of the 'normal
year' complemented McKenna's assumption that the war would be long.
On the other hand, it rested on a political assessment of the taxable capacity of the country. He believed that the country had reached the limits
of taxation:

it would be a mistake to drive this spirit of public sacrifice too hard . . . I know
there are advocates of heroic taxation . . . , but I am not sure that these persons
are fully apprised of the immense difficulty which large classes amongst us have
today in maintaining not the pre-War standard of their life, but such a standard
of life as is necessary in their circumstances for the maintenance of efficiency.[14]

[12] Morgan, *Studies*, pp. 92–3.
[13] *Parliamentary Debates, Commons*, 5th ser. 81, 4 Apr. 1916, cols. 1054–6.
[14] Morgan, *Studies*, pp. 92–3; M. E. Short, 'The politics of personal taxation: budget-
making in Britain, 1917–31', PhD thesis, Cambridge, 1985, p. 9; *Parliamentary Debates,*

He was applying peace-time assumptions about the even-handedness of the tax system and the need for equality in the burden of taxes between different classes and income levels. Of course, McKenna's argument was somewhat disingenuous, for reliance on loans and inflation produced massive distortions between interests and social classes which led to serious difficulties as the war progressed.

On the whole, the Treasury accepted McKenna's logic and John Bradbury,* the dominant voice at the Treasury during the war, did not provide a sustained argument in favour of orthodoxy. Bradbury accepted that additional taxation could provide only a 'relatively negligible' portion of revenue for the war, and that an increase in the rate of income tax would merely reduce the amount available for loans. He was not convinced that it was possible to increase taxation sufficiently to meet even the dictates of the normal year, for 'we are now approaching so nearly towards the limit of our taxable capacity'. The important point was to get as close as possible to the level of taxation required by the normal year 'in the interests of maintaining our credit with a view to future borrowing'. Bradbury was also concerned that civilian consumption in Britain had increased, placing strain on the economy's capacity to export in order to pay for goods from America. The solution adopted in the Second World War was to use taxes to remove excess civilian spending and to release production for war goods and exports – at the same time controlling inflation. Bradbury's approach was very different. He argued that *inflation* offered the best way of reducing consumption and releasing material resources for the war. Inflation would erode real earnings and therefore reduce civil consumption. He was confident that the sacrifices of inflation would be accepted – on condition that taxation of war profits created a sense of equity.[15]

Commons, 5th ser. 81, 4 Apr. 1916, col. 1055; on his assumption that the war would be long, see French, *British Strategy*, pp. 120–1.

[15] PRO, CAB37/126/12 and T171/110, 'The war and finance', J. Bradbury, 17 Mar. 1915; T171/138, budget 1917/18, J. Bradbury, 13 Apr. 1917; also see T172/274 for one dissenting voice in the Treasury in 1919; T170/84, J. Bradbury, 6 Jan. 1916.

* John Swanwick Bradbury (1872–1950) was born in Cheshire, the son of an oil merchant. He was educated at Manchester Grammar School and Brasenose College, Oxford, joining the Colonial Office in 1896 and then the Treasury. He became private secretary to Asquith in 1905, and in 1908 became head of one of the divisions of the Treasury. He worked on the 1909 budget, planned the finances of the health insurance scheme and served as insurance commissioner from 1911 to 1913. He was joint permanent secretary of the Treasury from 1913 to 1919, with responsibility for finance. He left the Treasury to serve as delegate to the Reparation Committee 1919–25; he was chairman of the Food Council 1925–9 and also a director (for the government) of the Anglo-Persian Oil Co. He was a member of the Macmillan committee on finance and industry 1929–31; his dissenting memorandum argued for strict economy in public expenditure. (*DNB, 1941–50*, ed. Legg and Williams, pp. 98–9.)

These hopes were soon disappointed, for the outcome was rampant inflation, a deterioration in labour relations as workers attempted to increase their wages and mounting resentment against war profiteers. Bradbury's easy acceptance of inflation was misplaced. Far from making resources available for the government, it simply forced the government to pay higher prices in competition with private consumers, and reliance on loans led to serious problems of servicing the debt after the war. The policy adopted by McKenna and Bradbury seems misplaced in the light of later experience in the Second World War, and it might be thought that criticism reflects the benefit of hindsight. However, the policy faced powerful criticism at the time, particularly from George Paish* and John Maynard Keynes† who urged the use of taxation or forced savings to reduce consumption. Keynes feared that inflation would be more disastrous for the 'open' British economy than the 'closed' German economy. The German government could obtain goods and labour by expanding credit, and prices could rise without a financial catastrophe. By contrast, additional spending power in the 'open' British economy would lead to an increase in imports or a cut in exports, and produce a serious problem in international finance. Keynes therefore advocated a tax on some basic necessity in order to remove the excess spending power of small wage-earners who did not contribute to loans and were not affected by direct taxation.[16] The pleas of Paish and Keynes were supported by a deputation of bankers, who argued for higher taxes to reduce consumption and to

---

[16] On George Paish, PRO, T171/110, 'The finance of Great Britain', G. Paish, n.d.; CAB37/134/12 and T170/85, 'Cabinet paper on financial prospects of this financial year', J. M. Keynes, 9 Sept. 1915; T170/73, 'The meaning of inflation', J. M. Keynes, 15 Sept. 1915; see also *The Collected Writings of John Maynard Keynes*, vol. XVI: *Activities 1914–1919: The Treaty and Versailles*, ed. E. Johnson (London, 1971), pp. 117–28; T171/116, 'A tax on meat', J. M. Keynes, 2 Sept. 1915. Note Keynes's proposals during the Second World War, below, p. 182.

* George Paish (1867–1957) was on the staff of the *Statist* from 1881, serving as joint editor from 1900 to 1916. He was a member of the departmental committee of the Board of Trade on railway accounts and statistics 1906–8, and adviser to the chancellor of the Exchequer and Treasury from 1914 to 1916. (*Who Was Who*, vol. V: *1951–60* (London, 1961), pp. 843–4.)

† John Maynard Keynes (1883–1946) was born in Cambridge, and educated at Eton and King's College, Cambridge. He worked in the India Office from 1906 to 1908, returning to Cambridge as a lecturer in economics from 1908, and serving as a member of the Royal Commission on Indian Finance and Currency in 1913–14. He joined the Treasury in 1915 and served at the peace conference in 1919, from which he resigned over the issue of reparations. He was involved with the Liberal party, in particular in the programme of public works and reform proposed in 1929; and he served on the Committee on Finance and Industry 1929–31. His *General Theory of Employment, Interest and Money* appeared in 1936. In 1940, he returned to the Treasury, and he played a leading part in the conference at Bretton Woods in 1944 which created postwar financial institutions. (*DNB, 1941–50*, ed. Legg and Williams, pp. 452–7.)

increase the share of taxation to a third of the cost of the war. As Bradbury remarked with sarcastic contempt, 'the Chancellor of the Exchequer can go cheerfully ahead knowing that for the first time in the history of his office he has been invited by the people to lay further fiscal burdens upon them . . . He cannot make a mistake, because if he taxes too much for revenue purposes he will thereby check spending all the more.'[17] It was a temptation which McKenna and the Treasury preferred to avoid.

The explanation was in part political expediency. Any scheme designed to remove spending power would necessarily apply to 'articles consumed by the many, not to the luxuries of the few'[18] and would immediately pose serious political problems. One method of taxing 'necessities' would be through 'a widespread customs tariff framed on "scientific" lines' which would reopen the contentious issues of free trade versus tariff reform. This was a defining issue in prewar politics, and it would be extremely difficult for the Liberals to surrender their cherished beliefs. Although McKenna did introduce some import duties in 1915, they were confined to specific goods and were justified as an attempt to ration the consumption of imported luxuries rather than to transfer spending power to the government. Indeed, McKenna claimed (perhaps disingenuously) that he was imposing the duties merely to expose the limitations of the policy of protection. He realised that the duties would neither reduce imports nor produce much revenue, and he hoped that their failure 'would be a good object lesson as to the impossibility of tariffs in this country'.[19] This might have been an astute and cynical attempt to justify his apparent breach of free trade – what is significant is that he needed the justification, and was limited in his freedom of action by the highly contentious nature of trade policy. As the Treasury realised, 'superfluous spending power' could only be removed by imposing either a general *ad valorem* duty on imports or a sales tax. Both were rejected because of doubts about administrative viability, the threat to consent and the problems of imposing duties at a time of rampant inflation with the prospect of further

---

[17] PRO, T170/88, 'Suggestions for further taxation'. This was sent in on the suggestion of Harmsworth, and submitted to Lloyd George by Hartley Withers of the Treasury: it proposed a doubling of all taxes and an excess profits tax of 10s or 15s in each £ of excess income.

[18] PRO, T171/117, 'Memorandum on the suggested increase of customs and excise taxation', H. V. R., 28 Aug. 1915; T171/126, 'Memorandum on the possibility of increasing the revenue from customs and excise duties', Aug. 1915; T171/130, 'Taxation aimed at reducing expenditure: suggestions by the Board of Customs and Excise', Dec. 1915.

[19] Churchill College Archives, McKenna MSS 5/10, Mond to McKenna, 14 Oct. 1915, f. 7. Mond was reporting McKenna's view and disagreeing with him, arguing both that the duties would offend free traders, and that their failure would have no impact on tariff reformers since they had not backed McKenna's duties.

Table 2.3 *Direct and indirect taxes, 1913/14 to 1929/30 (percentage)*

	Direct	Indirect
1913/14	57.5	42.5
1919/20	75.1	24.9
1924/5	66.9	33.1
1929/30	64.2	35.9

Source: PRO, T171/232, 235, and IR113/42.

Table 2.4 *Structure of central government revenue: net receipts due to the Exchequer, 1913/14 and 1919/20 (percentage)*

	1913/14	1919/20
Income tax and super-tax	29.0	35.9
EPD/munitions levy	–	28.9
Death duties	16.7	4.3
Stamps	6.1	2.3
House duty	1.2	0.2
Land tax/land value duties	0.9	0.1
Customs	21.8	14.9
Excise	24.3	13.4
Total	100.0	100.0

Source: PP 1914 L, *Finance Accounts of the UK for 1913–14*, pp. 20–1; PP 1920 XXVII, *Finance Accounts of the UK for the year ended 31 March 1920*, pp. 16–17.

deterioration in labour relations.[20] Consequently, the fiscal system was to shift even further towards direct taxes and away from indirect taxes (see tables 2.2 and 2.3).

The alternative to indirect taxation as a means of containing consumption and transferring surplus income to the government was to impose direct taxes on lower incomes. By reducing the level of exemption from income tax from £160 to £130 at a time of rapid inflation, a large number of lower-middle- and working-class incomes came within the reach of the Inland Revenue – an increase of more than six-fold in incomes above the

[20] PRO, T171/130, H. F., 14 Feb. 1916; T171/139, G. R. Hamilton to E. W. Hamilton, 9 Mar. 1917; LNG (Customs) to J. Bradbury, 12 Apr. 1917; Bradbury to Byrne, 7 Apr. 1917; 'Proposal to tax all retail purchases with certain exceptions', 12 Apr. 1917.

Table 2.5 *Income tax allowances and rate, 1913/14 and 1918/19*

	1913/14	1918/19
Exemption limit	£160	£130
Standard rate	5.8 per cent	30 per cent
Reduced rate	3.8 per cent on £160–£2,000	11.3 per cent on £130–£500
On earned income	5 per cent on £2,000–£3,000	15 per cent on £500–£1,000
	then normal rate	18.8 per cent on £1,000–£1,500
		22.5 per cent on £1,500–£2,000
		26.3 per cent on £2,000–£2,500
Surtax	Exceeding £5,000	Exceeding £2,000
	2.5 per cent above £3,000	5 per cent to £2,500
		7.5 per cent to £3,000
		10 per cent to £4,000
		12.5 per cent to £5,000
		15 per cent to £6,000
		17.5 per cent to £8,000
		20 per cent to £10,000
		22.5 per cent over £10,000
Abatements		£120 on incomes £130–£160
	£160 on incomes £160–£400	£120 on incomes £160–£400
	£150 on incomes £400–£500	£100 on incomes £400–£500
	£120 on incomes £500–£600	£100 on incomes £500–£600
	£70 on incomes £600–£700	£70 on incomes £600–£700
Children	£10 per child, incomes of	£25 per child, incomes £130–£800
	£160–£500	£25 on second child and above,
		incomes of £800–£1,000
Wife	None	£25 on incomes £160–£800
Dependent relatives	None	£25 on incomes £160–£800

Source: PP 1921 XIV, *64th Report of the Commissioners of Inland Revenue for the year ended 31 March 1921*, pp. 532–3, 540–1, 571.

threshold, and three and a half times in the number actually paying (see table 2.2). In 1919/20, of the 7,800,000 incomes above the exemption limit, 3,490,000 fell between the old and new limits, and 980,000 were actually liable to pay tax. Many of the smaller incomes were relieved of tax by various allowances, so that most of the burden fell on single incomes – but even so, more people came within the reach of the Inland Revenue. And those who paid tax did so at a much higher rate, which rose from a standard rate of 5.8 per cent in 1913/14 to 30 per cent between 1918/19 and 1921/2 (see table 2.5).[21]

[21] PP 1921 XIV, *64th Report of the Commissioners of Inland Revenue for the year ended 31 March 1921*, tables 67 and 68, pp. 550, 552; *Appendices to the Report of the Committee on National Debt and Taxation* (London, 1927), appendix XIV, 'Income tax and supertax structures

The extension of the income tax to more people and to small incomes meant that it might lose its widespread legitimacy and consent. The collection of tax from small incomes created difficulties, for manual workers were paid weekly, fluctuating wages. Clearly, collection of the tax in an annual lump sum would impose strains on working-class budgets and payment in instalments also created difficulties in estimating deductions and making adjustments at the end of the year. Since 1842, administration of the income tax relied heavily on commissioners drawn from the local middle class, which helped to create consent by taxpayers drawn from businessmen and professionals. But it was one thing for members of the local elite to assess each other in order to maintain consent; it was quite another to give local employers (or their associates) power over workers within the fiscal system. Any suggestion that tax should be deducted from wages was resisted by union officials as well as by employers who foresaw a threat to relations with the workforce as well as additional administrative burdens. The solution was to collect the tax directly from workers, and to involve their representatives in its administration. Nevertheless, serious problems of compliance ensued; in particular, miners in south Wales resented payment. In 1917, the miners' union demanded the reinstatement of the previous exemption limit of £160 in order to reduce the demands on working men at a time of inflation – and in at least one area of the coalfield, about 8,000 out of 71,000 miners refused to fill in their tax returns and withdrew the 'subcollectors' appointed to collect the tax. In 1919, the South Wales Miners' Federation voted for a tax 'strike'. Of course, the Inland Revenue and the chancellor of the Exchequer could argue that the children's allowances meant that most of the burden fell on bachelors who were able to pay – and also that they needed to show that all classes were contributing to the needs of the state. In fact, the problem largely disappeared after the war as the number liable to income tax was reduced.[22]

(1919–20) relating to various classes', pp. 128–9; Short, 'Politics of personal taxation', pp. 93–147; B. O. Mallet and C. O. George, *British Budgets, Second Series, 1913/14 to 1920/1* (London, 1929), pp. 320–33, 395–401.

22 PRO, T172/504, income tax: deputation from the Miners' Federation of Great Britain to the chancellor of the Exchequer, 29 Aug. 1917; T172/982, E. E. Nott-Bower and N. F. W. Fisher to chancellor, 20 Aug. 1917; G. R. Stenson, inspector of taxes, to chairman, Inland Revenue, 19 Aug. 1917; G. R. Stenson to deputy chairman, Inland Revenue, 7 Sept. 1917; income tax abatement: deputation from the South Wales Miners' Federation to the chancellor of the Exchequer, 20 Sept. 1917; G. R. Stenson to Verity, 3 Dec. 1919; T172/1000, deputation from the Triple Alliance to A. Chamberlain, 4 July 1919; PP 1920 xviii, *Report of the Royal Commission on the Income Tax*, pp. 211–13; Modern Record Centre, University of Warwick (MRC), TUC MSS 292/411/3, conference at Treasury, 4 Dec. 1915; R. C. Whiting, 'Taxation and the working class, 1915–24', *Historical Journal*, 33 (1990), 895–916.

The Labour party argued that expenditure should be covered from current income, but its support of Gladstonian fiscal orthodoxy created problems. What type of tax should be levied? Labour felt that the extraction of surplus spending power should not involve taxation of the working class – so contradicting the reasonable assumption of Keynes that it was the only way of removing excess consumption. Rather, Labour argued that industries should be controlled to prevent large private profits, with a higher level of tax on war profits of 80 per cent.[23] In 1916, Ramsay MacDonald* proposed a heavy graduated tax on large incomes, a special tax on land values, an increase in death duties on large estates, a graduated tax on capital and nationalisation of railways, mines, shipping, banking and insurance.[24] Meanwhile, the War Emergency Workers' National Committee (WEWNC) and the TUC developed the policy which formed the basis of Labour's postwar strategy: the conscription of wealth or a levy on capital.

The policy had its origins in 1915, when Ben Tillett[†] – the union leader and staunch supporter of the war – called for the 'conscription of riches' as a counterpoint to the sacrifices of men volunteering for the armed forces. 'The landed gentry had given their sons nobly and freely with the industrial classes', he argued, 'but the capitalist class were sitting at home in comfort and security behind the bodies of better men than themselves.'[25]

---

[23] J. C. Stamp, *Taxation during the War* (London, 1932), pp. 52–5, summarises Labour views in the Commons debate on the excess profits tax.

[24] *Report of the Annual Conference of the Labour Party 1916* (London, 1916), p. 135.

[25] 'Mr Ben Tillett's warning', *Times*, 26 July 1915, cited in R. Harrison, 'The War Emergency Workers' National Committee, 1914–20', in A. Briggs and J. Saville (eds.), *Essays in Labour History, 1886–1923* (London, 1971), p. 219.

* James Ramsay MacDonald (1866–1937) was born in Lossiemouth, the illegitimate son of a ploughman. He became a pupil teacher, moving to Bristol where he joined the SDF and then to London as a clerk. He was private secretary to a Liberal candidate from 1888 to 1891; he continued to be involved with the Social Democratic Federation (SDF), but also joined the Fabians in 1886 and the ILP in 1894. His marriage to the daughter of a leading scientist and philanthropist gave him financial independence and contact with the upper middle class. He was secretary of the Labour Representation Committee (LRC) from 1900, and treasurer from 1912 to 1924, and chairman of the ILP 1906–9. He was a Labour MP from 1906 to 1918, serving as leader of the parliamentary party from 1911. He opposed the war, and resigned as leader; he lost his seat in 1918. He returned to parliament in 1922 and became leader and first Labour prime minister in 1924 and 1929–31, before splitting the party over the formation of the national government. (*DNB, 1931–40*, ed. L. G. Wickham Legg (London, 1949), pp. 562–70; Robbins (ed.), *Biographical Dictionary*, pp. 277–81.)

† Ben Tillett (1860–1943) was the founder of the Dockers' Union in 1887, and was secretary until it became part of the Transport and General Workers' Union in 1922. He led the London dockers' strike in 1889, and was one of the creators of the National Transport Workers' Federation in 1910. He was a Labour MP from 1917 to 1924 and 1929 to 1931, and a member of the General Council of the TUC from 1921 to 1931. (*DNB, 1941–50*, ed. Legg and Williams, pp. 884–6.)

His case was strengthened by the introduction of conscription in 1916 which led the WEWNC to demand the 'natural corollary' of conscription of 'accumulated wealth' in order to pay for the war. Such a policy would 'avoid borrowing huge loans upon which enormous sums will have to be paid in interest by future generations, which will handicap the industries of the country in national and international competition, diminish trade, and impoverish the people'.[26] Their case rested on the contrast between conscripts who faced uncertainty in finding work, even assuming they escaped death or injury, and the rich who would enjoy their accumulated wealth as a result of the sacrifice of others. This inequity could only be made worse by burdening the working class with interest payments in order to sustain passive *rentiers*. As one union delegate informed the chancellor of the Exchequer, 'a great war loan is a wonderful system of outdoor relief for capitalist classes which does not carry with it a stigma of pauperism. It is a means whereby they can continue in their present position without having to do any more work than they and their descendants are disposed to do in the century to come.'[27] The capital levy formed a central element in Labour's election campaigns in 1919 and 1923: it was argued that a one-off graduated levy on personal capital in excess of £1,000 or £5,000 (the starting point was a matter for debate) would raise around £3,000m, reducing the cost of servicing the debt by about £150m, and allowing both a reduction in taxation and an increase in social expenditure.[28]

The proposal arose from war-time grievances against war profiteers and inflation, but owed much to Labour's prewar attack on 'accumulated' and socially created wealth. This rested on the notion of Rent, a concept developed by David Ricardo in the early nineteenth century with respect to land. As prices rose, farmers would move to marginal land with low productivity, and would pay just enough to their landlords to make a normal level of profits. Meanwhile, farmers on more fertile land would make a higher rate of profit – but this would soon pass to their landlords who would be able to charge more for the land as a result of competition from farmers. This difference between the normal and the higher rate of profit

[26] Harrison, 'War Emergency Workers' National Committee', p. 247; PRO, T172/639, copy of TUC resolution, Birmingham, Sept. 1916.

[27] PRO, T172/167, deputation from the TUC Birmingham to the chancellor of the Exchequer, 9 Feb. 1917; *Labour Party: Report of the Nineteenth Annual Conference, 1919* (London, 1919), pp. 146–9, 155.

[28] PRO, T172/167, deputation from the TUC Birmingham to the chancellor of the Exchequer, 9 Feb. 1917; *Labour Party Annual Conference, 1919*, pp. 146–9, 155; *Report of the Twenty-Third Annual Conference of the Labour Party, 1923* (London, 1923), pp. 177, 213–16; Labour Party Archive (LPA), JSM/FIN/23, G. D. H. Cole to A. Henderson, 28 May 1919; JSM/FIN/44, Labour Party Advisory Committee on Trade Policy and Finance.

was economic or Ricardian Rent, and was not 'earned' by the farmer or the landowner.[29] At the end of the century, Sidney Webb* extended this definition of Rent to cover interest, wages, salaries and profits as well as land, arguing that all were determined in the same way, and that all who drew such incomes were *rentiers*. The normal economic wage was derived by the most unskilled worker at the margin of cultivation with minimal capital; anything above this was Rent. Although the higher incomes of some workers might be explained in part by ability, any variation in the rate of return to *capital* was the result of 'opportunity' or chance, and was therefore an 'unearned' income received without commensurate work. In capitalist societies, many incomes were unethical and allowed consumption of goods and services without producing an equivalent amount for the community. Scarce ability was also socially created, so that solicitors received a higher income because of restrictions in the number of places for the children of the poor at grammar schools or university.[30] Webb's definition of Rent provided 'an ethical touchstone for evaluating the wealth and income of every man'. It was based upon 'a substitution of the motive of public service for the motive of self-enrichment . . . which will make "living by owning" as shameful as the pauperism of the wastrel'. On the one side, there was the socially undesirable, parasitic class made up of the 'functionless rich – of persons who deliberately live by owning instead of by working, and whose futile occupations, often licentious

[29] See D. Ricardo, *On the Principles of Political Economy and Taxation* (1817), ed. P. Sraffa (Cambridge, 1951).

[30] S. Webb, 'The rate of interest and the laws of distribution', *Quarterly Journal of Economics* 2 (1887–8), 200, 208, and 'The rate of interest', *Quarterly Journal of Economics* 2 (1887–8), 472. See also Thompson, 'Hobson and the Fabians', 203–20. For the development of Fabian notions of Rent, see for example Fabian Society, *Capital and Land* (Fabian Tract 7, London, 1888); *English Progress Towards Social Democracy* (Fabian Tract 15, London, 1890); *The Unearned Increment* (Fabian Tract 30, London, 1891); *The Difficulties of Individualism* (Fabian Tract 69, London, 1896); *Socialism and Superior Brains* (Fabian Tract 146, London, 1909); and S. and B. Webb, *Problems of Modern Industry* (London, 1898), p. 472.

* Sidney James Webb (1859–1947) was born in London; his father was a public accountant and his mother a hairdresser. He was educated at the Birkbeck Institute and City of London College, working as a clerk in the City in 1875–8 and then in the civil service 1878–91. He was called to the bar in 1885, when he joined the Fabian Society, and was a member of the London County Council (LCC) from 1892 to 1910. In 1892 he married Martha Beatrice Potter (1858–1943), the daughter of a wealthy industrialist. They wrote *History of Trade Unionism* (1894), *Industrial Democracy* (1897) and the history of English local government. They founded the LSE in 1895 and drafted the minority report of the Royal Commission on the Poor Laws, 1909. Sidney was on the executive of the Labour party from 1915 to 1925 and drafted *Labour and the New Social Order* (1918). He was a Labour MP 1920–9 and was then made a peer. He was president of the Board of Trade in 1924, and secretary of state for the dominions and colonies 1929–31. (*DNB, 1941–50*, ed. Legg and Williams, pp. 935–40; Robbins (ed.), *Biographical Dictionary*, pp. 411–14.)

pleasures and inherently insolent manners, undermine the intellectual and moral standards of the community'. These people had accepted the immoral and 'morbid obsession' which had dominated western Europe for the past 300 years, that 'man in society is and should be inspired, in the exercise of his function, by the passion for riches'. On the other side were people who made a contribution to society, to whom Rents should be reallocated. Ethically unearned income and wealth should be taken by the government, as the collective property of the English nation rather than individuals.[31]

In the nineteenth century, the concern of politicians was to ensure that the tax system was equitable, which was interpreted as imposing taxes according to ability or capacity. Of course, the definition of ability changed, away from an assumption that all should pay the same proportion of their income to a greater concern for the marginal burden of taxes at different levels of income. In the twentieth century, the Labour party was taking the argument a stage further, away from the equity of the tax system itself and the ability of citizens to pay, to a greater concern for the fairness of the distribution of wealth and income, and the morality of capitalism as an economic system. Attention turned from the equity of the tax system to issues of equality and the use of the fiscal system to alter the structure of society. The question facing the Labour party was the extent to which taxation could overcome the flaws of competitive capitalism, or whether the entire economic and social system should be reconstructed on a new basis. There was common agreement in the Labour party on the need to acquire unearned or socially created wealth for the community, and to bring remuneration into line with service. But members of the party differed over the extent to which reform was compatible with private ownership: should the taxes be used to create distributive justice within a free market; or were they to be used to *replace* the free market and capitalism by a new social order? The result was an unresolved ambiguity within the Labour party, which persisted throughout the rest of the century.

At the LRC's first annual conference in 1901, an ILP motion was accepted as a test for all candidates: privately owned capital had an inevitable tendency to monopoly, and private control was 'disastrous to the welfare of the consuming public, inimical to the social and political freedom of the people, and especially injurious to the industrial liberty and economic condition of the workers'. The solution proposed by the

---

[31] D. M. Ricci, 'Fabian socialism: a theory of rent as exploitation', *Journal of British Studies* 9 (1969–70), 105–21; also W. Wolfe, *From Radicalism to Socialism: Men and Ideas in the Formation of Fabian Socialist Doctrine, 1881–9* (New Haven, 1975); S. and B. Webb, *A Constitution for the Socialist Commonwealth of Great Britain* (London, 1920), pp. xii, 80, 350–1.

ILP was to transfer private monopolies to public control in 'an Industrial Commonwealth founded upon the common ownership and control of land and capital and the substitution of co-operative production for use in place of the present method of competitive production for profit'. The Marxist SDF added a further condition, that candidates should recognise 'class war as the basis of working-class political action'.[32] In 1909, one ILP MP adopted the labour theory of value, arguing that 'labour was the source of all wealth; and all the capital accumulated in private hands was the result of the unpaid labour of past generations of workmen and ought to be transferred to the National Exchequer'.[33] The rhetoric was dangerous, for it threatened to marginalise Labour as a special interest against the public and property; the success of the party was more likely to rest on its ability to portray itself as the guardian of the national interest against waste and exploitation. Party policy was therefore ambivalent.

The Labour party attempted to define its policy on taxation at the annual conference in 1906. Taxation to cover the costs of social reform should be shifted away from 'the industrious classes' to 'socially created wealth such as rent and interest', in order to 'secure for the community all unearned incomes derived from what is in reality communal wealth'. The ILP sponsor of the resolution went a stage further to suggest that taxation would help transfer capital and land to public ownership. A similar ambivalence appeared in January 1909 when Labour called a special conference to define tax policy more precisely. As Philip Snowden* argued,

Every question of reform was, at the bottom, a question of a more equitable and just distribution of wealth. What was meant by Social Reform, and what they who were Socialists meant by Socialism, was to secure for the wealth producers the use and enjoyment of the wealth which they produced. Our purpose, therefore, should be to see that social reforms were carried out in such a way that the people would receive the use and enjoyment of some part of that wealth which at the present time was unjustly taken from them; and . . . we had in the instrument of taxation a very potent means to that end.

---

[32] *Report of the First Annual Conference of the Labour Representation Committee, 1901* (London, 1901), pp. 20–1.

[33] *The Labour Party: Ninth Annual Conference, 1909* (London, 1909), appendix II, 'The incidence of taxation', report of conference, p. 109.

* Philip Snowden (1864–1937) was born in the West Riding of Yorkshire, the son of a weaver; he grew up in a radical, methodist *milieu* with strong admiration for Gladstone and Liberal radicalism. He became a pupil teacher and insurance clerk, before joining the excise service in 1886. He was invalided out of the service, and he became active in the ILP, serving as chairman of the party 1903–6 and 1917–20. He was MP for Blackburn from 1906 to 1918; he opposed the war, arguing for a negotiated peace and a capital levy. He lost his seat in 1918. He returned to parliament in 1922, and served as chancellor of the Exchequer in the first two Labour governments, and as lord privy seal in the national government. He remained a commited free trader. (*DNB, 1931–40*, ed. Legg, pp. 822–5; Robbins (ed.), *Biographical Dictionary*, pp. 378–82.)

Poverty was the direct result of the 'idle rich', drawing unearned rent, interest and profit. Did this entail an attack on all private property and capitalism? Ramsay MacDonald was careful to remove any such fear, arguing that the fundamental aim of Labour taxation was to 'tax the parasite and not persons who gave service'. In his view, the problem was not riches as such – it was whether the money was earned or acquired from the labour of others:

We wanted to divide the non-producing parasite dependent upon society from the producer and the service giver; and we wanted to direct our attention to the pockets of the person who did nothing and had much, and direct it away from the pockets of the person who might possess something but gave much service . . . [T]he Labour party stood for relieving as much as possible the financial burdens on industry.

Such an approach avoided a simple divide between workers and capital, and instead made a distinction between parasites who lived 'artificial lives' and producers, so converting the sectional interests of labour into the wider interests of the public at large. However, the rhetoric of a producers' alliance against parasites was weakened by the fear that it was simply a device to destroy private ownership, so alienating producers and driving them into the arms of the Conservatives in defence of property in general. There was an unresolved tension within the party about its desire to reform or to destroy capitalism and private property.[34]

The capital levy offered a means of implementing Labour's resolution in 1909 that 'taxation should aim at securing the unearned increment of wealth for communal use; therefore taxation should be levied on unearned incomes and should aim deliberately at preventing the retention of great fortunes in private hands'.[35] It also offered Labour and independent Liberals an issue which distinguished them from the coalition government. Far more than a means of obtaining revenue, it provided an emotive, moral attack on unearned wealth and on profiteers who remained at home under the protection of those who risked their lives in defence of their country. The rhetoric was particularly appealing as a way of defusing criticism of the Labour party as an unpatriotic party, for many members – including Ramsay MacDonald – opposed the war. The party was also open to the charge of being selfish in its pursuit of the interests of workers who were disrupting the war effort by strikes and wage demands. One response was to stress that workers made patriotic

[34] *Labour Party Annual Conference, 1909*, appendix II, 'The incidence of taxation', report of conference, pp. 104–8.
[35] P. Snowden, *Labour and National Finance* (London, 1920), p. 41.

sacrifices for victory and were morally superior to other selfish members of society.[36]

There was, therefore, a tension between three different views of war taxation. McKenna's 'normal year' was attacked from two directions. Paish and Keynes felt that taxation should be used to transfer excess spending from consumers to the government, which would entail higher taxes on the working class as the recipient of additional spending power. Such an approach made economic sense in controlling inflation and providing assets for the war effort, but was politically inexpedient. The second line of attack came from the Labour party, which argued that taxation should be used to reshape the economic and social structure, imposing much higher levels of taxation on capital, profits and large incomes. The outcome was that only one major tax was introduced during the war: the EPD.

The EPD was designed to provide a contribution to exceptional wartime expenditure rather than to cover the debt, so that it was excluded from calculations of the 'normal year' and was expected to disappear at the end of the war. Initially, the Treasury was reluctant to introduce a tax on excess profits. The Treasury's entrenched belief was that the tax system as it existed in 1914 was equitable, so that any change was a distortion of a 'neutral' fiscal regime which held the balance between all classes and interests. Since the income tax took a fair contribution from each level and type of income, the Treasury argued that the only justification for a specific tax on war profits was possession of a 'special ability' to bear taxation. In the early stages of the debate over profit taxes, the Treasury argued that this condition did *not* apply. Profits made through manufacturing and trading were 'earned' by owners who made an effort, and were 'precarious' rather than 'spontaneous'. The Treasury claimed that war profits were analogous to profits created by a sudden demand for goods in ordinary commerce which produced a quasi-monopoly for a short time before the normal operations of the market reduced profits – so there was no 'special ability'.[37] The underlying assumption was that the market could be left to allocate resources – an approach which was deeply flawed during the war when there was no chance of competition emerging and when war 'profiteering' was politically sensitive.

Taxation of 'excess' profits was soon reopened, for political as much as financial reasons. The Admiralty requisitioned ships for war needs, and

---

[36] On Labour and patriotism, see P. Ward, *Red Flag and Union Jack: Englishness, Patriotism and the British Left, 1881–1924* (Woodbridge, 1998), chapters 7 and 8; Harrison, 'War Emergency Workers' National Committee', pp. 217–24.

[37] PRO, T171/121, 'Memorandum on proposals for special taxation of incomes which show an increase during the war', 13 Apr. 1915.

consequently the freight rates paid by private traders rose; in order to mollify them, a substantial share of shipowners' profits was defined as having 'special ability' to pay taxes. Similarly, the failure of the government to control the price of bread led to complaints – and 'discontent, anger, anti-war feeling, determination to make trouble for the Government, is increased, and dangerously increased' by the announcement of large profits made by millers. It was also necessary to prevent a further deterioration in labour relations arising from 'the feeling that employers are making huge profits out of the war which they are being allowed to pocket'. The initial proposal was for a special war-time super-tax on all increases in any type of income, on the grounds that a doctor charging higher fees whilst his colleagues were away on military service was making a war profit as much as a munitions manufacturer. Such an approach was not politically defensible, and the tax was limited to trading concerns whether carried on by companies, private firms or individuals. A tax of 50 per cent was imposed on 'excess profits', defined either as an increase over the profit of the three years before the war or above 6 per cent on prewar capital.[38]

Not everyone was convinced by the equity of the tax, which was criticised by the financial secretary of the Treasury as 'special taxation of earned increment, – a tax on industry in exclesis'. He argued that firms providing armaments relied on low profits in peace and high returns in war; it was scarcely reasonable to impose punitive taxation because their previous investment allowed them to increase production in order to meet the needs of the state.[39] Further, the duty would fall not only on firms making an excess profit but also on firms gradually building up their trade so that their profits rose above prewar levels for entirely legitimate reasons.[40] But these doubts were swept aside. The Treasury came to justify the EPD as a corollary to the government's reliance on the market and higher prices as the main allocative device in rationing scarce goods. As Bradbury argued, 'So long as the production and distribution of commodities are left in the main to private enterprise, enormous war

---

[38] PRO, T171/121, 'Taxation of war profits', E. S. Montagu, 27 Apr. 1915; 'Taxing war profits', H. Withers, 16 June 1915; 'Proposed excess profits tax', [H. Withers, undated]; Acland to chancellor of the Exchequer, 29 Apr. 1915; 'Taxation of war profits: preliminary memorandum', E. E. Nott-Bower and N. F. Warren Fisher to chancellor, 18 June 1915; CH to chancellor, 16 June 1915. The various complaints are covered in Stamp, *Taxation during the War*, pp. 39–42: the milling firm of Spillers and Bakers made a profit of £89,352 in 1913 and £367,868 in 1914, which was taken up by Philip Snowden.

[39] PRO, CAB37/128 no. 3, 'Proposed taxation of war profits', F. D. A., May 1915 (financial secretary), which is also at T171/121, F. D. Acland to chancellor of the Exchequer, 29 Apr. 1915.

[40] PRO, T171/121, 'Memorandum on proposals for special taxation of incomes which show an increase during the war', 13 Apr. 1915.

profits are bound to accrue to a large number of trades and industries, and unless and until these trades and industries are brought under State management the only way of dealing with such war profits is by taxation.' The EPD complemented inflation and the free market in managing the war economy, as well as counteracting unrest caused by profiteering.[41]

By early 1916, McKenna lost his battle with the supporters of conscription into the army. The failure of the gamble that victory would be achieved by the end of 1916 led to the fall of Asquith, the resignation of McKenna and the creation of a new coalition government under Lloyd George. It also changed the nature of the war. The costs were high, for Britain was faced with 'the effort of being both the paymaster and economic powerhouse of the Entente and of raising a continental-scale army'.[42] It might have been expected that fiscal policy would now change, with a rejection of McKenna's 'normal year' and a shift to a much higher level of taxation. But the room for manouevre was also limited by a further feature of the new strategic policy. It was now crucial to maintain domestic support for the war, and to preserve the country's 'economic "staying power"',[43] which meant that the government had to show it was controlling profiteering and protecting workers and their families from higher levels of taxation. The political constraints on the tax system were in tension with the fiscal needs of the government. A more progressive tax system was needed for political reasons in order to secure popular support; it would not be effective in raising revenue or removing surplus spending power which was concentrated in the hands of the working class. The outcome was continued commitment to the 'normal year' in radically changed circumstances.[44]

The situation at the end of the war was a matter of considerable concern. Taxation reached a level not experienced since the Napoleonic wars, and was much higher than at the outbreak of war in 1914. Not only did the level of taxation increase, but there was also a change in the proportions of direct and indirect taxation. In 1913/14, the income and super-tax accounted for 27 per cent of tax revenues; in 1925/6, they provided 43 per cent of revenues.[45] Already before the war, many commentators felt that the trend towards direct taxes – the income tax, super-tax and

[41] PRO, T170/105, 'Profiteering', J. Bradbury, 12 Dec. 1916.
[42] French, *British Strategy*, pp. 244–9; French, *Strategy of the Lloyd George Coalition*, pp. 3–5.
[43] French, *Strategy of the Lloyd George Coalition*, pp. 6–7.
[44] French, *Strategy of the Lloyd George Coalition*, p. 208, on Mond's opposition to 100 per cent EPD which would remove capital needed for postwar reconstruction; Bonar Law sided with him and kept EPD at 80 per cent. See PRO, CAB24/34/GT2851; CAB23/4/WC305; CAB24/38/GT3253; T171/147, 150, 151, 154; CAB23/16/WC359A.
[45] Morgan, *Studies*, pp. 98–9; his figure differs from table 2.4 above.

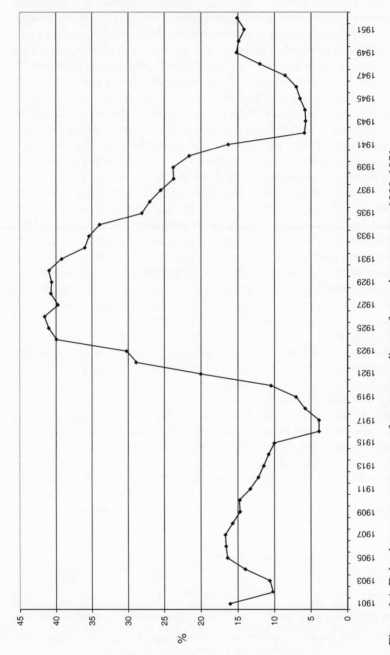

Figure 2.1 Debt charge as a percentage of gross expenditure of central government, 1900–1951
Source: B. R. Mitchell and P. Deane, *Abstract of British Historical Statistics* (Cambridge, 1962), pp. 398–9.

death duties – had reached its limit. In fact, the trend towards direct taxes went still further as a result of the political difficulties over free trade and the disinclination to impose taxes on working-class consumption. And just as striking as the level of taxation was the mountain of debt. The government neglected the principles of war finance laid down in the Crimean war and followed in the Boer war, and instead relied heavily on loans. Further, there was a shift early in 1917 from long-term funded loans to short-term 'floating' debt which had to be repaid very soon after the war, unless the government could re-borrow or convert the short-term into long-term loans. This floating debt was a serious danger to postwar financial stability, threatening a disruption of financial markets and a sudden increase in credit. The outstanding internal debt on 31 March 1914 was £694.8m; by 31 March 1919 it was £6,142.1m, including a 'floating' debt of £1,412m. Interest payments amounted to a quarter of all government revenue at the end of the war, rising to as much as 40 per cent in 1924/5.[46] The political problems of debt and transfer payments to *rentiers* caused serious difficulties in Britain after 1815, and in other European countries after 1918. How successfully did British politicians respond?

The concept of the 'normal year' assumed that 'ordinary' expenditure would return to prewar levels – an assumption which was soon to be tested in the new conditions of universal manhood suffrage and postwar political tensions. Here was the central issue of postwar politics: how far could taxation be reduced, and how much priority should be given to the costs of servicing the debt? Was taxation a drain on enterprise, so preventing economic recovery and harming the welfare of all members of society? Was the cost of the national debt preventing social reconstruction, placing a burden of taxes on the poor and producers in order to benefit *rentiers*? Should there be a readjustment in the proportions of direct and indirect taxation? The issues of distributive justice were presented in a stark way at the end of the war.

[46] Morgan, *Studies*, pp. 115, 117.

3 'This hideous war memorial': debt and taxation, 1918–1925

> ... debt and taxation lie like a vast wet blanket across the whole process of creating new wealth by new enterprise.
>
> Winston Churchill to Otto Niemeyer, 20 May 1927, in M. Gilbert, *Winston S. Churchill, Volume V, Companion Part I, Documents: The Exchequer Years, 1922–29* (London, 1980), p. 997

> ... one of the great constructive tasks in finance ... was to wipe off this burden of the War Debt, to abolish this hideous war memorial of capitalist finance and financial jugglery.
>
> Hugh Dalton, *Labour Party: Report of the 27th Annual Conference, 1927* (London, 1927), p. 246

Debt and taxation were at the heart of postwar politics, placing considerable strain on the fiscal constitution. One of the most pressing political issues after the First World War – as after the Napoleonic wars – was how to deal with the costs of servicing and repaying the immense burden of debt without alienating taxpayers and threatening the legitimacy of the state (see table 3.1). At the end of the Napoleonic wars, taxpayers *were* alienated and the legitimacy of the state *was* threatened. These problems were overcome in the mid-Victorian period, and by the late nineteenth century, the national debt was transformed into a symbol of British financial probity, a guarantee of British liberty by allowing the government to obtain large sums of money at short notice in order to defend the country from danger.[1] However, the scale of the debt at the end of the First World War now threatened a return to the sentiments of the early nineteenth century, when the debt was a symbol of waste, a burden on the forces of production to the benefit of the idle. A common trope in political debates after 1918 was an attack on parasitical *rentiers* who sucked resources from enterprise and prevented the government from providing welfare for more 'deserving' members of society. Debates over this issue were at the heart of postwar adjustments of political allegiances in response to the fourth reform act of 1918 and the realignment of the party system with the rise of Labour and the decline of the Liberals.

---

[1] See Daunton, *Trusting Leviathan*, pp. 119–123.

Much of the postwar debate employed a common rhetoric of opposition between active producers and passive *rentiers*, between risk-takers and parasites. The precise meaning of these terms was contested and formed one of the major fault lines in British politics in the decade after the war. Politicians do not simply appeal to pre-existing interest groups, by devising policies designed to meet their needs as expressed by various organisations. Rather, politicians attempt to define interest groups through a contested discursive process – and a crucial feature of the debate was where to draw the boundaries of production and useful enterprise. Should the definition unite active labour and capital, workers by hand and by brain, against passive, risk-free *rentiers*? Such an approach would create a common interest between workers, salaried members of the middle class and industrialists. This was one rhetorical strategy of the Labour party. After all, its very name might suggest a sectional concern for a specific and selfish interest rather than a principle (Conservativism, Liberalism). The party therefore needed to show that the interests of *labour* were those of the public in general.[2] The Conservative response was to define *all* capital and property as a common interest alongside the salaried middle class, in opposition to selfish members of the organised working class who were demanding high wages and welfare payments, and destroying the self-reliant and respectable middle class who had seen their standard of living and profits collapse during the war. Taxation was one significant element in parties' use of rhetoric to define the identities of their supporters – as well as providing a very immediate, material issue for 'real' interests.

Historically aware members of the Labour party were anxious that the precedents of debt service after the Napoleonic wars should not be repeated. In the opinion of F. W. Pethick-Lawrence,* the productive capacity

[2] For one approach to this issue, see J. Thompson, 'The idea of "public opinion" in Britain, 1870–1914', PhD thesis, University of Cambridge, 1999. For the Conservative attempt to define Labour as sectional and themselves as national or the public, see R. McKibbin, 'Class and conventional wisdom: the Conservative party and the "public" in interwar Britain', in his *Ideologies of Class: Social Relations in Britain, 1880–1950* (Oxford, 1990), pp. 259–93 and for a more subtle view, P. Williamson, *Stanley Baldwin: Conservative Leadership and National Values* (Cambridge, 1999). See also D. Jarvis, 'British Conservatism and class politics in the 1920s', *English Historical Review* 111 (1996), 59, 82.

* Frederick William Pethick-Lawrence (1871–1961) was educated at Eton and Trinity College, Cambridge, where he was a fellow from 1897 to 1903. He was called to the bar in 1899, and engaged in social work in the East End of London. He inherited the family fortune in 1900, and was adopted as a Liberal Unionist candidate in 1901. He married in 1901, adding his wife's name – Pethick – to his own family name. Both he and his wife advocated women's suffrage. He supported Labour; in the First World War he was a conscientious objector and stood as a candidate for peace by negotiation in 1917. He was a Labour MP from 1923 to 1931, serving as secretary to the Treasury from 1929 to 1931. He returned to the Commons in 1935, moving to the Lords in 1945 and serving

Table 3.1 *Debt charges as a percentage of total gross income of government, 1913/14 to 1930/1*

1913/14	9.7	1921/2	28.7
1917/18	26.9	1924/5	39.1
1919/20	24.8	1930/1	34.2

Source: B. R. Mitchell and P. Deane, *Abstract of British Historical Statistics* (Cambridge, 1962), pp. 394–5, 398–9.

of the nation was drained by interest payments, and to avoid a repetition, he favoured the proposal of David Ricardo: a once-and-for-all levy on capital to pay off the debt, so relieving enterprise and producers from the need to pay high taxes to passive *rentiers*.[3] But it was possible to draw a different lesson from the experience of the Napoleonic wars, stressing the cautious, sensible management of national finance by chancellors of the Exchequer who reduced the national debt through a commitment to the sinking fund, balanced budgets and the application of any surplus to debt redemption. Such an approach became a central element in the political culture of Victorian Britain, a defining feature of national identity and liberty in guaranteeing the credit-worthiness of the British state, and providing a 'war chest' in times of emergency. The more orthodox and prudent solution was to keep taxation at a high level, in order to permit a progressive reduction in the debt and to preserve the stability of the financial system – a policy which could be seen as favouring financial interests at the expense of enterprise and the working class, with serious risks of social tension, political unrest and economic depression. These dangers might justify, at least in the immediate aftermath of the war, the less orthodox approach of abandoning the sinking fund and balanced budgets, and giving priority to tax cuts as a way of stimulating economic recovery, regaining Britain's international trading position and sustaining the tax base.

The debate over taxation connected with a further strand in postwar economic policy: the attempt to reassert international economic stability by returning to the gold standard. This policy entailed a reduction in British prices and wages in order to restore prewar exchange rates. Interest payments on government loans were fixed, with the result that

---

as secretary of state for India from 1945 to 1947. (*DNB, 1961–70*, ed. Williams and Nicholls, pp. 835–7.)

[3] F. W. Pethick-Lawrence, *The National Debt* (London, 1924), p. 46; on Ricardo, see R. O. Roberts, 'Ricardo's theory of public debts', *Economica* n.s. 9 (1942), 257–66, who notes that Ricardo concluded that the proposal was not practical politics.

falling prices led to an increase in the real income of holders of government securities and in the real cost of servicing the debt. Although Winston Churchill accepted the restoration of the gold standard in his budget of 1925, he was alarmed at the dangers posed by the policy of deflation. He was well aware that the reduction of wages entailed 'fierce labour disputes' and pressure on industrial profits compared with the improved position of *rentiers*. Was this desirable on political grounds or as a means of stimulating economic recovery? Churchill feared that the outcome would be 'political reactions in the next ten years which may well undo what good has been achieved', with the worrying prospect that it would bring 'the forces creating new wealth into serious competition with the interests of the old wealth as represented by the bondholders'. He was particularly concerned that Britain was disadvantaged compared with Germany, where the real value of the government's debts was reduced by hyperinflation in 1923, amounting to 'a vast act of national repudiation extinguishing the *rentier* class'. Inflation allowed the government and business to pay off debts in worthless money, so freeing them from interest payments to *rentiers* and bankers.[4] The FBI also feared that German industrialists escaped from taxes to service the national debt, and that they could invest at low (or even negative) interest rates to recapture foreign markets. Britain might therefore have won the war on the battlefield only to lose it in trade.[5] The prospects filled Churchill with despair:

we may well see Great Britain with a debt still heavier – nominally and in reality – with crushing taxation, bad trade, high unemployment and great discontent; and on the other hand Germany with no internal debt, with reduced Reparations, with far lighter taxation, ever expanding trade and the contentment which comes from a sense of returning prosperity. That will be a strange contrast to be produced by military victory and financial orthodoxy on the one hand, and by decisive defeat and dishonourable repudiation on the other. It is a contrast from which most misleading deductions might easily be drawn by a democratic electorate.[6]

He was concerned that socialists could exploit the burden of the debt, turning an attack on passive wealth into a more general onslaught against capitalism and its evils.

[4] Gilbert, *Churchill, V, Companion I*, pp. 996–9, W. S. Churchill to O. Niemeyer, 20 May 1927.
[5] PRO, T172/5–7, excess profits duty: deputation from Central Council of Controlled Firms and Federation of British Industries to the chancellor of the Exchequer, 18 June 1917; T172/903, 'Federation of British Industries: peace aims', 12 Dec. 1918 and 30 Jan. 1919; T172/1193, deputation to Sir Robert Horne, chancellor of the Exchequer, from the FBI and Association of British Chambers of Commerce, 21 Apr. 1921. See R. P. T. Davenport-Hines, *Dudley Docker: The Life and Times of a Trade Warrior* (Cambridge, 1984), especially chapter 7.
[6] Gilbert, *Churchill, V, Companion I*, pp. 997–9.

Churchill had good reason to stress the capacity of the national debt to create political tensions and to provide Labour with an electoral issue. It is less clear that he was correct in his comparison between Britain and Germany. Although some historians share Churchill's view that the German hyperinflation was advantageous in reducing the burden of the national debt and external reparations, a good case can be made that it undermined political stability and confidence in the financial system, so that Germany was *less* able to face the strains of the slump. As Keynes pointed out, depreciation of the currency did indeed offer a means of reducing payments from active members of society and cutting the national debt: it meant that the debt was abolished in Germany, and reduced to under a third in France and a quarter in Italy. But the costs were also high. The result was to disorder the social and economic organisation of the country, impose an unfair burden on small savers, and let off the capitalist and entrepreneur. In Keynes's view, a capital levy would be fairer in spreading the burden, but the problem was political: it scared small savers and entrepreneurs preferred depreciation which did not affect them. The result was that 'a country will prefer the inequitable and disastrous courses of currency depreciation to the scientific deliberation of a levy'.[7] Although hyperinflation reduced the burden of debt and extinguished the *rentier* class, it equally destroyed the assets of institutions such as savings banks and voluntary associations with serious consequences for *bourgeois* culture. As Niall Ferguson has argued, hyperinflation expropriated savers who had been thrifty and parsimonious, and benefited those who consumed and borrowed. It threatened the sanctity of private property through a radical reordering of the worth of assets; it subverted legal contracts by allowing debtors to pay creditors in depreciated currency. Hyperinflation harmed small businesses, professionals and civil servants, and weakened the agencies of civil society. It brought large businessmen into disrepute and so prevented the emergence of a conservative alliance of property owners (as was to occur in Britain). Above all, hyperinflation sacrificed private savings as a necessary side-effect of liquidating the debts of the state, and it might as a result 'be said to have discredited the political authority of the Republic itself'. It was clear to contemporaries that a 'state which is no longer in a position to halt the collapse of its currency... necessarily loses its authority and ultimately its right to existence'.[8]

---

[7] J. M. Keynes, *A Tract on Monetary Reform* (London, 1923), in *Collected Writings of John Maynard Keynes*, vol. IV (London, 1971), p. 58 and chapter 2.

[8] Ferguson, *Paper and Iron*, pp. 18, 365, 418–19, 419–33. He returns to the criticism of hyperinflation in C. Bresciani-Turroni, *The Economics of Inflation: A Study of Currency Depreciation in Post-War Germany*, trans. M. E. Sayers (London, 1937), against the

The comparison with Germany could be rephrased in a more positive way than by Churchill and Keynes, to suggest that Britain won the financial peace as well as the military war. British politicians and officials were able to make difficult decisions with benefits for long-term stability. A central issue of postwar politics was the containment of tensions in order to preserve the legitimacy of the British state, the high degree of consent to taxation and the stability of the financial system. In these respects, British experience was different from that of Germany: the British financial system proved more resilient and the state did not lose its legitimacy. As Ferguson has argued, the German state had a long-term problem of 'a persistent discrepancy between the political demand for public expenditure, particularly on social welfare and defence, and the political tolerance of taxation'. The Reich financed militarism out of indirect taxation on working-class consumption prior to the war, and the political responsibilities of the Reich exceeded its fiscal resources. The result was fiscal laxity. These problems were intensified at the end of the war. The government failed to control expenditure, less as a result of the cost of reparations than domestic expenditure so that the budget fell into deficit and the debt rose. There was a breakdown in 'tax morality', and, meanwhile, financial markets were unable to absorb government bonds.[9] By contrast, the fiscal constitution was reasserted in Britain and the legitimacy of taxation preserved at a time of considerable tension. Although plans for postwar reconstruction were scaled down and expenditure reduced in order to balance the budget, the fiscal history of the period after the war was not simply one of retrenchment. Unlike in Germany, expenditure was kept under control; at the same time, a much higher level of extraction was maintained than before 1914, with an increase in expenditure on social policy and without a breakdown in 'tax morality'. The worst tensions over taxation were contained, which contributed to the restabilisation of British politics, and the ability of the tax system to produce more revenue helped to underwrite political and social stability during the depression. Conflict over taxation was therefore minimised and the worst fears of Churchill came to nothing, in part because of the policies he pursued at the Treasury. His great success was in creating a conservative alliance of property owners – an outcome helped

more optimistic view of K. Laursen and J. Pedersen, *The German Inflation, 1918–23* (Amsterdam, 1964). On the problems of financial stability, see H. James, 'The causes of the German banking crisis of 1931', *Economic History Review* 2nd ser. 37 (1984), 68–87, and *The German Slump: Politics and Economics, 1924–36* (Oxford, 1986).

[9] Ferguson, *Paper and Iron*, pp. 25, 91–2, 274, 277, 278–80, 319, 369, 446, 451. For the problems in Italy after the war, see D. J. Forsyth, *The Crisis of Liberal Italy: Monetary and Financial Policy, 1914–22* (Cambridge, 1993).

by the process of fiscal stabilisation pursued after the war.[10] Although fiscal stabilisation could not, in isolation, restore social stability and political legitimacy, it formed a crucial component of the wider project. Legitimacy and political stability could not be restored without removing the worst strains in the fiscal system which provided the state with finance for its policies, and stood at the heart of its relations with its citizens.

The capital levy and Labour

As we have seen, the Labour party devised one solution to the problems of war finance and postwar debt – a capital levy – which was a central element in the party's election campaigns of 1919 and 1923. A virtue of the proposal was that it could be used in different ways. It could be linked with a rejection of capitalism and acceptance of socialism. Rather than selling the assets surrendered to pay the levy, the state might hold them or vest them in co-operatives and local authorities, as a step away from private to socialised ownership. But initially, more emphasis was placed on the desire to secure the allegiance of disaffected 'new' Liberals. Before the war, the Labour party made little headway in areas where Liberalism was strong and a powerful 'progressive alliance' limited the scope of the party. The war led to a dissolution of the Edwardian progressive coalition and a weakening of new Liberalism, which created an opportunity for Labour to appropriate radical Liberal policies, and to lay claim to the Liberal party's role in preserving liberties which had been sacrificed as a result of the exigencies of war. The capital levy could be seen as part of the policy of 'moral reform' of new Liberalism, the desire to remove social and economic impediments to the self-sufficient and morally responsible citizen. A capital levy would fall more heavily on *rentiers* and 'dead' capital, allowing a reduction in the income tax on current earnings. By attacking passive *rentiers* and the unproductive rich who lived off the active enterprise of others, the capital levy could potentially attract Liberal support from the old progressive coalition. The growth of the Labour party outside its prewar power base was the result of its success in projecting itself as a modern version of Liberalism, based on a moderate moral reformism which was consonant both with progressive Edwardian hostility to unearned profits and with the Gladstonian emphasis on the virtues of

---

[10] On the wider Conservative response to class politics in the 1920s, see Jarvis, 'British Conservatism'. As he shows, the party moved away from fears of a monolithic proletariat to a more pluralistic understanding of politics, appealing to specific components of the working class, whether housewives, small savers or trade unionists hit by foreign imports.

debt redemption.[11] The policy therefore allowed moderates and radicals to come together, and placed Labour in a stronger position in competition with other parties. It was part of Labour's attempt to secure a wider electoral base than a simple divide between capital and labour which left it open to the charge of sectionalism and support for special interests. The capital levy continued the rhetorical strategy of defining the interests of Labour as those of the public, allowing Labour to position itself as the representative of both productive capital and labour against exploitation by passive *rentiers*, as the spokesman for the wider public against selfish interests. What was involved was a contest over the identity of property.

Before the First World War, parties were divided over the issue of land. The Liberal party argued that industrial, mercantile and finance capital were all productive and enterprising, and were opposed to landed property. By drawing a line between these types of property, the Liberal party could appeal to urban house owners and their tenants against aristocratic ground landlords, and could unite urban interests with the discontents of Scottish, Welsh and Irish farmers. On this view, miners and mineowners had a mutual identity against landowners who received excessive mineral royalties; workers and industrialists had a common interest in the development of industry which was frustrated by the high price of land for factories and houses. The removal of the unearned increment of Rent would therefore create a prosperous, free trade economy which would mitigate social problems of poverty and unemployment, and provide the tax revenue for social welfare. Here was a strategy both to contain the Labour party and to provide an alternative to tariff reform. In response, the Conservatives argued that the attack on land was an attack on property in general, so that mineowners and house owners should make common cause with landowners who supplied their building sites and mineral rights against radical attack on private ownership. Revenue should come from tariffs, in order to create a buoyant domestic market for industrialists, agriculturalists and workers. What was at stake was more than an attempt of Liberals and Conservatives to secure the allegiance of *existing* interests: it was an attempt to *construct* interests through a shaping of identities.[12]

---

[11] On moral reform, see P. F. Clarke, *Liberals and Social Democrats* (Cambridge, 1978), pp. 5, 15, which he defines as an attempt to remove the impediments to character and personal responsibility imposed by social conditions; D. Tanner, *Political Change and the Labour Party, 1900–18* (Cambridge, 1990), pp. 317–18, 347–8, 365–72, 381–3, 415–17, 426–30, 441–2.

[12] On debates over land, see Offer, *Property and Politics*, and, on the Conservative reaction to land reform as a threat to prosperity and a bureaucratic interference in private markets, M. Fforde, *Conservatism and Collectivism, 1886–1914* (Edinburgh, 1990), pp. 104, 133–58; on tariff reform, see Green, 'Radical conservatism', and *The Crisis of Conservatism: The Politics, Economics and Ideology of the British Conservative Party, 1880–1914* (London, 1995).

Labour's attack on the national debt after the war was part of its attempt to create a distinctive set of social identities. Interest on the debt was portrayed as a harmful transfer from active 'earned' incomes to inactive *rentiers* living in idleness, and misallocating labour from 'useful work' in order to provide personal services and luxuries. It diverted money away from 'current wealth production', from investment in productive enterprise and 'useful trade', and so prevented postwar recovery. A levy would pay off the debt and allow a reduction in taxes on new, active enterprises and production, so stimulating industry and creating a dynamic and competitive economy which would be better able to compete for world trade.[13] The levy was, therefore, part of a strategy of production which would be to the advantage

not of profits or fortunes but of the commodities and services by which the community lives. We can replace the material wealth destroyed in the wars only by new production. And we must therefore raise our national production – production, that is, of useful commodities and services – to its highest possible amount consistent with a humane and civilised life.[14]

It would free industry and the middle class from the burden of high taxes needed to support *rentiers*, and would unite workers, shopkeepers, the salaried and professional middle class, and businessmen with modest incomes, against 'men of great wealth and those living without personal exertion on the proceeds of their investment'.[15] Labour argued that recipients of unearned income from accumulated wealth would prefer a high income tax which would spread the burden to other forms of income; by contrast, earned incomes from salaries, professional fees and business profits would benefit from a reduction in the income tax made possible by a capital levy. The levy could therefore be presented as a measure of class co-operation between active, earned incomes of the middle class and 'the feeble-minded and the mothers of infants, the children and the slum-dwellers, the workers in the sweated trades, and generally all wage-earners'.[16]

Initially, the policy was supported by leading economists who felt that the issue came down to a pragmatic question of whether it was 'more to the national advantage to discharge a great slice of the debt by a single levy now, and so do away with the obligation to pay interest on it in the future, or to repay the debt gradually and face large interest charges for a long

[13] Pethick-Lawrence, *National Debt*, p. 61; Short, 'Politics of personal taxation', pp. 63–4, 38, 89–90; Snowden, *Labour and National Finance*, p. 55.

[14] S. Webb, *National Finance and a Levy on Capital: What the Labour Party Intends* (Fabian Tract 188, London, 1919), pp. 2–3.

[15] F. W. Pethick-Lawrence, *A Levy on Capital* (London, 1918), p. 77.

[16] Pethick-Lawrence, *Levy on Capital*, p. 77; *Labour Party Annual Conference, 1923*, pp. 177, 213–16.

term of years?' As Pigou remarked, a decision to opt for a levy 'is not red revolution'.[17] The Treasury, Inland Revenue and chancellor were initially sympathetic to a levy *after* the war. What they could not contemplate was conscription of riches *during* hostilities. There was no chance of compiling a census of wealth, and there would be serious problems of realising assets to pay the levy, which would distort capital markets and divert funds from war loans. The solution favoured by some advocates of the levy was to transfer shares and bonds to the government, but this would not provide immediate purchasing power to obtain commodities to fight the war. The Treasury argued that a voluntary loan was more effective in obtaining money from those who could spare it, with the least dislocation and without undermining confidence which was crucial for raising loans at home and abroad.[18]

Rejection of a war-time levy was therefore entirely understandable on pragmatic grounds. At the same time, a desire to sustain popular support for the war meant that a *postwar* levy could not be rejected by the government. In 1917, the chancellor assured the TUC that the cost of debt service 'is not likely to fall on the wage-earners as long as there is wealth which can be made to pay for it'. The implication was that the war-time shift to a more progressive tax system would be retained, and that 'whatever government is in power, whether we call ourselves Conservatives, Liberals or Socialists, the wealthy are going to bear a bigger proportion of taxation than they did after the Napoleonic wars'. As Bradbury commented, the *rentier* would not be able to shift the burden on to indirect taxes, and 'the masses may be trusted to see that the rich man's burden remains on his back'.[19] This assessment of political realities informed Bradbury's postwar recommendations and limited any shift towards a less progressive tax system.

Indeed, the Treasury was initially in favour of a postwar levy. In Bradbury's view, it was not 'a question which concerns the working classes against the financial classes'; it was a practical matter for property owners to decide whether they preferred a single heavy tax or an income

---

[17] A. C. Pigou, *A Capital Levy and a Levy on War Wealth* (London, 1920), pp. 12, 32, 43, and 'A special levy to discharge war debt', *Economic Journal* 28 (1918), 143, 156. See also *The Collected Writings of John Maynard Keynes*, vol. XVII: *Activities, 1920–22: Treaty Revision and Reconstruction*, ed. E. Johnson (London, 1977), p. 271; he argued in 1921 that a capital levy 'would transfer a part of the burden of taxation from new enterprise and current business, out of which the active elements of society, working men and business men alike, draw their rewards, to idle old-won wealth'. See also PRO, T170/125, Bradbury, 21 Feb. 1918.

[18] PRO, T171/167, E. E. Nott-Bower and N. F. Warren Fisher to chancellor, 9 Feb. 1917; Nott-Bower and Fisher to chancellor, 6 Nov. 1917; 'Memorandum', O. Niemeyer, 10 Nov. 1917; 'Conscription of wealth', J. Bradbury, 12 Nov. 1917.

[19] PRO, T171/167, deputation from the TUC etc., 14 Nov. 1917; 'Conscription of wealth', J. Bradbury, 12 Nov. 1917.

tax spread over a longer time.[20] The Treasury went some way to meet Labour's case for a levy as a means of stimulating production: it would fall only on wealth existing at the end of the war, so relieving *future* enterprise; and it would differentiate 'in favour of income derived from personal exertions and the investment of new savings'. Above all, a swift repayment of the debt was prudent:

the rentier will be the subject of perpetual jealousy and perpetual attack: the owner of other forms of capital wealth whose property could at any rate in the opinion of a large section of the public, be appropriated to meet the rentier's claims will be in a position scarcely less vulnerable . . . The rich will have to bear the main share of the burden of the national debt in any case: to take it frankly on his own back at the outset is in substance little more than a book-keeping adjustment but he will stand to gain politically by doing so, if the result is to remove it . . . from the national accounts, its presence in which will be a perpetual incentive to unrest and misconception.[21]

However, the Treasury soon realised that the choice between a levy and income tax *did* concern the working classes, and that it was more than a pragmatic issue for the propertied. At the very least, it offered a way of changing the balance between passive and active capital; and it might be a step in the direction of 'red revolution' rather than a means of preserving private property from attack.

The levy would be too large to be paid out of income, so that assets would need to be sold. An optimistic view was that resources would simply be transferred without disruption: assets would be sold to pay the levy, the proceeds would go to holders of government stock who would then buy the assets. More realistically, a sudden realisation of assets would disrupt capital markets and credit, with serious problems as a result of lags and the different preferences of investors.[22] One solution was obvious: the state could receive payment in land or shares, and take 'a direct financial interest in certain national public services . . . The interest thus acquired by the State in these concerns will be partial only, and can either be extended afterwards, by purchase to complete state ownership, or bought

[20] PRO, T171/167, deputation from TUC Birmingham to chancellor, 15 Feb. 1917.

[21] PRO, T171/167, 'Conscription of wealth', unsigned and undated memorandum; T171/167, 'Conscription of wealth', J. Bradbury, 12 Nov. 1917; see also IR63/47, 'The economic effect of estate duties upon capital', J. C. Stamp, 25 June 1914, which assessed the impact of estate duties on accumulation, and concluded that there was no evidence that it reduced potential fixed capital more than an income tax, except possibly to a small extent in the long term which might even be beneficial by preventing excessive accumulation and steadying production through increased consumption.

[22] Pigou, *A Capital Levy*, pp. 46–7, and 'A special levy', 149–50; see also S. Arnold, 'A capital levy: the problems of realisation and valuation', *Economic Journal* 28 (1918), 157–66.

out so as to restore full private possession.'[23] Here was the collectivist fist in the velvet glove of debt redemption, the spectre of red revolution within fiscal responsibility. There was a tension between Labour's ambition of constructing a producers' alliance and its potential for extending public ownership. Although Webb argued that a distinction should be drawn between the case for the capital levy as a means of debt redemption to the benefit of 'active' property, and the proposal for public ownership, in practice it was difficult to sustain. After all, nationalisation and taxation were both justified by the same ambition of preventing individuals from appropriating unearned wealth and income. Despite Webb's plea to draw a clear line between taxation and nationalisation, he remarked in 1919 that 'every form of unearned increment' should be intercepted so that the government shared as 'the sleeping partner in every undertaking, and the only righteous heir to every increment due to the progress of the nation in population and wealth'. Of course, he was a member of the Sankey Commission which recommended the nationalisation of the coal mines.[24]

Opponents of the capital levy could therefore present it as more than a means of aiding producers against *rentiers*. They could argue that the levy would hinder investment in industry by encouraging consumption rather than savings which would be liable to 'confiscation'. They could question the distinction between parasitical and productive, unearned and earned income. Why should retired professional men whose pensions came from their own savings be taxed, while retired civil servants with a state pension or barristers in employment escaped the levy? Further, the capital levy might always be used *in addition* to the income tax, not to redeem debt but to pay for social expenditure and to transfer income from rich to poor. It could therefore be criticised as a 'tricky device' to create socialism by subterfuge, by destroying the smooth operation of financial markets or by a surreptitious transfer of shares to public ownership.[25] The Conservatives were able to portray themselves as the defenders of property in general, fostering a common identity with great landowners and investors

---

[23] Pethick-Lawrence, *A Levy on Capital*, p. 73; Harrison, 'War Emergency Workers' National Committee', pp. 249, 251.

[24] Snowden, *Labour and National Finance*, p. 37; *Labour Party Annual Conference, 1916*, p. 135; see also *Report of the Annual Conference of the Labour Party and the Adjourned Conference, 1918* (London, 1918), pp. 133–4; *Labour Party Annual Conference, 1919*, pp. 146–9, 155; Webb, *National Finance*, pp. 4, 13, 19. On Webb's argument that conscription of riches should be separate from nationalisation, see Harrison, 'War Emergency Workers' National Committee', pp. 249–52, and J. M. Winter, *Socialism and the Challenge of War: Ideas and Politics in Britain, 1912–18* (London, 1974), p. 214.

[25] H. Cox, *The Capital Levy: Its Real Purpose* (National Unionist Association, n. d.), *passim* and p. 68. For a good example of the way the Conservatives used the levy to suggest that Labour threatened workers' property as well as the rich, see Waldorf Astor's comments of 1923 in Jarvis, 'British Conservatism', 82.

in the national debt. The strategy was denounced by Webb as a cynical manouevre in aid of the rich person who 'cowers behind the bulwark of the poor widow, the "lean annuitant", and the people who have laboriously accumulated a few hundreds in Government stock by way of provision for their old age'.[26] Although Webb stressed that Labour's ambition was to make small fortunes more secure by reducing their tax burden, middle-class electors were, not surprisingly, suspicious. The capital levy might have helped in attracting 'new Liberal' support for the progressive alliance, but it soon became a liability when the party had a realistic chance of forming a government.[27] The levy led to concerns whether Labour could be trusted and whether property was secure. The anti-*rentier* rhetoric failed, but as we shall see, this could not be taken for granted and has to be explained.

The Inland Revenue and Treasury were concerned that any attempt to value capital would lead to a repetition on a still larger scale of resistance to valuation for Lloyd George's land taxes. Consent and compliance would be threatened.[28] Indeed, recourse to a capital levy was interpreted as a sign that the relationship between the state and taxpayers or lenders had broken down. The introduction of the *Wehrbeitrag* (defence levy on property and income) in Germany in 1913 arose from the failure of a loan; in Britain, loans were readily accepted and a levy would simply undermine confidence in the government's trustworthiness.[29] Similarly, the proposed capital tax in France was seen as a sign of the failure of direct taxation and the slow development of 'scientific taxation'.[30] The capital levy was now defined by the Inland Revenue as a measure of desperation in the absence of consent to direct taxation and of confidence in lending to the government. It was not even clear that a levy would produce a large net annual saving, for the surrender of assets would reduce the future yield from the income tax and death duties. The net savings were reduced from the initial expectation of £115m to £200m to no more than

---

[26] Webb, *National Finance*, p. 14.

[27] Short, 'Politics of personal taxation', pp. 87–9, 248–9.

[28] J. E. Cronin, *The Politics of State Expansion: War, State and Society in Twentieth-Century Britain* (London, 1991), p. 83; PRO, IR75/110, 'The proposal of a capital tax with reference to its practical aspects' and 'General capital levy: note by the Board of Inland Reveue on the special difficulties introduced by the prevalence in this country of settlements and trusts', 19 May 1919; PP 1920 XIX, *Report from the Select Committee on Land Values*, 'Evidence given by Mr Percy Thompson, a commissioner of Inland Revenue, on the general position of the land values duties and the valuation under part I of the Finance (1909–10) Act, 1910', Sept. 1919, p. 783.

[29] PRO, T171/167, paper prepared at request of chancellor of the Exchequer on the German defence levy of 1913; for Germany's prewar difficulties, see Ferguson, 'Public finance and national security', 161.

[30] PRO, T171/167, Board of Inland Revenue, proposed capital tax in France, 15 Mar. 1919.

£42m to £50m, a modest figure which scarcely justified disruption of capital markets. The TUC and Labour party accepted these estimates, so that continued support of the levy rested less on its role in reducing taxes and freeing enterprise than on its use as a weapon against inherited wealth and private ownership.[31] The capital levy was transferred from pragmatic prudence to socialist menace.

The leadership of the Labour party felt retreat was expedient. The levy was marginalised in the 1923 election by promising that the Treasury would be consulted on its practicability in the event of forming a government. The king's acceptance of Labour as fit to govern in 1924 rested upon assurances that a commission would be established to consider means of dealing with the debt. The Committee on the National Debt and Taxation under the chairmanship of Lord Colwyn offered a means of avoiding action during its lengthy deliberations. It reported, eventually, in 1927. The majority report rejected the levy on the grounds that it would cause political upheavals for a small net saving; Labour's minority report suggested an alternative approach which became party policy. The income tax should be more steeply graduated and differentiated, with an additional surtax on unearned income above £500 a year. The surtax could be presented to the Labour party as a pragmatic and simple alternative to a levy: it was equivalent to a capital tax on estates of £10,000 without the need for new administrative machinery and a complicated valuation. But there was still a division of opinion over the use to which the revenue should be put. Should it be used for the reduction of debt and taxation in order 'to get this unproductive parasitic thing off the shoulders of the nation', or should it be used for the development of social services? The party's programme of 1928 presented the surtax as 'the closest approximation to equality of sacrifice', and made an appeal to *all* earned incomes – manual workers, clerks, teachers, doctors, shopkeepers and intellectuals – against owners of large unearned incomes in a further recension of the 'producers' alliance'.[32]

---

[31] For the high initial estimates, see Snowden, *Labour and National Finance*, pp. 76–8; H. Dalton, *Capital Levy Explained* (London, 1923), p. 33; and Labour party, *Labour and the War Debt: A Statement of Policy for the Redemption of War Debt by a Levy on Accumulated Wealth* (London, n.d.), p. 11. For revised estimates, see J. C. Stamp, *Studies in Current Problems in Finance and Government* (London, 1924), pp. 250–70; MRC, TUC MSS 292/411.27/4, General Council of TUC and Labour Party Executive Committee, Joint Research and Information Department, 'Note on net annual saving arising from a capital levy', Mar. 1925, and 'Draft answers to the committee's questionnaire upon the capital levy', Mar. 1925.

[32] *The Labour Party: Report of the 25th Annual Conference, 1925* (London, 1925), pp. 266–70; *The Labour Party: Report of the 26th Annual Conference, 1926* (London, 1926), pp. 267–8; *Labour Party Annual Conference, 1927*, pp. 244–55 and appendix x, 'Memorandum on the surtax on income from property and investments', pp. 330–1; Short, 'Politics of personal

The capital levy was contained by the mid-1920s, but the extension of the franchise, growth of the Labour party and concern about the burdens of the national debt placed civil servants and politicians in a difficult situation. Great care had to be taken to show that the tax system was fair and equitable *in the absence of* radical solutions. The attack on *rentiers* and the national debt might have renewed force if the strategies for the payment of interest were considered to be unjust. Promises were made to the TUC and WEWNC during the war that the costs would fall on wealth rather than on labour; any breach of these promises would threaten the legitimacy of the fiscal system, and increase the appeal of Labour's attack on parasitical *rentiers*. The political dangers were particularly acute because high levels of income tax at the end of the war created two possibilities. One was an alliance of labour and aggrieved middle-class taxpayers against war profiteers; the second was a populist attack on bureaucratic 'waste' and social expenditure which might alienate labour. The coalition government wished to avoid the first without playing into the hands of the second which would threaten policies of social reconstruction and stabilisation, and give more credence to Labour's attack on the national debt. A further major consideration was the need to maintain financial stability after the war, which meant that the government had to provide for the payment of interest on the debt, and tackle the problem of the short-term floating debt. How could financial stability be preserved without imposing a capital levy or alienating taxpayers?

Resisting the income tax and containing the floating debt

At the end of the war, the proportion of people paying income tax was higher than ever before, and the rate was at an unprecedented level. Both points had serious consequences for compliance and consent. Much of

taxation', pp. 246–51; T. Jones, *Whitehall Diary*, vol. I: *1916–1925*, ed. K. Middlemass (London, 1969), p. 260, T. Jones to Sir J. Chancellor, 20 Dec. 1923; M. Cowling, *The Impact of Labour, 1920–24: The Beginning of Modern British Politics* (Cambridge, 1971), p. 364, quoting Stamfordham to George V, 28 Dec. 1923 and 1 Jan. 1924; P. Snowden, *An Autobiography*, vol. II: *1919–1934* (London, 1934), p. 595; Barbara Wootton, who was working at the Joint Research Department of the TUC and Labour party, was a member and claimed to have written the minority report which drew attention to the high taxation of small incomes and criticised the incidence of indirect taxes. Although the case for a capital levy was admitted, she did not recommend its imposition and instead proposed a special charge on investment income and the adoption of the Rignano scheme advocated by Hugh Dalton: B. Wootton, *In a World I Never Made: Autobiographical Reflections* (London, 1967), pp. 65–6; for the debate on the capital levy prior to the election, see *Labour Party Annual Conference, 1923*, pp. 213–16; D. Marquand, *Ramsay MacDonald* (London, 1977), pp. 475–7; Labour party, *Labour and the Nation: Statement of the Labour Policy and Programme* (London, 1928), p. 37.

the outstanding liability of workers had to be written off, and trade unions were also pressing for the restoration of the prewar exemption limit in *real* terms with serious implications for yields and for the perceived 'fairness' of the tax between interests. Middle-class taxpayers might wonder why workers who secured higher wages should escape taxation, whereas the middle class which had not secured higher salaries was liable to heavier taxation. The government contained the demand for restoring the real level of prewar exemptions by increasing children's allowances and introducing wives' allowances in 1918/19. As a result, married men with three or more children had a higher exemption limit than before the war, and the burden fell on bachelors earning at least £3 a week.[33] Consequently, the Labour leadership was wary of pressing for a general restoration of the exemption limit which would benefit well-paid workers without family responsibilities.[34] In any case, union hostility to the income tax might be counter-productive, resulting in a shift to indirect taxation or a cut in social expenditure. It would also reinforce the populist campaign against 'waste' mounted by the press barons Northcliffe* and Rothermere.[†] Their rhetoric brought together idle bureaucrats, war profiteers and deceitful Germans who were gaining at the expense of the long-suffering, respectable and hard-working middle class. 'I, personally, have no intention of spending the rest of my life swotting to pay excess profits tax and supertax for the benefit of Germany, if I can help it', Northcliffe informed Rothermere in 1919, 'I do not believe the tales of German hard-up-ness.'[35] Many voters shared these sentiments, and they might well add 'selfish' trade unionists who had gained in

[33] Whiting, 'Taxation and the working class', 898; PRO, T172/504, income tax: deputation from the Miners' Federation of Great Britain to the chancellor of the Exchequer, 29 Aug. 1917; T172/982, E. E. Nott-Bower and N. F. Warren Fisher to chancellor, 20 Aug. 1917; income tax abatement: deputation from the South Wales Miners' Federation to the chancellor of the Exchequer, 20 Sept. 1917; T172/1000, deputation from the Triple Alliance to Austen Chamberlain, 4 July 1919.

[34] Snowden, *Labour and National Finance*, pp. 101–3.

[35] Quoted in C. J. Wrigley, *Lloyd George and the Challenge of Labour: The Post-War Coalition, 1918–22* (Hemel Hempstead, 1990), p. 188.

* Alfred Charles William Harmsworth, Viscount Northcliffe (1865–1922), was born in Ireland, the son of an unsuccessful barrister. He became a journalist, and with his brother Harold created Amalgamated Press in London in 1887. He appealed to the lower middle class with the *Daily Mail* and the *Daily Mirror*, founded in 1896 and 1903, and his pursuit of populist campaigns. He became the chief proprietor of *The Times* in 1908. He was director of propaganda to enemy countries in 1918. (*DNB, 1922–30*, ed. Weaver, pp. 397–403; Robbins (ed.), *Biographical Dictionary*, pp. 327–8.)

[†] Harold Sidney Harmsworth, Viscount Rothermere (1868–1940) was a clerk in the Inland Revenue before joining his brother; he provided the financial expertise for the business. He became director-general of the Royal Army Clothing Department in 1916, and air minister 1917–18. He controlled the newspaper business from 1922 to 1932. (*DNB, 1931–40*, ed. Legg, pp. 400–2.)

comparison with white-collar workers. Thrift and responsibility seemed to count for little.

As Ross McKibbin has commented, the immediate postwar years turned the panics and fantasies of Edwardian Britain into something like reality for the middle class, creating an 'active fear of the working class... the sense that there was a lower depth which could sweep away property, decorum, the constitution'.[36] The extension of the franchise to this 'lower depth' in 1918, the militancy of unions, and the demands for a capital levy, all contributed to the sense of panic which was expressed in the Rothermere and Northcliffe press, mobilised by the Anti-Waste League and provided an alternative to the anti-*rentier* rhetoric of labour. The League won three by-elections in 1921, and the coalition government feared that it was being deserted by middle-class voters. 'We must take counsel', Lloyd George warned Austen Chamberlain,* 'lest we find ourselves caught between labour in the North and anti-waste in the South.'[37] The government was in a difficult position, for it needed to maintain a high level of taxation both to pay for the national debt and to finance schemes of postwar construction such as the large-scale house-building programme and an increase in the school-leaving age. Abandonment of policies to create a 'land fit for heroes' would satisfy the adherents of 'anti-waste', at the cost of alienating the organised working class and giving credence to the Labour party's contention that the *rentier* class was being protected against the interest of the wider community. Postwar stabilisation was a formidably complicated task.

The problem was not simply the creation of balance between taxation and social expenditure, for there was a further serious issue: the huge postwar 'floating' debt threatened financial stability. There was a danger that short-term bills would not be renewed when they fell due, so driving the government to borrow from the Bank of England. Credit would expand, purchasing power rise and prices and wages spiral upwards in a vicious circle. Such a situation gave power to 'the holders of Treasury Bills – that is the banks, the market, and, to a certain extent, the investor generally – to force the Government at any time to create new credit,

---

[36] R. McKibbin, *Classes and Cultures: England, 1918–51* (Oxford, 1998), p. 67.

[37] Quoted in A. McDonald, 'The Geddes Committee and the formulation of public expenditure policy, 1921–22', *Historical Journal* 32 (1989), 650.

* Joseph Austen Chamberlain (1863–1937) was the son of Joseph and half-brother of Neville; he was educated at Rugby and Trinity College, Cambridge. He was a Liberal Unionist MP from 1892 to 1937: he was lord of the Admiralty 1895–1900, financial secretary to the Treasury 1900–2, postmaster general 1902–3, chancellor of the Exchequer 1903–5. He returned to office in the war as secretary of state for India 1915–17, a member of the War Cabinet in 1918, chancellor of the Exchequer 1919–21, and leader of the Conservatives in 1921–2. He was foreign secretary 1924–9 and first lord of the Admiralty in 1931. (*DNB, 1931–40*, ed. Legg, pp. 163–8; Robbins (ed.), *Biographical Dictionary*, pp. 89–92.)

and that means the whole cycle of inflation restarted'.[38] The Treasury believed that the dangers posed by the floating debt were so serious that it was necessary to keep taxes at a high level in order to reduce liability as fast as possible. The dangers of inflation were also stressed by the Treasury which believed that 'a general deflationary tendency is a very desirable one at the present time' as part of a strategy of price stability; the alternative was that 'the vicious circle will go on spinning and the crash will come'. In the opinion of the Treasury, inflation was like a drug which continued to stimuluate only with increased doses, until the economic health of the nation collapsed. The Treasury therefore preferred a small and controlled correction in order to avoid 'undue deflation' with harmful consequences for production. The Treasury's position was based on a realistic assessment of the dangers of the floating debt, as became clear in Germany where lack of demand for the 'floating debt' led to its monetisation, contributing to hyperinflation, to destabilisation of the economy and to a fundamental change in social relations between debtors and creditors.[39]

Avoidance of hyperinflation and economic crisis had a price, for the floating debt was in part transformed into long-term debt which *rose* between 1921 and 1923. When Churchill became chancellor in 1924, he feared that this policy was open to criticism as benefiting the City of London, and giving the impression that finance was exploiting producers. However, concern for the floating debt was much more complicated than a simple dominance by the City and finance over the Treasury and government policy. The City and Treasury agreed that the floating debt posed grave dangers, but their responses were fundamentally different. In 1920, the governor of the Bank of England, supported by the leading clearing banks, the Stock Exchange, the London Chamber of Commerce and the Accepting Houses Committee, proposed a reduction in the floating debt by imposing an additional income and super-tax for a period of up to three years, with the right to compound for a single payment.[40] The proposal was politically naive, and government policy was the outcome of

---

[38] The concern of Austen Chamberlain as expressed to the FBI and the Association of British Chambers of Commerce: PRO, T172/1164, deputation to the chancellor of the Exchequer from the Association of British Chambers of Commerce and the Federation of British Industries, 5 May 1920; Morgan, *Studies*, pp. 112–21, 140–56; T171/202, 'Budgeting for a deficit', B. P. Blackett, 24 Mar. 1924; PP 1920 VII, *Report from the Select Committee on Increases of Wealth (War)*, evidence of B. P. Blackett, Q.1533, and 'Memorandum by Mr B. P. Blackett, Controller of Finance in H.M. Treasury: deflation and the proposed levy on war time increases of wealth', Mar. 1920, pp. 370–3; see also PRO, T171/211, 'Budgeting for a deficit', B. Blackett, 23 Nov. 1921.

[39] Balderston, 'War, finance and inflation', 238–40, 224; Ferguson, *Paper and Iron*, pp. 17–27.

[40] PRO, T172/1105, 'Memorandum for the information of the chancellor of the Exchequer', 12 Apr. 1920; Montagu Norman to Austen Chamberlain, 17 Apr. 1920.

a more complicated interplay of interests between aggrieved campaigners against 'waste', the advocates of a capital levy with their animosity to *rentiers*, and industrialists who wished to be relieved of profits taxes. For its part, the Treasury was anxious to remove the real dangers posed by the floating debt, and the power it gave to the City over the state. The task was by no means easy.

A levy on war wealth and the Geddes axe

As we have seen, the coalition government initially favoured a levy on increases in war wealth as a politically safe alternative to a capital levy. It would contain the demands of Labour for a levy on *all* wealth; it would allow a reduction of profit taxes; and it would remove the danger of the floating debt. Above all, it would deal with the outcry against war profiteers which Lloyd George felt was 'a great danger to the state', uniting professionals and people on small incomes with the working class, and leading even army officers to talk 'wild bolshevism'.[41] In Austen Chamberlain's view, a levy on war wealth offered an insurance for property in general: 'the existence of large accretions of war wealth are not only a fair subject of taxation but . . . the prejudice created by them endangers all capital'.[42] Thus a levy on war wealth could be a measure of conservative restoration, innocent of the radical, redistributive ambitions of the capital levy. The logic of the levy on war wealth was explained by Herbert Samuel:*

[41] Wrigley, *Lloyd George and the Challenge of Labour*, p. 238, from PRO, CAB23/15, WC606A, 5 Aug. 1919.

[42] Birmingham University Library, Austen Chamberlain Papers (AC) 24/1/35, A. Chamberlain to J. L. Garvin, 31 Oct. 1919, quoted in Wrigley, *Lloyd George and the Challenge of Labour*, p. 237. See also his comment to the FBI, 10 Mar. 1920 – 'If these very great and sudden increases of wealth escape contribution, I think it will be at some cost to more hardly earned capital.' PP 1920 VII, *Report from the Select Committee on Increases of Wealth (War)*, 'Memorandum on the practicability of levying a duty on wartime wealth with suggestions as to the form which such a duty might take', Nov. 1919, pp. 297–305; 'Note by the Board of Inland Revenue on a scheme for levying a duty on war-time wealth', Mar. 1920, pp. 332–3; 'Note by the Board of Inland Revenue on the possible effects of a war levy upon businesses', Mar. 1920, pp. 340–2; 'Note prepared by the Board of Inland Revenue at the request of the Select Committee on Increases of Wealth (War) as to the possibility of avoiding valuation of capital for the purposes of a war levy', Mar. 1920, pp. 346–9. For Neville Chamberlain's comments that support of the levy was a sign of 'mental aberration' see Birmingham University Library, Neville Chamberlain Papers (NC) 18/1/242, Neville to Hilda Chamberlain, 1 Feb. 1920. He was referring to Keynes.

* Herbert Louis Samuel (1870–1963) was the son of a banker, inheriting a fortune in 1877 and marrying into another banking family. He was educated at University College School and at Balliol College, Oxford; he helped to formulate new Liberalism. He was a Liberal MP from 1902 to 1918, serving as under-secretary of state at the Home Office from 1905, chancellor of the Duchy of Lancaster in 1909, postmaster general in 1910, president of the Local Government Board in 1914, postmaster general in 1915, chancellor of the

the chief purpose of the tax is not financial but social. The working class will not settle down . . . so long as they have before their eyes the evidence of great fortunes made during the war. The contrast of riches and poverty tended to make our social system unstable before the war. The accentuation of those contrasts as a consequence of a war in which all classes were exhorted to make every sacrifice for the country, is likely to render it far more unstable. It is true that the total yield of such a tax cannot at present be foretold. But even if it were comparatively small, it is worth exacting as the only means of preventing the continuous growth of social discontent.[43]

It would help restore the prewar social hierarchy, for the levy would hit those who had done well out of the war, so removing the grievances of the professional and 'black-coated' middle class and the working class. It would contribute to returning prices to their prewar levels, so restoring the relative value of different forms of wealth, breaking the spiral of rising prices and easing a return to economic normality and the gold standard. A levy on war wealth therefore offered a means of removing the dangers of the floating debt, without succumbing to politically dangerous solutions of higher direct taxation favoured by the City. It was also preferable to continued reliance on the EPD, which would not produce any revenue in the event of a slump and falling profits.

In 1920, the Select Committee on Increases of Wealth (War) recommended a levy on war wealth which was expected to produce £500m. Although the Inland Revenue had anticipated a yield of £1,000m, Austen Chamberlain decided to opt for the smaller sum 'without undue friction, and without deleterious consequences to thrift generally, than double that sum with a rankling sense of injustice on the part of large numbers of taxpayers'. Accordingly, he proposed a duty on increases in war wealth in June 1920, with an immediate reduction of the EPD from 60 to 40 per cent and the prospect of its early termination. However, he was aware of the political difficulties of hostility from banks, commerce and the Stock Exchange. Austen informed his sister that 'If it were not for fear that the child would scream itself into fits, I would have the Levy and the child would be all the better for it. But it might die of fright before it found out that it was not hurt.' His support for the war levy was therefore half-hearted, and he was torn between his desire to contain Labour and his fear of the City:

Duchy of Lancaster in 1915 and home secretary in 1916 (resigning when Lloyd George became prime minister). From 1920 to 1925, he was high commissioner in Palestine; he returned to the Commons as a Liberal from 1929 to 1935, supporting the national government and serving as home secretary in 1931–2. (*DNB, 1961–70*, ed. Williams and Nicholls, pp. 918–22; Robbins (ed.), *Biographical Dictionary*, pp. 366–7.)

[43] Quoted in Wrigley, *Lloyd George and the Challenge of Labour*, p. 237, Samuel to Runciman, Newcastle University Library, Runciman Papers, box 2, 13 Oct. 1919.

I have felt throughout the danger of the present position of capital. We have for the first time a great political party organised on an anti-capital basis. They are a power and have violent views. The prejudice against great wealth in 'pockets' is a danger to all capital. The wealth has come to men too rapidly and they have waxed fat while the mass have grown poorer. This is felt among the whole of the professional classes and in black coated circles and by the squires who see new men in the country flinging wealth about extravagantly. A tax is the wise policy but for one thing – the panic. The City always has cold feet but this time they have frightened me. If there were a series of failures that would be attributable to us. It is monstrous that a sum like 500 millions should produce panic but there it is. If we do not do it we shall strengthen the socialist case and send new people to their side. I confess I fear the unreasoning fear of the City.[44]

Chamberlain's ambivalent support for the war levy turned to rejection as the postwar boom gave way to depression with the danger that a further deflationary measure on top of high interest rates would lead to serious economic problems.[45] This change in the economic climate, rather than a simple concern for City sentiment, contributed to a shift in Treasury and Cabinet attitudes to a war levy.

The only member of Cabinet who argued strongly in favour of the levy was Churchill. His advocacy was political rather than fiscal or economic, resting on the need to establish a 'democratic platform' and to undermine the socialists' case that the government was 'too tender to trusts, plutocrats and profiteers' and to secure 'the honest comradeship of the men who saved the country'. Failure to gain working-class support was the greatest danger to capital: 'It will be very hard anyway to hold this immense electorate by reason and not by force and still hold the capitalist system. If we cannot reason with them and convince them, we shall bring the very disaster which the City fears.' In other words, he was not following the dictates of the City, but devising policies to create stability. Other members of Cabinet were more impressed by the hostility of industrial

[44] PRO, T171/177, deputation to the chancellor from the Association of British Chambers of Commerce and the Federation of British Industries, 5 May 1920; Birmingham University Library, AC5/1/164, Austen Chamberlain to Ida Chamberlain, 27 May 1920, in R. C. Self (ed.), *The Austen Chamberlain Diary Letters: The Correspondence of Sir Austen Chamberlain with his Sisters Hilda and Ida, 1916–37* (Royal Historical Society, London: Camden 5th ser. 5, 1995), pp. 134–5; Birmingham University Library, AC25/4/24, Cabinet 31(20) conclusion 5, 2 June 1920.

[45] Birmingham University Library, AC5/1/165, Austen to Hilda Chamberlain, 6 June 1920, in Self (ed.), *The Austen Chamberlain Diary Letters*, pp. 135–6; PP 1920 VII, *Report from the Select Committee on Increases of Wealth (War)*, evidence of B. P. Blackett, Qq. 1546–7, 1631, and J. C. Stamp, Qq. 3169–70; Hopkins, Q. 1391; R. McKenna, *Post-War Banking Policy: A Series of Addresses* (London, 1928), p. 24, referring to the memorandum to the Select Committee on Increases of Wealth (War); Short, 'Politics of personal taxation', pp. 36, 68–84; House of Lords Record Office, Bonar Law Papers, BL99/1/15, George Younger to A. Bonar Law, 21 May 1920.

interests to the levy and the dangerous precedent for future attacks on capital. As Alfred Mond* argued, it was 'a great political mistake to play for the help of extremists' and to alienate the 'middle business class' whose electoral support was crucial. In Lloyd George's opinion, the best response was to mount a positive campaign stressing that a balance had been maintained between the rich and poor, and that the rich paid more than in other countries:

It is very important to give the impression we are not a 'class' Government. The strength of this Government must be that it holds the balance evenly between classes, and it is ready to face their opposition...We would lose the support of the professional classes, the small *rentier*, and the small property-owner. If we are impartial and fearless, we can carry conviction even to those we rule against...We must avoid the idea we are a capitalist conspiracy. But we will get nothing out of this tax except disturbance of trade.[46]

The rejection of the levy on war wealth therefore increased the need to show that the tax system was balanced *in its absence* and that the government was not a class conspiracy. This concern for equity and fairness was crucial to the failure of anti-*rentier* rhetoric, in marked contrast to the experience after the Napoleonic wars when the fiscal system was easily portrayed as inequitable and unfair, a system of transfer from poor to rich, from producers to parasites.

Rejection of the war levy did nothing to resolve the political problems of the coalition government. On the one hand, it gave renewed force to Labour's case for a capital levy which was contained so long as the Select Committee on Increases of Wealth (War) was deliberating. On the other hand, there was the 'anti-waste' campaign and the grievance of industry that the EPD was maintained after the war. As Chamberlain saw, the EPD was 'a weak reed' on which to rely for revenue, but there was no obvious alternative.[47] What was at stake in 1919 and 1920 was the

---

[46] Birmingham University Library, AC25/4/11, Austen Chamberlain to Sir John Anderson, 15 Mar. 1920; AC34/1/109, CP 1319, 'Levy on war wealth: memorandum by chancellor of the Exchequer, Austen Chamberlain, 20 May 1920'; AC25/4/24, Cabinet 31 (20), conclusion 5, 2 June 1920, and AC25/4/25, Cabinet 32 (20), 4 June 1920.

[47] Birmingham University Library, AC5/1/164, Austen Chamberlain to Ida Chamberlain, 27 May 1920, in Self (ed.), *The Austen Chamberlain Diary Letters*, pp. 134–5.

* Alfred Moritz Mond (1868–1930) was the son of Ludwig Mond, a German émigré and chemical manufacturer; he was educated at Cheltenham, Cambridge and Edinburgh. He was called to the bar in 1894, joining his father's business in 1895. He advocated industrial co-ordination and co-operation with labour; the firm became part of the new Imperial Chemical Industries in 1926. He was a Liberal MP 1906–23 and 1924–8, holding office as first commissioner of works 1916–21 and minister of health 1921–2. After the war, he supported protectionism and the Empire Economic Union; he became a Conservative in 1926 and a Zionist. (*DNB, 1922–30*, ed. Weaver, pp. 602–5; Robbins (ed.), *Biographical Dictionary*, pp. 304–6.)

assumption that industry alone had the capacity to pay, and that taxation of profits would provide sufficient respite to prevent the introduction of other, more divisive, means of extraction such as indirect taxation or a capital levy. Naturally, industrialists did not readily accept the conclusion that taxation of business profits was crucial to stabilisation. The FBI, for example, argued that politicians and civil servants could not be trusted to set the budget, and that an independent committee of financial and economic experts should establish the 'taxable capacity' of the country so as to protect industry and preserve funds for the renewal of capital.[48] Although the government would not cede power to a corporatist body, the appointment of a committee to review government expenditure and recommend savings had the virtue of strengthening the position of the chancellor and Cabinet in enforcing economy and removing attacks on the government as 'wasteful'.[49] In 1921/2, a committee on national expenditure met under the chairmanship of Sir Eric Geddes,* whose career in the railway industry before moving into politics in the war made him acceptable to business interests. The expectation that the 'Geddes axe' would cut waste and extravagance was a means of containing the populist challenge to taxation and the state.

The vigour with which the axe was wielded was a matter of fine judgement. Severe cuts would justify Labour's case for the capital levy and undermine the government's policy of social stabilisation. Superficial cuts would fail to contain the 'anti-waste' campaign. The savings could be used to reduce the national debt (as the Treasury preferred) or to conciliate middle-class voters by reducing taxes (as the Cabinet wished). The concept of the 'normal year' was useful to the Treasury in arguing for a reduction in expenditure, for it rested on the assumption that the normal year of the future would devote the same amount of money in real terms to social services as in 1914, with the cost of servicing the debt to be covered from ordinary taxation over the next fifty years. By

[48] PRO, T172/1164, R. P. Nugent to D. Lloyd George, 5 July 1920.
[49] PRO, CAB27/71, FC23, 22 July 1920, ff. 137–9.
* Eric Campbell Geddes (1875–1937) was born in India, where his father was a civil engineer. He was educated in Edinburgh and the Oxford Military College; he worked in the US on the railways and as a labourer in steel mills, before returning to India to run a forestry estate and as traffic superintendent on a railway. In 1906, he joined the North-East Railway, rising to deputy general manager in 1914. In 1915, he became deputy director-general of munitions supply, in 1916–17 inspector-general of transport in all theatres of war and in 1917 controller of the navy. He became a Unionist MP from 1917 to 1922, and served as first lord of the Admiralty in 1917–18, minister of transport 1919–21 where he carried through the amalgamation of railways. He returned to business as chairman of Imperial Airways and Dunlop Rubber. (*DNB, 1931–40*, ed. Legg, pp. 310–11.)

adhering to this definition of the normal year, the Treasury was able to give priority to the debt and constrain expenditure on social services. As Dr Short has said, the normal year provided 'an aura of an undeniable and timeless standard' in order to establish a ceiling on expenditure.[50] In fact, the 'normal year' was *not* achieved and social expenditure remained far above the real level of 1914; the normal year was at most a defence against any further increase, a device to protect debt service and redemption against pressure for a change in priorities. The outcome was a delicate balancing act which offered sufficient concessions to contain 'anti-waste' without 'any radical abandonment of social provision', and applied most of the savings to tax cuts rather than debt redemption.[51] The 'Geddes axe' was not a simple victory of the City and Treasury, but a more complicated and subtle process of mediation between a variety of concerns. Nobody was fully satisfied, no one was ignored; the crisis was contained, not solved. What was needed was a holding action which would see the government through the immediate alarms of the return to peace. The answer was a continued reliance on taxation of business profits.

Industry and the weight of taxation

Despite assurances that the EPD was an exceptional war tax, it was continued after the war: the government could scarcely surrender a net revenue of £284m, amounting to 36 per cent of the total revenue of central government in 1918/19.[52] At the end of the war, the high level of EPD was widely criticised for removing incentives to raise production, and reducing funds needed for expansion and postwar competition. The FBI argued that taxation ultimately fell on industry and on the costs of production, so that British industry was at a disadvantage in competing both with neutral countries and with enemy countries with a lower level of war taxation and a reserve of war profits. The result would be

---

[50] Short, 'Politics of personal taxation', pp. 28–9.
[51] McDonald, 'Geddes Committee', 672. For Labour's view of the cuts and support for the levy as an alternative, see National Joint Council of the General Council of the TUC, Executive Committee of the Labour Party and Parliamentary Labour Party, *Labour and National 'Economy'* (London, 1922), p. 7.
[52] PRO, T172/507, EPD: deputation from Central Council of Controlled Firms and FBI to chancellor of the Exchequer, 18 June 1917; T172/903, 'Federation of British Industries: peace aims', 12 Dec. 1918 and 30 Jan. 1919; T172/1193, deputation to Sir Robert Horne, chancellor of the Exchequer, from the FBI and Association of British Chambers of Commerce, 21 Apr. 1921; Mallet and George, *British Budgets*, pp. 328–31 and table xx.

'gradually-increasing industrial stagnation ending very possibly in complete economic ruin, in which all classes – employers and employed – will suffer'. Britain might win the war on the battefields and lose the peace in the marketplace; taxation might harm incentives and efficiency to the disadvantage of everyone.[53] The FBI was alarmed, complaining that 'any direct taxation upon production qua production is unsound', and that it was 'encroaching on capital or slaughtering assets, thus draining industry and commerce of the very resources which are essential to a revival of trade', and preventing an escape from 'the vicious circle of decreasing trade, decreasing national revenue, and increasing unemployment'.[54] The contention of the FBI was strongly supported by McKenna, that the capacity of industry to bear taxation was being exceeded, so that 'thrift, business enterprise, and needful capital development become seriously impaired'.[55]

This was more than special pleading, for profiteering was not a serious phenomenon. Before the war (1910–14), the rate of return on capital employed in a sample of industrial concerns, at current prices, was 8.2 per cent; the rate rose to 17.0 per cent in 1915–20, and fell to 6.3 per cent in 1921–4. Part of the capital employed by these firms was fixed interest loans, so that the return on *equity* capital was higher, at 10.1, 23.8 and 6.9 per cent. These figures give some credence to the widespread assumption that industry *was* profiteering during the war. However, the high rate of return to equity capital largely disappears when inflation and taxation are taken into account. The *real* return to equity capital after allowing for tax and inflation was actually lower during the war: it

[53] PRO, T170/105, 'Notes on the subject of "profiteering" during the war', R. V. N. Hopkins, 12 Dec. 1916; T171/141, EPD: note by the Board of Inland Revenue, 21 Dec. 1916; T172/903, FBI, peace aims, 12 Dec. 1918 and 30 Jan. 1919.

[54] MRC, FBI MSS 200/F/3/E4/1/1, 2 and 3, deputations to the chancellor of the Exchequer from the FBI, 7 Feb. 1919, 10 Mar. 1920 and 10 Dec. 1920; MRC, FBI MSS 200/F/3/E4/1/6, R. Nugent to R. Horne, 26 Apr. 1922; MRC, FBI MSS 200/F/3/E4/1/6, Nugent to chancellor, 26 Apr. 1922; PRO, T171/151, E. E. Nott-Bower and N. F. Warren Fisher to chancellor, EPD: proposal to increase the rate from 80 per cent to 100 per cent, 27 Dec. 1917, and War Cabinet: excess profits levy, note by Bonar Law, 7 Jan. 1918, circulating a memorandum by J. C. Stamp; T171/168, 'Points for discussion with the chancellor of the Exchequer: memorandum for the deputation of 18 June 1917'; Briden Scott, FBI, to Gower, 2 Oct. 1918; T171/176, A. Chamberlain to A. Bonar Law, 11 Mar. 1920; T171/177, 'Note in anticipation of the joint deputation from the Association of British Chambers of Commerce and the FBI', Inland Revenue, 3 May 1920; deputation to the chancellor of the Exchequer from the Association of British Chambers of Commerce and the FBI, 5 May 1920; T171/190, P. Rylands to chancellor, 10 Feb. 1921; T172/1432, report of proceedings at a deputation from the National Union of Manufacturers to the prime minister, 11 July 1922; T172/1205, deputation to the chancellor of the Exchequer from the FBI, 16 Feb. 1921.

[55] McKenna, *Post-War Banking Policy*, pp. 19, 35, 49–51.

stood at 10.0 per cent in 1910–14, 8.7 per cent in 1915–20 and fell to
3.1 per cent in 1921–4. These figures suggest that the FBI had a genuine
grievance: war profiteering was largely a monetary illusion, and profits
tax removed any remaining gains to equity capital. Returns were only
a third of prewar levels, yet companies maintained their distribution of
dividends with the result that retentions collapsed. Capital accumulation
over the transwar period was accordingly low, with serious consequences
for the competitiveness of British industry.[56]

The FBI had a number of possible solutions. One was to ensure that
the enemy paid for the war, and did not reduce its own internal debt before meeting the demands of the allies.[57] The Treasury accepted that the
tax treatment of German firms during the war was more generous than in
Britain and that large industrial firms were therefore able to accumulate
cash reserves. The Treasury interpreted generous treatment of German
industry as a conscious strategy to place firms in a strong position at
the end of the war, allowing them to accumulate reserves to maintain
postwar production, to preserve wages and dividends, and to secure foreign markets against their over-burdened British competitors.[58] In order
to improve the tax position of British industry, the FBI and McKenna
therefore argued that the national debt should be serviced by cutting
government expenditure and reducing taxes to stimulate recovery. Prices
should not be reduced through limits on credit; rather, any 'correction'
of price levels should be achieved through stimulating production and increasing the supply of commodities. The FBI's case was that maintenance
of trade depended upon fresh capital which could only be obtained from
the surplus of production over consumption. In its opinion, this surplus
was reduced by public expenditure and high taxation, leaving very little to
cover savings and industrial depreciation. Existing rates of tax, it seemed,

[56] A. J. Arnold, 'Profitability and capital accumulation in British industry during the trans-
war period, 1913–24', *Economic History Review* 52 (1999), table 3; S. N. Broadberry,
'The impact of the world wars on the long-run performance of the British economy',
Oxford Review of Economic Policy 4 (1988), 25–37.

[57] PRO, T172/903, FBI, peace aims, 12 Dec. 1918 and 30 Jan. 1919; also T172/1432,
report of proceedings at a deputation from the National Union of Manufacturers to the
prime minister, 11 July 1922.

[58] For example, PRO, IR63/80, E. E. Nott-Bower and N. F. Warren Fisher to chancellor,
27 Dec. 1917: EPD: proposal to increase the rate from 80 to 100 per cent; excess profits
duty: note by J. C. Stamp upon the suggestion that the rate should be increased from 80
to 100 per cent, 27 Dec. 1917. It was argued that at 80 per cent the duty was already
beyond its maximum productivity and was harming industrial output. PRO, T171/151,
'Resumé of the present German practice in connection with excess profits', H. Hirst,
10 Jan. 1918; IR64/41, N. F. Warren Fisher and H. P. Hamilton to chancellor, 15 Mar.
1919, and memorandum on French war profits tax, Inland Revenue, 15 Mar. 1919.

can only be paid in many instances by encroaching upon capital or slaughtering assets, thus draining industry and commerce of the very resources which are essential to a revival of trade. So long as industry is thus deprived by excessive taxation of the power to recover, the vicious circle of decreasing trade, decreasing national revenue, increasing unemployment, with its accompanying heavy charge upon the State, must continue.

What was needed, it seemed to the FBI, was a reduction in taxes and 'rigid restriction' of expenditure in order to reduce costs of production and leave more savings from which to provide capital.[59] An alternative suggestion put forward by the FBI was to abandon 'pedantic adherence to strict economic doctrine' in order to win the 'economic peace'. Budget deficits and suspension of the sinking fund were preferable to allowing industry to be 'absolutely crushed under a load they cannot carry . . . Face it that you have a cycle of three or four, or five years if you like over which you have to stand by industry and let it recover and not let it go under, and raise funds from other sources.' Reduction in taxation was given priority over redemption of the debt and a balanced budget in order to relieve the burden on industry and to increase domestic purchasing power as a stimulus to recovery. Above all, the FBI felt a reduction in income tax would provide 'a valuable psychological boost', and might justify a shift to indirect taxation.[60] The danger with these proposals was that an

---

[59] McKenna, *Postwar Banking Policy*, pp. 19, 35, 49–51; Short, 'Politics of personal taxation', pp. 153–9; on the FBI see MRC, FBI MSS 200/F/3/E4/1/3, draft memorandum for chancellor of the Exchequer, deputation of 10 Dec. 1920; MSS 200/F/3/E4/1/6, president of FBI to chancellor, 19 Dec. 1921, and R. T. Nugent, director of FBI, to chancellor, 26 Apr. 1922; MSS 200/F/3/E4/1/8, taxation policy, FBI memorandum to chancellor of the Exchequer, 27 Feb. 1924, also in T171/234, with comments by O. Niemeyer, 29 Feb. 1924, by R. G. Hawtrey, 3 Mar. 1924, and note by the Board of Inland Revenue, 13 Mar. 1924. See comment by J. Stamp, *Wealth and Taxable Capacity* (London, 1922), pp. 123–7, 136–7, on McKenna's argument to the National Union of Manufacturers in 1920 that the country was grossly over-taxed, leaving too little for industrial investment. McKenna claimed that savings and depreciation on industrial capital amounted to only a fifth of the prewar level; Stamp felt the figure was four-fifths. Nevertheless, Stamp was not optimistic, fearing that a fall in production and prices would remove the surplus of production over consumption which was available for savings and taxation, so that there could be little addition to capital and national wealth.

[60] Sir John Harmood-Banner, *Parliamentary Debates*, 5th ser. 128, 19 Apr. 1920, col. 121; MRC, FBI MSS 200/F/3/E4/1/2, deputation to chancellor of the Exchequer, 10 Mar. 1920; meeting of 6 May 1920 to discuss deputation to chancellor of Exchequer; MSS 200/F/3/E4/1/3, draft memorandum for the chancellor of the Exchequer (deputation of 10 Dec. 1920); deputation from FBI to chancellor, 10 Dec. 1920; MSS 200/F/3/E4/1/4, deputation to the chancellor of the Exchequer, 16 Feb. 1921; president of FBI to chancellor, 10 Feb. 1921; PRO, T171/177, deputation to the chancellor of the Exchequer from the Association of British Chambers of Commerce and the Federation of British Industries, 5 May 1920; T171/190, P. Rylands, FBI, to chancellor of the Exchequer, 10 Feb. 1921; T172/1205, deputation to the chancellor of the Exchequer from the FBI, 16 Feb. 1921; T172/1244, deputation to Sir Robert Horne, chancellor of the Exchequer

onslaught on expenditure or a shift to indirect taxation would threaten the consent of the working class, strengthen the case of the advocates of a capital levy and undermine financial confidence with the danger that would pose to the floating debt.

The Inland Revenue and Treasury were unmoved by these pleas, and opposed concessions to industry as a 'jerry-mandering of taxes' on the grounds that 'equality of treatment between taxpayer and taxpayer is a cardinal principle, the scope and conditions of liability are closely defined by statute and discretionary power is taboo'.[61] In any case, they were not convinced that the taxable capacity of industry *was* exceeded or that there was a shortage of capital. The Treasury argued that 'no section of society other than the industrial section can be pointed to as having or being likely in the immediate future to have a special ability to pay'. Although Otto Niemeyer* of the Treasury admitted that taxation in Britain was considerably higher than in other countries and that a reduction in taxation might stimulate trade, he was adamant that any tax cut should come from a surplus in revenue rather than suspension of the sinking fund. He opposed the FBI's plea that taxes be reduced in order to stimulate production and employment, and to provide savings for investment. The Treasury position was that tax cuts had a marginal impact on savings which would be more effectively increased by speedier redemption of debt. By using taxes to repay debt, money would be returned to investors in government bonds for use at a more profitable rate, so stimulating the recovery of trade and industry. The high level of taxation would therefore *increase* savings and augment 'the capital sources of the nation' by holding down consumption, and transferring money to the holders of securities who would undertake new investment. Consequently, the Treasury claimed that high taxation and debt redemption were a form of 'compulsory thrift' by 'mobilising – under the compulsion of the tax gatherer – capital for industrial investment'. Such logic led Hawtrey to argue that the aims of the FBI 'are best attained by the greatest possible reduction of expenditure and the highest possible

from the FBI, 15 Feb. 1922; Birmingham University Library, AC5/1/160, Austen to Ida Chamberlain, 25 Apr. 1920, in Self (ed.), *The Austen Chamberlain Diary Letters*, pp. 133–4.

[61] PRO, T171/141, Reconstruction Committee: encouragement of industries by means of remission of internal taxation: I, memorandum to the chancellor of the Exchequer from the Board of Inland Revenue, E. E. Nott-Bower and N. F. Warren Fisher, 30 Aug. 1916. The chancellor agreed it should be ruled out: II, minute of meeting of 27 Sept.

* Otto Ernst Niemeyer (1883–1971) was born in London, the son of a German merchant; he was educated at St Paul's and Balliol College, Oxford; in 1906 he entered the Treasury, and became controller of finance in 1922. He supported the return to gold in 1925, and left the Treasury to join the Bank of England as an adviser in 1927, and executive director from 1938 to 1952. (*DNB, 1971–80*, ed. Blake and Nicholls, pp. 631–3.)

taxation' in order to speed up debt redemption and release funds for investment.[62]

Above all, the Treasury believed that a sinking fund was essential for financial stability and that there should be no borrowing to meet peace-time expenditure. 'Most of the economic and financial ills of today (including the present trade depression in the United Kingdom)', argued Basil Blackett* of the Treasury, 'are in large part due to the inability or unwillingness of foreign governments to meet their expenditure out of taxation.'[63] As Niemeyer argued, the reduction of the national debt after 1815 created confidence in British government loans and credit which helped to preserve British freedom and liberty by providing a secure basis for war-time borrowing. This edifice of financial stability rested on

the British habit of meeting its expenditure (with something over for debt reduction) out of revenue. Nothing can be more dangerous for the State than to have the means of incurring expenditure without the need of imposing taxation to meet it. The present parlous condition of public finance in many European countries is largely due to the habit of their governments to spend money without covering their expenditure out of ordinary revenue.[64]

Any abandonment of the balanced budget would remove the model for other countries to follow, so that 'the hope of restoring sanity to public finance throughout the world would be long deferred'. It was also in the interest of industry to preserve constraints on expenditure: if they were relaxed to assist industry, they might be relaxed for other causes. The Treasury insisted that maintenance of a sinking fund and reduction in debt out of taxation were beneficial to industry in the longer term, allowing it to become competitive when the debt was paid off, and providing an insurance against forced loans or a capital levy.[65]

---

[62] PRO, T170/125, 'Reconstruction finance', J. Bradbury, 21 Feb. 1918; T171/190, 'Note on possible methods of replacing part of the revenue now drawn from the excess profits duty', 17 Dec. 1920; T171/202, 'Budgeting for a deficit', B. P. Blackett, 24 Mar. 1922; T171/214, Niemeyer to chancellor, 20 Mar. 1923; 'Sinking funds', Niemeyer to chancellor, 23 Jan. 1923; T171/222, budget memorandum by Niemeyer, n.d.; T171/226, Niemeyer to chancellor, 24 Jan. 1924, 10 Mar. 1924, 2 Apr. 1924; T171/234, note by O. Niemeyer, 29 Feb. 1924; FBI memorandum on taxation, R. G. Hawtrey, 3 Mar. 1924, and note by the Board of Inland Revenue, 13 Mar. 1924; T172/1237, memorandum by the Revenue Boards on a merchants' sales tax, 4 Mar. 1922; T172/1262, Chamberlain to Cecil, 2 Aug. 1920, and Cecil to Chamberlain, 3 Aug. 1920; IR74/231, CP3649, Cabinet: industry and the weight of taxation: memorandum written by the Board of Inland Revenue in consultation with the Board of Customs and Excise, Jan. 1922.

[63] PRO, T171/202, 'Budgeting for a deficit', B. P. Blackett, 24 Mar. 1922.

[64] PRO, T171/214, 'Funding pensions', Niemeyer to chancellor, 9 Feb. 1923.

[65] PRO, T171/202, 'Anti-Mond', O. Niemeyer?, n.d.; 'Budgeting for a deficit', B. P. Blackett, 24 Mar. 1922; T171/214, Niemeyer to chancellor, 20 Mar. 1923; 'Sinking funds', Niemeyer to chancellor, 23 Jan. 1923.

* Basil Phillott Blackett (1882–1935) was born in Calcutta where his parents were missionaries. He was educated at Marlborough and University College, Oxford; he entered

At the end of the war, the Inland Revenue proposed the replacement of the temporary EPD by a graduated tax on any profits above a standard rate on capital employed. Such a tax would mark a departure from the British approach to corporations as 'an aggregation of persons who may or may not be taxable', with the company merely withholding tax; it would entail a shift to the American approach to corporations as taxable entities in their own right.[66] The war-time EPD treated the business itself as taxable – a change which Josiah Stamp* felt should become permanent. In his view, the income of firms depended on public expenditures and the maintenance of the business environment so that they had a liability to taxation in addition to any liability as an aggregation of individuals.[67] His case was similar to J. A. Hobson's[†] distinction between 'costs' paid for the use of factors of production (which should be free of tax) and 'surplus' or

the Treasury in 1904, and was secretary of the Royal Commission on Indian Finance, 1913–14, Treasury representative in Washington 1917–19, controller of finance at the Treasury 1919–22, finance member of the Viceroy's Council in India 1922–8. He became a director of the Bank of England in 1929, and chairman of the Imperial and International Communications Co. from 1929 to 1932, when he joined De Beers Consolidated Mines. After the crisis of 1931, he supported planned money, the sterling area and deficit finance, in contrast to his classic statement against deficit finance of 1922. (*DNB, 1931–40*, ed. Legg, pp. 83–4.)

[66] K. K. Kennan, *Income Taxation: Methods and Results in Various Countries* (Milwaukee, 1910), pp. 280–2; PRO, T171/178, 'Report to the Board of Inland Revenue on the excess profits taxes imposed in Canada and the USA, with special reference to the imposition of a tax on business profits in the United Kingdom', G. B. Canny and W. F. Atkins, Jan. 1920; H. B. Spaulding, *The Income Tax in Great Britain and the United States* (London, 1927), pp. 35–6, 86–93; G. S. A. Wheatcroft, 'The tax treatment of corporations and shareholders in the United States and Great Britain', *British Tax Review* (1961), 41–61.

[67] PP 1920 VII, *Report from the Select Committee on Increases of Wealth (War)*, Q. 3133.

* Josiah Charles Stamp (1880–1941) was born in London, the son of a shopkeeper. He entered the Inland Revenue as a boy clerk in 1896, and took an external degree in economics from the LSE in 1911, followed by a DSc in 1916. He was assistant secretary of the Inland Revenue between 1916 and 1919, when he became secretary and director of Nobel Industries and in 1926 president of the London, Midland and Scottish Railway. He was a member of the Royal Commission on Income Tax of 1919/20 and the Committee on National Debt and Taxation of 1924–7, and he served on the Economic Advisory Council from 1930 to 1941, as well as becoming a director of the Bank of England in 1928. He was British representative on the Dawes (1924) and Young (1929) committees on German reparations. (*DNB, 1941–50*, ed. Legg and Williams, pp. 817–20.)

† John Atkinson Hobson (1858–1940) was born in Derby, the son of a newspaper proprietor. He was educated at Derby School and Lincoln College, Oxford; on graduating, he taught classics until 1887 and then worked as a university extension lecturer until 1897. He developed his idea of under-consumption (with A. F. Mummery) in *The Physiology of Industry* (1889), arguing for graduated taxation. He was influenced by Ruskin, and wrote a study of him in 1898, as well as a book on Cobden. He wished to nationalise monopolies and standardised industries, and retain individual enterprise where taste and skill were important to expressing the personality of the consumer and the producer. He believed that under-consumption led to over-saving and hence a flight of capital in search of imperialism; free trade would only lead to peace on condition that income was redistributed at home. (*DNB, 1931–40*, ed. Legg, pp. 435–6.)

'unnecessary and excessive payments' (which had a special ability to pay taxes). According to this approach, £1,000 obtained from speculation would have a large surplus whereas an income of £10,000 from house property or consols had no surplus. However, the income tax did not take account of the surplus; its only concern was the amount of income, so that the second was charged at a higher marginal rate than the first. Stamp followed Hobson's contention that a tax on profits was a better way of reaching the surplus and exempting costs. In particular, a progressive taxation of profits would hit profiteering, without discouraging ordinary business.[68]

The initial willingness of the Treasury and Inland Revenue to contemplate a graduated tax on profits was pragmatic, based on the belief that capital was resigned to a profit tax as preferable to 100 per cent EPD or a capital levy.[69] In 1919, Austen Chamberlain reduced the EPD to 40 per cent[70] and intimated that a revised profits tax would be less onerous and more equitable for industry. Consequently, officials were dispatched to report on the American and Canadian systems of taxation of profits above a fixed percentage on capital. Their response was guarded, stressing the difficulties of determining capital, and the discouragement to productivity and efficiency. At most, they were willing to concede that a profits tax offered a temporary solution 'in the present abnormal times as a matter of practical politics', when a limit had been reached in 'the rates of the regular and permanent taxes, which are fairer in their operation'. The attraction of a tax on profits in these extreme circumstances was three-fold. First, it secured revenue from those who had profits with which to pay. Secondly, it was an impersonal tax which was not a direct burden on any individual. Thirdly, and most importantly, it had the support of 'a large body of public opinion, comprising the bulk of the lower middle classes

---

[68] On Hobson's distinction between costs and surplus, see Daunton, *Trusting Leviathan*, pp. 344–6; he developed his case in *Minutes of Evidence Taken before the Committee on National Debt and Taxation* (2 vols., London, 1927), vol. I, Qq. 1555, 1578–649. For Stamp, see J. C. Stamp, 'The special taxation of business profits in relation to the present position of national finance', *Economic Journal* 29 (1919), 411–27, 'Taxation of capital and "ability to pay"', *Edinburgh Review* 20 (1919), and his memorandum in PRO, IR75/109, 'The levy on capital in its theoretical and academic aspects'. The issue of the best measure of ability – realised income, capitalised income or capital – is discussed in A. A. Mitchell, 'A levy on capital', *Economic Journal* 28 (1918), 268–75, which argues for realised income, as well as the problems of valuation and the 'ghastly fiasco' of the 1910 valuations; and in A. Hook, 'A tax on capital and redemption of debt', *Economic Journal* 28 (1918), 167–75.

[69] PRO, T171/151, 'Proposed compulsory limitation to dividends: note by J. C. Stamp, 9 February, 1919'; T171/162, N. F. Warren Fisher and H. P. Hamilton to chancellor of the Exchequer, 30 Nov. 1918; Stamp, 'Special taxation of business profits'.

[70] MRC, FBI MSS 200/F/3/E4/1/1, deputation to the chancellor of the Exchequer, 5 July 1919.

as well as labour' who believed that capital made excessive returns. The continuation of some form of profits tax offered a way of containing the pressure of Labour for a capital levy, of the middle class for a curtailment of profiteering, and of industry for the reform of the EPD. What was rejected by the Inland Revenue report was any *permanent* departure from prewar approaches to corporate taxation.[71]

Industrialists were not entirely convinced, arguing that any new tax should apply to *all* trades, including agriculture and the professions which had not been covered by the EPD.[72] However, any extension of the tax would make it difficult to distinguish from an increase in income tax. It would cover earned income, so undermining differentiation and contradicting 'the accepted trend of modern theories of equitable taxation ... which now firmly rests on the cardinal principle of ability to pay'. Above all, it would not resolve political hostility to excessive profits.[73] The budget of April 1920 therefore introduced a new corporation tax of 1s in £ (5 per cent) on the profits of limited liability companies. This could not contain public hostility to abnormally high returns during the postwar boom, so the EPD was retained at 60 per cent until excess profits disappeared; companies paid whichever tax was the higher. When profits returned to prewar standards and the EPD ceased to produce revenue, the possibility remained that the corporation profits tax could be retained. The tax could be justified on two grounds, as a payment for the legal privilege of limited liability, and as a measure of equity with private partnerships. Corporations paid the *standard* rate of income tax on *retained* profits; super-tax was only paid by shareholders who were liable when profits were distributed. Private partnerships paid super-tax on both distributed *and* retained profits.[74] The political case was overwhelming, and

---

[71] PRO, T171/178, 'Report ... on the excess profits tax imposed in Canada and the USA'; 'Memorandum by the Board of Inland Revenue as to the arguments which might be adduced for and against a tax on profits of corporate trading bodies, with suggestions as to the form which such a tax might take, February 1920'.

[72] PRO, IR63/84, A. Chamberlain to Fisher, 5 Feb. 1919; T172/1164, deputation to the chancellor of the Exchequer from the FBI, 10 Mar. 1920, also in MRC, FBI MSS 200/F/3/E4/1/2.

[73] PRO, T172/1164, and MRC, FBI MSS 200/F/3/E4/1/2, deputation, 10 Mar. 1920; PRO, T172/1164 and T171/177, deputation to A. Chamberlain, chancellor of the Exchequer from the Association of British Chambers of Commerce and FBI, 5 May 1920; T171/177, 'Note in anticipation of the joint deputation from the Association of Chambers of Commerce and FBI', 1 May 1920. The FBI complained that it was forced to chose between the EPD and a war levy; there was an alternative of a flat-rate tax: see MRC, FBI MSS 200/F/3/E4/1/2, director of FBI to Rylands, 23 Apr. 1920.

[74] PRO, T171/176, A. Chamberlain to A. Bonar Law, 11 Mar. 1920 (also in House of Lords Record Office, Bonar Law Papers, BL98/8/6); T171/178, 'Memorandum ... as to the arguments which ought to be adduced for and against a tax on profits of corporate trading bodies'; 'Note by the Board of Inland Revenue on alternative methods of securing

Chamberlain refused to bow to pressure from 'selfish, swollen' industrialists, urging them to remember the 'very dangerous feeling throughout the country' which threatened 'the security of more hardly earned
capital'. Reluctantly, the spokesmen for industry agreed that the EPD was
'a much safer tax' than a levy on war wealth which might 'produce a financial disaster of the most serious kind' by disrupting credit and providing
the precedent for a levy. As one Glasgow businessman put it, 'People hate
EPD as the devil hates holy water, but its strongest opponents would vote
for it to a man . . . as against a capital levy.'[75]

The EPD and corporation profits tax were therefore short-term expedients to cover the immediate postwar crisis. Much as industrialists might
protest, taxation of profits was preferable to the only other feasible tax: a
general indirect tax on sales. The chancellor, Robert Horne,[*] admitted
that the corporation tax was 'a bad taxation. It is a thing that has been
imported from America, and I have continued it because the man who
adopted it had to impose it to bring in the money.'[76] Horne was associated with the FBI and accepted that the taxable capacity of industry was
exceeded. He had the support of Winston Churchill, E. S. Montagu[†] and
Alfred Mond who were aware that reducing the income tax by deep cuts
in expenditure as proposed by the FBI would threaten the programme
of social reform and play into the hands of Labour. There seemed to be

a yield of revenue comparable with that offered by the existing EPD of 40 per cent';
Austen Chamberlain in *Parliamentary Debates.* 5th ser. 128, 19 Apr. 1920, cols. 96, 98–
9; T171/190, 'Note on possible methods of replacing part of the revenue now drawn
from the Excess Profits Duty', Inland Revenue, 17 Dec. 1920.

[75] House of Lords Record Office, Bonar Law Papers, BL99/1/15, Younger to Law, 21 May
1920; 99/1/26, H. Macgeorge to Law, 31 May 1920; see also 99/1/17, P. Woodhouse to
Law, 22 May 1920, on the same assessment by Lancashire businessmen.

[76] PRO, T172/1427, deputation to Robert Horne, chancellor of the Exchequer, from the
Association of British Chambers of Commerce, 14 Feb. 1922; see also T172/1319, note
by the Board of Inland Revenue in connection with the deputation of the FBI to the
chancellor on 30 Jan. 1923.

[*] Robert Stevenson Horne (1871–1940) was born in Stirlingshire, the son of a minister. He
was educated at George Watson's College in Edinburgh and the University of Glasgow,
and became an advocate in 1896. During the war, he was engaged in administration of
railways, materials and labour, in association with Geddes. He was a Unionist MP from
1918 to 1937, serving as minister of labour 1919–20, president of the Board of Trade
1920–1 and chancellor of the Exchequer 1921–2. He entered business as a director of
the Suez Canal, Lloyds Bank and P and O; he was chairman of the Burmah Corporation
and of the Great Western Railway. (*DNB, 1931–40*, ed. Legg, pp. 444–5; Robbins (ed.),
Biographical Dictionary, pp. 215–17.)

[†] Edwin Samuel Montagu (1879–1924) was the son of a leading financier; he was educated
at Trinity College, Cambridge, and served as a Liberal MP from 1906 to 1922. He
was private secretary to Asquith 1906–10, parliamentary under-secretary of state for
India 1910–14, financial secretary to the Treasury 1914–16, chancellor of the Duchy of
Lancaster 1915 and minister of munitions 1916. He resigned in December 1916, but
returned to office as secretary of state for India, 1917–22. (*DNB, 1922–30*, ed. Weaver,
pp. 607–10; Robbins (ed.), *Biographical Dictionary*, pp. 306–7.)

only one way of cutting income tax *and* maintaining expenditure: a budget deficit masked by raiding the sinking fund.[77] In the event, Horne's heresy went unnoticed and budgetary orthodoxy was preserved when economic recovery produced an unexpected surplus.[78] As a result, his successor as chancellor – Stanley Baldwin* – reduced the corporation profits tax to 2.5 per cent in 1923 and anticipated its demise. 'Everyone admits it is not a good tax', he informed the Commons, 'many think that it bears exceptionally heavily on enterprise and industry.'[79] The task of abolition was completed by Snowden in the first Labour budget of 1924.

Corporate taxation did not have a purchase in British fiscal policy, for it contradicted the assumption that firms were agents rather than taxable entities. Corporation taxation did not, as in the United States, connect with hostility to big business or with opposition to a federal income tax. On the contrary, the income tax was seen as the most equitable system of taxation. Although industry bore a large part of the fiscal burden immediately after the war, the chancellor accepted that taxation of business profits was not a normal part of the tax system and the existing fiscal constitution was reasserted as soon as circumstances permitted. More surprisingly, the Labour party rejected corporate taxation and dismissed Hobson's argument for taxation of 'surplus' profits. What was needed, so the party argued, was a direct attack on wealth *after* it was accumulated, rather than on the income which produced wealth.[80] In the opinion

---

[77] PRO, T172/1164, R. P. Nugent to D. Lloyd George, 5 July 1920; deputation to Austen Chamberlain from FBI, 10 Dec. 1920. For example, the National Union of Manufacturers urged a repeat of the Geddes Committee to cut expenditure in the 1923 budget: T172/1432, report of proceedings at a deputation from the National Union of Manufacturers to the prime minister, 11 July 1922; see also T172/1427, deputation to Robert Horne, chancellor of the Exchequer, from the Association of British Chambers of Commerce, 14 Feb. 1922.

[78] Short, 'Politics of personal taxation', pp. 151, 166–86; PRO, T171/202, memorandum by the secretary of state for India, E. S. Montagu, 9 Dec. 1921; memorandum by the minister of health, A. Mond, 'Reduction in Taxation', 30 Mar. 1922; Churchill to Horne, 30 Mar. 1922; T171/203, Hopkins to Grigg, 31 Aug. 1921; T171/205, Horne to G. V., 29 Apr. 1922; House of Lords Record Office, Lloyd George Papers, LGF/37/1/26, Mond to Lloyd George, 1 July 1921.

[79] U. K. Hicks, *The Finance of British Government, 1920–36* (London, 1938), p. 238; *Parliamentary Debates*, 5th ser. 162, 16 Apr. 1923, col. 1740.

[80] R. C. Whiting, 'The Labour party, capitalism and the national debt, 1918–24', in P. J. Waller (ed.), *Politics and Social Change in Modern Britain: Essays Presented to A. F. Thompson* (Brighton, 1987), p. 148, citing LPA, JSM/FIN/50.

* Stanley Baldwin (1867–1947) was the son of an ironmaster; he was educated at Harrow and Trinity College, Cambridge. He joined the family business, and was a Conservative MP from 1908 to 1937. He was private parliamentary secretary to Bonar Law 1916–17, joint financial secretary of the Treasury 1917–21, president of the Board of Trade 1921–2, chancellor of the Exchequer 1922–3, prime minister 1923–4 and 1924–9, lord president of the council 1931–5 and prime minister 1935–7. In 1919, he realised 20 per cent of his estate to cancel war debt. (*DNB, 1941–50*, ed. Legg and Williams, pp. 43–51; Robbins (ed.), *Biographical Dictionary*, pp. 30–3.)

of Dalton, taxation of profits was 'especially objectionable, discriminating against ordinary shareholders in joint-stock companies as compared with other property owners, and discouraging, in a specially high degree, the taking of business risks'. Company taxation contradicted Labour's strategy of taxing 'unearned' income and instead placed a tax on enterprise.[81] Pursuit of the chimera of the capital levy meant that the practical policy of taxation of company profits disappeared from the fiscal agenda until after the Second World War, and rejection of company taxation meant that the British fiscal regime, despite its heavily progressive income tax, did not tax corporate profits which were a major source of inequality of income.

Indirect taxation

Maintenance of high taxation and debt redemption did not necessarily imply taxation of profits or income: it could mean a shift to indirect taxation as suggested by the FBI.[82] During the war, the proportion of government revenue from indirect taxation fell from 42.5 per cent in 1913/14 to 24.9 per cent in 1919/20. Although the termination of the EPD and corporation tax led to a reversal in the trend to direct taxes, indirect taxes still accounted for only 35.9 per cent of revenue in 1929/30 (see table 2.3). Not surprisingly, many industrialists and income taxpayers felt they were bearing too great a burden and that indirect taxpayers were escaping a proper contribution to the costs of government. In 1922, Leo Amery* urged a 'rally against Socialism' designed to reverse current

---

[81] *Parliamentary Debates*, 5th ser. 141, 25 Apr. 1921, cols. 233 and 172, 29 Apr. 1924, cols. 1606–7; Dalton, *Capital Levy Explained*, p. 41. At this stage, capital gains from rising share prices were not considered. The concern for Rent and socially created value concentrated on the flow of unearned income rather than the underlying value of the asset which was left to the operation of death duties or to nationalisation. Concern for capital gains did not arise until after the Second World War, when high levels of income tax opened the possibility of tax avoidance through untaxed capital gains in the value of shares rather than taxed dividends. Further, in 1947 Dalton turned to higher taxation of distributed profits to encourage retentions.

[82] For example, PRO, T171/190, P. Rylands to chancellor of the Exchequer, 10 Feb. 1921, and T172/1205, deputation to the chancellor of the Exchequer from FBI, 16 Feb. 1921.

* Leopold Charles Maurice Stennett Amery (1873–1955) was born in India, where his father was in the Indian civil service. He was educated at Harrow and Balliol College, Oxford, becoming a fellow of All Souls. He was a journalist on *The Times* from 1899 to 1909, and was called to the bar. He supported tariff reform and conscription, and opposed home rule. He was an MP from 1911 to 1945. After a period in the army, he became a political secretary of the War Cabinet; in 1919 he was parliamentary undersecretary at the Colonial Office, and in 1921 parliamentary and financial secretary to the Admiralty. He was first lord of the Admiralty 1922–4, and colonial secretary from 1924

policies of 'discouraging thrift in every class and breaking down the whole capitalist or individualistic economic system under the burden of excessive direct taxation'. His solution was an immediate cut in income tax and an increase in taxes on consumption, in the form of a revenue tariff or a tax on sales at each stage of production and distribution. Here, it seemed to Amery, was 'a policy with a definite appeal to interest and sentiment, something to fight for'.[83] However, the election of 1923 suggested that such a protectionist programme was unpopular. The possibility of introducing a new indirect tax was seriously considered on two occasions at the end of the war when the merits of three indirect taxes were assessed: a tax on retail turnover; a general excise on successive turnover of goods at each stage from raw material to the consumer; and a merchants' sales tax levied when the commodity passed beyond a 'ring fence' of extractors, manufacturers and wholesalers to a retailer or consumer.[84] Each faced opposition from the tax authorities as posing too great a threat to consent.

A tax on retail turnover would lead to price increases at a time when the government was anxious to deflate the economy, and it would fall disproportionately on the poor. The Inland Revenue also argued that it would fall more heavily on heads of families who were less able to save or to spend money on untaxed services, which contradicted the policy of relieving heads of families from direct taxation. Moreover, the tax would be difficult to collect, for it would entail dealing with 850,000 retailers which would lead to hostility and undermine the existing good relations in the collection of excise duties.[85] Taxation of goods at each stage of production

to 1929. He then turned to business, backing Churchill over rearmament but differing from him over self-rule for India. He was secretary of state for India 1940–5, where his attempts to win nationalist support were undermined by Churchill. After the war, he continued to support imperial preference. (*DNB, 1951–60*, ed. Williams and Palmer, pp. 16–19; Robbins (ed.), *Biographical Dictionary*, pp. 9–12.)

[83] Birmingham University Library, AC24/4/1, L. S. Amery to Austen Chamberlain, 26 Jan. 1922.

[84] PRO, T171/203, 'Possible increase of existing customs and excise taxation: note by the Board of Customs and Excise', 20 Jan. 1922; IR74/245, 'New Taxation Sub-Committee II to consider (a) separately (b) in conjunction an individual expenditure tax and an annual tax on capital of individuals in supplement to or part substitution for the income tax'; 'New Taxation Sub-Committee G, to examine suggestions arising in any quarter not covered by the other sub-committees and to explore any proposals which seem worthy of consideration'. PRO, T171/203, 'Note of interview with the chancellor of the Exchequer, 29 August 1921', R. V. N. Hopkins, 30 Aug. 1921.

[85] PRO, T171/176, 'A tax on turnover: memorandum submitted by the Board of Inland Revenue with the concurrence of the Board of Customs and Excise, 10 November 1919'. On the reconsideration in 1922, see T171/204, 'Note by the Revenue Boards: tax on turnover', H. P. Hamilton and P. Thompson to chancellor, 18 Jan. 1922, and 'Notes by the Board of Inland Revenue on turnover and sales taxes abroad'; T172/1237, 'Memorandum by the Revenue Boards on a tax on turnover', 18 Jan. 1922.

and distribution magnified these criticisms, and added a further problem. Imports would have an unfair advantage unless there was a protective or countervailing tariff; and exports would suffer unless there was a 'drawback' of duty. Other countries with a turnover tax already had protection, which was a highly contentious issue in Britain.[86] A merchants' sales tax would reduce some of the difficulties of collection, for it was levied only once and was usually paid by larger wholesalers and manufacturers rather than small shopkeepers. Imported goods would be on an equal footing to domestic goods as they moved from the wholesaler or importer to the retailer, and exports could easily be exempted. The merchants' sales tax was therefore practicable, and it was more or less identical to the purchase tax introduced in the Second World War.[87] Even so, it was rejected as contradicting the high level of consent achieved by the British tax regime. The argument against indirect taxes rested upon the legitimacy of direct taxation in Britain in comparison with other, less fortunate, countries which were obliged to rely upon indirect taxation. The Inland Revenue adopted a self-congratulatory attitude, that its efficiency reduced public toleration of evasion and inequality in fiscal administration below the level of other countries.[88]

Sales taxes on all or a wide range of commodities were common in other European countries. These could take the form of a single-stage tax imposed only once on a commodity as it passed through the chain of production and distribution, or a multiple or 'cascading tax' which was levied at each stage. Germany adopted a 'cascading' turnover tax (*Umsatzsteuer*) in 1918, in place of a stamp duty on sales in 1917 which produced little revenue. The turnover tax played a major role in the finances of the central state; indeed, the federal state in West Gemany did not have a direct tax and over half of its revenues came from the *Umsatzsteuer*. This tax favoured large integrated concerns where goods remained within a single firm as they moved from process to process, in comparison with small firms where goods were bought and sold at each stage. In Germany, this point was much less important than in France – and there might even be some support for integration as efficient. In France, it did create political difficulties. The French government also introduced a stamp duty in 1917, with the same disappointing yield as in Germany. In 1920, it was replaced by a turnover tax (*taxe sur le chiffre d'affaires*) of

---

[86] PRO, T172/1237, 'Memorandum by the Revenue Boards on a tax on turnover', 18 Jan. 1922.
[87] PRO, T172/1237, 'Memorandum by the Revenue Boards on a merchants' sales tax', 4 Mar. 1922.
[88] PRO, T172/1237, 'Memorandum by the Revenue Boards on a tax on turnover', 18 Jan. 1922.

2 per cent, except on luxuries which paid more and food which was exempt. This tax was highly contentious, both because it favoured integrated concerns and because it was regressive; its revenue was also crucial for the government. Although the radicals and socialists were committed to abolishing the tax, their room for manouevre was limited when they came to power in 1924. They retained the tax, but added a new duty on the production of specified goods – a complicated system which was reformed by the Popular Front government in 1936 with a single-stage tax on production, with an exemption for small artisans. This new *taxe à la production* remained in force until 1954, but it did not produce sufficient revenue and the turnover tax (*taxe sur les transactions*) was reintroduced in 1939. The structure of the tax remained highly divisive in France throughout the interwar period, and was eventually reformed with the introduction of a new form of tax – the *taxe sur la valeur ajoute* or VAT – in 1954 which was to provide the basis of fiscal harmonisation within the EEC.[89]

The Treasury and revenue departments were concerned that a sales tax would exacerbate already strained social and economic relations. A sales tax implied that wage-earners were under-taxed compared with industry, a proposition not entirely accepted by the Inland Revenue. It also doubted whether indirect taxes would assist industry, for the burden would be shifted from consumers and 'largely thrown back on the stream of production'. Sales taxes could only relieve industry where unions were weak and wages did not rise. However, 'the power of Labour organisation vis a vis both the State and employers, is much more developed in Great Britain than anywhere else in the world, with the exception of Australia, where there is no turnover tax'. Higher prices would simply lead to demands for higher wages, so transferring the burden from wage-earners to industrial capital, and intensifying the struggle over the division of the product of industry. Whether or not labour was successful, wage disputes would increase the costs of production. If labour succeeded, industry would not escape taxation; if labour failed, real wages would fall, workers would be less productive and the loss of output would be greater than the gains from lower taxes. Further, there would be inequities between organised workers able to obtain higher wages and those who could not increase their incomes (the unemployed, pensioners and recipients of fixed interest investments). The Inland Revenue concluded that it was much better for industry to accept existing taxes (which only fell on profits

[89] J. F. Due, 'Sales taxes in western Europe, II', *National Tax Journal* 8 (1955), 300–21; C. S. Shoup, *The Sales Tax in France* (New York, 1930), pp. 3–4, 7–37, 354; Maier, *Recasting Bourgeois Europe*, pp. 466–506; F. M. B. Lynch, 'A tax for Europe: the introduction of value added tax in France', *Journal of European Integration History* 4 (1998), 67–87.

after they had been made and which did not raise costs) than to opt for indirect taxes.[90]

The Inland Revenue was led to the conclusion that industry had no particular grounds for complaint, and that taxation of profits was the best means of dealing with the immediate postwar crisis, less on grounds of intrinsic merit than the greater objections to alternatives. Although an increase in the income tax might be more 'scientific' and more attuned to ability to pay, it was best avoided because any rise 'would increase the burden of the tax to a small but appreciable extent upon an enormous number of manual and other small wage earners'. By contrast, the merit of a profits tax was that its 'ultimate incidence is obscure'.[91] Rejection of the levy on war wealth and the capital levy increased the need for some other means of taxation. It was difficult to increase indirect taxes, after the war-time assurances to labour; a retreat from this promise would cast doubt on the legitimacy of the postwar settlement and the 'fairness' of the state. It was also imperative to show that something was being done to control profiteering, which was resented both by wage-earners and members of the middle class. The answer was the maintenance of the EPD and corporation tax until the worst problems of the floating debt were resolved and revenues recovered.

Preserving the fiscal constitution

The end of the First World War marked a critical phase in British history which has been neglected in comparison with the drama of 1931. In reality, the options available in 1931 were largely determined by the negotiations at the end of the war, when policy discussions were foreclosed and the fiscal constitution re-established.[92] It was a period marked by a radical demand for a capital levy, with its potential for transforming British society, and by bitter middle-class resentment expressed in the anti-waste campaign and a sense of grievance at the gains of labour. Ross McKibbin has argued that the settlement reached by the mid-1920s subordinated the working class and enthroned the middle class, whose interests were served by the political economy of the interwar period.[93] But this is only partially true. Despite the containment of the capital levy,

[90] PRO, T172/1237, 'Memorandum by the Revenue Boards on a tax on turnover', 18 Jan. 1922; 'Memorandum by the Revenue Boards on a merchants sales tax', 4 Mar. 1922; IR74/231, 'Industry and the weight of taxation'.

[91] PRO, T171/190, 'Note on possible methods of replacing part of the revenue now drawn from the Excess Profits Duty', Inland Revenue, 17 Dec. 1920.

[92] A point well made by S. Pedersen, 'From national crisis to "national crisis": British politics, 1914–31', *Journal of British Studies* 33 (1994), 327–8, 332.

[93] McKibbin, *Clases and Cultures*, pp. 54, 59–60, and 'Class and conventional wisdom'.

fiscal extraction remained more than twice the prewar level and there was a further shift in favour of direct taxation. Of course, a large part of the increased government revenue went to service the national debt, but expenditure on social welfare also rose. Reliance on the income tax meant that the tax base was relatively narrow and prone to electoral pressure, so creating an incentive to ensure that the high level of income tax did not alienate an important constituency. Consequently, there was a need to reduce the burden of the income tax on particular sections of the middle class, especially families in receipt of modest incomes and with children to support. The political economy of the interwar period largely served their interests, but not necessarily at the expense of the working class. The attack on wages largely stopped after the general strike, and falling prices led to considerable gains for those in employment. The careful handling of the floating debt meant that Britain escaped the financial problems of Germany, where the failure of the money market to absorb short-term government debt contributed to hyperinflation and depression.[94]

Obviously, there is a danger of exaggerating the sophistication of the Treasury's management of the economy and its care in establishing fairness and balance. All the same, the Treasury and government were not simply obeying the wishes of the City against productive industry, or of the middle class against the working class. A central feature of the process of 'recasting bourgeois Britain' was success in preserving the legitimacy of the state and of taxation at a higher level of extraction. It was a hardwon achievement, which differed from the corporatism of continental Europe with its 'constant brokerage' between organised interests outside the legislature, and a displacement of power from elected representatives, parliament, political parties and the career bureaucracy.[95] By contrast, parliamentary government was accepted in Britain, and organised business was obliged to join rather than to reject the party-political system. Interests (whether constructed through political rhetoric or real and material) remained within the parliamentary arena. The state reacted to the strains of the war and postwar readjustment by 'a determination to build a national consensus in which the government would accommodate all the major economic and political interests'. Deputations from organised pressure groups of industry and labour presented their case to the chancellor, and their arguments were carefully considered by the Treasury and Inland Revenue. Nevertheless, these bodies were not part of the process of policy formation which remained in the hands of politicians. They received advice from career bureaucrats who remained extremely

[94] See Balderston, 'War finance and inflation', 238–40, 224.
[95] Maier, *Recasting Bourgeois Europe*, pp. 4, 8–10, 580–1.

powerful, constraining what was permissible and shaping the reaction to external pressure. Rather than corporatist brokerage, there was a process of 'reassertion' which stressed 'the "naturalness" of the existing system', and propagated an aura of neutrality and fairness, a rhetoric of concern for abstractions of legality and constitutionality.[96] The state had its autonomous interests, such as the need to deal with the floating debt in order to maintain financial stability, and it had some capacity to implement its goals in the face of opposition from powerful groups, whether the City, industrialists, organised workers or middle-class opponents of 'waste'.

How should the outcome be judged? Care was taken that no single interest was given preferential treatment or suffered undue hardship so that the legitimacy of the tax system and the state were accepted at a much higher level of extraction. The result was the survival of a higher level of transfer payments to the unemployed and a more generous system of welfare provision during the depression than would otherwise have been possible. But was the outcome so equitable as the rhetoric of the Treasury and Inland Revenue claimed? It could be that consent was created to a fundamentally *inequitable* system, and that the implications of a widening of the franchise in 1918 were contained. In Macnicol's opinion, the Treasury succeeded in limiting the threat of mass democracy to a capitalist social order, turning aside the threat of redistributive taxation of social welfare into contributory insurance.[97] On such an account, defeat of the capital levy meant that the existing distribution of income and wealth was preserved, which was as much a political decision as the attempt by Labour to use the capital levy to create a more egalitarian social structure.

Nevertheless, the actions of the Treasury and Inland Revenue should not simply be viewed as the successful propagation of a spurious equity in order to contain change. After all, there was a major shift in the distribution of national income in favour of labour since 1914. Smaller incomes gained as a result of the narrowing of wage differentials during the war, and indirect taxes were not drastically increased on working-class consumption. Better-paid workers came within the income tax during the war, but thresholds were adjusted after the war to remove most of them from the scope of the tax. Rather surprisingly, the redistribution of income towards less well-off members of society was not reversed after the

---

[96] This approach is found in Turner, 'The politics of "organised business"', pp. 48–9, and *British Politics and the Great War: Coalition and Conflict, 1915–18* (New Haven and London, 1992), p. 369; McDonald, 'The Geddes Committee', 648, 673–4; Nottingham, 'Recasting bourgeois Britain?', 244–7.

[97] Macnicol, *Politics of Retirement in Britain*, pp. 3–6.

war.[98] It is not clear that the containment of change was entirely in the interests of capital and the middle class. A distinction should also be drawn between 'pragmatic' and 'principled' equity. The revenue authorities were concerned to achieve the former, by balancing interests in a way which secured their consent to providing revenue to the state. They did not seek 'principled equity' by using the tax system to adjust other social inequities, with the danger that the tax system would be viewed as a political device, so undermining its legitimacy and making it more difficult to extract revenue. Officials held that it was essential to maintain the high degree of consent achieved by the British tax system, which could supply politicians with the revenue for public policies. By removing the danger that the fiscal system would be a source of conflict, the postwar settlement enabled rather than constrained the British state. As a result, the level of spending was maintained between the wars with a minimum of resistance compared with France or Germany. But we should also note the basic assumptions of the Treasury and politicians, for legitimacy and stability rather than incentives and growth – unlike in the United States where Andrew Mellon tried both to make the Treasury non-partisan and to grant concessions to business as a source of prosperity.[99] The concerns of the FBI for economic efficiency were marginalised – a point all the more apparent after the Second World War. The demands of Labour for major structural change were also contained – yet without turning back the considerable war-time shift towards greater equality of income distribution. A new standard of distributive justice emerged from the war and postwar debates.

The main concern of officials and politicians was financial and political stability: the need to remove the danger of the floating debt, and to contain the challenge both of Labour's capital levy and of the populist campaign against 'waste'. The policies adopted by the government were designed to negotiate between these conflicting nostrums, without appearing too blatantly in the interest of any one group. A general sales tax would merely suggest that workers were suffering in order to hand money to parasitical *rentiers*, so increasing support for the capital levy as a way of removing their burdens. The levy could also be presented as a way of relieving active enterprise from taxes – but might scare all

[98] C. Feinstein, *Statistical Tables of National Income, Expenditure and Output of the UK, 1855–1965* (Cambridge, 1972), T44. In 1913, income from employment amounted to 54.7 per cent of GDP and in 1920, 65.5 per cent; meanwhile, gross trading profits fell from 15.4 to 11.8 per cent and rent from 11.7 to 4.3 per cent.

[99] W. E. Brownlee, 'Economists and the formation of the modern tax system in the US: the World War I crisis', in Furner and Supple (eds.), *State and Economic Knowledge*, pp. 428–31, and *Federal Taxation in America: A Short History* (Cambridge, 1996), pp. 60–6.

owners of property into a defensive alliance. At the heart of the debate over distribution was the definition of producers versus parasites or property versus socialism. Would individuals define themselves as producers whose efforts were hampered by payments to *rentiers* and passive capital? In that case, incentives and growth would be encouraged by high levels of taxation on accumulated capital. Or would they define themselves as owners of property who were threatened by taxation of any form of capital, whether passive or active? The task of politicians was to define these identities through their rhetoric and their normative definitions of society. Although the debate started from a concern for stability, it soon involved consideration of the impact of different fiscal systems on incentives and economic growth.

Officials had their own perceptions of how the economy functioned, which stressed the need for a stable and efficient system of public finance. In their view, the economy could not operate effectively if financial relations were threatened: the state would not be able to borrow on favourable terms, and a loss of confidence would threaten the stability of the economy. Hence they emphasised the need to deal with the national debt, less out of subservience to the City of London than from an appreciation of the need for financial stability for economic recovery. Their concern was not unreasonable, and Britain avoided both hyperinflation and the worst problems of financial collapse in the slump. It also meant a policy of deflation in the 1920s, and the maintenance of high levels of taxes to reduce the debt. Here the Treasury justified its policies through its analysis of investment: by reducing the national debt, money would be returned to investors who would place the money in industrial securities. Hence high taxation was in the interests of industrial recovery – a proposition with which industry did not necessarily agree. As we shall see in the next chapter, between 1924 and 1929, Winston Churchill used the fiscal system in a creative way to respond to these issues, in order to foster a sense of balance between groups and interests which would encourage enterprise and growth. He moved away from his earlier Liberal onslaught on the idle rich, realising that the result might be a wider attack on property. Instead, he shaped the tax system to benefit the moderately affluent and above all middle-class families with children, with an extension of pensions to widows.

4 'Adjusting the particular turns of the different screws': reforming the income tax, 1920–1929

> Pressing as was the need for reform before the war it is even more imperative now. Taxation has so greatly increased since 1914 that it is more than desirable, it is vital to our country's future, that now, when the national burden is at its heaviest, it shall be fairly distributed, and the individual share fitted with sympathy and with discrimination to the back that will for many years have to bear it.
>
> PP 1920 XVIII, *Report of the Royal Commission on the Income Tax*, p. 107

> The doctrine of ability to pay, worked on no definite principle except perhaps political pressure, may become a gigantic instrument of doles...The doctrine of ability to pay would, if carried to its logical conclusion, resolve itself into a series of hidden subsidies in the shape of allowances given by rule of thumb to certain favoured classes.
>
> Lillian Knowles, PP 1920 XVIII, *Report of the Royal Commission on the Income Tax*, p. 257

Since its reintroduction in 1842, the income tax evolved through small-scale adjustments designed to meet political and financial exigencies. Thus differentiation, graduation and child allowances were grafted on to a different system based on abatements from the standard rate of tax, without rethinking the income tax as a whole. Reform was imperative when tax rates rose during the war and more people became liable. In 1919, the coalition government responded by appointing a Royal Commission to undertake the first survey of the income tax as a whole since 1842. Its main recommendations were implemented in the Finance Act of 1920, and contributed to reasserting the legitimacy of the fiscal system and, above all, preserving consent to a still greater reliance on direct taxes and a much higher marginal rate.[1] Indeed, the elasticity of growth in total government expenditure relative to GDP at current prices was higher between 1924 and 1937 (at 1.64) than after the Second World War (1.24 from 1951 to 1979). Despite the usual emphasis on parsimony and balanced budgets, the elasticity of government expenditure between the wars

[1] The best discussion of the Royal Commission is in Short, 'Politics of personal taxation', pp. 93–147.

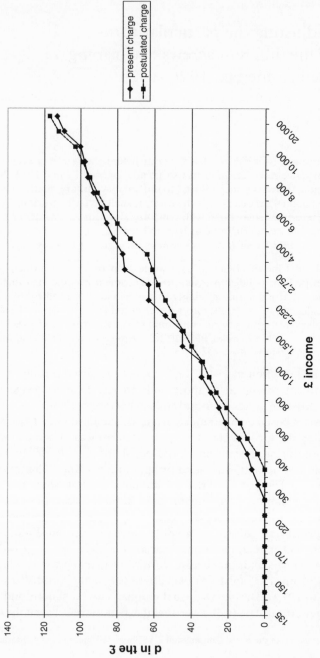

Figure 4.1 Effective rate of tax (d in the £) on earned income of married couples with three children, before and after the Royal Commission on the Income Tax

Source: PP 1920 XVIII, *Report of the Royal Commission on the Income Tax*, appendix II, tables 3 and 6.

was historically high.[2] The Treasury's repeated stress on the need for restraint in the 1920s and 1930s was less a sign of its *success* in containing expenditure than of its attempt to instil prudence and economy at a time of high spending in relation to economic growth.[3] The major issue is not how expenditure was contained (as after the Napoleonic wars) but how spending and taxation remained so high without serious political tensions.

An appeal to continuity was central to the rhetoric of the Royal Commission, based on respect for an 'old-established system' which had proved its worth in times of national danger. Acceptance of the income tax was a symbol of British liberty, and it 'should be judged not by a theoretical standard of possible excellence, but by the results which it has achieved'. What was needed was further 'natural development . . . on sound and politic lines' to remove any blemishes and distribute the tax 'more fairly over the whole taxpaying community'.[4] The strategy adopted by the Royal Commission was to remove the basic structure of the income tax from contention in order to secure widespread acceptance at a much higher rate of extraction, and to limit discussion to narrower, technical issues of marginal changes in tax rates.

Although the Royal Commission and the coalition government were concerned to establish the legitimacy of the fiscal system by an appeal to equity and fairness, their claims should not be taken as proof that the tax system was in reality neutral between classes and interests. The definitions of 'sympathy' and 'discrimination' were far from value-free. Political parties do not simply appeal to existing social or economic interests; they try to define interests through their rhetoric, and taxation was one element in this discursive formation of political identities. The definition of identities was particularly pressing at a time when the franchise was extended to all adult men and party structures were in flux, with many middle-class voters cut adrift from the Liberal party. Politicians responded to concerns about war wealth, profiteering and *rentiers* in an attempt to appeal to, and if possible shape, interests and identities. Another significant theme in defining political identities was the family, which became particularly important after 1918 with the extension of the vote to women over the age of thirty meeting a property qualification, who formed two-thirds of the new voters. The strategy of the Conservatives moved from an earlier appeal to working-class male voters threatened by the Liberal attack on 'historic male pleasures', to an appeal to the family in order to attract the

[2] Middleton, *Government versus the Market*, table 3.13 and p. 118.
[3] For the argument about containing expenditure, see Cronin, *Politics of State Expansion*, pp. 13, 87–92.
[4] PP 1920 xviii, *Report of the Royal Commission on the Income Tax*, p. 107.

votes of housewives (the dominant perception of women enfranchised in 1918) and their husbands who paid the taxes. The Conservatives portrayed themselves as a bulwark against socialism which could be linked with domesticity, and the sanctity of the family and home – a rhetoric more relevant to the 'feminised' franchise after 1918. Women were portrayed as the real locus of power in the household, as family 'chancellors' who were distinct from male trade unionists and strikers, as level-headed and instinctively anti-socialist. The existence of children's and marriage allowances gave chancellors a means of shaping the tax system to benefit, above all, middle-class families with modest incomes – a central theme in the realignment of politics between the wars.[5] As Lillian Knowles,* a member of the Royal Commission, pointed out, the tax system could provide hidden subsidies to favoured interests. Politicians had to draw a very careful balance. On the one hand, they wished to make concessions to particular groups in order to secure electoral advantage for their party or to shape society in pursuit of their prescriptions. On the other hand, preservation of a high degree of consent to taxation was crucial to the legitimacy of the state and its ability to extract revenue. If the tax system were blatantly biased between interests, the willingness of taxpayers to pay would be weakened: they would not have trust in each other or in the state.

Officials at the Inland Revenue and Treasury had a greater interest in the preservation of consent, and were always wary of the more adventurous schemes of chancellors in pursuit of electoral gain or ideology. Of course, politicians are (usually) coalition builders, wishing to secure support from the largest possible portion of the electorate, so that politicians and officials were not necessarily at odds. Chancellors were usually aware of limits to the use of taxation for electoral advantage and social change. Blatant concessions to particular interests would call into question the supposed neutrality of the state above politics and class interests, so creating greater difficulties in preserving consent and raising revenue for the state, and reducing the effectiveness of the tax system as a way of financing policies designed to shape society. The difference between civil servants

---

[5] Turner, *British Politics and the Great War*, chapter 11; J. Lawrence, 'Class and gender and the making of urban Toryism, 1880–1914', *English Historical Review* 108 (1993), 629–52; D. Jarvis, 'Mrs Maggs and Betty: the Conservative appeal to women voters in the 1920s', *Twentieth Century British History* 5 (1994), 129–52, and 'British Conservatism'.

* Lillian Charlotte Anne Knowles (d. 1926) was educated at Truro Grammar School and Girton College, Cambridge; she was lecturer, reader and professor of economic history at the LSE from 1904. She was a member of the departmental committee on the rise in the cost of living to the working classes in 1918, and of the Royal Commission on Income Tax in 1919–20. (*Who Was Who*, vol. II: *1916–28* (London, 1929), p. 459.)

and politicians was therefore a matter of emphasis – but the difference was important in the peculiar conditions of electoral realignment in the 1920s. Both Churchill (for the Conservatives) and Snowden (for Labour) had ambitions to use the income tax to reshape British society by benefiting particular groups; officials at the Treasury and Inland Revenue were anxious to moderate their schemes, so as to prevent the fiscal system from becoming too politicised. Officials saw their role as protecting the fiscal *status quo*, and any change was interpreted as upsetting a carefully achieved balance. But there was a danger that the official appeal to tradition could make the tax system appear anachronistic or inequitable, as assumptions about equity changed and the structure of society shifted. Their emphasis on consent through stasis could become self-destructive by removing flexibility. Astute politicians were aware that preservation of consent at higher levels of extraction required adjustments to the taxation of different interests and classes, with the danger that taxation might become highly contentious, so undermining compliance and weakening the state's capacity.

The successful re-establishment of the 'fiscal constitution' rested upon two strands. One was the initial success of the Royal Commission in reasserting the income tax as fair between classes and interests. The second was the willingness of successive chancellors to operate within the terms of this fiscal constitution in a creative way to secure the support of important social groups without alienating other interests. Taxation was contentious, yet never destructive of political stability. As a result, the legitimacy of the tax system was preserved, so allowing a much higher level of extraction of GNP and a more generous provision of welfare benefits than before the First World War, with surprisingly little dissent and without a loss of consent and legitimacy.

The Royal Commission on the Income Tax: reasserting the fiscal constitution

The main technical concern of the Royal Commission was to remove the confusion of combining the older system of 'degression' – reductions for smaller incomes – with the newer pattern of graduation for higher incomes, differentiation between 'earned' and 'unearned' incomes, and allowances for family responsibilities (see table 4.1). The result was sudden jumps in the 'slope' of graduation, so that a small increase in income could produce a disproportionate addition to tax liability (see figure 4.1). The Commission aimed to create a smooth line of graduation in order to remove resentment at 'inequities', stressing the technical nature of the exercise and excluding the political issue of the *steepness* of the line of graduation and the maximum rate of tax. Richard Hopkins* adopted a pragmatic approach, starting from the amount of revenue required from the income tax (about £350m) which severely limited the scope for altering the gradient of progression. As he pointed out, consent to the high rates of taxation could only be secured by removing resentment at anomalies through an adjustment to the 'particular turns of the different screws upon different sections of income'. Once the slope of graduation had been fixed, the Royal Commission argued that it should not be constantly adjusted so that it was taken for granted and beyond dispute. The intention was to exclude the slope of the gradient from political discussion as far as possible and to make it an integral and natural part of the fiscal constitution.[6]

The necessary changes were matters of numbing technical tedium, and the Commission set three tests to assess any reform: was it practicable; would it create a smooth gradient; and was it simple to understand? The creation of a smooth gradient proved relatively simple, through a technical change in the procedure for calculating an individual's tax liability after taking account of the tax-free limit, earned income and allowance for wife and children. This was introduced in 1920, and in theory the new line of graduation was taken out of politics; in practice, the reform of the method of calculation allowed chancellors to tinker with allowances and benefits more easily than before. But other changes proved more contentious, and the requirements for simplicity and practicability could not always be reconciled – at least in the opinion of the Inland Revenue. As far as officials were concerned, the main practical need was to preserve deduction of income tax 'at source', which they saw as crucial to easy administration. In other words, interest on government stock (schedule C) or rent on property (schedule A) was handed over to the recipient net of tax, which was passed on to the Inland Revenue by the Bank of England or tenant – a painless and efficient way of collection. But the tax was charged at a single standard rate, and the taxpayer subsequently reclaimed any

---

[6] PP 1919 xxiii, Part i, *Royal Commission on Income Tax First Instalment of Minutes of Evidence*, evidence of R. V. N. Hopkins, Qq. 4072, 4232; PP 1920 xviii, *Report of the Royal Commission on the Income Tax*, pp. 106–7, 132–9.

* Richard Valentine Nind Hopkins (1880–1955) was educated at King Edward VI School, Birmingham, and Emmanuel College, Cambridge; he entered the Inland Revenue in 1902, becoming a member of the Board in 1916 and chairman in 1922. He moved to the Treasury in 1927 as controller of finance and supply services, rising to second secretary in 1932 and permanent secretary from 1942 to 1945. The author of his entry in the *DNB*, another leading Treasury official, remarked that Hopkins was inclined to his master's view, but insisted on two secrets of the Inland Revenue: what could be managed and how far the taxpayer could be pushed. (*DNB, 1951–60*, ed. Williams and Palmer, pp. 500–1.)

over-payment if he were below the tax threshold, or made a supplementary payment if he were liable to super-tax at a higher rate. As far as the Inland Revenue was concerned, the super-tax was a separate tax, and needed an entirely separate form for assessment of liability to the higher levels of graduated tax; in this case, simplification was not possible on grounds of administrative practicality.

Another area of confusion or complexity was the variation in the period of assessment of different forms of income, even within the same schedule. Thus in schedule A, covering income from real property, rent received from tenants paid on the year of assessment, whereas profit on railways paid on the preceding year, and on coal mines on the average of the preceding five years. In schedule D, income from trade, manufactures, professions and employment paid on the average of the three preceding years; and schedule E (salaries of public employment) paid on the year of assessment. Many people received income under different schedules on different time scales, and there were glaring anomalies. The Royal Commission recommended simplification in this system of assessments. In 1842, taxation of regular salaried employment was relatively insignificant, and schedule E of the income tax initially applied to salaries from public office, which was extended in practice at least to senior positions in corporate bodies and limited companies. By 1920, salaried employment was much more important, and the distinction between employment in schedules E and D was anomalous. The Royal Commission therefore recommended that *all* employees of government, public bodies, firms and individuals should be transferred to schedule E and assessed on the current year, leaving schedule D for income from business, professions and self-employment. At the same time, the Commission proposed that schedule D profits should be charged on the preceding year rather than the average of the last three years – so removing the opportunity to offset losses or low profits in bad years against profits in good years.[7] These proposals would ease the process of assessment of the income tax – but they ran into serious political difficulties.

'Simplification' of administration of the income tax was linked with another and, from the taxpayers' point of view, alarming proposal at a time of serious concern over 'waste'. The Royal Commission proposed the transfer of assessment to the staff of the Inland Revenue. When the income tax was reintroduced in 1842, much of the administration was left to local lay commissioners, collectors and assessors, an approach

[7] The reforms are discussed in Short, 'Politics of personal taxation', chapter 3; PP 1920 XVIII, *Report of the Royal Commission on the Income Tax*, pp. 132–42, 158–60, 162–7, 177–191, 208–11, 214–15; PP 1919 XXIII Part II, *Royal Commission on Income Tax, Fifth Instalment of Minutes of Evidence*, evidence of E. R. Harrison, annexe 1, p. 12.

widely seen as a protection of the taxpayer from 'inquisition'.[8] The Royal
Commission argued, with some justice, that the system offered little real
protection to the taxpayer, for in practice most of the work was undertaken
by officials and simply approved by the lay commissioners. The Royal
Commission believed that taxpayers would have greater protection if the
local commissioners were confined to an appellate function as umpires
in disputes with the Inland Revenue. However, the Revenue Bill of 1920
ran into considerable opposition as a threat to lay control. As a result,
both the transfer of assessment to officials and the reform of its basis were
abandoned – somewhat to the relief of the coalition government, for the
three-year average protected the revenue from a serious fall with the onset
of the slump.[9]

The Inland Revenue's wish to change the system of assessment was
linked with its realisation that higher levels of income tax increased the incentive for evasion or avoidance. In its evidence to the Royal Commission,
the Inland Revenue tried to place legal avoidance within the same
category as illegal evasion, and was concerned both by its own lack of
investigative powers, and the taxpayers' lack of a sense of social disgrace –
not least because they assumed that other taxpayers were doing the same.
Indeed, Stamp feared that improvements in 'tax honesty' before 1914
had suffered a 'bad relapse'. The Inland Revenue therefore wished to
strengthen its powers of locating inaccurate returns, which helps to explain
the attempt to shift to more professional assessment – and the taxpayers'
resistance. During the war, taxpayers were prosecuted for inaccurate or
fraudulent returns, but there were many legal ways of avoiding tax. One
response to the higher rate of tax was the development of more sophisticated tax advice by accountants who became more adept at finding
loopholes in the tax code, not least the use of settlements and trusts in
favour of members of the family. Thus a father could settle a sum of
money in trust for his children to pay for their maintenance and education; the income of the trust would be free of tax, so reducing the
father's tax liability on the money he spent on their up-bringing. The
assets were not permanently alienated and the trust could be revoked at
any time; the Inland Revenue felt that the income should be treated as
belonging to the person making the transfer unless the assets were absolutely alienated. Legislation was introduced in 1922, but the loophole
was not entirely closed and accountants soon publicised ways of avoiding
its provisions. Although a Cabinet committee considered tax avoidance

[8] This is discussed in detail in Daunton, *Trusting Leviathan*, pp. 186–204.
[9] Short, 'Politics of personal taxation', pp. 103, 114–19, 141–4, 146–7; PP 1920 xviii,
Report of the Royal Commission on the Income Tax, pp. 177–91.

in 1927, it decided not to take further steps and simply asked the Inland Revenue to keep the situation under review. In 1933, the Inland Revenue was so concerned that a committee was set up, which found that something like £8m a year was lost in the income and surtax, mainly through settlements and trusts in favour of children (£1.25m), covenants to charities (£1m) and the use of foreign holdings (£2.75m). Little could be done about foreign avoidance, for the issue came down to one of motive: were assets held overseas for genuine trading reasons or for avoidance? In the case of charities, a proposal to tighten up tax relief failed in 1927, and the loss of revenue continued to mount until 1946, when covenants in favour of charity were only relieved of income and not surtax. Any further attack proved difficult – and what had once been seen as a loophole in the tax system became an accepted, and even desirable, element. Action *was* taken on settlements and trusts in 1938 which removed some of the opportunities for avoidance.[10]

During his tenure of the chancellorship between 1924 and 1929, Churchill concentrated on other areas of reform to the tax system. He succeeded in pushing through 'simplification' of the income and super-tax by his tenacious bullying of a reluctant Treasury and Inland Revenue. He insisted that the income and super-tax should be combined, and different sources of income assessed on the same basis in order to achieve 'the Sovereign Principle . . . to get the money, as near as possible to the moment when it is received by the taxpayer'. As he remarked with exasperation, the Inland Revenue assumed that the present system had no anomalies and was 'the last word in efficiency and simplicity', and therefore concentrated on raising every possible objection to change whilst overlooking the fact that the current system was 'so complicated and elaborate that very few taxpayers can understand it'. Churchill had no patience for the Inland Revenue's argument that the income tax and super-taxes were separate taxes, developed at different times and with different graduation. 'This "conception" argument is of no importance', he insisted. 'The point is the effect upon the taxpayer who has to pay under various heads . . . a certain aggregate sum in a given year. From his point of view the burden is already united but he has to sign different

---

[10] On charities, see Daunton, *Trusting Leviathan*, pp. 211–17; and D. Stopforth, 'Charitable convenants by individuals – a history of the background to their tax treatment and their cost to the Exchequer', *British Tax Review* (1986), 101–16. Avoidance is dealt with by D. Stopforth, 'Settlements and the avoidance of tax on income – the period to 1920', *British Tax Review* (1990), 225–50, 'Sowing some of the seeds of the present anti-evasion system – the 1920s', *British Tax Review* (1985), 28–38, and '1922–36: halcyon days for the tax avoider', *British Tax Review* (1992), 88–105. The quote from Stamp is from his *Fundamental Principles of Taxation in the Light of Modern Developments* (London, 1921), p. 107; the figures on avoidance are in PRO, T171/318.

sets of forms because there are two histories about his burden.' A single graduated scale was introduced in 1928, with a single return.[11]

In his battle with the Inland Revenue, Churchill had support from the Income Taxpayers' Society which welcomed a uniform system of assessment as a means of reducing the number of bureaucrats and preserving local control. The Inland Revenue had a different order of priorities, and felt that any change to the system of assessment should be linked to a change in the administration of income tax. Churchill played the two groups against each other. The Income Taxpayers' Society was a useful ally against the Inland Revenue's hostility to simplification; once this was achieved, Churchill abandoned the Society as soon as he won this battle and transferred assessment under schedules D and E to the inspectors. Churchill therefore achieved both simplification of the income tax *and* a weakening of local lay administration. Only someone with Churchill's bloody-mindedness and tenacity would have persevered – even if his private secretary, James Grigg,* doubted that the effort was worthwhile.[12]

This conversion of the local commissioners into adjudicators between the Inland Revenue and taxpayers raises a major point about the structure of the British state. In the past, the commissioners were associated with the collection of taxes on behalf of the state, and might therefore be the body against whom the taxpayer wished to appeal. Now they were transformed into independent adjudicators between taxpayers and the Inland Revenue, without a change in their formal status. Much as they claimed to be independent, taxpayers were inclined to see the local commissioners as part of the Inland Revenue and the state. Here was a general theme in the history of the British state: the delegation of duties to bodies

---

[11] Short, 'Politics of personal taxation', pp. 211–23; PRO, T171/255, Winston Churchill to Richard Hopkins, 27 Dec. 1925, commenting on Inland Revenue report of 18 Dec. 1925; Hopkins to Churchill, 5 Jan. 1926 and 19 Feb. 1926; report of 17 Mar. 1926 on the 'Suggested proposals by the Income Taxpayers' Society for the simplification in the assessment of income tax and supertax', and Churchill's marginal comment; Inland Revenue, 'Report of a committee appointed to consider the simplification of the income tax and super tax', Oct. 1926; Hopkins to Churchill, 27 Oct. 1926. The super-tax was renamed the surtax.

[12] P. J. Grigg, *Prejudice and Judgment* (London, 1948), p. 199; also PRO, T171/255, Hopkins to Grigg, 27 Oct. 1926; Short, 'Politics of personal taxation', pp. 216–17.

* Percy James Grigg (1890–1964) was educated at St John's College, Cambridge, and entered the Treasury in 1913. He was private secretary to five chancellors of the Exchequer between 1921 and 1930; in 1930, he became chairman of Customs and Excise, moving to be chairman of the Inland Revenue from 1930 to 1933. He was finance member of the vice-roy's executive council for India, 1933–9, and permanent secretary of the War Office from 1939 to 1942, when he became an MP and secretary of state for war from 1942 to 1945. In 1946, he became a director of the International Bank for Reconstruction and Development; in 1947 he joined the Imperial Tobacco Co.; and in 1959 he became chairman of Bass, the brewer. (*DNB, 1961–70*, ed. Williams and Nicholls, pp. 460–2.)

such as the Law Society or General Medical Council which lacked independence of the bodies they were supposedly regulating. Arguably, a
more independent system of regulation would offer greater protection
to the citizen.[13] The danger was not only from despotic bureaucrats but
also from the low levels of accountability of bodies outside the formal
machinery of the state.

The adoption of a more centralised and bureaucratic system of administration prepared the ground for another reform rigorously opposed
by the Inland Revenue: the introduction of Pay As You Earn (PAYE)
in 1942, which allowed employers to deduct tax on monthly salaries or
weekly wages.[14] Churchill's campaign of simplification was part of an
attempt to bring the Inland Revenue to terms with the fact that most
taxed income was no longer drawn from land and government stocks as
in 1842. Although the deduction of income at source had the great virtue
of minimising tension in tax collection, it became less relevant with the
changing pattern of employment: the threat to consent was more likely
to come from the Treasury's and Inland Revenue's attempts to maintain
the principles of 1842 rather than to respond to changing economic reality. Above all, how could tax be collected from modest salaries or wages,
without causing difficulties for the taxpayer by claiming a lump sum at
the end of the year?

The collection of tax from weekly wage-earners first became a matter
of concern in 1915, when the exemption limit was cut and the number
caught by the income tax rose. The use of a three-year average was impracticable for workers who were liable to shift jobs and suffer periods
of unemployment, and they could not set aside money to pay income
tax at the end of the year. The Inland Revenue therefore introduced an
assessment every three months in order to spread the liability of tax. At
the end of the first quarter, the taxpayer completed a form on which any
allowance was claimed; at the end of each quarter the employer informed
the inspector of the worker's wages; assessment of tax liability was made
by the inspector with a right of appeal to the general commissioners; and
the tax was paid directly by the worker at the end of each quarter. The
Royal Commission felt that deduction of tax from wages by the employer
was impracticable because of taxpayers' hostility and administrative difficulties, and it recommended the continuation of quarterly assessments.
The difficulties were removed as manual workers dropped out of liability
in the 1920s, but the issue returned during the Second World War when

---

[13] C. Stebbings, '"A natural safeguard": the General Commissioners of income tax', *British
Tax Review* (1992), 398–406.
[14] See below, pp. 179–80.

a large part of the working class again came within liability.[15] As we shall see, the problem was solved with the introduction of PAYE.

Revision of the level of allowances and differentials was another controversial issue faced by the Royal Commission. The exemption limit was reduced from £160 to £130 during the war, and restoration of the prewar level in real terms to take account of inflation would entail an increase to £250, which would exempt 2.2m of 3.4m income taxpayers. Such a change would seriously threaten the government's revenue, and the Royal Commission refused to accept that the prewar threshold was sacroscant. After all, the exemption limit of £160 was fixed in 1894 for all taxpayers regardless of family responsibilities, before the introduction of allowances for wives and children. The Commission therefore recommended that the new personal allowance should be set at £135, with an allowance of £90 for married men, £40 for the first child and £30 for subsequent children. As a result, single taxpayers were liable on incomes below the prewar threshold even in *money* terms, and the greatest benefit went to married men with large families. Although the Royal Commission attempted to take the slope of graduation out of politics, the new administrative procedure for calculating tax liability gave chancellors greater freedom to adjust tax breaks to married men compared with single taxpayers, or married couples with children compared with childless couples.[16] The fiscal system came to benefit married couples with children, and these families were defined in a patriarchal way.

Although wives could opt to be separately assessed from their husbands, their incomes were added together to calculate the marginal rate on the assumption that the couple had a single income. The procedure was open to the obvious objection that married women could own property and vote, yet were still denied equal civil rights in the tax system, for the income tax return still stated that 'the income of a married woman living with her husband is deemed by the Income Tax Acts to be his income'. However, the Commission justified its patriarchal assumptions by appealing to *social* equity. Separate treatment of husband and wife as single persons would allow wealthy couples to divide their assets in order to remain below the super-tax threshold, and so shift the burden on to poorer taxpayers. The issue, as the majority report of the Royal Commission saw it, was fiscal justice rather than any desire to subordinate women:

[15] Short, 'Politics of personal taxation', pp. 104, 136–8; PP 1920 xviii, *Report of the Royal Commission on the Income Tax*, pp. 211–14; G. R. Carter and H. W. Houghton, 'The income tax on wages by quarterly assessment', *Economic Journal* 28 (1918), 30–42.

[16] Short, 'Politics of personal taxation', pp. 126–7; PP 1920 xviii, *Report of the Royal Commission on the Income Tax*, p. 135.

The aggregation for Income Tax purposes of the income of husband and wife is not dependent upon any medieval conception of the subordination of women . . . The incomes are aggregated because the law of taxable capacity is the supreme law in matters of taxation, and taxable capacity is, in fact, found to depend upon the amount of the income that accrues to the married pair, and not upon the way in which that income happens fortuitously to be owned by the members of the union.[17]

Not everyone was convinced by this logic.

One view was that married couples should be taxed separately. Lillian Knowles argued that the contention of the majority report was spurious: a brother and sister might share a house and contribute to a single budget without being taxed as a unit. She argued for separate taxation of husbands and wives as if unmarried.[18] An alternative approach, favoured by Sidney Webb, was to adopt a 'family basis'. He started from the assumption that any income for maintenance and improvement of the family was a cost, so that the surplus available for taxation varied with the size of the family and its needs. Webb proposed that the entire family income should be divided by the number of family members it maintained, with each receiving the full allowance. He proposed tax breaks for middle-class families with incomes up to £1,500 or £2,500, to continue while children were in full-time education. In Webb's opinion, a flat-rate relief did not assist middle-class families in the production and education of children. These approaches were rejected by the Inland Revenue and Royal Commission, and flat-rate allowances were adopted on the grounds that they gave more benefit to families with smaller incomes, where the burden of children was greater. Of course, the burden of supporting children was still greater in families below the income tax threshold, who received no assistance from the state until the introduction of family allowances after the Second World War.[19]

In 1907, the Liberal government introduced differentiation of the income tax between earned and unearned income, so that the latter paid a higher rate to reflect the existence of an asset producing a flow of income apart from the risks of unemployment or ill-health, and free of the need to set aside savings for retirement. The majority of the Royal Commission agreed that differentiation between earned and unearned income was 'desirable and just', or at least that there was a 'deeply-rooted

---

[17] PP 1920 xviii, *Report of the Royal Commission on the Income Tax*, p. 162; Daunton, *Trusting Leviathan*, pp. 218–22.

[18] PP 1920 xviii, *Report of the Royal Commission on the Income Tax*, pp. 255–6.

[19] Short, 'Politics of personal taxation', pp. 97, 122–6, 129–35; PP 1920 xviii, *Report of the Royal Commission on the Income Tax*, pp. 132–9, 158–66, 255–64; for Webb, see PP 1919 xxiii pt i, *Royal Commission on the Income Tax, Third Instalment of Minutes of Evidence*, Qq. 6885–8; J. A. Hobson, *Taxation* (London, Labour Party, n.d.), p. 5.

conviction...in the public mind that there is a real difference in taxable identity between the two classes of income in question'.[20] However, a minority dissented from what they saw as a moral attack on certain forms of wealth. To them, the distinction between earned and unearned income was artificial. Why should a private trader who owned a cotton mill pay tax at a lower earned rate, while the same investment in shares in a neighbouring mill paid the higher unearned rate? Was it desirable to tax savings at a time when capital was required for reconstruction? Differentiation was criticised as a tax on thrift and self-reliance. A large part of 'unearned' income rested on savings from earned income designed to provide for retirement and dependants. Why should a widow with a modest investment income derived from her husband's savings pay a higher rate of tax than a neighbour with a large earned income? On this view, the only consideration was the amount of income and not its source. Any legitimate complaint, so it was argued, was against *inherited* wealth which was already dealt with by death duties. It could even be argued that tax should be *reduced* on income from savings made from earnings, as morally and economically beneficial.[21]

Of course, the distinction between earned and unearned incomes was by no means clear cut. It was strongly resisted in the 1850s and 1860s, and its acceptance in 1907 was linked to the re-emergence of radical attacks on Rent. After the war, Lloyd George had to accept the abandonment of his prewar schemes of land taxation as a price for Conservative support. But it was more difficult for critics of differentiation to win their argument given the ferocity of attacks on the war debt and the *rentier* class. Any reduction in the level of differentiation would be seen as an attempt to adjust the tax system in favour of holders of the national debt with their unearned income. Stability required the maintenance of differentiation as a symbol of the equity of the fiscal system, and as a means of blocking a more radical onslaught on property. A modest differential in favour of earned income defined as '*active* agency in the partnership between capital and labour in producing income' was a measure of prudential conservatism. However, differentiation *was* modified in order to benefit small unearned incomes which were usually pensions derived from savings out of incomes. In 1907, differentiation took the form of a flat-rate reduction of tax on earned income, so that small unearned incomes paid proportionately more than large unearned incomes which were more likely to come from inherited wealth. The Royal Commission accepted the need for some concession to these smaller unearned incomes, and

[20] PP 1920 xviii, *Report of the Royal Commission on the Income Tax*, p. 128.
[21] PP 1920 xviii, *Report of the Royal Commission on the Income Tax*, pp. 251–3.

Table 4.1 *Income tax paid on wholly earned income, 1918 and 1920*

	Single person		Married, no children		Married, 3 children	
	1918	1920	1918	1920	1918	1920
£150	£3.38	–	–	–	–	–
%	2.3	–	–	–	–	–
£250	£14.63	£13.5	£11.31	–	–	–
%	5.9	5.4	4.5	–	–	–
£350	£25.88	£27.0	£23.6	–	£13.5	£14.63
%	7.4	7.7	6.6	–	3.9	4.2
£450	£45.0	£60.75	£39.94	£33.75	£31.5	£20.25
%	10.0	13.5	8.9	7.5	6.9	4.5

Source: M. E. Short, 'The politics of personal taxation: budget-making in Britain, 1917–31', PhD thesis, Cambridge, 1985, pp. 97, 127.

recommended a reduction of a tenth of earned income. Further, moral opprobrium was removed by a change of terminology, so that 'unearned income' became 'investment income'.[22] These modifications were introduced in the Finance Act of 1920, with the result that taxation of single persons rose on all except the lowest incomes; couples without dependent children secured more benefit, especially on the lowest incomes; and the greatest gain went to couples with three children (see tables 4.1 and 4.2).

Calculation of the incidence of *all* taxes on different classes of society and levels of income is highly problematic, for much depends upon the consumption of taxed commodities (especially tobacco and alcohol) and the ultimate incidence of indirect taxes; the burden of death duties needs to be converted into an annualised tax on different levels of unearned income; and local rates on housing must be taken into account. One of the first attempts to calculate the incidence of both central and local taxation was made by Bernard Mallet.* His estimates rested on a crude distinction between the income tax paying and non-income tax paying classes. He estimated that in 1903/4, 950,000 families with an income of £750m paid £81.4m or 61.3 per cent of national taxes; 8,160,000 did

[22] Short, 'Politics of personal taxation', pp. 119–21; PP 1920 xviii, *Report of the Royal Commission on the Income Tax*, pp. 129–31; PP 1919 xxiii pt i, *Royal Commission on Income Tax, First Instalment of Minutes of Evidence*, appendix 7(b), historical note on differentiation, Board of Inland Revenue, pp. 172–3.

* Bernard Mallet (1859–1932) was the son of the permanent under-secretary of state for India; he was educated at Clifton and Balliol College, Oxford; he entered the Foreign Office in 1882 and transferred to the Treasury in 1885. He was a commissioner of Inland Revenue from 1897 to 1909, and registrar-general for England 1909–20. He was president of the Royal Statistical Society 1916–18 and of the Eugenics Society in 1929. (*Who Was Who*, vol. iii: *1929–40* (London, 1941), p. 894.)

not pay income tax and were responsible for £51.2m or 38.6 per cent of taxes. His conclusion was simple: income taxpayers handed over 10.8 per cent of their income, compared with 5.6 per cent by other families. The implication of his figures was that the better-off members of society were heavily burdened.[23] These figures were the best official estimates available to prewar politicians, and it was perfectly possible to conclude that the fiscal system was already sufficiently progressive. However, they were open to criticism for failing to estimate the incidence of taxation at different levels of income, which produced a picture of a regressive tax system falling heavily on the unskilled working class. Shortly before the war, R. H. Tawney's* research foundation at the LSE found that indirect taxes were regressive on the poor: a family with a weekly income of 18s paid 2.8 per cent of its income in food taxes and 7.1 per cent in food, alcohol and tobacco taxes; a family with 24s paid 2.1 per cent and 5.3 per cent respectively. By contrast, a family with £2 a week paid 1.3 per cent and 3.2 per cent. Regression at the lower levels of income was intensified by local rates and the flat-rate insurance contributions. Indeed, the main beneficiaries of the Liberal fiscal reforms were middle-class men with families; taxes on the poor were not reduced, and on the rich were increased by the super-tax and differentiation.[24]

At the end of the First World War, Herbert Samuel analysed the shape of the tax system in 1903/4 and 1913/14 (see figure 4.2). His figures of the incidence of taxation by income level established the basis for later calculations, and allowed politicians to assess the impact of their policies. He discovered that between 1903/4 and 1913/14, taxation of working-class incomes fell slightly with the reduction in the sugar duty, and taxation of earned incomes up to £2,000 also fell by a modest amount. In the decade before the war, taxation of unearned incomes above £500 and of earned incomes above £2,000 increased, to a maximum of 18.1 per cent

---

[23] PRO, IR74/82, B, 'Incidence of public burdens', B. Mallet, Mar. 1902; IR74/83, 'Incidence of imperial revenue taxation (budget estimate for 1903/4) on income tax and non-income taxpaying classes respectively', B. Mallet, Jan. 1904.

[24] F. W. Kolthammer, *Memorandum on Problems of Poverty No. 1: Some Notes on the Incidence of Taxation on the Working-Class Family* (Ratan Tata Foundation, London, 1913?).

* Richard Henry Tawney (1880–1962) was born in Calcutta, where his father was principal of Presidency College. He was educated at Rugby and Balliol College, Oxford. He taught at the University of Glasgow 1906–8, and for the Workers' Educational Association 1908–14, when he became director of the Ratan Tata Foundation at the LSE. He joined the army in 1915, and became a lecturer at the LSE in 1917, fellow of Balliol 1918–21 and lecturer, reader and professor of economic history at the LSE from 1920 to 1949. In 1919 he was a member of the Royal Commission on the Coal Industry, and 1912–31 a member of the consultative committee of the Board of Education. He was a major influence on Labour thinking on education and equality, not least through his books on *The Acquisitive Society* (1921) and *Equality* (1931). (*DNB, 1961–70*, ed. Williams and Nicholls, pp. 994–8.)

on unearned incomes and 8.4 per cent on earned incomes of £50,000. During the war, taxation of the working class and lower middle class doubled as a proportion of income; it rose three-fold on earned incomes of £1,000 and even more on earned incomes of £2,000 to £5,000. The tax system in 1918/19 was much more progressive than before the war, with a 'dip' around an earned income of £200. As Samuel noted, 'the British system of taxation is regressive in the lower stages; the classes with the smallest incomes pay a larger proportion of them in contributions to the revenue than the classes immediately above them'. The explanation was the reliance on a narrow range of indirect taxes on sugar, tea, alcohol and tobacco which formed a large proportion of working-class expenditure; the implication, which Samuel did not draw, was that a more widely based indirect tax would have been less regressive by tapping more middle-class consumption.[25] Liberal and Labour hostility to protection meant that there were few revenue duties, strictly limited to non-protective tariffs on basic commodities with a low or negative income elasticity of demand. The tax system would be less regressive if duties were extended to commodities with a high income elasticity of demand – a strategy adopted in one case with the duty on petrol. But the implication drawn by Winston Churchill from these figures was a different one, that the class which was most in need of assistance was the lower levels of liability to super-tax.

The aim of the Royal Commission and the coalition government was to re-establish the social contract of the fiscal system, at a time of immense political tension over the payment of the war debt, an increase in the number of people liable to income tax and a much steeper graduation. The Royal Commission removed some of the 'sore points' of the prewar income tax, but taken in isolation it was a technical exercise which needed to be given political force. The dry details required a creative spark. Dr Short has suggested that there was a major change in the basis of taxation at the end of the war, when universal manhood suffrage and the demise of property qualifications severed any remaining connection between political rights and taxation which lay at the heart of Gladstone's fiscal constitution. The principle was weakened by Disraeli's extension of the franchise in 1867 and by the third reform act of 1885; it was finally jettisoned in 1918. Taxation was no longer seen as an insurance premium for the defence of property and protection by the state; it was firmly linked with welfare politics.[26] The danger now was that middle-class taxpayers might revolt against high levels of direct taxation as they did in other European countries. By contrast, the consent of middle-class taxpayers

[25] H. Samuel, 'The taxation of various classes of the people', *Journal of the Royal Statistical Society* 82 (1919), 143–82.
[26] Short, 'Politics of personal taxation', p. 147.

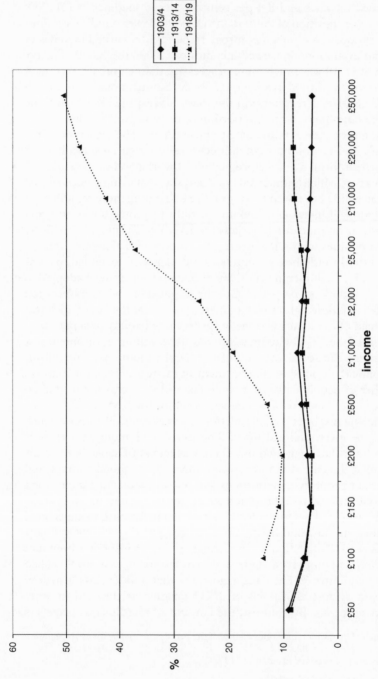

Figure 4.2 Direct and indirect taxation as a percentage of earned income, married men with three children, 1903/4, 1913/14 and 1918/19

Note: excluding local taxes and insurance contributions, and EPD in 1918/19.

Source: H. Samuel, 'The taxation of various classes of the people', *Journal of the Royal Statistical Society* 82 (1919), 176–7, 179.

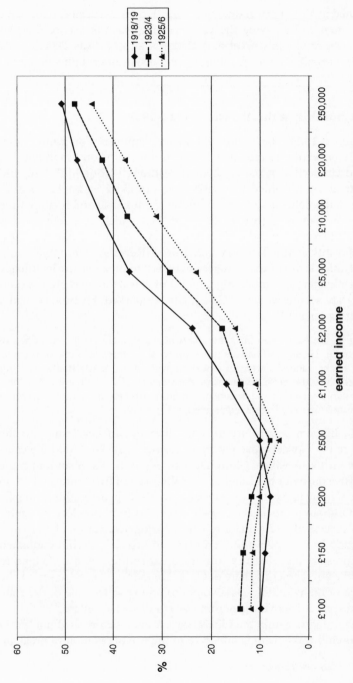

Figure 4.3 Incidence of national taxation (direct and indirect), married men with three children, 1918/19, 1923/4 and 1925/6

Source: G. F. Shirras and L. Rostas, *The Burden of British Taxation* (Cambridge, 1942), p. 58.

was retained in Britain, by reducing the burden on a crucial constituency of family men and allowing the Conservative party to secure their allegiance. Above all, this fiscal and electoral strategy was exploited by Winston Churchill who forged a new fiscal constitution in his budget of 1925.

Churchill at the Treasury, 1924–1929

In November 1924, the minority Labour administration came to an end, the Conservatives returned to office and Winston Churchill was appointed chancellor of the Exchequer. Although Churchill's long and eventful tenure of the office up to 1929 is notorious for his fateful decision to return to the gold standard in 1925, he spent considerably more time and effort on plans for reform of the income tax which were central to his vision of British society and of the Conservative party. Despite the alarm of civil servants at the Treasury and Inland Revenue, Churchill had a strong intuitive sense of the changes necessary to preserve the legitimacy of the fiscal system at a much higher level of extraction and progression. As his private secretary, James Grigg, later remarked, his budgets had a consistent pattern:

In spite of all the Keynesian jibes, his main object was always the reduction of unemployment. He showed himself much under the influence of the 20 years he had spent in the Liberal Party, for it was he who impelled Mr Baldwin's Tory Government into the great advances in the scheme of Contributory Pensions, and he certainly exercised all his skill and might to oppose any serious departure from our fundamentally Free Trade system.[27]

Above all, his aim was to secure the adherence of key groups to the state and to the Conservative party, providing an alternative to the campaign for tariffs to which Churchill was opposed. He abandoned the Conservative party for the Liberals over the issue of free trade; he had no intention of returning to the Conservatives at the expense of this principle. Although Labour politicians naturally dissented from his electoral ambitions, his success played a major role in securing acceptance of high rates of extraction based upon a limited range of taxes. Churchill contained the ambitions of the Treasury to reduce expenditure and so helped to preserve the government's share of GNP. He managed both to secure the adherence of many middle-class voters to an expanded role of the state and to preserve a relatively generous system of social welfare.

As a major figure within the Liberal government before the First World War, Churchill was a leading advocate of the use of taxation to break up

[27] Grigg, *Prejudice and Judgment*, p. 194.

accumulations of 'dead' capital by attacking the unearned increment and the acquisition of wealth by 'plunder'. His aim was not to destroy capitalism and competition, but rather to preserve them from socialist attack by creating an active, dynamic society based upon *current* wealth.[28] These 'new Liberal' policies connected with the ambitions of financial experts within the Labour party, who wished to encourage production and break up passive wealth through the use of the capital levy. However, there were significant divergences between the position adopted by Labour politicians and by Churchill. Both Philip Snowden (chancellor in Labour's first administration) and Hugh Dalton (the leading authority on finance within the party and chancellor after the Second World War) were more concerned with equality and the appropriation of socially created wealth by the state.[29] When Churchill joined the Conservatives, his 'maturer views of life'[30] led him to abandon a frontal attack on accumulated wealth for a more gradual and muted policy of adjustments to the tax system designed to create incentives for the pursuit of personal ambition.

He was concerned that debt should be paid off as soon as possible, for large payments of interest 'will not be allowed to continue indefinitely in a country based on an adult suffrage'.[31] He had serious reservations about the entire thrust of postwar economic policy which was based upon 'deflation, debt repayment, high taxation, large sinking funds and Gold Standard'. Although credit improved, the exchange rate strengthened and the cost of living fell, he was aware that the policy also led to 'bad trade, hard times, an immense increase in unemployment'. The result was 'a complete impasse'. Although taxpayers were making sacrifices, the nominal total of debt was growing and the real value of bonds increasing as the cost of living fell. He feared the prospect of 'gigantic taxation and an enormous rentier class' which would 'lie like a vast wet blanket across the whole process of creating new wealth by new enterprise':

I shall certainly have to meet the criticism that the policy of the Treasury and the bank favours the Capitalists' interests and in particular the rentier class to such an extent that the nation will never be free from the debt in any period which can be foreseen ... The fact that such a policy obtains keen approval among the banking classes and in the City of London is no answer. Indeed, it might be considered quite natural that they should welcome a policy which undoubtedly tends to foster to its highest point the interests of creditors and inert citizens of

---

[28] M. Gilbert, *Churchill's Political Philosophy* (Oxford, 1981), p. 43; W. S. Churchill, *Liberalism and the Social Problem* (London, 1909), pp. 336, 377–8.

[29] See, for example, P. Snowden, *Labour and the New World* (London, 1921); H. Dalton, *Some Aspects of the Inequality of Incomes in Modern Communities* (London, 1920), and *Practical Socialism for Britain* (London, 1935).

[30] Gilbert, *Churchill, V, Companion I*, p. 297, Churchill to Lord Salisbury, 9 Dec. 1924.

[31] PRO, T176/28, Churchill to R. V. N. Hopkins, 26 Jan. 1927.

all kinds at the expense of all those forces which by fresh efforts are perennially replacing what is consumed. Everything in fact under this system is consumed and replaced except the debt which towers up higher and higher.

Churchill was anxious to position the Conservatives as a party of production and enterprise, and he was acutely conscious of the dangers of appearing to favour passive wealth and financial interests.[32]

In 1924, Churchill warned his colleagues against defensive and paternalistic justifications of wealth and urged the adoption of a more aggressive and positive argument, that the capitalist system and private property provided the foundation of civilisation and material security:

an attempt to hunt down 'the idle rich', whoever they are, wherever they may be found, might be attended with so much friction and injury to the general system of capital and to the freedom arising under a capitalist system that it would be more trouble than it is worth. The existing system of death duties is a certain corrective against the development of a race of idle rich. If they are idle they will cease in a few generations to be rich. Further than that it is not desirable for the legislature to go.[33]

Churchill's ambition was to channel the progressive rhetoric of production versus plunder away from Labour's policies of nationalisation and the capital levy into the maintenance of a competitive economy. Above all, he needed to present a policy for industrial recovery and economic prosperity based on the maintenance of free trade.

Churchill's vision of British society emerged in his first budget of 1925, which ranks as a major restatement of fiscal policy. Churchill's ambitions were 'the appeasement of class bitterness, the promotion of a spirit of co-operation, the stabilisation of our national life'.[34] At first sight, these sentiments do not sit well with the return to the gold standard and the crisis in labour relations culminating in the general strike of 1926. In the eyes of many trade unionists, Churchill was a class warrior rather than a mediator. However, Churchill's opposition to the strike was complemented by a more constructive policy resting on the view that social harmony and political stability required a dynamic, competitive economy which would be destroyed by high taxes and industrial militancy. Churchill's vision of co-operation and stabilisation depended upon a reduction in the taxation of active wealth at the expense of inherited wealth, a cut in the tax burden on moderately well-to-do middle-class families and the extension of pensions. His concern was for incentives and growth in a capitalist economy, always provided that the result was social integration. In his intuitive way

[32] Gilbert, *Churchill, V, Companion I*, pp. 924–5, Churchill to O. Niemeyer, 26 Jan. 1927, and p. 997, Churchill to O. Niemeyer, 20 May 1927.

[33] Gilbert, *Churchill, V, Companion I*, pp. 297–8, Churchill to Salisbury, 9 Dec. 1924.

[34] Quoted in Gilbert, *Churchill's Political Philosophy*, p. 53.

and with his penchant for dramatic gestures, he was developing a vision of British society and of the electoral strategy of the Conservative party which was to assist in the stabilisation of political and social relations up to 1939.

Churchill's flamboyant approach was complemented by the more low-key style of leadership of Baldwin who was less concerned with specific policies than forging links between Conservatism and his vision of national values. Some historians argue that the Conservatives were pursuing a strategy which set the selfish interests of unions and Labour against the public. More accurately, Baldwin attacked strikers, socialists and intellectuals, and stressed that workers, despite party differences, shared the same basic cultural assumptions and national characteristics as self-reliant, sturdy Englishmen joining in voluntary activities and service. In this way, he was able to appeal to the middle ground, from a high moral position rather than as a divisive politician. He differed from Churchill in defining the Englishman as concerned with home and the countryside rather than the empire; where he agreed with Churchill was in the definition of capitalism as democratic and not simply the possession of the rich. In his view, industry and commerce were social products, and capital was made up of the savings of rich and poor, created 'by the coppers as much as by the sovereigns', through co-operative and friendly societies and union funds. Rather than high taxes to seize socially created capital from a narrow group of exploiters, Baldwin stressed that capital was spread throughout society, and that the correct policy was a 'multiplication of capitalists'. Similarly, high taxation would be felt throughout society, for it 'has an astonishing way, like water . . . of filtering down and down till it bears on the backs of every class of the people'. Hence workers were interested in low taxation as employees and as small savers or members of clubs and societies. As Philip Williamson argues, these arguments were much more sensitive and subtle than the crude campaigns against waste, for Baldwin was anxious to maintain social expenditure in order to avoid alienating workers and to create a sense of fairness. Such an approach turned aside the more divisive possibilities of cutting spending and taxation. It was left to Churchill to turn Baldwin's homilies into action.[35]

One of the crucial issues was the treatment of the national debt. Churchill feared that the Treasury's policies of maintaining taxes and a budgetary surplus in order to redeem debt could lead to accusations that the government was exalting the Money Trust in preference to other 'social, moral or manufacturing' interests, and he argued that 'there is more in the life of a nation than the development of an immense rentier

---

[35] Williamson, *Stanley Baldwin*, pp. 171, 180–1, 336, 338–41, 343, 353, 358; the alternative view of a simple opposition between the public and Labour is expressed in McKibbin, *Ideologies of Class*, pp. 271, 275, 281–2, 292–3, 299.

class quartered in perpetuity upon the struggling producer of new wealth'.[36] Churchill was anxious to remove the political danger posed by high levels of debt service, and at the end of 1924 he asked the Treasury to consider two possibilities: a conversion of the debt to a lower rate of interest; and a reduction in the sinking fund. In 1927, he made a further proposal – a forced loan at a low rate of interest. 'I am quite sure', he informed Niemeyer, 'that a really well argued political campaign to get clear of a process by which the total of the debt is continually increasing would be irresistible if it were launched with sufficient knowledge and skill. And I do not want to see such a development against us.'[37]

The Treasury took a different view, that such measures were quite unsuited to Britain. The Treasury had no difficulty in accepting the desirability of conversion, which had been used in the past and was compatible with fiscal orthodoxy, offering a safe alternative to a capital levy. The problem was how to make the holders of government stock accept a lower rate of interest. One possibility was to create an incentive through the tax system, on the lines of Dalton's suggestion of an additional death duty or an increase in taxation of unearned income, with the opportunity of conversion into tax-free annuities payable for twenty years. Although this scheme would produce an immediate saving, it would cost more over the whole period of the annuities. The use of penal taxation to force people to take up the new assets also troubled the Treasury. There was, argued Niemeyer, simply no need for extreme measures such as in France with its unbalanced budgets, a huge floating debt and high interest rates of 8 per cent. 'We are not desperate men: we cannot justify, and we need not incur the enormous risk of, desperate measures.' The alternative was to make conversions from time to time in the market, which depended upon balancing the budget, maintaining a sinking fund and ensuring that expenditure did not rise. The task might be encouraged by an *increase* in the sinking fund, possibly through the introduction of a special, short-term tax. Indeed, in 1925 Niemeyer contemplated a tax on the annual return of capital.

There seems to me to be a good deal to be said for the proposition that compared with other persons the Rentier is getting too much, and I have been wondering whether we could devise a tax to fall on the Rentier while possibly giving him a chance to escape by conversion into a lower interest stock free, not from taxation in general, but from this particular tax.

The crucial point, in Niemeyer's opinion, was to increase the sinking fund, if necessary by imposing a new tax, in order to convert the debt as

[36] PRO, T176/39, W. S. Churchill to O. E. Niemeyer, 26 Jan. 1927.
[37] PRO, T171/577, W. S. Churchill to P. J. Grigg and O. Niemeyer, 26 Nov. 1924; T176/39, Churchill to Niemeyer, 26 Jan. 1927.

soon as possible and to avoid more serious financial measures such as a capital levy.[38]

It followed that the Treasury rejected Churchill's proposal to reduce the sinking fund. During the nineteenth century, only a few compulsory sinking funds were included with the budget estimates; otherwise, debt was reduced by means of budget surpluses remaining at the end of the year. The convention established in 1829 was that any surplus left at the end of the financial year should be used to reduce the national debt, and should not be carried over to the next year. In the absence of such a rule, the Treasury feared that unscrupulous chancellors might accumulate a fund for reducing taxation before the general election, which would turn the tax system into a gigantic system of jobbery, so making it highly politicised and challenging the legitimacy of the fiscal system.[39] It was therefore essential, in the Treasury's opinion, to use any surplus to redeem the debt – always assuming that the chancellor budgeted for a surplus rather than increasing spending or reducing taxes. In order to create more discipline, in 1923 Stanley Baldwin made a definite commitment of £50m a year for debt redemption so that the budget would only balance if this sum were taken into account.[40] As Niemeyer argued, redemption of the debt was a definite contract when the loans were issued and must be preserved. Further, government borrowing took money from the investment market and depressed the value of stocks, so that any additional borrowing would be at increasingly unfavourable rates. In his view, there was no scope for making economies on redemption; the choice was between maintaining a sinking fund or incurring extra debts which would absorb a substantial part of the country's savings.[41] The Treasury argued that strict adherence to redemption was beneficial to industry by releasing funds from government loans and making them available for investment and economic recovery. The Treasury position was therefore to maintain a high level of taxation and to increase the sum available for debt redemption through cuts in expenditure.[42]

[38] PRO, T176/39, 'Conversion', O. E. Niemeyer, n.d.; O. E. Niemeyer to R. V. N. Hopkins, 12 Nov. 1925; O. E. Niemeyer to D. Veale, 13 Mar. 1926; Niemeyer to chancellor on Colwyn Committee, 22 Nov. 1926; on Dalton's scheme, see below, pp. 147–52.

[39] PRO, T171/9, Basil Blackett's memorandum on Finance Bill 1909, 22 Nov. 1910.

[40] PRO, T171/578, F. Phillips to R. V. N. Hopkins, 24 Oct. 1927; see also T171/579 on the technical issues of showing debt above and below the line.

[41] PRO, T171/577, Niemeyer to chancellor, 1 Dec. 1924.

[42] PRO, T171/214, O. Niemeyer to chancellor, 20 Mar. 1923, and 'Sinking funds', O. Niemeyer to chancellor, 23 Jan. 1923; T171/222, budget memorandum, O. Niemeyer, n.d.; T171/226, O. Niemeyer to chancellor, 24 Jan. 1924, 10 Mar. 1924 and 2 Apr. 1924; T171/234, note by O. Niemeyer, 29 Feb. 1924, and R. G. Hawtrey, 3 Mar. 1924. On the Treasury view, see G. C. Peden, 'The Treasury view in the interwar period: an example of political economy?', in B. Corry (ed.), *Unemployment and the Economists* (Cheltenham, 1996), pp. 69–88, and G. C. Peden, 'The "Treasury view" on public works

The Cabinet's committee on expenditure took a similar line to the Treasury, arguing for a cut in spending. The committee had the 'gravest apprehension' about spending on social services, fearing that it 'constitutes a future menace of a most serious character'. It was also alarmed by grants to local government, arguing for an end to the existing system by which the central government covered a fixed percentage of local expenditure, without adequate control.[43] Churchill's approach to the financial situation was more creative. Rather than reducing expenditure on social services, he introduced a new form of widows' pension that was linked with a rhetoric of assistance to respectable and hard-working members of society. He also readjusted the income tax in order to benefit married, family men in a creative shaping of the electoral identity of the Conservative party.

Churchill took a different view of economic recovery from that of the Treasury. His priority was to stimulate enterprise which would be achieved most effectively by reducing the amount of income tax paid by active members of society – even if it meant subverting the Treasury's definition of fiscal probity. Churchill's policy required him to escape from long-established Treasury constraints, not least because economic stagnation and the impact of the general strike reduced the yield of taxes. There was a danger that an increase in taxes to cover any deficit would check a revival of trade. Despite Baldwin's insistence that at least £50m be allowed for debt redemption, in reality the chancellor had more power to incur a deficit than before the war. Treasury bills could not be used to cover a deficit before 1914, for they had to be repaid by the end of the financial year with no power to renew. Similarly, 'Ways and Means' advances had to be repaid within three months of the end of the financial year. These restrictions fell into abeyance during the war and the War Loan Act of 1919 gave the government more discretion in provision for debt.[44] Churchill exploited this freedom to the full. During his period as chancellor, the rate of redemption of the national debt was much slower, and Churchill used a number of creative accounting devices in order to

---

and employment in the interwar period', *Economic History Review* 2nd ser. 37 (1984), 167–81; P. F. Clarke, 'The Treasury's analytical model of the British economy between the wars', in Furner and Supple (eds.), *The State and Economic Knowledge*, pp. 171–207.

[43] PRO, CAB27/304, Standing Committee on Expenditure, 17 Dec. 1926, f. 7; 5 Apr. 1927, f. 21; CAB27/305, CP54(26), Standing Committee on Expenditure, report 9 Feb. 1926.

[44] On the restoration of the sinking fund in 1923, see PRO, T171/214, Niemeyer to chancellor, 'Sinking funds', 23 Jan. 1923; T171/578, F. P. to R. V. N. Hopkins, 24 Oct. 1927; on treatment of debt charges above and below the line, see the explanation in T171/584, unsigned and undated note; Short, 'Politics of personal taxation', pp. 208–9. The budget of 1930 restored the prewar rule and removed Churchill's freedom.

give the appearance that the budget was in balance when he was, in reality, running a deficit which gave him room to modify the tax system.

An apparently trivial stratagem adopted in 1925 was to give the net rather than gross expenditure of the government. In fact, this was a serious breach of the Gladstonian fiscal constitution which scandalised the Treasury. As Frederick Leith-Ross* remarked, 'it will be a bad day for British finances when, for the sake of a little window-dressing, aimed at appeasing the appetite of the ignorant, the Treasury is prepared to throw over the main principle of the Gladstonian reforms'. He argued that the 'fundamental basis' of public finance was the payment of gross revenue into the Exchequer; Leith-Ross feared that 'netting' the budget marked a return to pre-Victorian practice and would give departments more control over their finances. Leith-Ross stressed the inviolability of the Gladstonian system which gave constant control over spending and prevented any recurrent item of expenditure from becoming stereotyped; it allowed the Treasury to use balances to finance any area of expenditure which was not possible if funds were earmarked; and it provided a clear picture of expenditure as a whole. As Leith-Ross argued,

The rapidity with which British finances were restored to order after the war as compared, for example, with those of France or other Continental countries, is largely due to the corrective effect of this system. The special accounts which result from the system of assignments, are the curse of the Continental Budget, as they afford a ready means of cloaking Government liabilities and concealing deficits in a Budget, which balances on paper; but if Parliamentary assent must be obtained for the application of all public resources, it is impossible to disguise the situation.

Churchill's decision to give the net rather than gross expenditure of the government gave him the freedom of appearing to reduce the scale of government spending.[45]

Churchill also embarked on a number of schemes to boost his income. He 'raided' the sinking fund, taking some of the money set aside for debt redemption.[46] He looked to the surplus on the National Health Insurance

---

[45] PRO, T171/582, Leith-Ross to W. S. Churchill, 13 Aug. 1927; Grigg, *Prejudice and Judgment*, pp. 196–7; on netting the budget, see T171/578, budget 1928, vol. 1, general and netting the budget which deals with ways of showing net expenditure.

[46] Short, 'Politics of personal taxation', pp. 209–10.

* Frederick William Leith-Ross (1887–1968) was educated at Merchant Taylors and Balliol College, Oxford. He entered the Treasury in 1909, and was private secretary to Asquith from 1911 to 1913. He served as British representative on the Finance Board of the Reparations Commission, 1920–5; was deputy controller of finance at the Treasury 1925–32; chief economic adviser to the government 1932–46; and director-general of the ministry of economic warfare 1939–42. (*Who Was Who*, vol. VI: *1961–70* (London, 1972), p. 666.)

Fund, which gave him scope to announce a new social policy at the end of the parliament, when he had funds in hand to use with dramatic effect.[47] And in 1926 he turned to the reserve of the Road Fund. This separate fund was an anomaly, a breach in the Treasury's distrust of hypothecation. Its origins are to be found in the reform of local government finance in 1888, when a number of 'assigned revenues' or licence duties were handed to local authorities, in an attempt to limit their demand for constant grants from central government. One of these assigned revenues was the licence on carriages, which was replaced in 1909 by a new tax on petrol and a duty on the horse power of motor vehicles. The revenue was paid to a new Road Improvement Fund as part of the Liberal government's policy of national development, with a fixed payment to the local authorities in place of the income from carriage licences. During the war, the petrol duty was diverted to the Exchequer, and in 1920 it was abolished in response to problems in defining fuel used for motor cars rather than heating or lighting, and because of difficulties created by exemptions to farmers or trawlers. At the same time, the minister of transport struck a deal with the chancellor that the proceeds of the vehicle duty should be paid to the Road Fund (less the fixed payment to local authorities), on condition that no claim was made on the Exchequer for road building. As a result, the revenue of the Fund rose faster than expenditure, and a large surplus was accumulated. The Treasury was highly critical of this hypothecation of revenue, arguing that the Fund was outside parliamentary control and that it resulted in lavish spending on wide roads on which cars drove at excessive speeds, at a time when industry was burdened with taxes and other forms of spending were being cut. As Churchill argued, it was 'nonsense' to argue that motorists were excused from any contribution to the general revenue of the country:

Who ever said that, whatever the yield of these taxes and whatever the poverty of the country, we were to build roads and nothing but roads, from this yield? We might have to cripple our trade by increased taxation of income. We might have to mutilate our Education for the sake of economy. We might even be unable to pay for the upkeep of our fleet. But never mind, whatever happens, the whole yield of the taxes on motors must be spent on roads! . . . Such contentions are absurd and constitute at once an outrage upon the sovereignty of parliament and upon commonsense.

Of course, the motor lobby argued that the Fund was 'their' money and that any surplus should be devoted to a reduction in motor taxation. One way of circumventing their protests was to divide the duty, at least

---

[47] PRO, CAB27/305, NE29, Standing Committee on Expenditure, National Health Insurance, memorandum by chancellor of the Exchequer, 8 Jan. 1926.

notionally, into a payment for 'wear and tear' on the roads and a 'luxury' or pleasure tax on private cars to be paid into the Exchequer. In 1926, Churchill took £7m from the surplus of the fund, and a further £12m in 1927. In 1926, he assigned a third of the revenue from private cars as a tax on luxury and pleasure uses. In addition, Churchill proposed a tax on imported petrol, which he justified as an encouragement to the extraction of fuel from domestic coal, and as a way of putting competition between road transport and railways on a fair basis. Churchill felt that a tax on motor fuel 'is from every point of view desirable and in harmony with the largest and longest conceptions of the national interest'. Accordingly, he imposed a tax on petrol in 1928, which would produce sufficient revenue to reduce the burden of local rates on industry. This was the only significant new indirect tax until the introduction of the purchase tax in 1942.[48] By these means, Churchill was able to create sufficient freedom of action to adjust the income tax in pursuit of his vision of economic recovery and political stability.

Not surprisingly, senior officials at the Treasury were scandalised by Churchill's creative accounting. As Montagu Norman* of the Bank of England remarked, Churchill was the Blondin of finance, a great escape artiste. Churchill himself did not dissent, remarking that his budget of 1927 was 'as good a get-out as we could get'. Even the prime minister had the honesty to inform the king that Churchill's budget was 'a mischievous

[48] *Parliamentary Debates*, 5th ser. 194, 26 Apr. 1926, cols. 1710–15; 205, 28 Apr. 1927, cols. 94–5, 1153–4; 216, 24 Apr. 1928, cols. 854–9, 861–3; PRO, T171/250, Cabinet Economy Committee, Road Fund, memorandum by the home secretary, 16 Oct. 1925; memorandum on Road Fund, G. Barstow, 30 Oct. 1925; W. S. Churchill to Barstow, 30 Oct. 1925; W. S. Churchill, 2 Nov. 1925; minute dictated by chancellor, 20 Nov. 1925; memorandum on Road Fund by W. S. Churchill, 22 Nov. 1925; memoranda in regard to the Road Fund prepared by the Treasury, prefaced by memorandum by chancellor of the Exchequer, 16 Dec. 1925; Standing Committee on Expenditure: the Road Fund, memorandum by the minister of transport, 17 Dec. 1925; Standing Committee on Expenditure, 18 Dec. 1925; report of Standing Committee on Expenditure CP54/26; T171/251, memorandum: motor taxation – Road Fund; Customs to chancellor 1 Jan. 1926; meeting of Application Committee, 7 Jan. 1926; Churchill to Horace Hamilton, 7 Mar. 1926; G. Barstow to chancellor, 9 Mar. 1926, treatment of the Road Fund; CP150(26), the taxation of motor vehicles: memorandum prepared by the Treasury and the Customs. Much of this material may also be found in CAB27/305–6, Standing Committee on Expenditure, reports and memoranda. See T171/264 for discussions of motor spirit tax; and Short, 'Politics of personal taxation', p. 210.

* Montagu Norman (1871–1950) was the son of a director of Martin's bank, and on his mother's side connected to the merchant bank Brown Shipley. After education at Eton and King's College, Cambridge, he joined Martin's in 1892 and Brown Shipley in New York in 1894, becoming a director in 1907. He left the firm in 1915 to join the Bank of England. He rose to deputy governor and was governor from 1920 to 1944 – the first permanent central banker. He stressed the independence of the Bank and its links with an international network of central bankers, but also its advisory role to the government. (*DNB, 1941–50*, pp. 633–6; Robbins (ed.), *Biographical Dictionary*, pp. 326–7.)

piece of manipulation . . . a masterpiece of ingenuity'.[49] The question was whether his escape was to be applauded as an act of showmanship, or decried as the trick of a charlatan.

Churchill emphasised a creative revision of taxation, and was fully aware that the Treasury's approach, for all its financial probity, posed other dangers in alienating two extremely important interests: taxpayers aggrieved by the high level of extraction; and the poor and unemployed who would suffer hardship from reductions in welfare expenditure. The concern of the Treasury was predominantly with debt redemption and financial stability; Churchill was aware that these were only part of a larger issue of the legitimacy of the state and its fiscal system. A loss of consent to taxation, and in particular to high levels of income tax at a progressive rate, would undermine the Treasury's strategy and create a 'legitimation deficit'.

In his creative approach to reforming taxation, Churchill started from a simple, pragmatic issue. Should death duties on large fortunes be reduced from the high level to which they were raised in 1919? The line adopted by the Treasury was that no reduction was necessary, for duties paid at death were 'psychologically a much less onerous charge' than an annual income tax and had little effect on enterprise. Richard Hopkins went so far as to suggest that an increase in the rate on small and moderate estates might finance a cut in income tax.[50] Churchill seized upon the thought and erected it into a political principle. His initial concern was to assist the lower level of super-tax payers. Despite war-time inflation, the threshold of the super-tax remained at its prewar level of £2,000 which meant that many members of the middle class were liable. His starting point was to leave the burden of income tax and super-tax on the very largest incomes more or less at the existing level, without any increase in the incidence of death duties on the very largest estates above £1m. He could then increase death duties on estates of £12,500 to £1 million to yield £10m in a full year. As a result of this revision of the death duties, earned incomes would be treated more favourably than inherited wealth which was liable both to a higher rate of income tax on unearned income and to death duties. Such a policy could be presented as an incentive to creators of wealth, appealing to the 'highly paid brain worker who has nothing behind him but his earnings' compared with those who received income from investments. He could claim to remove 'a grave discouragement to enterprise and thrift' and 'relieve the pressure

[49] Short, 'Politics of personal taxation', p. 210, from T. Jones, *Whitehall Diary*, vol. II: *1916–1930*, ed. K. Middlemass (London, 1969), p. 98, entry for 28 Apr. 1927; and Baldwin to George V, in Gilbert, *Churchill, V, Companion I*, p. 986.

[50] PRO, T171/239, R. V. N. Hopkins to Churchill, 14 Nov. 1924 and 18 Dec. 1924.

upon the highly-creative faculties of the community'. In his view, direct taxation on enterprise led to a reduction of effort and a loss of savings which harmed all members of society. 'It is an undoubted fact that the country with the highest rate of unemployment is also the country where the taxes on income are at the highest level, and where at the highest level they are collected in full. Are you sure it is only a coincidence? I am sure it is not.'[51] He therefore presented the adjustment of income and super-tax as an incentive to growth and dynamism.

The revenue from death duties, as well as his creative finances and economic recovery, gave Churchill scope to reform the income tax and super-tax. His strategy was to leave the very rich 'stranded on the peaks of taxation to which they have been carried by the flood'. Cuts in taxation should concentrate on

the lower and medium classes of Super Tax payers, giving the greatest measure of relief to the lowest class comprising professional men, small merchants and businessmen – superior brain workers of every kind. Where these classes possess accumulated capital in addition to their incomes, the increase of Death Duties operating over the same area will reclaim a substantial portion of the relief afforded by the reform of the Super Tax. The doctor, engineer and lawyer earning 3 or 4 thousand a year and with no capital will get the greatest relief; the possessor of unearned income derived from a capital estate of 2 or 3 hundred thousands, the smallest relief; while the millionaire will remain substantially liable to the existing scales of high taxation.

Churchill also aimed to reduce the standard rate of income tax in order to benefit the lower ranges of earned income, and especially the 'very large class of deserving people who have to maintain a certain status of living, who are sometimes called "the black coated working men"'.[52] His intention was to gain the allegiance of a crucial section of the electorate for the Conservative party, and at the same time to establish the legitimacy of the state and secure consent to the fiscal system at a higher level of extraction.

Churchill's aim was clear, but it was not without its technical difficulties. A concession to the super-tax would be criticised by Labour as benefiting the rich. In any case, it would not produce the results sought by Churchill: a simple reduction in super-tax would benefit the largest incomes with the greatest proportion of their income above the super-tax threshold. Here was the virtue, in Churchill's eyes, of simplification

[51] *Parliamentary Debates*, 5th ser. 183, 28 Apr. 1925, cols. 64–5, 85–6; Gilbert, *Churchill, V, Companion I*, p. 466, Churchill to George V, 23 Apr. 1925; PRO, T171/239, Churchill to R. V. N. Hopkins, 14 Dec. 1924; T171/247, W. S. Churchill, remarks to a deputation from the National Conference of Employers' Organisations, 4 Mar. 1925.

[52] PRO T171/239, Churchill to R. V. N. Hopkins, 28 Nov. 1924; Gilbert, *Churchill, V, Companion I*, p. 467, Churchill to George V, 23 Apr. 1925.

by combining the income tax and super-tax, and levying the super-tax on the *net* income after payment of income tax. This change would help those with a small proportion of the income above the threshold. But Hopkins realised that this approach was still open to attack by Labour as an underhand way of assisting the rich. Accordingly, he suggested that a concession to super-taxpayers should be linked with a concession to 'the great mass of reasonably successful professional men and other similarly circumstanced' who fell just below the threshold. He therefore proposed a return to the prewar level of differentation in favour of earned income. This would, argued Hopkins, meet Churchill's 'essential condition of relieving successful professional men and businessmen', extending concessions from the lower and medium super-taxpayers on incomes of £3,000 to £4,000 to incomes of £500 to £1,000. His solution better fulfilled Churchill's aim of assisting 'superior brain workers' and was less open to political challenge as merely assisting the rich. It also had the virtue of being a restoration of the prewar scale of differentiation rather than a new departure, an act of restitution rather than a disruption of social relations.[53]

Churchill claimed that the combined effect of his proposals was a budget balanced both in the narrow sense of ensuring that revenue covered expenditure, and in the wider sense of ensuring that 'the scales of justice between one class and another in our varying community' were fairly weighted:

a scheme which has both unity and combination, which is national and not class or party in its conception or intention, which seeks to give to every class the assistance it most requires in the form most acceptable to the individual and most useful to the State – a scheme from which no class of men or women in the country, from the poorest to the richest, is excluded, and in which the proportion of advantage or relief progressively increases as the ladder of wealth is descended. I cherish the hope that by liberating the production of new wealth from some, at least of the shackles of taxation, the Budget may stimulate enterprise and accelerate industrial revival; and that, by giving a far greater measure of security to the mass of the wage-earners, their wives and children, it may promote contentment and stability, and make our island more truly a home for all its people.[54]

It was an appeal from the rhetoric of conflict associated with the capital levy to a vision of integration and class harmony in a prosperous, dynamic economy.

Churchill's adjustment of taxes was part of a creative interpretation of social identities and political allegiances. His strategy offered the same

[53] PRO, T171/239, memorandum from the Board of Inland Revenue upon the proposal to place super-tax upon the net income, 25 Nov. 1924; R. V. N. Hopkins to Churchill, 12 Dec. 1924.

[54] *Parliamentary Debates*, 5th ser. 183, 28 Apr. 1925, col. 89.

results as Labour promised by the more contentious capital levy: a gain for members of the middle class living on earned incomes. Churchill's approach offered a much more comforting appeal to enterprising members of the middle class, promising them that their needs would be considered without setting them against large property. To use Churchill's metaphor, millionaires were left stranded at the high-water mark as the tide of taxation receded, and ordinary super-taxpayers were pulled further down the beach as the water went out. However, the greatest gains would be experienced by 'the great mass of the Income Tax payers [who] subside into the refreshing waters of the sea'. The revision of death duties allowed him to emphasise that higher unearned incomes were paying more, and he widened the distinction between earned and unearned income. He claimed that the result would be

an encouragement to people to bestir themselves and make more money while they are alive and bring up their heirs to do the same. The process of the creation of new wealth is beneficial to the whole community. The process of squatting on old wealth though valuable is a far less lively agent. The great bulk of the wealth of the world is created and consumed every year. We shall never shake ourselves clear from the debts of the war and break into a definitely larger period except by energetic creation of new wealth. A premium on effort is my aim and a penalty on inertia may be its companion.[55]

Churchill was holding out the prospect of freedom from the burden of the national debt by a policy designed to appeal to enterprise and to reassert the benefits of capitalism, based on co-operation in a hierarchical society rather than class conflict. He was in agreement with Labour on the burden of the debt and its drain on enterprise, but departed from Labour's solution of an attack on the *rentier* class through socialisation of property and a tax on wealth. The postwar government had mounted a successful holding operation; Churchill embarked on an ideological counter-attack.

Churchill's strategy did not stop with a revision of tax rates, for he was also concerned to spend in order to create social cohesion and to encourage enterprise. Churchill consciously seized the mantle of David Lloyd George, with whom he had been closely involved in the introduction of non-contributory old age pensions in 1908 and contributory health and unemployment insurance in 1911. He was aiming to appropriate the ideology of 'new Liberalism' which had, to a large extent, migrated into the Labour party with its attempt to claim socially created wealth for the community. But Churchill felt that Labour's development of 'new Liberal' ideology would destroy rather than preserve enterprise and competition.

[55] PRO, T171/239, Churchill to R. V. N. Hopkins, 28 Nov. 1924; Churchill to Hopkins, 14 Dec. 1924; *Parliamentary Debates*, 5th ser. 183, 28 Apr. 1925, cols. 63–4.

Churchill claimed that he was the true heir to the approach of 1911, extending 'modern conceptions of scientific State organisation' in a way which preserved rather than challenged a sense of personal responsibility. He was offering support for the 'cottage home' against misfortune:

Inconceivable waste, degenerating into havoc, takes place all over the country, and is taking place whenever a lamentable catastrophe of an exceptional character falls upon the otherwise happy, free and prosperous workman's home ... It is not to the sturdy marching troops that extra rewards and indulgences are needed at the present time. It is to the stragglers, to the exhausted, to the weak, to the wounded, to the veterans, to the widow and the orphans that the ambulance of the State and the aid of the State should, as far as possible, be directed.[56]

He was continuing the argument he used before the First World War to justify social insurance as a way of mitigating the consequences of failure in a competitive society and of encouraging risk-taking:

We want to draw a line below which we will not allow persons to live and labour, yet above which they may compete with all the strength of their manhood. We want to have free competition upwards; we decline to allow free competition downwards. We do not want to pull down the structures of science and civilisation: but to spread a net over the abyss.

There was, he remarked, no chance of making people self-reliant by confronting them with problems beyond their capacities; personal responsibility would best be achieved by the state providing an assurance that efforts would succeed.[57] The budget of 1925 built upon this approach, by arguing that a society of self-reliant individuals would be encouraged by an extension of state support for pensions, and by a reduction in punitively high levels of direct taxation which led to a lessening of effort, loss of savings and economic stagnation. He presented a reduction in income and super-tax as a way of releasing enterprise, boosting savings and consequently increasing the yield of taxes which would reduce the debt and support expenditure.

Churchill was also pursuing a strategy adopted by earlier Liberal chancellors to retain support from modest middle-class incomes. When William Harcourt introduced graduated death duties in 1894, he used part of the revenue to reduce income tax on the lowest level of liability. Similarly, Lloyd George's fiscal strategy increased the tax burden on super-taxpayers, unearned incomes and large estates; by contrast, a man with two children and an earned income of £300 paid no more in 1913/14 than in 1892/3. The budget, and the social reforms it financed, were therefore designed to 'promote the welding together of a progressive coalition

[56] *Parliamentary Debates*, 5th ser. 183, 28 Apr. 1925, cols. 71–2.
[57] Churchill, *Liberalism and the Social Problem*, pp. 82–3, 376.

for reform that encompassed both the middle and working classes'.[58] Lloyd George was aiming to retain middle-class voters for the Liberal party by showing that a fiscal policy based on free trade would not hit their pockets.[59]

Churchill was well aware of the incidence of taxation and of its electoral implications. The result of his adjustments was that the 'dip' in the proportion of income taken in taxation became deeper, and it moved up the income scale so that family men earning £500 paid the lowest contribution in proportion to earnings.[60] These changes had obvious political overtones, for the main beneficiaries of changes in the structure of taxation were the upper range of the working class and the lower middle class who amounted to about 1,350,000 taxpayers earning between £300 and £600[61] (see figure 4.3). Their allegiance was crucial to electoral success in interwar Britain – a point Churchill fully realised in his desire (as Grigg saw it) 'of making the Treasury an active instrument of Government social policy instead of a passive concomitant or even, as it sometimes was, an active opponent'. As Grigg remarked,

The plan is quite obvious – to transfer some of the burden of direct taxation from the active to the inactive, and at the same time to start it on a definitely downward trend; to stiffen the indirect taxation on luxuries; and to carry on the Lloyd George traditions of making and helping industry provide for those who have fallen by the wayside or grown old in its service.[62]

His later budgets were marked by 'an obstinate refusal to go back on the carefully thought-out scheme of 1925'.[63]

Should these changes to the tax system be seen as a cynical device to benefit groups who provided the electoral base of the Conservative party? The tax system had a 'regressive tail', with a higher level of extraction from lower than middle incomes, which was open to the criticism that it transferred income from poor working-class families to the modestly affluent middle class. But the issue is not so straightforward, for funds were also transferred from the rich, and social expenditure might transfer more funds to the poor. It could be argued that stabilisation of the fiscal system maintained a higher level of extraction than before the First World War, so permitting an increase in transfer payments, and producing a social-fiscal system which was more progressive. The significant issue was the

[58] Balderston, 'War finance and inflation', 233; Murray, *People's Budget*, p. 5.
[59] Samuel, 'Taxation of various classes', 177.
[60] Short, 'Politics of personal taxation', p. 204.
[61] Hicks, *Finance*, p. 274.
[62] Grigg, *Prejudice and Judgment*, pp. 174, 196; Short, 'Politics of personal taxation', pp. 211, 225.
[63] Grigg, *Prejudice and Judgment*, p. 199.

Table 4.2 *Structure of income tax, 1920/1*

Standard rate	30 per cent
Earned income allowance	one tenth of earned income, up to allowance of £200
Personal allowances	married £225
	other £135
	increased allowance where wife has earned income:
	up to £45
Children, under 16 or in full-time education	£36 for first child
	£27 for each subsequent child
Tax rate	on first £225 of taxable income (after allowances) 15 per cent
	remainder 30 per cent
Super-tax	exceeding £2,000
	on incomes £2,000–£2,500 7.5 per cent
	£2,500–£3,000 10 per cent
	£3,000–£4,000 12.5 per cent
	and then by steps of 2.5 per cent to 30 per cent above £30,000

Source: PP 1921 xiv, *64th Report of the Commissioners of Inland Revenue for the year ended 31 March 1921*, pp. 529, 570.

preservation of a high level of extraction without facing a taxpayers' revolt or de-legitimising the state. Although the Conservative electoral strategy was self-interested, it could be argued that it also contributed, and not entirely unwittingly, to a larger project of stabilisation which formed a counterpoise to the attack on organised labour during the general strike. Above all, it was possible to maintain reliance on a peculiarly narrow fiscal system based on a progressive income tax (see table 4.3).[64] Rather than stressing, as do some historians, the successful campaign of taxpayers and bureaucrats against public expenditure,[65] it makes more sense to point to powerful forces leading to an increase in expenditure with only a partially successful rearguard action. The battles fought in the 1920s and 1930s took as given a level of fiscal extraction at least double the prewar figure. It is not helpful to view the 1920s and 1930s simply as a taxpayers' campaign against spending. There were different groups of taxpayers with different interests, and those groups and interests were themselves defined, at least in part, by the fiscal policies of the government. At the end of the war, working-class resistance to imposition of taxes on their incomes and goods posed problems for the government; the result was

[64] Hicks, *Finance*, p. 272, argued that there was little progression, for 'the increase of social expenditure is largely negatived by taxation'. This could be expressed more positively: the working class received more in transfer payments than they paid in indirect taxes: see McKibbin, *Ideologies of Class*, p. 273. This point deserves closer analysis than is possible here, for it is also necessary to add local taxation and insurance contributions.

[65] Cronin, *Politics of State Expansion*, pp. 4–13, 93.

not simply a reduction in expenditure but also a relocation of incidence to other groups and interests which were less able to defend themselves, and which were considered by the government to have a greater capacity to bear taxes. The issue was the relative power of these groups, and the assessment by politicians and civil servants of electoral considerations and the needs of the state. Churchill's strategy offered more groups in society a claim on welfare, and the self-interest of the beneficiaries could convert state welfare from a threat to self-reliance into a social right. The significant feature was less the imposition of limits on expenditure than a major shift in attitudes to the scope of public welfare.[66]

Labour's critique of Churchill's policy was weakened by the large number of electors who gained from pensions and tax cuts, as well as by Churchill's rhetoric of growth and dynamism after a period of depression and gloom. Even Neville Chamberlain,[*] who was not usually an admirer of Churchill's grandiose schemes, was convinced that the link between taxation and pensions was 'a bold and singularly attractive proposition' which created popularity amongst 'black-coated' and manual workers. 'There is no doubt', he informed his sister, 'that the Labour party are thoroughly sick. Their faces are the picture of gloom and we hear from various sources how thoroughly they have been disconcerted.'[67] The gloom extended beyond the Labour party to the Treasury, where Warren Fisher[†] castigated the chancellor as an irresponsible child who rejected

---

[66] Widows' pensions were contributory and may be interpreted as an attempt by the Treasury to limit the redistributive thrust of taxation – yet this is to ignore the creative use of welfare policy as a means of social cohesion. For the assessment of the scheme as designed to contain redistribution, see Macnicol, *Politics of Retirement in Britain*, pp. 184–193, 200–24; R. Lowe, 'Taxing problems', *Labour History Review* 57 (1992), 47; see also Baldwin, *Politics of Social Solidarity*, especially pp. 3–31, on the creation of middle-class commitment to state provision as efficient and fair, which created support for benefits for the poor.

[67] Birmingham University Library, NC 18/1/483, Neville to Hilda Chamberlain, 2 May 1925; NC 2/21, entries for 26 Nov. 1924, 26 Mar., 1 May and 9 Aug. 1925.

[*] Arthur Neville Chamberlain (1869–1940) was the son of Joseph and half-brother of Austen. He was educated at Rugby and Mason College, Birmingham. He ran an unsuccessful plantation in the Bahamas to 1897, when he entered business and local politics in Birmingham, becoming lord mayor. In 1917 he was invited to become director-general of national service but he found it impossible to work with Lloyd George. He was elected to parliament in 1918, and became paymaster general in 1922. In 1924, he turned down the chancellorship of the Exchequer in preference to being minister of health to 1929, undertaking major reforms in local government. In 1931 he was chancellor in the national government, until he became prime minister 1937–40. (*DNB, 1931–40*, ed. Legg, pp. 155–63; Robbins (ed.), *Biographical Dictionary*, pp. 155–63.)

[†] Norman Fenwick Warren Fisher (1879–1948) was the son of a gentleman of independent means; he was educated at Winchester and Hertford College, Oxford. He joined the Inland Revenue in 1903 and dealt with the introduction of super-tax; in 1912–13, he was seconded to the new National Health Insurance Commission for England; he was appointed deputy chairman of the Inland Revenue in 1914 and chairman in 1918. In 1919, he became permanent secretary to the Treasury and head of the civil service.

Table 4.3 *Structure of central government revenue: net receipts due to the Exchequer, 1928/9 (percentage)*

	1928/9
Income tax and super-tax	42.8
EPD/munitions levy/corporation tax	0.3
Death duties	11.8
Stamps	4.4
Land tax/mineral rights duty	0.1
Motor vehicle duty	3.7
Customs	17.3
Excise	19.5
Total	100.0

Source: PP 1929–30 XVIII, *Finance Accounts of the United Kingdom for the year ended 31 March 1929*, pp. 16–17.

caution in favour of spectacular schemes which would merely get the national finances into a mess.[68] Of course, Churchill believed that budgetary prudence as preached by the Treasury was equally dangerous in alienating crucial interests from the state and fiscal system, and that the best way of preserving stability might well be boldness rather than timidity.

Certainly, Churchill wished to take his policy further after 1925. In 1926 he enthusiastically seized upon an 'extremely revolutionary scheme': a national register of taxpayers with investment income in order to introduce separate taxation of earned and unearned income.[69] The scheme was soon abandoned, and in 1927 Churchill hit upon yet another proposal: a forced loan, by which taxpayers would be obliged to take a graduated amount of government bonds at a low rate of interest. In effect, the proposal would impose a new tax amounting to the difference between the value of bonds at par and their market price. The intention of the scheme was to free Britain from the drain of the national debt and payments to a *rentier* class, in order to stimulate economic recovery.[70] It had disturbing echoes of the capital levy and was soon abandoned. Churchill then turned to another proposal – the 'small fry' concession. His initial intention was to cut the income tax on small incomes, especially

(*DNB, 1941–50*, ed. Legg and Williams, pp. 252–5; Robbins (ed.), *Biographical Dictionary*, pp. 152–3.)

[68] His views were reported by Neville Chamberlain, who was a biased witness: Birmingham University Library, NC 2/21, 1 Nov. 1925.

[69] Gilbert, *Churchill, V, Companion I*, pp. 626–9; PRO, T171/255, Churchill to R. V. N. Hopkins, 7 Jan. 1926; Hopkins to Churchill, 23 June 1926; Inland Revenue Committee report on proposal of 7 Jan. 1926, 10 June 1926.

[70] PRO, T176/39, miscellaneous papers about the debt, 1925–7.

of married men, in order to remove between 300,000 and 350,000 entirely from liability. This scheme would be financed by an increase in the upper levels of super-tax, but was abandoned because it 'is somewhat smirched by the Socialist surtax stunt' (see chapter 5). The loss of additional revenue limited Churchill to modest changes in child allowances which removed 60,000 households from the income tax. Churchill was pursuing the fiscal policy of a showman who understood political and electoral realities, making easily grasped and dramatic concessions which would amaze the audience at small cost.[71]

Not everyone at the Treasury was impressed by his feats, but Neville Chamberlain, who was so suspicious of Churchill's ill-considered gestures, could at least agree that he had correctly identified the crucial group to which the Conservative party should appeal. As he commented in 1925, 'Our policy is to use the great resources of the State, not for the distribution of an indiscriminate largesse, but to help those who have the will and desire to raise themselves to higher and better things.' These paragons of self-help had incomes of between £500 and £5,000 a year, both from earned income and retired people living on saved income. The concessions could be justified as the counterpoise to contributory pensions to the poor, which themselves encouraged self-help. In other words, public expenditure could become a support of self-reliance rather than a threat. 'All MPs', as Ross McKibbin has remarked, 'think there is a class which cannot be deserted without dishonour or whose interests are in some fundamental sense inseparable from those of their party.' Most Conservative MPs between the wars had a clear notion of who made up this class: the family man on £500 a year.[72] The question to be addressed in the next chapter is how far Labour was able to develop a response to Churchill's strategy. Could it fill the gap left by the demise of the capital levy by a fiscal policy which would appeal to activists without alienating moderate opinion? And how did the national government of 1931 amend Churchill's schemes under the pressure of depression and, eventually, rearmament?

[71] PRO, T171/255, Churchill to Hopkins, 27 Dec. 1925; T171/257, Hopkins to Churchill, 31 Jan. 1927 and comment by W. S. C. 6 Mar. 1927; IR64/70, E. A. G. to chancellor, 1 Nov. 1928; T171/271, W. S. C. to Gowers, 7 Jan. 1928; Gowers to Churchill, 13 Jan. 1928 and 16 Feb. 1928; Inland Revenue to chancellor, 16 Apr. 1928; Short, 'Politics of personal taxation', pp. 232–4.
[72] Lowe, 'Taxing problems', 47; *Parliamentary Debates*, 5th ser. 184, 18 May 1925, col. 92; McKibbin, *Ideologies of Class*, p. 269.

5 'The great conflict of modern politics': redistribution, depression and appeasement, 1929–1939

> To spend liberally upon services which release new energies and cultivate powers hitherto not fully used is, not extravagance, but economy. To permit a small group of rich men to appropriate, for such purposes as they deem most conducive to their own interests, the wealth without which the elementary needs of the community must be starved is, not economy, but extravagance.
>
> Labour Party, *Labour and the Nation: Statement of the Labour Policy and Programme* (London, 1928), p. 37

Despite Churchill's creative use of the fiscal and welfare systems, the Conservatives did not secure a majority in the general election of 1929, and Labour formed its second minority administration. The Conservative slogan in the elections was 'safety first', an appeal to orderly reform and stability as a basis of economic recovery. By contrast, Lloyd George and the Liberals fought on a radical programme of public works and economic reform – *We Can Conquer Unemployment* (London, 1929). The traumas of the general and miners' strikes, the difficulties created by the return to gold and the persistence of unemployment seemed to contradict the Conservative claims, yet without convincing the electorate of the desirability of Lloyd George's panacea. The question was: how would the new Labour administration react as economic recovery faltered after 1929, and the country moved into financial crisis and slump in 1931?

The economic policy of the second Labour government has been a matter of controversy between those who feel that Labour adopted a cautious policy, neglecting schemes of public works and expansion, and those who stress the difficulties faced by the government. In the opinion of Ross McKibbin, the government did 'about as well as a "progressive" party could do in a mature capitalist economy that was showing no signs of cyclical recovery'. In his view, other countries followed even more deflationary policies, so that by comparison British policy 'appears generous and almost unorthodox'.[1] Much of this debate is cast in terms of the

---

[1] R. Skidelsky, *Politicians and the Slump: The Labour Government of 1929–31* (London, 1967);

failure to adopt Keynesian remedies, but Labour's policies should be understood in terms of its own ambitions and ideologies, in order to see how these shaped the government's response to the depression, and how the depression impacted on the economic policies of the party after the crisis of 1931.[2]

Labour's fiscal policy

Not surprisingly, Labour was highly sceptical about Churchill's strategy of encouraging enterprise and production, and suspicious about the redistributive consequences of his pension scheme. Snowden castigated the budget of 1925 as 'the worst rich man's Budget that was ever proposed', on the grounds that compassion was confined to 'the poor, overburdened, starving, unemployed Super-tax payer'.[3] Labour denounced the budget as far removed from Churchill's rhetoric of integration and balance, and pointed to an alternative relationship between taxation and society as a means of stimulating production and financing social welfare.

Labour attacked the pension proposals of 1925 because flat-rate insurance contributions were regressive, a feature of the prewar health and unemployment insurance schemes criticised by Labour in 1912.[4] H. B. Lees-Smith* argued that employees' contributions were 'a poll tax of the old, obsolete kind which throughout the whole of the rest of the realm of taxation we have abandoned'. In Dalton's view, the funding of pensions came

from those who will benefit, and by taxation of wages and employment, and taxation in a very special sense on industry . . . these are the worst possible ways to raise funds for a scheme of this character. The right way to raise this money is by general taxation adjusted to individual ability to pay and to the wealth of the individual taxpayer.

R. McKibbin, 'The economic policy of the second Labour government, 1929–31', *Past and Present* 68 (1975), 120–1, 123.

[2] For an important study of Labour's fiscal policy from 1929 to the war, see R. C. Whiting, *The Labour Party and Taxation: Party Identity and Political Purpose in Twentieth-Century Britain* (Cambridge, 2000), pp. 34–60.

[3] *Parliamentary Debates*, 5th ser. 183, 29 Apr. 1925, cols. 179, 182.

[4] On Labour's criticism of the 1911 schemes, see *Report of the 12th Annual Conference of the Labour Party, 1912* (London, 1912), pp. 96–7.

* Hastings Bertrand Lees-Smith (1878–1941) was born in India, the son of an army officer; he resigned his cadetship at the Royal Military Academy and attended Queen's College, Oxford. He was a Liberal MP from 1910 to 1918, when he stood as an independent radical. He joined the Labour party in 1919, sitting as an MP in 1922–3, 1924–31 and 1935–41. He was postmaster general 1929–31 and president of the Board of Education in 1931. (*Who Was Who*, vol. IV: *1941–50* (London, 1952), p. 674.)

He denounced concessions to income and super-taxpayers as 'enormous doles given to the wealthier members of the community' without any assurance that they would save the windfalls received from the chancellor. On this view, a better way of ensuring that savings *did* increase was through higher levels of debt redemption, for bondholders would reinvest most of the money they received from the repayment of loans. To this extent, Labour was close to the Treasury view that surpluses should be directed to debt redemption rather than tax cuts. The major difference was that the Treasury was eager to *cut* expenditure as a means of speeding up debt redemption, whereas Labour wished to reduce the debt in order to *sustain* expenditure on welfare, even at the cost of higher taxes. Labour was sceptical that a reduction in direct taxation would stimulate enterprise as Churchill claimed. In Lees-Smith's opinion, a large part of the remission of taxes would go to elderly ladies living on income from low-risk debentures and to the recipients of fixed salaries, so offering little incentive to enterprise.[5]

Labour argued for a different method of stimulating production and financing welfare, by extracting a 'vast amount of unappropriated revenue' from parasites who extorted 'an annual tribute from contemporary labour'. Death duties were 'one of the most legitimate and socially beneficial forms of taxation', and would allow tax breaks for wage-earners – rather than middle-class families – in order to increase their purchasing power and stimulate industry.[6] Labour's fiscal policy assumed that greater equality would lead to more demand and economic recovery; the problem was devising proposals which could be presented as stimulating recovery without alienating a significant proportion of the electorate or shaking financial confidence. The abandonment of the capital levy meant that Labour needed to find an alternative source of revenue and another means of attacking 'dead' capital. A commonplace of Labour rhetoric was that the *rentier* class gained, for interest payments were the first charge on the economy and their real value had risen as a result of deflationary policies. Meanwhile, other groups in society suffered from the fall in prices and return to gold at a high exchange rate which overpriced British goods in export markets. In 1929 Pethick-Lawrence claimed that the *rentiers'* share of national income had risen by 40 to 50 per cent. 'What this passive element has gained the active producing element has lost. This is at once the cause of the poverty of the workers and of the slump in trade.'[7]

[5] *Parliamentary Debates*, 5th ser. 183, 29 Apr. 1925, cols. 229–30, 232, 30 Apr. 1925, cols. 418–20.

[6] *Parliamentary Debates*, 5th ser. 183, 29 Apr. 1925, cols. 184, 189, 229–33, 30 Apr. 1925, cols. 418–20.

[7] F. W. Pethick-Lawrence, *National Finance* (Fabian Tract 229, London, 1929), p. 3.

Philip Snowden was chancellor in Labour's first minority administration in 1924, and again in 1929–31. He was widely attacked after the collapse of the Labour government in 1931 as a stalwart of Treasury orthodoxy. Indeed, Churchill remarked that Snowden and his Treasury officials were like-minded spirits who 'embraced themselves with all the fervour of two long-separated kindred lizards'.[8] The Treasury found him more biddable than Churchill – but that could be said of most chancellors of the twentieth century. In fact, Snowden retained a measure of independence and remained convinced of the need to capture socially created, unearned wealth for the community. He realised that the capital levy alienated middle-class voters, yet he did not simply become a conservative exponent of Treasury orthodoxy convinced of the need to balance the budget and redeem the national debt in preference to the creation of a socialist society.

Snowden's approach to taxation rested on the attack on Rent developed before the First World War. In his view, 'private property is a public trust and must be surrendered at the demands of the State' – and all unearned incomes should be taken by the government, on condition that the money would 'confer greater social benefits than have been derived from the private expenditure of the income previously untaxed'. His aim was 'to relieve productive industry and to relieve the burdens which are at present upon the shoulders of the poorer part of our population. We believe that National Revenue should be raised in the main from profits, realised profits, from large incomes and accumulated wealth, and from sources which are socially created.' In Snowden's opinion, the tax system was already capable of implementing such a policy, so that 'I do not think that anything special and new in the machinery of taxation is at all necessary, unless it is to be used for some very special purpose.' The existing surtax allowed differentiation between earned and unearned income, and could be complemented by higher death duties on inherited wealth to raise revenue and relieve social inequalities. Although Snowden rejected novelty, he had not rejected his earlier radical views. He continued to claim that 'all wealth is produced by the labour of hand and brain, and the wealth which is appropriated by the idle rich is a deduction from the just share which should go to the remuneration of industry in all its forms'. Taxation of inheritance was morally justified, for living without working 'is a violation of the first obligation which should attach to every member of society, namely to work for his own maintenance. It violates, too, the fundamental basis of a just social order, namely that no person should be able to live by appropriating wealth which has been created

[8] Quoted in R. Skidelsky, *Oswald Mosley* (London, 1975), p. 181.

by others.' The existence of a few large incomes, largely spent on luxury, took support away from 'really useful and productive employment'.[9]

The attack on socially created wealth was complemented by suspicion of an active capital market. In Snowden's view, corporate and national savings were more important than individual savings, for they were more easily directed to socially useful purposes:

The taxation of the rich for purposes of national reconstruction and for social reforms is a means of redistributing the national income so as to lessen social evils of the slums, physical deterioration, diseases, inadequate education and the lack of industrial training, and industrial inefficiency, and the existence of unemployment are things that must be removed, and the cost of doing that must be paid for by the people who are responsible for the existence of the evils, and who are the people who have the financial means to do so. The Labour party does not overlook the need for capital saving. The Labour party's schemes would require more saving, not less. But a nation can save as well as an individual. When we spend public money wisely in schemes for improving the health of the people, in education, in national development, and in new construction which will be remunerative, we are saving in the best sense.

New capital is provided today mainly by corporate and not by individual saving. When the nation spends revenue or loan capital on useful works there is the assurance that it is saved, whereas if it is left with the individual there is no such assurance.[10]

Nationalisation or public investment should be combined with corporate savings, in preference to individual savings which produced inequalities of income and wealth. Snowden had a clear vision of how society should develop, yet he was wary about innovations in taxation as the instrument for change. He adhered to the line of the Inland Revenue and Treasury that it was dangerous to use taxation too explicitly to reshape society, for this would weaken acceptance of the fiscal system as equitable in extracting revenue for social services. The tax system should be administratively practicable and acceptable to the electorate, or there would be little chance of gaining office and, once in office, of obtaining revenue to carry out the government's policies. Snowden's pragmatic approach seemed cautious and negative to many members of the party, reflecting a constant tension in the history of Labour between ministers aware of practical constraints and those who wished a fundamental reconstruction of society, using taxation itself as a means of social engineering.

After the fall of the first minority Labour administration in 1924, the party needed an electorally attractive package of taxes which would go

[9] *Report of the Twenty-Eighth Annual Conference of the Labour Party* (London, 1928), pp. 228–30; P. Snowden, *Wealth or Commonwealth: Labour's Financial Policy* (London, n.d.), pp. 3, 11, 14, *Labour and the New World*, pp. 134–7, and *Labour and National Finance*.

[10] Snowden, *Wealth or Commonwealth*, p. 15.

some way to fulfilling its social aims of equality and social justice. One approach was developed by the ILP, reflecting the influence of J. A. Hobson and his theory of Rent. Hobson drew a distinction between costs and surpluses. The costs of production were the minimum payment to provide savings for industry, income for professionals and above all wages for labour; they were needed for the productive use of any factor and had no ability to pay tax. The surplus or Rent was any interest, profit or salary in excess of what was needed to make capital or ability available: it was social in character and provided a fund on which the state could draw. Hobson accepted that social ownership offered a means of diminishing the unproductive surplus, but he gave it much less weight than Sidney Webb and the Fabians. This difference of emphasis reflected a disagreement over the role of the market. Although Hobson and Webb both assumed that a large element of profit was socially created and should be acquired by the community, they differed on the extent to which competition and individuality in consumption were to be welcomed. To the Fabians, the market meant waste; they assumed the inevitable concentration of production in large units as a step towards replacing private ownership and irrational consumer choice. By contrast, Hobson assumed that differentiated individual needs would become *more* important and would check the emergence of monopolies; private enterprise had a role in responding to individuality in consumption as an agent of moral and aesthetic advance. In Hobson's view, acquisitiveness should be accepted rather than denied; the market would generate incentives and any predatory gain could be captured through a 'surplus profits tax'. He saw the market as leading to a dynamic, flexible economy, transmitting a more accurate idea of social need and allowing an efficient allocation of resources – always on condition that the distribution of wealth was equitable and working-class purchasing power increased. But Hobson's political economy was rejected at the Labour party conference of 1928 and Webb's approach was contained in the party's manifesto, *Labour and the Nation*. The decision was crucial to the future shape of Labour's fiscal and economic strategy, with its greater stress on bureaucratic management of the economy, and suspicion of private profits, consumption and the market.[11]

In the late 1920s and 1930s, Hugh Dalton was emerging as the leading financial expert in the Labour party, building on his training as an economist and academic at Cambridge and the LSE. After the First World War, he advocated both the capital levy and, when it lost favour, the scheme of the Italian economist Eugenio Rignano. Rather than sweeping

---

[11] Daunton, *Trusting Leviathan*, pp. 342–6; Hobson, *Taxation*, pp. 3–4; H. N. Brailsford, J. A. Hobson, A. Creech Jones and E. F. Wise, *The Living Wage* (ILP, London, 1926); Labour party, *Labour and the Nation*; Thompson, 'Hobson and the Fabians'.

nationalisation, Rignano argued that the provision of new capital and
the production of commodities should be left to individual initiative and
competition. Once the instruments of production had been created, their
future management could be left to a variety of public bodies which would
acquire the assets by a gradual, automatic transfer through death duties.
The rate of death duty would vary according to the number of transfers: the first transfer by the person who accumulated the wealth would
pay a modest duty, and subsequent transfers to heirs more distant from
the formation of the enterprise would pay a progressively higher rate. As
a result, the machinery of economic production would not be harmed,
and a bourgeois state based on private ownership would be succeeded
by a liberal-socialist shareholding state, with taxation gradually replaced
by revenue from publicly owned assets. Rignano's scheme therefore differentiated between earned wealth acquired as a result of initiative, and
inherited unearned wealth. In this sense, it took the older Liberal views
of J. S. Mill or Gladstone, and added a greater concern for creating a
socialist or corporatist society. Dalton argued that the Rignano scheme
would stimulate enterprise and provide incentives, for heavy taxation of
unearned wealth would create 'a stronger inducement to work and save
in order to provide for his heirs, and making it less easy for him to rest
on his oars and allow the dead hand to propel his boat'. Further, the tax
would reduce the likelihood that prospective heirs would be disinclined
to work and save. 'An inheritance tax . . . by reducing these expectations,
stimulates work and saving by prospective inheritors and, the heavier the
tax, the greater the stimulus.'[12]

The problem with the Rignano scheme was that it would not provide additional income until the second heir inherited. How could the
state acquire revenue in the interim? Dalton suggested that the first heir
should immediately surrender part of the inheritance in return for ter-
minable annuities, so that the state got money at once and the heir would
'be stimulated, by the prospect of the annuities running out, to work and
save in order to make good the prospective loss of income'. Not surprisingly, Dalton's proposal met with little enthusiasm in the Treasury,
for there were major administrative difficulties in drawing a distinction
between saved and inherited wealth over the generations. In any case,
the government would gain little from the scheme, for the debt would
not be reduced until the annuities ran out. As Niemeyer pointed out, an

[12] For an English version, see E. Rignano, *The Social Significance of Death Duties, Adapted
from Dr Shulz's Translation from the Italian by J. Stamp* (London, 1925). On Dalton, see
H. Dalton, *Principles of Public Finance* (6th edn, London, 1930), pp. 114–15, and
Inequality of Incomes, pp. 311–43. Rignano was also discussed by J. Wedgwood, *The
Economics of Inheritance* (London, 1929).

ordinary tax would be less harmful for the taxpayer and make a greater contribution to the reduction of debt.[13]

Of course, Dalton was not simply attempting to pay off the debt, for he was committed to equality. He posed the question: 'How far, without damage, and if possible with benefit, to productive power, can inequality be deliberately reduced?' Dalton did not give a precise answer, but he made two points which suggested that there was considerable room for change. Economic forces were the result of human desires and activities which were not fixed; and there was no imminent prospect of harming production.

How far along the road to complete equality it is desirable to travel, it is not necessary in present circumstances to decide. For that road is far longer than this generation will have power or time to cover. It is enough to know that to travel a long distance along it, without back-slidings in productive power, will open out new prospects and opportunities of unprecedented promise, and will modify profoundly the present class structure of society.[14]

Dalton argued for equality on ethical grounds and as a means of stimulating production; he gave little attention to any possible loss of welfare as a result of equality blunting incentives and efficiency. In Dalton's view, great inequality of incomes meant a loss of 'potential economic welfare', for an individual's marginal economic welfare declined as income increased and total welfare would therefore reach its maximum 'when all incomes are equal'.[15]

The problem was how to reconcile equality with increased production, which needed the motive of personal profit. Dalton accepted that private property could serve as 'an extension of human personality' so long as it was not anti-social. Dalton's hostility was directed against 'private property in excess and in socially undesirable forms' which meant an attack, above all, on inherited wealth which provided the basis for most

[13] Dalton, *Practical Socialism*, pp. 341–2, and *Public Finance*, pp. 116–17; he made this suggestion in *Minutes of Evidence Taken Before the Committee on National Debt and Taxation*, vol. II, evidence-in-chief 393–6, especially paras. 18–20, and discussion at Qq. 5545–53. A similar proposal was made by H. D. Henderson, *Inheritance and Inequality: A Practical Proposal* (London, 1926). For Niemeyer's scepticism, see *Minutes Taken Before the Committee on National Debt and Taxation*, vol. II, Q. 8821; PRO, T176/18, ff. 39–41, undated and unsigned memorandum for Colwyn Committee (drafted by Niemeyer), and ff. 53–7, Committee on National Debt and Taxation: note by the Board of Inland Revenue on Dr Dalton's scheme in connection with the death duties; see also *Appendices to the Report of the Committee on National Debt and Taxation*, appendix XXVI, 'The Rignano scheme of death duty taxation: note by the Board of Inland Revenue', pp. 175–7.

[14] Dalton, *Inequality of Incomes*, pp. 352–3. His views should be placed in the longer development of thinking on equality: see Daunton, *Trusting Leviathan*, pp. 138–47.

[15] H. Dalton, 'The measurement of the inequality of incomes', *Economic Journal* 30 (1920), 348–9.

large fortunes created by 'passive acquisition divorced from the active performance of any social function'. An attack on inheritances was therefore
needed 'to carry the inner citadel of Capitalism, to complete the work of
Socialisation, and to sublimate the individual justice of Compensation in
the higher social justice of Equality'. As the party's memorandum on the
surtax on income from property and investments put it, the attraction
of death duties was their ability to raise revenue 'without imposing any
additional burden on any struggling business, without injuriously affecting the accumulation, by saving, of the additional capital required by the
nation's industries, and without impinging with regard to any individual on any socially-desirable standard of life'.[16] Clearly, the emphasis on
death duties provided a link with earlier Liberal attacks on passive wealth
and land, but went much further in the direction of equality.

Opponents of Labour's strategy pointed to the dangers of 'insular socialism', fearing a flight of capital as a result of heavier taxation than in
other countries.[17] They feared, in the words of Josiah Stamp, that 'The
economic millennium does not lie along the line of redistribution and
equalising the present total. The effect of this course is a percentage
addition to the lower level – which compares unfavourably with the automatic additions that came in two or three decades of industrial peace
and progress in the Victorian era.'[18] In other words, the poor were more
likely to benefit from an increase in the size of the economy created by the
pursuit of profit than from a redistribution of *existing* wealth and income.
On such a view, the redistribution of income might have gone too far,
despite Dalton's confidence that the point was still far off. The supporters of redistribution could even respond that a flight of *rentiers* might be
beneficial. After all, active businessmen were not likely to migrate with
their plant and machinery; the loss of 'wealthy but inactive *rentiers*' would
create a healthier political and social system.[19] Of course, the argument
on the costs and benefits of overseas export of capital had a long history,
and opinions continued to be divided. On one side, it could be claimed
that capital exports were beneficial in stimulating the export industries.[20]
On the other hand, Josiah Wedgwood* was in favour of an embargo on

---

[16] Dalton, *Inequality of Income*, pp. 281–3; Dalton, *Practical Socialism*, pp. 330, 335–7;
Labour Party Annual Conference, 1927, appendix x, 'Memorandum on the surtax on
income from property and investments', p. 331.

[17] See [H. D. Henderson], 'The limits of insular socialism', *The Nation* 46 (30 Nov. 1929),
306–7.

[18] J. C. Stamp, *The Christian Ethic as an Economic Factor: The Social Service Lecture* (London,
1926), p. 44.

[19] J. Wedgwood, 'How far can a Labour budget go?', *Political Quarterly* 1 (1930), 26–37.

[20] C. K. Hobson, *Is Unemployment Inevitable? The Export of Capital in Relation to Unemployment*, pp. 165–78, cited by Wedgwood, 'How far can a Labour budget go?', 33.

* Josiah Clement Wedgwood (1872–1943) was a descendant of the great pottery
manufacturer. He was educated at Clifton; he trained as a naval architect; he served

foreign loans, with encouragement to home investment through a strategy of equality. Wedgwood challenged the assumption that inequality
was essential for enterprise, incentives, industry and growth. In his view,
a policy which stressed individual enterprise and neglected the condition
of 90 per cent of the population 'is at least as unfavourable to the human
factor in productivity as it is unfavourable to the accumulation of capital'.
Individual savings were simply less important:

the supply of capital to British industry need not and does not depend exclu-
sively or even mainly on the private income and private desires of the individual
investor . . . Egalitarian taxation can and should certainly be framed so as not to
remove or diminish the natural desire of the healthy citizen to be generous in
his industry and economical in his expenditure. But it is bound to cut down
the private surplus incomes available for private saving; and our modern Income
Tax, Super Tax and Death Duties have already done so to an appreciable extent.
Hence, the Labour Party, if it is not entirely to abandon its Socialist aims, must
recognise in a practical manner the increasing responsibility for financing British
industry which devolves on the Labour Government and on public and private
corporations.

In other words, egalitarianism meant that more weight should be given
to bureaucratic control of investment by the state and by the managers of
large corporations.[21] Rather than accepting that the pursuit of equality
might harm incentives in a capitalist economy, the answer was to reform
the operation of capitalism so that it was less dependent on selfish individual gain. Such an approach had major implications for Labour's fiscal
strategy after the Second World War.

The solution preferred by the party was the policy put forward in the
minority report of the Colwyn Committee on the National Debt and
Taxation: to 'soak the rich' by an additional, graduated surtax on all investment income over £500, which was equivalent to a capital tax on
estates of £10,000. The surtax was justified to the party (and to the electorate) as a pragmatic alternative to the capital levy. The rationale was
that it would benefit clerks, teachers, doctors, shopkeepers and intellectuals who would gain as much as manual workers from ensuring that
large fortunes and unearned incomes contributed to national needs. After
all, *rentiers* with fixed interest securities were gaining from falling prices,
whereas workers, producers and the holders of risk capital suffered from
the depression. The proposal offered a way of combining equality with
the encouragement of production, uniting workers and active members

in the Boer war and stayed as a resident magistrate in the Transvaal 1902–4. He was an
MP from 1906 to 1942, initially as a Liberal and from 1919 Labour. He was chancellor
of the Duchy of Lancaster in 1924. As his sister pointed out, he was 'devoted to causes',
and not least the taxation of land values as well as Indian independence and a Jewish
national home. (*DNB, 1941–50*, ed. Legg and Williams, pp. 941–3.)

[21] Wedgwood, 'How far can a Labour budget go?', 34.

of the middle class in a productive alliance.[22] It was a key element of the programme set out in the manifesto for the 1929 election which proposed to raise revenue from 'those elements in the income of society which contribute little to social efficiency, and which too often are squandered in unproductive waste', by means of duties on inherited wealth, taxation of land values and a graduated surtax. This revenue would be devoted to social expenditure rather than debt redemption, and the result would be greater efficiency:

The idea that all public expenditure is burdensome – the idea that the nation is richer if less is spent on public objects that are beneficial to all, and taxation on large incomes is accordingly reduced, and that it is poorer if more is spent on such objects, and taxation on large incomes is increased – is an elementary fallacy.[23]

These additional taxes would raise considerable sums without (so it was claimed) placing a burden on business or lowering anyone's reasonable standard of living; it would curb ostentation rather than savings. It would also, in the opinion of Lees-Smith, be a retrospective act of justice for the war. In his view, the wealthy received back from the state in interest as much as they paid in taxes, and then used the high taxes as an argument against social expenditure. As Lees-Smith remarked, *'Behind the Surtax... lies the great conflict of modern politics – whether the war shall be paid for by taxing wealth or stunting the lives of the poor.'*[24]

Despite the endorsement of the surtax at the party conference in 1927 and its incorporation into the manifesto in 1928, Snowden was loath to implement the proposal when he became chancellor in 1929.[25] Of course, the Treasury and Inland Revenue were adept at blocking novelty. In their view, the surtax would provide 'the engine for an orgy of new expenditure' rather than debt redemption, a 'calamity' which would breach the fiscal constitution and set interests against each other. The Inland Revenue's notes for a speech by a Conservative politician in 1928 seem to express the department's own view:

Taxation must be ruled by justice. The state has no authority to use the taxation machine as an instrument for the distribution of wealth. To take away from A by a tax in order to give to B requires not merely an appreciation of B's necessity

---

[22] MRC, TUC MSS 292/411/1, TUC General Council Research Department, 'The possibility of further direct taxation', 25 Mar. 1931; *Labour Party Annual Conference, 1927*, pp. 244–9, 250–5, for the discussion of appendix x, 'Memorandum on the surtax on income from property and investments', pp. 330–1; Labour Party, *Labour and the Nation*, pp. 37–9.

[23] Labour Party, *Labour and the Nation*, pp. 36–7.

[24] H. B. Lees-Smith, *The Surtax* (London, 1928), pp. 2–7 (italics in the original); also Pethick-Lawrence, *National Finance*, pp. 5, 9.

[25] Short, 'Politics of personal taxation', pp. 252–6.

but also a just consideration of the extent, if any, to which A can be called upon to contribute towards the alleviation of that necessity, and if A is already heavily taxed and B is already the recipient of his bounty the just exercise by the state of its taxing powers is the more important.

Certainly, the Inland Revenue feared the potential impact of the surtax on savings, which already formed a lower proportion of national income than before the war.[26]

Such arguments might be dismissed as simply designed to preserve the existing social structure against a radical threat. However, there was a genuine concern that savings and investment were too low. The statistics produced by the Inland Revenue marked a significant attempt at analysing the performance of the economy, providing a new form of economic knowledge. On their estimates, annual savings by individuals and companies amounted to £400m before the war, or £650m at the price level of 1927; in fact, savings were about £475m, and they feared that an attack on the wealthy would produce a further drop. In any case, the surtax seemed an unnecessary complication to officials, for investment income could be taxed more easily by increasing differentiation between earned and unearned income, or by higher death duties. Indeed, the Treasury and Inland Revenue feared that the surtax would be particularly harmful, for it would apply to the undistributed profits of companies and the investment income of insurance funds which paid the standard rate of tax and were not liable to the 'ordinary' surtax or death duties. The point of detail was important, for the Inland Revenue argued that retained profits were an important source of savings for the expansion of industry:

In the case of investment income of individuals the argument can be made . . . that the capital behind the income gives greater taxable capacity; but the capital behind the profits and the undistributed income of trading companies is the factory and the workshop, and it cannot seriously be argued that the possession of the plant and machinery for manufacture represents greater taxable capacity; such an argument would almost lead to the penalisation of industry . . . the saving represented by the reserves of Companies is . . . intimately connected with development of industry and of production, and any action prejudicial to it cannot but be prejudicial in the long run to the national prosperity.

Heavy taxation of large incomes reduced the margin for personal saving, and a further tax on 'those forms of income which furnishes the life blood of trade . . . at a time when the industry of the country is still struggling to loose itself from the bonds of depression which have bound it, surely surpasses the ordinary limits of folly'. Investment would be checked, industry

[26] PRO, IR113/21, memorandum on surtax, unsigned and undated, ff. 229–30; draft suggestions for speech by Lord Birkenhead, 30 Jan. 1928; 'The surtax', E. A. G., 22 Nov. 1927.

would stagnate and unemployment would continue.[27] Indeed, the FBI pressed for a reduction in the taxation of reserves – a proposal rejected by Churchill and the Treasury who argued that the EPD and corporation profits tax had already been abolished. In their opinion, it would not help those industries most in need of assistance, where the problem was the *absence* rather than taxation of profit. Any concession to reserves would benefit relatively prosperous sectors of the economy with reasonable profits rather than depressed industries. Instead, Churchill's strategy was to relieve industry of local rates, which hit the old staple industries more than newer industries in more prosperous districts with lower rates.[28]

Lower taxation of retained profits was eventually introduced by Dalton after the Second World War, complementing Labour's policy of encouraging large-scale, bureaucratic control over investment in preference to an active capital market and personal gain. By limiting dividends through higher taxation on distributed profits, Dalton hoped to prevent inequalities of income and to check conspicuous consumption; by encouraging retentions, he hoped to stimulate investment and economic growth. After the Second World War, a *lower* rate of tax on retained profits was justified on the grounds that capitalism had a long-term future, and that large-scale, bureaucratic ownership was efficient and responsible. By contrast, many members of the Labour party in the 1920s and 1930s felt that private ownership and capitalism should be limited to the initial stages of active risk-taking, with established concerns passing into the hands of public bodies. Indeed, Dalton was critical of the corporation tax on the grounds that it fell on a particular class of property – ordinary shares in joint-stock companies – and so diverted capital from risky to safe

[27] PRO, IR113/21, 'The surtax', E. A. G., 22 Nov. 1927; draft suggestions for speech by Lord Birkenhead, 30 Jan. 1928; memorandum on surtax, unsigned and undated, ff. 229–30. See the data in IR74/238, Inland Revenue Report on National Income, Feb. 1929, which compare national income and savings before and after the First World War.

[28] The case was made by Horne, *Parliamentary Debates*, 5th ser. 172, 30 Apr. 1924, cols. 1685–6. He felt it was essential not to 'cripple the very springs of energy and enterprise', and he proposed reducing income tax on reserves which 'really form the fund by which industry is replenished in this country'. See also MRC, FBI MSS 200/F/3/E4/1/9, notes on the taxation policy of the FBI, n.d., and FBI to Churchill, 6 Mar. 1925; FBI MSS 200/F/3/E4/1/10, deputation of the FBI to the chancellor of the Exchequer, 12 Mar. 1926; FBI MSS 200/F/3/E4/1/11, deputation of the FBI to the chancellor, 9 Mar. 1927; FBI MSS 200/F/3/E4/1/12, deputation to the chancellor of the Exchequer, 15 Mar. 1928; FBI MSS 200/F/3/E4/1/13, letter to chancellor, 12 Feb. 1929. For the official reaction, see PRO, IR64/24, 'Savings through the medium of reserves of companies', 3 June 1925, and R. G. H. to O. Niemeyer, 15 May n.d.; response to question of A. Steel-Maitland on 22 Apr. 1931; for the Colwyn Committee's opposition to relief on reserves, see PP 1927 xi, *Report of the Committee on National Debt and Taxation*, pp. 346–8. The derating of industry is discussed below, pp. 343–7.

investments.[29] At this stage, Dalton was implying that dividends should be *relieved* of taxation in order to encourage socially beneficial risk-taking; after the Second World War, he took a different view. Apparently narrow, technical arguments over the taxation of company reserves were therefore linked with much larger issues of the future economic and social structure of Britain.

Snowden was well aware that grand gestures would be electorally counter-productive, without much benefit to the revenue. His budgets were cautious, yet their implications were very different from Churchill's fiscal strategy. When Snowden presented the first Labour budget in 1924, he was dependent on Liberal support and he was concerned to show that Labour was fit to govern. He therefore wished to portray his measures as 'vindictive against no class, and against no interest', and he offered a carefully balanced set of concessions. The complaints of industry were met by repeal of the corporation profits tax; Liberal free traders were satisfied by removal of the war-time 'McKenna duties' and a reduction in duties on sugar, tea, coffee and tobacco. Like Churchill, he was seeking the support of modest middle-class incomes and denying that Labour was embarking on class warfare. 'A black coat and fustian jacket are not the marks of class distinction', he remarked. 'Neither does the difference between £2 a week and £500 a year, when both incomes are earned, make the difference between those who would receive the consideration of a Labour government.'[30] He was laying claim to represent all active and earned income. Where he differed from Churchill was in reducing taxes on the lower levels of income *without* making concessions to the well-to-do.

In his next budget in 1930, he raised the level of surtax on large incomes (by 3d on the initial band and 1s 6d on the top rate) and imposed a higher level of death duties. Although he increased the standard rate of income tax by 6d, he took care not to hit modest middle-class incomes. He extended the range of incomes covered by the lower band so that a third of taxpayers (750,000 out of 2,250,000) paid no more tax than before. As a result, the increase in taxes mainly hit incomes above £10,000, and taxpayers with modest middle-class incomes of £430 to £880 largely escaped. Unlike Churchill, and against the advice of the Inland Revenue, he *increased* taxation of the rich. Indeed, the Inland Revenue calculated that an investment income of £50,000 derived from a capital of £1 million would pay 26s 4d in the pound when the income tax, surtax and death

---

[29] Dalton, *Public Finance*, pp. 122–3.
[30] *Parliamentary Debates*, 5th ser. 172, 29 Apr. 1924, col. 1610; C. Cross, *Philip Snowden* (London, 1966), p. 177, quoting Snowden's article 'If Labour rules' in the *Morning Post*, a Conservative paper, in 1923.

duties were combined.[31] The Inland Revenue felt that direct taxation had reached or even passed its limit, leading to evasion, with the danger that the tax authorities would need 'the inquisitorial powers of a Star Chamber'. At the beginning of 1931, officials at the Treasury and Inland Revenue feared a further increase in the surtax and death duties, which they felt would threaten compliance. 'Occam's razor might well be added to the canons of income taxation as an objection to this proposal', remarked Cornelius Gregg* of the Inland Revenue. 'One has only to consider the extent to which the taxation of the capital by Death Duties is lost sight of by advocates of taxation of investment income to realise the way in which the right hand may seize regardless of what the left hand is already taking.'[32] Snowden, it seems, was not entirely a kindred spirit of Treasury officials: in 1930 he went further than his officials would have liked. Did he then succumb to official conservatism in 1931, ignoring more radical proposals in the face of the financial crisis?

Whatever the left wing of the Labour party thought in 1931, Snowden had to consider whether he could go much further without threatening a loss of middle-class consent to taxation, and of confidence in the national finances. He was well aware that many of Labour's core supporters *did* wish to go further in 1931, with another increase in the surtax or a special tax on *rentiers* who were – so it was argued – gaining from an increase in the purchasing power of fixed interest securities. Such a tax did not appeal to the Treasury. As Hopkins argued, government stock was not held by a distinct class of the community, and other groups benefited from falling prices, such as investors in savings banks, pensioners, recipients of unemployment and health benefits, and wage-earners on fixed rates. Similarly, those who suffered from falling prices were a mixed bag of businessmen, owners of ordinary shares or workers in industries experiencing world competition. What was at stake was the definition of social divisions: was there a binary split between *rentiers* and the rest of society, or did falling prices have a much more complex and varied impact on all sorts of groups? The Gladstonian fiscal constitution rested on the assumption that a complex society created blurred, overlapping and varied identities. On this view, the more radical proposals of the Labour party threatened a serious fiscal crisis and consent to taxation,

---

[31] Jones, *Whitehall Diary*, vol. II, 14 Apr. 1930, pp. 252–3; *Parliamentary Debates*, 5th ser. 237, 14 Apr. 1930, cols. 2675–8; PRO, IR64/83, 'Note on the incidence of taxation on wealthy persons', May 1930.

[32] PRO, IR113/42, P. J. Grigg and R. V. N. Hopkins, 2 Mar. 1931; C. J. Gregg, 13 Feb. 1931; memorandum by C. Gregg, 17 Mar. 1931.

* Cornelius Joseph Gregg (d. 1959) was born and educated in Ireland, where he attended University College Dublin; he joined the Board of Inland Revenue and was chairman from 1942 to 1948. (*Who Was Who*, vol. v, p. 454.)

with potentially damaging repercussions on the economy and social stability.[33]

Snowden faced a serious problem as he prepared for the budget in 1931: it was in deficit, largely as a result of the costs of unemployment relief. He accepted the Treasury's view that the budget should be balanced, and that the sinking fund should not be raided or suspended. Such proposals were, in his view, misguided, simply leading to a loss of confidence and a financial crisis with serious consequences for the economy. He argued that a breach of contract with lenders would undermine the government's credit and lead to a fall in the price of government securities, so increasing the costs of borrowing and delaying conversion which offered the best way of reducing expenditure. A balanced budget was therefore crucial to sound state finance. Neither was Snowden willing to increase the income tax or surtax, or to impose a tax on *rentiers*, and he accepted official criticism of the party's more radical proposals. Instead, he confined his tax increases to a rise of 2d in the petrol tax and a tax on land values which would, he claimed, be 'a landmark on the road of social and economic progress'. A land value tax was considered in 1924; now, Snowden announced a tax of 1d in the £ on land values to deal with 'the scandal of the private appropriation of land values created by the enterprise and industry of the people and by the expenditure of public money'. But his claim that it marked 'one further stage towards the emancipation of the people from the tyranny and the injustice of private land monopoly' no longer had the resonance of the prewar period. Lloyd George's electoral strategy of uniting active industry and labour against parasitical landowners made little sense when landowners and industrialists were already allies in the Conservative party, and many in the Labour party saw the tax as merely part of a wider campaign against socially created wealth. Certainly, the proposal could do nothing to provide revenue to meet immediate financial difficulties. The new tax was a feeble and relatively harmless sop to demands for action against parasitical capital; it was suspended in 1932 and abandoned in 1934.[34]

---

[33] PRO, T171/287, 'Memorandum for consideration of Cabinet through Consultative Committee, on proposals arising out of unofficial party meeting on February 25th 1931, further to consider financial policy', 26 Feb. 1931; R. V. N. Hopkins to Warren Fisher and Fergusson, 4 Dec. 1930; 'The effect of price changes on the burden of the national debt', F. Phillips, 2 Dec. 1930; Fergusson to chancellor, 6 Feb. 1931; T171/288, P. J. Grigg, Board of Inland Revenue to chancellor, 17 Aug. 1931; IR 63/132, budget (no. 2) resolutions, 1931: note on resolutions, Board of Inland Revenue, paras. 28–31 on 'special tax on fixed interest securities'.

[34] PRO, T171/287, CP (3) Cabinet: the financial situation: memorandum by the chancellor of the Exchequer, Philip Snowden, 7 Jan. 1931; *Parliamentary Debates*, 5th ser., 172, 29 Apr. 1924, cols. 1608–9, and 251, 27 Apr. 1931, cols. 1409–11; Short, 'Politics of personal taxation', pp. 259, 279–80. On debates in 1924, see T171/234, R. V. N. Hopkins

During 1931, the financial crisis deepened. The deficit on the unemployment insurance fund led to a loss of international confidence, and compelled Snowden to introduce an emergency budget. His plans split the Labour government in August 1931. Snowden was caught between two opposing views: should the budget be brought into balance by economy or by taxation? On the one hand, many Labour ministers and MPs opposed cuts in expenditure, especially on unemployment pay. On the other hand, officials warned that Snowden's plans to increase taxes would not succeed 'unless the whole Government plan is received as a fair and just plan demanding equal sacrifices from all sections of the community'. The Inland Revenue and Treasury were adamant that direct taxation had reached its limits, and that any further increase would 'lose that willing co-operation of the great majority of taxpayers on which the success of the tax machine depends, with disastrous results on the yield of revenue'. The Treasury preferred to raise taxes on the lower middle class who benefited from Churchill's budgets, and to impose indirect taxes on the working class who were relatively lightly taxed. At this point, the Treasury and Inland Revenue *are* open to the charge of advocating a politically biased policy, reflecting sympathy with the plight of 'over-taxed' surtax payers and seeking to pass the costs of the depression to small income taxpayers who were better off than before the war.[35]

In fact, Snowden did not entirely follow their advice and he produced a somewhat more balanced package of measures in the supplementary budget he eventually introduced in September 1931, after the formation of a 'national' government. He imposed additional indirect taxes, increased the standard rate of income tax and reduced income tax allowances so that a further 1,250,000 people paid income tax. Consequently, the group hit most heavily was the lower middle class that had been cosseted

to chancellor, 26 Sept. 1924. For Snowden's views on the land question, see his *Labour and the New World*, chapter 5. The leading, obsessive, campaigner was Josiah Wedgwood: see J. Wedgwood, *The Land Question: Taxation and Rating of Land Values* (London, TUC and Labour Party, 1925). For conference support of land taxation and nationalisation, see *Labour Party Annual Conference, 1919*, pp. 170–1; *Labour Party Annual Conference, 1923*, pp. 242–3; *The Labour Party: Report of the 24th Annual Conference, 1924* (London, 1924), p. 174; *Labour Party Annual Conference, 1925*, pp. 271–5.

[35] On the supplementary budget of September 1931, see Short, 'Politics of personal taxation', chapter 7; PRO, T171/288, NE(31)2, Cabinet Committee on the report of the Committee on National Expenditure: forecast of the budget position in 1931 and 1932: note by the chancellor of the Exchequer; N. F. Warren Fisher, R. V. N. Hopkins, P. J. Grigg and A. J. Dyke to chancellor, 18 Aug. 1931; P. J. Grigg, Inland Revenue, to chancellor of Exchequer, 17 Aug. 1931; IR64/83, P. Thompson to R. V. N. Hopkins, 10 Aug. 1931; obiter dicta of Somerset House: weight of direct taxation: note on taxation borne by the wealthy, Statistics and Intelligence Division, Inland Revenue, 10 Aug. 1931; IR63/132, note by R. V. N. Hopkins: economy or taxation, undated; Board of Inland Revenue, budget (no. 2 resolutions), 13 Aug. 1931.

by Churchill. Snowden justified the adjustments to allowances on the grounds that the cost of living was lower than when they were last fixed in 1920, and that taxation of small incomes was still lower than at the end of the war. Further, he rejected official advice and increased surtax by 10 per cent. Even so, the outcome was not fundamentally different from the Treasury's advice. Between 1930 and 1932 the effective rate of income tax rose by only 11 per cent on incomes of £50,000, compared with an increase of 380 per cent on earned incomes of £500 received by a married man with three children. A large part of Churchill's 'dip' in the incidence of taxes was removed, and Snowden secured 70 per cent of additional revenue from direct taxes.[36]

Snowden's critics argued that his response to the crisis of 1931 marked a surrender to the Treasury and a rejection of a more adventurous policy of public works financed by budget deficits, with tax cuts and a redistribution of income to increase demand. But Snowden's response to the crisis was not unusual compared with other countries. The only other social democratic party in power, the Labour government in Australia, also turned to deflation; and the social democratic government in Sweden adopted similar policies to Britain when it came to office in 1932. In McKibbin's view, Snowden lacked alternative models abroad, and realised that the problems of the British economy were structural, and that it was heavily dependent on the international economy. A policy of reflation might simply make British goods still more uncompetitive, creating a balance of payments deficit, a loss of confidence and flight of capital. In fact, Labour was *less* deflationary than most governments: it allowed unemployment pay on easier terms in 1930 which resulted in a deficit on the fund; and it did not reduce government spending until July 1931. Snowden did not simply surrender to the Treasury: he contained their pressure for deeper cuts in expenditure and increases in indirect taxes, and he did impose higher taxation on the wealthy, so reversing the trend of Churchill's budgets by reducing the 'dip' in middle-class incomes. What stands out is not simply the cuts in public expenditure but also the steep taxation of large incomes and the maintenance of the government's share of the GNP.[37]

Whatever the arguments in favour of Snowden's response to the unprecedented financial and economic crisis, the collapse of the second Labour government and the creation of the national government were widely

---

[36] On the details of the second budget, see Short, 'Politics of personal taxation', pp. 289–93; PRO, IR63/132, budget (no. 2) resolutions, 1931: note on resolutions, Board of Inland Revenue.

[37] Short, 'Politics of personal taxation', p. 285; McKibbin, 'Economic policy', 97–8, 101–23, 105, 112–14.

seen within the rump of the party as a sign of failure which demanded a fundamental reassessment of policy. The immediate response of the Labour party and TUC was to reassert old nostrums of suspending the sinking fund, taxing fixed interest securities or even conscripting wealth. But the crisis could also be seen as proof of the failure of capitalism and of taxation policies which assumed the continuation of private enterprise. In the 1930s, many on the left agreed that taxation was a second-best policy, a mere palliative; it was preferable to cut off the flow of income from private ownership which led to large fortunes and unequal incomes. In the opinion of many in the Labour party, taxation was much less important after the crisis, for reasons explained by Herbert Morrison:[*]

I do not believe that you can get an effective redistribution of wealth within the capitalist order of society, and if you go upon the assumption that you can and there is no limit to public expenditure, then repeatedly you will come up against crisis after crisis and difficulty after difficulty, leading our people to disillusionment and disappointment.

The emphasis therefore shifted from taxation to nationalisation as a way of creating a just society. At the party's conference in 1934, the aims of socialism were defined as socialising industries and services in order to replace private profit as the motive for production, and removing inequality in the distribution of wealth. The apparent collapse of capitalism in 1931 showed that taxation and social services could not achieve distributive justice without a fundamental change in the capitalist economy; socialisation was therefore essential.[38] This shift was expressed in a particularly

---

[38] *Report of the 31st Annual Conference of the Labour Party* (London, 1931), p. 177 for Morrison and pp. 5–6 for 'Manifesto of the Trades Union Congress General Council, the National Executive Committee of the Labour party, and the Consultative Committee of the Parliamentary Labour party'; *The Labour Party: Report of the 33rd Annual Conference* (London, 1933), p. 236; *The Labour Party: Report of the National Executive Committee* (London, 1934), appendix III, 'Public ownership and compensation', pp. 106–8, which was discussed at *The Labour Party: Report of the 34th Annual Conference, 1934* (London, 1934), pp. 191–9.

[*] Herbert Stanley Morrison (1888–1965) was born in south London, the son of a policeman; he left school at the age of fourteen and worked as an errand boy and shop assistant. From 1912 to 1915 he was circulation manager of a Labour newspaper, and in 1915 became part-time secretary of the London Labour party. He was largely responsible for building up the party in London. He was elected to the LCC in 1922; as leader of the LCC from 1934, he pursued progressive policies in health, education and housing. He was an MP in 1923–4, 1929–31 and 1935–59. As minister of transport in the second Labour government, he created the London Passenger Transport Board as a public corporation which set the pattern for postwar nationalisation. He was minister of supply in 1940, and from 1940 to 1945 home secretary and minister of home security, taking a major role in shaping plans for postwar reconstruction. In the Labour government of 1945–51, he was deputy prime minister and lord president of the Council and

stark way by Robert Hall,* a young Oxford academic who reappears after the war as a leading Treasury official with very different attitudes.
In 1937, he argued that 'no practicable taxation will produce sufficient
economic equality to be acceptable to Socialists'. Hall's heroic suggestion was to end private property in the means of production, and to limit
private ownership to consumption goods.[39]

The problem faced by advocates of nationalisation was that the acquisition of private firms would increase the burden of debt to be serviced
by the community. One solution to the dilemma was simple confiscation,
on the grounds that private ownership and property rights ultimately derived from the community and could be taken back by the community.
As Stafford Cripps[†] argued,

the capital value of industry is created solely by community action . . . If we are
really going out for a planned Socialist State we have definitely to take up the
point of view that the capital value of industries has been created by the workers
of this country, and they are not going to pay for them when they take them back
into their own ownership . . . the community are not prepared to load up the new
Socialist State . . . with this vast load of capital debt which will for many years not

leader of the Commons, playing a central role in debates over policy. In 1951, he was
appointed foreign secretary. (*DNB, 1961–70*, ed. Williams and Nicholls, pp. 769–73;
Robbins (ed.), *Biographical Dictionary*, pp. 310–14.)

[39] R. L. Hall, *The Economic System in a Socialist State* (London, 1937), pp. 42–4, 60, 63.

* Robert Lowe Hall (1901–88) was born in New South Wales. He was educated at the
University of Queensland as a civil engineer, before attending Oxford as a Rhodes scholar
and reading politics, philosophy and economics. He was a fellow of Trinity College,
Oxford, from 1927 to 1950, and Nuffield College from 1938 to 1947. In the 1930s, he
was a member of the Economists' Research Group, working on how business behaved in
fixing prices and responding to price signals. He spent the war in the ministry of supply;
after the war he divided his time between Oxford and the Board of Trade. In 1947
he succeeded James Meade as director of the Economic Section of the Cabinet Office,
transferring to the Treasury in 1953 as economic adviser to the government. He retired
in 1961, and became principal of Hertford College, Oxford, in 1964. He maintained
contacts with Whitehall, as well as taking positions as advisory director to Unilever
from 1961 to 1971, and adviser to Tube Investments 1961–76. (*DNB, 1986–90*, ed.
Nicholls, pp. 177–8.)

† Richard Stafford Cripps (1889–1952) was born in London, the son of a barrister and
Tory MP who joined Labour and served in the governments of 1924 and 1929–31. He
was educated at Winchester and at University College London as a chemist; he was called
to the bar in 1911. He joined the Red Cross in the war, and in 1915 became assistant
superintendent of an explosives factory. He returned to the bar after the war, joining
Labour in 1929; in 1930 he was found a safe seat and appointed solicitor-general. He
moved to the left after 1931; he was expelled in 1939 and was only readmitted in 1945. He
went on a mission to Russia in 1940, and in 1942 became leader of the Commons and lord
privy seal; he moved to be minister of aircraft production. In the Labour government,
he was initially president of the Board of Trade; in 1947 he moved to the new post
of minister of economic affairs and later that year chancellor of the Exchequer until
he resigned in 1950. (*DNB, 1951–60*, ed. Williams and Nicholls, pp. 270–4; Robbins
(ed.), *Biographical Dictionary*, pp. 108–11.)

only perpetuate a class of capitalists within society, but which will also lead to such a large burden on those industries that they will be unable for many years to come to give any better terms either to the producer or to the consumer.

But confiscation also posed problems, of disrupting industry, creating unemployment and losing votes. Accordingly, the Labour party accepted that compensation *should* be paid, based on a recondite formula of the 'net sustainable revenue' of the business. This sum was defined as the reasonable 'net maintenance' of the undertaking, with regard to the financial benefit of tariffs and other government measures; it would be paid in fixed-term bonds, so preventing the growth of a permanent *rentier* class; and the necessary funds would be obtained by a tax on capital in general. Although the exact meaning of this formula was (to say the least) opaque, it served its political purpose within the party.[40]

Not everyone in the party was convinced that nationalisation was a sufficient response. During the 1930s, a group of democratic socialists – Evan Durbin,* Douglas Jay[†] and Hugh Gaitskell,[‡] with support from Dalton – tried to show how nationalisation could be combined with private ownership and control over private investment. They stressed the need to take charge of the main levers controlling the economy, through a combination of nationalisation and new institutions such as a National

---

[40] MRC, TUC MSS 292/560.1/1, Labour party Policy Committee, 'Public ownership and compensation', June 1934; *The Labour Party: Report of the National Executive Committee*, appendix III, 'Public ownership and compensation', and discussion, pp. 191–9.

* Evan Frank Mottram Durbin (1906–48) was the son of a clergyman; he was educated at Taunton School and New College, Oxford, where he read politics, philosophy and economics. He lectured in Oxford and the LSE, joining the Economic Section of the War Cabinet in 1940, and becoming personal assistant to the deputy prime minister (Attlee) in 1942. He was elected a Labour MP in 1945, and parliamentary secretary to the ministry of works from 1947. (*Who Was Who*, vol. IV, p. 340.)

† Douglas Jay (1907–96) was educated at Winchester and New College, Oxford. He was a fellow at All Souls 1930–7 and 1968–96. He worked as a journalist on *The Times*, *Economist* and *Daily Herald* 1920–40, and then joined the ministry of supply and Board of Trade 1940–5. He was personal assistant to the prime minister in 1945/6, and sat as a Labour MP 1946–83. He was economic secretary of the Treasury 1947–50, financial secretary 1950–1, and president of the Board of Trade 1964–7. He was a director of Courtauld's 1967–70. (*Who's Who 1996* (London, 1996), p. 1007.)

‡ Hugh Gaitskell (1906–63) was born in London; his father was in the Indian civil service. He was educated at Winchester and New College, Oxford, where he read politics, philosophy and economics. He worked in adult education and taught economics at University College London from 1928 to 1939. During the war, he joined the ministry of economic warfare, and moved to the Board of Trade as personal assistant to Dalton. He was elected a Labour MP in 1945; he became parliamentary secretary to the ministry of fuel and power in 1946, and was appointed minister in 1947. In 1950 he moved to the Treasury as minister of state, and in 1950 he became chancellor of the Exchequer. He succeeded Attlee as leader of the party in 1955, and after the election defeat of 1959 he started to question clause IV. (*DNB, 1961–70*, ed. Williams and Nicholls, pp. 413–15; Robbins (ed.), *Biographical Dictionary*, pp. 163–5.)

Investment Board (NIB). In their view, it was not enough simply to adopt Keynes's policy of deficit finance and borrowing in a recession, for there was a danger of creating a *rentier* class. A similar problem arose with nationalisation, that payment of compensation to private owners would increase government debt and so 'create a permanent rentier class claiming for ever from the community a tribute of a large share of the productive effort of the people'. Consequently, higher direct taxes and death duties were needed to take 'unearned' and undeserved income and wealth, which could be used to finance generous social services. Redistribution of income from the rich to the poor would maintain spending power and remove the tendency to over-saving which led to economic depression. Further, the Bank of England should be nationalised in order to control credit and stabilise purchasing power; and control over investment should be transferred from Stock Exchange speculators to a NIB which could direct savings to the areas of greatest social need. The result, so it was hoped, would be 'a far greater transfer of wealth than any yet attempted, without any dislocation of the community's economic life'. As Jay remarked, 'Labour's ultimate objective in economic policy is the removal of unjustifiable inequalities of wealth and opportunity by the transfer of private unearned income and capital into public hands.'[41]

The case for the NIB was developed in the 1930s and was eventually adopted as Labour party policy in the manifesto for the 1945 election. As Dalton put it in 1932, the NIB 'is an essential instrument... in carrying out our policy of socialist planning. We must exercise control over the direction and over the character of new capital issues on the money market, and of new capital developments in different parts of the country, and in different industries.' New housing, for example, should be given priority over dog tracks: the market could not be allowed to make decisions over the allocation of resources. There were, however, significant exceptions. The NIB 'would not deal with the private investment of savings in private business, nor with the re-investment of undistributed profits by public companies in their own businesses'. The scheme could be associated with the continuation of a large private sector to provide

---

[41] D. Jay, *The Nation's Wealth at the Nation's Service* (London, 1938); C. Clark, *A Socialist Budget* (London, 1935), produced for the New Fabian Research Bureau; Nuffield College, Oxford, Fabian Society Papers, J26/7, New Fabian Research Bureau, Financial Policy Committee, memorandum on the official and unofficial material dealing with the Labour party's financial policy, C. P. Mayhew. This summarises Clark's memorandum 276 on budgetary considerations, which argued that the use of taxes to finance an investment programme would reduce spending, and borrowing would build up the *rentier* class with its demands for interest. His solution was to start with borrowing until unemployment was reduced, and then to turn to taxation; a tax on capital or even a capital levy would provide the best of both worlds.

the dynamic element in economic growth, and the NIB could be limited to removing socially created value *after* capital had been accumulated through a competitive market economy. As we shall see, the NIB was not introduced by the postwar Labour government. However, Dalton did introduce other elements of the policy. He attempted to encourage private investment through retained profits in large firms, in the belief that they were bureaucratically efficient rather than the source of large private fortunes. Private ownership would continue to play an important role in the economy, but only on condition that it did not produce inequality. In Dalton's vision of society, incentives and growth did not rely on the pursuit of personal profit and gain; rather, efficiency and growth rested on long-term rational management by large concerns.[42] The dominant assumption of the Labour party after the crisis of 1931 was therefore scepticism that the free market was a prerequisite for liberty and efficiency, and confidence that equality should be pursued as far as possible. Disagreement was mainly over the extent of private ownership and the means of extracting socially created surpluses.

Keynes, the Treasury and taxation

More immediately, the problem facing the national government in the 1930s was how to respond to the depression. Economic policy in the 1930s is usually seen as a conflict between the 'Treasury view' and Keynes on public expenditure, demand management and deficit finance – a contest with major implications for the tax system. In 1933, Keynes argued that a reduction in taxation would be recouped in the future by a higher yield from economic recovery; he favoured deficit funding to increase consumption and employment. The Treasury was dubious, arguing that tax cuts would be of little help, for 'things throughout the world are so radically and utterly wrong that the expedient is quite incapable of correcting the maladjustment'. Major structural problems in the world economy meant that a reduction in taxation in Britain would provide at best a short-term psychological boost which would soon be overwhelmed by a new problem somewhere in the world. The Treasury and Inland Revenue officials had a more cynical (and perhaps realistic) view of the politics of taxation than Keynes, fearing that an initial cut in taxes would

---

[42] J. Tomlinson, 'Attlee's inheritance and the financial system: whatever happened to the National Investment Board?', *Financial History Review* 1 (1994), 140–4; *Labour Party: Report of the 32nd Annual Conference 1932* (London, 1932), p. 184; Labour party, *Currency, Banking and Finance* (London, 1932); E. Durbin, *New Jerusalems: The Labour Party and the Economics of Democratic Socialism* (London, 1985).

be followed by further demands for reduction. They were also sceptical about the effectiveness of cutting the income tax to encourage profit and business performance: they kept to the line of argument developed after the First World War, that 'in no other way could an equally important sum be raised with less depressing effect on industry than by taxation levied on profits'.[43]

Indeed, the Treasury officials were not particularly concerned about the impact of taxation on business and efficiency. Their position was explained in its most developed form in their evidence to the Colwyn Committee on the National Debt and Taxation in 1927, which was incorporated into the report. On this view, the income tax did not enter into the price of goods, for this was set by the marginal cost of production which did not have any element of profit. Since the income tax was not passed on in prices, the ability of the public to buy goods was not affected. Neither was the income tax particularly harmful to savings. Despite the burden on individual taxpayers, the reserves of public companies were maintained and redemption of the national debt from taxation helped industry by releasing funds for investment. The Committee was also relaxed about the impact of taxation on enterprise. According to the Committee, public companies were more concerned with the general prospects of trade: their managers were not troubled by the impact of tax on shareholders' dividends, and money put to reserve only paid the standard rate of income tax. Private traders were more affected by the psychological impact of high taxes, but even so there was no sign that their level of activity was affected. The impact of high taxes was therefore considered to be relatively harmless. 'Wider causes than taxation . . . and particularly the dislocation of our old export markets, must be held mainly responsible for the lack of buoyancy in recent years. Relatively, income taxation has not been a factor of high importance.' Although the FBI dissented, its concerns received less attention than the Treasury's stress on maintaining the integrity of the fiscal constitution. Such an approach may be read by some historians as an example of the hostility of the City and Treasury to industry. However, the situation was more complex. After all, the position of the City was itself eroded in the 1930s, and the Treasury was concerned that the repayment of debt should provide funds for industrial investment. Financial stability was not simply a concern of the City, for the stability of the British financial system moderated the impact of the world depression. Above all, the Treasury was concerned

---

[43] PRO, T171/309, 'Mr Keynes' articles' and 'Memorandum on article in Daily Express, 28 Feb. 1933'; 'Arguments against unbalancing the budget', R. V. N. Hopkins, 7 Apr. 1933.

to preserve the integrity of the tax system as a precondition for political stability and order.[44]

A potential alternative to public expenditure as a means of stimulating recovery was an income tax allowance for any company profits ploughed back into development – a suggestion made in 1931 by Herbert Samuel, the home secretary, and in 1933 by Keynes. The Treasury was hostile and Grigg complained angrily of the time he was forced to spend on Samuel's 'silly nonsense'. Grigg appealed to the classic official response that any concession to help in the depression would simply provide the 'thin end of the wedge', opening the way for two general claims. First, industry would argue that *all* capital expenditure out of savings was a charge against revenue; and, secondly, *all* savings might claim tax relief:

The concern which raises its capital in the market out of the savings of other taxpayers will have no corresponding relief and will be correspondingly prejudiced. The reserves made by a Company out of its income are really the savings of the shareholders. They are, no doubt, the most important element in National Savings but it is only in degree of importance and not in character that they differ from any other kind of saving. If they are to enjoy in the future any substantial measure of relief, there will be continuous pressure for a general allowance for savings.

Keynes's scheme had a similar response. The Treasury argued that it would simply benefit more prosperous concerns which were making a profit. It would not stimulate new expenditure, and would not turn losses into profits in depressed industries. The Treasury argued that the concession would have a minimal impact on employment, yet have a serious effect on the budget. In the Treasury's view, the 'very first principle of the taxation of income' was that it was concerned only with 'annual income as represented by the surplus of receipts over current expenditure'. It should not be concerned with capital expenditure or appreciation, or with the purposes to which income was applied. The Treasury feared that any departure from this principle would affect the yield of income tax and its wide acceptance, which was 'so securely based upon the principle of absolute fairness between taxpayers that, despite the extremely high present rates, it has remained the most important tax in our fiscal system.

---

[44] PP 1927 XI, *Report of the Committee on National Debt and Taxation*, pp. 486–547; *Minutes of Evidence Taken Before the Committee on National Debt and Taxation*, vol. I, evidence-in-chief of W. T. Layton, 177, Q. 2543; *Appendices to the Report of the Committee on National Debt and Taxation*, E. R. A. Seligman, 'Income taxes and the price level', appendix XII, pp. 114–26. For a discussion which disagreed with the logic but accepted the conclusion, see D. H. Robertson, 'The Colwyn Committee, the income tax and the price level', *Economic Journal* 37 (1927). The FBI dissented from the assumption that taxation was not harmful to industry: see MRC, FBI MSS 200/F/3/E4/1/11, deputation to chancellor of Exchequer, 9 Mar. 1927.

It is therefore the one tax which ought to be immune from experiments unrelated to revenue considerations.' In the opinion of Richard Hopkins, the time for risks was *after* recovery had started, when 'a large and striking remission of taxation might be a powerful and sustained psychological stimulus which would accelerate the recovery', and allow the chancellor to be 'hailed as the greatest financier of the age'.[45] An unorthodox budget in the depths of the depression would be ineffective and might well threaten acceptance of the fiscal system and the political credibility of the government. The Treasury's emphasis on the inviolability of the income tax, the need to ensure that it was a legitimate source of income for government policies, was essential to an understanding of the fiscal constitution of Britain. In fact, industry was compensated for the increase in the standard rate of income tax by a special allowance for depreciation of plant and machinery, which mainly helped depressed industries using large amounts of plant and machinery.[46]

Snowden's successor as chancellor in the national government – Neville Chamberlain – accepted the force of the Treasury's arguments. He rejected fiscal innovation in favour of reducing taxes from the peak of the emergency budget of 1931 – on condition that he could also restore cuts in welfare benefits. He had to decide between two options, with different implications. A reduction in the standard rate of income tax would benefit *all* taxpayers, including industry and large taxpayers. On the other hand, restoration of personal allowances would help individuals rather than industry, and small incomes more than large.[47] Chamberlain opted for the second approach, increasing married men's and children's allowances. He also offered a concession to small investment (unearned) incomes by abolishing differentiation where total income was £500 or less. This could be justified as an act of justice to small *rentiers* who were hit by the conversion of the national debt to a lower rate and by low interest rates. Chamberlain therefore undid some of Snowden's changes to the curve of graduation, restoring a 'dip' in the incidence of taxation on middle-class incomes of between £300 and £1,000 (see figure 5.1). In 1937/8,

---

[45] PRO, IR63/132, P. J. Grigg to N. Chamberlain, 5 Sept. 1931; 'Note by Inland Revenue on Sir Herbert Samuel's scheme', P. J. Grigg, 5 Sept. 1931; P. J. Grigg to chancellor, 7 Sept. 1931; increase in standard rate of income tax: companies' reserves, 29 Aug. 1931; T171/288, Grigg to Fergusson, 5 Sept. 1931; T171/309, 'Income tax and development expenditure. Mr Keynes: *The Times*, 13 March 1933', Inland Revenue, 15 Mar. 1933; Hopkins to Fergusson, 7 Apr. 1933. See below, pp. 200–4, for the adoption of the scheme by Dalton.

[46] PRO, IR63/132, budget (no. 2 resolutions), 1931: notes on the resolutions, Board of Inland Revenue, paras. 19–24; effect on industry of the increase of 6d in the standard rate.

[47] PRO, T171/590, income tax: personal allowance, note concerning deputation of 12 Mar. 1934.

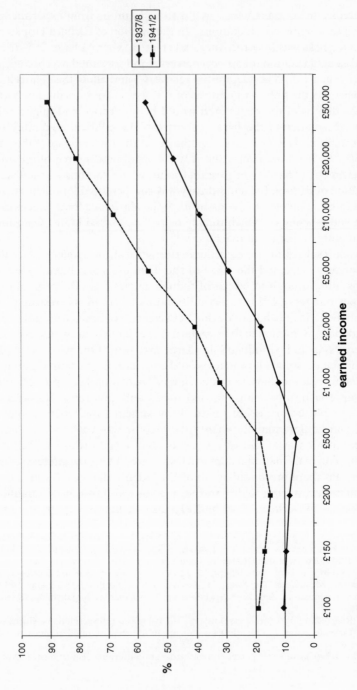

Figure 5.1 Incidence of national taxation (direct and indirect), married men with three children, 1937/8 and 1941/2
Source: G. F. Shirras and L. Rostas, *The Burden of British Taxation* (Cambridge, 1942), p. 58.

the combined weight of direct and indirect taxes on earned incomes of
£150 a year was 9.5 per cent, falling to 5.6 per cent on £500 and then
rising to 56.7 per cent on £50,000. The distribution of the tax burden
was progressive above £1,000 and regressive below £300, with a lighter
burden on middle incomes of between £300 and £1,000. The Second
World War overturned this pattern, for the budget of 1941 removed the
'dip' in middle-class family incomes.[48]

Preparing for war

In addition to economic depression, British governments in the 1930s
faced new threats from Nazi Germany and Japan. The question was how
to secure the necessary funds for rearmament without weakening the
economy or provoking tax resistance which would simply undo any de-
terrence offered by stronger armed forces. During the First World War,
the principle of the 'normal year' and reliance on loans resulted in a massive postwar debt with problems of financial and political stabilisation.
Between the wars, this policy was widely seen as mistaken and most informed opinion held that in any future conflict taxation should be set
at higher levels. However, the Treasury faced a serious dilemma in the
later 1930s as hostilities became more likely and the need to rearm more
urgent. On the one hand, it was necessary to provide financial and physical resources for defence; on the other hand, it was essential to stimulate
economic recovery and create a strong balance of payments in order to
sustain the armed forces in a protracted war. Could the resources for
rearmament be made available without weakening the economy, and so
making it difficult to provide the necessary funds and materials?

The Treasury was firmly committed to balanced budgets in the 1930s
and opposed Keynes's proposal for a deficit as a way of stimulating the
economy. Treasury officials had a coherent case for rejecting his advice.
They blamed Britain's economic difficulties on a lack of industrial competitiveness as a result of high labour costs and low productivity, and
believed that industry would become more competitive by complementary policies of threat and encouragement. The threat came from a harsh

[48] PRO, T171/317, memorandum by P. Thompson to chancellor, 2 Mar. 1935; McKibbin,
Ideologies of Class, pp. 269–70; G. F. Shirras and L. Rostas, *The Burden of British Taxation*
(Cambridge, 1942), pp. 25, 58; PRO, T171/317, P. Thompson to chancellor, 22 Mar.
1935; N. Chamberlain, 24 Mar. 1935; Forber to chancellor, 29 Mar. 1935 and 3 Apr.
1935; Fergusson to chancellor, 30 Mar. 1935. There are also some figures, on different
assumptions, in D. Caradog Jones, 'Prewar and postwar taxation', *Journal of the Royal
Statistical Society* 90 (1927), which compared 1913/14 and 1925/6: he concluded (706–7)
that while it was possible to defend a higher proportion from those with large fortunes,
or a uniform percentage, it was difficult to defend what was found at the lowest levels.

market environment where only the fit could survive, combined with a strategy of rationalisation to create larger, more efficient units. But the Treasury did not simply wish to bludgeon industry into efficiency, for low interest rates also offered an incentive to invest and re-equip. On this view, deficit finance would be counter-productive, for it would artificially stimulate the domestic economy and remove the motivation for competitiveness. Over-expansion of the domestic market would lead to a misallocation of resources, and a further deterioration in the balance of payments that was crucial to Britain's ability to rearm and sustain a long war.

The Treasury argued that so long as a combination of threat and encouragement worked, there was no need to adopt the proposals of Keynes. It followed that rearmament should not place too much strain on the budget, with the dangers of higher taxes or budget deficits. Higher taxes might undermine the legitimacy of the fiscal system, so creating an impression in Berlin that the government did not have popular support for its policy. The alternative strategy of a deficit might result in a loss of business confidence and misallocation of resources. The Treasury therefore argued that rearmament must *follow* economic recovery, for there was no point in rearming to deter aggressors only to convey an impression of economic vulnerability. Above all, the Treasury's attitude to rearmament was influenced by a concern for the balance of payments, for it would be impossible to fight a major war without the ability to purchase raw material and food from overseas. Accordingly, an improvement in Britain's economy and a restoration of international competitiveness were the 'fourth arm of defence'.[49]

A careful line had to be drawn. It was necessary to rearm sufficiently to deter Germany, while avoiding any repeat of the financial crisis of 1931 which would simply make Britain appear vulnerable. The difficulty in devising a strategy was that it was not clear when war would start. As the chancellor, Sir John Simon,* remarked in 1938, 'we are in the position of a runner in a race who wants to reserve his spurt for the right time, but does not know where the finishing tape is. The danger is that we might knock our finances to pieces prematurely.'[50] From 1932 to 1934, the

[49] R. Middleton, *Towards the Managed Economy: Keynes, the Treasury and the Fiscal Policy Debate of the 1930s* (London, 1985); Peden, *British Rearmament*, pp. 63–4.
[50] Quoted in Peden, *British Rearmament*, p. 66.
* John Allesbrook Simon (1873–1954) was born in Manchester, the son of a Congregationalist minister; he was educated at Fettes School, Edinburgh, and Wadham College, Oxford. He was a fellow of All Souls, and was called to the bar in 1899. In 1906 he became a Liberal MP, and was appointed solicitor-general in 1910 and attorney-general in 1913. He became home secretary in 1915, but resigned in 1916 over the introduction of conscription. He lost his seat in 1918, returning to the Commons in 1922. He declared the general strike illegal; and he moved away from free trade. In 1927, he became chairman of the Indian Statutory Commission. In 1931, he took a group of Liberals into the national government. He was home secretary 1935–7, chancellor of the Exchequer

dread of financial collapse was uppermost in the minds of the Treasury, and priority was given to restoring the economy through bolstering business confidence, and removing the emergency tax increases of 1931. The needs of defence were more pressing by 1937, and coincided with a check to economic recovery. The Treasury's strategy was no longer working, and Germany would not be deterred if the British economy was weak *and* defences were inadequate. At this point, the Treasury's approach was more pragmatic than its critics allowed. Indeed, Warren Fisher was concerned about the dangers of war as early as January 1934, and he argued that British taxpayers should be educated into the need for higher taxation for defence. By 1935, he was aware of the extent of German military expenditure and was willing to sacrifice orthodox finance, on the grounds that a policy of financial caution might be more dangerous than unorthodox finance. By the end of 1935, the Treasury and Inland Revenue accepted that the defence programme could not be reduced, whatever the dangers of diverting resources and weakening the balance of payments. Priorities were reversed: rather than defence spending being set by financial constraints, it was now necessary to determine financial policy by the needs of defence.[51]

Defence costs could be covered by borrowing, with the danger of harming confidence at home and diminishing Britain's reputation abroad. The Treasury was willing to compromise, relying on borrowing to cover exceptional rearmament over the next five years, with taxes to cover permanent expenditure on maintenance and replacement in a 'normal' year, plus the additional annual cost of debt. This scheme spread the high cost of rearmament over a longer period, but breached the Gladstonian principle that all expenditure should come from the revenue of the year. However, Richard Hopkins accepted that 'the country is taxed to full capacity' so that strict orthodoxy was impossible.[52] Warren Fisher took a similar position. He was deeply sceptical of Keynes's panacea, yet he saw still greater dangers in a rigid commitment to sound finance at a time when the public was insufficiently aware of dangers looming abroad. The safety and independence of the state were the supreme considerations, and the slow process of educating the public to foreign threats would not be helped by the 'tax-collector ramming his hand still further into their pockets'. Fisher therefore argued that a balance needed to be drawn between two considerations. Rapid rearmament was crucial, for he feared that completion of

---

1937–40 and lord chancellor 1940–5. (*DNB, 1951–60*, ed. Williams and Nicholls, pp. 892–4; Robbins (ed.), *Biographical Dictionary*, pp. 374–5.)

[51] Peden, *British Rearmament*, pp. 74–9.

[52] Peden, *British Rearmament*, pp. 89–90 and 74, quoting Hopkins in 1935; see also PRO, T171/324, general note by Sir F. Phillips on methods of financing the defence programme, 29 Nov. 1935; memorandum by R. Hopkins, 2 Dec. 1935; F. Phillips to Hopkins, 8 Apr. 1936.

Germany's rearmament programme would coincide with a crisis caused by unsound finance, and so lead Hitler to diversionary military adventures. At the same time, care had to be taken not to jeopardise Britain's rearmament by antagonising the public by high taxes:

The supreme interest of the stockholders is the integrity of the State – not merely meaning thereby 'sound finance' – but also, and much more, in the sense of preservation from destruction by external force . . . In all the circumstances, therefore, and particularly because of the dangerous ignorance and illusions prevalent in the country, I think it would be most unwise to increase taxation next year.

The Treasury was therefore moving towards a rejection of 'sound' finance and the acceptance of a deficit in order to overcome the fiscal constraints on rearmament.[53]

Despite the willingness of senior Treasury officials to condone borrowing, Chamberlain preferred to rely on taxation with the risk of alienating taxpayers and creating an impression that rearmament was unpopular. In 1937, he raised the standard rate of income tax and introduced the national defence contribution (NDC), a new tax specifically ear-marked for rearmament over the next five years. As he remarked in his diary, the NDC was both a surprise and a severe shock. His initial proposal took the form of a graduated tax on any increase in profits in excess of £2,000 compared with the average profits of 1933–5 or a return of 6 per cent on the capital of companies and 8 per cent on the capital of private firms. Chamberlain justified the NDC on the grounds that the increase in profits 'has come about largely through the policy of the Government in creating the conditions under which improved trade is possible, and also in consequence of direct expenditure by the State . . . by reason of the Defence programme'. The political consideration was that it would help to placate labour and reassure small taxpayers. But his proposal soon ran into difficulties.[54]

It was not clear that profits *had* increased, and the standard was in any case inequitable between industries. In prosperous sectors, profits were fairly constant so that the firms least affected by the depression would pay no or little tax. By contrast, firms severely hit by the depression would be taxed as they recovered and profits rose. The proposed tax

---

[53] PRO, T171/324, Warren Fisher to chancellor, 2 Dec. 1935. See also Hopkins to Fisher and Fergusson, 3 Apr. 1936 and comment by Fisher, 4 Apr. 1936, setting out the argument which could be made against borrowing by Labour, and how to respond to their case that the government was practising unsound finance. As Fisher pointed out, it was a sad but true reflection that borrowing for unemployment was unacceptable when on the gold standard, whereas borrowing for rearmament was acceptable.

[54] Birmimgham University Library, NC2/24A, 24 Jan. 1937, 12, 21, 23, 29 Apr. 1937, 29 May 1937.

was also complicated to administer, with the need to establish average profits or capital. The NDC faced strong opposition from industry and Chamberlain was forced to convert it into a profits tax of 5 per cent paid by *any* business making a profit. This simple, flat-rate tax caused less alarm to business, and marked a major change in the fiscal constitution, for this short-term expedient to finance rearmament became a major element in postwar fiscal policy.[55] In 1942, the NDC was continued 'until such date as Parliament might determine' and in 1947 it became a permanent tax on profits.

The yield of the profits tax fell far short of the additional sums needed for rearmament in 1938/9 and 1939/40, and the standard rate of income tax was again increased in 1938. Perhaps the limits of taxation had been reached, and the Treasury was divided on how to proceed. Hopkins opposed further increases in taxes, fearing that consent was already threatened by the transfer of income 'from the rich and moderately wealthy to the indigent and the relatively poor. We cannot for ever solve our problem by raising the Income Tax... At some point a limit will be reached where the taxpayer will revolt or confidence will be undermined.' Hopkins was pessimistic about any major increase in taxation, which might mean 'heroic measures' such as a turnover tax; he saw no escape from borrowing.[56] However, it could be argued that the ever growing threat from Hitler changed the psychology of taxpayers. Fisher's earlier doubts on raising taxes gave way to a belief that the wealthy were now willing to pay. In his opinion, higher taxes on the better-off would have a salutary effect in contributing to a change in attitudes, encouraging unions to reform and so improving efficiency. As Fisher complained in 1939, Britain continued

To amble along in our old and well-tried and (for the small minority) very comfortable economic paths, which means... business... profiteering out of the occasion of the country's need, and, with this patriotic example before him, the workman... stimulated to insistence on some improvement in his rather shabby lot in life.[57]

[55] On the NDC, see PRO, T171/336 on the first version: E. L. Forber to chancellor, 11 Feb. 1937 and 31 Mar. 1937; note by R. V. N. Hopkins, 31 Mar. 1937; note by Neville Chamberlain, 1 Apr. 1937; Forber to chancellor, 6 and 8 Apr. 1937; Forber to Woods, 14 Apr. 1937; R. V. N. Hopkins, 15 Apr. 1937; J. Simon to chancellor, n.d.; Hopkins to Fisher, 4 May 1937; NDC, Hirst, Plender and Stamp, 4 May 1937. On the revised version, T171/337, outline of the scheme of the proposed new NDC, Inland Revenue, 7 June 1937; E. Forber to chancellor, outline of alternatives to NDC, n.d.; Forber to chancellor, 3 June 1937.

[56] PRO, T171/341, R. Hopkins to Warren Fisher and chancellor, 24 June 1938, and Hopkins, 3 Jan. 1939.

[57] Peden, *British Rearmament*, p. 105, quoting British Library of Political and Economic Science, Fisher Papers 2/11, Fisher to Simon, 3 Jan. 1939; also in PRO, T171/341.

On this view, the tax system could be used in a creative manner to forge a cross-class patriotic alliance, without provoking resistance from the affluent or giving an impression that Britain lacked the will to resist Hitler. The outbreak of war soon transformed the debate: resistance was imperative, and the crucial issue was where the costs should be allocated.

Taxation and distribution

What stands out in the interwar period is not simply the containment of the radical threat from Labour and the dominance of the Treasury.[58] Such an account is one-sided, for there was a remarkable increase in the level of government expenditure without a loss of consent. The tax system remained heavily dependent on direct taxes at much higher levels and with a steeper graduation, despite the concern expressed before the First World War that the fiscal system was becoming unbalanced and rigid. Before the First World War, indirect taxes did not attach effective 'handles' to economic growth, for they were largely levied on items of consumption with a low income elasticity of demand. Overall, excise duties formed a declining share of government revenue, falling from 20.1 per cent of gross income in 1913 to 16.9 per cent in 1925 and 13.0 per cent in 1935. Pressure for a general sales or turnover tax was contained at the end of the First World War, and did not reappear until the outbreak of the Second World War. Despite the introduction of protective duties in the 1930s, the revenue from customs did not increase to any great extent. Customs duties accounted for 17.7 per cent of the gross income of central government in 1913, falling to 12.4 per cent in 1925 before rising to 23.0 per cent in 1935. The combined total of customs and excise duties was therefore remarkably stable, at 37.8 per cent of the gross income of central government in 1913 and 36.0 per cent in 1935.[59] The decline in the contribution of indirect taxation had virtually stopped, but was not reversed between the wars (see tables 5.1 and 5.2).

Reduction of taxation of the 'middling' middle class removed the threat of an electoral revolt and helped to secure political stability and a reasonable level of welfare provision. The transfer of income was largely from the rich to the poor, leap-frogging the 'middling' middle class who were crucial to the electoral base of the Conservative party. However, electoral self-interest on the part of Conservative chancellors was probably beneficial to lower incomes in providing the basis for a high level of fiscal extraction. Since the bulk of unemployment was amongst the

[58] As argued by Cronin, *Politics of State Expansion*, pp. 13, 87–92.

[59] B. R. Mitchell and P. Deane, *Abstract of British Historical Statistics* (Cambridge, 1962), pp. 394–5.

Table 5.1 *Direct and indirect taxes as a percentage of national revenue, 1913/14 to 1931/2*

	Indirect	Direct
1913/14	42.5	57.5
1924/5	23.1	66.9
1929/30	35.9	64.1
1931/2 (second budget)	33.8	66.2

Source: PRO, IR63/132, budget (no. 2) resolutions, 1931: notes on resolutions, Board of Inland Revenue.

Table 5.2 *Structure of central government revenue: net receipts due to the Exchequer, 1938/9 (percentage)*

	1938/9
Income tax and super-tax	44.5
NDC	2.5
Death duties	8.6
Stamps	2.4
Other Inland Revenue	0.2
Motor vehicle duty	4.0
Customs	25.2
Excise	12.7
Total	100.0

Source: PP 1938–9 XVI, *Finance Accounts of the UK for the year ended 31 March 1939*, pp. 14–15.

working class and transfer payments were largely confined to the poor, they probably received more than they paid in indirect taxation.[60] An established and legitimate tax system provided the basis for an expansion of welfare measures. However, changes in taxation during the Second World War posed a possible danger to this balance of interests. Higher levels of marginal taxation were imposed further down the income scale. Could the allegiance of the 'middling' middle class to higher taxes be preserved? The fiscal sociology of the interwar period would need to be reconsidered.

[60] McKibbin, *Ideologies of Class*, p. 273.

6 'The exigency of war': taxation and the Second World War, 1939–1945

> ...whether we remain at home in relative safety, or whether we pass across the narrow water to fight, we must all live and work with a responsibility for the continuation of the struggle upon our shoulders. I can only hope that the careful reflection of the economist and the financial expert...may help, in some tiny degree, to sustain our common burden.
>
> E. F. M. Durbin, *How to Pay for the War: An Essay on the Financing of War* (London, 1939), pp. 20–1

The First World War marked a major increase in fiscal extraction, yet the main features of the fiscal constitution survived – dependence on progressive direct taxation and the rejection of both a sales tax and taxation of business profits. The outbreak of the Second World War placed new strains on the fiscal constitution. As with the First World War, the level of taxation was displaced with a further increase from 25.2 per cent of national income in 1938 to 44.7 per cent in 1944; it was still 44 per cent in 1948/9.[1] This increase in the level of extraction was linked with a renegotiation of the fiscal constitution. During the First World War, the government was heavily dependent on loans, which led to inflation and to difficulties of postwar debt service. Could these issues be averted during the Second World War, by a greater reliance on taxation and lower levels of debt? However, reliance on taxation posed other problems. How far could income tax be increased and tax thresholds reduced without provoking political problems? Would a new indirect tax be needed, both to provide revenue and to remove spending power? And should business be taxed, to prevent attacks on war profiteers? The response to these questions would shape the postwar fiscal constitution: the difficulties of debt service might be avoided, only to create new problems (in the eyes of Conservative politicians) that high levels of taxation damaged incentives and efficiency. Of course, Labour politicians could argue that a high level of redistributive taxation would create a more just society, stimulating

---

[1] These are the contemporary estimates in PRO, T230/145, draft budgetary prospects and policy, 1948/52.

a prosperous home market in place of the unemployment of the 1920s and 1930s, and replacing the pursuit of private gain by the efficiency of a planned economy.

The finance of the Second World War was strikingly different from the First World War, for the relative shares of loans and taxes were reversed. However, there was a period of 'phoney' taxation as well as 'phoney' war before the levels of taxation were increased as far as Keynes and others wished. At the start of the war, the chancellor, Sir John Simon, introduced an excess profits tax of 60 per cent, but he was cautious in other respects and relied on existing taxes, particularly increases in the rate of income tax and reductions in allowances. At the same time, Simon introduced subsidies for essential goods in order to hold down the cost of living and to prevent an inflationary rise in wages – so releasing consumption for other goods in short supply. Keynes was highly critical of Simon, pointing out that 'by depending so largely on existing taxes you have shot your last bolt and have done nothing to appeal to the imagination; whereas it would have been possible to lay new foundations which would prepare the way for important further developments'.[2] Keynes had no problem in devising a package of measures designed to finance the war and contain inflation, to reform British society and to manage the economy. He was now an insider and could not simply be ignored, much to the annoyance of Treasury officials who felt that many of his ideas were administratively impracticable and politically inept. In any case, the pressures of war meant that Simon's caution soon gave way to a searching debate on the structure of taxation that marked a major shift in the fiscal constitution.

As in the First World War, the reduction in income tax allowances and exemptions led to a massive increase in the number of people liable to pay the tax. Cornelius Gregg realised in 1940 that the whole method of collection would need to change to allow a deduction from wages and salaries month by month.[3] Generally, working-class families paid their rent or rates at shorter intervals than the middle class, reflecting the economic realities for people living on narrow margins. The movement of income tax further down the social scale was likely to cause problems, and to create pressure for the payment of tax in regular instalments, rather than the system of payment in two instalments of three-quarters and one quarter. During the 1930s, the Inland Revenue was reluctant to change

---

[2] PRO, T160/993/F17281, Keynes to chancellor, 24 July 1940; for Simon's war budgets of 1939 and 1940, see *Parliamentary Debates*, 5th ser. 351, 27 Sept. 1939, cols. 1361–80, and 360, 23 Apr. 1940, cols. 51–88. On Keynes, see R. Skidelsky, *John Maynard Keynes*, vol. III: *Fighting for Britain, 1937–46* (London, 2000), p. 71.

[3] PRO, T160/993/F17281, note by the Board of Inland Revenue on possible expedients for increased yield of income tax, C. J. Gregg, 1 June 1940.

to monthly instalments, arguing that the precedents were not good. It cited the existing system by which taxpayers could buy stamps to stick on cards which could then be set against their liability. Not only was the system costly to administer, but it did not make collection any easier:

The reality of collection is not a passive organisation engaged merely in receiving moneys and issuing receipts but an active organisation which has to seek its money . . . If payment by means of stamps should appeal to anyone it would appeal to the wage earner who lives on a weekly budget. In fact, less than one-fifth of the liable weekly wage earners elect to use cards . . . Large numbers of those who take cards do not stamp them.

Monthly instalments were ruled out on similar grounds, that it would increase the cost of collection: 'The idea assumes that the collection machine has nothing to do but receive money thrust upon it by the taxpayer. In fact, the taxpayer does not pay up immediately but has to be induced to pay.' In 1933, the Inland Revenue stood firm on the general principle that it was 'the duty of the taxpayer to meet his obligations to the Exchequer when they fell due and make every provision in advance that may be necessary for the purpose'. Even so, the Inland Revenue accepted the problems of finding the initial instalment of three-quarters of the tax, and attention turned to a scheme to allow employees of local authorities and large industrial firms to pay by weekly or monthly deductions from their wages.[4]

Problems remained for deductions were based on *previous* earnings. The Inland Revenue informed employers of the amount to be deducted from each weekly wage or monthly salary over the next six months, based on the income of the previous six months. Delays in making assessments meant that employers were only told of the amount to deduct *after* the start of the period, and the weekly deductions were increased in the remaining weeks to clear liability. The system was, as the Inland Revenue admitted, 'unintelligible to the average working man', and a simpler procedure would reduce dissatisfaction.[5] Ernest Bevin,* who moved

[4] PRO, IR64/91, 'Income tax instalments, half and half up to £750 only', 18 May 1933, and IR64/92, discussion of income tax instalments, May 1933.
[5] PRO, T171/360, 'Note on the position reached with regard to working of the scheme for deducting tax from wages'.
* Ernest Bevin (1881–1951) was born illegitimately, in Somerset; he left school in 1892 and became a van driver. He joined the Bristol Socialist Society and became chairman of the carters' branch of the Dockers' Union. In 1914, he became a national organiser and in 1920 assistant general secretary of the union. He was instrumental in the formation of the Transport and General Workers' Union in 1922, becoming the first general secretary. He was a powerful figure in the Labour movement during the 1930s and in 1940 Churchill invited him to become minister of labour, when he became an MP. He was foreign secretary from 1945 to 1951. (*DNB, 1951–60*, ed. Williams and Nicholls, pp. 102–10; Robbins (ed.), *Biographical Dictionary*, pp. 53–5.)

from the Transport and General Workers' Union to become minister of labour, pointed to 'growing resentment' with serious consequences for production.

The wage earner budgets on the basis of his weekly earnings. He judges the operation of the Income Tax system by its immediate effect on his weekly pay packet and he is not consoled by assurances that, taken over a period of six or twelve months, the British system of taxation is the most equitable that can be devised.

In particular, Bevin feared difficulties at the end of the war, when incomes might fall but tax would be deducted on the basis of peak war-time earnings. As an official warned, the result might be the collapse of 'the whole wage-earners' tax system', with serious consequences for postwar finance. The precedent of the First World War gave weight to these concerns, for working-class resistance to the income tax and direct collection meant that the level of compliance was low and much tax was simply written off.[6]

Although the Inland Revenue raised administrative objections to any change, a solution was found in 1942 – the 'very ingenious scheme' of PAYE which allowed deduction of tax on the basis of *actual* earnings each week. Before the start of each tax year, the tax-free income of each taxpayer was calculated and a code number assigned. Employers were given a book of tables which indicated the tax liability for each code on the income paid to date over the year, and gave the amount of tax to be deducted from each weekly wage or monthly salary. The system was simple to administer: the employer looked up the relevant table, checked the amount of income received in the period, and deducted the tax. Since the code was set by the Inland Revenue on the basis of information supplied by the taxpayer, the employer did not have access to personal information. And the employee was protected from over- or under-payment, with the need for adjustments at the end of the year.[7]

[6] PRO, T171/360, WP(42)78, 'Effect of income tax on the weekly wage earner: memorandum by the Minister of Labour and National Service, 13 February 1942'; T171/363, P. D. Proctor to chancellor, 6 Mar. 1943; Whiting, 'Taxation and the working class'.

[7] PRO, T171/360, 'Income tax on weekly wage earners', J. M. Keynes, 9 Jan. 1942; 'Note by the Board of Inland Revenue on Keynes' paper', 28 Jan. 1942; E. Bevin to K. Wood, 3 Dec. 1941; 'Note on the deduction of income tax from wages paid to manual wage earners employed in seasonal industry', G. Canny, 11 Dec. 1941; 'Note on the position reached with regard to working of the scheme for deducting tax from wages'; Gregg to chancellor, 10 Feb. 1942; Catto to chancellor, 'Income tax on weekly wage earners', 30 Mar. 1942; notes by financial secretary, 11 Feb. and 31 Mar. 1942; WP(42)78, War Cabinet: effect of income tax on the weekly wage earner: memorandum by the minister of labour and national service, 13 Feb. 1942; WP(42)89, War Cabinet: incidence of income tax on weekly wage earners, 17 Feb. 1942; 'Note of a deputation to the Board of Inland Revenue from the British Employers Confederation', 11 Mar. 1942; T171/366, C. J. Gregg to chancellor; Catto to chancellor, 12 July 1943; Keynes to Padmore, 12 July 1943.

Table 6.1 *Individuals with income above the exemption limit for income tax, United Kingdom, 1937/8 to 1947/8 (000)*

	Entirely relieved of tax	Chargeable with tax	Total
1937/8	6,000	3,700	9,700
1940/1	6,000	6,000	12,000
1944/5	5,250	13,000	18,250
1947/8	6,500	14,500	21,000
PAYE 1944/5			
Number of employees	16,750		
Number of employers	687		

Source: PP 1938–9 xii, *82nd Report of the Commissioners of Inland Revenue for the year ended 31 March 1939*, p. 57; PP 1948-9 xvii, *91st Report of the Commissioners of Inland Revenue for the year ended 31 March 1948*, pp. 21, 33.

The system of PAYE was crucial in adjusting the administration of the income tax to changes in the economic and social structure, and extending the income tax to small salary and wage-earners. In the nineteenth century, deduction at source was crucial to the success of the income tax, which was most easily achieved in the case of rent, interest and dividends. PAYE provided a means of extending deduction at source and ensured that compliance was much higher than during the First World War. As Douglas Houghton* later remarked, 'there can be not the slightest doubt that the retention of PAYE has enabled successive governments since the war to tax earnings far more heavily than would have been possible otherwise'.[8]

Consent to taxation not only required administrative changes in the system of collection, but also a reassessment of graduation and differentiation to meet new political circumstances. The 'dip' in the middle ranges of income for married men with children was crucial to the sociology of taxation between the wars. It was removed during the Second World War,

---

[8] Whiting, *Labour Party and Taxation*, pp. 63–4; D. Houghton, 'The futility of taxation by menaces', in A. Seldon (ed.), *Tax Avoison: The Economic, Legal and Moral Inter-relationships between Avoidance and Evasion* (Institute of Economic Affairs, London, 1979), p. 97.

* Arthur Leslie Noel Douglas Houghton (1898–1996) was born in Derbyshire, and was a clerk in the Inland Revenue from 1915 to 1922. From 1922 to 1960, he was secretary of the Inland Revenue Staff Federation. He was an alderman on the LCC 1947–9, and a Labour MP from 1949 to 1974. He chaired the Public Accounts Committee in 1963–4, and served as chancellor of the Duchy of Lancaster 1964–6, minister without portfolio 1966–7, chairman of the Parliamentary Labour party 1967–74. (*Who's Who 1996* (London, 1996), p. 945.)

both to improve the yield of the income tax and because heavy taxation of single taxpayers was causing discontent and loss of production. The removal of tax benefits for married, middle-class men caused some disquiet to members of the Eugenics Society who feared that childbearing would be discouraged 'among the higher intellectual levels of the population, represented on the average by the section of it which pays Income Tax'.[9] As Keynes – himself a member of the Society – put it, 'the strengthening of the economic position of the family unit should be a main purpose of social policy now and after the war'.[10] Of course, such an ambition could lead in a different direction, not to income tax allowances for the better-off but to family allowances paid in cash to families below the tax threshold. Attitudes to tax breaks for middle-class families started to shift, as a result of concern about the low birth rate in the 1930s and the realisation that poverty was related to family size.

Exclusion of the poor from any support was, in the words of one adviser to the Treasury, 'wrong and indeed inhuman'.[11] One possible solution was to pay family allowances in cash to everyone with children, and to abolish income tax allowances for children. The difficulty was that abolition of tax allowances would place middle-class parents in a worse position than childless couples or the single. The economist H. D. Henderson[*] argued that middle-class families should be protected because 'their ways of life, their standards of values and their ideas exert a strong influence, both direct and indirect, upon their fellow citizens'. On these grounds, Henderson argued that family allowances designed to help those on low incomes should be combined with more generous tax allowances for families with children, and that the cost of tax relief could be covered by narrowing the differential between earned and unearned income.[12] In other words, support for families was becoming

[9] PRO, T172/1901, E. S. Goodrich, professor of zoology and comparative anatomy, and E. B. Ford, reader in genetics, to Lord Horder, 5 Oct. 1939.

[10] PRO, T171/360, notes on the budget, J. M. Keynes, 3 Nov. 1941.

[11] PRO, T171/363, memorandum by Lord Catto, budget: taxation, 30 Nov. 1942.

[12] PRO, T171/363, 'Family allowances: note by H. D. Henderson', 12 Aug. 1942.

[*] Hubert Douglas Henderson (1890–1952) was born in Beckenham; his father was London manager of the Clydesdale Bank. He was educated at Rugby and Emmanuel College, Cambridge; he read for the bar while teaching economics at Emmanuel. During the war he joined the statistical section of the Board of Trade, and in 1917 became secretary of the Cotton Control Board in Manchester. After the war, he became a fellow of Clare College, Cambridge, and a lecturer in economics. In 1923, Keynes invited him to edit the Nation, a Liberal journal. He opposed the return to gold, and helped write Britain's Industrial Future (1928) and Can Lloyd George Do It? (1929). In 1930, he left the Nation to become assistant (later joint) secretary of the Economics Advisory Council; in 1934 he became a research fellow at All Souls, Oxford. During the war, he assisted Stamp in the survey of economic and financial plans and he also advised the Treasury. In 1945, he was elected professor of political economy at Oxford, and he was a member (and later chairman) of the Royal Commission on Population. In 1951, he became warden of All Souls. (DNB, 1951–60, ed. Williams and Nicholls, pp. 470–2.)

more important than differentiation in favour of earned incomes. An alternative solution was to pay family allowances to everyone and to treat it as taxed income so that the well-to-do would pay some of it back. In 1943, the Inland Revenue proposed that all contributions should be set against tax and all benefits liable to tax, but this neat solution was not adopted and the connection between the tax system and social benefits was to provide a continuing problem after the war.[13]

Above all, Keynes linked family allowances with a wide-ranging package of measures designed to pay for the war and 'to snatch from the exigency of war positive social improvements'. His aim was 'to devise a means of adapting the distributive system of a free community to the limitations of war', in order to preserve incentives for risk-taking and to offer the maximum choice in spending income. He argued that consumer choice and a relatively free market could be preserved by removing excess spending power and deferring the receipt of some earnings until after the war. This deferred pay could be paid to bodies under working-class control, such as friendly societies or trade unions, as 'a big constructive working-class policy'. Keynes suggested that the support of these bodies could be secured by offering family allowances and a postwar capital levy or annual capital tax to cover the costs of returning the deferred pay. As a result, the debt 'will be widely distributed amongst all those who are foregoing immediate consumption, instead of being mainly concentrated ... in the hands of the capitalist class', so that animosity against a small group of *rentiers* would be avoided. Further, the timing of repayment of deferred pay would allow the government to stimulate demand in the event of the onset of depression. Keynes's proposals were designed to create social integration and economic stability within a dynamic free market. Rather than controlling consumption by rationing and planning, he wished to control *aggregate* spending and then give individuals freedom to determine their own consumption, by their own preferences. He argued that his scheme had greater political and popular appeal than 'tinkering' with the income tax. 'What the public require is a sense that imagination has been used, that a novel fiscal instrument has been forged, that social justice has been preserved, that a basis for further social improvement has been laid.'[14]

[13] PRO, T161/1242, Proctor to chancellor, 21 May 1943; C. J. Gregg to Hopkins and chancellor, 13 Feb. 1943; 'National insurance and income tax', A. T. Haynes and R. J. Kirton, 30 Nov. 1944; T161/1250, B. W. G. to Bridges, 28 Jan. 1946; C. J. Gregg to chancellor, 25 Jan. 1946.

[14] J. M. Keynes, *How to Pay for the War* (London, 1940), pp. iii, 7, 10–11; PRO, T171/355, 'Note by the Board of Inland Revenue on the proposal to treat part of an income tax payment as a deferred credit available to the taxpayer at the end of the war', G. B. Canny, 6 Jan. 1941; IR64/100, 'Revised proposals for a war surcharge', J. M. Keynes, 5 Jan. 1941; for a recent assessment of the scheme, see R. Toye, 'Keynes, the Labour

These proposals were adopted in a truncated manner. Although surveys of working-class savings carried out by Mass-Observation suggested that workers preferred compulsory savings to taxation, trade unions were sceptical.[15] They viewed family allowances as a threat to the male wage, and saw deferred pay as 'an interference with the normal liberties of citizens of a democracy', a deception to make the working class pay for the war, and a device to reduce real wages. The capital levy was supported by some unions, but even this was muted. The Economic Committee of the TUC came to the conclusion that 'a Capital Levy is not a suitable instrument for raising, during the war, the money necessary to pay for the war'. It preferred voluntary to compulsory savings, and taxation of unearned incomes.[16] The TUC's caution was understandable, for deferred pay did not provide savings in any meaningful sense: there was no interest, no date for repayment and it was not transferable. Indeed, the failure to repay postwar credits until their value was seriously reduced by inflation meant that workers paid a form of levy, whereas holders of government bonds were able to secure repayment and received interest.[17] Neither were the Treasury and Inland Revenue convinced, viewing both deferred pay and a capital levy as 'an unwelcome appendage to a simple scheme of direct taxation', introducing complexities without necessarily securing the support of workers for higher taxation. The Inland Revenue saw any attempt to shape savings and consumption as an unwelcome departure. As Gregg commented at the end of the war:

I regard it as fantastic for the state to assume control of the individual to the point of making him save when the state thinks he ought to save and trying to make him spend when the state thinks he ought to spend. I regard that as a totalitarian interference with human liberty.[18]

movement and how to pay for the war', *Twentieth Century British History* 10 (1999), 255–81.

[15] PRO, T171/355, J. M. Keynes to H. Wilson Smith, 'Mr Madge's latest report on savings in four Yorkshire towns', also in *The Collected Writings of John Maynard Keynes*, vol. XXII, *Activities, 1939–45: Internal War Finance*, ed. D. Moggridge (London, 1978), pp. 274–6.

[16] MRC, TUC MSS 292/402, 2/2, meeting between trade union side of the National Advisory Council to the minister of labour and Keynes, 24 Jan. 1940; Electrical Trades' Union Walthamstow to TUC, 19 Mar. 1940; London Trades Council, 12 July 1940; TUC MSS 292/402, 2/3 Economic Committee 3/1, TUC Economic Committee, resolutions on compulsory savings and capital levy; conscription of wealth; stabilisation of prices; and postwar planning; resolutions on savings, taxation, prices, etc., 12 Mar. 1941; Economic Committee, resolutions on savings, taxation, stabilisation of prices etc.

[17] J. S. Flemming, 'Debt and taxes in war and peace: the case of a small open economy', in M. J. Boskin, J. S. Flemming and S. Gorini (eds.), *Private Savings and Public Debt* (Oxford, 1987), p. 386.

[18] PRO, T171/372, Gregg to Hopkins, 9 July 1945; he remarked that he expressed the same sentiment in 1939 when Keynes first proposed compulsory savings. IR64/100, 'Notes on Mr Keynes' scheme', 18 Apr. 1940; 'Note by the Board of Inland Revenue on Mr Keynes' revised proposal for a war surcharge', 15 Jan. 1941.

The outcome was a modest scheme of deferred pay or postwar credits, held by the government rather than by working-class bodies. There the scheme stopped, without the payment of family allowances or the promise of a capital levy.

Interest in the scheme did not entirely disappear, for in 1943 the Economic Section suggested that deferred pay should continue after the war in order to collect tax credits at periods of excess demand, and to repay them in times of depression. Indeed, the Economic Section extended the argument to investment demand as well as personal consumption. In 1941, steps were taken to redress the problems created by the excess profits tax of 100 per cent. In his economic survey, Stamp found that the 100 per cent excess profits tax set the private interest of the manufacturer against the public interest in stimulating production: why would industry take risk for little return? As he remarked, 'patriotism and peril are curiously transient as complete substitutes for the old incentives'; the result was a 'gradual decline of zeal, and energy and enterprise, a growing bias against the adoption of new methods'. As Keynes remarked, the 100 per cent rate was unjust between firms. It benefited firms whose profits were no higher than before the war; it hit new and growing firms, and so 'stops dead the process of survival of the fit which is the main justification of private enterprise, and replaces this process by nothing whatever'. The tax was, in his view, the result of 'confusing the prevention of profiteering with the doctrine that in time of war no-one shall be rewarded for energy, extra work, exceptional efficiency or courageous risk-taking'. And was it logical to prevent industry from making a higher profit, when the same principle did not apply to workers who secured higher wages? Of course, the rationale was simple, as the Inland Revenue pointed out: it was to secure the maximum effort from *labour*, which meant a strict limit of profits. Churchill went too far in his comment on the excess profits tax, when he said that it showed 'deference not to sound financial canons but to harping and insatiable left-wing propaganda'. Rather it reflected a desire to secure support from workers as a pragmatic response to managing the economy.

The eventual solution was to convert 20 per cent of the tax into a deferred credit to be repaid after the war. In Bevin's view, repayment should be permitted upon certain conditions; the Inland Revenue protested that it could not sit in judgement, on the grounds that the money was essentially a compulsory loan. But there was another way of using deferred credits. Here, it seemed to the Economic Section, was a way of managing the economy and maintaining full employment, by removing excess demand in periods of boom and offering tax breaks to industry in periods of recession, provided that the funds were used for capital developments. The Inland Revenue remained doubtful, fearing that the dual system of tax credits and changes in the rate of income tax would create complications. After all, personal consumption could just as easily be adjusted through changes in the rate of tax. But it was not accepted by everyone at the Inland Revenue that taxes should be used for *any* purpose except to obtain the revenue needed for government expenditure. The purists argued that its use to regulate consumption would 'prejudice the whole tax structure and bring the Income Tax into discredit'. As they realised, there was a major psychological difference between taking money during the war and promising its return in peace, and taking money in periods of prosperity with a promise to repay on some vague date in the future unrelated to any obvious event. Neither was the Inland Revenue convinced by the use of the tax system to influence the timing of capital investment. Here the common trope of fairness and equity was called into service. The income tax rested, so it was argued, on the taxable capacity of the taxpayer, and allowances and reliefs were designed to measure ability to pay. Was it fair and equitable to allow tax breaks to some firms making investments at a certain time; or to offer tax breaks which would only go to firms making a profit?[19]

The 'inflationary gap' of excess spending was not controlled by deferred pay as Keynes hoped, for rationing and indirect taxes were also needed. Here was a further breach in the fiscal constitution, for the share of indirect taxation started to rise for the first time in a century. The 1941 budget marked the limit of reliance on direct taxes, and in 1942 the emphasis shifted to indirect taxes with higher rates on 'optional expenditure' on beer, tobacco and entertainment, and the introduction of the purchase tax. The purchase tax was similar to the wholesale tax considered at the end of the First World War, which was relatively easy to collect from a small number of wholesalers or suppliers at the point the commodity was sold to a retailer. It was also applied in 'bands' of zero to 100 per cent,

---

[19] PRO, T171/356, W. S. Churchill to chancellor of the Exchequer, 19 Feb. 1941; T171/357, War Cabinet: survey of economic and financial plans: excess profits tax and production: memorandum by the Survey, 30 July 1940; J. Stamp to K. Wood, 30 July 1940; Canny to H. Wilson Smith, 5 Aug. 1940; EPT, J. M. Keynes, 21 Oct. 1940; excess profits tax: note by the Board of Inland Revenue on Mr Keynes's memorandum of 21 Oct. 1940; L. Amery to K. Wood, 8 Jan. 1941; draft memorandum, R. V. N. Hopkins, 8 Jan. 1941; War Cabinet: excess profits tax: memorandum by the chancellor of the Exchequer, 13 Jan. 1941; A. Greenwood to K. Wood, 14 Jan. 1941; note by the Board of Inland Revenue: EPT: deferred credit proposal, G. Canny, 29 Jan. 1941; E. Bevin to K. Wood, 27 Jan. 1941; G. Canny to R. V. N. Hopkins and Wilson Smith, 5 Feb. 1941; excess profits tax: the proposed 'withholding' arrangement, 11 Feb. 1941; excess profits tax: the 20 per cent 'withholding' arrangement, R. V. N. Hopkins, 11 Feb. 1941; G. Canny to Wilson Smith, 27 Mar. 1941; T161/1137/S52098/03, H. Brittain to S. P. Chambers, 8 Sept. 1943; income tax deferred credits; C. Gregg to W. Eady, 13 Oct. 1943; covering note, Inland Revenue, 13 Oct. 1943, on the Economic Section's memorandum on the maintenance of employment; taxation of industrial policy [*sic*], Board of Trade, Nov. 1943.

allowing the consumption of different goods to be manipulated. Above all, 'utility goods' did not pay the tax, so encouraging the purchase of standardised commodities. As Hopkins argued, 'it is only by taxing articles the consumption of which is the taxpayer's own choice, that it is possible to strike at the surplus purchasing power of those with rising or casually inflated incomes without inflicting hardship on those classes whose contribution to the national Exchequer is already at its maximum'.[20]

Of course, indirect taxes were traditionally opposed by Labour and the trade unions. Not surprisingly, Pethick-Lawrence complained that it meant 'putting the burden on the backs of the poorer people . . . it would be very disastrous if the war were used as a means of permanently fastening any such tax as this on the country . . . there is a very very strong case for this not being a permanent part of the fiscal system of the country'.[21] More surprisingly, most Labour and trade union opinion accepted that the situation had changed. In 1943, some members of the Labour party argued that the payment of income tax by a large proportion of the population meant that it no longer made political sense to oppose indirect taxes and favour direct taxes. Rather, greater discrimination was needed about precisely which direct and indirect taxes were desirable, and which should be opposed.[22] The postwar Labour administration retained the purchase tax which was too useful to abandon, both for its yield and as a tool of economic planning. This was not what Keynes wished: it marked a continued reliance on planning and intervention in consumers' preferences.

At the end of the First World War, Labour and the unions opposed any extension of indirect taxes and pressed for a capital levy. During the Second World War, they acquiesced in the purchase tax and expressed little support for the capital levy. Pethick-Lawrence did seize on the introduction of conscription of labour in 1939 as an argument in favour of conscription of wealth; and Chamberlain responded to these concerns, linking his announcement of conscription with the promise of a study of taxation of war wealth.[23] Nevertheless, the issue was much less important than during the First World War and many Labour commentators pointed to other, more effective, means of avoiding a massive postwar debt. Durbin,

[20] PRO, T171/363, R. V. N. Hopkins to chancellor, 13 Feb 1943; T171/367, Hopkins to Chancellor, 10 Feb. 1944.

[21] PRO, T172/1974, deputation to the chancellor of the Exchequer from Labour Members of Parliament and representatives of the co-operative movement to urge the abolition of the purchase tax, 28 May 1941.

[22] PRO, T172/1972, note of a deputation to the chancellor of the Exchequer from the National Council of Labour, 18 Dec. 1941; W. Emy to Wilson Smith, 17 Dec. 1941.

[23] LPA, Home Policy Committee, Box I, minutes, Nov. 1937 – Sept. 1953, Labour Party Policy Committee, 'Labour's home policy', Mar. 1940; PRO, T230/94, National Debt Enquiry, first meeting 19 Feb. 1945.

Table 6.2 *Structure of central government revenue: net receipts due to the Exchequer, 1945/6 (percentage)*

	1945/6
Income tax and super-tax	44.9
NDC/excess profits tax	14.5
Death duties	3.7
Stamps	0.8
Motor vehicle duty	1.4
Customs	17.8
Excise	16.9
Total	100.0

Source: PP 1945–6 xv, *Finance Accounts of the UK, for the year ended 31 March 1946*, pp. 12–13.

for example, suggested a combination of taxation (including an annual tax on capital), direct control of industry and borrowing at low interest rates.[24] Members of the Economic Section – Keynes, Hicks* and Meade – discussed the impact of a capital levy in 1942 and 1943, but the most serious consideration of the levy was undertaken by the National Debt Enquiry of 1944, which arose from Clement Attlee's[†] suggestion that the Economic Section might prepare a note on the subject.[25]

[24] E. F. M. Durbin, *How to Pay for the War: An Essay on the Financing of War* (London, 1939), pp. 75–83.

[25] PRO, T230/94, Meade to Hicks, 18 Aug. 1942; Hicks to Meade, 26 Aug. 1942; note by Meade and comment by J. M. Keynes; 'A capital levy and incentive', R. C. [?] to Meade, 4 June 1943; on Attlee's suggestion, see J. E. Meade to secretary, 12 July 1944.

* John Richard Hicks (1904–89) was born in Warwick, the son of a newspaper editor. He was educated at Clifton College and Balliol, Oxford, where he read politics, economics and philosophy. After a period in journalism, he became a lecturer in economics at the LSE in 1926, moving to Cambridge in 1935 and Manchester 1938–46. He was a fellow of Nuffield College, Oxford, from 1946 to 1958, and professor of political economy from 1952 to 1965. He won the Nobel prize for economics in 1972. (*DNB, 1986–90,* ed. Nicholls, pp. 200–2.)

† Clement Richard Attlee (1883–1967) was born in London, where his father was a solicitor in the City. He was educated at Haileybury and University College, Oxford. When he joined chambers in London, he visited Stepney and went to live in a settlement house in the East End. He joined the Fabians in 1907 and the ILP in 1908. In 1912, he joined the department of social science and administration at the LSE. After the war, he was mayor of Stepney and was elected MP for Limehouse in 1922. He immediately became one of MacDonald's parliamentary private secretaries; in 1924 he was under-secretary at the War Office, in 1930 chancellor of the Duchy of Lancaster and 1931 postmaster general. He was leader of the party from 1935 to 1955. He joined the coalition government in 1940, and was deputy prime minister from 1942 to 1945, and Labour prime minister from 1945 to 1951. (*DNB, 1961–70,* ed. Williams and Nicholls, pp. 46–55; Robbins (ed.), *Biographical Dictionary,* pp. 25–8.)

Meade seized the opportunity to consider the economic impact of postwar debt. He was concerned that the high rates of tax needed to service the debt might harm incentives to work and take risk, and so stifle recovery. Could a capital levy be used in order to reduce taxation and increase incentives? The Economic Section embarked on a major enquiry by a group of leading economists as well as representatives of the Treasury and Inland Revenue. The agenda was set out by Meade:

In what sense is the transfer of debt payments from the taxpayer to the debt holder a burden on the community? Can we rely upon a secular rise in the national income as the main way of reducing the burden of the debt? What future relief can we expect from conversion operations? What is the role which might be played by a Sinking Fund? Should a Sinking Fund be fixed in amount in view of the type of budgetary policy suggested by the White Paper on Employment? Could a Capital levy be usefully employed for the reduction of debt?[26]

The answer of the enquiry was that a capital levy did *not* provide a useful device to reduce the debt.

The general feeling of the National Debt Enquiry was that a levy offered few benefits, but would create serious administrative problems and dislocate capital markets. The levy had less attraction than in the 1920s, for war wealth was more widely distributed, borrowing was at a lower interest rate and taxation prevented the accumulation of fortunes by 'war profiteers'.[27] More emphasis was given to 'cheap money' as a way of reducing the costs of debt service and stimulating recovery. Keynes lectured the enquiry on the main point of his *General Theory*, that growth was not dependent on the level of savings and its encouragement by high interest rates; rather, the driving force was the investment needs of industry which would be encouraged by cheap money. Interest rates should therefore fall as far as possible, with the proviso that there should be a 'socially desirable reward for saving, with its implications regarding the provision for families, the working of charitable institutions, and other aspects of social life'. The burden of debt could therefore be reduced by a

---

[26] The papers of the enquiry are in PRO, T230/94 and T230/95. See especially, T230/94, J. E. Meade to secretary, 12 July 1944; 'The postwar treatment of the national debt: the capital levy'; 'The postwar treatment of the national debt: the fiscal problem set by the debt'; 'The postwar treatment of the national debt: debt repayment and employment policy'; minutes of meetings 8 and 27 Mar., 5 Apr. 1945; T230/95, 'The control of inflation: the three alternatives: note by the Economic Section', J. E. Meade and L. C. Robbins, 3 May 1945; National Debt Enquiry: summary by Lord Keynes of his proposals, 18 Apr. 1945; 'National Debt Enquiry: first report: the question of future gilt-edged interest rates', 15 May 1945; meetings of 10, 18 and 19 Apr., 18 and 24 May 1945.

[27] The final report is in PRO, T230/95, 'The capital levy' which was reissued in the later debates: T171/395, capital levy, 15 June 1945; see also T230/94, National Debt Enquiry: the capital levy, historical note.

low rate of interest to hold down the cost of borrowing, and by economic growth to reduce its real value.[28]

The potential net yield of the levy was even less at the end of the Second World War than at the end of the First World War, for low interest rates reduced the savings from debt redemption, and higher levels of taxation at progressive rates increased the loss of revenue from death duties and income tax on assets surrendered to the state. A reasonable return could only be achieved by imposing a heavy levy on small property, which would be politically dangerous and do little to improve incentives. Meade did try to rescue the proposal by arguing that the levy would reduce incomes so that they would be liable to a lower marginal rate of tax, which was as good as a reduction in the tax rate. But as Hicks commented, the real problem was taxation of business profits, which would only be affected by an alteration in the standard rate of tax. In Keynes's opinion, there was more to be said for an annual capital tax than a 'catastrophic capital levy' as a means of off-setting the disincentive of high income and surtax rates.[29]

Labour opinion was shifting in the same direction. A levy was not necessary to fulfil Labour's ambition of redistributing wealth and breaking up accumulations of capital. After the First World War, annual taxes did not touch capital; during the Second World War, high levels of income tax were a form of capital levy, forcing the rich to live on their capital assets and removing unearned incomes as they arose. Consequently, the yield of a levy and its potential impact on wealth could not justify the political danger of offering the Conservatives 'a great opportunity to terrify the electorate'. As one Labour party document commented, the capital levy would be 'an even poorer election cry than it was last time, alienating at once a large proportion of the "black coated workers"!' Labour policy moved from a capital levy towards an annual tax on capital. It would offer a way of coping with any increase in debt after the war to pay for public services; and it would ensure that payment of interest did not distort the distribution of the national income and increase the power of privately owned banks.[30] However, even this proposal was not

[28] PRO, T230/94, National Debt Enquiry, second meeting 8 Mar. 1945; third meeting 22 Mar. 1945; fourth meeting 27 Mar. 1945.

[29] PRO, T230/94, EAS 12/01/A, Meade to Hicks, 18 Aug. 1942, Hicks to Meade, 26 Aug. 1942, R. C. to Meade, 'A capital levy and incentive', 4 June 1943; Keynes to Meade, 28 July 1944; National Debt Enquiry, first meeting 19 Feb. 1945.

[30] LPA, LP/CL/22/9, 'A capital levy after this war – or not?', n.d.; F. W. Pethick-Lawrence, *An Emergency Tax on Wealth* (London, 1939), p. 4; Durbin, *How to Pay for the War*, p. 109. Douglas Jay also proposed an annual capital tax of 2 per cent on £10,000, but in conjunction with a capital levy after the war. D. Jay, *Paying for the War* (London, Labour party, 1940); LPA, Home Policy Committee, box 1, minutes, Nov. 1937 – Sept. 1953, 31 July 1939, 8 Feb. 1940, 14 Mar. 1940.

central to policy after 1945, for an annual tax on capital would involve serious problems of valuation and would potentially harm savings and enterprise.

In many ways, Labour lacked a clear fiscal strategy by the end of the war. The nearest to a general statement came from the Home Policy Committee in 1940, which reiterated the old nostrum of an attack on unearned wealth through death duties, an increase in the graduation of the income tax and a capital levy in order to break 'that ugly tradition which binds poverty in one generation to poverty in the next, and perpetuates great fortunes by unearned inheritance'. The general approach reflected continuity with the debates in Edwardian Britain:

Any great effort at social reconstruction necessarily requires a wise administration of the national income; and no administration is wise that is not founded also in justice. The Labour Party differs from its critics in its test of fiscal wisdom. They believe that the less the income of the rich is reduced, the more prosperous is the community... This view, Labour emphatically condemns... It is both economically right and socially just to raise the sum required for a vigorous social policy from those elements in the nation who contribute relatively little to social efficiency and too often waste their resources unproductively. A Socialist policy in public finance is not less vital to the clerk and the teacher, the professional man and the technician, than to the wage-earner...

The Labour Party does not seek to treat harshly those who have profited by an outworn and unjust system. But we are convinced that the existing vast differences in wealth poison the relation between classes in a way that is incompatible with the achievement of a common good. They increase every difficulty in meeting the needs of a rapidly changing world. They make privilege ever less conscious of social obligation.[31]

However, high levels of income tax and restrictions on profit during the Second World War blunted the electoral and economic force of these attacks on socially created wealth and unearned incomes. There was something of a policy vacuum, and the matter was not seriously considered beyond a commitment to steeply graduated taxation and a high level of differentiation as a means of attacking 'functionless ownership'. There was no serious discussion of the future shape of the taxation of profits and companies, and it was assumed that the NDC and the excess profits tax would expire at the end of the war. The war-time debates on taxation were inconclusive, and Labour did not have a clearly formulated policy when it formed its first majority government in 1945 – and neither, for that matter, did the Conservatives.

Above all, taxation became a device for economic management and planning as well as a means of financing the government. The principle

---

[31] LPA, Labour Party Policy Committee, 'Labour's home policy', Mar. 1940.

that taxes should be 'scientific' and equitable between interests according to ability to pay became less insistent. In 1943, Keynes firmly rejected

the spurious doctrine that the sole purpose of taxation policy is to apportion the costs of government equitably without *arrières pensées* as to the effect of the particular method or formula in stimulating industrial enterprise and employment. If there ever was such an orthodoxy, it was abandoned many years ago. Almost everyone, whether in the Civil Service or in Parliament or amongst the general public, would be surprised and indeed shocked, if they were to be told on high authority that this was an operative orthodoxy of government.[32]

Keynes exaggerated, for many officials in the revenue departments and Treasury *did* believe that taxes were simply to secure revenue for the purposes of government. Nevertheless, their position was weakened, and they were on the defensive. Fiscal policy was no longer dominated, as after the First World War, by the sinking fund and debt redemption; taxes could be used more actively to shape the economy. Of course, the change of emphasis was highly contested, for it was by no means agreed *how* taxes should be used to manage the economy, and for what ends. The relationship between equality and efficiency, the nature of incentives and the role of the market in allocating resources were at the heart of war-time and postwar politics.

Keynes's own approach depended on the use of taxes to balance the economy over the trade cycle, by removing inflationary pressure through higher taxes and injecting demand at times of depression. His emphasis was therefore on stabilising the economy by measures designed to adjust the aggregate level of personal consumption and investment demand. Once the economy had been brought into equilibrium, and the perils of inflation or depression had been avoided, the allocation of resources could be left to the free market. However, taxation could also be used in a much more directive way in order to change the structure of the economy, both as a tool of planning to encourage or discourage investment, and to create equality by removing wide differentials of income and wealth. The balance between these different uses of taxation was at the centre of political debates during and particularly after the war. At the two extremes were Friedrich von Hayek and the so-called 'gosplanners' on the left of the Labour party.

In the 1930s, Hayek raised the issue of how resources could be allocated in the absence of information on prices and costs generated by a competitive market. This so-called 'calculation debate' might lead to a commitment to a free market economy; by contrast, the 'gosplanners'

32 PRO, T161/1137, Keynes to Eady, 'Industrial enterprise and employment and the tax system', 16 Dec. 1943.

rejected the market as a means of allocating resources, arguing that the market was wasteful and inefficient and that more power should be given to government departments and to nationalisation in shaping the economy. Of course, most opinion fell somewhere between the two extremes. Hayek's stress on the need for price information to guide the efficient allocation of resources influenced democratic socialists such as Durbin, Meade and Jay who combined commitment to a degree of nationalisation and the need for regulation of private investment with a belief that markets should allocate resources. They were therefore closer to Keynes's position, with planning largely confined to macroeconomic adjustment of demand and investment over the trade cycle, largely by means of taxation and the budget. Once the total level of consumption was adjusted, the market would play the major role in the allocation of resources. But many members of the Labour party placed more weight on the use of taxation as a means of shaping the structure of the economy and the distribution of income and wealth, and wished to limit the role of the market to a greater or lesser extent.[33]

A related issue was the relationship of the tax system to incentives, efficiency and equality. Should taxation be used in order to reduce income and wealth differentials, and remove socially created wealth, as means of creating a more equal society on grounds of equity and efficiency? One way of proceeding was to replace private ownership by state enterprise. Another strategy was to retain a large element of private enterprise, but to limit the distribution of business profits to wealthy shareholders and to encourage companies to retain profits for investment and higher productivity. Opponents of such a view argued that high levels of taxation meant a loss of incentives for risk-taking, so leading to economic rigidities and stagnation. By encouraging reliance on the reserves of existing companies, risk-taking by new firms was discouraged. At the heart of these debates was a fundamental disagreement over the means of creating an active, dynamic economy. Put in its starkest form, should the tax system give priority to equality or to incentives?

There was an uneasy tension between the use of taxation for demand management, as a device to create social equity, and as an incentive for

---

[33] On Labour and planning, see Tomlinson, 'Planning'; S. Brooke, 'Problems of "socialist planning": Evan Durbin and the Labour government of 1945', *Historical Journal* 34 (1991), 687–702; R. J. Toye, 'The Labour party and the planned economy, 1931–51', PhD thesis, University of Cambridge, 1999. On the 1930s and different approaches to planning, see D. Ritschel, *The Politics of Planning: The Debate on Economic Planning in Britain in the 1930s* (Oxford, 1997). Contemporary writings are extensive: see for example J. E. Meade, *Planning and the Price Mechanism* (London, 1948); and E. F. M. Durbin, *Problems of Economic Planning: Papers on Planning and Economics* (London, 1949). On Hobson versus the Webbs, see above p. 147.

enterprise. A desire to remove excess spending power could result in higher indirect taxes on the less affluent which might be considered inequitable; or it could result in higher levels of income tax which might blunt the motivation for additional effort and risk. The exact balance between these conflicting considerations depended on assumptions about the nature of society and personality: were people driven by individual material gain or encouraged by 'fairness' and equity? Further, the change in the level and uses of taxation might affect compliance and acceptance of the fiscal system. The use of high levels of progression to create equality or to adjust demand might create resentment to the tax system and encourage evasion with additional costs of compliance. In the 1920s and 1930s, the 'dip' in tax liability on modest middle-class families with children helped to secure the consent of an important block of voters; its removal during the Second World War altered the politics of taxation and might weaken support for fiscal extraction in the future.

7 'The mortal blows of taxation': Labour and reconstruction, 1945–1951

> If we ... want to remain a private enterprise country, we must not kill the goose (which is what our tax-system is doing) ... The grievance, which is stated by business in terms of a shortage of working capital, would be expressed by an economist as the result of a deprivation of real resources through the mortal blows of taxation.
>
>   PRO, T171/369, B(45)3, note by Lord Keynes: Budget Committee: EPT and changes in stock values, 16 Jan. 1945

> The influence which taxation can have on economic development is purely negative. By its nature it cannot be creative; it can be more repressive or less according to its design in relation to the matter which is taxed. Like the brake to the vehicle, it can be applied so hard as to stop further progress, or it can be applied so lightly as to produce nothing more serious than light friction, but it can never assist in propelling the vehicle.
>
>   MRC, FBI MSS 200/F/3/S1/16/23, 'Notes on taxation in relation to post-war planning', 3 July 1945

The national debt was a major issue at the end of the First World War; it was much less important at the end of the Second World War, reflecting the differences in war finance. Much more pressing was the need for economic recovery in order to restore Britain's international trading position. How could Britain regain export markets in order to improve its balance of payments, and hence to deal with its external debts and buy essential goods for reconstruction? Meanwhile, pent-up demand at home and the continuation of full employment after the war threatened to crowd out exports, suck in imports and drive up prices. The new Labour government had to grapple with these serious problems of increasing production to meet demand, especially for exports, which meant raising productivity and holding down domestic consumption, prices and wages. At the same time, it was constructing the welfare state and pursuing a policy of equality.

Taxation was central to these concerns. Labour policy after the war used taxation to stimulate production and increase productivity – less by offering incentives to risk-takers than by encouraging large-scale firms to

194

Table 7.1 *Income and profits tax, 1939–1950*

Excess profits tax

1 April 1939 to 31 March 1940	60 per cent
1 April 1940 to 31 December 1945	100 per cent; postwar refund of 20 per cent
1 January to 31 December 1946	60 per cent

Profits tax

	Distributed	Not distributed
To 30 September 1949	25 per cent	10 per cent
From 1 October 1949	30 per cent	10 per cent

Standard rate of income tax

1940/1	8s 6d in the £ (42.5 per cent)
1941/2 to 1945/6	10s in the £ (50 per cent)
1946/7 to 1949/50	9s in the £ (45 per cent)

Source: PP 1950–1 XVI, *Report of the Commissioners of Inland Revenue,* pp. 256, 208.

Table 7.2 *Structure of central government revenue: net receipts due to the Exchequer, 1950/1 (percentage)*

	1950/1
Income tax and super-tax	41.2
Profits/special contribution	7.3
Death duties	5.0
Stamps	1.5
Motor vehicle duty	1.7
Customs	24.1
Excise	19.3
Total	100.0

Source: PP 1950–1 XXI, *Finance Accounts of the UK for the Financial Year 1950–1*, pp. 14–15.

retain and invest profits. Taxes could also be used to hold down domestic consumption and control inflation, by discouraging the payment of high dividends and salaries and by taxing goods – especially 'luxuries'. Such a policy might absorb excess spending power and create the political conditions for wage restraint. Of course, it also posed the danger of removing incentives and creating rigidities in the economy. There was a real concern that both the high *level* and the *form* of taxation were blunting efficiency and incentives. Incomes were more equal, but at what cost to incentives and economic growth? Of course, Labour politicians had their own ideological assumptions about the nature of incentives and the determinants of economic growth, rejecting the pursuit of personal gain as the only route to efficiency. What did seem obvious by the late 1950s and 1960s, regardless of political persuasion and ideology, was the low level of British growth compared with other countries. The postwar fiscal constitution, so it appeared, produced inflexibility and uncompetitiveness, and needed major reform to assist in the modernisation of Britain. These debates over modernisation of the fiscal system are the subject of later chapters; the point to consider here is why the fiscal constitution took the form it did after 1945. The best place to start is with the taxation of business profits, which now came to play a larger role in fiscal policy.

Taxing profits

At the end of the Second World War, as after the First, industry faced the problem of postwar reconstruction and the replacement of worn-out plant. At the same time, the government had to reach a decision on the future of war-time taxes on company profits, and to find an alternative source of revenue. During the Second World War, profits were much more rigidly controlled, with a higher level of income tax and an excess profits tax at 100 per cent. At the end of the war, there was much less room for complaint about *rentiers* or profiteers. But the high level of profits tax also created problems for business and the government. Industry escaped the charge of profiteering, only to find it had fewer resources to respond to the needs of postwar reconstruction; and government might not be able to dispense with the revenue from the profits tax. The political circumstances in 1945 were different from 1918. The concern of the government was less with the attack on *rentiers* than with the desperate attempt to hold down domestic consumption and to control inflation and wages in order to release goods for export markets. The Labour government was also committed to a programme of equality and social justice, to implement the redistribution which had been contained after the First World War.

Not surprisingly, the taxation of industry was a major concern to the FBI. At the end of the war, business was liable to the full standard rate of income tax on both distributed and retained profits; when shareholders received their dividends, they paid any higher rate to which they might be liable or reclaimed any over-payment. In addition, companies paid the NDC on all profits, and a tax on their excess profits above a prewar standard at a rate of 100 per cent. These taxes imposed a considerable burden on industry which was exacerbated by two other features of the tax system: the definition of profit and the treatment of inflation. Trading profit was defined in the income tax as the surplus of current trading receipts over trading payments. Strictly speaking, only payments relating to operations of the year could be set against tax, which led to problems in the treatment of depreciation of capital assets. Taxation was levied on a figure in excess of commercially understood profits, and industrialists argued for a wider definition, based on the actual expenditure needed to produce a profit. Furthermore, the tax system did not recognise changes in price levels. Inflation was not a problem in itself, for it was possible to make 'substantial additions to reserves out of enhanced profits'. The FBI realised that the difficulty arose from a combination of inflation and high taxation. The profits tax was levied on *money* profits which were falling in real terms, given the higher price of replacement plant and machinery which was not taken into account by depreciation allowances. Consequently, taxation was eroding industrial capital and diverting profits to the state for current government expenditure. The FBI argued that taxation should fall on profits *after* provision for the maintenance and replacement of raw materials, buildings and plant, by shifting depreciation allowances from historic to replacement costs.[1]

Industry's claim for allowances on capital expenditure went back to 1931 and 1933, when the Inland Revenue opposed any concession on the grounds that existing depreciation allowances were adequate, and that it was wrong to charge a capital item against one year's expenditure. As the Inland Revenue pointed out, an allowance against tax would not help firms without profits and so would not assist depressed industries. The Inland Revenue also feared that any concession to capital investment

---

[1] Daunton, *Trusting Leviathan*, pp. 107–210; MRC, FBI MSS 200/F/3/D2/1/19, Taxation Committee, 6 Dec. 1940, 24 Feb. 1941, 17 Dec. 1942, 31 Dec. 1942; memorandum on EPT, 16 Jan. 1941 and 24 Feb. 1941; report of Taxation Committee, Jan.–Feb. 1942; note by W. H. Coates, industry and finance, 11 Feb. 1942; financing of industry by retention of profits: deputation to the chancellor of the Exchequer, 1943; 'Inflation and British taxes on profits', F. Bowers, 1943; evidence of the Association of British Chambers of Commerce and the FBI to the Committee of the Board of Inland Revenue, Aug. 1943; FBI MSS 200/F/3/S1/16/20, Association of British Chambers of Commerce and FBI, 'Taxation', 6 Apr. 1943; FBI MSS 200/F/3/S1/16/4, distribution of war profits, 31 Aug. 1945; Taxation Committee, 27 Nov. 1945, 14 Nov. 1946; budget, 1946; taxation, 1947–8: policy, 19 Dec. 1946; FBI MSS 200/F/3/E6/3/1, representations to the chancellor of the Exchequer, 2 Feb. 1948; 'Taxation and shortage of industrial capital', 15 Dec. 1948; 'The profits tax: the incidence of the tax on ordinary shareholders', 20 Dec. 1948; FBI MSS 200/F/3/E5/6/4, 'Taxation and capital requirements', C. D. Hellyar, 4 Aug. 1948; S. P. Chambers, 'Taxation of the supply of capital for industry', *Lloyds Bank Review* n.s. 11 (1949), 1–20; Whiting, *Labour Party and Taxation*, pp. 83–90 and 'Taxation policy', in H. Mercer, N. Rollings and J. D. Tomlinson (eds.), *Labour Governments and Private Industry: The Experience of 1945–51* (Edinburgh, 1992), pp. 117–34.

would be extended to tax relief on reserves which were used for capital expenditure. In their view, the income tax did not take account of *personal* savings and it was not fair to give a concession to *company* savings. As they saw it, the income tax was a tax on income without consideration of the uses to which income was put, and the tax system should not be used to shape investment.[2] Such views were restated in the war, in response to the Economic Section's proposal to use the tax system and deferred credits to influence investment demand and stabilise the economy after the war.[3] However, this attempt to limit the role of taxation simply to the collection of revenue was not to survive. The Treasury was not entirely convinced by the Inland Revenue, and wished to find some way of helping industry after the war. In 1943, attention turned to the possibility of a lower rate of tax on reserves or undistributed profits – and Keynes's opinion was sought. He agreed that the most promising approach was not to vary business taxation over the cycle, but to develop a scheme for the differential taxation of profits. This might be done in one of three ways. The first was to tax *all* undistributed profits at a lower rate regardless of their use, which might be deflationary in withholding dividends for hoarding rather than use. The second possibility was to provide an allowance for capital expenditure, whether from profits or borrowed money. Keynes rejected this approach, on the grounds that it gave new businesses relief on the *whole* of their capital in competition with established companies which would only have relief on *increments* to capital. He favoured the third option: restricting relief to any retained profits employed within the business.[4]

Company taxation emerged as a central theme in Labour's economic policy in response to economic circumstances at the end of the war rather than as the result of careful thought. As Whiting has remarked, Labour was much better prepared for dealing with the capital wealth of *individuals*, and above all inheritances, which were now 'marginal to the questions of incentive and economic management which surrounded fiscal policy after 1945'.[5] Before 1939, Labour thinking stressed taxation of unearned income and socially created wealth in order to remove a burden from other members of society and to release enterprise. Labour policy therefore emphasised a surtax on large incomes and death duties to break up large fortunes. These policies continued at the end of the

[2] On 1931, see above, p. 166; on 1933, PRO, T172/1805, P. J. Grigg to Fergusson, 2 Feb. 1933, and Inland Revenue note on *The Times* campaign and in particular the suggestions in the letters of the marquis of Lothian and the Associated Chambers of Commerce.

[3] See above, p. 184.

[4] PRO, T161/1137, Eady to Keynes, 14 Dec. 1943; Keynes to Eady, 'Industrial enterprise and employment and the tax system', 16 Dec. 1943.

[5] Whiting, 'Taxation policy', p. 117; Whiting, *Labour Party and Taxation*, pp. 83–90.

Second World War, with a radical attack on socially functionless wealth. Cheap money would encourage the 'euthanasia of the *rentier*' – a phrase Dalton borrowed from Keynes. In Dalton's budgets of October 1945 and April 1946, redistribution of wealth was taken still further by increases in both the surtax on large incomes and in death duties on larger estates.[6] So far, he was merely following the well-trodden path of Labour attacks on unearned income. However, he also adopted a policy which had not previously formed part of Labour's thinking, and which now became central to issues of equality, incentive and economic management: company taxation.

Labour's thinking on taxation, incentives and social justice in the 1920s and 1930s rested on two themes. First, the tax system should remove socially created wealth, after it had been produced by the market, through death duties and surtax; secondly, the ability of individuals to appropriate socially created wealth should be removed by the socialisation of industry. Some members of the party wished to extend the socialisation of industry in order to remove the profit motive as the governing force in the economy. But there was also a realisation after 1945 that a large part of business would remain in private hands, whether as a matter of pragmatic reality or a positive commitment to a modified form of private ownership. Indeed, there was considerable ambivalence within the party concerning the role of private profit and property. This was apparent in the debate over the capital levy which was torn between two different rationales: should it be used as a means to transfer the ownership of industry to public bodies so that private industry would wither away; or to reduce transfer payments to *rentiers* paid by active, dynamic enterprise, where a reasonable level of profit was acceptable unless it contained an element of unearned Rent. Labour politicians and economists between the wars showed little interest in the taxation of business profits at the point of creation: their concern was to remove unmerited, inactive, inherited wealth with high death duties, or to destroy excess levels of personal (and especially unearned) income through the surtax. Hence Snowden confirmed, and Dalton approved, the abolition of corporation tax in 1924 which hit business profits at the point of creation. Profits could be seen as a return to enterprise in order to create an alliance between 'active' capital and labour. Dalton's support of the Rignano scheme rested on the belief that wealth became more reprehensible as it was further removed from its active creation. Other members of the party were more hostile to profits and private property, wishing to nationalise industry. Nicholas Davenport, a

---

[6] H. Dalton, *Financing Labour's Plan* (London, 1946); *Report of the 45th Annual Conference of the Labour Party, 1946* (London, 1946), p. 200; on the budget, see *Parliamentary Debates*, 5th ser. 414, 23 Oct. 1945, cols. 1894–5, and 421, 9 Apr. 1946, cols. 1834–7.

Labour sympathiser in the City, criticised members of the party for assuming that profits were 'reprehensible if not immoral'. When Labour came to power in 1945 and Dalton became chancellor, the government had scarcely considered its policy towards private industry and profit. Indeed, Harold Wilson remarked in 1950 that it was 'almost a vacuum in Socialist thought', and in the words of one recent study of Labour's thinking on private industry, it had an 'almost schizophrenic attitude to the role of the market, competition and free enterprise'.[7] These confusions had to be worked out in government in response to the pressure of political and economic events. Did the market and profits provide the most efficient way of allocating resources, or might they simply lead to new accumulations of wealth? Should the private market be replaced by collective ownership; or should private enterprise now be controlled in order to reconcile incentives for economic growth with the desire to prevent the reappearance of large fortunes? The outcome was Dalton's differential profits tax of 1947.

When he became chancellor, one of Dalton's pressing needs was to encourage savings in order to hold down domestic consumption, to release goods for export, contain inflation and stimulate investment. Initially, his thoughts ran towards an excess dividends levy which would control inflation by removing purchasing power as well as creating the political context for wage restraint. In the event, Dalton relied on voluntary dividend restraint, and he urged industry to plough back profits in order to finance reconstruction. Meanwhile, Bevin called on the TUC to take 'a sensible view about profits ... Some of your best firms are the firms who pay the highest wages and make the biggest profits and they very often adopt the method of putting those profits back into improvements.' However, the government's plea for wage restraint by organised workers depended on 'fiscal justice', the imposition of a tax on the better-off and socially functionless wealth to counterpoise the sacrifices of the working class. Taxation of profits was 'the ideal complement, by way of social justice, and political practicability, for any sacrifices that must be asked from the wage earners as a whole'. Accordingly, when Dalton abolished the excess profits tax with effect from the end of 1946, he continued the NDC as a profits tax at the existing rate of 5 per cent. In 1947, he went a stage further and differentiated the tax. He adopted the first of the three options considered by Keynes, of providing relief to *all* retentions regardless of their use: the rate remained at 5 per cent on retained profits but was raised to 12.5 per cent on distributions. The rates were doubled later

[7] M. Francis, 'Labour policies and socialist ideas: the example of the Attlee government, 1945–51', DPhil thesis, University of Oxford, 1993, pp. 221–32; Whiting, 'Taxation policy', pp. 120–39; N. Davenport, *Memoirs of a City Radical* (London, 1974), pp. 149–50.

in the year to 10 per cent on retentions and 25 per cent on distributions. Differential taxation of profits became a major strand in Labour policy.[8]

On one level, differential taxation of profits was a pragmatic response to postwar difficulties. It had the practical virtue of creating a major source of revenue and filling the gap left by the excess profits tax. It would also remove inflationary pressures, both directly by holding down distributions to shareholders and indirectly through wage restraint. It also had a wider ideological purpose, as a means of defining the purpose of the market, the nature of incentives and the desire for equality in an economy with a continuing role for free enterprise. Differential taxation of profits was linked with a commitment to a 'supply-side' or production-ist approach to restructuring the economy which combined equity for workers with a commitment to business efficiency. Dalton's attack on distributions continued his earlier hostility to large fortunes and socially created wealth. Although socially created value could be captured by nationalisation, the bulk of industry would still remain in private hands. Accordingly, socially created wealth would pass to individuals and dis-tort the economy until it was eventually removed by death duties. The attraction of taxation of distributions was that it would block the private, or at least individual, ownership of socially created value; a lower tax on retentions would offer incentives to industry to invest in new plant and machinery without creating inequality of income from high dividends. It combined efficiency with egalitarianism. As Roy Jenkins* argued, dis-tributions would create high levels of unearned income whereas 'frozen profits' were irrelevant. High personal incomes and individual material gain were castigated as the source for luxury, idleness and economic dis-tortions rather than a means of creating incentives. In Dalton's view, efficiency, investment, innovation and incentives were linked to rational,

[8] PRO, T172/2033, discussions with the TUC, 17 Nov. 1947; T171/386, Dalton to Bridges, 17 Nov. 1945; note of discussion between chancellor, Edward Bridges, Keynes, Richard Hopkins and Bernard Gilbert on the scope of the budget, 20 Feb. 1946; T171/388, B(46)5, proposal for excess dividends tax, 7 Jan. 1946; B(46)7, substitutes for the excess profits tax; flat-rate tax on profits; T172/2033, discussion with the TUC, 17 Nov. 1947; T171/392, 'Budget and food subsidies', D. Jay, 10 Oct. 1947; *Parliamentary Debates*, 5th ser. 436, 15 Apr. 1947, cols. 83–5.

* Roy Harris Jenkins (b. 1920) was born in Pontypool, where his father was a miner, union official, Labour MP and private parliamentary secretary to Attlee. He was educated at Abersychan Grammar School and Balliol College, Oxford. He became a Labour MP in 1948. He saw Labour as non-doctrinaire and appealing to all non-Conservatives. He sup-ported Gaitskell, except over Europe where Jenkins was more enthusiastic. In 1964, he was appointed minister of aviation and then home secretary. In 1967, he become chancellor of the Exchequer, and 1970 deputy leader, but he was isolated as the party moved to the left. In 1971, he voted against the party over Europe and in 1972 resigned as deputy leader. In 1974, he returned to the Home Office before moving to the presidency of the European Commission. In 1981, he returned to British politics and was involved in the formation of the Social Democratic party. (Robbins (ed.), *Biographical Dictionary*, pp. 229–31.)

economic decision making by large, bureaucratic concerns under the control of salaried managers who would use retained profits more rationally than an active external capital market operated by financiers and speculators. Large private concerns and nationalised enterprises were both distinguished from rapacious personal capitalism, and retained profits were acceptable because they could be used for production rather than stimulating inflation, conspicuous consumption, personal fortunes and inequality.[9]

Of course, Labour proposed the creation of the NIB as a means of shaping investment. However, the NIB was not created, and differential taxation of profits offered an alternative means of shaping the capital market without the need for a new financial institution. In 1948/9, about a quarter of investment was made by central and local government, and a quarter by nationalised industries; a further 15 per cent was in areas susceptible to government influence. The remaining 35 per cent was private, and would gradually escape from government regulation with the removal of physical controls imposed during the war. What was needed, it seemed, was an alternative means of controlling private investment in place of physical controls, and without the difficulties of creating the NIB. The solution was to use *fiscal* devices in order to influence investment by companies. A higher rate of tax on distributed profits and a more favourable treatment of depreciation would encourage retentions and investment. After all, 25 per cent of gross investment in 1948 came from undistributed profits and 12.5 per cent from company reserves; a further 41.25 per cent came from depreciation allowances. The underlying assumption was that large-scale industrial concerns were less prone to influence from financiers and speculators: they were similar to bureaucratic public corporations, and more amenable to reasoned discussion with the government. Attention turned away from the NIB and direct control over the allocation of finance towards fiscal manipulation of levels of retained profits and depreciation allowances.[10]

Dalton's policy rested on the use of profits taxation as an instrument of planning on the supply side of the economy. Others were less convinced by his approach. Meade preferred to use differential taxation of profits as a tool for economic management on the lines proposed by the Economic Section in 1943. At times of inflationary pressure, taxation should be

[9] On the supply-side approach, see J. Tomlinson, 'Mr Attlee's supply-side socialism', *Economic History Review* 47 (1993), 1–23; R. Jenkins, 'The investment programme', *Socialist Commentary* 13 (1949), 177, cited in M. Francis, 'Labour policies and socialist ideas', p. 229.

[10] Tomlinson, 'Attlee's inheritance', 147–51; the data on investment is from PRO, T230/143, Economic Section, 'Alternative methods of controlling investment', cited by Tomlinson, 'Attlee's inheritance', 147–8.

increased on distributed profits in order to encourage retentions; at times of deflation, reserves should be taxed at a higher rate in order to encourage distributions. Meade claimed that such a policy would both control inflation and preserve incentives by retaining profits for later distribution. In addition, Meade suggested that new capital investment should be delayed during periods of inflationary pressure and encouraged in periods of deflation by varying the initial allowance on plant and buildings. Such an approach did not imply ideological aversion to profits and distributions, and simply argued for a variation over the cycle in order to maintain stability.[11]

The proposal was not adopted, and the Treasury and Inland Revenue remained doubtful about too great an involvement in the internal affairs of industry. Their attitude was clear: discrimination in the level of profits tax over the cycle or according to the use of reserves 'would mean, in effect, that the government would take over the running of industry' and that state control over savings and spending amounted to a 'totalitarian interference with human liberty'. These fears misunderstood Meade's intention of using taxation as an *alternative* to direct controls, by influencing demand and investment to create stability in a free market. The point was realised by Robert Hall in 1950, who had abandoned his earlier socialist hostility to free enterprise. As he pointed out, the government had more effective means of influencing consumer than investment demand, and the government might turn to crude and damaging direct controls if the Treasury did not provide its own solution. One possibility was the Swedish approach, which drew a distinction between ordinary reserves to be used at any time, and special reserves which formed an investment fund to be used at times and for purposes laid down by the government. Whether British officials would devise a scheme remained doubtful, given the resistance to a selective or discriminatory use of the tax system.[12]

Meanwhile, Keynes took a different line from his position in 1943, when he favoured a higher tax on distributions than on retentions, on condition that the money retained was used within the business. After the war, he felt that retentions were *not* to the benefit of the economy:

[11] PRO, T171/391, B(47)9, 'Stabilisation and the taxation of company profits, J. E. Meade', and B(47)13, 'Differential taxation of undistributed profits: note by J. E. Meade, statistical annex by Board of Inland Revenue'.

[12] PRO, T171/392, notes on discussion, 16 Oct. 1947; T171/404, BC(50)33, Budget Committee: taxation and the control of investment: note by the director, Economic Section, R. L. Hall, 24 Nov. 1950, covering 'Taxation and the control of investment by companies', 7 Nov. 1950; BC(51)17, initial allowances: note by the Board of Inland Revenue; T171/420, 'Control of investment: note on proposal to give relief from tax on earmarked funds', 27 Sept. 1950.

the whole bias of big business and of the managerial economy is not to over-declare, but to under-declare dividends . . . Where a company is under the control of surtax payers, there is, of course, a strong and obvious motive for declaring as low dividends as possible. Where, as is increasingly the case, these matters are settled by managements who are not primarily shareholders, there is also a tendency to under-declare, since a conservative policy provides a marvellous margin for subsequent inefficiency. A manager who keeps a wide margin, especially if it is a concealed margin, is in a far better position for covering up subsequent inefficiency than if such inefficiency has to be reflected in a reduction of dividends.

In the United States this bias has now reached quite extravagant lengths. The New Dealers have tried to devise all sorts of ways of encouraging *larger* declaration of dividends. And as soon as one moves into the period when more purchasing power is advisable, one can see, as has happened in the United States, what a potent influence towards over-saving under-declaration of dividends can prove.[13]

In other words, incentive and efficiency might be created by means of an active external capital market stimulating change and creating new, dynamic enterprises.

Certainly, attitudes within the Labour party to private profits and incentives were somewhat confused. As Whiting remarks, the attack on inherited wealth and on unearned income through death duties and a higher rate of income tax 'sanitised business profits' which were not a matter for concern until transformed into passive, *rentier* capital. However, the issue was somewhat more complicated than he allows: did business profits paid in dividends constitute a morally justified earned reward for dynamism, or a morally suspect unearned income and socially created wealth? In the nineteenth and early twentieth centuries, advocates of differential taxation of income defined dividends from shares as *unearned* income liable to a higher rate of tax. Their logic was that whilst shares were susceptible to risk, they did not involve personal decision making and management, unlike partners in a private firm. A higher tax on distributions in the differential profits tax was therefore compatible with higher taxation of dividends in the differential income tax. But there was also a difference from earlier assumptions. In the nineteenth century, advocates of differential taxation of income wished to encourage competitive private firms in comparison with large-scale corporate firms which might behave in an irresponsible manner. By contrast, Dalton's differential profits tax assumed that large, corporate concerns were *more* responsible.

[13] PRO, T171/388, 'The dividend policy of companies', Keynes, 31 Mar. 1946. Keynes pointed out (T161/1137, 'Industrial enterprise and employment and the tax system', 16 Dec. 1943) that the American tax system partially exempted profits put to reserve, and led to hoarding rather than their use in the business. On the debate over taxation of undistributed profits in the United States in the 1920s and 1930s, see W. E. Brownlee, 'Tax regimes, national crisis, and state building in America', in Brownlee (ed.), *Funding the Modern American State*, pp. 67, 79–80, 82–3.

Not everyone in the Labour party agreed with Dalton's strategy. The left saw large concerns as a source of monopoly capital and exploitation to be swept aside in the creation of a socialist economy. Others feared that retentions would blunt the efficiency of private enterprise. Even the advocates of differential taxation of profits had a nagging doubt about its effectiveness in creating equality and efficiency. Might retained or 'frozen' profits increase the earning power of the company and its capacity to pay dividends? Might retentions simply increase the value of shares and hence of the capital assets of the rich? Although Jenkins claimed that frozen profits were irrelevant, he also realised that retentions might 'lead to greater inequality not of income today but of property in the future'. The policy might simply create equality of income at the expense of inequality of capital. Others expressed reservations about the attack on profits. In 1951, Gaitskell commented that 'There are some who disapprove of profits in principle. I do not share their view. In an economy three quarters of which is run by private enterprise, it is foolish to ignore the function of profits as an incentive.' The TUC also expressed doubts whether retentions led to efficiency, for much depended on whether the retained profits were invested in plant and machinery, and the extent to which the firm relied on borrowed capital. The TUC favoured more generous depreciation allowances on *actual* investment, yet remained cautious about any increase in profits. As the TUC realised in 1948, 'if wage demands are not to be stimulated not only should prices be limited, but private *profits* should not be excessive'. Perhaps it is not surprising that Anthony Crosland* complained in 1956 that failure to agree a coherent policy on profit taxation was 'the central economic dilemma facing contemporary social democracy'. Differences over the moral and social desirability of private profit and ownership exploded in the debate over clause IV at the Labour party's conference in 1959, where Gaitskell's attempts to move away from a commitment to public ownership were defeated.[14]

[14] Francis, 'Labour policies and socialist ideas', chapter 6, pp. 221–32; Whiting, 'Taxation policy', pp. 120–39; Gaitskell in *Parliamentary Debates*, 5th ser. 486, 10 Apr. 1951, col. 854; Crosland, *Future of Socialism*, p. 415; Jenkins, 'The investment programme', 177; D. Seers, 'Undistributed profits', *Socialist Commentary*, 15 July 1951, 152; Jenkins, *Report of the 48th Annual Conference of the Labour Party, 1949* (London, 1949), p. 143. On the TUC, MRC, MSS TUC 292/401.2/1, report of meeting with the chancellor of the Exchequer, 2 Nov. 1945; TUC: considerations affecting the 1947 budget, 7 Feb. 1947; TUC: notes on the 1947 budget, 10 May 1947; TUC: brief note on the budget, 22 Apr. 1948.

* Charles Anthony Raven Crosland (1918–77) was the son of a senior civil servant and lecturer in Old French; the family were Plymouth Brethren and he remained something of a puritan with a strain of self-indulgence. He was educated at Highgate School and Trinity College, Oxford; after war service, he was a lecturer in economics at Oxford from 1947 to 1950, when he was elected to the Commons. He lost his seat between

Many economic historians now argue that the poor performance of British industry after the war was in part the result of limiting competition which harmed efficiency. The government felt that it should work with unions and organised industry in controlling inflation, which made it difficult to reform the structure of industrial relations. Further, about 60 per cent of manufacturing output was covered by some form of agreement on prices, and there was strong opposition from both industry and unions to anti-trust policies. An alternative approach was problematic, for liberalisation would imply an increase in prices, a balance of payments crisis, depreciation of the pound and labour unrest. Indeed, in the short term the policy controlled inflation – at the cost of locking the economy into an institutional and policy structure which inhibited productivity growth.[15] Certainly, the FBI argued that high taxation blunted the expectations of businessmen and their capacity to invest, and that conditions had changed since the Colwyn Committee on the National Debt and Taxation reported that industry alone had the capacity to bear taxation.[16] The problem was in deciding how exactly to respond to Labour's policy, and in the event they concentrated on narrower, technical problems than a major reduction in the tax burden on industry. In the event, they went along with differential taxation of profits as part of the agreement with the government and unions.

During the war, the FBI pressed for two changes in the tax system: relief on undistributed profits; and more generous treatment of depreciation so that plant could be written off more quickly. These proposals

1955 and 1959. He wrote *The Future of Socialism* (1956) which assumed the triumph of Keynesianism and economic growth; he argued for social equality and liberty in an affluent society, based on a greater enjoyment of pleasures and an end of class barriers. He supported Gaitskell in his battles over clause IV. In the government of 1964–70, he served in the Department of Economic Affairs, and as secretary of state for education and science, president of the Board of Trade and secretary of state for local government. After 1970, he pressed for a reconsideration of policy, and published his thoughts in *Socialism Now* (1974). He was secretary of state for the environment 1974–6 and foreign secretary 1976–7. (*DNB, 1971–80*, ed. Blake and Nicholls, pp. 193–5.)

[15] S. N. Broadberry and N. F. R. Crafts, 'British economic policy and industrial performance in the early post-war period', *Business History* 38 (1996), 65–91; J. Tomlinson and N. Tiratsoo, '"An old story, freshly told?" A comment on Broadberry and Crafts' approach to Britain's early post-war economic performance', *Business History* 40 (1998), 62–72; and S. N. Broadberry and N. F. R. Crafts, 'The post-war settlement: not such a good bargain after all', *Business History* 40 (1998), 73–9.

[16] MRC, FBI MSS 200/F/3/E5/6/4, inflation and capital for industry: report and recommendations of the Home Economic Committee to the Grand Council; capital requirements: effects of inflation and heavy taxation, 29 Oct. 1948; FBI MSS 200/F/3/E5/6/5, taxation and capital requirements, C. D. Hellyar, 4 Aug. 1948; 'Report of Costs and Taxation Panel', 21 Apr. 1950.

were considered by a committee of the Inland Revenue, which (again) rejected relief on retained profits on the grounds that the principle could be extended to *any* form of savings out of income, and that it would not help firms which were not making a profit. The committee argued that the aim was to encourage reconstruction of industry rather than saving, so that it made more sense to give relief to actual expenditure on new plant and machinery. As the Board of Trade remarked, the American tax code wrote off plant and machinery in half the time allowed in Britain, where there was accordingly a temptation to keep obsolescent plant in operation. In addition to more generous depreciation allowances, the Inland Revenue proposed an 'initial allowance' on actual investment in new plant and machinery to encourage re-equipment. Industries could set a larger part of the cost of buildings, plant and machinery against tax at the time the investment was made, rather than depreciating it over a longer period; in effect, it was an interest free loan. The cost of these concessions would be considerable, amounting to the equivalent of 6d in the £ off the income tax. The initial allowances were indeed introduced in 1945, at 20 per cent, and increased in 1949 to 40 per cent – and were to be complemented by differential taxation in favour of retained profits.[17]

In 1945, the FBI proposed some general principles for postwar taxation. It accepted that taxes would need to remain at a high level in order to remove surplus spending, and tax cuts would only be possible as consumer goods became available. Within this general constraint, the FBI argued that the general principle in shaping the tax system should be

the encouragement of production. Those taxes which most discourage work and enterprise should be discarded first, those which increase costs of production and the cost of living should go next, and the last reductions should be in those taxes which are selected to be retained as the main sources of permanent revenue because they least impede the productivity of the nation.

The FBI was reconciled to high levels of state expenditure and even accepted that it might contribute to efficiency. However, the FBI opposed the use of taxes to redistribute wealth or to influence economic development, for 'it can only repress to a greater or less degree but it can never activate'. Above all, 'taxation can best be adapted to conscious planning

[17] PRO, T171/367, R. V. N. Hopkins to chancellor, 10 Feb. 1944; G. L. Wilkinson to C. J. Gregg, 1 Apr. 1944; Gregg to Padmore, 10 Mar. 1944 and 4 Apr. 1944; report of Committee of Enquiry to the Board of Inland Revenue, 9 Mar. 1944; Inland Revenue, 'Postwar industrial taxation: note on the amount of income tax involved', S. P. Chambers, 17 Apr. 1944. The initial allowances were introduced in the Income Tax Act, 1945: for details, see PP 1950–1 xx, *Report of the Committee on the Taxation of Trading Profits*, p. 41.

for prosperity by lifting it from the actual production of wealth wherever possible, and placing the main burden at the point where income enters into consumption after it has been produced'. Consequently, the FBI argued for reliance on income tax on the grounds that it reflected the ability of individuals to pay, as well as committing the state to growth of the national income which affected the yield of the tax.[18]

Nevertheless, the FBI realised that, unlike after the First World War, abolition of taxation of profits was not feasible. Although industrialists resented being selected for higher taxation, and some called for cuts in social services and food subsidies, the leading figures in the representative organisations were more politically astute. In many cases, they had worked with civil servants and politicians during the war, and they realised that policy options were limited by the need to contain inflation and maintain wage restraint. They accepted that it was more sensible to accept the profits tax, which was in reality much less onerous than appeared at first sight, for payments of the profits tax were set against income tax. As *The Accountant* pointed out in 1949 when the profits tax was again raised, it was a political gesture 'simply to induce the mass of the workers to refrain from making higher wage claims'. The profits tax therefore struck a balance between the need to show equity and justice, while preserving business incentives.[19]

Rather than pressing for repeal of taxation of profits, the FBI stressed the need to restore incentives for wage-earners to work overtime and for salaried staff to assume additional responsibilities:

The wage earner feels that the net reward for his last unit of effort is so much smaller than for those that went before that it is not worth while to make that effort. It is true that the lack of goods on which to spend money is one of the causes of unwillingness to earn more, but that in turn can only be cured by greater production. It is therefore necessary to devise means for sharpening incentives.

The FBI therefore proposed a reduction in the standard rate of income tax (which would benefit companies as well as individuals) and an increase in personal allowances to remove as many as possible from liability.[20] Of course, this demand for reductions in the income tax limited the FBI's ability to argue for a reduction in the profits tax and it was more inclined to accept a lower rate on retentions, which it had itself advocated during the war. Many businesses were concerned by the low level of postwar reserves, at a time when high personal taxation reduced external sources

---

[18] MRC, FBI MSS 200/F/3/S1/16/23, 'Notes on taxation in relation to post-war planning', 3 July 1945.
[19] *The Accountant*, 8 Oct. 1949, cited in Whiting, 'Taxation policy', p. 131.
[20] MRC, FBI MSS 200/F/3/D2/1/23, taxation 1947/8: policy, 3 Dec. 1946.

of funds from private savings. Although the FBI was concerned by 1950 that the level of distributions was penalising 'venture capital', and argued that savings should be encouraged by a decent return for risk, at the same time it accepted that industry would rely more on its own retained profits. It was difficult to break free from the existing system to argue for an end to differential taxation, when retained profits seemed so important.[21]

By pressing for lower taxation of reserves, industrialists effectively surrendered the case for repealing profits taxation, and Labour could argue that differentiation between distributions and retentions took account of industrial needs. Instead, industry turned to two narrower, technical issues which became matters of accounting practice rather than a more politically contentious claim for relief from taxation. One was to bring the definition of income in tax law into line with business practice; the other was to take account of changing price levels. Industrialists were fully aware that any success in reducing their tax burden rested on their ability 'to locate relief in that part of the tax system which had not been politicised by the policy of wage restraint'.[22] As Frank Bower* of Unilever argued,

If industry went forward with a plain plea for the reduction of taxation on the grounds that it could not stand the present level and if the Government agreed, the TUC would immediately feel free to advance claims for higher wages. The argument in favour of inflation allowances provided a method of getting a reduction of taxation which would not start a new wave of wage demands. It was an argument which the TUC could accept without appearing to have conceded relief of taxation.[23]

The case was the best industry could devise in the circumstances – and it did not entirely work. After all, it could be claimed that industry was also *gaining* from inflation, for machinery and plant bought at lower prices in the past were now making high profits.[24] Industrialists also found it difficult to reach agreement on highly technical accounting principles,

---

[21] Whiting, 'Taxation policy', p. 126; MRC, FBI MSS 200/F/3/E5/6/4, 'The profits tax: the incidence of tax on ordinary shareholders; capital requirements: effects of inflation and heavy taxation', C. D. Hellyar, 29 Oct. 1948.

[22] Whiting, 'Taxation policy', p. 127.

[23] MRC, FBI MSS 200/F/3/E5/6/4, Taxation Committee minutes, 8 Nov. 1948. The issues of taxation and profits were considered in PP 1950–1 xx, *Report of the Committee on the Taxation of Trading Profits*.

[24] T. Barna, 'Those "frightfully high profits"', *Oxford Bulletin of Statistics* 11 (1949); also N. Kaldor, *An Expenditure Tax* (London, 1955), pp. 154, 156.

* Frank Bower (1894–1982) was educated at Lancaster Royal Grammar School and St Catharine's College, Cambridge. He became an inspector of taxes from 1920 to 1924, before joining Unilever as taxation officer from 1924 to 1959. (*Who Was Who*, vol. VIII: *1981–90* (London, 1991), p. 82.)

and the Inland Revenue stressed the administrative problems of valuing plant and machinery every year. Instead, officials in the revenue departments suggested that industrialists' complaints could be met by a simpler expedient of increasing the 'initial allowance' for new plant and machinery, in order to encourage re-equipment and efficiency.[25]

Far from declining, the taxation of profits increased over the period of the Labour government. Cripps increased the rate of tax on distributions to 30 per cent in 1949, on the grounds that profits were 'frightfully high'. This claim was supported by estimates that the profits of private enterprise in 1948 were two and a half times as high as in 1938 – a somewhat doubtful proposition when the impact of inflation and taxation is taken into account.[26] But the need to hold down dividends was crucial to attempts to control inflation and to secure wage restraint. Indeed, the government became more dependent on taxation as time passed. The removal of physical controls meant that more emphasis was placed on taxes, which were expected to meet the competing needs of economic management, equity and efficiency. The pressures of rearmament for the Korean war created further difficulties. One response was a renewed interest in taxation of capital; another was Nicholas Kaldor's proposal to move from a negative and temporary policy of freezing wages and dividends to a more sophisticated and flexible system – or to his critics, an unrealistically complex and overly ambitious scheme. His proposal was designed both to give an incentive to efficient firms and to satisfy the TUC. Wage claims would be considered by a Wages Board, and dividends would be set by the current average rate of distribution. Firms below the standard level of distribution had an incentive to increase their dividends to the permitted level – and as they increased their distribution, the standard would rise as the economy prospered. Kaldor was well aware that his proposals contradicted the Treasury's and Inland Revenue's long-established principles of even-handedness and equity, and used the tax system to shape the internal affairs of companies. He argued that such a change in emphasis was desirable. 'The social justification of dividend payments is as a reward for risk-bearing; it is the essence of this reward that it should

[25] MRC, FBI MSS 200/F/3/E5/6/4, 'Inflation – finance for industry'; 'Inflation and capital for industry: report and recommendations of the Home Economic Policy Committee to the General Council'; 'The depreciation of fixed assets by reference to increased replacement costs: the case for recognition for tax purposes'; 'Capital requirements: effect of inflation and heavy taxation', 29 Oct. 1948; FBI MSS 200/F/3/E5/6/5, discussion on Taxation Panel. PRO, T171/398, PB(48)13, depreciation allowances and replacement of plant, Inland Revenue, 7 Oct. 1948; PB(48)15, depreciation of plant: special replacement allowance, 1 Nov. 1948; BC(49)9, depreciation allowances and replacement of plant: note by Sir John Woods, Board of Trade, 14 Jan. 1949.

[26] Francis, 'Labour policies and socialist ideas', p. 224; Barna, 'Those "frightfully high profits"', 219.

be apportioned by the criteria of success, rather than by some criteria of "fairness" or "equity".' The Treasury and Inland Revenue were not convinced, arguing that any benefits would be offset by further rigidities as a result of perpetuating the existing pattern of dividend distribution. The new chancellor, Hugh Gaitskell, complained that the scathing criticism of officials crossed the line into political advocacy. In the event, he opted for a further increase in the profits tax on distributions to 50 per cent in 1951, and he proposed a statutory limitation of dividends which was not implemented before the government lost power.[27] Despite Gaitskell's claim that profits were a justified reward, the Labour government left office with a high level of profits taxation.

Profits taxation was part of a strategy designed to tackle the major issue at the end of the war: the reduction of consumer demand at home in order to prevent inflation and to ensure that production was concentrated on exports. But there was a danger that taxation of profits and high levels of income tax would be counter-productive through a loss of incentive, with harmful effects for productivity and competitiveness. High taxes might reduce savings, or even lead to 'dissaving' through spending out of capital. How could the government reconcile the need to hold down domestic consumption with its desire to increase production and encourage efficiency and growth? And how could these ambitions be reconciled with the use of taxation to create a fairer, more equitable society? A major element in the ideology of the Labour government was an ethical commitment to a reduction of 'morally unjust' inequalities in the distribution of income and wealth. Further, equality was defended on grounds that it would remove 'over-saving', class envy and social waste, and so stimulate economic efficiency.[28] Redistribution of income and wealth ended

[27] PRO, T171/403, 'A positive policy for wages and dividends', N. Kaldor, 21 June 1950; BC(51)21, Budget Committee, dividend limitation, 5 Feb. 1951; 'Dividend limitation and the profits tax', E. E. Bridges, 12 Jan. 1951; dividend limitation, D. Jay, 7 Nov. 1950; BC(50) 6th meeting, Budget Committee, 17 Oct. 1950; chancellor to Bridges; budget prospects: note by chairman of the Budget Committee, E. E. Bridges, 27 Nov. 1950; BC(51) 2nd meeting, 12 Jan. 1951; BC(51) 5th meeting, 6 Feb. 1951; the general budgetary problem, 1951: note by the chairman of the Budget Committee, covering note to BC(51)16 second revise on general budgetary problem in 1951; BC(51) 7th meeting, minutes of meeting held at Roffey Park, 17 and 18 Feb. 1951; BC(50)22, Budget Committee, limitation of dividends, 26 Oct. 1950 with note by Gaitskell; T171/417, BC(50) 5th meeting, 27 Sept. 1950. PRO, T171/424, dividend limitation, n.d.; E. E. Bridges, 14 July 1951.

[28] Labour party, *Labour Believes in Britain: A Statement of Policy* (London, 1949), p. 3; Francis, 'Labour policies and socialist ideas', chapter 6; Ellison, *Egalitarian Thought*, refers to three 'visions' of equality: technocratic socialists were concerned with equality and public ownership as a means towards productive efficiency; Keynesian socialists favoured redistribution and social equality over public ownership; and qualitative socialists sought 'fellowship' or fraternity (pp. ix–x). For a discussion of the interplay between these visions from the 1930s to the end of the Attlee government, see chapters 1 and 2.

the curse of unemployment; the unresolved problem was how to reconcile equality with the control of inflation and the encouragement of a
productive, dynamic economy. Would redistribution increase the level of
consumption by lower incomes and reduce over-saving and accumulation
by the better-off? Or would it blunt incentives for risk-taking and enterprise? In the opinion of Martin Francis, these debates raised questions
about the traditional ideology of the Labour party, which had 'ultimately
failed to devise any coherent answers, let alone any effective alternative
strategies'. There was continued tension between the need to preserve
profits in order to provide an incentive for entrepreneurs, and the desire
to prevent accumulations of socially created wealth. Francis argues that
Labour politicians failed to agree over the best approach, so that 'Labour
left office without finding a means to resolve the dilemma that while the
limits of income re-distribution had been reached, vast inequalities of
wealth still remained in Britain.'[29] Perhaps the answer would be found in
the taxation of capital.

Capital taxation

Capital taxation offered an alternative means of controlling consumption
and creating equality or opportunity. As Roy Jenkins pointed out, the government had made a great advance towards equality of income, and little
more could be achieved. However, the trend to equality might be stopped
or even reversed unless there was an onslaught on inequality of *property*
where 'we have hardly yet scratched the surface'. Jenkins stressed the
need for equality – but taxation of capital could also create opportunity,
by taxing existing accumulations of capital and encouraging higher risk.
The tax fell on capital values and not on the flow of income so that there
was every reason to maximise the income by shifting from safe, cautious
investments. Thus plant valued at £500,000 in a low-risk trade might
produce a profit of £25,000, and would pay the same capital tax as in a
new, high-risk trade where it produced a profit of £50,000; by contrast,
a profits tax fell more heavily on the high-risk trade and acted as a disincentive. Taxation of capital had different motivations, and could take
different forms. The first type of tax was the long-established method of a
duty on estates at death. The second was an annual capital or wealth tax
at a modest rate on all holdings of capital. The third was a capital gains

[29] On discussion of dividend limitation, see PRO, T171/403, Budget Committee, 17 Oct.
1950, 12 Jan. 1951; 'Dividend limitation', D. Jay, 7 Nov. 1950; 'Dividend limitation and
the profits tax', E. E. Bridges, 12 Jan. 1951; BC(50)22, Budget Committee, limitation
of dividends, 26 Oct. 1950, and marginal comment by Gaitskell; BC(51)21, Budget
Committee, dividend limitation, 5 Feb. 1951; 'A positive policy for wages and dividends',
N. Kaldor, 21 June 1950; Francis, 'Labour policies and socialist ideas', pp. 255–6.

tax on the increased value of an asset at the time of its realisation. The fourth was the old nostrum of a capital levy, a one-off tax at a high rate on all assets. Although capital taxation attracted increasing attention, there was disagreement over the form it should take, and very little progress up to 1945.

Death duties were the traditional answer favoured by Dalton. In 1946, he adjusted the death duties by exempting smaller estates and reducing the rate on estates up to £7,500. He then increased the rate on estates over £21,500 to a maximum of 75 per cent, which was raised to 80 per cent in 1950. The problem with taxation of inheritances was that it would be slow, and could be avoided by gifts during life.[30] Dalton also claimed that low interest rates offered a simpler way of reducing the income of large *rentiers*, as well as holding down the costs of servicing the national debt and stimulating investment by industrialists.[31] There seemed to be little more scope for squeezing large fortunes through the death duty.

The case for an annual tax on capital was made by Keynes and Meade, who argued that it was preferable to a profits tax. They felt that it was more equitable to assess an individual's tax liability on the basis of both the ownership of capital *and* the flow of income. Further, a tax on the underlying asset would encourage more risky investments with higher yields, and lead to greater dynamism.[32] What was involved, in other words, were two different visions of the British economy. Dalton looked to internal investment by responsible managers, concerned for efficiency and long-term growth; Keynes argued in favour of risk and enterprise, with a greater reliance on the distribution of profits. Indeed, a wealth tax was to play a central role in the 'tax package' devised by the Conservatives in opposition between 1964 and 1970, as part of its attempt to create a more dynamic society based on opportunity and incentives.

Although some Labour politicians did support a capital tax after the war, it was not central to debates within the government. There was more discussion of a capital gains tax, again without any practical outcome. In

---

[30] Whiting, 'Taxation policy', p. 119; Francis, 'Labour policies and socialist ideas', p. 244; M. Francis, 'Economics and ethics: the nature of Labour's socialism, 1945–51', *Twentieth Century British History* 6 (1995), 227–8.

[31] Francis, 'Labour policies and socialist ideas', pp. 244–7. On cheap money, see S. Howson, 'The origins of cheaper money, 1945–7', *Economic History Review* 40 (1987), 433–52, and C. M. Kennedy, 'Monetary policy', in G. D. N. Worswick and P. H. Ady (eds.), *The British Economy, 1945–1950* (London, 1952), pp. 188–207.

[32] J. M. Keynes, *The Collected Writings of John Maynard Keynes*, vol. XXVII: *Activities 1940–46: Shaping the Post-War World: Employment and Commodities* (London, 1980), J. E. Meade to J. M. Keynes, 25 June 1942, p. 214; PRO, T230/94, Keynes to Meade, 28 July 1944; PRO, T230/94, National Debt Enquiry, first meeting, 19 Feb. 1945; T171/389, note by Mr Meade, 25 Apr. 1946. Note also that Douglas Jay favoured an annual capital tax as a way of preventing a large war-time debt and to reduce their claims on the community's future income: see Jay, *Paying for the War*, pp. 10–11.

the British tax code, income was defined as annually recurring so that a one-off gain from the sale of an asset was tax free. After the Second World War, high levels of tax on income flows created an incentive to take gains through appreciation of the value of shares, which was untaxed at the point of realisation. In other words, generous retention of profit might increase the value of shares, and so provide a means of tax avoidance and the accumulation of private fortunes through untaxed capital apprecia-tions rather than taxed incomes. As a result, some economists realised that high levels of income tax and differential taxation of profits created a need for a capital gains tax. Even before the introduction of differentiation, H. D. Henderson noted that war taxation created a new phenomenon, of rich individuals living on their capital so that 'the suppposedly sharp and clear-cut distinction betwen capital and income, upon which so many of our economic generalisations rest, is becoming blurred'. And after the war, John Hicks pointed out that taxation restricted spending out of income, but did nothing to limit spending out of capital.[33]

A capital gains tax had some support within the Labour party and TUC in order to 'increase the measure of justice afforded to workers as against property owners as a whole'. The appeal was both emotional and pragmatic. In the words of R. H. Tawney, 'the immunity from taxation which . . . such speculative plunder continues to enjoy has as much jus-tification as a close season for sharks'. More practically, high levels of taxation might fail to reduce consumption and merely lead to low levels of saving or even encourage 'dissaving' by the rich who maintained their spending out of capital. As Attlee remarked,

We have, I think, always recognised that restrictions on purchasing power by a high rate of taxation was [sic] to some extent nullified by the use of savings for current ex-penditure on consumption goods. It is, for instance, not possible for some sections of the community to maintain their high standard of expenditure out of income. In fact they do so by drawing on their capital resources. It seems to me, therefore, that to some extent our present policy affects not the total purchasing power, but its distribution. The very wealthy section living on capital take up the demand which would otherwise come from a less wealthy section who live on income.

However, a capital gains tax did not offer a solution to the much greater need, as many members of the party saw it, to alter the existing distri-bution of wealth. As Roy Jenkins pointed out, the capital gains tax in the United States had not produced a more socialistic distribution of

---

[33] PRO, T161/1137, H. D. Henderson, 'Cheap money, trade activity and inflation', 20 Oct. 1943; J. R. Hicks, 'The empty economy', *Lloyds Bank Review* n.s. 5 (1947), 9. On the definition of income, see Daunton, *Trusting Leviathan*, pp. 204–10. In the United States, capital gains *were* defined as income, a point which was sometimes made by British advocates of the tax: see W. W. Brudno and L. D. Hollman, 'The taxation of capital gains in the United States and the United Kingdom', *British Tax Review* (1958), 26–48.

property. Indeed, the tax would hit active producers at the expense of passive capital. 'If our object is to promote as much equality as is compatible with the maintenance of reasonable incentive', remarked Jenkins, 'a capital gains tax is indeed the least desirable of all forms of attack upon property.'[34]

The Inland Revenue also stressed the administrative problems of a capital gains tax, which they claimed would bring the whole tax system into disrepute – a common trope in opposing any new tax. The Inland Revenue argued that a capital gains tax was only feasible where taxpayers made a voluntary statement of liability, which was consistent with the American system of self-assessment monitored by spot checks to keep evasion within limits. By contrast, the Inland Revenue informed British taxpayers exactly how much was owed, and 'it was contrary to previous practice to impose a tax the yield of which depended on how much the taxpayers concerned wanted to offer'. The Inland Revenue feared that the yield of the tax would be 'very capricious', the legislation highly contentious, the administrative strain immense and the taxpayers' resentment formidable. As the Inland Revenue argued, a capital gains tax 'would have to be regarded as a "luxury" rather than as an important source of revenue', and the effort would be better expended in improving the collection of existing taxes.[35]

Eventually, the Conservatives introduced a tax on short-term or speculative capital gains in the take-over and property booms of the early 1960s, and Labour introduced a tax on all capital gains in 1965. The Labour government of 1945–51 did not pursue the idea and returned, atavistically, to a capital levy. The case was not financial, for the costs of debt service were much lower than after the First World War. Rather, the levy offered two benefits. The first was as a means of creating equality, which was stressed by Jenkins. He argued that 'the present distribution of property is not only unfair as between rich and poor; when combined with the present rate of surtax, it is also unfair as between the rich man who gets his income from work and the rich man who gets it from a store of wealth'. Inequality of property had become an obstacle to redistribution,

---

[34] Hicks, 'Empty economy'; PRO, T171/400, memorandum, Addison to Cripps on budget proposals, 10 Mar. 1950; Attlee to Cripps, 11 Mar. 1950; Whiting, 'Taxation policy', pp. 129–30, and Francis, 'Labour policies and socialist ideas', pp. 249–51; R. H. Tawney, *Equality* (London, 1952 edn), p. 243; R. Jenkins, *Fair Shares for the Rich* (Tribune pamphlet, London, 1951), pp. 9–16.

[35] PRO, T171/391, BC(47)5, note by the Board of Inland Revenue covering memoranda on the profits tax and on the question of the taxation of gifts and capital gains; 'Taxation of capital gains in the United States'; 'Note by Board of Inland Revenue: taxation of capital gains', 1 Nov. 1946; T171/400, BC(50)2, 'Taxation of capital gains', Inland Revenue, 12 Jan. 1950; BC(50)2 revise, 'Taxation of capital gains', Inland Revenue, 27 Jan. 1950; T171/403, Budget Committee, minutes of meeting at Roffey Park, 17 and 18 Feb. 1951.

and death duties would take a long time to have any impact – and were easily avoided. Jenkins therefore turned to the capital levy to curb spending by the wealthy and to encourage equality.[36] The second benefit was control of what Hicks called 'suppressed inflation'. The problem, as he saw it, was that the economy was 'empty': goods were in short supply and controls prevented prices from rising. The removal of controls would cause serious inflation, and an increase in taxation would simply reduce savings or stimulate 'dissavings' from capital. A capital levy could remove suppressed inflation, preventing consumption out of capital and above all encouraging unions to accept a wage freeze and higher indirect taxes.

Inflationary pressure mounted in 1948 and created considerable problems for Stafford Cripps. Attention turned to the capital levy as an anti-inflationary device to reduce cash balances and as a political counterpoint to the wage freeze, possibly linked with control of dividends and a capital gains tax.[37] Cripps was wary: a levy would entail a valuation of capital; and control of dividends implied a contentious decision on the 'fair' level of profit. As he now accepted, private enterprise would continue to exist. Consequently, it was necessary to reward efficiency with higher profits and to give management freedom in allocating the gains from efficiency to wages or profits. He therefore argued that price controls were preferable, for they were more compatible with 'traditional methods of private enterprise finance' than were limits to profits. Cripps's policy rested on an attempt to combine incentives with controls on inflation. Incentives would be offered to lower incomes by applying the reduced rate of income tax to more taxpayers. Spending power would then be removed by an increase in indirect taxes, balanced by a 'special contribution' from investment incomes – an emergency '"once for all" levy'. Cripps's aim was to offer incentives to wage-earners without damaging business confidence, to remove inflation from the economy without destroying the profit

---

[36] Jenkins, *Fair Shares for the Rich*, pp. 9–16. Jenkins hoped that the levy would remove the 'last traces of Whiggery' and the power of great magnates; a powerful central state had been constructed to control them, and could not be replaced by a more decentralised system of municipalities and co-operatives. Jenkins was linking the capital levy with the arguments of Michael Young for a less intrusive state: see M. Young, *Small Man: Big World: A Discussion of Socialist Democracy* (London, 1949).

[37] Hicks, 'Empty economy', 2–13; PRO, T171/395, the capital levy, 15 June 1945; BC(48)7 revise, note on capital levy; BC(48)11, a capital levy and deflation: note by the director of the Economic Section; BC(48)13, note on a capital levy, 14 Jan. 1948; BC(48)17, Budget Committee: special contribution payable by surtax payers, C. J. G., 23 Jan. 1948; BC(48)13, note on capital levy, 14 Jan. 1948; BC(48)20 final, proposals for a special levy, 5 Feb. 1948; BC(48)22, Budget Committee: special contribution charged on investment income, C. J. G., 2 Feb. 1948; BC(48)35, Budget Committee: special levy, 2 Mar. 1948. Dividend limitation was also discussed by Dalton in 1947, but not proceeded with in the autumn budget: T171/389, Inland Revenue: limitation of dividends, 20 Sept. 1947; limitation of dividends, n.d., and marginal comment by H. Dalton, 10 Dec. 1947.

mechanism essential for the survival of a free market. It was an attempt to combine efficiency and equality in a particular way – not by means of tax breaks to higher incomes or reductions in the taxation of profits, but by rewarding the efforts of the less affluent, within a free enterprise economy based on a sense of equity.[38] This shifts attention to another area of the Labour government's approach to taxation, on personal income and consumption.

Direct and indirect taxes

Inflation could be contained through direct controls, by rationing goods and subsidising basic necessities (especially food) in order to stabilise the cost of living and limit pressure for higher wages. Of course, subsidies might simply release consumer demand for other goods, and weaken the price mechanism in allocating resources. Consequently, economists such as Meade argued that subsidies should be cut, the price mechanism restored, and fiscal policy used to control demand. But Dalton was not convinced, arguing that subsidies offered a means of helping the poor, stabilising the cost of living and containing wage inflation. There was, therefore, continued reliance after the war on direct controls as one means of controlling inflation, with the danger that the economy would become inflexible. Dalton viewed fiscal policy as part of a 'supply-side' approach designed to stimulate production through the use of differential profits taxation, rather than as a tool of demand management.[39] Much the same may be said of the use of indirect taxes after the war.

[38] PRO, T171/394, BC(48)12, subsidies and prices: memorandum by the chancellor of the Exchequer, 13 Jan. 1948; T171/394, BC(48)23 final, special measures to counter inflationary pressure: memorandum by the Treasury, 5 Feb. 1948; T171/394, note on discussion at Roffey Park, 14 and 15 Feb. 1948, between chancellor and officials; why tax increases are necessary: note by R. Hall, 13 Mar. 1948; revised Chequers brief; T171/395, BC(48)13, 'Note on capital levy', 14 Jan. 1948; T171/395, BC(48)17, Budget Committee: special contribution payable by surtax payers, C. J. G., 23 Jan. 1948; BC(48)20 (final), proposals for a special levy, 5 Feb. 1948; BC(48)22, special contribution charged on investment income, C. J. G., 2 Feb. 1948; BC(48)35, Budget Committee: special levy, 2 Mar. 1948; T171/395, Plowden to Cripps, 31 Mar. 1948.

[39] Meade, *Planning and the Price Mechanism*, pp. 9–11, refers to the pricing system and money as 'among the greatest social inventions of mankind ... combining freedom, efficiency and equity in social affairs'; PRO, T171/389, post-budget reflections, Keynes; 'The economic crisis and the budget for 1947/8: note by J. E. Meade', and B. W. S. to Bridges, 14 March 1947; T171/391, BC(47)9, 'Stabilisation and the taxation of company profits: note by J. E. Meade; T171/392, Autumn budget, E. E. Bridges, 23 Sept. 1947; budget, 30 Sept. 1947: discussion between chancellor and officials; 'Budget and food subsidies', D. Jay, 10 Oct. 1947; E. E. Bridges to chancellor, 22 Oct. 1947; memorandum by H. Dalton, n.d.; memorandum on subsidies by E. E. Bridges, n.d.; T171/393, memorandum from Budget Committee to chancellor, 2 Sept. 1947; T171/394, Parliamentary Labour party, Finance Group: note of discussion on 11 Feb. 1948, and also minutes of meeting; BC(48)12, subsidies and prices: memorandum by the chancellor of the

Although Labour long opposed indirect taxation, it rose from about a third of revenue in 1945/6 to three-sevenths in 1949.[40] Indeed, Dalton argued that the income tax was 'more disliked, and is a greater discouragement to productive effort, than taxes on commodities'. He justified the change in the structure of the fiscal system by arguing that progressive direct taxes were no longer so necessary as a result of the reduction in inequality. As Roy Jenkins remarked in 1949, 'even the complete obliteration of all upper and upper-middle incomes would produce nothing sensational for the wage-earner'. Higher rates of progressive income tax, whatever their ethical attraction, simply would not produce enough revenue. Further, the increase in the number of taxpayers and in the rate of income tax meant that political sensitivity to direct taxes was now potentially as great as to indirect taxes. Accordingly, the Labour government opted to retain the purchase tax after the war. As the TUC argued, it was impossible to raise sufficient revenue for the government without a major contribution from indirect taxation. The emphasis should therefore shift from simple hostility to indirect taxes to ensuring that concessions in both indirect and direct taxes were 'justified on grounds on incentive' – a word open to various interpretations.[41]

The purchase tax was compatible with the government's emphasis on the supply side and the desire to contain consumption through direct controls. It could be used to extract spending power, and at the same time provide a device for planning the economy through variation in rates on different goods. Punitive rates of tax were imposed on luxuries, lower rates on necessities and 'utility' goods were exempted. The purchase tax was expected to fulfil two, potentially contradictory, tasks: on the one hand, controlling domestic consumption and encouraging exports; and on the other hand securing revenue for the government. These two purposes required different forms of tax. The attempt to shape domestic consumption suggested high rates on particular classes of goods, with

Exchequer, 13 Jan. 1948; T171/403, minutes of meeting held at Roffey Park, 17 and 18 Feb. 1951; J. Tomlinson, *Democratic Socialism and Economic Policy: The Attlee Years, 1945–51* (Cambridge, 1997), pp. 214–15, 217–20; H. Dalton, *Parliamentary Debates,* 5th ser. 414, 23 Oct. 1945, cols. 1878–80.

[40] D. Bruce, 'A review of socialist financial policy, 1945–49', *Political Quarterly* 20 (1949), 315.

[41] Dalton's lecture to the Fabians on 13 Nov. 1946, quoted in Francis, 'Labour policies and socialist ideas', pp. 234–5; on the limited yield from higher levels of income tax, see pp. 240–1, citing Jenkins's comment to the 1949 conference on 'Problems ahead'; on the TUC, see MRC, TUC MSS 292/410.2/1, TUC Economic Committee: report of a meeting with the chancellor of the Exchequer, 24 July 1946; TUC MSS 292/410.2/1, TUC considerations affecting the 1949 budget, 24 Feb. 1949; TUC summary of the budget, Apr. 1949, 11 Apr. 1949; TUC the 1949 budget: report of a meeting between the Economic Committee with other members of the General Council with the chancellor of the Exchequer on 13 Apr. 1949.

lower rates or exemptions for others. But revenue would be most easily obtained by a standard, moderate tax on a wide range of goods, without seriously distorting consumption. After the war, the purchase tax followed the first pattern of widely divergent rates in order to shape the economy. The Board of Trade was sceptical, fearing that the purchase tax and 'utility' scheme were harming the export drive rather than releasing goods from the domestic market. Domestic consumers were encouraged to buy utility goods which were exempt from purchase tax, so that industry lost the ability to develop more expensive, high-quality goods suitable for export. The high level of purchase tax on some goods, and frequent changes in the rates and classification of goods, were criticised for distorting the economy. Consequently, some officials argued for a shift to the second form of tax, by introducing a general sales tax or at least widening the range of the purchase tax to produce a reasonable return at a more moderate rate. Of course, the problem was political: could the Labour government reduce the tax on luxuries and impose it on basic necessities? Even some industrialists had their doubts about a move to a general sales tax. The virtue of the purchase tax was that it did not fall particularly heavily on working-class families; by contrast, a wider retail tax would enter into the cost of living 'in a very direct and forcible manner' and so stimulate wage demands.[42]

The Labour government's reliance on profits taxes and purchase tax left the question of what to do with the income tax, which many industrialists and some Labour politicians felt was the greatest threat to incentives. Any concession to the income tax could take one of two forms, with different ideological assumptions and social implications. A reduction in the standard rate would benefit large incomes, unearned incomes, single people, childless couples and businesses; on the other hand, tax allowances could benefit smaller incomes, earned incomes and married people with children. The Inland Revenue favoured a reduction in the standard rate and surtax, on the grounds that larger incomes paid more during the war, and that distributive justice required concessions to them. Above all, the Revenue stressed the need for incentives to earned incomes

---

[42] PRO, T171/369, B(45)8, purchase tax policy: memorandum by the Board of Customs and Excise, 23 Jan. 1945; B(45)11 revise, Budget Committee, purchase tax, 10 Feb. 1945, and see annex D, L. C. Robbins to R. V. N. Hopkins, 8 Feb. 1945; T171/395, BC(48)19, purchase tax: review of schedules and rates, note by Customs and Excise; T171/398, PB(48)11, purchase tax: memorandum by the Board of Customs and Excise, Sept. 1948; T171/400, BC(50)7, purchase tax: joint note by Board of Trade and Customs, 7 Feb. 1950; C&E(50)1, purchase tax: Customs and Excise, 12 Feb. 1950. On the FBI, see MRC, FBI MSS 200/F/3/D2/1/23, Purchase Tax Committee, 2 Jan. 1945 and 12 Dec. 1946; FBI MSS 200/F/3/S1/16/25, 'Demobilisation of war taxes'; FBI MSS 200/F/3/D2/1/24, Purchase Tax Panel, 20 Jan. 1950; replacement of purchase tax by a sales tax; Purchase Tax Panel, 22 Mar. 1950.

of £5,000 to £10,000 from professional and commercial activities, both to stimulate economic recovery and to preserve compliance. The Inland Revenue argued that the differential between the earnings of a manager or technician and an unskilled worker was simply too small. The government was not convinced. Ernest Bevin and the TUC stressed the need for incentives further down the social scale, arguing that there was little point in a worker putting in extra effort, only to lose the additional income in taxation. Lower-middle earned incomes had deteriorated compared with unearned incomes during the war, and the TUC called for a restoration of the earned income allowance and the removal of as many workers as possible from the system of PAYE.[43]

In his first postwar budget, Dalton reduced the standard rate from 10s (50 per cent) to 9s (45 per cent), and he increased personal allowances and earned income relief. As a result, he took 2 to 2.5 million entirely out of the income tax, and reduced the burden on the remainder. At the same time, he retained the existing surtax on incomes up to £10,000 with a further increase on larger incomes. The line of graduation was steeper, and Dalton remarked that he had 'swung the curve round on a hinge' as part of his attempt to create economic and social equality.[44] The aim of the Attlee administration was to restore incentives by concessions to earned income and the lower level of earnings, rather than to larger incomes and profits. The standard rate was not changed for the remainder of the Labour government, and most concessions were directed to the reduced rates of tax and earned incomes.[45] As Cripps explained, concessions should be given mainly to earned incomes up to £2,000, 'because we were anxious to get in the technicians and scientists and people of that class who are quite important to production, to give them some encouragement as well as other people, and we did that quite consciously if it is an earned income'. Cripps realised that taxation could not equalise all incomes, but he did claim that 'we have telescoped the whole thing

[43] PRO, T230/282, E. M. Nicholson to lord president, profits and dividends, EPC (47)27, 4 Dec. 1947; T172/2029, Bevin to Dalton, 15 Oct. 1947; MRC, TUC MSS 292/410.2/1, report of a meeting with the chancellor of the Exchequer, 2 Nov. 1945.

[44] H. Dalton, 'Our financial plan', in H. Morrison et al., Forward from Victory! Labour's Plan (London, 1946), p. 48.

[45] PRO, T171/372, Hopkins to Gregg, 2 July 1945; 'Income tax allowances after abolition of the postwar credits'; [Gregg] to Hopkins, 4 July 1945; [Gregg?] to Bridges, 9 July 1945; Gregg to Hopkins, 9 July 1945; Gregg to Bridges, 21 July 1945; 'Income tax credits', J. E. Meade, 20 July 1945; Hopkins, 25 July 1945; B2(45)3, note by Gregg on income tax; note by Dalton, 9 Sept. 1945; 'Income tax', Gregg, 13 Sept. 1945; minute on budget, B. Trend, 17 Sept. 1945; Gregg to Trend, 29 Sept. 1945; T171/388, J. Simon, Royal Commission on Population, to chancellor, n.d.; Gregg to chancellor, 22 Jan. 1946; T171/389, 'The economic crisis and the budget for 1947/8: note by Mr Meade'; E. F. M. Durbin to Dalton, 21 Feb. 1947; G. Benson, chairman of Finance Group, to Dalton, 21 Feb. 1947; E. E. Bridges to chancellor, the budget.

tremendously' by reducing income differentials from about £100,000 to a maximum of £6,500.[46]

The strategy created problems. The failure to reduce the standard rate hit business which paid the tax on both distributed and undistributed profits. The middle class could claim that it was over-burdened, not just by high levels of taxation but also by the difficulties experienced by salaried staff. The Inland Revenue calculated that wages (after tax) rose in real terms by 21 per cent between 1938 and 1949, whereas salaries dropped by 16 per cent. The result, as one Labour MP remarked, was that middle incomes of £750 to £2,000 were badly affected:

the honest, capable, intelligent and hard-working professional men, technicians, managers, Civil Servants, Ministers of Religion, and the like, have to struggle to survive. Added to this they get little or no leisure to study . . . This state of things, if allowed to continue will destroy the backbone of the country.

As he informed Cripps, 'the middle class are being rapidly eliminated and I have never understood that to be any part of the Labour Party policy'.[47]

The political implications were obvious, and go some way towards explaining growing middle-class disenchantment with Labour. Certainly, there was concern amongst some Labour politicians that taxation was damaging both the economy and electoral support. Herbert Morrison feared that 'the incentive to effort for workers as well as professional and technical people and employers is seriously affected by this burden, which, in turn, reacts on our costs, and on our capacity to earn dollars. Sooner rather than later the taxpayer will rebel verbally and at the ballot box.'[48] Although the Royal Commission on the Taxation of Incomes and Profits found that income tax affected the actual productive behaviour of fewer than 5 per cent of its sample, it was widely considered to be a deterrent and a source of discontent.[49]

The limits of fiscal policy

Strains were appearing in Labour's fiscal policy, with a clear sense that the government had reached the limits of its fiscal strategy. By 1950, there was general acceptance both in the civil service and in the Labour

[46] MRC, TUC MSS 292/410.2/1, TUC note on the Apr. 1948 budget, 10 Apr. 1948; TUC brief note on the budget, 22 Apr. 1948; meeting between the chancellor of the Exchequer and the TUC, 22 Apr. 1948.

[47] PRO, T171/400, BC(50)5, taxation of the middle classes, Inland Revenue, 12 Jan. 1950; R. R. Stokes to S. Cripps, 28 Nov. 1949; *Times*, 29 Dec. 1949; T171/403, 'Memorandum on the plight of the middle classes', R. R. Stokes, 12 Oct. 1950.

[48] PRO, PREM8/1415, CP(49)159, 'The economic situation: memorandum by the lord president of the Council, H. Morrison', 21 July 1949.

[49] PP 1953/4 xx, *Royal Commission on the Taxation of Profits and Income, Second Report*, appendix 1, 'PAYE and incentives', pp. 291–324, at 292.

government that a long-term review of the tax system was needed to moderate the competing needs of social justice and equality on the one hand and efficiency and incentives on the other. Taxation of unearned income and inherited wealth, complemented by retentions within firms, were intended to create a dynamic and buoyant economy. In the opinion of the FBI, the result was very different: a 'lack of flexibility has become a chronic condition of the British economy'. The FBI complained that the 'vast and menacing' level of expenditure and taxation hindered the accumulation of capital, and removed incentives to work harder or to take risks on new enterprise. Controls over prices, profits and wages contained inflation, at the cost of using the market to attract more resources. As a result, the search for new markets, goods and techniques depended on existing large firms with accumulated reserves, and new firms were penalised by their need for external finance:

There is too much emphasis on safety and too little on enterprise. To remain vital, enterprise needs hope and imaginative vision. Our young men and women must be given an opportunity of recapturing that self-reliance and audacity that existed in the Elizabethan era, and to a lesser degree in the Victorian era. Adventure, even though linked with folly, is better than any amount of austerity unrelieved by hope.[50]

The problem, as expressed in a paper to the Budget Committee in 1950, was that reliance on the reserves of existing companies meant that 'new developments, fostered by private "risk-money" will be at a disadvantage, at a time when the balance of payments problem demands the maximum flexibility in the industrial structure'.[51] These concerns were shared by at least some economists associated with the Labour government. Kaldor was alarmed that 'the egalitarianism of the *status quo* will ossify the economic structure'. The limitation of dividends and high levels of profit tax were preventing change, and he characterised the government's policy as 'the Socialist version of Baldwinism' – of safety first.[52]

The issue was how to escape from 'safety first' in order to create a more dynamic and flexible economic system. Should the free market be embraced, or should the government develop a more discriminating means of encouraging growth? Labour's fiscal strategy and wider economic policy started to face criticism within the civil service as well as from the

[50] MRC, FBI MSS 200/F/3/E6/3/1, 'British industry and the crisis', R. G., 13 Dec. 1949.
[51] PRO, T171/400, BC(50)13, 'The 1950/1 budget', 16 Feb. 1950.
[52] Letter in the *Economist*, 5 Apr. 1947, p. 493, cited in Whiting, 'Taxation policy', p. 130; and N. Kaldor, 'A positive policy for wages and dividends', reprinted in N. Kaldor, *Essays in Economic Policy*, vol. I (London, 1964), p. 127. See also A. Rogow and P. Shore, *The Labour Government and British Industry* (Oxford, 1955), pp. 128–9.

Conservative opposition and industrialists. One of the leading critics was Paul Chambers,* formerly a senior official at the Inland Revenue who became chairman of ICI. He argued that too much reliance was placed on price controls and interest rates which could not be used for their normal purposes of allocating resources. Although cheap money might reduce the cost of debt service, the cost was the misdirection of the entire capital programme. As Chambers argued, low interest rates and high marginal taxation meant that 'there is little incentive to work, little incentive to save, and hardly any incentive at all to work and save at the same time, which is what is vitally needed'.[53] Chambers therefore suggested a reduction in high marginal rates of taxation to provide incentives and an increase in interest rates to encourage savings.

Here was an approach to the problems of excess demand which the Labour government had not contemplated: stimulating economic growth to meet demand through a free market economy based on the lure of higher incomes and profits. Labour attitudes to profit were ambivalent, and the same could be said of its attitude to savings. Labour rhetoric stressed that 'unearned income' was morally flawed in comparison with earned income, but Labour also claimed it would protect widows and pensioners living on small sums saved from earnings. Indeed, Jay linked the creation of the NIB with the encouragement of small savings in unit trusts as part of the planned investment of the nation's savings; the NIB could even act as the trustee of all unit trusts. But the distinction between moral and immoral, beneficial and parasitical unearned income was not pursued in a systematic way. The Inland Revenue pointed out that differential taxation of retained profits implied, by analogy, a lower rate of tax for personal savings from earned income. The Attlee government did not admit the analogy. Higher tax rates remained on *all* unearned incomes, and tax breaks on savings from earned incomes were limited to life insurance premiums.[54] The emphasis on retained profits rested in part on a belief that future investment would be undertaken by large corporations and nationalised industries rather than by individual savers. Labour's concern for taxation of profits, nationalisation and low interest rates left little or

[53] PRO, T172/2023, 'The economic crisis', S. P. Chambers, 1 Nov. 1947; also S. P. Chambers, 'Taxation and incentives', *Lloyds Bank Review* n.s. 8 (1948), 1–12; Ferguson, *The Cash Nexus*, p. 124.

[54] On Jay, *Nation's Wealth at the Nation's Service*, pp. 7–8; on Inland Revenue, see above, p. 166.

* Stanley Paul Chambers (1904–81) was born in Edmonton; he was educated at the City of London School and LSE. He became a tax inspector in 1927; in 1935 he served on the Indian income tax enquiry committee, becoming the adviser to the Indian government on the income tax in 1937. In 1940, he returned to London to help introduce PAYE. In 1945, he was appointed finance director of the British section of the control commission for Germany. In 1947 he became a director of ICI and chairman 1960–8. (*DNB, 1981–5*, ed. R. Blake and C. S. Nicholls (Oxford, 1990), pp. 80–1.)

no scope for the encouragement of small savers as a means of absorbing excess demand and providing incentives.

Increasingly, the Treasury and the government's economic advisers argued that Labour's economic and fiscal polices were creating a vicious circle of stasis and inflexibility. In 1948, a Treasury paper provided a depressing analysis of the prospects over the next five years. The income tax now covered nearly 12 million people compared with 4 million in 1938, and the standard rate of tax was higher. Not only was the incidence of the tax a deterrent, but the redistribution of about 60 per cent of private taxes in social benefits weakened the connection between real incomes and output. The 'free' social services were paid from high taxes on marginal earnings, and reduced the gains of working harder. Further, the fiscal system affected the structure of private enterprise. Small businesses had difficulties in growing since profits were taxed so heavily and private investors were no longer so important. Instead, existing large concerns were strengthened through access to retained profits and institutional investors. As a result, work and enterprise were hampered. What was needed, according to this analysis, was a reduction in the total tax burden and a cut in expenditure, so as to reduce inflationary pressure and encourage private savings. Instead of relying on high taxation and budgetary surpluses to check inflation (and so reduce private savings), expenditure and taxes should be reduced in order to stimulate private savings and investment.[55]

On this view, the lack of incentives to private enterprise meant that 'we are trying to put altogether too heavy a load on the economy and that this will produce a continuous tendency towards inflation which can only be checked by taxation so severe as to dishearten the community'. High taxes were 'a strong deterrent to risk-taking' as well as leading to increases in costs and demands for higher wages and dividends. In any case, the deflationary impact of taxation was offset by a reduction in savings, so that 'to increase taxes still further would be self-defeating from the point of view of inflation, as it would merely lead to more dis-saving by private individuals or less saving by business'. There was an urgent need for an economic and fiscal policy to break the vicious downward spiral, and to start a virtuous circle of growth which would maintain employment, create a surplus on the balance of payments and provide revenue for government policies. The Treasury increasingly stressed the need for 'large and sustained industrial investment' which would reconcile 'the need for reduced costs and the demand for a relatively high wage level supported by a rather rigid industrial structure'. Rapid growth and higher productivity were needed to make British goods competitive in overseas markets

[55] PRO, T230/145, 'Draft, budgetary prospects and policy 1948/52'.

and to meet the demand for higher wages. Senior officials at the Treasury started to press for a fundamental change in economic and fiscal policy.[56] It remained to be seen whether the Conservative governments after 1951 would be able to reshape fiscal policy on these lines.

Of course, one way of reducing taxes *and* avoiding inflation would be a cut in government expenditure, particularly on social security and the National Health Service. Further, the redistributive consequences of the welfare state cannot be separated from the way in which it was financed: were benefits to be funded from contributions with limited redistribution, or from general taxation with more possibility of redistribution? Would high levels of general taxation harm incentives and lead to lower growth which would hit the poor? And might the middle class secure tax breaks and make greater use of the 'free' social services, especially health and education? Obviously, the costs of the welfare state could not be separated from the success of economic policies in providing jobs and generating tax revenues.[57] The issue facing the Labour government was how to conceptualise the links between the welfare state and a dynamic economy. On the one hand, investment in welfare could be a means towards an efficient economy, a point argued by Aneurin Bevan* and in part conceded by the FBI. On the other hand, the costs of welfare might be seen as a burden on industry and productive efficiency. As Tomlinson has argued, the Treasury and the economic advisers to the government tended to interpret welfare as a 'burden' on production, so that 'the question was always posed in terms of how much welfare the country could afford, not how far welfare could contribute to the economy'. The priority

---

[56] PRO, T171/397, R. Hall to E. Plowden, 19 Mar. 1948; outline of the problems of a four-year budgetary policy, E. E. Bridges, 10 Sept. 1948; T171/400, BC(50)2, the budget position 1950/1: memorandum by the Budget Committee; BC(50)13, the 1950/1 budget, 16 Feb. 1950, and BC(50)15, the budget position 1950/1: memorandum by the Budget Committee, 22 Feb. 1950.

[57] R. Titmuss, *Essays on the Welfare State* (London, 1958), chapter 2; C. Pond, 'Tax expenditure and fiscal welfare', in C. Sandford, C. Pond and R. Walker (eds.), *Taxation and Social Policy* (London, 1980), pp. 47–63.

* Aneurin Bevan (1897–1960) was born in Tredegar, the son of a miner; he went down the pit at the age of thirteen, and became involved in union and local politics. He opposed the war, and from 1919 to 1921 the South Wales Miners' Federation sent him to the Central Labour College in London. In 1921, he was unable to get a job in the coalfield, but in 1926 be became disputes secretary for his union lodge. He was elected a Labour MP in 1929 and was expelled from the party in 1939 for supporting a popular front. During the war, he criticised Churchill and Labour's subordination in the coalition; to Churchill, he was a 'squalid nuisance'. In 1945, he was appointed minister of health and created the National Health Service (NHS). He was soon disillusioned with what he saw as the government's lack of commitment to socialism. In 1951, he moved to the ministry of labour, and resigned when Gaitskell proposed charges on teeth and spectacles. He was in conflict with the leadership, and out of sympathy with affluence and the need to adjust policy. Nevertheless, in 1956 he became shadow colonial and then foreign secretary, and broke with the left over disarmament. (*DNB, 1951–60*, ed. Williams and Nicholls, pp. 99–102; Robbins (ed.), *Biographical Dictionary*, pp. 46–9.)

was to raise output and increase exports, with private and collective consumption kept under strict control.[58] Of course, this raises the issue of *how* to increase output and exports. As far as the Labour government was concerned, there was a close ideological connection between welfare spending and management of the economy. Taxes were designed to create equality and to replace the pursuit of individual profit by a more bureaucratic system of managerialism. Much the same applied to the administration of welfare systems such as the National Health Service (NHS) which was run by 'experts' rather than (as in the 1911 insurance schemes) by 'approved societies'. The welfare system was also financed by central taxes to a much greater extent than in the past or in other European countries, reflecting the animosity of Labour to contributory insurance.

The case against welfare spending on the grounds that it imposed a burden on the economy was made by Robert Hall and Edward Bridges* at the Treasury who stressed the harmful effects of high spending from taxation:

The social services are part of the citizen's real income; but a part that is independent of his output and service to the community. The money to pay for them, however, has largely to be collected in taxes that fall, directly or indirectly on marginal earnings. From both sides, therefore, 'free' social services narrow the comparative advantage of working harder. The tax structure reduces the advantages obtainable from extra income and the expenditure of the taxes removes the most serious penalties which would otherwise attend inefficiency. The full benefits of the policy of full employment can only be secured if labour is responsive to incentives to earn more and to move freely between occupations. Our financial policy at present produces the opposite effect.

Further, they argued that the marginal rate of tax rose steeply above £2,000 so that there was little incentive to increase income by senior managers who were responsible for improvements in production and the efficient allocation of resources. Risk was unattractive, for high marginal rates of tax reduced the gains from successful innovation; the profits tax made the situation worse by suggesting that profits were objectionable rather than a motive for efficiency. The result, so they claimed, was the diversion of energy away from improvements in production. In Hall's view:

Most management in this country is done by Companies. The 'lethargy' of British industry is undoubtedly caused in part by the weight and incidence of taxation. High progressive taxation is an inducement for corporate management to seek

---

[58] J. Tomlinson, 'Welfare and economy: the economic impact of the welfare state, 1945–51', *Twentieth Century British History* 6 (1995), 217, 219.

* Edward Ettingdene Bridges (1892–1969) was the son of the poet laureate, and was educated at Eton and Magdalene College, Oxford; he was a prize fellow of All Souls and joined the Treasury. He was secretary of the Cabinet 1938–46, and permanent secretary to the Treasury and head of the civil service from 1945 to 1956. (*DNB, 1961–70*, ed. Williams and Nicholls, pp. 132–6.)

security rather than risk... It must be mainly to industrial and commercial enterprise that we look for the generation of income to maintain the necessary expenditure including 'social' investment.

Officials at the Treasury and Inland Revenue rejected the assumptions of the Colwyn Committee on the National Debt and Taxation after the First World War, and were challenging the fiscal strategy of Labour.[59]

By the last year of the Labour administration, a number of civil servants and advisers were anxious to provoke a public debate on these issues, allowing their concerns to move from internal memoranda within Whitehall to a wider audience. As Hall remarked,

there is undoubtedly a conflict between the objective of social equality and that of industrial efficiency. There is room for instance, for a considerable alteration in super tax rates with very little effect on the Revenue, but probably with enormous effect on efficiency and enterprise. At present, however, we cannot do very much because it is politically so difficult to lower the top levels of taxation. In the same way, it may be that considerable concessions could be made in the field of company taxation with no real effect on our overall Budget objectives, if we could only get over the political difficulties of doing anything at all for the capitalist. I feel convinced that we ought to work for something which will bring this issue into the open... What I really want is an authoritative and impartial statement, to which everyone in the country will have to pay attention, to the effect that there are features in our present system which in the long run are very likely to damage our industrial efficiency, and that the price of removing these features is fairly small, whereas the price of keeping them may in the long run be fairly heavy.[60]

These officials were formulating a fiscal policy with obvious attractions to a Conservative administration committed to a free market and incentives.

Hall realised that reform of the fiscal system could not come about simply by internal criticisms within the civil service. He hoped that a narrow, technical discussion of the administration and operation of the income tax could be used to bring the real problem into the open: the effect of taxation on enterprise and efficiency.[61] The central issues were

[59] PRO, T171/397, PB(48)3, outline of the problems of a four-year budget policy, and outline of a four-year budgetary policy, E. E. Bridges to chancellor, 10 Sept. 1948; 'Budgetary prospects and policy, 1948–52', R. Hall.

[60] PRO, T171/427, enquiry into the taxation of income: review of the field; Hall to Plowden, 'Taxation enquiry', 18 May 1950.

[61] PRO, T171/397, R. Hall to E. Plowden, 19 Mar. 1948; 'Budgetary prospects and policy, 1948–52', R. Hall, n.d.; Budget Committee, 20 Apr. 1948; budgetary problems and disinflation, 9 Dec. 1948; PB(48)6, Budget Committee, memorandum on tax revision, received by Sir E. Plowden from a non-official source; PB(48)8, comments by the Board of Inland Revenue on the paper received by Sir E. Plowden, E. StJ B., 24 Dec. 1948; PB(48)2, 'Simplifying the income tax', 7 Aug. 1948; E. E. Bridges to chancellor, 10 Sept. 1948; T171/420, reform of the tax system, 8 Dec. 1950; paper 1, 'Simplification of the income tax', 8 Dec. 1950; paper 2, 'Further proposals for simplifying the tax system', 8 Dec. 1950; T171/419, E. E. Bridges to chancellor, 23 Jan. 1951; Gaitskell, 25 Feb. 1951; T171/398, BC(49)29, 'Enquiry into the taxation of industry: note by the

set out by Arthur Cockfield,* an official of the Inland Revenue who went on to join the Conservative Research Department. Was the existing level of taxation excessive; was the balance between direct and indirect taxes acceptable; what was the relationship between taxes and social services; what were the effects on incentives and risk-bearing for workers, professionals, managers and businesses; and what was the impact on savings and capital expenditure?[62] The Labour government accepted the need for an enquiry into the vexed question of the impact of the *form* of taxation on economic behaviour and incentives, and appointed a committee to consider the taxation of trading profits; and a Royal Commission was established to advise on the taxation of profits and income.

The Labour government lost power at the start of a far-reaching debate over the fiscal constitution. Essentially, the fiscal system was part of the low-effort, low-productivity system which marked post-war Britain. The pursuit of growth by means of retained profits, the sacrifice of profits to secure wage restraint by organised labour, the weakness of an active capital market, complemented the low level of price competition. As Broadberry and Crafts comment, workers and managers settled for a quiet life.[63] This was underwritten by a trade-off between profit taxation and wage restraint, a means of controlling inflation at the expense of productivity. An escape from the low-effort, low-productivity world would demand a change in competition policy, an attack on the power of unions and industrial associations and a willingness to condone higher profits. It remained to be seen whether the Conservatives were able to make any major changes to the fiscal system, or whether they were so constrained by circumstances that little was achieved before they lost office in 1964.

Board of Inland Revenue', E. St J B., 3 Mar. 1949; T171/427, Hall to Plowden, 'Taxation enquiry', 18 May 1950.

[62] PRO, T171/427, enquiry into the taxation of income: review of the field (first draft, Feb. 1950).

[63] Broadberry and Crafts, 'British economic policy', 83.

* Francis Arthur Cockfield (b. 1916) was educated at Dover Grammar School and the LSE; his father was killed on the Somme in 1916. He joined the Inland Revenue in 1938, and was called to the bar in 1942; he was assistant secretary to the Board of Inland Revenue in 1945, director of statistics and intelligence 1945–52 and a commissioner of Inland Revenue in 1951–2. He left to become finance director of Boots 1953–61, and managing director 1961–7. He was a member of the NEDC 1962–4 and again from 1982 to 1983, adviser on tax policy to the chancellor of the Exchequer 1970–3, and chairman of the Price Commission 1973–7. He was made a life peer in 1978, and served as minister of state of the Treasury 1979–82, secretary of state for trade and president of the Board of Trade 1982–3 and chancellor of the Duchy of Lancaster 1983–4. He became vice-president of the European Community 1985–8. (*Who's Who 2001* (London, 2001), p. 415.)

8 'A most injurious disincentive in our economic system': Conservatives and taxation, 1951–1964

A high rate of taxes reduces incentive – whether it is an incentive to work a bit more overtime or the incentive to exercise business initiative. A high rate of tax militates against personal saving and leaves companies with less funds to invest in the expansion and modernisation of their business. A high rate of tax inevitably leads to wasteful expenditure and a waste of technical expertise in thinking up new methods of tax avoidance.

> Bodleian Library, CPA, CRD 2/10/11, notes for Mr Heathcoat Amory, 27 Apr. 1959 (B. Sewill)

The system for financing public expenditure is a product of history. It is not necessarily what would have been devised for an efficient economy under circumstances of full employment and still capable of sustained growth.

> PRO, PREM11/3304, note to prime minister on Treasury paper on 'Economic growth and national efficiency', 12 July 1961

... the effect of taxation on economic development needs a thoroughly new approach. Much of the current talk about the effect of taxation on the economy ... is conducted in terms of nineteenth century equity rather than in terms of the effect of taxation on economic development. Discussion of broad issues should no longer be confined to the Revenue and Customs; operational changes must of course be conducted behind closed doors, but this is no reason for failing to look at the wider long-term issues.

> PRO, T230/579, 'Elements of a policy for economic growth', F. R. P. Vinter, 27 Feb. 1961

'A long, slow grind'

When the Conservatives returned to power in 1951, the government was taking an unprecedented proportion of the GNP; marginal tax rates were as high as 98 per cent; death duties were as much as 80 per cent; the purchase tax continued; and a new differential profits tax at a high rate was in force. How should the new Conservative administration respond to these major changes in the fiscal constitution? Would the government embark on an overhaul of the tax system to create incentives and efficiency, as various Treasury officials desired at the end of the Labour administration – or would the system prove remarkably resilient?

The immediate issue facing Churchill's new administration was very similar to the issue he tackled at the Treasury in the 1920s: how to distribute tax cuts to the maximum electoral advantage and to stimulate the economy. Churchill no longer had the energy to set out a striking new vision of British society, and his chancellor, R. A. Butler,* was less creative in the early 1950s than Churchill had been in 1925. The diagnosis of the failings of the current tax system (at least in the eyes of the Conservatives) was easy. In the words of John Boyd-Carpenter:[†]

the present situation is not the result of an attempt to lay burdens fairly. Over the last six years the bias has been against 'the higher income groups'. Large sections of industrial workers are better off than they have ever been. Other sections of the community are much worse off. The present basis is not a fair 'taking-off point'.[1]

It followed that the budget should redress the 'bias' of Labour's fiscal policy: organised workers gained from increased wages, and the middle class was hit by inflation and high taxation. The limit for surtax had not been changed since 1918, so that the 'most valuable managerial and professional men' were liable to surtax on incomes of £2,000 – a much

---

[1] PRO, T171/409, J. A. Boyd-Carpenter to chancellor, 18 Feb. 1952, standard rate of income tax.

* Richard Austen Butler (1902–82) was born in India where his father was in the Indian civil service. He was educated at Marlborough and Pembroke College, Cambridge; he became a fellow of Corpus Christi, Cambridge, and married into the Courtauld family with an income for life. He entered politics, sitting as a Conservative MP from 1929 to 1965. He was under-secretary of state for India from 1932 to 1937, parliamentary secretary in the ministry of labour, and in 1938 under-secretary of state at the Foreign Office, where he was an appeaser. In 1941, he became president of the Board of Education and chairman of the Conservative Postwar Problems Committee. He was minister of labour in 1945; in opposition as chairman of the Conservative Research Department (CRD) he helped to reshape policy. He was chancellor of the Exchequer from 1951 to 1955, when he became lord privy seal and leader of the House. In 1957 he became home secretary, and from 1959 to 1961 he was also chairman of the party and to 1961 leader of the House. He was also in charge of the Cabinet committee overseeing negotiations for entry to the EEC. In 1962, he was removed from the Home Office and became first secretary of state with responsibility for central Africa; he was foreign secretary in 1963–4. He was master of Trinity College, Cambridge, from 1964 to 1977. (*DNB, 1981–5*, ed. Blake and Nicholls, pp. 62–8; Robbins (ed.), *Biographical Dictionary*, pp. 62–8.)

† John Boyd-Carpenter (1908–98) was educated at Stowe and Balliol College, Oxford. He was called to the bar in 1934 and became a Conservative MP 1945–72. He was financial secretary to the Treasury 1951–4, minister of transport and civil aviation 1954–5, minister of pensions and national insurance 1955–62 and chief secretary to the Treasury and paymaster general 1962–4. He was opposition spokesman on housing and local government 1964–6 and chairman of the public accounts committee 1964–70. He was a director and later chairman of Rugby Portland Cement from 1970 to 1984, and chairman of the Civil Aviation Authority 1972–7. (*Who's Who 1998* (London, 1998), p. 222.)

lower real income than before the war.[2] More significantly, married couples on modest middle-class incomes of £500 to £2,000 experienced a
decline in their relative position since 1938.

Certainly, some members of Churchill's administration were concerned
at the stultifying effects of high taxes. In 1954, Woolton* argued that the
issue of taxation was 'more urgent and deep seated than any others with
which the government is faced', and that it should be reduced in order to
maintain enterprise, competition and employment. In his view, prosperity
depended on the willingness of a large number of companies and a relatively small number of highly able people to take risks. These individuals
exploited new inventions and opened up markets; and trade depended on
profits. In Woolton's opinion, it was 'not reasonable to expect the fires of
adventure to continue to burn very brightly' when taxes took over 50 per
cent of any increase in profit and 19s in the £ of additional income. Here
was a plea to reduce taxation to encourage initiative and to provide incentives, by a gradual process of cutting taxes to a maximum of 15s in
the £ (75 per cent). However, Cabinet discussion was rather cautious.
The economic case was accepted, but Butler was well aware of the rising
costs of government policies. He feared still higher taxes in 1955 unless
spending plans were reduced, and he was not confident that substantial
or swift cuts could be made unless the Cabinet was willing to 'slash' social
services. Since this was not politically expedient, his policy was 'a long,
slow grind' over many years. On the one hand, this meant resisting increases in services and cutting costs; on the other hand, it meant a steady
growth in productivity to reduce the real burden of spending. 'This is not
a pleasant prospect', he admitted, 'but it is the only course open to us.'[3]

The implications were clear to one Conservative MP: Labour assumed
that no one should have a net income of less than £500 or more than

---

[2] PRO, T171/422, draft paper on budget policy, Anthony Barber, 11 Jan. 1952; see also
J. Downie, 15 Jan. 1952, who claimed the deterioration was overstated.

[3] PRO, PREM11/653, C(54)22, 21 Jan. 1954, Cabinet: government methods of financing
and effects of taxation: memorandum by the chancellor of the Duchy of Lancaster and the
minister of materials; C(54)83, 2 Mar. 1954, Cabinet: government methods of financing
and effects of taxation: memorandum by the chancellor of the Exchequer; CC(54), 14th
conclusions, minute 7, 3 Mar. 1954.

* Frederick James Marquis, earl of Woolton (1883–1964), was born in Salford, the son
of a saddler. He was educated at Manchester Grammar School and the University of
Manchester; he became a teacher and warden of a settlement house in Liverpool. During
the war, he worked in supply organisations; after the war, he joined the board of Lewis's,
the department store, where he rose to be joint managing director and chairman. In the
1930s, he was a commissioner for areas of special distress, and he served on committees to
consider bombing and the aircraft industry. In 1939, he devised a programme of clothing
a mass army and became director-general of the ministry of supply. He was created a
peer in 1940 and appointed minister of food and, in 1943, minister of reconstruction.
He joined the Conservative party in 1945 and served as party chairman 1946–55; he was
a Cabinet minister from 1951 to 1955 in non-departmental posts. (*DNB, 1961–70*, ed.
Williams and Nicholls, pp. 728–31; Robbins (ed.), *Biographical Dictionary*, pp. 292–3.)

£2,000, on the basis that most needs could be supplied more efficiently and cheaply by the state. But the result was tax evasion and avoidance, with serious consequences for business morality, a loss of incentive for hard work and commercial risks and a threat to private savings. Butler's willingness to face a long, slow grind therefore filled him with dread, and he warned Churchill that it implied 'that a Conservative government must perpetuate, or at least is powerless to alter, the pattern of society which the Socialists set out deliberately to create. It may be that this is inevitable. But Ministers should look this prospect squarely in the face before deciding that it is so.'[4] On the whole, ministers *did* accept the inevitability of high levels of spending and adopted Butler's strategy of a long, slow grind. Tax cuts would be the *consequence* of steady growth, rather than a means of stimulating growth through incentives to commercial risk and individual initiative.

Usually, changes in the fiscal constitution arose from strong-willed chancellors battling with the innate caution of officials who wished to preserve the existing structure of taxation. Most chancellors were emasculated by the technical authority of the Treasury and Inland Revenue, with their ready explanation of why change was impossible – until a dominant figure with a clear vision such as Lloyd George, Churchill or Dalton could impose their wishes. The pattern between 1951 and 1964 was somewhat different. At least some officials, such as Robert Hall, argued for change in the fiscal constitution but they were stymied by the authority of the revenue departments and by the procedures for considering fiscal policy which limited the scope for long-term, strategic discussion. The operation of the government machinery meant that major reconsideration of the structure of taxation was difficult. Each year from the end of the war, a Budget Committee was established, with leading officials from the Treasury, Inland Revenue, Customs and Excise and Board of Trade; most of the discussions took place in the absence of ministers whose opinions were usually sought by the chairman of the committee. Within the Treasury, the Economic Section proferred advice and opinions, often in tension with officials more concerned with administration. Essentially, the Budget Committee considered two factors: the state of the economy and the need to control demand; and the requirements of the government for revenue. Its main concern was the shape of the next budget. Although it considered the general structure of taxation – the proportions of direct and indirect taxation; the use of investment allowances to stimulate productivity; or the possibility of export incentives – in most cases these issues were handed back to individual departments for report. The usual outcome of these departmental reports was a conservative defence of the

---

[4] PRO, PREM11/653, Norman Brook to prime minister, 2 Mar. 1954, taxation.

status quo. The Board of Customs and Excise would almost certainly report that the existing structure of indirect taxation was preferable to any radical change; and the Inland Revenue would start from the assumption that any change would upset the relationships with the taxpaying public. Neither the Inland Revenue nor Customs and Excise had a professional economist; and they did not really consider advice on the economics of taxation to be part of their concern. Their attitude was typified by the response to the chancellor's request for a report on the economic effects of a wealth tax. As D. J. S. Hancock* remarked, the Inland Revenue's comments were written by a detached administrator reporting on what economists said, with a clear impression that such matters were none of his business.[5] The result was a neglect of the large picture and of long-term change. The failures of this system were realised by the early 1960s when some tentative and inadequate steps were made to consider the long-term effects of taxation on the economy.

Between 1951 and 1964, chancellors were cautious, fearing the political consequences of radical change. There was a sense of being trapped by the existing institutional structures and trade-offs. As Hall pointed out in 1951, there was little hope that 'we could make new Ministers, if they are Conservative, take painful decisions. They are very nearly pledged to do little about the social services, they certainly do not want to produce more unemployment, and they cannot really start by making taxes much more regressive.'[6] In many ways, Hall and other officials at the Treasury had a clearer vision of how to change the tax system to create incentives. By contrast, chancellors did not hold office for long enough, or have the technical expertise, to impose a radical change in the tax system – and in any case they feared the political consequences.

During the thirteen years of Conservative government, six chancellors passed through the Treasury, and the only one with a clear agenda for reform – Peter Thorneycroft[†] and his team of Enoch Powell[‡] and

---

[5] PRO, T320/18, minute of D. J. S. Hancock, 1 Nov. 1963.

[6] A. Cairncross (ed.), *The Robert Hall Diaries, 1947–1953* (London, 1989), p. 174.

[*] David John Stowell Hancock (b. 1934) was educated at Balliol College, Oxford. He joined the Board of Trade in 1957, moving to the Treasury in 1959, Cabinet Office in 1982 as deputy secretary and Deparment of Education and Science as permanent secretary, from 1983 to 1989. (*Who's Who 2001*, p. 887.)

[†] George Edward Peter Thorneycroft (1909–94) was called to the bar in 1934, and was a Conservative MP from 1938 to 1966. He served as president of the Board of Trade 1951–7, chancellor of the Exchequer 1957–8, minister of aviation 1960–2 and defence 1962–4. He was shadow home secretary 1964–6. When Mrs Thatcher became leader, she invited him to become chairman of the party from 1975 to 1981, recognising him as her forerunner in monetary and financial stringency. (Robbins (ed.), *Biographical Dictionary*, pp. 400–2.)

[‡] John Enoch Powell (1912–98) was born in Birmingham and educated at King Edward VI School and Trinity College, Cambridge, where he was a fellow before moving to the University of Sydney as professor of Greek. He worked in the CRD after the war. He was

Nigel Birch* – resigned. The longest serving chancellor, Butler, soon disappointed any expectation of radical departure from Labour's fiscal policies when he took over the office in 1951. His overwhelming sense of complexity resulted in a cautiously balanced package of measures, and more adventurous spirits at the Treasury soon complained that he was 'not unlike a defective petrol gauge on the dashboard of a motor car. He wobbles in different sectors and gives no clear indication of the depth of feeling.' Hall despaired of his 'hesitations and wavering' and 'strong streak of moral cowardice'. Edwin Plowden[†] was no more complimentary of his 'incompetence and vacillation'.[7] Of course, these criticisms of Butler partly missed the point: permanent officials might devise imaginative fiscal strategies; politicians had to win elections and placate different interests. Might concessions to middle-class incomes simply play into the hands of Labour, justifying their claims that the Conservatives were selfishly helping the affluent at the expense of the poor? Might trade unionists pursue inflationary wage claims? What was needed was some wider rhetoric, such as Churchill devised in 1925. Above all, changes in tax rates had implications for incentives and investment, for economic

a Conservative MP 1950–74. He opposed involvement in the Korean war, membership of the European Coal and Steel Community and withdrawal from Suez. He was parliamentary secretary to Housing and Local Government in 1955, and financial secretary to the Treasury in 1957–8. He was appointed minister of health in 1960–3. He joined the shadow Cabinet but was dismissed in 1968 over his speech about immigration. In 1974, he left the Conservative party and became an Ulster Unionist MP from 1974 to 1987. (Robbins (ed.), *Biographical Dictionary*, pp. 344–6.)

[7] PRO, T171/423, ? to Bridges, 15 Feb. 1952: budget 1952; Cairncross (ed.), *Hall Diaries, 1947–1953*, pp. 254, 271. Nevertheless, Hall admitted that he liked Butler, 'presumably because of his personal charm as I cannot really make out what he thinks' (p. 191).

[*] Evelyn Nigel Chetwode Birch (1906–81) was the son of a general; he was educated at Eton and became a stock broker. He was a Conservative MP 1945–70; he was a critic of Keynesianism and advocated what he termed 'strictly honest public finance'. He was parliamentary under-secretary at the air ministry in 1951 and defence in 1952; in 1954 he was minister of works and 1955 secretary of state for air; he was secretary to the Treasury in 1957–8. He never held office again, and became a critic of what he saw as Macmillan's lax and inflationary policies. (*DNB, 1981–5*, ed. Blake and Nicholls, pp. 37–8.)

[†] Edwin Noel Plowden (1907–2001) was educated in Switzerland and at Pembroke College, Cambridge. After a period out of work and in manual jobs, he joined a firm of City commodity dealers. During the war, he joined the ministry of economic warfare and from 1940–6 the ministry of aircraft production. He came into contact with Cripps, who appointed him chief planning officer in 1947, working in conjunction with Robert Hall as the director of the Economic Section. They had a powerful joint influence on Cripps which continued with Gaitskell, but there were some tensions with Butler. In 1953, he moved to the Atomic Energy Organisation and was chairman of the Atomic Energy Authority 1954–9. He returned to business, as a director of the National Westminster Bank 1960–77 and president of Tube Investments 1976–90, but spent much time in government service. He chaired the Treasury Committee of Enquiry into the Control of Public Expenditure in 1959–61. (*Who's Who 2001*, p. 1654; obituary by Alec Cairncross, *Guardian*, 17 Feb. 2001.)

growth and competitiveness. Conservative ministers needed to develop a view on the extent to which high personal taxes blunted incentives and personal savings. Should tax cuts be concentrated on higher earned incomes and on the encouragement of savings? Or was the real problem in corporate taxation? Perhaps the tax system should be changed in order to encourage firms to become more capital intensive; and it might be wondered whether Labour's strategy of encouraging retentions was the most sensible way of stimulating investment. Such issues required more than marginal tinkering with tax rates, but the discussion of fiscal policy within the government machinery was highly routinised and overwhelmed by short-term considerations.

This situation caused considerable despondency within the Conservative party, not only because taxes were 'a most injurious disincentive to our economic system' but also because resentment among the middle class might 'drag us the same way as its precursor dragged the Labour party'. In 1954, the Conservative Research Department (CRD) argued that taxes on the middle class must be cut as a matter of urgency:

Invest in success means not only investment in capital equipment: it must also be investment in the man behind it. We seek to give greater incentives to effort, to the skilful, the trained and the responsible, and to put a premium on ability. And we want to make it possible for these people to save and invest.[8]

Butler's policy of 'long, slow grind' meant that little was done, and there was concern by 1957 that the growing discontent of middle-class voters might threaten electoral success.

In January 1957, Harold Watkinson* warned the new prime minister, Harold Macmillan,[†] that a new approach was needed to remove the

---

[8] PRO, T171/422, draft paper on budget policy, A. B., 11 Jan. 1952; CRD2/10/12, James Douglas to Fraser, 25 Sept. 1956: draft reply for chairman to Lord Clitheroe; CRD 2/10/8, note on tax concessions, 21 Dec. 1954.

* Harold Arthur Watkinson (1910–95) was educated at Queen's College, Taunton, and King's College London. He was a Conservative MP from 1950 to 1964, serving as parliamentary private secretary to the ministry of transport and civil aviation 1951–2, parliamentary secretary to the ministry of labour and national service 1952–5, minister of transport and civil aviation 1955–9 and minister of defence 1959–62. He left politics for business in 1963, as group managing director and later chairman of Cadbury Schweppes 1963–74, a director of BICC 1968–77 and of the Midland Bank 1970–83; he was president of the Confederation of British Industry in 1976–7. (*Who's Who 1996*, p. 2018.)

[†] Maurice Harold Macmillan (1894–1986) was the son of a publisher, and was educated at Eton and Balliol College, Oxford. After war service, he became aide-de-camp to the governor-general of Canada, the duke of Devonshire, and married his daughter. He entered the family publishing firm, but he had a taste for politics and aristocratic society. He was a Conservative MP 1924–9 and 1931–64. In the 1930s, he attempted to develop a middle way of a mixed economy and planning. He was parliamentary secretary to the ministry of supply 1940–2, under-secretary of the colonies in 1942 and minister of state

bitterness felt by middle-class incomes of £500 to £2,000. He informed Macmillan that the primary aim of his 'new tough leadership' should be

to give back incentive and a sense of purpose to this section of our people. This means that we should have to concentrate more of our domestic policy towards the support of private enterprise in trade, commerce and industry . . . and that we should try to give a chance to the middle classes to keep a somewhat larger share of the money that they earn by their skill and enterprise.

If we can make everybody anxious to belong to a broadly based and prosperous middle class, we shall also bring a great many of the more successful Trade Unionists to our side. I believe in this way we could lay the foundations for a new up-swing in output and efficiency which we shall certainly need if we are ever to become really prosperous again.[9]

Would Macmillan and his new chancellor, Peter Thorneycroft, rise to the challenge?

The plea led Macmillan to write, with patrician hauteur, to the CRD. 'I am always hearing about the Middle Classes', he remarked. 'What is it they really want? Can you put it down on a sheet of notepaper, and then I will see whether we can give it to them.' This was scarcely the basis for a fundamental reconsideration of the tax system and its impact on the economy, and the CRD's response was limited to minor concessions to assist the elderly living on small fixed incomes.[10] One backbench MP had a much clearer sense of what the middle class wanted. As he informed Thorneycroft, the entire tax system should be reshaped to assist middle-class taxpayers:

Let the forthcoming budget be the first instalment of a comprehensive recasting of our tax system and of tax reduction, like the trailer to a great Hollywood epic! The Prime Minister and the Chancellor have already given us the political theme – 'opportunity and justice'. Opportunities must cover companies and institutions, as well as individuals. The current obsession with arithmetical equality is destructive both of opportunity and of justice.[11]

Thorneycroft saw the force of the argument, but more cautious members of the government believed it was not politically feasible to roll back the fiscal structure created during the war and confirmed by the Attlee administration. The result was a 'B' movie rather than a blockbuster.

in north Africa 1942–5. He was minister of housing 1951–4, minister of defence 1954–5, foreign secretary 1955, chancellor of the Exchequer 1955–7 and prime minister 1957–63. (*DNB, 1986–90*, ed. Nicholls, pp. 276–82; Robbins (ed.), *Biographical Dictionary*, pp. 287–91.)

[9] PRO, PREM11/1816, minister of transport, H. Watkinson, to prime minister, 11 Jan. 1957.
[10] PRO, PREM11/1816, Macmillan to Michael Fraser, 17 Feb. 1957; Fraser to Macmillan, 25 Feb. 1957; Macmillan to chancellor, 25 Feb. 1957.
[11] PRO, T171/479, David Price to Thorneycroft, 7 Feb. 1957.

Change was contained, and strict limits were set to reform between 1951 and 1964. In the circumstances, was there much that chancellors could do except behave like defective petrol gauges?

Indirect taxes and export incentives

One possible reform was to reshape the purchase tax and increase the share of indirect taxes in order to reverse the long-term reliance on high direct taxation. The change would help exporters by bringing the British tax system more in line with broadly based indirect taxes in continental Europe. The overall level of indirect taxation as a proportion of government revenue and GNP was actually slightly *above* Germany and considerably below France in 1959, at respectively 48.4, 46.6 and 59.7 per cent. What stood out was the different form of indirect taxes. The British taxes were highly dependent on a few duties on beer, spirits, tobacco and petrol, and on the purchase tax with its narrow coverage and wide variation in rates. By contrast, the French and German systems were more dependent on general turnover taxes, which amounted to 25.3 per cent of revenue in Germany and 34.7 per cent in France.[12] British officials, politicians and economists became concerned that the fiscal system distorted the economy by unduly affecting the relative prices of goods and by increasing the costs of exports. Perhaps they exaggerated, placing too much emphasis on the impact of taxes compared with other reasons for the low rate of growth of productivity. Nevertheless, there was a widespread belief that convergence with the fiscal system of continental Europe would help create a competitive economy. In the first place, reliance on indirect taxes would allow a reduction in direct taxes on incomes and profits, so encouraging risk-taking and savings which would make Britain more competitive and productive. As Frank Bower remarked, 'it is illogical to devise taxes which take an increasing share of the reward of successful creation. It is better policy to make expenditure on personal satisfaction more expensive and to encourage savings.' In the second place, a greater reliance on indirect taxes offered a way of increasing British competitiveness in export markets. The General Agreement on Trade and Tariffs (GATT) banned any remission of direct taxes on exports, but *did* allow remission of indirect taxes. Consequently, British exporters liable to high levels of direct tax argued that they were at a disadvantage compared with their competitors. Of course, the argument against indirect taxes was that they were regressive – a point countered by Bower who pointed to payment

---

[12] I am grateful to Frances Lynch for the French and German figures from Archives National, Min. Fin. B25335, EEC Comm. Directive, 31 Oct. 1962; the British figure is from PRO, T171/593. See also table 10.1 below.

of social benefits to the poor and to the relative decline in the position of
the capital-owning classes. Would the government have the political will
to change the balance of the fiscal system from direct to indirect taxes?[13]

Certainly, the purchase tax was far from perfect either as a source of
revenue or as a means of controlling the economy. Frank Lee* of the
Board of Trade argued the case for reform of the purchase tax on pragmatic grounds, that it was 'a hotch-potch without any logical or defensible
basis'. In 1957, Thorneycroft castigated the purchase tax as 'thoroughly
unsatisfactory: it is incoherent and discriminatory: it is too narrowly
based: at the top levels it is penal: its general effect on industry is to distort the natural pattern of production: it is a heavy and uncertain burden
upon retailers who suffer when it changes'. Purchase tax rates were high
and the differentials were wide. In 1954, 'utility' goods were exempt, the
basic rate was 33.3 per cent, the semi-luxury rate 66.7 per cent and the
luxury rate 100 per cent. The result was to distort the market. In particular, the Board of Trade complained that the high price of non-utility goods
reduced domestic demand for better quality production with serious
implications for export markets.[14]

The purchase tax was used for contradictory purposes, as a planning
tool to direct consumption in particular directions and as a source of revenue. The origins of the purchase tax in the Second World War involved a
conflict over the role of the market. Keynes opposed the tax, preferring to
remove excess spending by taxation and deferred pay, and to leave individuals to purchase goods according to their own preferences. By contrast,
the purchase tax was linked to a controlled consumers' market, with rationing, utility goods and a wide range of tax rates to shape consumption.
Unlike the purchase tax, a flat-rate sales tax would raise substantial revenue and remain neutral between commodities so that consumers could
make their own choice within the market. The point was made most
clearly by the FBI in 1963, when it argued that a shift to indirect taxes
made more sense in an affluent society with high levels of discretionary
expenditure:

[13] F. Bower, 'Some reflections on the budget', *Lloyds Bank Review* n.s. 65 (1962), 36–7.

[14] PRO, T171/434, F. Lee to E. Plowden, 21 Oct. 1952; F. Lee to Bridges, 10 Apr. 1953;
T171/484, F. Lee to R. Makins, 5 Nov. 1956; T171/479, note by P. Thorneycroft,
indirect taxation, n.d.

* Frank Godbould Lee (1903–71) was born in Colchester, the son of school teachers. He
was educated at Downing College, Cambridge, and passed for the Indian civil service.
He entered the Colonial Office, moving to the supply side of the Treasury in 1940; in
1944, he went to Washington as deputy head of the Treasury delegation. In 1946, he
was deputy secretary of the ministry of supply and permanent secretary at the ministry
of food in 1949, moving to the Board of Trade in 1951 and to the Treasury between
1960 and 1962 as joint permanent secretary in charge of financial and economic policy.
He became master of Corpus Christi College, Cambridge, in 1962. (*DNB, 1971–80*, ed.
Blake and Nicholls, pp. 493–4.)

The principles on which the present British tax system is based and the conceptions behind them are largely a legacy of the nineteenth century, when the mass of the working population was still at or near the subsistence level. With the increasingly broadening affluence of the present age and the ever-widening field of choice in personal expenditure which is being opened up, the time has come for a reappraisement of the older concepts. We hope for the abandonment of some of the old prejudices against indirect taxes as such.[15]

On this view, an affluent consumer market changed the character of the fiscal system, and permitted a shift from direct taxes which blunted incentives. Such a change would seem to hold attractions to Conservative politicians committed to an affluent consumer society, in addition to securing substantial revenue with less harm to incentives and exports.

The Board of Trade's solution was to sweep away the ramshackle structure of the purchase tax and to replace it with a general turnover tax on retail sales, at a low rate over a wide range of goods, to be collected by retailers. Any attempt to plan the economy by differential rates of tax between commodities should be abandoned; instead, the level of the flat-rate sales tax could be varied over the trade cycle to influence consumption and inflation in a market economy.[16] A strong case was therefore made for a reform of indirect taxes, yet little was achieved before the Conservatives lost power in 1964. Adoption of a sales tax would amount to a fundamental change in the fiscal constitution, and there was considerable inertia within the machinery of government. The Board of Customs and Excise would have responsibility for collecting the tax, and continued to support the purchase tax as easy to administer, involving a relatively small number of wholesalers. It insisted on the 'insuperable' administrative difficulties of dealing with large numbers of retailers, and the likelihood of evasion and low yields. Consequently, there was little chance of extending the range of the existing purchase tax to other goods, and certainly not to services which formed an increasing share of consumption.[17]

[15] MRC, FBI MSS 200/F/3/E7/1/4, report of the Committee on the Balance of the Fiscal System; FBI MSS 200/F/3/E7/1/5, Taxation Committee, 1963: the budget 1964: the balance of the fiscal system.
[16] PRO, T171/434, 'The future of the purchase tax: note by the Board of Trade', n.d.; F. Lee to E. Plowden, 21 Oct. 1952; note for the record, 12 Nov. 1952; F. Lee to Bridges, 10 Apr. 1953; T171/438, purchase tax: note of meeting in chancellor of Exchequer's room, 30 Nov. 1953. On the use of a sales tax as a better means of regulating the economy than the purchase tax or hire purchase restrictions, see T171/484, F. Lee to R. Makins, 5 Nov. 1956; T171/492, notes of a meeting in Sir R. Makins's room, 26 Nov. 1957. For a more cautious view on the introduction of a sales tax, see T171/434, 'The future of the purchase tax', IM General, Board of Trade, 8 Oct. 1952; 'The future of purchase tax, Part I', IM General, Board of Trade, 25 Aug. 1952; 'The future of purchase tax, Part II', IM General, Board of Trade, 30 Aug. 1952.
[17] PRO, T171/414, BC(52)34, 'The future of the purchase tax: note by Customs', 23 Dec. 1952; BC(53)9, 'Purchase tax in the next budget, note by Customs', 4 Feb. 1953;

Many Conservative politicians shared the caution of Customs and Excise, fearing that even a modest shift to a more broadly based system of purchase tax with lower rates and narrower differentials between goods would overstep the limit of what was 'just or practicable'. A reduction in the top rate on luxury goods would benefit affluent consumers, and they would also gain from cuts in income tax made possible by a greater reliance on indirect taxes.[18] Meanwhile, food subsidies were to be removed from the poor, and the extension of indirect taxes would further increase prices. When the Conservatives took office in 1951, the combination of subsidies to basic foods, of welfare benefits and taxes led to a highly complex pattern of gains and losses for individuals, with the danger of distortions to the economy. As Customs and Excise pointed out in 1952, large sums of money were collected and then repaid; the outcome was simply a cumbersome transfer of money which distorted the economy. First, relative prices were affected through the payment of subsidies to some goods and the imposition of high levels of purchase tax on others. Secondly, incentives were affected, for a basic, subsidised standard of living was easily attained and an improvement was difficult as a result of heavy taxes. The reduction of food subsidies might make economic sense, at least to politicians and officials eager to use price signals in allocating resources, but the task was not easily achieved. A cut in subsidies would need to be offset by benefits to those losing from higher food prices. Of course, the political problem for Butler was that a cut in subsidies, and the use of the revenue to make concessions to the income tax, could be portrayed as socially divisive and benefiting the rich. As one participant in the discussion remarked, 'we won't get away on food subsidies unless we at least go through some pretty energetic motions of penalising the rich rentier'.[19] The desire to cut food subsidies made any increase in indirect taxes all the more difficult. It could be denounced by Labour as socially divisive and selfish. Indeed, the TUC argued that 'on grounds of equity a cut in purchase tax is preferable to a general cut in income tax because purchase tax is not related to an individual's capacity to pay'.[20] Certainly, a shift to indirect taxes would threaten the policy of wage restraint, for workers would demand higher wages to cover the increase in the price

T171/452, C&E(54)1, purchase tax, 12 Nov. 1954; T171/475, 'Taxation of consumer goods, Customs note, 5 Dec. 1955; H. Brooke to economic secretary and chancellor, 6 Dec. 1955.

[18] PRO, T171/414, economic secretary to chancellor, 16 Feb. 1953.

[19] PRO, T171/422, C&E(52)1, 'Food subsidies, welfare payments and taxation', 8 Jan. 1952; T171/422, ? to Bridges, 15 Feb. 1952: budget 1952. On the debates over cuts in food subsidies ('Diogenes') and benefits to those who lost ('Senegold'), see papers in T171/409; Peden, *Treasury and British Public Policy*, p. 476. Treasury officials with a classical education would know that Diogenes argued that happiness was achieved by satisfying natural needs in the cheapest way.

[20] PRO, IR63/209, TUC: the economic situation and the 1959 budget.

of goods. The need to keep wages under control effectively limited the chancellor's room for manoeuvre.

A major shift in the balance of direct and indirect taxation would require a politician of considerable courage (or foolhardiness) to implement change against these administrative and political doubts. The only chancellor prepared to contemplate radical changes was Thorneycroft, who insisted in 1957 that the Budget Committee should consider a turnover tax covering food and services on the lines of the German 'cascading' tax which was paid on each turnover from raw material to finished product. The Budget Committee virtually mutinied, refusing to proceed unless Thorneycroft explicitly stated that he was willing to accept the political consequences. As he complained, civil servants were adept at defending the *status quo* by stressing the dangers of change without making comparison with the distortions of the existing system.[21]

Opponents of the 'cascading' turnover tax had a point, for a tax on each stage of production created problems of equity between firms. The incidence of the tax depended on the degree of integration: a firm purchasing components from *outside* producers paid the tax and was at a disadvantage compared with highly integrated concerns relying on internal supplies. Eventually, harmonisation of indirect taxes within the EEC was on the basis of the French *taxe sur la valeur ajoutée* or TVA rather than the German cascading tax.[22] The TVA was adopted in France in

[21] PRO, T171/479, note by Thorneycroft, indirect taxation, n.d.; T171/487, Budget Committee meeting, 13 Sept. 1957; meeting in chancellor's room, 4 Dec. 1957; T171/488, 'A broader base for indirect taxation', EWM, 11 Oct. 1957; BC(M)(57)14, R. Makins to chancellor, 20 Sept. 1957; T171/492, 'Sales tax', T. Padmore to R. Makins, 6 Dec. 1957; note of a meeting in Sir Roger Makins's room, 26 Nov. 1957; T171/492, indirect taxation, P. Thorneycroft, 9 Sept. 1957. Thorneycroft wished to cut public expenditure by £153m in order to deflate, even at the expense of unemployment; he only secured Cabinet agreement to a cut of £105m. His main concern was the impact of inflation on the middle class, caused not only by the demand for higher wages (a common complaint) but by high public spending and lack of control over the money supply. See E. H. H. Green, 'The Treasury resignations of 1958: a reconsideration', *Twentieth Century British History* 11 (2000), 409–30; Peden, *Treasury and British Public Policy*, pp. 486–93. The importance of his resignation was that attempts to control inflation were subsequently dominated by concerns for wage restraint, which Hall felt was much more important than the money supply. Hence changes in the fiscal system had one eye on the attitudes of trade unions in order to 'purchase' wage restraint. Inflation also meant a lack of competitiveness, and a concern for export incentives, which dominated much of the discussion of taxation at the end of the Conservative government. For comments on wage-push inflation, see T. W. Hutchison, *Economics and Economic Policy in Britain, 1946–66* (London, 1968), pp. 138–50; and E. H. H. Green, 'The Conservative party, the state and the electorate', in M. Taylor and J. Lawrence (eds.), *Party, State and the Electorate in Modern Britain* (Aldershot, 1996), pp. 176–200; Lowe, 'Resignation at the Treasury', sees the resignation as reflecting the refusal of the Treasury to engage in constructive debate.

[22] On the effect of the German system on integration, see PRO, T171/492, 'A cumulative turnover tax: note by Customs and Excise', 17 Dec. 1957. The existence of two fiscal systems created problems for firms within the European Coal and Steel Community, and contributed to harmonisation: see Lynch, 'A tax for Europe', 82.

1954 as a means of resolving the problems of existing taxes on sales (1920) and production (1937). The political background was very different from Britain, where a general sales tax was open to the charge of favouring the rich and harming the poor. In France, it was a considerable improvement on the existing fiscal system, which had been highly contentious since the First World War. Both the communist unions and the United States Economic Co-operation Administration agreed that the existing sales tax was inequitable, imposing too great a burden on industrial labour. The proposal for a tax on value added came from the communist unions in 1947, and was taken up and modified by advocates of modernisation. The 'modernisers' argued that the TVA would give more favourable treatment to investment than the existing production tax, helping to raise productivity and growth. The burden of taxes would then fall as a proportion of national income.[23] The introduction of the tax in France therefore arose from a highly specific set of circumstances, reflecting the need to resolve a serious problem with existing taxes and indicating the power of 'modernisers' within the French state.

The situation in Britain was very different. British officials did not have the power of their French counterparts to impose a policy, and the machinery of government was more likely to block change than to force through major reform. Of course, the British tax system was not facing the same strains as in France, where the sales tax was a matter of contention from 1920 and unions were hoping to replace an unacceptable indirect tax. In Britain, the unions opposed a shift to indirect taxes, which they saw as less fair than direct taxes, and the purchase tax was accepted as a means of taxing 'luxuries' rather than basic necessities. Certainly, a higher level of indirect taxes would threaten the fragile policy of wage restraint which was crucial to controlling inflation. Neither was the FBI entirely convinced of the case for a value added tax (VAT). The FBI's concern over the harmful impact of taxes led it to establish a working party on the balance of the fiscal system in 1961. Its main concern was that 'future fiscal policy should constantly bear in mind the inherent anti-growth nature of direct taxes and the necessity for avoiding forms of taxation, which markedly discourage productive effort, saving and investment'. The report was concerned about the overall level of taxation, and in particular argued for a cut in the profits and income taxes in order to create efficiency and incentives. There was also support for a shift towards indirect taxes, despite some alarm at the impact on the cost of living and wage restraint. One advantage of indirect taxes in comparison with a profits tax was that they could be rebated on exports. But the adoption of VAT

[23] See Lynch, 'A tax for Europe', 74–6, 80–7.

offered no advantage compared with the purchase tax, where exports remained within the tax-free 'ring' of producers and wholesalers, and did not pay the tax. The FBI therefore argued that a more broadly based tax with a higher yield could just as easily be achieved by reform of the purchase tax, with its simplicity of collection and administration compared with the complexities of VAT. The FBI accepted that reform of the purchase tax would only be possible if low incomes were compensated by improved social benefits and a cut in national insurance contributions. Consequently, an additional tax was needed to compensate low incomes, and to provide revenue to allow a cut in the profits tax – and the FBI proposed a new wealth tax on individuals. The FBI felt that its package of measures was preferable to a 'fundamental reconstruction of our fiscal system which would be involved in the replacement of profits tax by a turnover tax'.[24] In reality, the package was intensely controversial and politically naive. But it did suggest a major difficulty: could a shift to indirect taxes be made without compensation to poorer members of society who would suffer, at least in the short term, before the economy grew as a result of incentives and competitiveness?

The Conservatives achieved little change in the structure of indirect taxes or in the balance between direct and indirect taxes from 1951 to 1964. More radical change was debated, especially as a result of the growing awareness of Britain's lack of competitiveness and the need for tax incentives to exporters. The case for and against VAT was tied up with this narrower question which diverted attention from other justifications for change. In 1960–1, discussion of tax incentives for exporters by the Treasury, Inland Revenue, Customs and Excise and Board of Trade found that the existing tax system did not give any scope for export incentives compatible with GATT; the only possibility was a major shift of taxation to a sales or turnover tax. At first, the president of the Board of Trade, Reginald Maudling,* accepted the case for change. As he remarked, a

---

[24] MRC, FBI MSS 200/F/3/E7/1/4, report of the Committee on the Balance of the Fiscal System; Taxation Committee, 12 Oct. 1961; FBI MSS 200/F/3/E7/1/5, Taxation Panel, 1 Nov. 1961, 1 Dec. 1961, 11 Apr. 1962, 9 Oct. 1962, 14 Feb. 1963, and 'Memorandum on the replacement of purchase tax and/or profits tax by a tax on added value, 28 February 1963', 14 Mar. 1963; Taxation Committee, 9 Oct. 1962, 23 Oct. 1962.

* Reginald Maudling (1917–79) was born in London; he was educated at Merchant Taylor's School and Merton College, Oxford. He was called to the bar in 1940; he worked in the CRD after the war, and was elected to the Commons in 1950. In 1952, he was parliamentary secretary to the ministry of civil aviation, economic secretary to the Treasury 1952–5, minister of supply 1955–7, paymaster general 1957–9, president of the Board of Trade 1959–61, colonial secretary 1961–2 and chancellor of the Exchequer, 1962–4. Although he was deputy leader, he played little role in rethinking policy under Heath, and he was out of sympathy with the ideologies of free markets and monetarism. He resigned in 1972 as a result of his ill-advised business contacts. (*DNB, 1971–80*, ed. Blake and Nicholls, pp. 556–9; Robbins (ed.), *Biographical Dictionary*, pp. 297–9.)

variable turnover tax would provide a better way of regulating consumer demand, as well as allowing tax rebates to exporters. But the chancellor was wary on practical and political grounds, preferring some simpler means of regulating demand which led to the adoption of the surcharge (see below, pp. 267–9). A gradual process of adjustment and simplification of the purchase tax by lowering rates and narrowing differentials offered an easier way of making it a permanent source of revenue on 'defensible principles', while gradually increasing the proportion of indirect taxation. A complete recasting of the tax system simply seemed too complex for the possible benefit to exporters – as well as posing serious political problems.Further, officials on the Budget Committee warned that any shift to regressive indirect taxes would create difficulties when the government was 'trying to secure the co-operation of the trade union movement in establishing a more realistic system of wage determination and a new planning organisation'. Caution was the watchword of the Budget Committee, a sense that the scope for change was 'strictly limited'. Any desire of the chancellor for a more radical change encountered considerable official opposition.[25]

Of course, the alternative approach was to revise the fiscal system to benefit efficiency and growth in general, rather than to provide specific benefits for exporters. As Alec Cairncross* commented, the best way of

[25] PRO, T171/438, purchase tax: memorandum by the chancellor of the Exchequer, 27 Nov. 1953; T171/467, 'General revview of purchase tax', 27 July 1955; financial secretary (H. Brooke) to chancellor, purchase tax, 29 June 1955; C&E(55)12, general review of purchase tax, 17 June 1955; T171/478, Budget Committee, 30 Jan. 1957, and note of meeting in chancellor's room, 6 Feb. 1957; T171/479, BC(57)7, purchase tax: possible further broadening of the tax: customs note, 25 Jan. 1957; EWM to chancellor, indirect taxation, 2 Feb. 1957; T171/484, taxation of consumer goods: Customs note, 5 Dec. 1955; T171/488, C&E(58)1, purchase tax, 26 Feb. 1958; BC(57)22, a broader base for indirect taxation, Customs and Excise, 19 Aug. 1957; T320/58, president of the Board of Trade to chancellor, 29 Nov. 1960; note by T. Padmore, 1 Dec. 1960; W. Armstrong, brief for prime minister's meeting on exports, 6 Dec. 1960; tax incentives for exporters: first draft report to ministers; T171/515, meeting in chancellor's room, 22 Dec. 1960; T320/61, tax incentives for exporters: meeting in chancellor's room, 11 Dec. 1961; T171/592, Budget Committee, 12 June 1961, 8 Sept. 1961, 17 Oct. 1961, 2 Nov. 1961, 22 Feb. 1962; export incentives: note of a meeting held in Sir F. Lee's room, 16 Mar. 1962; BC(61)31, indirect taxation: note by Customs and Excise, 23 Sept. 1961.

* Alexander Kirkland Cairncross (1911–98) was born in Lesmahagow, near Glasgow, the son of an ironmonger and teacher. He was educated at Hamilton Academy, the University of Glasgow and Trinity College, Cambridge, where he studied British foreign investment before 1914. He became a lecturer at Glasgow in 1935, and joined Stamp's team of economists at the Cabinet Office in 1940. He transferred to the Board of Trade in 1941 and then to the ministry of aircraft production up to 1945 when he went to Berlin as Treasury representative to draw up plans for reparations, which were soon abandoned. He joined *The Economist* in 1946, and served on the Board of Trade's working party on wool which brought together employers, unions and outsiders to recommend policies of reconstruction – an experience which led to scepticism of the value of such an approach.

assisting exporters was through a reform of the tax system to secure industrial efficiency, and to promote enterprise and adaptability, without creating obstacles to growing firms using new technology. Such an approach required a general assessment of the economic consequences of the fiscal system rather than the short-term pragmatism which marked the 1950s.[26] A committee was indeed appointed to undertake a fundamental, long-term review of tax policy in 1962; as we shall see, it lacked the time and expertise for its task. The report proved disappointing to Cairncross, for it was still dominated by a concern for export incentives, and it tamely concluded that the purchase tax was superior to any alternative with, at most, an extension to other goods and the addition of a complementary tax on services. As the chairman of the committee pointed out, indirect taxes would do little to help exports, but a regressive tax regime would create other dangers. Indeed, he suggested that indirect taxes might be *abolished* in order to bring relative prices into line with relative costs.[27]

Of course, this argument could be turned around, for a uniform tax on all goods and services would have the same effect of bringing relative prices into line with relative costs. As Cairncross and the Economic Section pointed out, the existing tax system with its wide differentials between goods led to a misuse of resources in relation to consumer preference; a tax on all forms of consumption at the same rate would produce the same revenue and increase consumers' satisfaction. Above all, he argued that the existing tax system taxed consumer durables and left services largely untouched. In his view, taxes should be reduced on consumer durables, in order to encourage the development of new goods for the home market, which could then be exported. The production of these goods had high economies of scale, so that a larger home market would reduce their price. In other words, a successful exporter needed to have the most modern and desirable goods, which high levels of purchase

He joined the Board of Trade as an adviser, accepting the department's general approach of free trade, markets and consumer choice. In 1949, he went to Paris as an economic adviser to the Organisation for European Economic Co-operation. From 1951 to 1961 he was professor of applied economics at Glasgow. In 1961, he replaced Hall as chief economist at the Treasury and head of the Economic Section. In 1964, confusion arose as a result of the competing sources of economic advice, with Neild as economic adviser to the Treasury, Kaldor as adviser on taxation and Balogh advising the prime minister. He remained head of the government economic service, leaving at the end of 1968 and becoming master of St Peter's College, Oxford, from 1969 to 1978. (T. Wilson and B. Hopkin, 'Alexander Kirkland Cairncross, 1911–1998', *Proceedings of the British Academy* 105, *1999 Lectures and Memoirs* (Oxford, 2000), pp. 339–61.)

[26] PRO, T320/59, Cairncross to Lee, 11 Oct. 1961, and T171/592, BC(61)42, taxation and exports: note by the director, Economic Section, 5 Dec. 1961.

[27] PRO, T320/51, T. Padmore to J. Crosbie, 26 Feb. 1962; D. J. S. Hancock to T. Padmore, 27 Feb. 1962; RTP(62)5 (Final) Committee on the Review of Taxation Policy, interim report: structure of direct taxation, 4 Apr. 1962; T320/52, meeting, 8 Mar. 1962.

taxes made more difficult. Taxes could then be shifted to services, where Cairncross assumed there were no economies of scale. Above all, he argued that a shift from direct to indirect taxes was essential for incentives, both for individuals and companies. In his view, an increase in indirect taxation was 'unlikely to be such a disincentive unless the effect on the distribution of income were so great as to poison the social atmosphere':

In a society whose wealth was high and increasing it should be possible to raise a larger proportion of tax revenue in indirect forms without causing hardship, but in this country we had not so far made a deliberate attempt to achieve a higher proportion of indirect taxation. One reason for this was that we tend to pay greater attention to social justice and less to economic incentive than other countries ... It would not be an exaggeration to say that the only arguments for direct taxation were the social ones and that we are faced with a choice between social justice and economic growth.

Perhaps, as Frank Lee argued, the benefits of a radical reshaping of the tax system could justify the difficulties.[28]

The possible introduction of a value added tax therefore remained on the agenda, alongside other reforms of the fiscal system. However, little progress was made by the committee of officials appointed by the chancellor in 1962. Customs and Excise stressed the difficulties of collection of VAT and the virtues of the purchase tax. The economic secretary and chancellor agreed, preferring to adjust the purchase tax by extending its range and simplifying the rates. They were cautious, fearing the political dangers of an increase in indirect taxes on poorer families – not least in the light of Richard Titmuss's* writings on the regressive effects of the fiscal-welfare system. But they did now accept that the reform of the purchase tax was merely a step towards the introduction of the VAT, possibly as early as 1964.[29] At the same time, the EEC was moving towards tax

[28] PRO, T320/51, comments on the report by A. Cairncross, 5 Apr. 1962, and Lee, 13 Apr. 1962; T320/52, review of taxation policy, meetings, 27 Mar., 14 May 1962; T. Padmore to F. Lee, 'Review of taxation policy', 4 Apr. 1962; RTP(62)9, 'The loss on consumers imposed by unequal rates of indirect taxation: note by the Economic Section', 8 May 1962.

[29] PRO, T320/51, review of taxation policy, F. Lee, 13 Apr. 1962; D. F. Hubbard, programme of work for the Budget Committee, 17 Apr. 1962; T320/52, review of taxation policy, meeting with chancellor of the Exchequer, 17 May 1962; RTP meeting, 23 July 1962; RTP(62)15 (final), review of taxation policy: the added value turnover tax: note by Customs and Excise, Aug. 1962; T320/53, W. Armstrong, 17 May 1962; 'The French value added tax', T. Padmore, 12 Oct. 1962; economic secretary to the Treasury to chancellor, 19 Nov. 1962, and comment on this by Maudling; economic secretary to chancellor, 19 Dec. 1962.

* Richard Morris Titmuss (1907–73) was born in Bedfordshire, the son of an unsuccessful farmer and haulier; he was educated at a small preparatory school and took a commercial course in book-keeping. He worked as an office boy and clerk, writing in the evenings. His first book, *Poverty and Population*, appeared in 1938, and he was invited to join the

harmonisation on the basis of VAT, with a draft directive at the end of
1962 which was approved at the beginning of 1964. Sentiment was shifting within the government, for it was committed to seeking membership
of the EEC. A committee of enquiry was appointed in 1963, again with
disappointing results: in 1964 its report recommended *against* the introduction of VAT. As the British delegation to the EEC pointed out, the
report barely considered the issue of harmonisation.[30]

The Conservative government drew to a close without a major change
in indirect taxation, but with a dawning realisation that the VAT was likely
to come. The issues raised during these tentative discussions continued
in opposition, when the Conservative party grappled with the issue of
how to make a radical change in the tax system to benefit enterprise, and
at the same time ensure that poorer families did not suffer in the short
term before the benefits of growth were apparent. Cairncross's comment
on the balance between economic growth and social justice was central to
these debates. As we shall see, the attempt at creating a balance between
these two *desiderata* failed and VAT was eventually introduced *without*
countervailing measures to protect the poor. Meanwhile, the Labour government of 1964 to 1970 developed some of the themes which emerged
in the discussions of the early 1960s. Labour was anxious to create a modern, efficient economy, and to improve competitiveness. Cairncross offered one approach: an attempt to boost manufacturing industry with its
economies of scale, and to check services, where economies were less apparent. Similar thoughts were running through the fertile mind of Kaldor,
and were to be implemented when Labour narrowly won the election
of 1964. The Conservatives' failure to reform the tax system before
they lost office cleared the way for Labour to develop some of the same
ideas – and to give them a distinctive ideological twist.

Profits and the economy

The Conservative government failed to make any radical change to the
relationship between direct and indirect taxation, but growth could also
be encouraged by changes *within* direct taxation, through the shifting
impact of different forms of profits and income tax on investment and
incentives. The precise structure of direct taxes, and especially of profits
taxes, entailed different normative assumptions about Britain's economic

---

team writing the civil history of the war. His *Problems of Social Policy* appeared in 1950,
when he was elected to the chair of social administration at the LSE. (*DNB, 1971–80*,
ed. Blake and Nicholls, pp. 849–50.)

[30] PP 1963–4 XIX, *Report of the Committee on Turnover Taxation*, conclusions on pp. 377–81;
PRO, T320/226, C. O'Neill to H. Keeble, Foreign Office, 24 Mar. 1964.

future. These debates were technical and were largely carried out within the machinery of government or amongst economists rather than in the public arena. Nevertheless, they were significant in prescribing different visions of a modern, efficient Britain. Should growth and efficiency depend on creating nationalised industries or large public companies with retained profits, linked with planning and economies of scale? Were high salaries and profit margins a sign of socially created wealth and greed, at the expense of social integration and equality? Or should growth and efficiency rest on an active capital market designed to stimulate new concerns and technical change, encouraged by high profits and incomes for risk-taking? Should the wider public participate through popular share ownership and savings?

The Labour government of 1945 to 1951 stressed the importance of large public companies, state corporations and managers in creating an efficient, productive economy, and used differential taxation to encourage retentions. This approach rested on hostility to high distributions and an active capital market, which would lead to large incomes and socially created wealth in the hands of individuals. Differential profits tax offered a way of raising the amount and quality of investment. Large firms, with professional advice and research capacity, were more likely to diversify into new lines than 'private citizens advised by stockbrokers and solicitors at second-hand through favouring certain shares'. On this view, the most efficient way of allocating resources was through the rational decisions of company executives rather than financiers in the capital market. An increase in dividends would simply lead to higher personal consumption, to 'unearned' profits and inequality and to wage demands leading to inflation and a drop in investment.[31] Would the new Conservative administration take a different line, arguing that economic efficiency depended upon a dynamic private sector and capital market, encouraged by distributions and the profit motive? The implication might be an encouragement of private savings, as a way of providing funds for new concerns and dealing with social risks.

Leading officials were eager to abandon central features of Labour policy: they were pressing for a reconsideration of policy before Labour left office in 1951 – and they were scarcely less critical of the new Conservative administration. In 1954, Robert Hall, Edward Bridges and other officials set out their 'underlying philosophy': the economy depended on efficient and energetic industries, best encouraged by private initiative and increasing levels of investment. In turn, these depended on reasonable returns on risk capital. Although they admitted that retentions were

---

[31] T. Balogh, 'Differential profits tax', *Economic Journal* 68 (1958), 528–33.

an important source of funds, they were concerned that they favoured investment in existing production, with the dangers of inertia and lack of initiative. They therefore stressed the need for a 'free' supply of capital for new ventures, drawn from higher dividends paid to shareholders and directed to dynamic concerns in a flexible, responsive economy.[32] As the Royal Commission on the Taxation of Income and Profits argued, retentions did not necessarily increase net savings, for individuals could draw on the capital to maintain their consumption. Indeed, retentions might lead to a misallocation of resources: firms with internal sources of capital had less stringent conditions for investment; firms without large reserves had greater difficulties in securing external capital; and capital was not allocated to produce the highest marginal return. For these reasons, the Commission recommended the abolition of differentiation.[33]

The Labour government's preference for retentions rested not only on its approach to economic growth, but also on a more pragmatic consideration: low distributions would check inflation and encourage wage restraint. However, Hall doubted whether the policy *was* effective. In his view, the implication of Labour's policy was 'to encourage workers to think that there is something wrong about dividends ... It suited the Labour Party that dividends were apparently regarded as wrong. From an economic point of view I think this is a pity.' Neither did retentions do much to contain inflation, for increased share values allowed spending from capital gains, and the large reserves of companies weakened the government's ability to influence the timing of investment.[34] Opinion among some Treasury officials was therefore moving in the direction of using dividends as a reward for initiative and risk in a free enterprise economy, permitting the optimal allocation of resources and maximising growth. It followed that the high level of profits tax should be reduced and differentiation ended, in order to encourage private enterprise and investment, and to give companies freedom to make their own decisions about the allocation of profits within a free market. The technicalities of company taxation reflected contested attitudes to the financing of productive investment, and the means to achieve high rates of economic growth.

Once again, the policy of the Conservative government was rather half-hearted, with considerable uncertainty and lack of consistency.[35] Despite the recommendation of the Royal Commission to move to a single rate

[32] PRO, T230/282, EAS 34/296/01, 'Underlying philosophy', B. Gilbert, H. Brittan, R. Hall, S. C. Leslie and E. E. Bridges, 20 Oct. 1954; T230/282, EAS 34/296/01, S. C. Leslie to R. Hall, 7 Jan. 1955.

[33] PP 1955–6 xxvii, *Royal Commission on the Taxation of Profits and Income, Final Report*, pp. 887–92.

[34] PRO, T171/471, Hall to Petch, 22 Mar. 1956.

[35] See M. A. King, *Public Policy and the Corporation* (London, 1977), p. 42.

of profit tax,[36] Butler and Macmillan *widened* differentiation in favour of retentions in 1955 and 1956, more out of despration than ideological commitment. In 1955, concern about inflation forced the government to cut consumption, and officials felt this 'might need to be accompanied by a political *quid pro quo* in the form of a move to restrict profits'. Cabinet agreed, stressing the need for balance between classes in order to reduce wage demands, and to show that the government was committed to economic stability. The alternative was dividend limitation, but as Bridges pointed out 'it involves something tantamount to socialisation of all capital, leading perhaps to some horrid bureaucratic control to decide what rate of interest is allowable on particular types of risk bearing capital'. By comparison, an increase in the profits tax on distributions seemed 'a good suggestion' to the prime minister, Anthony Eden,[*] as part of a wider package of reforms, involving an end of subsidies on housing and food, and an increase in relief on earned income to assist the 'managerial and professional classes'. As Eden remarked, 'It may be that it is only by taking action against profits that it will be politically possible to eliminate some of the other pressures which are distorting the economy.'[37] The decision was intended as the least harmful of various ways of controlling profits, and as crucial to creating an acceptable package. It was precisely the sort of pragmatic calculation which limited the scope for fiscal reform, and helped to lock the economy into low effort and low productivity.

[36] PP 1955–6 xxvii, *Royal Commission on the Taxation of Profits and Income, Final Report*, p. 896.

[37] PRO, T171/456, note of meeting in Sir Edward Bridges's room, 28 July 1955; note for the record, meeting of chancellor of the Exchequer with junior ministers, advisers and Hancock and Miller of the Inland Revenue, 15 Aug. 1956; note of meeting in Sir Edward Bridges's room, 16 Aug. 1955; E. E. Bridges to chancellor, 19 Aug. 1955; Eden to chancellor, 19 Aug. 1955; H. Brook to chancellor, 22 Aug. 1955; note for the record, meeting of prime minister and chancellor, 23 Aug. 1955; B. Gilbert to Bancroft, 'Dividend limitation', 24 Aug. 1955; CM(55) 29th conclusions, Cabinet, 26 Aug. 1955; R. Hall to Bridges, 'The economic situation', 30 Aug. 1955; Bridges to chancellor, 30 Aug. 1955; Eden to chancellor, 3 Sept. 1955; note of meeting in chancellor's room, 5 Sept. 1955; CM(55) 30th conclusions, Cabinet, 5 Sept. 1955; note of meeting in Sir Edward Bridges's room, 6 Sept. 1955; Eden to chancellor, 8 Sept. 1955; chancellor to prime minister, 8 Sept. 1955; note of meeting in chancellor's room, 20 Oct. 1955; Bridges to chancellor, 21 Oct. 1955; T171/457, H. D. H. to chancellor, increase in the tax on distributed profits, 5 Oct. 1955; Bridges to chancellor, 6 Oct. 1955.

[*] Robert Anthony Eden (1897–1977) was born in Co. Durham, the son of a landowner; he was educated at Eton and Christ Church, Oxford. He was elected to the Commons in 1923; he was private parliamentary secretary in the Home Office in 1924, and Foreign Office in 1926. In 1931, he was appointed parliamentary under-secretary in the Foreign Office, becoming lord privy seal with duties in the Foreign Office in 1933, minister without portfolio for the League of Nations in 1935 and Foreign Secretary from 1935 to 1938, when he resigned over Chamberlain's foreign policy. He became secretary of state for the dominions in 1939, war secretary in 1940, foreign secretary 1940–5 and 1951–5, and prime minister 1955–7. (*DNB, 1971–80*, ed. Blake and Nicholls, pp. 262–72.)

Harold Macmillan succeeded Butler as chancellor in December 1955. Even before he moved to the Treasury, he was feeling his way towards a fiscal strategy designed to encourage economic growth, based on a policy of 'savings and incentives'. As he saw it, there were two ways of dealing with the inflationary pressure of full employment. One was physical controls, which Labour could do better. The other was to encourage production by tax cuts designed both to give incentives to the managerial and entrepreneurial class, and to encourage savings. Heavy taxation of the managerial and professional classes was seen as the root cause of economic and political problems, reducing incentives and leading to resentment by middle-class voters who felt that their interests were neglected. He explained to the Cabinet,

Lloyd George's 1909 Budget had as it theme 'Slosh the Landlord'; Dalton's Budget was 'Slosh the Rentier'. Had we been able to make a Capital Gains Tax our theme could have been 'Slosh the Speculator'. But since this cock won't fight, we must think of another. I think the theme might be ... entitled – *Savings and Incentives*.

Macmillan's aim was to create a politically acceptable package which could contain wage demands and reduce taxation on the managerial classes.[38] In the first place, he hoped to encourage production by a reduction in taxation, especially on earned income as an incentive to 'the managerial and entrepreneur class', linked to a cut in purchase tax to lower the cost of living. Secondly, he wished to stimulate saving, both by companies (through reducing or abolishing tax on retained profits and increasing the tax on distributions) and by individuals through schemes to make saving more attractive.[39] In 1956, he increased the profits tax on distributions in order to provide relief to the income tax. His programme was, in many ways, ill-considered – as David Eccles* informed the prime minister. In his view, discrimination against distributions would merely encourage companies to be extravagant, paying higher salaries with the money they would otherwise distribute, and at the same time increasing

---

[38] PRO, T171/457, CP(55)11, 'Dizzy with success', H. Macmillan; T171/473, the budget: Harold Macmillan to Sir E. Bridges, 31 Jan. 1956; note for the record, L. P., 2 Feb. 1956.

[39] PRO, T171/471, increase in profits tax: note by Inland Revenue, 21 Mar. 1956; Hall to Petch, 22 Mar. 1956; T171/457, CP(55)111, 'Dizzy with success', H. Macmillan.

* David McAdam Eccles (1904–99) was born in London. He was educated at Winchester and New College, Oxford. He worked in the City and in the war he joined the ministry of economic warfare and the ministry of production; he was elected a Conservative MP in 1943. In 1951, he called on the Conservatives to support those who increased rather than owned wealth; he was appointed minister of works in 1951, moving to education in 1954 and the Board of Trade in 1957, before returning to education 1959–62. He moved to the Lords and entered business, returning to politics as paymaster general with responsibility for the arts, 1970–3. He became chairman of the British Library 1973–8. (*Who's Who 1999* (London, 1999), p. 596; *Guardian*, 27 Feb. 1999.)

the value of shares. Consequently, trade unions could complain about the blatant prosperity of a few people, which was usually based on capital gains. By contrast, 'the modest rise in dividends after tax which has helped so many of our supporters has bought no one a Bentley'. The answer, it seemed to Eccles, was a capital gains tax to deal with the few people able to secure large untaxed incomes out of capital, rather than still greater discrimination against dividends:

The salaried man with no capital cannot easily save today. Indeed he is finding it harder and harder to pay school and university fees. The owner of capital at least keeps afloat and may become very much richer. It is this increasing differential between the man with and without capital that is going to cause us so much trouble.[40]

This logic was to lead to a shift in profits taxation.

Attention started to turn to reforming the profits tax, possibly in conjunction with a capital gains tax. Under the existing British fiscal regime, companies paid both the differentiated profits tax *and* the standard rate of income tax, which was set against the shareholders' liability on distributions. The initial idea was to separate corporate and personal taxation, so that the income tax only applied to dividends received by shareholders; the company would then pay a tax on its profits, either in their entirety or simply on retentions. The Inland Revenue and Treasury were uneasy at this separation of taxation of income and profits, and objected to both possibilities. Any decision to impose a profits tax on *retentions* and leave distributed profits to the income tax could be challenged as a tax on funds for investment, and would help firms with high distributions. The alternative was to tax the company's entire profit and impose an income tax on the dividends; the objection was that it would be seen as double taxation of shareholders. As a result of these arguments, both the income tax *and* profit tax continued to apply to *all* profits, which was the approach recommended by the Royal Commission. The new corporation tax would be set at a single rate on both retentions and distributions – a proposal which caused the Inland Revenue and Treasury concern that it would be inequitable between firms. The new unified rate would be fixed somewhere below the existing rate of 30 per cent for distributed and somewhere above the existing rate of 3 per cent for retained profits. Consequently, firms with high retentions (including export industries such as engineering, motor vehicles and aircraft) would face an *increase* in their liability for tax. Meanwhile, firms with high distributions would pay *less* – and they included sectors such as food, drink and tobacco which were less important for exports. The Treasury and Inland Revenue insisted that implementation of the proposal should wait until the government

[40] PRO, T171/457, David Eccles to prime minister, 1 Sept. 1955.

could afford to set the unified rate at a sufficiently low level to ensure that *no* firm paid more tax. A low rate of corporation tax posed other problems, in stimulating wage demands. In the event, a flat-rate profit tax of 10 per cent was introduced in 1958 and Dalton's differential profits tax was abandoned. Although this rate hit firms with high retentions, it seemed desirable to maintain wage restraint. The firms would then be compensated by 'initial allowances' on new capital equipment.[41]

In 1961 and 1962, the proposal to replace the profits tax and income tax on companies with a single corporation tax, distinct from the personal income tax, resurfaced. This could take one of two forms. The first was to impose a corporation tax on *all* profits and then set it against the income tax liability of shareholders. In the budget of 1961, the chancellor hinted that the government might adopt a corporation tax on these lines, but the Inland Revenue claimed it was simply too complex to administer. The alternative was to levy a corporation tax on all profits, without any credit for the income tax on distributions. This approach was recommended by Kaldor in the minority report of the Royal Commission, and it would reintroduce differential taxation of profits: firms with high distributions would pay more tax and firms with high retentions would pay less. As a result, nothing was done – and the way was left for the Labour government to adopt Kaldor's approach and so restore differential taxation in a new guise.[42]

---

[41] PRO, T171/473, note for the record, L. P., 2 Feb. 1956; T171/478, note for the record, 29 June 1956; Budget Committee, 26 July 1956, 27 Nov. 1956, 30 Jan. 1957, note for the record, 13 Sept. 1956: chancellor with economic and financial secretaries and Hancock on Inland Revenue proposals for the budget; note of meeting in chancellor's room, 17 Jan. 1957, 27 Feb. 1957; T171/480, Macmillan to Hancock, 2 May 1956; profits tax, H. D. H. to chancellor, 23 Jan. 1957; Makins to chancellor, 1 Feb. 1957; E. W. M. to chancellor, 1 Mar. 1957; corporate and personal taxation: note by the Board of Inland Revenue, 12 Nov. 1956; T171/487, meeting in chancellor's room, 12 Feb. 1958; R. M. to chancellor, 28 Feb. 1958; direct taxation: note of meeting in chancellor's room, 10 Mar. 1958; T171/489, H. D. H. to chancellor, 2 May 1957; BC(58)3, 17 Jan. 1958, Budget Committee: corporation taxation: note by the secretary; H. D. H. to chancellor, 11 Feb. 1958: profits tax; R. M. to chancellor, 1 Feb. 1957; H. D. H. to chancellor, profits tax, 23 Jan. 1957; note to chancellor, profits tax, 19 Feb. 1958; BC(M)(58)9, Budget Committee, profits tax, R. Makins, 27 Feb. 1958; E. W. Maude to Robertson, Inland Revenue, 12 Mar. 1958; E. W. M. to chancellor, 13 Mar. 1958; R. W., Inland Revenue, 14 Mar. 1958; note to chancellor by financial secretary, 21 Mar. 1958; profits tax, J. E. S. Simon, 19 Feb. 1958; IR63/207, H. D. H., Inland Revenue, 11 Feb. 1958; profits tax, R. M., 1 Feb. 1957; profits tax, H. D. H., 23 Jan. 1957; profits tax, J. E. S. Simon, 19 Feb. 1958; BC(M)(58)8, Budget Committee: profits tax, R. M., 27 Feb. 1958. For the recommendations of the Royal Commission, see PP 1955–6 XXVII, *Royal Commission on the Taxation of Profits and Income, Final Report*, pp. 887–98. See also the Inland Revenue's defence of the existing system in T171/508, Board of Inland Revenue: a corporation tax, 30 Dec. 1959.

[42] PRO, T171/595, corporation tax: economic secretary (Anthony Barber) to chancellor, 9 Jan. 1962; M294, corporation tax, A. Johnston, Inland Revenue, 4 Jan. 1962; M295, taxation of companies, A. Johnston, Inland Revenue, 18 Jan. 1962; PP 1955–6 XXVII,

The attitude of the Treasury and Inland Revenue provides a further example of their ability to frustrate change, and their concern for somewhat small issues of equity at the expense of the wider picture. As in the case of indirect taxation, many officials took a hostile attitude to change, failing to consider the wider implications of the tax system for growth and social justice. Ministers were also concerned that their actions should not alienate unions and stimulate wage demands: they were anxious that any concessions to larger earned incomes or changes in the profits tax would not be interpreted as 'selfish' or divisive. Despite their ideological commitment to incentives, they were hampered by pragmatic electoral considerations and alarm at wage inflation. Underlying these somewhat myopic concerns of officials and ministers was a basic structural flaw: the machinery of government did not provide a forum to consider the wider issues and implications of the tax system for growth until the final years of the Conservative administration.

The reform of the profits tax in the budget of 1958 started to move away from Dalton's strategy of increasing investment in industry by encouraging existing, large firms as rational and efficient. At the same time, the government started to encourage competition. More consideration was now given to the role of the external capital market in creating flexible and responsive enterprise, with a realisation that British economic performance suffered from low productive investment. As Edwin Plowden explained, policy 'is directed towards the strengthening of productive industry under free enterprise conditions – a vital need in our present situation. To achieve this two main things have to be done: we must use every means of ensuring that industry is better equipped and we must ensure that enterprise is rewarded.'[43] How should this be done? Did it simply mean the removal of differential profits taxes, or should it involve a more active policy of encouraging savings, investment and profits? And if it did, should this be achieved through changes in the tax position of *corporate* investment or through the provision of incentives to *individuals*?

In fact, the debate within the machinery of government concentrated on *corporate* investment decisions through tax breaks to plant and machinery, reflecting the concern of officials to revise and adjust the existing tax code. 'Initial allowances' were introduced in 1945; in 1954, they were replaced by 'investment allowances' which gave companies *more* tax relief than the cost of the plant and machinery. Investment allowances were in turn abolished in 1956, and reintroduced in 1959 alongside a lower

Royal Commission on the Taxation of Profits and Income, Final Report, memorandum of dissent, pp. 1114–22.

[43] PRO, T171/435, W. Strath to E. Plowden, 25 Nov. 1952; Plowden to chancellor, initial allowances, 8 Apr. 1953.

initial allowance.[44] Much effort was expended on the debate over initial and investment allowances in the early 1960s, a sign of concern for detail at the expense of larger strategic issues.

Others saw these allowances as a means of modernising the economy – or at least, as the Board of Trade argued, of providing a more politically acceptable way of reducing taxation of industry than a direct cut in the profits tax 'at a time when we are striving to mobilise support for our wages policy'. The TUC accepted the case for investment allowances as 'a more effective method of assisting investment than a reduction in profits tax or in the standard rate of income tax, as the tax relief from the latter may be used to increase dividends rather than to increase investment'.[45] Hall and the Economic Section took a somewhat similar line, arguing that investment allowances offered a way of encouraging the external capital market and flexibility – especially if the allowances were funded from an *increase* in the profits tax. Although it might seem curious to encourage enterprise by a higher taxation of profits, Hall argued that funds would be taken from firms with accumulated profits and transferred to firms in expanding sectors in need of investment. In his view, investment allowances gave more incentive to actual investment than the differential profits tax or initial allowances.[46] Hall's approach therefore continued to use taxation to shape corporate investment rather than returning decisions to the market.

The Inland Revenue was sceptical, arguing that any concession would be costly and ineffective, mainly benefiting short-lived assets which would be replaced in any case, without raising total investment which depended on the conditions of trade. The Treasury and Inland Revenue were concerned that allowances also breached the impartiality of the tax system by granting subsidies to particular taxpayers. Of course, insistence that the tax system should be 'fair' might simply result in the 'continued rigidity of the productive machine', denying the possibility that taxation should stimulate productivity and efficiency.[47] Furthermore, the allowances were used for different, not entirely compatible, purposes: to stimulate investment and to regulate its timing. If allowances were used mainly to regulate

---

[44] See table 5.4 of Steinmo, *Taxation and Democracy*; the changes are outlined in PRO, IR63/209, BC(59)27, Budget Committee: report of the Committee on Incentive Allowances, 24 Feb. 1959, and BC(M)(59)10, report of the Committee on Incentive Allowances, R. M., 27 Feb. 1959.

[45] PRO, IR63/209, TUC: the economic situation and the 1959 budget.

[46] For Hall and the Economic Section, see PRO, T171/439, BC(54)19, Budget Committee: incentives for investment: note by the director, Economic Section, 11 Feb. 1954; A. Cairncross and N. Watts, *The Economic Section, 1939–1961: A Study in Economic Advising* (London, 1989), pp. 132, 264.

[47] PRO, T230/328, EAS 31/02/A, 'Selective investment and discriminatory tax policies'; 'Taxation and incentives'; 'Obstacles to efficiency', 5 Dec. 1952.

investment over the cycle, they would be less effective in raising the level of investment as a whole. Perhaps the answer was to introduce yet another form of regulator, so that the allowances could be used to stimulate investment. The outcome was a further change – the replacement of the dual system of investment and initial allowances with a single initial allowance alongside a regulator.[48]

Much time and energy was spent to little practical effect, for business decisions could not rely on these constantly changing allowances. Adjustments arose from short-term political expendiency rather than consistency, from a desire to reduce company taxation by sleight of hand. The government offered a tax concession – and then made an adjustment to compensate firms with different levels of retention, or to placate the TUC. In one sense, the result was balance – the watchword of the British fiscal system. But in another sense, the pursuit of equity led to complexity, confusion and inconsistency which might start to undermine consent. Much effort was spent in debating small changes in the company tax code with only a modest impact on behaviour, at the expense of serious consideration of strategic shifts in the fiscal system. As in the case of the purchase tax, action was limited by established structures with many small-scale, inconsistent adjustments within their confines. Structural stasis was linked with incessant tinkering.[49]

Personal taxation: incentives and savings

The concern for company taxation and the importance of retentions also had implications for another element of the tax system: the treatment of personal savings and incentives. There was an alternative to adjustments to the tax position of corporate investment, which would entail a more radical shift in policy: encouragement of *individual* savings, linked to a rhetoric of popular capitalism and privatisation. In order to pursue such a policy, the government would need to decide, in the first place, on the priority for tax cuts. Should the emphasis be on concessions to companies or to individuals? The stress on corporate investment had major implications for the definition of incentives, suggesting that tax cuts should be granted to companies to encourage capital investment and profitability

[48] PRO, T171/592, Budget Committee, 15 Dec. 1961, 16 Mar. 1962; president of the Board of Trade to chancellor of the Exchequer, 5 Mar. 1962; 'Investment and initial allowances: note by R. Turvey, Economic Section', 6 Nov. 1961; T171/595, Economic Section to chancellor, 19 Mar. 1962; BC(62)10, 'Tax reliefs on industrial investment: a note by the Board of Trade', Feb. 1962; BC(62)12, tax depreciation allowances: memorandum by the Board of Inland Revenue, 8 Mar. 1962.

[49] PRO, T320/219, 220 and 221, provides the papers on 'Effect of incentive tax allowances upon capital investment: Tax Incentive Committee'.

rather than to individuals to encourage effort and enterprise. A cut in the standard rate would benefit companies, whereas an adjustment in income tax allowances and thresholds would help individuals. Allowances and thresholds could also be manipulated in order to benefit particular groups, such as family men on modest incomes or those paying surtax. These debates had major ideological implications, resting on different assumptions about the sources of growth and incentives to shape Britain's economic future. They implied particular visions of human motivation, as well as self-interested electoral calculation.

The scope for concessions was not great, for major reductions in expenditure were unlikely, given the government's caution about cutting social services. The limited scope for concessions created difficulties: should they be concentrated on one striking remission; or should they be spread over a wide area in order to satisfy everyone (and perhaps failing to please anyone)? Should tax cuts be given to higher incomes as an encouragement to incentives and growth? In Hall's view, the high marginal rates gave a greater incentive to evade than to produce, which was 'an economic loss to the country and, in the long run, a source of corruption, tending to bring all payment of taxes into disrepute'.[50] Or should concessions go to lower incomes to secure support for wage restraint?

One view was that concessions should be concentrated on surtax payers. It was, as Eden put it, 'in the interest both of social justice and of incentives' to extend earned income relief to higher incomes in the managerial and professional class. Macmillan agreed, arguing for 'income tax relief as *incentives* to productivity and effort. This really amounts to doing *as much as we can possibly get away with* politically for the "executive" in the £2000 pa and above class. At present they find it more profitable to gamble than to work.'[51] Not everyone agreed, arguing that the gravest problem was further down the income scale amongst the 'promising executives' on £200 to £500. They could be helped by a sizeable cut in the standard rate of income tax, which would benefit higher and middle incomes more than small incomes, and would also relieve companies. In 1954, the CRD argued that a striking reduction in the standard rate of income tax would provide a psychological boost:

It helps the saver, the better paid worker, the middle classes, the surtax payer and industry. I am convinced that we must try to reduce the standard rate by at least 1s before the next election. This would mark the essential difference between Conservative and Labour financial policies and would make things difficult for

[50] T171/515, Budget Committee, 22 Sept. 1960.
[51] PRO, T171/456, Eden to chancellor, 19 Aug. 1955 and 3 Sept. 1955; T171/470, H. Macmillan to financial secretary, 1 Jan. 1956. The surtax threshold was £2,000, as at the end of the First World War.

the Socialists should they be returned to power. If we reduce the profits tax, the first thing the Socialists will do will be to restore it, and they will incur no unpopularity in doing so. But if we reduce the standard rate and they raise it again, everyone will be hurt, and there will be a universal groan.[52]

The alternative to a sizeable cut in the standard rate was a more modest reduction, linked with an increase in the earned income and child allowances. Such an approach would offer more to smaller incomes and less to companies.[53]

The balance between these different claims for tax relief was difficult to strike, and had obvious political repercussions. Concessions to surtax payers would expose the Conservatives to charges of favouring the rich to the detriment of the poor. Meanwhile, inflation was taking more and more people above the threshold for payment of income tax, with the dangers of a 'poverty' trap. And there was always the threat of middle-class resentment towards the Conservatives. Whatever the impact on economic incentives, the CRD was clear about the political consequences of high taxation on the middle class. 'There is a strong feeling among many middle class supporters that their interests are not being looked after by the Government ... In considering any future tax changes those reductions which will most help the middle classes should be given particular emphasis.'[54] In 1960, the Conservative party's Taxation Policy Committee reached a similar conclusion when it considered where the burden of taxation 'pinched'. The standard of living of the working classes had risen; those earning the lowest wages were helped in other ways:

The worst pinch was in the £1000–2000 a year level, and perhaps a little above. These include a large number of middle-class professional people who have not yet escaped from family responsibilities. In these cases there is not only an actual pinch, but a relative pinch in relation to the big rise in the standard of life of the working population since before the war. For this deserving and important class, a reduction in the standard rate of income tax, and to a lesser extent a reduction in surtax, would be the most useful relief.[55]

Here was a narrow, electoral approach to taxation – even if the CRD had sufficient self-awareness to admit that it was 'a little blatant' to suggest that those most in need of assistance were people like the members of the committee.[56]

---

[52] PRO, T171/437, 'Note on the various proposals for tax reductions', CRD, 16 Feb. 1954.
[53] PRO, T171/515, BC(60), 4th meeting, 22 Sept. 1960; for FBI support see, MRC, FBI MSS 200/F/3/E7/1/4, Tax Committee, 12 Oct. 1961.
[54] PRO, T171/470, note on tax concessions, CRD, 12 Jan. 1956.
[55] CPA, CRD 3/7/26/2, TPC (60)5, minutes of 3rd meeting of Taxation Policy Committee, 30 June 1960; indeed, the starting point for payment of surtax had not been raised since 1920, when it was set at £2,000.
[56] CPA, CRD 3/7/26/2, memorandum by James Douglas, 13 July 1960.

These issues were central to Selwyn Lloyd's* budget of 1961. In the run-up to the budget, considerable attention was paid to the best means of providing incentives. Should concessions be given to the highest levels of income, or to incomes around £2,000 at the threshold for the surtax? Should the standard rate be reduced, and allowances increased? And how should the cost of any concessions to the surtax be covered? Lloyd was anxious to offer considerable concessions to surtax, arguing that it 'would produce the dramatic effect which was needed to bring a real change in outlook among those whose additional efforts and energies could lead to a marked growth of the economy'. Officials were more wary, concerned at the 'political and social limit' of action as a result of the need to find revenue from other sources. Should a new tax be imposed on capital gains, the profits tax raised, indirect taxes extended or duties on oil and motor vehicles raised? The eventual outcome of the convoluted discussions was an increase in the threshold for the payment of surtax from £2,000 to £4,000 for earned income, to be covered by an increase in the profits tax and various indirect taxes. The failure to introduce a capital gains tax, and the recent increases in insurance contributions, led to political outcry. The budget was, in the words of Harold Wilson,[†] the shadow chancellor, 'class legislation of the most blatant type'. As the *New Statesman* put it, the budget was 'part of a deliberate strategy to make private enrichment rather than collective endeavour the economic main-spring of our society'. The attempt to 'balance' the budget by raising the profits tax was not welcomed by industry – and the budget was compromised by confusion over the imposition of a 'regulator'. Above all, it seemed to offer tax cuts for the rich rather than a carefully considered strategy for economic efficiency. As the Budget Committee remarked, the budget of 1961 offered 'appreciable concessions to the upper income groups but none at all for the lower income

---

* John Selwyn Brooke Lloyd (1904–78) was born on the Wirral. He was educated at Fettes and Magdalene College, Cambridge. In 1929, he stood as a Liberal but he soon became a Conservative. He was called to the bar in 1930 and became a Conservative MP in 1945. In 1951, he became minister of state at the Foreign Office, moving to be minister of supply in 1954, minister of defence in 1955 and foreign secretary in 1955. He was chancellor of the Exchequer 1960–3 and leader of the Commons 1963–4; from 1971 to 1976 he was speaker of the Commons. (*DNB, 1971–80*, ed. Blake and Nicholls, pp. 511–15.)

† Harold Wilson (1916–95) was born in Huddersfield; he studied politics, philosophy and economics at Jesus College, Oxford, and taught and worked as an assistant to Beveridge. In 1940, he joined the War Cabinet secretariat. He became a Labour MP in 1945, and was parliamentary secretary at the ministry of works, and from 1947 to 1951 president of the Board of Trade, resigning with Bevan. From 1955 to 1963, he was successively shadow chancellor and foreign secretary, leading the party from 1963 to 1976, and serving as prime minister 1964–70 and 1974–6. (Robbins (ed.), *Biographical Dictionary*, pp. 425–8.)

groups'; indeed, later in the year Customs and Excise duties were raised by 10 per cent.[57]

Conservative chancellors were acutely conscious of the need to secure the TUC's co-operation in wage restraint and reduction of consumption by action against excessive profits and speculative capital gains. The capital gains tax was also expected to appeal to salaried men conscious (so it was claimed) of the widening gap with those who had capital gains. It marked a further stage in the old story of earned versus unearned, industrious versus spontaneous income: capital gains provided an income which was not taxed in any way, and was derived from speculation. As Eden explained,

a basic cause of the sense of unfairness which exists in the country today arises from the difference of opportunity which exists between those who happen to possess capital and those who do not. With the present rate of taxation, the earning of a high income does not enable anyone to enjoy blatant luxury. Only capital gains and perhaps a generous expense account can do that. It is this type of spending that is resented not only by industrial workers but by many middle class and professional people as well. I am convinced that the gesture would out-weigh the dangers and even the inefficiency of the tax.

Thus taxation of capital gains would balance concessions to (earned) surtax, and counter criticism of the Conservatives as the party of speculators and shady financiers. The capital gains tax could be justified as a measure of social equity in taxing a major source of wealth, and at the same time the surtax threshold could be raised, the standard rate of income tax cut and allowances increased to help small incomes. As Lee remarked, the capital gains tax would not provide a source of revenue

[57] H. Pemberton, 'The 1961 budget', MA dissertation, University of Bristol, 1991, pp. 35–43; the relevant files are in PRO, T171/515, Budget Committee meetings, 15 June, 12, 22 Sept., 12, 26 Oct., 20, 22 Dec. 1960, 10, 31 Jan., 3, 24, 27, 28 Feb., 1, 6, 20 Mar. 1961; 'Possible long-term programme of tax changes': note by F. Lee, BC(M)(60)4, 1 Nov. 1960, covering BC(60)43, revised, memorandum by Board of Inland Revenue, 'Long-term programme of tax changes', 28 Oct. 1960; 'The shape of the budget', F. Lee, 9 Mar.1961; E. Boyle to S. Lloyd, 14 Mar. 1961; T171/517, A. Johnston to Hubback, 1 Feb. 1961; 'Surtax relief', A. Johnston, 23 Feb. 1961; 'Surtax reliefs', A. Johnston, 28 Mar. 1961; F. Lee to Hubback, 'Proposed surtax concessions', 9 Mar. 1961; 'Surtax and profits tax', A. Barber to S. Lloyd, 13 Mar. 1961; T171/520, FBI to S. Lloyd, 4 May 1961; Institute of Directors to Lloyd, 21 Apr. and 18 May 1961; T171/526, T. Padmore to F. Lee, 16 Mar. 1961; T171/592, Budget Committee meeting, 17 Oct. 1961; T230/493, 'Supplementary note for the chancellor: taxation', F. Lee, 27 July 1960; PREM11/3762, Brook to Macmillan, 23 Feb. 1961; A. Cairncross (ed.), *The Robert Hall Diaries, 1954–1961* (London, 1991), pp. 259–60. The quotations from Wilson and the *New Statesman* are from Pemberton, 'The 1961 budget', p. 42, citing *The Times*, 19 Apr. 1961, and *New Statesman*, 21 Apr. 1961. I would like to thank Hugh Pemberton for making available his dissertation and material arising from his subsequent PhD thesis.

or means of regulating the economy; rather, it was a political act and a measure of social justice to ease strains with the unions.[58]

In the opinion of the Inland Revenue, any capital gains tax was administratively complex and impractical.[59] Eventually, Lloyd announced in 1961 his intention of introducing a tax on *short-term* or speculative capital gains, as a way of dealing with resentment against speculators in the take-over and property booms. As Maudling, the president of the Board of Trade, argued, a tax on speculation and a reduction in the surtax on earned incomes was

a fundamental act of justice in a society where the rewards for ownership are disproportionate to the rewards for effort. It would have a tonic effect upon management and upon professional classes; and incidentally I think it would be politically very welcome to many of our supporters.

It was introduced in 1962, in response to political sensitivity over some of the spectacular fortunes in the property and take-over boom.[60]

The failure to introduce a full capital gains tax contributed to the wider difficulties of Macmillan as chancellor and prime minister in redefining taxation policy and creating a new vision of the economic future. How far was he able to go in his strategy of reducing taxation of the managerial classes to encourage incentives to promote individual savings? His strategy would require an end of differentiation against 'unearned' or investment income. Macmillan felt that the situation had changed since differentiation was introduced in 1907, when

it represented a kind of moral judgement ... wages, salaries, and the profits of professional men were regarded as somehow more meritorious than the income of the rentier, large or small. I feel now that the boot is rather on the other leg. It is quite easy to earn large wages and salaries in an inflationary period – almost too easy. The difficulty is to save. There are no great attractions to it, either to the small saver, the middle saver, or the large saver. The moment that earnings

[58] PRO, T171/515, BC(60)43, revised, possible long-term programme of tax changes, and covering note by F. Lee, 1 Nov. 1960; T230/493, supplementary note for the chancellor, taxation, F. Lee, 27 July 1960.
[59] PRO, PREM11/4769, capital gains tax: philosophy of the tax system, n.d.; T171/518, Board of Inland Revenue, taxation of short-term capital gains, 16 Feb. 1961. The tax was rejected by PP 1955–6 xxvii, *Royal Commission on the Taxation of Profits and Income, Final Report*, pp. 757–9.
[60] PRO, T320/58, Maudling to Lloyd, 29 Nov. 1960; T171/600, short-term capital gains: note by the Board of Inland Revenue, 7 Sept. 1961; see Lloyd's speech in *Parliamentary Debates*, 5th ser. 638, 17 Apr. 1961, cols. 821–2, which rejected the tax in the budget; he announced the short-term capital gains tax in 648, cols. 833–4, 7 Nov. 1961, and introduced it in *Parliamentary Debates*, 5th ser. 657, 9 Apr. 1962, cols. 978–80; also Bower, 'Some reflections on the budget', 29–32.

are turned into savings by some mysterious alchemy they lose their respectability. The interest on savings is unearned.

When you think of how most of these unearned incomes, at least up to £1000 or £1500 a year, have really come about, this is somewhat absurd. They represent in many cases years of genuine sacrifice, for a man trying to build up a nest egg for his wife or his children; or, in many cases, insurance premiums which require real effort to keep up.

All this leads me to say that I believe that it is more important to encourage savings than it is to encourage earnings, and that the whole system discriminates against savings. Therefore if, as I hope, you can do something for unearned incomes (which would certainly help the so-called 'middle classes' a good deal) you can provide a good moral argument for it. It is also of course good economics because savings are the things we are trying to get. We also know in our hearts that in a period where inflation cannot be stopped, at the most controlled, savings are becoming less attractive.[61]

Of course, two forms of savings *did* have tax benefits. One was life insurance premiums, which were granted tax relief by Gladstone in 1853. The other was owner-occupied housing. In theory, the imputed income of a house was taxed under schedule A, so removing much of the benefit of tax relief on mortgage interest. In practice, valuations had not changed since before the war, so that the imputed income was unrealistically low. In the early 1960s, a decision was needed to reform or abolish schedule A tax. Clearly, many middle-class voters would gain from abolition – and the revaluation of property for the local rates in 1963 made some concession politically desirable.[62] As a result, owner-occupied housing and life insurance absorbed a high proportion of middle-class savings, and distorted the capital market. The question posed by Macmillan was whether incentives to savings should be widened.

The attraction of the policy was political and social as much as economic, reinforcing the party's commitment to private ownership compared with Labour's stress on public ownership. 'The social reasons are obvious', remarked the economic secretary to the Treasury:

On the political side ... we are specifically pledged to a property owning democracy ... I am confident we could work out a scheme which would benefit a wide range of savings institutions from Building Societies and Unit Trusts, to the Joint Stock Banks. Not only would this be sensible but it would be very popular with our own people.[63]

[61] PRO, T171/479, Macmillan to Thorneycroft, 2 Mar. 1957; also in PREM11/1816.
[62] On schedule A, see PRO, PREM11/4191, chancellor to prime minister, 17 June 1960; PREM11/3763, schedule A, 26 Mar. 1962; CRD 2/10/19(1), taxation policy – 1960 and after, 22 Jan. 1960; CRD 2/10/19(4), TPC(64)8, the 1964 budget, 23 Oct. 1963; TPC(63)3, Taxation, 1963, 10 Dec. 1962; TPC(64)2, Taxation Policy Committee, 1963: stable savings, 10 Sept. 1963; TPC(64)4, Taxation Policy Committee, 1963, earned income relief, 9 Sept. 1963.
[63] PRO, T171/607, economic secretary to chancellor, 6 Feb. 1963.

The Conservative party's enquiry into economic growth, chaired by Paul Chambers, proposed tax breaks for 'contractural' savings, as part of a general package to increase incentives. Little was done. In 1963, the proposal of the Wider Share Ownership Group for tax relief on some forms of contractual saving was firmly rejected by the Inland Revenue as 'inequitable'. Taxation was determined by 'capacity to pay' – and what better measure of capacity could there be than a surplus for savings after meeting other expenses? Such arguments took no account of the need – as the NEDC saw it – for higher investment and savings to stimulate economic growth. In the chancellor's opinion, there was no reason why the tax system should not be used for this desirable national objective.[64]

The Inland Revenue was not convinced. 'It is surely wrong', argued the chairman of the Inland Revenue, 'to regard the tax structure as a kind of Christmas tree to be festooned with small presents for worthy causes. We shall never be able to streamline and simplify taxation if that point of view prevails.'[65] His comment mixed good sense and naivety. The tax system was indeed a Christmas tree, festooned with incentive or investment al-lowances, short-term capital gains tax, tax breaks for charities and life insurance – with little coherence. There was nothing 'natural' about the existing tax advantage to earned income or to certain forms of saving; and the Inland Revenue had no expertise in assessing the economic impact of the existing tax system or of any reforms. Its concern remained the narrow – and important – one of ease of collection and administration, with a predilection for balance defined in terms of the *status quo*.

The wider (and different) packages of fiscal reforms towards which Macmillan and Thorneycroft were groping were not implemented. Thorneycroft's policy of cutting expenditure and controlling money was dismissed by the Cabinet. The second approach was devised by Macmillan: a reversal of both the differentiation of income tax and profits tax; and a shift from the egalitarian thrust of the recent past to a commit-ment to incentives for production and enterprise. His strategy depended on incentives to both firms *and* invididuals rather than a stress on one at the expense of the other. It was based on investment allowances and a flat-rate profits tax for firms, allied with concessions to middle-class in-come taxpayers and tax breaks for savings. At the same time, the less successful would be protected by welfare benefits. The full implications of this approach were not worked through before the end of Macmillan's

[64] PRO, T171/607, minute by J. Crawley, Inland Revenue, 22 Jan. 1963; chancellor to A. Johnston, 27 Jan. 1963 and 4 Feb. 1963; A. Johnston to chancellor, 1 and 8 Feb. 1963; CPA, CRD 2/9/47, 'Report of the Policy Committee on Economic Growth', May 1962; NEDC, *Conditions Favourable to Faster Growth* (London, 1963).
[65] PRO, T171/607, A. Johnston to chancellor, 'Contractural savings', 8 Feb. 1963.

premiership in 1963 or the end of the Conservative government in 1964. Changes in fiscal policy between 1951 and 1964 were modest, leaving the major elements of the fiscal constitution intact. Indeed, the containment of inflation rested much more on an attempt to control wage inflation, which meant that the tax system was used to secure the support of the unions rather than provide incentives. Much of the serious thinking about a new fiscal strategy was carried out in opposition between 1964 to 1970 – at the same time as Labour was implementing major changes in the fiscal system. Labour politicians were reacting to similar concerns about the inflexibility of the tax system and the need to encourage growth and modernisation. In some cases, they even turned to similar taxes which were incorporated into a different ideology. As a result, the Conservative government in 1970 had to undo the errors (in their view) of Labour, as well as tackle the unresolved problems of 1951–64.

Funding welfare and the economic regulator

The reform of taxation was linked to welfare in a number of ways. First, welfare was a major item of expenditure, and the question arose whether spending could be reduced as a means of cutting taxes. Secondly, encouraging enterprise through tax changes might require an increase in welfare spending to compensate the losers, and to sustain political support for wage restraint. Thirdly, there was the question of how money was secured. In Britain, more of the cost of welfare fell on progressive general taxation than in other members of the EEC where social services were funded to a greater extent from social security contributions. In 1938/9, the finance of the health services came from insurance contributions (17.0 per cent), central taxation (4.5 per cent), local taxation (61.1 per cent) and voluntary sources (17.4 per cent). Labour's plans for the new NHS entailed a major change. In 1945, Aneurin Bevan estimated that insurance contributions would rise modestly to 24.6 per cent, local taxation would drop dramatically to 4.1 per cent and voluntary payments to nil. Meanwhile, national taxation would rise to 71.2 per cent.[66] In reality, reliance on general taxation proved to be still higher when Labour left office (see table 8.1). A similar pattern applied to finance of other social security: in 1960, only 14 per cent of the finance of social services in the United Kingdom came from contributions, compared with over 50 per cent in France and nearly 75 per cent in Italy.[67]

Here, it seemed to many commentators, was a possible explanation for the lag of British labour productivity behind other countries and the

---

[66] C. Webster, *The National Health Service: A Political History* (Oxford, 1998), p. 23.
[67] PRO, T227/1357, R. W. B. Clarke, 19 Dec. 1960.

Table 8.1 *Sources of finance for the NHS, 1950/1 to 1974/5 (percentage)*

	Taxation	Insurance	Charges
1950/1	87.6	9.4	0.7
1956/7	88.7	6.4	4.7
1962/3	77.1	17.2	5.5
1974/5	91.3	5.7	2.6

Source: A. Leathard, *Health Care Provision* (London, 1990), p. 38, cited in R. Lowe, *The Welfare State in Britain since 1945* (2nd edn, Basingstoke and London, 1999), p. 187.

'hoarding' of labour by firms in response to full employment. In effect, employers paid below the full costs of labour and passed much of the welfare bill to general taxpayers. An increase in their contributions would, so it was argued, make them more efficient in the use of labour, encouraging a shift to capital-intensive production and shedding workers who could be used more effectively elsewhere in the economy. A tax-funded system of welfare was open to the charge that the active, productive population was paying for non-active members of society; a contribution-based welfare system would allow benefits to be concentrated on the working population. A shift from general taxation to insurance and charges for the use of services would permit a reduction in taxes and hence (so it was claimed) an improvement in incentives. Of course, Labour opposed the use of contributions since their introduction in 1911, arguing that the employees' flat-rate insurance payment was regressive and pressing instead for general, progressive taxation.[68] The funding of welfare, and particularly of the NHS, was a major issue of contention between Labour and the Conservatives.

A change in the funding of the welfare state was under consideration in 1957, both by officials and leading Conservative politicians. Robert Hall argued that 'a tax on labour employed would be the right way to proceed' as an incentive to firms to economise on the use of labour and to invest in capital intensive production. In Hall's view, a tax on employment should replace the profits tax which weakened the use of profit as a reward for efficiency.[69] Such a view commanded wide support in the late 1950s

---

[68] J. Harris, 'Enterprise and the welfare states: a comparative perspective', *Transactions of the Royal Historical Society* 5th ser. 40 (1990), 175–95.

[69] PRO, T171/478, Budget Committee meeting, 19 Feb. 1957, discussing T171/480, 'Taxation for increased production: note by R. L. Hall', 18 Feb. 1957.

and early 1960s. The Association of British Chambers of Commerce urged Thorneycroft to control expenditure on social services as a way of cutting taxes, which could be achieved by a shift to contributions and to selective benefits.[70] The CRD recommended that 'we should try and find means of hiving off some of the responsibility for social services on to contributions as most of the non-Socialist European countries have already done'.[71] Similarly, the NECD's report on faster economic growth proposed a shift from taxation of profits to a combination of a value added tax and a wage-related social security scheme.[72]

Change in the funding of welfare commanded wide support within the government and civil service, and a shift to higher levels of insurance contributions or the introduction of a new payroll tax were seriously considered. The line of argument did not necessarily entail a reduction in *total* welfare spending (as Thorneycroft proposed). The dangers of a cut in social spending was obvious to civil servants: it would alienate trade unions and make wage restraint more difficult. As Hall commented, any prospect that the welfare state was in danger 'might lead to a general hardening of attitudes'.[73] What was needed was a shift in the *structure* of finance. The aim was to reduce general taxes which hit incentives, and to pass costs on to employment as an encouragement to efficiency. At the same time, the beneficiaries would be insured workers so that welfare was, in effect, an investment in human capital. This was the strategy pursued by Macmillan. He rejected Thorneycroft's proposals of cuts in spending, arguing that government had an 'inescapable obligation to large sections of the community, the evasion of which would be both inequitable and unacceptable to public opinion'.[74] Although Macmillan was not willing to cut welfare spending in the late 1950s, he did attempt to shift towards contributory insurance.

The chancellor, Derick Heathcoat Amory,* wished to ensure that any increase in the costs of the NHS should automatically lead to an increase

---

[70] PRO, IR63/207, Association of British Chambers of Commerce to Thorneycroft, 12 Dec. 1957.

[71] CPA, CRD 2/10/15, 'The level of taxation here and abroad', J. Douglas, 30 Sept. 1960; CRD 2/10/15, J. Douglas to Fay, 7 Oct. 1960.

[72] For the NEDC, see A. Ringe and N. Rollings, 'Responding to relative decline: the creation of the National Economic Development Council', *Economic History Review* 52 (2000), 331–53.

[73] See, for example, PRO, T171/478, 'The budget and the TUC', S. C. Leslie, 4 and 11 Mar. 1957, and R. Hall, 'The budget and the TUC', 7 Mar. 1957.

[74] Quoted in Lowe, *Welfare State*, p. 82.

* Derick Heathcoat Amory (1899–1981) was educated at Eton and Christ Church, Oxford; he went into the family textile business in Devon. He was elected a Conservative MP in 1945; he was minister of pensions 1951–3, minister of state at the Board of Trade 1953–4, minister of agriculture 1954–8 and chancellor of the Exchequer 1958–60, when he retired from politics. (*DNB, 1981–5*, ed. Blake and Nicholls, pp. 10–11.)

in charges and contributions. An interdepartmental working party was established to consider NHS finance, which suggested that the contributory element might take one of two forms: an insurance 'stamp' for health; or a separate income tax which would make taxpayers aware of the cost of the service, rather than seeing it as something 'free', hidden in general taxation. Of course, a tax ear-marked for one service fell foul of Treasury hostility to hypothecation. Rather than creating sensitivity to the cost of the NHS, it might force the government to spend the available revenue on health, regardless of other circumstances – much the same as with roads in the 1920s. The proposal seemed particularly dangerous as a result of the administrative structure of the health service. Services were provided by local health authorities, which were not concerned about the increase in costs which were met from central government revenues. The working party was therefore hostile to any hypothecated health tax.[75] Nevertheless, the government did raise the 'health contribution', and the increase of 1961 marked the high-water mark of reform of the finance of the health service. Enoch Powell was now minister of health, and his decision to increase the NHS contribution, and at the same time to raise charges for prescriptions, dentistry and ophthalmic services, caused political outcry and the abandonment of the policy.[76]

At the same time, the government was anxious to devise an 'economic regulator', a 'new, flexible and convenient measure' to adjust demand. Although the government had a variety of methods of boosting demand, it lacked the ability to fine-tune the economy. In the words of Edward Boyle,* the financial secretary, 'one can use the accelerator with greater confidence if one knows the brakes are in good order'. The existing taxes were not appropriate: changes in the income tax created political problems; the purchase tax was unfair in its incidence; and other indirect taxes were at high levels. As Lee commented, the obvious solution was a new indirect tax with a wide coverage which could affect consumer demand

---

[75] PRO, T227/137, T. Padmore, 8 July 1960; R. W. B. Clarke, NHS Finance Working Party, 8 Feb. 1960; R. W. B. Clarke, health service finance, 12 May 1960; draft section on hypothecation.

[76] Webster, *National Health Service*, p. 37. For a detailed analysis of the 1961 budget, see Pemberton, 'The 1961 budget'.

* Edward Charles Gurney Boyle (1923–81) was born in Kensington; he was educated at Eton and Christ Church, Oxford. He went into journalism, and was elected a Conservative MP in 1951. In 1952, he was parliamentary private secretary to the under-secretary of air; he became parliamentary secretary to the minister of supply in 1954, and economic secretary to the Treasury 1955–6. In 1957, he returned to office as parliamentary secretary to the minister of education, and in 1959 as financial secretary to the Treasury where he supported indicative planning and an incomes policy. He became minister of education in 1962 and minister of state for higher education in the new department of education and science. He served as an opposition spokesman, and in 1970 became vice-chancellor of the University of Leeds. (*DNB, 1981–5*, ed. Blake and Nicholls, pp. 49–51.)

immediately and effectively through small changes in the rate. It was also necessary to change the tax outside the budget, as an anti-cyclical measure rather than a source of revenue. Difficulties of introducing a general sales tax meant that consideration turned to another device, a payroll tax which offered the additional advantage of encouraging employers to use labour more effectively. Despite its attractions, the political difficulties of such a major reform turned attention to two other, more feasible, proposals. One was a surcharge on excise duties and the purchase tax, which could be adjusted to stabilise the economy. The second was a surcharge on employers' insurance contributions. At this point, the search for a regulator met the attempt to shift the funding of social services. The result was confusion and incoherence, an attempt to use a modest change in insurance contributions for two distinct purposes. The minister of pensions was strongly opposed to using an insurance surcharge as a regulator, on the grounds that it would increase prices and lead to a demand for more benefits. The chancellor argued that it could regulate the economy *and* induce employers to invest in labour-saving machinery. The outcome was a compromise or – perhaps more accurately – a decision to temporise. In 1961, Lloyd took powers to impose a surcharge on both Customs and Excise duties *and* employers' insurance contributions. He also announced that the insurance regulator would expire at the end of the financial year, so that some other device would be considered for the future years.[77] The government was, again, tinkering with modest changes in response to major problems. No sooner was the employers' surcharge introduced than the search started for another measure. The employers' surcharge seemed neither a good regulator nor an effective incentive to the efficient use of labour – and, to make matters worse, it added to export costs. Once again, a permanent payroll tax was considered as a means of encouraging efficiency in the use of labour and passing some of the costs of social security to employment. The proposal foundered, for it would

---

[77] PRO, T230/493, 'Supplementary note for the chancellor: taxation', F. Lee, 27 July 1960; for support of a sales tax as a regulator and incentive to exports, see T320/58, Maudling to Lloyd, 29 Nov. 1960; T171/521, BC(60)37, note of conclusions, Budget Committee, 3rd meeting, 15 June 1960; BC(60)38, 'A wages of payroll tax: note by the Economic Section', 22 July 1960; T171/516, BC(M)(60)5, 'Possible economic regulators', F. Lee, 8 Nov. 1960; BC(60)38, revise, 'A wages or payroll tax, note by Economic Section, Treasury', 20 Oct. 1960; BC(60)41, budget ideas: note by Customs and Excise, 19 Sept. 1960; 'Possible economic regulators' BC(M)(60)5, E. C. G. B. to chancellor, Nov. 1960; BC(M)(61)7, 'A possible economic regulator: the special surcharge scheme', 3 Jan. 1961; BC(60)49, 'Economic regulator: proposed special surcharge on Customs and Excise duties and purchase tax', 16 Dec. 1960; note by T. Padmore, 13 Feb. 1961; A. J. Collier to T. Padmore: employer's surcharge, 10 Feb. 1961; BC(M)(61)10, Budget Committee: economic regulators: the employers' surcharge scheme, 17 Mar. 1961; note of meeting in chancellor's room, 30 Mar. 1961; chancellor to Macmillan, 7 Apr. 1961. The issue is discussed in Pemberton, 'The 1961 budget'.

increase prices, make exports less competitive and hit some firms more than others.[78]

Discussion was trapped in an endless round of indecision, resulting in minor tinkering which reflected short-term compromises and poorly conceived economic analysis. Consideration of large-scale changes in the fiscal system – whether a reform of indirect taxes, the treatment of companies, the finance of social security or the taxation of employment – was swamped by detail, by pettifogging as well as sensible administrative objections, and by political pragmatism. Extremely minor changes, such as an adjustment in initial allowances or a surcharge on employers' contributions, were expected to produce results far beyond any realistic expectation. Indeed, some reforms were expected to produce more than one result, which were often incompatible. Could a surcharge on employers' contributions regulate the economy *and* encourage efficiency? The outcome was minor changes without the political will to introduce major reforms in the tax system, or in economic management and institutions. The problems of the 1961 budget indicated the need for a more coherent assessment of the economic impact of the fiscal system and its connection with growth. By the early 1960s, political debate was dominated by a concern for growth, a realisation that Britain was falling behind in productivity. In 1962, Macmillan remarked that 'every budget acquired a title . . . It would be right to try and introduce the idea of growth into this year's Budget – "Platform for Growth" would be the right line to try and get across.'[79] But how were the new ideas to be developed and implemented in order to break out of the low-effort, low-productivity economy? The search for growth implied a change in the machinery of government in order to articulate new policies and to escape from established routines.

Modernising the machinery of government

By the early 1960s, the failings in the machinery of government were apparent. One problem was the difficulty experienced by more radical voices – both officials and politicians – in convincing the Inland Revenue,

---

[78] PRO, T171/592, Budget Committee meetings, 12 June, 8 Sept. and 2 Nov. 1961; BC(61)31, indirect taxation: note by Customs and Excise, 23 Sept. 1961; BC(61)32, permanent payroll tax: the economic outlook: note by Sir T. Padmore, 14 June 1961; T171/595, a permanent payroll tax, F. Lee, 14 Nov. 1961; T171/594, permanent payroll tax: memorandum by Board of Inland Revenue, 25 Oct. 1961. On the Research Department's support for a payroll tax, see CPA, CRD 2/10/15, note on a payroll tax, 7 June 1961; and on the doubts of the FBI, MRC, FBI MSS 200/F/3/E7/1/4, Tax Panel, 21 Dec. 1960; report of the Committee on the Balance of the Fiscal System.

[79] PRO, PREM11/3763, budget 1962: note of discussion, prime minister and chancellor, 23 Mar. 1962.

Customs and Excise and Treasury of the possibility of change. The existing fiscal system was taken as the norm, with any changes criticised for overturning a carefully wrought balance. The position was most clearly put by the Inland Revenue in 1952:

> The Inland Revenue reputation for fair dealing with all classes of citizens … rests upon the even handed dispensation of justice according to the rule of law. If particular discrimination entered the income tax system … there would be a serious danger that the good relations between the Department and taxpayers generally would suffer.

Consent to payment of taxes was vital, and no changes should be made which would 'lower its efficiency, detract from the certainty of its yield, or impair the public faith in its justice'.[80] Here was an all-encompassing argument against change. In 1952, the Inland Revenue's target was egalitarianism which was criticised for upsetting the balance of society. But it was easy to change the argument, and to defend the distribution achieved by the Attlee government as 'natural' compared with earlier 'misappropriation' of socially created wealth. The Inland Revenue's ingrained reaction to any change was to see it as an unwarranted and politically motivated attack on the social order – forgetting that they had also attacked the fiscal policies which shaped the existing structure of society. This conservatism was reinforced by the fact that the Budget Committee was overwhelmed by immediate concerns, without the time or expertise to assess the overall impact of the tax system.

These shortcomings were admitted by the Budget Committee by the early 1960s. F. R. P. Vinter* argued that the broad issue of the impact of taxation on economic growth needed to be considered more systematically. His plea led Frank Lee to appoint a working party on growth and taxation, under Vinter's chairmanship and with representatives from the Board of Trade, Treasury and ministry of labour. Their report on economic growth and national efficiency was highly critical of the existing tax system, and argued the case for 'a more fundamental study, so that in later years the effects of the financing operations of public authorities on efficiency and growth may be more clearly understood than they are today'. The problem, in their opinion, was that the tax system was the product of history, shaped by a concern for individual equity, the pressures of war finance and economic stabilisation. The result was complexity and

---

[80] PRO, T171/434, 'General note by the Board of Inland Revenue on the equitable distribution of direct taxation', 11 Dec. 1952.

* Frederick Robert Peter Vinter (b. 1914) was educated at Haileybury and King's College, Cambridge. He joined the ministry of economic warfare in 1939, moving to the Cabinet Office in 1943, the Treasury in 1945; he was deputy secretary of the ministry of technology and the department of trade and industry from 1969 to 1973. (*Who's Who 2001*, p. 2136.)

incoherence, with little sense of the connection between individual taxes or of the impact of the entire fiscal system on efficiency and growth. Even the Royal Commission on the Taxation of Profits and Income failed to consider the wider picture, concentrating instead on the effect of individual taxes on particular types of taxpayers from the standpoint of accountants and tax lawyers. What was needed, the report concluded, was a wide-ranging enquiry 'on the economic effects of taxation from the point of view of efficiency and adaptability'.[81]

As a result, Lee suggested that the Budget Committee should establish a committee staffed by officials with less concern for daily affairs, which could consider taxation in relation to growth and social objectives. The Review of Taxation Policy Committee was established, and was presented with a formidable list of topics. How were exports to be encouraged; what was the case for or against a shift to indirect taxation or taxation of companies? Which taxes should be raised or introduced to provide for increased public expenditure and to control demand? Should taxes be used to stop a drift to the south-east; to provide an incentive for investment; or to act as an economic regulator? This was a large task, largely ignored: the committee did not have the time, resources or intellectual formation to consider such fundamental issues. The result was disappointing, for the committee's interim report in 1962 was largely confined to indirect taxation and rejected any major change.[82]

The review was not integrated with discussions of the Budget Committee, and was made up of officials without any input from politicians. There was little sense of connection between these deliberations within the machinery of government and the more ideological or political discussions of ministers and their advisers. Was it really possible for *officials* to analyse long-term taxation policy and its impact on the economy apart from political ideology and normative assumptions about the future shape of society? The deliberations of the committee were marginalised. Although it continued to meet, it had virtually no impact on policy. In 1965, Vinter felt that its conclusions should not be presented to ministers; reform was, he suggested, a long-term issue and it would be a diversion to imply to ministers that it could be dealt with quickly.[83]

---

[81] PRO, T230/579, 'Elements of a policy for economic growth', F. R. P. Vinter, 27 Feb. 1961; 'Economic growth and national efficiency: report by officials to the chancellor of the Exchequer, July 1961' (this report is also in CAB129/105, C(61)94, 10 July 1961). See T230/524 and 525 for working papers.

[82] PRO, T171/592, Budget Committee meeting, 8 Sept. 1961; for the deliberations of the committee, see T320/51, T. Padmore to J. Crosbie, 26 Feb. 1962; D. J. S. Hancock to T. Padmore, 27 Feb. 1962; RTP(62)5, final, review of taxation policy, 4 Apr. 1962; and T320/52, review of taxation policy, meetings, 8 and 27 Mar., 14 and 17 May, 23 July 1962.

[83] PRO, T320/392, F. R. P. Vinter, 9 June 1965.

Not surprisingly, politicians had a different perception of time scales. The Labour government proceeded with its own distinctive fiscal policies, and the Conservatives developed their own ideas in opposition. The formulation of new structures of taxation was largely undertaken apart from the deliberations of officials within the government machinery, which created other difficulties. Officials were obsessed with administrative detail and maintenance of the existing system; by contrast, politicians might overlook administrative practicability, and lurch from one policy to another as parties gained and lost power. An attempt was made to deal with some of these problems of co-ordination in 1965, when the Budget Committee was restructured. One committee would consider the short-term economic forecast and what was needed in the next budget; a second body, chaired by the chancellor, would consider new taxes already announced; and a third, chaired by a senior civil servant, would consider new proposals for structural change.[84] This reform highlights the serious shortcomings of policy discussions between 1951 and 1964, when the Budget Committee dealt with *all* of these issues and was usually so concerned with immediate difficulties that long-term change was neglected. The failure of the machinery of government allowed more ideological and contradictory approaches to fill the gap. The outcome was unfortunate, for any prospect of agreement on the reform of the fiscal system was lost. Rather than consensus emerging under the guidance of officials concerned with the long-term efficiency of the tax system, each party adopted its own particular strategy which was then condemned by the opposition – despite its own support for a broadly similar tax within a different set of normative assumptions.

Meanwhile, the Treasury was restructured in 1962 in an attempt to co-ordinate thinking on the economic impact of policies. A Public Income and Outlay Division was established at the Treasury with a new post to consider tax policy. The task of this official was to review the structure of taxation in order to improve long-term growth. It was not clear that the experiment worked, for the resources were minimal and the Economic Section continued to function as an alternative source of advice. In any case, consideration of economic growth was moving to the National Economic Development Office, where it was felt that taxation might offer the key to growth. Rather lamely, the Treasury asked that it should be involved in the discussions at some future stage.[85] This response reflects D. J. S. Hancock's admission that the Treasury lacked resources to consider taxation policy – and he doubted that it mattered,

[84] PRO, T171/803, CM(0), 1st meeting, 22 Jan. 1965.
[85] PRO, T320/233, D. J. S. Hancock, 7 June 1963.

for the chancellor in the next government, of whatever party, would probably prefer a proper tax unit. Meanwhile, the Inland Revenue took steps towards considering the impact of the fiscal system on the economy. Hancock was highly sceptical whether its initiative would be sufficient, given the absence of economists within the revenue departments. Accordingly, in 1963 he recommended reforms to permit a proper consideration of taxation policy. He suggested that the revenue departments should employ professional economists working alongside officials; the Treasury should then co-ordinate thinking in a coherent assessment of the impact of taxes on the economy.[86] Although the Treasury had a clear sense of its traditions and was concerned to preserve stability and balance, it was also intellectually cautious, aware of its need to provide advice to different governments. Despite its claims to omniscience, it relied heavily on the functional departments such as the Inland Revenue, not only for the machinery of policy implementation but also for the analysis of policy – a task for which they were ill-suited.

The chancellor agreed that relations between the revenue departments and Treasury needed to be improved in order to foster a more creative attitude towards taxation policy – a suggestion which immediately provoked a demarcation dispute. Was this the role of the Inland Revenue; or could the task be left to the Budget Committee and working parties on particular problems? The chancellor realised, with some justice, that more radical change was needed. As he remarked, the revenue departments and Treasury reacted to external forces rather than actively considering ways of adapting the tax system to the needs of the economy. What was needed was not simply discussions on the Budget Committee, but closer contact at the working level between those concerned with taxation and economic policy. In 1963, the chancellor realised – it is tempting to say at last – that the Treasury and revenue departments should think more actively about taxation in relation to the needs of the economy. Certainly, after the failed application for entry to the EEC, a number of Conservative politicians insisted that a change in the structure of taxation was all the more necessary to provide the incentives which were not available from the Common Market.[87]

The machinery of government did not help in the formulation of long-term reforms to the tax system, so producing a lack of consistency. But it would be unfair to civil servants in the 1950s and early 1960s to criticise

[86] PRO, T320/18, minute of D. J. S. Hancock, 1 Nov. 1963; notes of a meeting in the chancellor of the Exchequer's room, 30 May 1963.
[87] PRO, T320/18, note of a meeting in the chancellor of the Exchequer's room, 30 May 1963; CCO4/9/440, letter to *The Times*, 18 Feb. 1963 – including Paul Channon and Robert Carr.

them for failing to take the initiative. Could Treasury officials really follow, for example, the implications of Cairncross's case in favour of indirect taxes? It was not a technical economic issue, for it posed major political issues. Would Labour and the general public really accept that a wider sales tax would be less disruptive of consumer preference and so improve overall welfare? Thomas Padmore* had a point: it was not for officials to take the initiative, and they lacked clear direction from ministers who were more concerned with daily events and electoral realities. Chancellors were aware that any reform would cause immense controversy, and there was not a huge demand for change within the Conservative party. In January 1960, at least one member of the CRD basked complacently in the satisfaction that taxes had fallen in nine Conservative budgets. The tax structure, it seemed, was more tolerable with a reduction in punitive marginal rates of income and surtax, and most people seemed more interested in *increasing* government expenditure than in reducing tax rates.[88]

Of course, the inertia of the civil service had been shifted before and there were voices arguing for change *within* the Treasury. The problem was just as much the lack of nerve on the part of ministers, an inability to cut through the debates over fiscal policy and carry through a consistent vision. Politicians were transfixed by the difficulties of their situation, the constraints on their action. A central element in Thorneycroft's resignation was the government's desire to retain trade union co-operation to control wage inflation and rising costs which would be jeopardised by cuts in social expenditure and tax concessions for the middle class. In the opinion of one Treasury official, unions were suspicious that the government's tax concessions were designed to increase middle-class consumption rather than offering incentives for production. The answer, he felt, was to produce a package of measures to show it was 'genuinely interested in incentive rather than easement'. The important point was to 'show that the Government really wants middle-class incentives for the sake of the whole economy, and not as a bonus for the "haves" '. The task was not easy, for the unions were 'suspicious of a fiscal policy designed to provide better incentives: they think of it not as an industrial dynamic but as class politics, likelier to increase middle-class consumption than general production. They tend to react accordingly, and it will be very hard to persuade them otherwise by words alone, however, cogent.' Hall was more

[88] CPA, CRD 3/7/26/1, 'Taxation policy, 1960 and after', 18 Jan. 1960.
* Thomas Padmore (1909–96) was educated at Queens' College, Cambridge, and joined the Inland Revenue in 1931, transferring to the Treasury in 1934; in 1962 he moved to the ministry of transport as permanent secretary, retiring in 1968. (*Who's Who 1996*, p. 1470.)

sceptical, arguing that the unions were more likely to support Labour, and that it was embarrassing to place them in a position of approving Conservative policies. Perhaps it was simply better for the Conservatives to pursue with conviction the things they believed in – and to ignore the concerns of the unions.[89] This exchange was crucial to fiscal policy: how to reconcile incentives and growth with social justice or, more cynically, with winning the next election?

Little could be done until the government opted for one of two policies. The first policy was to devise a package of measures to provide incentives for profits, savings and earnings, alongside more generous welfare for low incomes. This was the approach adopted by the Conservatives in opposition after 1964. The second policy was simply to ignore the unions and concern for the construction of an even-handed package, on the ground that slow growth harmed everyone. This policy was pursued after 1979, when the balanced package fell apart and Mrs Thatcher embarked on a policy of incentives *without* social integration. Of course, her ability to adopt such an approach was not really feasible in the 1950s or 1960s: the budgets of 1958 and 1961 were modest steps in this direction, but the political dangers seemed too great. Why did it enter the realms of practicable fiscal politics? It meant breaking with established institutions and interests, which often failed to deliver what was expected, whether wage restraint or productivity growth. The government might be able to ignore organised interests such as the TUC or FBI by redefining them as working against the public as agents of selfishness and inflexibility rather than forces for order and stability. At the same time, other interests might emerge as the result of social change and political rhetoric, whether the affluent consumer or the popular capitalist. The government could respond to these social developments, but also encourage and help to define the new interests. There was, in other words, a complex interplay between real and constructed interests and identities. Above all, the shift in policy may be understood in terms of the sense of crisis in the performance of the economy and the operation of the tax system between 1964 and 1979. The initiative in taxation policy passed to Labour, which embarked on a sweeping reform of the tax system in Callaghan's first budget of 1965. Although Labour's strategy had some elements in common with Conservative thinking, such as the introduction of a capital gains tax and a tax on employment, its fiscal policies were embedded in a radically different set of assumptions about the conditions for economic growth and social equity.

[89] PRO, T171/478, 'The budget and the TUC', S. C. Leslie, 4 Mar. and 11 Mar. 1957; 'The budget and the TUC', R. Hall, 7 Mar. 1957.

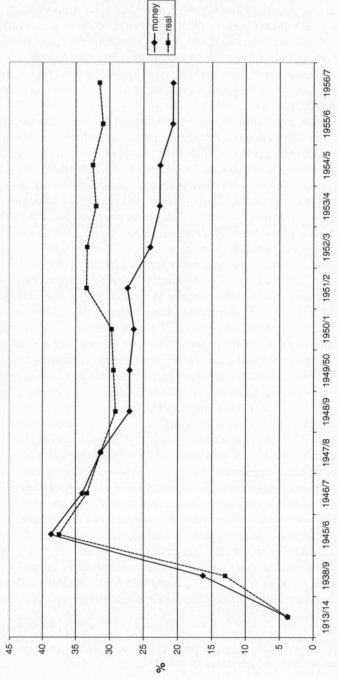

Figure 8.1 Percentage of money income (£2,000) and equivalent real income (1947/8 prices) paid in income tax and surtax, married men with two children, 1913/14 to 1956/7.

Source: F. W. Paish, 'The real incidence of personal taxation', *Lloyds Bank Review* (1957), 4–5.

Conservative tax policy between 1951 to 1964 was characterised by tinkering, a process of 'continual movement and little change'.[90] There was a general downward drift in tax rates, made possible by economic growth and reduced spending on defence and food subsidies, but no consistent line in reshaping the *structure* of taxation. Thus the rate of profits tax was reduced, and the treatment of allowances for purchases of new plant and machinery was changed in eleven out of thirteen budgets.[91] Similarly, policy towards the income tax was one of 'spasmodic remission and retrenchment in both rates and allowances'.[92] The standard rate of income tax was lower in 1964 than in 1951, and married men with children, in receipt of earned income, paid less tax than in the past. However, much of the reduction in income tax was illusory, for inflation took more people across the tax threshold or into higher tax rates, so that the effective tax rate rose (see figure 8.1 and table 8.2).[93] Little was done to pursue the strategy of incentives, or to encourage personal savings through tax incentives. Indirect taxes were not fundamentally changed, either in their structure or in their contribution to revenues. Although the purchase tax was modified in various ways, it had many of the same shortcomings in 1964 as in 1951, and the overall contribution of indirect taxes remained largely unchanged (see tables 7.2 and 8.3). When the Conservative government took office in 1951, it inherited unresolved problems of taxation; when it left office in 1964, it had done little to remove the difficulties.

The willingness of Conservative chancellors to work within the existing fiscal structure meant that it had become sclerotic by the late 1950s. By then, it was increasingly clear that fundamental change was needed. First, the tax system needed to be more flexible in producing revenue to meet the demands for public expenditure, and especially on welfare. One response might be to *cut* welfare spending, but the dominant view within the party was that welfare spending was sacrosanct, and in many ways the late 1950s marked the entrenchment of the welfare state at higher levels of expenditure. Secondly, there was a growing realisation by the late 1950s that Britain was experiencing relative economic decline, and the tax system was widely criticised for creating distortions and inefficiencies. Indeed, the problem was not so much the level of taxation (which was not out of line with other European countries) as the form of taxation which

[90] Steinmo, *Taxation and Democracy*, p. 149.
[91] Steinmo, *Taxation and Democracy*, pp. 150–1.
[92] B. E. V. Sabine, *A History of Income Tax* (London, 1966), p. 230.
[93] F. W. Paish, 'The real incidence of personal taxation', *Lloyds Bank Review* n.s. 43 (1957), 1–16; Steinmo, *Taxation and Democracy*, p. 152. As Paish pointed out, there was also a fall in the share of total incomes received by the highest income groups, which reduced the proportion of incomes paying the highest rates (7–14).

Table 8.2 *Percentage of money and equivalent real income (1947/8 prices) paid in income tax and surtax, married men with two children, 1938/9, 1945/6, 1950/1 and 1956/7*

	1938/9		1945/6		1950/1		1956/7	
	Money	Real	Money	Real	Money	Real	Money	Real
£600	3.7	–	20.2	15.4	6.5	8.4	0.5	6.9
£1,000	10.2	1.5	30.1	25.4	16.9	19.3	8.5	16.7
£1,500	13.5	10.0	35.1	30.3	23.2	24.6	16.6	24.0
£2,000	16.3	13.0	38.8	37.5	26.4	29.7	20.7	31.5
£5,000	28.3	24.0	55.2	53.3	47.8	50.8	43.9	53.4
£10,000	38.6	33.5	67.8	65.9	63.2	66.0	60.0	68.6

Source: F. W. Paish, 'The real incidence of personal taxation', *Lloyds Bank Review* (1957), 4–5.

Table 8.3 *Structure of central government revenue: net receipts due to the Exchequer, 1962/3 (percentage)*

	1962/3
Income tax and super-tax	45.7
Profits	5.8
Death duties	4.1
Stamps	1.5
Motor vehicle duty	2.4
Customs	24.9
Excise	15.7
Total	100.0

Source: PP 1962–3 XXVI, *Finance Accounts of the UK for the Financial Year 1962–3*, p. 5.

was attacked for blunting incentives and eroding profit and enterprise. These concerns were coming to the fore in the late 1950s, but it was really after 1964 that serious discussion of policy started. The Labour government of 1964–70 implemented a series of changes, reflecting its internal debates in opposition since 1951; and the Conservatives mounted their own enquiry into the shape of the fiscal system. The next two chapters explore these different visions of fiscal policy between 1964 and 1979.

9 'Modern and dynamic economic policy': Labour and taxation, 1951–1970

> Many people think of the Labour Party as a 'higher taxation' Party... It is very important that we should establish the fact that we stand for the more *equitable* distribution of taxation; this means easements for some as well as heavier (but fairer) burdens for others.
>
> LPA, Finance and Economic Policy Sub-Committee, RD139/Apr. 1961, 'Taxation of profits and income proposals for reform': memorandum by D. Houghton

> There was no evidence that high taxation had a disincentive effect.
>
> George Woodcock of the TUC: MRC, TUC MSS 292/410.2/2, 'Report of a meeting between the Economic Committee, the chancellor of the Exchequer and the minister of labour, 1 Apr. 1952', 4 Apr. 1952

By the time Labour lost power in 1951, leading civil servants felt that Labour's fiscal policy was threatening economic growth and efficiency. Although Labour politicians were less inclined to accept the need for a shift to a free market economy with incentives for higher incomes, many members of the party admitted that the tax system should be reassessed. The Attlee government established a Royal Commission on the Taxation of Profits and Income in 1951.[1] The main lines of Labour's fiscal policy emerged from the memorandum of dissent to its report (largely the work of Nicholas Kaldor), and from a series of internal working parties. When it returned to power in 1964, Labour introduced a major series of reforms to the tax system, escaping from the constraints of the Conservative government, and adding a layer of complexity to the fiscal system. Labour devised policies independently of civil servants with their stress on the difficulties of administrative change and the need to preserve a carefully crafted balance in the tax system. The solidity of official cultures meant that new ideas were slow to penetrate the civil service; rather, new ideas emerged from outside, entering into policy with the backing of a parliamentary majority, and without much consideration by officials, on the floor of the Commons, or in consultation with professional bodies or trade associations. The official emphasis on continuity therefore gave way

---

[1] The three reports are in PP 1952–3 xvii, PP 1953–4 xix and PP 1955–6 xxvii.

to a sudden, and perhaps ill-considered, lurch in policy – and the same might happen with a further change in government. The administration acted as a dam, holding back reform up to 1964 rather than attempting to shape fiscal policy; after 1964, the dam broke and officials were unable to direct the flow of new ideas. Instead of a consensus emerging on the basis of technical advice, the result was complexity and even incoherence by the late 1970s. The fiscal system was starting to lose its legitimacy and trust – at least in part because of the failure of the Treasury and revenue departments to reassess their assumptions in the light of changing conditions.

Debates over fiscal policy between 1964 and 1979 can only be appreciated in the light of the failure of radical change between 1951 and 1964. Little had been achieved, despite the realisation that the tax system needed reform to deal with increases in public spending and to assist economic growth. Debates over the relationship between direct and indirect taxes were inconclusive; and there was no clear strategy on investment or the finance of social security. There was a policy vacuum at the heart of government – or a sense of fatalism that the room for change was limited. The strongest case for reform came from a small number of officials within the Treasury, but they were opposed by colleagues and by ministers who were more concerned with ease of collection of taxes, the maintenance of existing patterns of incidence and the need to limit inflationary wage pressure. The failure of the Conservative government to propose a coherent and electorally attractive package of measures gave Labour an opportunity to introduce its own fiscal policies, with a particular definition of incentives and social justice, and a distinctive approach to encouraging economic growth.

Meanwhile, loss of office in 1964 stimulated the Conservative party to a searching analysis of fiscal policy, in an attempt to escape from the constraints of the 1950s and to devise an alternative to Labour's innovations. During the 1960s and 1970s, fiscal policy became a topic of controversy within and between the major political parties, closely linked with debates over economic decline and the needs for 'modernisation'. This context created further difficulties, for the tax system was viewed less as a source of revenue than as a means of shaping the economy and society according to contested prescriptions. Both major parties saw the virtues of similar taxes – on valued added, wealth, capital gains and payrolls – which were connected with different social visions and became the subject of conflict rather than consensus. The failings of the machinery of government meant that officials blocked change and allowed more ideological approaches to emerge, creating complexity and confusion rather than rationalisation and consistency. At one end of the spectrum, the free market

Institute of Economic Affairs complained that the pervasive concern with vertical and horizontal equity was leading to over-refinement, threatening compliance because of the complexity of legislation, and destroying incentives. Nigel Lawson* denounced the 'social justice mongers of all parties and none' on the grounds that excessive government spending and high taxation meant 'the certainty of misallocation of resources, economic and social debilitation, excessive state power, and – very far from least – the erosion of personal freedom'.[2] At the other end of the spectrum, members of the Labour party believed that redistribution had not gone far enough, and that taxation (and other policies) should be used to create a more egalitarian society where profit was no longer supreme. Between 1964 and 1970, both parties attempted to devise integrated packages of reform, especially in the proposals of Nicholas Kaldor for Labour and the Conservative working party on future economic policy. Neither package was implemented in full; instead, partial solutions with their own distinctive ideologies were superimposed on one another. Adversarial politics did huge damage in the 1960s and 1970s, creating a palimpsest of different approaches and principles which contributed to a growing loss of legitimacy for the tax system.

Redefining taxation policy, 1951–1964

Labour's fiscal strategy denied (with greater or lesser vigour) that the pursuit of personal gain was the driving force for economic growth, and stressed the virtues of equality for social justice and economic efficiency. Equality would help to resolve conflicts over productivity, for workers would not accept changes in work practices if they felt that they were working harder merely to increase the dividends of shareholders. Many Conservative politicians in the 1950s and early 1960s similarly accepted the need for a trade-off between profits and productivity; Labour went further in doubting the desirability of the profit motive. Indeed, Labour

---

[2] A. R. Prest, 'What is wrong with the UK tax system?', in Institute of Economic Affairs, *The State of Taxation* (London, 1977), pp. 4, 11; W. Elkan, 'A public sector without bounds', in Institute of Economic Affairs, *The State of Taxation*, p. 42; N. Lawson, 'Taxation or government expenditure?', in Institute of Economic Affairs, *The State of Taxation*, pp. 30–1.

* Nigel Lawson (b. 1932) was educated at Westminster and Christ Church, Oxford, where he read politics, philosophy and economics. He was a financial journalist 1956–63, and speech writer for Alec Douglas-Home as prime minister in 1963–4, returning to journalism before becoming special political adviser at party headquarters 1973–4. He was a Conservative MP from 1974 to 1992, serving as financial secretary to the Treasury 1979–81, secretary of state for energy 1981–3 and chancellor of the Exchequer 1983–9. He then went into the City. (*Who Was Who 2001*, pp. 1211–12; Robbins (ed.), *Biographical Dictionary*, pp. 259–61.)

could argue that greater equality created the prosperity of the postwar world. Before the First World War, Labour argued that inequality of wealth led to under-consumption, waste and unemployment. The strategy seemed to work after the Second World War, when the reduction in gross disparities in income and wealth, and the attack on socially created wealth, formed the basis for affluence and full employment.[3]

In the opinion of some members of the Labour party, the economic case for equality was compatible with a social order based on free market capitalism, always provided that benefits were spread widely and not appropriated as 'unearned' income or socially created wealth. Other members of the party felt that equality could only be achieved by abolishing, or at least strictly limiting, private ownership. The difference of emphasis had implications for fiscal policy. Could inequality be kept in check by using the tax system to ensure that the flow of income and wealth was shared between members of society; or was it necessary to nationalise industry in order to remove the flow of income and wealth at its origin? The answer might depend on another major question: was the aim equality of *opportunity*, so that everyone had an equal chance of developing their talents, or was it equality of *outcome*, so that everyone ended up equal? An emphasis on opportunity gave more weight to access to education than to equality of income as an end in itself. The definition of equality was bitterly contested in the Labour party in the 1950s. The concept was at the heart of politics – and it was difficult for *any* politician to argue for a degree of inequality as a source of growth. Disagreements within the Labour party were over the best way of creating equality, not over its desirability as the major aim of Labour policy.

Most Labour commentators could admit that the existing tax and welfare systems were no longer creating equality of opportunity or of outcome. Disparities of wealth had not narrowed, and the trend towards greater equality of income was in danger of being reversed. During the 1950s, income differentials before tax started to widen, and Richard Titmuss and others suggested that the combined impact of the tax and welfare systems did not narrow the gap. Although the nominal rate of taxation was high, many middle-class taxpayers reduced their liability through tax breaks on pensions, insurance policies and mortgage interest. Middle-class families were also beneficiaries of the welfare state, obtaining secondary education and health care which they had previously purchased. The 'fiscal welfare state' was less redistributive than appeared at first sight.[4]

---

[3] On Labour thinking on equality, see Ellison, *Egalitarian Thought*, chapters 3–5.

[4] R. M. Titmuss, 'The social division of welfare: some reflections on the search for equity', in his *Essays on the Welfare State*, pp. 34–55; F. Field, M. Meacher and C. Pond, *To Him*

Discussion of taxation policy started within the context of debates over equality in 1955/6. The study group on equality departed from the basic assumption that unearned incomes provided the source of inequalities, and that highly concentrated ownership of wealth made any further redistribution of income difficult. These attacks on 'unearned income' and a misuse of resources in 'irrational' consumption looked back to Edwardian debates rather than to the affluent Britain of the 1950s. Revisionists took a somewhat different line, arguing that equality was a matter of opportunity in an affluent society where workers wished to join in the world of consumption and to accumulate assets. The study group posed the question of how an equal, classless society should be created, which in turn raised another major issue:

how far do we wish to maintain private ownership? In particular, how far do we wish to maintain private ownership of industrial wealth, which is the most important source of new wealth? Sooner or later there must be a decision between a further extension of state ownership and a wider distribution of property among individuals. It may be a valid criticism of Labour policy proposals that they do not make it clear which of these is our ultimate goal.[5]

The study group was divided over the weight to be given to two strands of policy.

Fiscal policy reduced inequality in incomes, and steps should now be taken to reduce inequality in wealth by taxes on capital gains, a capital levy, reform of death duties or a tax on all forms of spending power. It was also necessary to extend state ownership, not simply through nationalisation in the hands of monolithic state corporations but also by devising new forms of industrial organisation: 'While in the interests of equality big differences of wealth must be abolished, in the interests of freedom and initiative ownership and control must be made more widespread.' The study group's initial draft gave considerable weight to fiscal policy; some members dissented, arguing that a just and equal society could not be achieved by using taxation to 'correct' the injustices of private ownership. Rather, public ownership was needed to sweep away private profit and fortunes amassed from socially created wealth. The study group struggled to reconcile the two positions in its final report, which eventually accepted that an extension of public ownership *was* a prerequisite for a just and equal society. Taxation became a means of extending public

Who Hath: A Study of Poverty and Taxation (Harmondsworth, 1977); Meade, *Efficiency, Equality and the Ownership of Property*; Baldwin, *Politics of Social Solidarity*.

[5] LPA, Working Parties, Finance, Box 1, Re5/Nov. 1955, Home Policy Committee, 'A synopsis for the research project on equality'. The study group was chaired by Gaitskell; other members included Hugh Dalton, Barbara Castle, Roy Jenkins, Ian Mikardo, Harold Wilson, Barbara Wootton and W. A. Lewis.

ownership and transferring socially created wealth from individuals to
the state. The deliberations of the study group exposed, once again, the
tension in Labour's thinking. Was taxation a means of preserving socially
responsible private property and raising revenue for welfare; or should it
be used as a device to create public ownership, which offered the only
effective way of removing the injustices of capitalism?[6]

Despite these differences of emphasis, the main lines of fiscal strategy
were agreed in the late 1950s and early 1960s. In many ways, the problem
was the same as at the end of the First World War. The question then was
whether the capital levy offered a means of extending public ownership
and replacing capitalism, or of breaking down accumulations of passive,
socially created wealth and releasing active, widely diffused ownership.
The capital levy appealed on both grounds. Similarly, the Labour party
created a fiscal policy by the early 1960s which secured a wide measure
of support within the party, for different and even contradictory reasons.
It could be linked to a rhetoric of modernisation and economic growth,
or to the extension of public ownership and the destruction of socially
created wealth. The fiscal strategy offered a means of solving the internal
divisions within the party, and overcoming the difficulties experienced
by the Conservative government in reforming the fiscal system. Indeed,
there was overlap between the fiscal programme of Labour and the 'tax
package' devised by the Conservative working party in the 1960s, with
a common interest in taxes on wealth, capital gains and employment.
Where they differed was in the wider rhetorical justification as a means
of creating incentives and enterprise or justice and equality.

The starting point of Labour's fiscal policy was traditional and, arguably, dated: an attack on unearned income and socially created wealth.
Since large fortunes could not be accumulated from income, by definition
they were not the outcome of 'a virtuous alliance of personal worth with
thrift'. High levels of progressive income tax did not touch accumulated
fortunes and could not produce a more equal society. What was needed
was more taxation of capital and business profits, and less of personal
incomes and consumption, to take account of changes in the processes
of accumulating large fortunes and securing excessive incomes through
non-taxed capital appreciation. 'We are deceiving ourselves', argued Roy
Jenkins,

by having nominally very high rates of income tax and surtax erected on an
artificially narrow basis of income so that it bears hard on some people and not
nearly so hard on other people. I think that this system of taxation is today not

[6] See the three versions of the report in LPA, Working Parties, Finance, Box I, Re36/Mar.
1956, subject group on equality: preliminary memorandum on equality; Re54/Apr. 1956,
subject group on equality: equality (second draft) and Re69/May 1956, subject group on
equality: equality. See also the minutes for 10 Apr. and 1 May 1956.

only unfair but is widely felt to be unfair, and that we can use this widespread feeling as an impetus behind us to carry out a great measure of taxation reform which will also carry us a long way towards greater social equality . . . the principle of this measure of taxation reform should be this, that the best measure of a man's taxable capacity is the standard of living which he feels able to sustain for himself, whether it comes from ordinary income, whether it comes from capital gains, whether it comes from the dissipation of capital gains or tax fiddles of one sort or another. That is the best and truest and fairest measure of his taxable capacity.[7]

In other words, what was needed was a tax on all forms of *spending* from whatever sources. As James Callaghan commented, the distinction between taxation of income during life and of capital at death was 'an unreal golden curtain'. In the words of one delegate to the party conference in 1963, 'The standard of fairness we ought to adopt should be to shift the burden of taxation from those who earn their living by work by hand or by brain, to those who derive their income from speculation or title to wealth.' By these means, it was hoped to replace Labour's reputation as a 'high tax Party', and to 'establish the fact that we stand for the more *equitable* distribution of taxation; this means easements for some as well as heavier (but fairer) burdens for others'.[8]

In the 1959 election, Labour argued that its taxation policy offered greater equity, relieving wage- and salary-earners in contrast to the Conservatives' policy which 'gives the "expense account" man an easy run, and lets the spiv and the speculator off scot free . . . Labour policy will make the wealthiest pay their fair share by shifting the burden back from earned to unearned income, and from personal taxation to taxation on profits.'[9] The party's defeat in 1959 made the search for a coherent fiscal policy all the more urgent. Douglas Houghton was confident that 'a more effective network of taxes to fit more closely and more fairly the shoulders of those who have to bear them would make considerable appeal, especially if it could be shown that the result would not be heavier taxation but fairer distribution of the burden'.[10] The policy took shape in extended discussions between 1959 and 1964, starting wth a working party on profits taxation, continuing in the Finance and Economic Affairs Sub-Committee and culminating in the working party on taxation in 1963/4.

[7] LPA, Finance, Box I, Study Group on Equality, Re69/May 1956, 'Equality'; *Report of the 55th Annual Conference of the Labour Party, 1956* (London, 1956), pp. 117–32.

[8] *Report of the 62nd Annual Conference of the Labour Party, 1963* (London, 1963), pp. 252–6; LPA, RD139/Apr. 1961, taxation of profits and income proposals for reform: memorandum by D. Houghton. See also *Report of the 60th Annual Conference of the Labour Party, 1961* (London, 1961), pp. 145–52.

[9] Labour party, *Your Personal Guide to the Future Labour Offers You* (London, 1958).

[10] LPA, RD139/Apr. 1961, taxation of profits and income proposals for reform: memorandum by D. Houghton.

Central to these debates was Nicholas Kaldor's 'integrated' tax system. Ideally, Kaldor wished to introduce a new personal expenditure tax on the ability to spend from all sources, but he realised that the same results could be achieved with fewer administrative and political difficulties by a range of new taxes on each source of spending power. He therefore proposed capital gains tax, an annual wealth tax and a gift tax. His approach reflected a desire to create a modern, flexible and efficient economy, for the revenue from these new taxes would permit the abolition of surtax and the disincentive effects of high marginal taxation. He hoped to encourage saving, risk-taking and the opportunity to earn money through personal effort. Thus a tax on net wealth would encourage the productive employment of capital, for assets of equal value would pay the same tax, irrespective of the income.[11] The package was linked with a rhetoric of modernisation; it was designed to appeal to productive, salaried members of the middle class against speculators and recipients of socially created wealth. Labour's fiscal strategy therefore rested on reform of the tax system in order 'to ensure that the burden of taxation falls less heavily upon those who earn their money the hard way and which ensures that those who get their money the easy way by capital gains, by inheritance, by speculation, pay their fair share'.[12] These proposals could also be justified on more pragmatic grounds, that they would

---

[11] LPA, Finance, Finance and Economic Affairs Sub-Committee, Box II, minutes, 25 Nov. 1958–12 Sept. 1966, RD100/Dec. 1960, Sub-Committee on Finance and Economic Policy: draft programme of work; RD139/Apr. 1961, taxation of profits and income: proposals for reform: memorandum by D. Houghton (this summarises earlier papers); RD178/Nov. 1961, draft programme of work; RD222/Mar. 1962, capital gains tax, D. Houghton; RD470/May 1963, NEDC report on conditions favourable to faster growth; RD579/Nov. 1963, draft programme of work for 1963/4 and minutes of 1 Dec. 1961, 16 Mar. 1962, 29 Nov. 1963, 1 May 1964; Finance, Box IV, Working Party on Profits Taxation: papers and minutes, 13 May–21 July 1959, Re556/May 1959, the case for an integrated tax structure: N. Kaldor, for meeting of 2 June 1959; Re560/June 1959, issues concerning the taxation of capital gains, N. Kaldor; Re567/June 1959, tax policy for investment, P. Streeten; Re589/July 1959, wealth tax; Re605/Oct. 1959, report on the working party on the shape of taxation with particular reference to the taxation of profits; minutes, 13 May, 2, 9, 19 and 29 June, 7, 14 and 21 July 1959; Finance, Box IV, Taxation Working Party, minutes and papers, 17 Dec. 1963–19 Mar. 1964, RD623/Jan. 1964, the taxation implications of an incomes policy; RD635/Jan. 1964 (revise), report on taxation and industrial planning; RD636/Jan. 1964, report on taxation and regional planning; RD637/Jan. 1964, a note on the wealth tax, T. Balogh; RD677/Feb. 1964, annual wealth tax, N. Kaldor; RDR695/Feb. 1964, draft report on taxation and incomes policy, and RDR695/Mar. 1964 (second revise); N. Kaldor, a positive policy for wages and dividends: memorandum submitted to the chancellor of the Exchequer, 21 June 1950, and minutes, 17 Dec. 1963, 13, 24 and 31 Jan., 7, 14, 21 Feb., 19 Mar. 1964. The proposal for an expenditure tax was put forward in Kaldor, *An Expenditure Tax*; for an assessment of the likely impact on equity and savings, see A. R. Prest, 'A tax on expenditure?', *Lloyds Bank Review* n.s. 42 (1956), 35–49.

[12] *Labour Party Annual Conference, 1961*, p. 152.

foster a climate of social justice in order to contain wage pressure and inflation.[13]

The proposals were designed to achieve equity and also to stimulate economic growth. The problem with Kaldor's tax package, in the opinion of some other economists associated with Labour, was that it might *harm* rather than stimulate economic growth. Would the pursuit of equality reduce investment by shifting income from people with a greater propensity to save and giving it to people with a greater likelihood to spend? Thomas Balogh* feared that the study group of 1963/4 was only concerned with social equity and failed to consider the impact on investment and growth. As he saw the situation,

If we were already on an incontestable equilibrium growth path, with the entrepreneurs convinced that they can make money and that their risks are being reduced by careful governmental management of economic affairs, the proposals would not seem to me ill-conceived. I feel, however, that the *overwhelmingly important first policy goal is to reach this path of harmonious growth*. Taxation of capital gains and of wealth in the way envisaged, even if a modified expenditure tax is introduced and the savings allowances are granted, seems to me contrary *in this first period of heightened risk feeling* to this overriding aim.

Balogh felt that the issue was how to combine faster economic growth with more desirable distribution. His answer was to increase the role of the state.[14]

In Balogh's view, nationalisation would allow a more effective control of prices than any attempt to contain inflationary pressure through wage restraint. It would reduce excessive incomes and create equality; it would give more control over investment policy. The most important benefit of social ownership, he argued, was the elimination of a senseless stimulation of demand. In common with many earlier Labour intellectuals, Balogh viewed consumption as in some sense irrational; he felt that investment

[13] R. C. Whiting, 'The boundaries of taxation', in S. J. D. Green and R. C. Whiting (eds.), *The Boundaries of the State in Modern Britain* (Cambridge, 1996), p. 156.

[14] LPA, Box II, Finance, Finance and Economic Affairs Sub-Committee minutes, 25 Nov. 1958–12 Sept. 1966: RD764/Apr. 1964, note of dissent from report on taxation and incomes policy, T. Balogh.

* Thomas Balogh (1905–85) was born in Budapest, where his father was director of the transport board. He was educated at Budapest, Berlin and Harvard Universities. He worked in the research departments of the Banque de France, Reichsbank and Federal Reserve and then in the City of London before joining University College London as a lecturer from 1934 to 1940. He moved to Oxford where he taught from 1939 to his retirement in 1973. He worked with Harold Wilson in the 1950s and early 1960s, devising a policy for growth, linked with an incomes policy and intervention in industry; he proposed a separate ministry of expansion or planning. In 1964, he joined the Cabinet office to advise on economic affairs. In 1974, he took office as minister of state at the Department of Energy, and he was deputy chairman of the British National Oil Corporation 1976–8. (*DNB, 1981–5*, ed. Blake and Nicholls, pp. 25–6.)

should not be determined by the mere pursuit of profit at the expense of social spending on schools or hospitals. Balogh was critical of the profit motive, private investment and high levels of personal consumption:

Without a better balance between leisure and increase of collective or private consumption, satisfaction from higher income is illusive. But such better balance cannot be achieved without limiting the impact of the profit motive on resource distribution. Profit can be earned not merely by satisfying long felt wants more efficiently and in a better fashion, but also by creating new wants through artificially engendered satisfaction and the suggestion of status symbols.[15]

These proposals were intended as an alternative to entry to the Common Market, which many Conservative and some Labour politicians saw as the best hope for Britain in gaining access to a large, sophisticated market which would stimulate demand and efficiency. To Balogh, the EEC implied a loss of freedom to reshape the British economy in a collective, socialist way.

Kaldor's 'package' was attacked by adherents of collectivism and planning – and also on diametrically opposite grounds that it was *too* collectivist. W. Arthur Lewis,* a leading economist who served on the working party on equality, argued for a wider diffusion of ownership and greater equality by encouraging small savers rather than imposing additional taxes on capital:

All new property is created out of saving. The inequality of property ownership is due to the inequality of saving, that is to the fact that most saving is done by the rich (or by the companies whose shares they own). Hence the only way to alter the distribution of property in the future, other than confiscation, is to alter the distribution of saving: there must be relatively less saving by the rich, and relatively more saving by the poor and by public authorities . . . It is a complete illusion to suggest that you can alter the future distribution of wealth by a capital gains tax or by more death duties or capital levies, *if the future distribution of savings remains the same.*

Lewis linked equality with a positive encouragement of saving by as many people as possible rather than a simple destruction of existing

---

[15] LPA, RD360/Nov. 1962, the alternative to the common market, T. Balogh.

* W. Arthur Lewis (1915–91) was born in St Lucia, the son of teachers. He won a scholarship to the LSE, where he taught from 1938 to 1948. He joined the Fabians. In 1948, he moved to Manchester as professor of economics. He criticised planning as leading to standardised, low-quality goods. He argued that prices and money flows should be manipulated to harness the market and ensure that the benefits of growth were widely shared. He was principal of University College of the West Indies from 1959 to 1963, when he moved to Princeton. He won the Nobel prize for economics in 1972. (*American National Biography*, vol. XIII, ed. J. Garraty and M. C. Carnes (New York, 1999), pp. 609–11.)

accumulations of wealth. Such views were shared by few in the Labour party, but they do indicate that policies more closely associated with the Conservatives could fit into a social democratic vision of society. Lewis combined ownership of property with egalitarianism, unlike the Conservative stress on the pursuit of private gain as the major incentive for economic growth.[16] Houghton had similar doubts about the taxation of capital. 'To bring within our traditional *income* tax system the ultimate product of self-sacrifice and prudent investment (made out of income which has already been taxed) during the lifetime of the taxpayer will strike a lot of people as being objectionable. Capital to many self-employed persons is what pensions are to executives and managerial staffs.' Here was an alternative to public ownership and investment; to encourage small savings by promoting a wider diffusion of ownership, reducing the amount taken in taxation, exempting earnings from new investment in selected industries and encouraging unit trusts.[17] In the event, many of the ideas were developed by the Conservative administration of Mrs Thatcher in a different ideological context.

These debates over fiscal policy were grappling with the basic dilemma of how to reconcile equality with growth and investment. The search for a coherent policy on taxation became more pressing as alternative – and unacceptable – approaches emerged in the early 1960s. In 1963, the NEDC suggested that a value added tax and wage-related social security system should be adopted to stimulate economic growth. Both proposals were attacked by Labour. The VAT was easily criticised as a regressive tax, especially when the NEDC linked it with the abolition of the profits tax. The result, it was feared, would be an increase in inequality. Any move from tax-funded welfare to social security contributions was firmly rejected on the grounds that 'reliance on a flat rate poll-tax falls very heavily indeed on the low-paid worker'. In 1963, the Labour party conference resolved that a pressing need for the next Labour government was a system of taxation which would combine 'incentive, growth and a fairer allocation of national income'.[18] When Labour won the election in 1964 by a narrow margin, it had the chance to shape the fiscal system on these lines.

[16] LPA, Finance, Box I, Study Group on Equality, Re58/May 1956, W. A. Lewis to B. Robertson, 27 Apr. 1956. In the final report, the study group hoped to improve the distribution of wealth through an extension of public ownership and socially owned wealth through more extensive public savings; encouragement of small and medium individual savings through occupational pensions, home ownership and contractual savings was mentioned as an afterthought.

[17] LPA, Finance, Box II, RD222/Mar. 1962, capital gains tax, D. Houghton.

[18] NEDC, *Conditions Favourable to Faster Growth*; *Labour Party Annual Conference, 1963*, pp. 225, 252.

Labour in office, 1964–1970

The basis for Labour's thinking on taxation was provided by Kaldor's integrated package, and above all by the budget of 1965 when Callaghan reformed the tax system as part of a 'modern and dynamic economic policy'. It was, as Richard Crossman remarked, the most complicated fiscal reform for thirty years.[19] The chancellor's stated aim was to ensure that 'those who earn high rewards through skill and enterprise should enjoy the benefit of them – but they must be earned'.[20] Kaldor provided the logic, setting his approach soon after the election when he proposed a corporation profits tax, wealth tax, long-term capital gains tax, gift tax (possibly with a reform of death duties), and new taxes to improve the balance of payments. As we shall see, the corporation tax and capital gains tax were introduced in 1965, but not the wealth tax to which he attached considerable importance.[21]

A change in the taxation of company profits was central to Kaldor and Callaghan's policy. Although the Conservatives ended differentiation of the profits tax in 1958, they did not merge the income tax on company profits with the profits tax in order to create distinct taxation of companies and individuals. Instead, all profits paid a tax of 15 per cent, plus the standard rate of income tax on retentions and whatever rate applied to individual shareholders for distributions. In 1965, Callaghan announced that he would combine the profits tax and income tax on company profits into a single corporation tax of somewhere between 35 and 40 per cent on retentions and distributions. When shareholders received their dividends, they paid income tax *without a tax credit* for the corporation tax already paid. The corporation tax, Callaghan claimed, was 'the most fundamental of the tax reforms in this Budget. It is a new landmark in our fiscal history, such as we have rarely been able to create in this country save under the stringent needs of war.'[22] Why did he attach such importance to the tax?

The change implied a return to Dalton's differential profits tax of 1947 by another route. Taxation on retained profits fell, for they only paid the 35–40 per cent corporation tax; it rose on distributions which also paid the income tax on individuals. The aim was to encourage plough-back of profits, both to encourage economic growth and to help wage restraint. The logic was explained by Balogh when he attacked the Conservatives'

---

[19] R. Crossman, *Diaries of a Cabinet Minister*, vol. i: *Minister of Housing, 1964–66* (London, 1975), p. 228.

[20] *Parliamentary Debates*, 5th ser. 710, 6 Apr. 1965, col. 245; A. R. Ilersic, 'Taxes, 1964–66: an interim appraisal', *British Tax Review* (1966), 365–73; R. C. Whiting, 'Ideology and reform in Labour's tax strategy, 1964–70', *Historical Journal* 41 (1998), 1121–40.

[21] PRO, T171/804, 'First memorandum on tax reform', N. Kaldor, 29 Oct. 1964.

[22] *Parliamentary Debates*, 5th ser. 710, 6 Apr. 1965, col. 254.

removal of differentiation. He assumed that small, dynamic firms had greater difficulties in obtaining funds from the London capital market than large concerns. Further, the amount of capital available would *fall* as a result of an encouragement of distributions, for shareholders would consume part of their dividends. A reduction in retentions would make firms more dependent on the capital market – and that would increase the advantage of large firms over small in securing funds from the reduced supply of savings. Balogh also denied that retentions led to a less efficient use of funds than the capital market: companies with expert technical advice would make better judgements about the development of new products and technologies than private investors advised by stock brokers. Above all, he claimed that expanding firms in new sectors grew as a result of high retentions. In Balogh's opinion, differentiation was a policy for growth – and also for managing the economy. In his view, higher dividends and upper-class consumption would merely stimulate wage demands. Balogh's paper followed the logic of the memorandum of dissent to the report of the Royal Commission on the Taxation of Profits and Income.[23]

Kaldor was largely responsible for the dissenting memorandum, and he continued to press for a return to differentiation in the party debates of the late 1950s and early 1960s. In his view, Britain had an active capital market, so there was no need to encourage distributions as in Germany where the market was weak and rapidly growing firms had problems in securing finance. In Britain, the result would simply be higher dividends and a Stock Exchange boom without any significant change in the source of finance. Kaldor denied that the policy was designed to discourage the capital market; it was to increase the rate of growth of dynamic firms which relied on loans or plough-back rather than external capital. In Kaldor's view, a lower rate of tax on retained profits would help new and successful firms to a much greater extent than the Conservative policy of high dividends, which set the private interest of the shareholder against the national interest by stimulating inflation and destroying wage restraint. A separate corporation tax also fitted with Labour's stress on economic planning, for it could be varied independently of personal income tax in order to influence investment and the amount of retentions or distributions.[24] Here was the rationale of Callaghan's corporation tax in

[23] Balogh, 'Differential profits tax', 528–33; see LPA, Finance, Box IV, Working Party on Profits Taxation, minutes, 19 June 1959; the memorandum is in PP 1955–6 XXVII, *Royal Commission on the Taxation of Profits and Income, Final Report*, pp. 1086–202.

[24] PRO, T171/806, 'Brief for the financial secretary: corporation tax', N. Kaldor, 8 Apr. 1965; T171/807, 'Double taxation', N. Kaldor, 1 June 1965. In Germany, companies paid 56 per cent on retained and 25 per cent on distributed profits which were then liable to income tax.

a modern and dynamic economy: the burden of taxation could be shifted away from faster-growing companies which were low distributors; and all companies would have an incentive to retain profits for expansion and efficiency. The Conservative policy of 1958 would be reversed, and Dalton's approach of using differential taxation to favour large firms would be restored.[25]

The Balogh–Kaldor–Callaghan policy rejected the majority view of the Royal Commission, that high retentions simply led to wasteful expenditure and over-expansion in existing lines. In their opinion, low distributions depressed share values and hindered the capital market. Rather than encouraging investment, the result was to distort the market by driving a wedge between external and internal rates of return. A firm could use its retained profits on less stringent terms and get a higher return than a firm obliged to use more costly external capital.[26] Similarly, the Inland Revenue remained sceptical about the case for a corporation tax. Might the outcome be retention of profits rather than investment; and if companies did invest, was there any guarantee that they would make rational decisions in the absence of the constraints of the capital market? Might the result be to stimulate take-overs in order to obtain reserves rather than to rationalise? On this view, profits would be used more efficiently as dividends in the hands of shareholders and an active, external capital market. In any case, investment in Britain was not significantly below the level in Germany; the basic problem was the lower level of *efficiency* of investment, reflecting low effort and low productivity which required more drastic solutions than mere tinkering with company tax rates.[27]

The corporation tax was linked with a long-term capital gains tax which was introduced in 1965. Callaghan wished to encourage retentions as a means of stimulating efficiency and a 'sensible and equitable' wages policy – but he also had to reassure the unions that dividend restraint would not simply lead to capital gains. The capital gains tax would 'provide a background of equity and fair play' for the government's wages policy. In Kaldor's opinion, the main justification of the tax was equity, but this connected with economic benefits. The ability to secure capital gains amounted to discrimination in favour of property

[25] *Parliamentary Debates*, 5th ser. 710, 6 Apr. 1965, col. 255.
[26] The argument of the final report as outlined in Balogh, 'Differential profits tax', 528–9; for the report, see PP 1955–6 xxvii, *Royal Commission on the Taxation of Profits and Income, Final Report*, pp. 890–2.
[27] PRO, T171/806, corporation tax, A. Johnston, Inland Revenue, 6 Nov. 1964; N. R. F. Crafts, 'Economic growth', in N. R. F. Crafts and N. Woodward (eds.), *The British Economy since 1945* (Oxford, 1991), pp. 276–7, 289–90.

owners and against wages and salaries; and encouraged speculation at the expense of production. A long-term capital gains tax would make rewards more proportionate to the social value of services, and improve the allocation of scarce labour. The policy was designed to contain inflation through limits on dividends and wages, as part of an attempt to placate the unions and make them accept a voluntary incomes policy, rather than what Balogh termed the 'Quixotic argument' that the economy could be controlled by monetary means. Indeed, high retentions meant that companies had large cash reserves which reduced the role of monetary policy. At the most basic level, the debate was over the use of monetary policy or direct controls over the economy.[28] The debate over company taxation also had implications for the nature of incentives, profits and the external capital market. Although Kaldor claimed that the policy was not intended to discourage the capital market, Labour remained ambivalent towards profits and the allocation of resources by the market. High profits and distributions were viewed with some disquiet. The option of encouraging small savings and diffusing ownership as a means of increasing investment was not adopted, and many members of the Labour party were still wedded to the policies pursued between 1945 and 1951, of public ownership combined with encouragement of retentions by private concerns.

The introduction of the corporation tax and capital gains tax in 1965 did not end the innovations of Callaghan and Kaldor, for in 1966 a new, and highly controversial, tax was introduced: the selective employment tax (SET). Like the innovations of 1965, this tax aimed to encourage economic growth by stimulating structural change in the economy, rather than by offering personal incentives. It must also be placed in the context of concerns over the lack of competitiveness of British industry in export markets which had so troubled the previous Conservative administration. When Labour took office, it was faced with the immediate prospect of a serious balance of payments deficit, and an obvious response was to restore competitiveness by devaluing sterling. Wilson initially decided to maintain the existing exchange rate, and an alternative response was needed. Attention initially turned to VAT – a tax not usually associated with Labour.

---

[28] PRO, T171/804, note of meeting between the chancellor of the Exchequer and the TUC Economic Committee, 3 May 1965; T171/805, 'Arguments for and against the long-term capital gains tax', N. Kaldor, 24 May 1965; *Parliamentary Debates*, 5th ser. 710, 6 Apr. 1965 col. 245; Crossman, *Diaries of a Cabinet Minister*, vol. I, p. 228. See Balogh, 'Differential profits tax', 533; P. Streeten and T. Balogh, 'A reconsideration of monetary policy', *Bulletin of the Oxford University Institute of Statistics* 19 (1957), 336–7; P. Streeten, 'Report of the Royal Commission on the Taxation of Profits and Income', *Bulletin of the Oxford University Institute of Statistics* 17 (1955), 341–2.

In the early 1960s, VAT was considered as a way of offering incentives to exports – a case not sustained by internal debates within the civil service or the report of the Committee on Turnover Taxation. Although VAT could be returned to exporters, it was no improvement on the existing purchase tax where exports did not pay at all. Indeed, firms would have to pay tax before securing a refund, and would incur additional costs of administration. The case for replacing the profits tax by VAT was rejected, for the committee feared that the tax would be passed on in prices rather than absorbed in profits, so making exports still less competitive and undermining wage restraint.[29] Consequently, the case for VAT did not rest on the encouragement of exports – and the alternative rationales had some appeal to Labour. VAT offered a solution to the pressing need for more revenue. The Department of Economic Affairs pointed out that any increase in direct taxes would face resistance. Further, the existing indirect taxes fell on a narrow range of goods, distorting consumer choice and production, and making large increases in revenue difficult. The purchase tax did not cover services which formed a larger part of expenditure; and it was politically difficult to extend its coverage with the need to justify an extension to each exempt good. Politically, it was easier to treat untaxed goods as one *bloc*, and to bring in a broadly based tax at a low rate. This could be justified on the grounds that a tax on expenditure was as logical as a tax on income: it would reduce the disparities between goods which were taxed and untaxed; and it would make the tax system more responsive to future changes in spending.[30] As we have noted, Cairncross informed the outgoing Conservative administration that VAT might actually *increase* consumer welfare by reducing taxes on highly desired consumer durables.

Above all, Kaldor advocated the introduction of VAT as a means of modernising and regulating the economy. He started from a pessimistic view that British industry had lost its competitiveness; he then argued that it was unlikely that the position could be restored either by a faster rate of growth in productivity or a slower rate of growth in wages. At most, further deterioration might be prevented. He rejected the use of devaluation to restore competitiveness; the only remaining possibility was to reduce labour costs by a combination of taxes and subsidies. Hence his interest in VAT as a solution to the balance of payments crisis. In 1964, he suggested that the VAT could be used to replace social security contributions; the tax could then be used to finance regional payroll

---

[29] On the report of the Committee on Turnover Taxation, see above p. 247.
[30] PRO, T320/455, indirect taxation: note by the DEA, draft, n.d.

subsidies, social security benefits and export incentives, as well as regulating the economy. The attraction of VAT, as Kaldor saw it, was that export costs would be reduced by cutting the employers' insurance contribution which raised labour costs and could not be refunded. Further, the funding of social security could be shifted from a flat-rate 'poll tax' to VAT which was less progressive than the income tax, but less regressive than existing indirect taxes and insurance contributions. The tax would raise large sums without distorting production and consumption. In addition, the new tax had a major advantage over devaluation: it could be linked with a subsidy to payrolls in order to reduce labour costs and increase competitiveness. As far as the domestic consumer was concerned, the payroll subsidy would be offset by payment of VAT; as far as export markets were concerned, costs would fall and there was no liability to VAT. The result would be to reduce profits on domestic sales and increase profits on exports. Further, the subsidy could be varied between regions in order to assist depressed areas.[31] This 'modified universal' VAT combined technical brilliance with a scant regard for political and administrative practicability.

The case for replacing social security contributions by VAT did not convince the PSI committee of the Treasury, nor a committee of officials from the Treasury, Customs and Excise, Board of Trade and Department of Economic Affairs which reconsidered VAT and indirect taxation at the end of 1965. Social security contributions were already a smaller proportion of GNP in Britain than in West Germany and France, and there was a strong argument in favour of *increasing* taxes on labour in order to force employers to use their workforce more efficiently and to invest in capital equipment.[32] Officials were concerned about the social consequences of a change in welfare funding. Insurance contributions fell on heavy users of labour; a shift to VAT would increase prices and move the costs of welfare from the employed who paid insurance contributions to the non-employed (mainly married women and pensioners) paying VAT. Of course, the Treasury and other departments were anxious to maintain a link between benefits and contributions. In the absence of contributions, how could eligibility be established or earnings-related benefits

[31] PRO, T320/455, review of direct taxation policy, 1965–6: PSI(64)7, 'A tax instrument for adjusting the balance of payments, note by N. Kaldor, 25 Oct. 1964', and developed further in PSI(64)10, Public Sector Income Committee: the case for a value added tax as an additional instrument of taxation: note by Nicholas Kaldor (also in T171/802).

[32] PRO, T320/455, PSI(64)8, Treasury: Public Sector Income Committee: Richardson revisited, 18 Dec. 1964; T320/382, Public Sector Income Committee, D. J. S. Hancock, 21 Dec. 1964.

paid without a means test?[33] For its part, Customs and Excise were hostile to any move from the existing purchase tax and excise duties, which were administratively simple.[34] The official view on Kaldor's scheme was blunt: 'There can be few whose immediate reaction to a proposal to tax consumption to finance wages will not be "this is bonkers".'[35]

The PSI committee continued to consider various proposals to assist exports in 1965. Should the purchase tax or corporation tax be replaced by VAT? Should the national insurance contribution be abolished in favour of the VAT? Should the revenue from VAT be used to provide a payroll subsidy? Or should a payroll tax be imposed in booming regions in order to subsidise employment in depressed regions? Alternatively, the existing investment allowances might be replaced by subsidies to users or producers of plant and equipment. The first three proposals were rejected by the PSI committee as simply too large a task for the civil service and firms, and because of the political dangers of extending indirect taxes. Instead, attention turned to some form of subsidy. The committee considered the case for a payroll tax, either on the prosperous regions or on service employment. In particular, attention turned to the so-called 'northern regulator', a temporary subsidy paid to all employment in the north and Scotland when unemployment rose above a certain level. The problem of existing policies of economic management was that measures to contain inflation created unemployment in these regions.[36] Kaldor and Balogh were not impressed, arguing that their policy had been 'emasculated'.[37]

Despite official opposition, Callaghan was planning changes in indirect taxes and in April 1966 Wilson asked for a scheme to be prepared to implement VAT. Their motivation was the urgent need to allow tax rebates on exports, and to relieve pressure on other taxes which had reached their limit. At this point, Kaldor modified his proposal. Rather than using the

---

[33] PRO, T320/455, PSI(65)4, replacement of National Insurance contributions by a major extension of indirect taxation: note by the secretaries, 13 Jan. 1965.

[34] PRO, T320/455, W. Armstrong, 26 Nov. 1965; future work on indirect taxation, 6 Dec. 1965; further work on indirect taxation: minutes of meeting, 7 Dec. 1965; future work on indirect taxation, 15 Dec. 1965; VAT: supplementary comments by Customs and Excise, 14 Dec. 1965; review of indirect taxation policy: minutes of meeting, 16 Dec. 1965; minute by Kaldor, 29 Dec. 1965; indirect taxation, D. McKean, 15 Mar. 1966; indirect taxation, W. W. M., Customs and Excise, 12 Apr. 1966; note for the record, 25 April 1966; VAT: note of a meeting, 26 May 1966.

[35] PRO, T320/382, 'Payroll subsidy financed by VAT rebateable on exports imposable on imports', Jan. 1965.

[36] PRO, T171/813, PSI(65)7, final, fiscal incentives for exports: progress report by the PSI committee, 3 Feb. 1965, and Sir Richard Clarke, Plans D, E and F, 14 July 1965, covering report by a group of officials, 14 July 1965.

[37] PRO, T171/813, Kaldor to chancellor, 16 July 1965, and Balogh to prime minister, 15 July 1965.

revenue from VAT to reduce employers' contributions and cut labour costs, he now proposed an additional payroll tax on services. The revenue would then be used to subsidise manufacturing costs by remitting the employers' contributions. He argued that his proposal would help exports by reducing costs by 4 per cent; it would also check the movement of labour into services. Over the previous ten years, 80 per cent of additional employment was in the service sector, and Kaldor argued that economic growth and an improved trade balance depended on increased manufacturing output and employment. He argued that productivity in the service sector was low and difficult to increase; economic growth depended on shifting labour into industry, where productivity was higher and capable of improvement through investment in more advanced capital plant. The introduction of a new tax was likely to be time-consuming, so Kaldor proposed an interim measure of raising the employers' national insurance contribution and rebating it on exempted sectors such as manufacturing. In Callaghan's opinion, this proposal would create price stability; reduce the over-taxing of manufactures and the under-taxing of services; and economise on labour in unproductive services.[38] In the event, it was again modified to remove the problem of collecting and returning large sums. Instead, a SET was levied on employment in service industries. Callaghan argued that it would contribute to long-term structural change as well as supplying a major new source of revenue. Expenditure on services amounted to £7,000m, with taxes of only 1 per cent; consumers spent £6,000m on goods liable to customs and excise, with taxes of 40 per cent. The result was to distort consumption and employment, and a differential tax on employment would correct the imbalance by increasing the costs of labour in services and reducing it in industry.[39]

The introduction of SET in 1966 continued the approach of the budget of 1965: encouraging growth through structural change rather than personal incentives and enterprise. The SET seemed, at least to Kaldor, to have an important advantage over VAT which would equally well widen the tax base and avoid distortions to consumer choice and production. It

---

[38] For the argument on growth, see N. Kaldor, *Causes of the Slow Rate of Economic Growth of the United Kingdom: An Inaugural Lecture* (Cambridge, 1966); for a discussion of the impact of the tax, see B. Reddaway, *First Report, on the Effects of Selective Employment Tax: The Distributive Trades* (London, 1970); and J. D. Whitley and G. D. N. Worswick, 'The productivity effects of select employment tax', *National Institute Economic Review* 56 (1971), 36–40; and comments in N. Woodward, 'Labour's economic performance, 1964–70', in R. Coopey, S. Fielding and N. Tiratsoo (eds.), *The Wilson Governments, 1964–70* (London, 1993), pp. 88–9. PRO, T171/813, N. Kaldor to chancellor, 6 Apr. 1966, 'The case for a payroll tax and for a new incentive for exports'; A. K. Cairncross, 18 and 19 Apr. 1966; I. P. Bancroft to Vinter, 5 Apr. 1966; note of a meeting 19 Apr. 1966; note for record: payroll levy, 18 Apr. 1966.

[39] *Parliamentary Debates*, 5th ser. 727, 3 May 1966, cols. 1453–4.

would encourage the redeployment of labour from services. Further, he realised the political dangers of VAT, for many members of the Labour party and the electorate were instinctively hostile to a shift towards indirect taxes.[40] But Kaldor's enthusiasm for his new tax was shared by few other people. Indeed, the introduction of SET bears some resemblance to later experience with the poll tax – the adoption of a new tax with little consideration within the machinery of government or consultation with external bodies. Crossman pointed to the constitutional issue that the simple announcement of the tax as a *fait accompli* without an opportunity for discussion 'makes an absolute mockery of Cabinet government and Cabinet responsibility'.[41] Officials were adept at blocking reforms of the tax system; the result was to leave the chancellor susceptible to Kaldor's clever impracticalities. Although the SET did not provoke civil disobedience as did the poll tax, within a few weeks of its introduction, officials were already debating a possible replacement.

The VAT now seemed so much more appealing as a way of taxing services and raising revenue – not least with the prospect of entry into the EEC. As the Inland Revenue pointed out, the SET was too arbitrary to provide the basis for heavy taxation, and its yield was likely to be modest.[42] Certainly, there was a pressing need for additional taxes. In 1967, Kaldor argued that the UK was not heavily taxed and that since 1959 taxation was too low by about 3 per cent of GNP to sustain a healthy economy. His fellow economist, Robert Neild,* claimed that the tax base was too narrow and should be widened by the introduction of payroll or indirect taxes, if development of the economy and social fabric were not to be damaged. The case for VAT shifted from export incentives to the need to increase the buoyancy of the revenue and to raise the proportion of

---

[40] PRO, T320/455, tax on value added: proposal of the DEA, N. Kaldor, 12 May 1966; export incentives and the VAT, memorandum by the director-general of the National Economic Development Office, N. Kaldor, 18 May 1966.

[41] Crossman, *Diaires of a Cabinet Minister*, vol. I, p. 511.

[42] PRO, T320/455, VAT: note of a meeting, 23 May 1966; A. Johnston, Inland Revenue, to Armstrong, 24 May 1966; VAT: note of a meeting, 26 May 1966; T320/456, R. Powell, Board of Trade, to Armstrong, 3 June 1966; draft brief for first secretary for meeting of NEDC, 15 June 1966; VAT memorandum by director-general, R. J. S. Corry, 6 June 1966.

* Robert Neild (b. 1924) was educated at Charterhouse and Trinity College, Cambridge. From 1947 to 1951 he was on the secretariat of the United Nations Economic Commission for Europe; he was in the Economic Section of the Cabinet Office and Treasury from 1951 to 1956. He was a lecturer in economics and a fellow of Trinity College, Cambridge, 1956–8, and a member of the National Institute of Economic Research from 1958 to 1964. He returned to Whitehall as economic adviser to the Treasury from 1964 to 1967, leaving to be director of the Stockholm International Peace Research Institute 1967–71. He returned to Cambridge as professor of economics from 1971 to 1984. (*Who's Who 2001*, p. 1515.)

taxation in GNP.[43] When VAT was introduced by the next Conservative government in 1974, the ideological context was somewhat different for it was linked with a shift to a more regressive tax system, and encouraging growth through personal incentives. As Kaldor noted in 1968, 'The strong advocacy of the value added tax by the Tory Party and business circles is really an attempt to shift the balance of taxation from direct to indirect taxes. This of course would not be acceptable from a socialist point of view.'[44]

The reforms of 1965 and 1966 marked the high point of Labour's fiscal strategy. Devaluation was forced on the government in 1967, and Callaghan resigned. The new chancellor, Roy Jenkins, was cautious about any further changes after the excitement of the Callaghan–Kaldor reforms: 'there is a limit to the amount of change which the Revenue Departments, individuals, companies and their professional advisers can reasonably absorb'.[45] He blocked pressure for an annual wealth tax, despite the attraction of broadening the tax base without increasing income tax on middling incomes. Arguably, a wealth tax offered a better way of giving incentives to 'middle management' than a general reduction in income tax rates which would also relieve *rentiers*. In fact, little was done apart from the 'special charge' of 1968, a measure akin to the special contribution of Cripps.[46]

The Callaghan–Kaldor reforms were disappointing, for they produced little revenue and did not stimulate economic growth to any discernible extent. They did very little to resolve the growing problem of the burden of income tax on low incomes. The concern for the regressive impact of *indirect* taxes obscured serious problems with the income tax. Average wages were rising, and a larger number of people were crossing the income tax threshold. When Labour came to office, the tax threshold for a married man with two children was 78.1 per cent of the average earnings of an adult male manual worker (1964/5); when it left office, the figure had dropped to 56.1 per cent (1969/70). The result was alarming: people in lower income brackets faced large increases in their liability to income tax compared with those further up the income scale.[47] Here was an attraction of a wealth tax or even VAT in increasing the buoyancy of

---

[43] PRO, T171/820, 'The budgetary outlook in the longer term setting', N. Kaldor, 17 Mar. 1967; R. R. Neild, 22 Mar. 1967; T171/821, 'Value added tax and alternatives', 10 Aug. 1966.

[44] Quote by Whiting, *Labour Party and Taxation*, p. 201 n. 89 from King's College, Cambridge, Kaldor Papers, 3/30/209.

[45] *Parliamentary Debates*, 5th ser. 761, 19 Mar. 1968, col. 274.

[46] Whiting, *Labour Party and Taxation*, pp. 190–5.

[47] Whiting, *Labour Party and Taxation*, pp. 185–7.

the tax system. The legitimacy of the tax system was threatened, and for all their sophistication the reforms of 1965 and 1966 did little to meet the real difficulties. The Labour government went into the 1970 election facing criticism from the progressive left, concerned about the impact on equality and poverty, as well as from the right.

The innovations of the Labour government did influence thinking within the Conservative party, giving new force to the view that retentions might simply 'make life too comfortable for inefficient managements'.[48] Growth depended on obtaining capital in the market, which required distribution of dividends for reinvestment. The underlying assumption of SET was attacked by Norman St John-Stevas* and Iain Macleod[†] as a sign that Labour was wedded to the past and a 'ludicrously old fashioned view of the structure of our economy'. As they pointed out, services were not separate from and inferior to industry which relied on an efficient banking or insurance sector. An expanding service sector was a sign of a prosperous economy, and the tax was derided as an expression of 'old fashioned cap and muffler Socialism'.[49] Certainly, the fiscal policy of Kaldor and Callaghan made the merits of VAT more apparent as a way of raising revenue and converging with Europe. The SET also foreclosed other options for the Conservatives, for their pledge to repeal the tax made it more difficult to advocate a payroll tax. Could they remove a tax on *some* forms of employment, only to introduce a tax on *all* forms of employment?

Callaghan's budgets forced the Conservatives to define their position, with a greater emphasis on the need for distributions and small savings, and a shift to a higher proportion of indirect taxes. During the years of

[48] E. Boyle, *Parliamentary Debates*, 5th ser. 710, 12 Apr. 1965, col. 978.
[49] *Parliamentary Debates*, 5th ser. 727, 3 May 1966, cols. 1511–12, 4 May 1966, 1648, 1655.
* Norman Anthony Francis St John-Stevas (b. 1929) was educated at Fitzwilliam College, Cambridge, and Christ Church, Oxford. He was called to the bar in 1952, and taught at the University of Southampton 1952–3 and King's College London 1953–6. He joined *The Economist* in 1959, and was a Conservative MP from 1964 to 1987. He served as parliamentary under-secretary of state at the Department of Education and Science 1972–3, as minister of state for the arts 1973–4, chancellor of the Duchy of Lancaster, leader of the Commons and Minister of Arts 1979–81. He was Master of Emmanuel College, Cambridge, 1991–6. (*Who's Who, 2001*, p. 1823.)
† Iain Norman Macleod (1913–70) was born in Skipton; he was educated at Fettes and Gonville and Caius College, Cambridge. He joined the CRD in 1946 and became an MP in 1950. He was a leading figure in the 'One Nation' group. He became minister of health in 1952, moving to be minister of labour in 1955 and secretary of the colonies in 1959, and in 1961–3 chancellor of the Duchy of Lancaster, leader of the Commons and chairman of the party. He then edited the *Spectator* and became a director of Lombards Bank, as well as joining the opposition front bench. In 1970, he was appointed chancellor of the Exchequer, but died very soon afterwards. (*DNB, 1961–70*, ed. Williams and Nicholls, pp. 700–4.)

opposition between 1964 and 1970, the Conservative party attempted to develop a package of tax measures which would resolve the difficulties it experienced in office, as well as providing an alternative to Labour. By the time Labour returned to power in 1974, some of Callaghan's schemes had been swept away and a major change had been implemented in the form of VAT. However, the Conservative administration of 1970 to 1974 failed to implement the wider package of reforms developed in opposition, which would fulfil Macmillan's ambition for a tax policy combining revenue for socially integrative welfare with a pursuit of enterprise. Instead, the emphasis shifted to encouragement of incentives without a concern for those who would suffer, at least in the short term before economic growth led to general prosperity. The approach to distributive justice changed in a fundamental way, with less concern for the extent to which the worst-off members of society suffered, and a much greater sense that the middling and upper incomes were being treated in a punitive way.

10 Rethinking taxation policy: from an opportunity state to an enterprise society, 1964–1979

> ... take the whole tax system to pieces and put it together again in a way
> that will radically alter the economic climate – the framework of rewards
> and penalties in which personal and corporate decisions are taken within
> the economic system.
>
> Bodleian Library, CPA, CRD 3/7/6/6, 'Swinton policy weekend 1967:
> report', J. Douglas, 26 Sept. 1967

> ... there are two well-established Conservative principles which ought
> to be applied to personal taxation. One is to improve personal incentives;
> the other is to encourage the broader ownership of capital.
>
> Bodleian Library, CPA, CRD 3/7/6/9, Policy Group on Future Economic
> Policy, 'Personal taxation: An agenda', William Rees-Mogg

> There may well be a good case for the euthanasia of the share-holder
> as well as the rentier; equally, high net incomes may have no place in a
> Socialist society. These are all legitimate objectives. But it is the height of
> folly, while pursuing these objectives, to pay lip-service to the merits of
> private enterprise and then simultaneously, ensure that the forces which
> make such an economy tick are suppressed. Only when the [Labour]
> Government makes up its own mind as to the type of society and econ-
> omy it wants to create will it be possible to evaluate the relevance and
> adequacy of its fiscal policy.
>
> A. R. Ilersic, 'Taxes, 1964–66: an interim appraisal', *British Tax Review*
> (1966), 373

'A kind of tax prison': Conservatives in opposition and government, 1964–1974

Conservative fiscal strategy rested on the assumption that economic
growth was promoted by personal risk-taking and enterprise in a free
market. Inequality was therefore defensible, a reward for those who created wealth and prosperity. However, in the 1950s and early 1960s, many
Conservatives still believed that the pursuit of self-interest should be
carefully contained within an integrated, cohesive society which would
be better able to respond to economic problems and define agreement
between different interest groups. In part, this was a pragmatic response

to the need for wage restraint. By 1964, only tentative steps had been taken in pursuit of incentives for risk and profit. Concessions to salaried, managerial and technical staff might offer incentives and secure votes for the Conservatives, but threatened to alienate the unions and undermine wage restraint. The task of the Conservatives in opposition from 1964 to 1970 was to devise a policy offering greater incentives and encouraging risk in an 'opportunity state' – without threatening social integration and cohesion. The failure to resolve the tension between these two ambitions provided the background for the Thatcher administration's pursuit of opportunity at the expense of integration. The attempt to maintain social integration might be at the expense of economic growth which left everyone poorer – or so the more radical Conservatives came to believe.

The British welfare state was characterised by a high reliance on funding from central government taxation. By the 1960s, both the Labour and Conservative parties were forced to consider whether the welfare state and the fiscal constitution could continue to be compatible, or whether the relationship would become increasingly strained. The legitimacy of central government taxation meant that other methods of funding welfare atrophied; a fiscal system which for so long secured a high degree of consent to taxation, might start to appear rigid as the costs of welfare increased and more taxpayers became liable to pay income tax at higher marginal rates (see table 10.2). A major political problem, at the centre of discussions within the Conservative party in the 1960s, was how to renegotiate the fiscal constitution. The conflicts over tax policy within the party during the 1960s, and particularly in the years of opposition between 1964 and 1970, entailed a debate over fundamental assumptions and a battle for the ideological heart of the party.[1] Although the Heath government of 1970 to 1974 avoided many of the most contentious issues, the ground was laid for the Thatcher project after 1979.

In 1960, Edward Boyle accurately predicted that taxation 'would turn out to be the main bone of contention inside the party during the 1960s'. There were two causes for concern. Boyle realised that reductions in taxation during the 1950s depended upon special factors which were no longer present. A fall in defence expenditure, and the end of food subsidies and housing grants, allowed higher social expenditure *and* tax cuts in the 1950s. Boyle feared that government spending in the future would increase at a faster rate than the GNP.[2] There was also an increasing realisation that there was a crisis in the *structure* of taxation which would

---

[1] For a brief account of the review of 1964 to 1970, see J. Ramsden, *The Making of Conservative Party Policy: The Conservative Research Department since 1929* (London, 1980).

[2] CPA, CRD 3/7/26/2, TPC(60)7, minutes of 4th meeting of Taxation Policy Committee, 15 July 1960.

require the fiscal constitution to be recast. A comparison between Britain and other countries suggested that the divergence was not the high proportion of GNP taken by the government, but *how* it was taken – as indicated in the comparative figures for 1962 presented in the report on turnover taxation (table 10.1). On the surface, the British tax system was reassuringly average: the level of taxation was broadly in line with other countries in western Europe, and it stood eighth out of fifteen major economies in the Organisation for Economic Co-operation and Development in 1974. Further, there was a similar balance between direct and indirect taxes. But the Economist Intelligence Unit argued that this 'averageness' concealed defects in the constituent parts of the tax regime. Indirect taxes were highly selective, falling on a limited range of goods through the purchase tax or excise duties on tobacco, beer and petrol; as a result, saturation point was reached more quickly than in countries with a general sales or turnover tax. Direct taxes were heavier, over a wider income range, than in other countries in western Europe. As a result of rising real incomes, many people passed through the reduced rates of income tax into the standard rate, so that 'the buoyancy in our tax system is derived from the high marginal rates of direct tax on middle and upper incomes', with a consequent 'pinch' of taxation on middle-class professional families. Further, the contribution of general taxation to welfare expenditure was much greater than elsewhere in western Europe, where social security contributions were more important and funding of social services fell on labour costs rather than taxation of profits and personal income. In 1974, social security contributions were only 6.1 per cent of GNP in Britain, compared with 13.3 per cent in Germany and 15.7 per cent in France. An increase in expenditure on welfare would therefore impose strains on an inflexible system of general taxation which lacked 'buoyancy'. In a 'buoyant' tax regime, a rise of 1 per cent in national income produces an increase of more than 1 per cent in government revenue, as incomes move into higher tax brackets or more taxed commodities are consumed. As a result, any increase in government expenditure was painless, and there was a prospect of a reduction in tax rates. In the 1960s, the tax regime lost its 'buoyancy', and Labour's fiscal reforms merely made a bad situation worse, for its new taxes did not have a greater ability to tap economic growth.[3] Economic growth was itself a major problem, for British rates of growth of GDP in the 1950s

[3] CPA, CRD 3/7/26/26, Economist Intelligence Unit report, 'Comparative studies in taxation: United Kingdom, France, West Germany, Sweden and USA: a summary report', Apr. 1967; CRD 3/7/6/1, EPG/66/44, Economic Policy Group, first draft of Swinton discussion weekend document, 2 June 1967, and CRD 3/7/26/38, EPG/66/114, Economic Policy Group, first draft of the final report on the reform of taxation, 16 Jan. 1969. Figures for 1974 are from Kay and King, *British Tax System*, pp. 238–9.

Table 10.1 *Taxation as a percentage of GNP and composition of tax revenues in the United Kingdom, France and Germany, 1962*

Taxation as a percentage of GNP

	Total	Direct	Social security	Indirect, including rates
United Kingdom	34.3	13.8	4.8	15.7
France	41.1	6.9	14.6	19.6
West Germany	41.0	15.6	11.6	13.8

Composition of tax revenues (percentage)

	UK	West Germany	France
Direct taxes			
Individuals	29.2	26.8	10.8
Companies	11.2	11.2	6.1
Social security contributions	14.0	28.2	35.5
Payroll taxes	–	0.8	4.5
Indirect taxes			
Turnover and sales	6.7	16.1	22.7
Tobacco	10.3	3.5	2.1
Alcohol	5.5	1.8	1.5
Hydrocarbon oils	6.4	3.1	5.5
Other (including local rates)	16.7	8.5	11.3
	100.0	100.0	100.0

Source: PP 1963–4 xix, *Report of the Committee on Turnover Taxation*, pp. 307, 309.

and 1960s were below those of France and Germany, so that government demands for revenue seemed more onerous. The tax system could be seen both as a cause of the slow growth and as a device to create faster growth.

Awareness of a structural problem in the British fiscal system transformed the debate in the 1960s, which became all the more intense because of the Conservatives' need to counter the innovations of the Labour government. The party's Taxation Policy Committee realised before 1964 that something more appealing than a series of 'standstill budgets' was needed to prevent dissatisfaction. A fiscal policy was needed to appeal to the electorate, and the committee tentatively hinted at various changes: shifting the cost of the NHS to employees' and employers' contributions; requiring nationalised industries to finance more of their development; encouraging the private provision of welfare services; and charging tolls on new roads and bridges.[4] Both the Taxation Policy Committee and a

[4] CPA, CRD 3/7/26/3, 'Expenditure and taxation', 30 Aug. 1960.

sub-committee of the (Conservative) Parliamentary Finance Group set up to consider direct taxation started to discuss a payroll tax or sales tax, the desirability of reforms of company taxation and the finance of social services.[5] The proposals were not developed before the loss of office exposed the need to make difficult decisions over taxation, with wide implications for many areas of policy and for existing electoral alliances. What was needed was not mere tinkerings within the existing fiscal constitution, but a fundamental review which would 'displace income tax from the pinnacle it had occupied for the last 100 years'.[6] The proposed changes needed to be formed into a coherent package, extending beyond rebarbative technicalities to create a new vision of the future of British society – much as Churchill had done in 1925. This was the task for the Policy Group on Future Economic Policy set up in 1965, and especially its sub-committee on taxation.

There was a growing sense in the Conservative party of the 1960s that the tax system was blunting efficiency and enterprise. The solution was a major restructuring of the tax system – a formidable undertaking, for it rested on a complex balance of interests which would be politically dangerous to dismantle and reconstruct.[7] There were two equally important requirements. On the one hand, the Conservatives needed to link the technicalities of taxation to a wider rhetoric of the transformation of British society which could justify a major reshaping of the fiscal regime, help to redefine interests around new identities, and re-establish legitimacy and consent on a new basis. On the other hand, interests were not simply imagined: the adherence of organised, material interests had to be obtained in order to construct a new coalition. Progress was made in constructing a new rhetoric of an 'opportunity state' which promised more rapid growth by offering greater incentives and encouraging efficiency in the use of labour. Everyone would benefit in the medium to long term, both from the proceeds of growth and from restoring buoyancy to

---

[5] There is a long list of discussion papers: see CPA, CRD 3/7/26/3, TPC(62)4, 'A payroll tax' (undated); TPC(62)5, 'A payroll tax', 24 July 1961; 'Note on the French payroll tax', 27 July 1961; TPC(62)7, 'A payroll tax?', 27 Sept. 1961; TPC(62)6, 'Indirect taxes', 26 Sept. 1961; J. Douglas to B. Sewill, 27 Oct. 1961; TPC(62)12, 'Note on payroll tax: David Dear', 1 Nov. 1961; 'Payroll tax: a rejoinder by James Douglas' (undated); TPC(62)13, 'Taxation policy 1962', final draft, 1 Nov. 1961, and TPC(62)14, redraft of section on payroll tax, 7 Nov. 1961. For the Sub-Committee on the Structure of Direct Taxation, see CRD 2/10/17, 'Note on how to finance the social services for discussion on 12 April 1961'; 'Note on a payroll tax', 7 June 1961; 'Note on a sales tax for discussion on 28 June 1961'; 'The need for a corporation tax and a graduated income tax', R. Gresham Cooke, 14 Jan. 1961; 'A corporation tax', 1 Dec. 1960.

[6] CPA, CRD 3/7/6/1. A. Cockfield at 8th meeting, Economic Policy Group, 13 Apr. 1967.

[7] On the problems of remaking 'distributional coalitions', see Olson, *Logic of Collective Action*, and *Rise and Decline of Nations*.

government revenues. In the short term, anyone who suffered should be compensated by improved, selective, welfare benefits. The problem was that these radical proposals developed in the internal policy debate were not accepted as politically expedient by the leadership. The implications of reforming the tax system were not carried through into the related area of welfare,[8] and the dangers of alienating existing interests were considered to be too great. Radical proposals for reform were not fully implemented by the Heath government, and it was left to Mrs Thatcher to implement a different – arguably narrower and socially divisive – version of the rhetoric after 1979.

The rhetoric was articulated by William Rees-Mogg,* who argued for an improvement in personal incentives and a broader ownership of capital. As he pointed out, Conservative governments paid some attention to incentives since 1951, but they ignored property ownership and the encouragement of savings. A change in emphasis required a shift from direct to indirect taxation, and from taxation on income and capital to taxation on expenditure:

The chief means of encouraging the extension of capital must include the encouragement of home ownership, of the establishment and expansion of small businesses, and of personal saving, particularly through unit trusts ... For professional men and business managers, there is now great difficulty in forming even quite small capital after tax. Yet capital is usually a stronger incentive than income ... We are now in a situation where a reasonably successful professional man could well earn £250,000 in his lifetime and yet leave no more than a tenth of that sum on his death. For economic and social reasons this should be put right.[9]

High rates of personal taxation prevented salaried and professional men from accumulating capital; if they did save, penal rates of differential taxation on investment income and heavy death duties undermined their efforts. By contrast, anyone with an existing large fortune was able to avoid paying taxation, so that 'the present system is weighted against the modest capitalist or would be capitalist compared to the man with

---

[8] The discussion of welfare is covered by R. Lowe, 'Social policy', in S. Ball and A. Seldon (eds.), *The Heath Government: A Reappraisal* (London, 1996), pp. 191–214.

[9] CPA, CRD 3/7/6/9, PG/8/65/7, 'An agenda', William Rees-Mogg (undated).

* William Rees-Mogg (b. 1928) was educated at Charterhouse and Balliol College, Oxford, and was a journalist 1952–67; he stood as a Conservative candidate in 1956 and 1959. He edited *The Times* 1967–81, and his politics shifted from moderate Heathite Conservatism to Thatcherite monetarism. On leaving *The Times*, he was vice-chairman of the BBC 1981–6; chairman of the Arts Council 1982–9; chairman of the Broadcasting Standards Council 1988–93; and a director of GEC 1981–97. (Robbins (ed.), *Biographical Dictionary*, pp. 355–6; *Who's Who 2001*, p. 1728.)

a very large fortune'.[10] In effect, Macmillan's thoughts on 'savings and incentives' were being developed, and the Conservatives were rejecting Labour policy of increased taxation of capital.

Members of the policy group also claimed that high levels of income tax led to a bunching of incomes, so that Britain had a relatively egalitarian income distribution. However, the lack of incentives to save meant that the distribution of *wealth* was still highly skewed.[11] The Labour party reached the same conclusion, but its approach – with few exceptions – was to attack large fortunes rather than to encourage small fortunes. The Conservative policy group felt that what was needed was a tax system which would allow the accumulation of up to £25,000 without penalty, so that 'for the first time there will be real and positive encouragement to the acquisition of a modest capital'. Advocates of this policy hoped it would transform the British economy:

Economic growth depends fundamentally upon human ingenuity, upon energy, effort and enterprise. These are the true conditions of growth and where they exist the means of achieving the growth will always be found. It is because increasingly as a nation we have lacked these qualities that the British economy has become stagnant and unprogressive. There is no single factor which bears a heavier responsibility for this than our tax system. Too much has been taken and the dice has been too heavily loaded against initiative and enterprise. The proposals we put forward are designed to produce a fundamental change and to recreate in our economy the conditions in which growth will flourish.[12]

Here was the vision of an 'opportunity state' which would lead to a greater sense of initiative. The aim was easily defined: to find 'so large a revenue raiser that one could take the heat off the income tax'.[13] More difficult to achieve was agreement on the best alternative source of revenue, and whether the proposal would secure the allegiance of interest groups or the backing of the party leadership.

A major concern was the funding of social welfare which connected with another serious difficulty: the relationship between the tax system and welfare benefits. The British welfare state was constructed on the

[10] CPA, CRD 3/7/6/10, PG/8/A/65/34, Policy Group on Future Economic Policy Sub-Group A, Taxation, draft report, 23 Sept. 1965; see also CRD 3/7/6/9, PG/8/65/28, 3rd meeting of Policy Group on Future Economic Policy, 30 June 1965; CRD 3/7/6/1, EPG/66/44, Economic Policy Group, first draft, Swinton discussion weekend document, 2 June 1967.
[11] CPA, CRD 3/7/26/38, EPG/66/114, Economic Policy Group, first draft of the final report on the reform of taxation, 16 Jan. 1969.
[12] CPA, CRD 3/7/6/10, PG/8/A/65/34, Policy Group on Future Economic Policy, Sub-Group A, Taxation, draft report, 23 Sept. 1965.
[13] CPA, CRD 3/7/6/1, EPG/66/33, A. Cockfield to 8th meeting of Economic Policy Group, 13 Apr. 1967.

basis of contributory insurance for health and unemployment. The exception was old age pensions, which were funded from taxes on their introduction in 1908. In John Macnicol's view, the Treasury contained the threat (as they saw it) to government finances by the introduction of contributory pensions in 1925 and a contributory welfare state in the Beveridge reforms which was designed to constrain government expenditure and to limit redistribution.[14] If that was the intention, something went seriously awry, for the British welfare state became *less* reliant on contributions than other European countries.

Beveridge's support for contributory insurance was more than a cynical Treasury ploy to contain expenditure; it had a clear philosophical basis. Beveridge wished to permeate a seemingly solidaristic welfare policy with notions of liberalism and individualism. By emphasising contributions paid by all members of society, the middle class was brought within the welfare system, and at the same time the poor were converted into upright, self-maintaining members of society. Both were brought together in the welfare state: benefits were legitimised, the stigma of dependence removed and collective action accepted.[15] The strategy also had serious disadvantages, which became apparent by the 1960s. Alongside contributory insurance, Beveridge offered tax-funded means-tested benefits to support marginal members of society. The relationship was soon upset, for the means-tested benefits became ever more important, and changed the welfare state towards a tax-funded, targeted system. At the same time, insurance benefits were inadequate. Flat-rate contributions gave flat-rate benefits, and private or company pensions became the norm for the middle class with the result that their support for the contributory system declined, and it no longer fulfilled its role of integration between rich and poor.[16] Indeed, taxation could now be seen as a means of supporting members of society who were *not* self-maintaining and respectable – a view that conveniently overlooked the tax breaks given to private pension schemes or owner-occupied housing.

The Beveridge scheme failed to consider the interrelationship between the tax system and welfare, a shortcoming which caused problems. The threshold for payment of the income tax did not rise in line with inflation

---

[14] J. Macnicol, 'Beveridge and old age', in J. Hills, J. Ditch and H. Glennester (eds.), *Beveridge and Social Security: An International Perspective* (Oxford, 1994), pp. 74, 79–80, and *Politics of Retirement*; on the shift to taxes, see J. Harris, 'Political thought and the welfare state, 1870–1940: an intellectual framework for British social policy', *Past and Present* 135 (1992), 116; and Daunton, 'Payment and participation'.

[15] P. Baldwin, 'Beveridge in the *longue durée*', in Hills, Ditch and Glennester (eds.), *Beveridge*, pp. 45–6.

[16] H. Glennester and M. Evans, 'Beveridge and his assumptive worlds: the incompatibilities of a flawed design', in Hills, Ditch and Glennester (eds.), *Beveridge*, p. 70.

or wage increases, and resulted in a 'poverty trap' or 'poverty surtax' (see table 10.2). The low threshold for income tax meant that low earners became liable to income tax despite falling below the minimum earnings for supplementary benefits. A small increase in earnings could take poor working-class families into the tax system, imposing a high marginal tax rate and creating 'fiscal diswelfare'. The British income tax had a low threshold and high initial rate, and rose to higher levels of marginal taxation at lower incomes than in other countries. No real attempt was made to define the minimum taxable income, and the Royal Commission on the Taxation of Profits and Income realised in 1954 that taxation was being levied on income which was insufficient to provide subsistence. Despite this realisation, the Royal Commission feared that an increase in tax-free allowance would be expensive in giving relief to *all* taxpayers at their highest marginal rate.[17] The technical solution was simple: the benefit to larger incomes could be clawed back by reducing the thresholds for the higher rates of tax, or tax-free allowances could be confined to the standard rate of tax.[18] The real issue was political and ideological: it was a matter of to whom tax concessions should be granted, in pursuit of what social vision and electoral calculation. Proposals were floated to integrate the welfare and tax systems, by both Conservative and Labour politicians and advisers. One idea, associated with Lady Juliet Rhys Williams* and rejected by the Royal Commission, was a 'social dividend' or 'negative income tax'. Everyone would receive a cash allowance, and all income would then be taxed, so reducing the various cash benefits and allowances against tax into a single measure.[19] Little was achieved, as a result of the

[17] PP 1953–4 XIX, *Royal Commission on the Taxation of Profits and Income, Second Report*, pp. 248–9.

[18] J. Hills, *Changing Tax: How the Tax System Works and How to Change It* (Child Poverty Action Group, London, 1988).

[19] J. Rhys Williams, *Something to Look Forward To: A Suggestion for a New Social Contract* (London, 1943); Meade, *Planning and the Price Mechanism*, pp. 42–6; PP 1953–4 XIX, *Royal Commission on the Taxation of Profits and Income, Second Report*, pp. 205–14; D. Lees, 'Poor families and fiscal reform', *Lloyds Bank Review* (1967), 10–15; A. B. Atkinson, *Poverty in Britain and the Reform of Social Security* (Cambridge, 1969); A. R. Prest, 'The negative income tax: concepts and problems', *British Tax Review* (1970), pp. 352–65; A. W. Dilnot, J. A. Kay and C. N. Morris, *The Reform of Social Security* (Oxford, 1984); H. Parker, *Instead of the Dole: An Enquiry into the Integration of the Tax and Benefit System* (London, 1989); chancellor of the Exchequer and secretary of state for social services, *Proposals for a Tax Credit System* (London, 1972); D. Piachaud, 'Taxation and social security', in C. Sandford, C. Pond and R. Walker (eds.), *Taxation and Social Policy* (London, 1980), pp. 68–83; Lowe, 'Social policy', pp. 201–2.

* Juliet Rhys Williams (1898–1964) was the daughter of the popular novelist Elinor Glyn; she held secretarial posts in various government offices, and was active in charity, standing as a Liberal candidate in 1938 and 1945. At the end of the war, she was active in the Liberal party and increasingly in the United Europe Movement. She was a governor of the BBC 1952–6, and chair of the Cwmbran Development Corporation 1955–60. (*Who Was Who 1961–70*, vol. VI, p. 951.)

Table 10.2 *Income tax, married couple with two children, 1955/6, 1965/6 and 1979/80*

| | Tax threshold as percentage of | | | Standard rate threshold as |
	Average male full-time earnings	Supplementary benefit level	First rate payable	percentage of average earnings
1955/6	96.0	224.6	9p in the £	179.3
1965/6	70.5	137.5	15p in the £	109.8
1979/80	46.8	96.9	25p in the £	62.6

Source: D. Piachaud, 'Taxation and social security', in C. Sandford, C. Pond and R. Walker (eds.), *Taxation and Social Policy* (London, 1980), p. 69.

technical complexities of reform and the strong motivation for inertia, for fiscal drag provided an easy way of securing more revenue. A revision of thresholds and a search for alternative sources of finance would be more difficult and contentious.

Of course, the change in perceptions of the tax system and collective consumption reflected far more than the relationships between the distribution of income, taxation and the electoral system. There was also a growing concern from the late 1950s to modernise the British economy and improve productivity. As we have seen in the previous chapter, the tax system played a significant role in controlling inflationary pressure after the war by securing the co-operation of trade unions. Taxation might also be used to modernise the economy, perhaps by raising productivity through passing costs on to the employment of labour and so encouraging investment in labour-saving plant. At the same time, it was hoped to provide incentives to the better-off members of society – but not at the expense of the poor. The aim of the Conservatives was to create social integration: a reduction in the higher levels of income tax or of profits tax and a shift to indirect taxes or contributions would hit the poor, who would be compensated by more generous welfare provision. Incentives should not be at the expense of social disruption and exclusion.

Attention turned to a proposal considered in the late 1950s: to transfer the costs of social services from general taxation to a payroll tax on the lines of West Germany and France. The rationale was that high direct taxes on profits and personal income blunted incentives, and implicitly subsidised labour so weakening the motivation of employers to increase labour productivity and resist wage demands. Financing social security from general taxation was estimated to be equivalent to a subsidy of £1,000m to labour costs in 1962, or 6.5 per cent of the total wage and salary bill. A comparison with Germany suggested that a payroll tax to finance social services would save £647m from general taxation, allowing the reduction of income tax by 6d in the £, and the abolition of profits tax. In Arthur Cockfield's opinion, it was 'neither morally justifiable nor economically desirable that those who employed large numbers should be able to shift on to the general body of taxpayers part of the indirect costs of their labour force'. Here, it seemed to the CRD, was a major reason for the less efficient use of labour than in Europe: 'There is no doubt that British industry is more wasteful of labour than some of our overseas competitors. One of the reasons for this is probably that so high a proportion of the national cost of labour falls on the general taxes such as Income and Profits Tax instead of being collected in social security contributions.' Removal of the subsidy would encourage industrialists to use labour more effectively, and to develop capital-intensive production on which the future prosperity of the country depended. Since revenue from the payroll tax would rise with wages, it would also solve the problem of financing social services and restore buoyancy to the tax system.[20]

Not everyone was convinced by these radical proposals. Was it wise to hypothecate taxes by assigning revenue to particular expenditure? Was it advisable to increase costs in labour-intensive industries, with the danger of increases in politically sensitive prices? Were the prospects of economising on the use of labour realistic unless the payroll tax was much higher? Employers would be faced with an increase in labour costs which were already high, with consequent difficulties in international competition in the short term. Supporters of the proposal were confident that the results would have long-run benefit by shifting the balance between labour- and capital-intensive industries, increasing the incentive to invest and generating growth.[21] The immediate political problems were more apparent

[20] CPA, CRD 3/7/26/3, TPC(62)4, 'A payroll tax', n.d.; TPC(62)5, 'A payroll tax', 24 July 1961; TPC(62)7, 'A payroll tax?', 27 Sept. 1961; TPC(62)12, 'Note on payroll tax', D. Dear, 1 Nov. 1961; J. Douglas to B. Sewill, 27 Oct. 1961; 'Payroll tax: a rejoinder', J. Douglas (undated); CRD 2/10/17, 'Note on how to finance the social services for discussion on 12 April 1961'; 'Note on a payroll tax', 7 June 1961; CRD 3/7/6/11, PG/8/B/65/2, Future Economic Policy Sub-Group B, 'Effects of method of financing social security services', J. Douglas, 22 Mar. 1965; PG/8/B/65/4, 'Notes on second meeting of Sub-Group B'; PG/8/B/65/28, Policy Group on Future Economic Policy Sub-Group B, interim report from Sub-Group B to main group, 30 June 1965; PG/8/B/65/9, K. Joseph to E. Heath, 1 Apr. 1965; A. Cockfield, CRD 3/7/6/1, EPG/66/43, 10th meeting of Economic Policy Group, 11 May 1967; CRD 3/7/26/18, SET, 30 Nov. 1966.

[21] The dangers of the payroll tax are discussed in the material cited in the previous note; it might also be noted that there was concern in the USA that the payroll tax had been the most rapidly growing tax since 1945. There was little resistance to the tax, for it was assumed by the taxpayers that it offered benefits; and it was considered to be less onerous than the income tax. In fact, about half the employers' contribution fell on workers, and it was regressive for there were no exemptions. See J. A. Brittain, *The Payroll Tax for Social Security* (Brookings Institute, Washington DC, 1972).

than these putative benefits, and it was not clear *how* the revenue from the payroll tax would be used. It could pay for higher expenditure on social services; it could reduce income tax; or it could reduce company taxation in compensation for the increased burden of the payroll tax. The policy group on the reform of the social services abandoned the notion of a social security tax on the grounds that it would merely allow a temporary reduction of other taxes before they returned to their previous level; in effect, a new tax would simply be imposed.[22] The payroll tax was also fatally weakened by Labour's introduction of the SET, which the Conservatives were committed to repeal: it would be difficult to explain why a tax on service employment was repealed only to be replaced by a *general* tax on employment. The proposal was therefore curtailed, to a more modest increase in employers' national insurance contribution to 7.5 per cent of labour costs, which amounted to a marginal reform of the existing fiscal system rather than a fundamental change in its structure.[23]

The policy group turned in another direction, to a new indirect tax on sales, turnover or value added. There was considerable scepticism in the party in the early 1960s. An increase in the cost of living as a result of higher indirect taxes would hit the poor and recipients of fixed incomes, and would provide political capital for Labour. The existing purchase tax also had the advantage of administrative convenience, for it was collected from about 70,000 wholesalers; any replacement would be more complicated and impose strain on relations between the revenue authorities and taxpayers. The simplest tax to administer would be a flat-rate duty at the point of final sale, which would involve about 500,000 shopkeepers. Still more complicated was the German 'cascading' turnover tax which imposed a tax each time a good changed hands during its passage from raw material to the final consumer. The disadvantage of such a tax, apart from administrative complexity, was that it would encourage vertical integration and monopoly, for goods were not liable to taxation so long as they remained within a *single* firm. The alternative was the French system of VAT which had its own administrative complexities.[24]

---

[22] CPA, CRD 3/7/6/11, PG/8/B/12, notes of the 4th meeting of Future Economic Policy Sub-Group B, 14 Apr. 1965, and PG/8/B/17, notes of the 6th meeting of Future Economic Policy Sub-Group B, 12 May 1965; CRD 3/7/26/33, PG/13/65/41, 4th meeting of Policy Group on National Insurance Scheme, 6 May 1965; PG/13/65/56, 7th meeting of the Policy Group on National Insurance Scheme, 7 Oct. 1965.

[23] CPA, CRD 3/7/26/38, EPG/66/114, Economic Policy Group, first draft of the final report on the reform of taxation, 16 Jan. 1969.

[24] Conservative party, *The Campaign Guide 1964: The Unique Political Reference Book* (London, 1964), p. 35; CPA, CRD 2/10/17, Conservative Parliamentary Finance Committee, Sub-Committee on the Structure of Taxation, 'Note on a sales tax for discussion on 28 June 1961'; CRD 3/7/26/3, TPC(62)1, 'Indirect taxation', 18 May 1961; TPC(62)2, 'Indirect taxation', 19 June 1961; TPC(62)6, 'Indirect taxes', 26 Sept. 1961.

No definite decision was made by the Conservative government about the replacement of the purchase tax before its defeat in 1964, when the context was changed by Labour's radical agenda of tax reform and by the need to find a replacement to the payroll tax in the Conservative 'tax package'. The attraction of VAT compared with the profits tax or payroll tax was that it could be rebated on exports, which was seen to be crucial in view of the concern for international competitiveness and the balance of payments. Further, advocates of the VAT argued (with somewhat strained logic) that it offered at least a partial improvement upon taxation of profits, for it would fall on profits *plus labour costs*, and there was an incentive to cut costs in order to reduce tax liability. The argument ran as follows: if a firm became more efficient and reduced its prices, there would be less value added and the tax would be reduced, even if the profit remained the same or rose. By contrast, a tax on profits meant that any gains in efficiency, with an increase in the profit margin, would increase tax liability. Such arguments placed too much weight on changes in the tax system, as a means of stimulating productivity, when the problem was much more deep-seated. A further attraction of VAT was that it would create fewer distortions in the market than the purchase tax, which fell on a narrow range of goods at relatively high rates. The purchase tax was progressive, for the rate was highest on luxury commodities, and exempted necessities; it also excluded services. Although the SET taxed services, it hit employment of the lowest paid workers and was regressive. By contrast, the policy group suggested that the VAT would be neutral between incomes, for it would not be imposed on food, fuel and rent which formed a larger proportion of expenditure of the poor, and it would tax services purchased by the affluent. Above all, the policy group was confident that a shift in the relative importance of direct and indirect taxes would restore buoyancy to the tax system: 'increased revenue for bigger public spending would be generated by the buoyancy of taxes which people did not expect to be cut (mainly indirect taxes). At the same time, other taxes (mainly direct) could be cut periodically . . . this would have the effect over the years of shifting the tax burden from direct to indirect taxes.' Moreover, indirect taxes were 'less damaging than the deadening effect of heavy direct taxation on energy, enterprise and efficiency'. The introduction of VAT would therefore provide the basis for a major reform of other elements in the tax system, permitting a reduction in personal and company taxation. Obviously, the choice of VAT was encouraged by a desire to conform to the EEC, but the shift to indirect taxes also had domestic origins. Of course, the introduction of VAT would also have a major disadvantage: it would increase the cost of living, and impose a new burden on members of society who would not benefit from cuts in personal taxes. During the discussions of the later 1960s, the policy group felt that further changes to the fiscal system were crucial in order to preserve the sense of equity and justice which underwrote consent and legitimacy. An opportunity state for some should not entail harm to others.[25]

The creation of an opportunity state begs an important question: what were the best incentives to offer, in order to encourage what type of opportunity? The ability to accumulate a small capital might offer a greater incentive than income, and it was necessary to allow salaried and professional men to build up a modest capital sum out of income and savings, as 'an essential part of the Conservative doctrine of a property owning democracy'.[26] The aim was to encourage the establishment of new, modest fortunes rather than the survival of old money. Such a change in the pattern of wealth distribution, it was assumed, would release enterprise from the dead-hand of accumulated capital. This ambition was a constant theme in debates on taxation, and produced a number of divergent solutions. It provided the justification for differential taxation of unearned income from property and investments (which arose 'spontaneously' from accumulated assets) and earned income from trades, professions and employment (which were 'precarious' and disappeared in ill-health or unemployment). Advocates of differential taxation of income were not opposed to the accumulation of capital, but aimed to relieve precarious incomes of risk-takers in trade and the professions so that they could save to provide for themselves and their dependants when earned income ceased. Once they started to receive unearned income from these savings, the higher tax rate would come into force.[27] Members of the

---

[25] CPA, CRD 3/7/6/10, PG/8/A/65/1, notes on 1st meeting of Sub-Group A; PG/8/A/65/28, 'Note by Nigel Lawson on value added tax', 9 July 1965; PG/8/A/65/34, Policy Group on Future Economic Policy Sub-Group A, Taxation, draft report, 23 Sept. 1965; CRD 3/7/6/1, EPG/66/33, 8th meeting, Economic Policy Group, 13 Apr. 1967; EPG/66/43, 10th meeting, Economic Policy Group, 11 May 1967; EPG/66/44, Economic Policy Group, first draft, Swinton discussion weekend document, 2 June 1967; CRD 3/7/6/3, EPG/66/87, Economic Policy Group, minutes of 25th meeting, 13 June 1968; EPG/66/103, Economic Policy Group, minutes of 27th meeting, 11 July 1968; EPG/66/85, Economic Policy Group, revised report on the reform of taxation, 30 May 1968; EPG/66/95, Economic Policy Group, 'Relative merits of the value added tax and the retail sales tax: a note by Professor A. R. Prest', 4 July 1968; CRD 3/7/26/36, minutes of the working conference on VAT, 16–18 June 1969; CRD 3/7/26/5, two-way movement: questions for discussion in the future policy of the Conservative party, no. 4, Apr. 1965; CRD 3/7/26/16, VAT, CD, 22 Nov. 1968. On the connection between VAT and profits taxation, see A. R. Prest, 'A value added tax coupled with a reduction in taxes on business profits', *British Tax Review* (1963), 336–47. Prest (who was a member of the sub-committee) was sceptical about VAT and preferred to extend the purchase tax and reform company taxation by confining it to undistributed profits or by imputing retained profits to shareholders and taxing them as income tax.

[26] CPA, CRD 3/7/26/16, CRD: Conservatives and capital tax, T. E. B., 8 Aug. 1968.

[27] See Daunton, *Trusting Leviathan*, pp. 83–5, 91–101.

Conservative tax committees in the 1960s felt that differentiation was no longer working: far from encouraging enterprise and dynamism, it was frustrating risk-takers. High levels of income tax prevented individuals from exercising their fundamental right to accumulate capital which was seen as an integral part of Conservative philosophy, and the best way of creating incentives and enterprise. In order to allow an ever-widening circle of people to acquire capital, it was necessary to reduce the income tax and remove the differential against investment income which 'falls upon the income from savings and thus penalises the very virtues that we seek to encourage'.[28] These propositions were readily accepted; what was *not* accepted was the initial proposal of the policy group to make good the loss of revenue – an annual tax on wealth or capital which was, in the opinion of one member of the policy group, 'really the keystone of the arch'.[29]

At first sight, the proposal seemed perverse. Why encourage a wider ownership of capital, and then tax it? The rationale was provided by a report by the NEDC, which argued that such a tax 'may have a useful role in a major review of taxation related to a programme of growth'. A tax on wealth fell on the value of assets rather than their yield, so that it would 'encourage capital to be more productively used' by offering an incentive to invest in high-risk, high-yield stock. The underlying capital would be taxed regardless of its yield, and the income derived from the asset would be less heavily taxed than in the past. 'The present structure of tax acted as a disincentive to risk-taking . . . the object of the shift was to place more burden on the static existing accumulations of wealth and thus to avoid the present concentration of the burden of tax on the creation of wealth.' The revenue from the wealth tax would permit the replacement of the surtax on incomes and provide recipients of earned income with an incentive to greater efforts. The wealth tax was also politically necessary in order to offset the concessions to high incomes and *rentiers*. This argument appealed to some members of the Conservative committees, who wished 'to tax capital in future, in such a way as to create the conditions for the accumulation of capital', giving an incentive to *create* wealth by making it easier to save out of income. The existing levels of income tax were 'near farcical in any system which does not actively regard private incomes as evil', in effect giving an advantage to those who currently held capital which was protected by trusts. The Conservative party should not, it was argued, merely defend existing wealth. An annual capital or wealth

[28] CPA, CRD 3/7/26/38, EPG/66/114, Economic Policy Group, first draft of the final report on the reform of taxation, 16 Jan. 1969.

[29] CPA, CRD, 3/7/6/9, PG/8/65/34, Policy Group on Future Economic Policy, 6th meeting, 27 Oct. 1965, comment of Angus Maude.

tax would reduce income tax rates and so allow accumulation; other taxes on capital could be moderated by removing the differential against investment income, reducing the capital gains tax introduced by Labour, and cutting death duties. The total burden of taxation on capital would not be reduced so much as redistributed in a way which would encourage accumulation. The overall result, argued Nigel Lawson, was a distinct improvement, for 'the present tax structure redistributed wealth but did it illogically. Their proposals would do it logically.'[30]

It was one thing to be logical; it was another to be politically acceptable, particularly when the economic case was open to question. It was doubtful whether a modest reduction in the marginal rate of tax on earned income would affect enough people to make a difference. The impact of the wealth tax on investment decisions was also likely to be small, since most assets were held by the elderly who were more interested in security than risk. Any economic benefits would probably be modest, and could just as easily be achieved less contentiously by ending the distinction between earned and unearned income, or by a change in the surtax threshold. Indeed, the case for a wealth tax made more sense on other grounds, as a measure of social reform designed to reduce the high degree of inequality of wealth and to attack a 'property-owning gerontocracy'. Although some Conservatives supported such reform as a means of generating opportunity, it had a suspiciously socialist tinge. After all, Bruce Millan,* a Labour MP, advocated a wealth tax as a means of producing a 'radical distribution of wealth'. Rees-Mogg was horrified by the proposal, and appealed to William Pitt's maxim that taxation should fall on the fruit and not the tree. Income taxes and the capital gains tax fell on the fruits of property; a capital tax was 'a direct invasion of the right to hold private property without disturbance ... such a tax goes against what I believe to be an essential element in our Party's character ... The essence of this tax is that it is an annual capital levy. The Conservative Party has always

[30] NEDC, *Conditions Favourable to Faster Growth*, section E, especially para. 170; the case is assessed in R. C. Tress, 'A wealth tax is a wealth tax', *British Tax Review* (1963), 400–9, and A. Peacock, 'Economics of a net wealth tax for Britain', *British Tax Review* (1963), 388–99; CPA, CRD 3/7/6/9, PG/8/65/28, 2nd meeting of Policy Group on Future Economic Policy, 30 June 1965; CRD 3/7/6/10, PG/8/A/65/8, 'Note for Sub-Group A' (undated); PG/8/A/65/10, 3rd meeting of Sub-Group A, 14 Apr. 1965; PG/8/A/65/12, 'The taxation of capital', F. A. Cockfield (undated); PG/8/A/14, 4th meeting of Sub-Group A, 28 Apr. 1965; PG/8/A/65/34, 'Policy Group on Future Economic Policy, Sub-Group A, Taxation, draft report', 23 Sept. 1965.

* Bruce Millan (b. 1927) was educated at Harris Academy, Dundee; he was a chartered accountant, and Labour MP from 1959 to 1988. He served as parliamentary under-secretary of state for defence 1964–6, and for Scotland 1966–70. He was minister of state in the Scottish office 1974–6 and secretary of state for Scotland 1976–9. He was a member of the Commission of the European Community from 1989 to 1995. (*Who's Who 2001*, p. 1433.)

opposed capital levies and could hardly introduce a regular and progressive one without gross inconsistency.' Rees-Mogg feared that a wealth tax had similar, dubious antecedents to a capital levy; it 'creates a powerful agency of socialism' and egalitarianism, offering an open invitation to Labour to introduce a more far-reaching socialist fiscal policy. He also doubted the economic benefits of encouraging high-yield, high-risk investment. 'We wanted to encourage people to invest in long term schemes which often involve locking capital up for a considerable time before yielding a return ... a wealth tax would encourage investment that was highly speculative and encourage people to hold their capital in relatively liquid form switching it frequently.' Certainly, it would be difficult to convince the electorate that the benefits of capital ownership would be extended by the seemingly perverse means of taxing capital. The committee was split, and the Shadow Cabinet eventually abandoned the wealth tax proposal in 1968. It would, as John Biffen* remarked, 'seriously shatter the political morale of a Conservative administration', and Iain Macleod felt that 'the important things on which the Conservative party ought to be concentrating attention were earning, owning, saving and learning. A proposal to introduce a wealth tax would distract from these objectives.'[31]

The attempt to encourage personal accumulation of modest amounts of capital as a major incentive in an opportunity state came into conflict with the existing structure of company taxation. Labour's corporation tax of 1965 meant that a higher rate of tax was imposed on distributed profits: company profits were taxed at 40 per cent, and the individual recipient of dividends paid income tax without any credit for the corporation tax. The justification was that shareholders would either spend their dividends on extravagant consumption or accumulate passive *rentier* capital. The corporation tax was complemented by a capital gains tax which taxed any gains realised by shareholders from the sale of shares

[31] Peacock, 'Economics of a net wealth tax', 396–7, 399; Tress, 'A wealth tax is a wealth tax', 406–7; J. R. S. Revell, 'Assets and age', *Bulletin of the Oxford Institute of Statistics* 24 (1962), 363–78; B. Millan, *Taxes for a Prosperous Society* (Fabian Research Series, London, 1963); CPA, CRD 3/7/6/9, PG/8/65/26, 'Comments by Mr William Rees-Mogg on Sub-Group A's interim report to the main group on personal taxation', 28 June 1965; PG/8/65/28, Policy Group on Future Economic Policy, 3rd meeting, 30 June 1965; CRD 3/7/6/10, PG/8A/65/35, 'Comments by William Rees-Mogg on Sub-Group A's draft report', 27 Sept. 1965; CRD 3/7/6/10, PG/8/A/65/27, W. J. Biffen, 7 July 1965; CRD 3/7/6/3, EPG/66/87, minutes of 25th meeting, Economic Policy Group, 13 June 1968.

* William John Biffen (b. 1930) was educated at Dr Morgan's School, Bridgwater, and Jesus College, Cambridge. He worked for Tube Investments 1953–60 and the Economist Intelligence Unit 1960–1; he was a Conservative MP from 1961 to 1997. He served as chief secretary to the Treasury 1979–81, secretary of state for trade 1981–2, lord president of the council 1982–3, leader of the Commons 1982–7 and lord privy seal 1983–7. In 1987, he returned to business. (*Who's Who 2001*, p. 173.)

whose price rose as a result of the retention of profits. The dominant
Labour view was that retention of profits should be encouraged in order
to provide funds for investment which would lead to growth, and that
taxation should then hit individual gains. The policy was open to criticism, for individual incentives were blunted and it was by no means clear
that there was a correlation between retention and growth.[32] Distribution
was not necessarily harmful, for a large proportion of dividends went to
institutional shareholders who reinvested, and retention might lead to the
accumulation of assets in large firms which perpetuated old and inefficient industrial concerns and distorted the capital market as an allocator
of resources. The technical complexities of company taxation implied a
divide between two views of society. Labour wished to cut off the flow
of income to private owners of assets as a means of preventing the accumulation of large fortunes, and preferred to leave investment decisions
to the deliberations of corporate managers rather than to the external
market.[33] By contrast, the Conservative approach was more inclined to
favour allocation by the market, without any attempt to divert the flow of
dividends away from shareholders. Growth was more likely to be encouraged by offering incentives to the accumulation and investment of small
amounts of capital, rather than by encouraging retention in existing corporations. As Edward Heath remarked, reliance on retentions 'does not
produce the system of the survival of the fittest. It produces the system of
the survival of the fattest.'[34] Nevertheless, some doubts were expressed
about going too far in the direction of positive encouragement of distributions. Maudling felt that companies already distributed generously,
and that encouragement of distributions contradicted the proposals on
savings – why encourage private savings and discourage corporate savings
at the same time? There was also the danger that increased distributions
would stimulate inflation by making wage restraint more difficult, and by
increasing consumption.[35]

The outcome was a proposal to introduce the German system of corporation taxation, which was emerging as the model for the EEC.[36] In
Germany, the corporation tax had a split rate, of 51 per cent on retained
profits and 15 per cent on distributions which were also liable to income

[32] Whiting, 'Taxation policy'; I. M. D. Little, 'Higgledy piggledy growth', *Bulletin of the Oxford Institute of Statistics* 24 (1962), 387–412.

[33] See CPA, CRD 3/7/26/5, two way movement: questions for discussion in the future policy of the Conservative party, no. 4, Apr. 1965; CRD 3/7/26/7, CRD: capital gains tax, 21 Jan. 1969.

[34] *Parliamentary Debates*, 5th ser. 710, 7 Apr. 1965, col. 497.

[35] CPA, CRD 3/7/26/6, Maudling to Macleod, 31 Mar. 1969.

[36] *The EEC Reports on Tax Harmonisation: Report of the Fiscal and Financial Committee* (Amsterdam, 1963).

tax in the hands of the recipients. Retained and distributed profits paid the same total rate when the corporation tax and income tax were combined; as far as companies were concerned, their tax liability was reduced if they made more distributions. The FBI favoured the German system, on the grounds that it helped companies which needed to raise funds on the capital market and penalised companies which relied on retentions. In the opinion of the FBI, the tax system should now favour distributions. The proposal would mean that the tax on distributed profits would fall and on undistributed profits rise, so removing the incentive to plough back earnings into reserves and exposing them to the discipline of the market – a different approach from Labour's corporation tax. A technical change in company taxation was, therefore, an integral part of the vision of an opportunity state which would permit greater incentives and faster growth.[37]

The tax package sought to achieve three aims: a reduction in the proportion of taxation falling on profits and an increase in the proportion on costs in order to increase efficiency; less reliance upon the finance of welfare from general taxation which implied a subsidy to employment; and a lower rate of taxation of earnings and distributed profits which discouraged incentives. Although the payroll tax and wealth tax were dropped, it was hoped that the aims would still be achieved by introducing VAT and removing differential taxation on investment income and distributed profits, so that it would be easier to accumulate a small fortune. The buoyancy of the tax system would be restored, and high marginal rates of income tax reduced in order to encourage incentives. There was, however, a major problem: how to deal with those members of society who would be hit by VAT without benefiting from lower income tax?

The ambition was to provide incentives to the energetic and enterprising in order to create faster growth which would benefit everyone. The tax package rested upon a desire to change the basis of British society from equality to equity, from stasis to dynamism. However, care should

---

[37] MRC, FBI MSS 200/F/3/E7/1/6, 'A UK corporation tax'; Taxation Committee, 5 Nov. 1964, Taxation Panel, 17 Nov. 1964; CPA, CRD 3/7/6/3, EPG/66/85, 'Revised report on the reform of taxation', 30 May 1968; EPG/66/87, Economic Policy Group, minutes of 25th meeting, 13 June 1968; EPG/66/88, 'The reform of corporation tax and capital gains tax', J. F. Chown, 17 June 1968; EPG/66/90, 'Revised report on the reform of taxation: note by Mr Cockfield: II: the "balance" of the package: investment income – the taxation of companies', 18 June 1968; CRD 3/7/6/10, PG/8/A/65/3, 'Notes on company taxation', A. R. Prest, 23 Mar. 1965; PG/8/A/65/7, 'The taxation of companies', A. Cockfield (undated); PG/8/A/65/34, 'Policy Group on Future Economic Policy, Sub-Group A, Taxation', 23 Sept. 1965; PG/8/A/65/17 and 18, minutes of 6th meeting of Sub-Group A, 12 May 1965; CRD 3/7/26/38, EPG/66/114, Economic Policy Group, first draft of the final report on the reform of taxation, 16 Jan. 1969.

be taken that no group suffered. 'It is not our aim to favour any single broad section of the community at the expense of another (where the section of community is defined along conventional lines – e.g. middle income earners, pensioners, lower paid workers). Our intention is to favour the energetic, resourceful, enterprising and hard-working against the lazy, cautious and complacent.'[38] By providing incentives to those who created the nation's wealth in the middle and higher ranges of income, faster growth would be achieved by a new climate of competition, efficiency and productivity so that everyone would be better off in the longer term. 'The policy of trying to improve living conditions by a more even distribution of income has, in our view, been pressed over recent years to an extreme at which it becomes self-defeating.'[39] However, the policy group stressed that no one should suffer in the short term. Price increases would hit everyone, and those who paid little or no direct taxes would not have any recompense. The balance of the tax package was distorted by the rejection of a wealth tax and the replacement of the payroll tax by VAT which hit the poorest members of society. In order to preserve balance, it was necessary to offer welfare benefits to those who would be hit by the shift to indirect taxation, which had major implications for the future structure of the welfare state. Did it entail a move from universal provision to selectivity? 'A package of tax reforms designed to increase incentives to those who produce the Nation's wealth cannot at the same time make adequate provision for those who must receive a greater share than they earn, except through a departure from the principle of universality. The attempt to adjust the balance would otherwise dissipate the very incentives we seek to introduce.'[40] The replacement of universalism by selectivity was crucial to the viability of the scheme: compensating the poor through a higher level of universal benefits would destroy the finances of the tax package.

The package of reforms which emerged during opposition was coherent and comprehensive. It offered an opportunity state based on economic growth and on incentives for the accumulation of small capital, from which no one would lose. It claimed to offer an alternative to socialist intervention and bureaucratic planning. Buoyancy and flexibility would be restored to the tax system, so that chancellors were freed from the ever-increasing rates of income tax, which could be reduced to a 'smaller, more reputable and less harmful tax'. Economic growth and buoyant tax

[38] CPA, CRD 3/7/6/3, EPG/66/85, revised report on the reform of taxation, 30 May 1968; see also speech by Macleod to the Institute of Directors in 1969, CRD 3/7/26/38.

[39] CPA, CRD 3/7/26/38, EPG/66/114, Economic Policy Group, first draft of the final report on the reform of taxation, 16 Jan. 1969.

[40] CPA, CRD 3/7/6/3, EPG/66/85, revised report on the reform of taxation, 30 May 1968.

revenues would permit reduction in the rate of tax and a higher level of welfare spending. The result would be beneficial for all:

This does not mean that in the long run we will be able to spend less on socially desirable objectives. On the contrary, we shall be able to spend more. Once a proper balance can be re-established in the community between the share of our resources taken by the Government and the share which is left for the people, we shall be able to achieve a higher rate of growth. Out of the greater national income generated in this way we shall be able to spend more, not less, without at the same time any of the strains to which the present policy gives rise.[41]

The policy was not based upon the crude anti-statism which developed in the 1980s, and it tried – in Rodney Lowe's words – to link competition and compassion.[42] It offered an alternative to Labour's rhetoric of modernisation and meritocracy based on equality and public ownership.

The package started to unravel. Macleod realised that abandonment of the wealth tax made it impossible to afford all the 'plums' initially proposed (abolition of the differential taxation of unearned income, reduction in death duties and introduction of a split rate of company taxation). The room for manoeuvre was further limited by the pledge to replace the SET and by a slow-down in economic growth. In particular, Keith Joseph* was concerned that the revised package gave too much relief to larger investment incomes, with 'very little benefit to the upper-medium earned incomes, which were the ones that affected middle management'.[43] Despite his reputation as a die-hard free-marketeer and proto-Thatcherite, Joseph was alarmed that the package would be interpreted as benefiting wealthy investors, and regretted the rejection of the wealth tax which 'gave a morally defensible package in a way the present package did not'.[44] Joseph had a point, for an estimate of the impact of the package commissioned by the CRD produced a worrying result: the tax cuts would favour the rich, welfare benefits would assist the poor, but family men on an income of £560 to £1,750 would lose. These middle-class family men were crucial to the electoral success of the

[41] CPA, CRD 3/7/26/38, EPG/66/114, Economic Policy Group, first draft of the final report on the reform of taxation, 16 Jan. 1969.
[42] Lowe, 'Social policy', p. 213.
[43] CPA, CRD 3/7/6/3, EPG/66/93, Economic Policy Group, minutes of 26th meeting, 27 June 1968; see also EPG/66/97, 'Note by Mr Cockfield', 8 July 1968.
[44] CPA, CRD 3/7/6/3, EPG/66/108, Economic Policy Group, 28th meeting, 26 July 1968.
* Keith Sinjohn Joseph (1918–94) was minister of housing 1962–4, and social services minister 1970–4; in both positions, he was a spending minister before shifting to – or even defining – Thatcherism in 1974. He always believed in the virtues of free enterprise; after 1974, he argued that the poor would not be helped by spending public money, and that only entrepreneurs could create wealth. He developed this theme from 1974 to 1979 through the Centre for Policy Studies. He was secretary for industry 1979–81 and education 1981–6. (Robbins (ed.), *Biographical Dictionary*, pp. 233–5.)

party, and were precisely the group that it was hoped would participate in a new, dynamic opportunity state.[45]

The demise of the payroll tax meant that more weight was given to VAT and cuts in government expenditure. The tax system would be less buoyant than anticipated, for VAT would not produce revenue for several years, and the shift of funding of social services from general taxation was slight. The immediate prospect of a reduction in direct taxes was therefore remote, and meanwhile rising prices would lead to unpopularity. Despite the need for selective help to target those who would suffer from rising prices and cuts in government expenditure, there was a lack of serious thought about such a radical change in policy.[46] Indeed, the policy group on social services, of which Joseph and Thatcher were leading members, backed away from selectivity, which they realised was a prerequisite for tax reform.[47]

Another possible way of squaring the circle was a negative income tax or tax credit, which would ensure that no one lost from changes in the fiscal system. Some Labour commentators proposed the abandonment of selective, means-tested benefits so that payments were not lost when income increased. Surprisingly, some Conservatives agreed. John Nott* argued (somewhat eccentrically) that selectivity 'is inherently bureaucratic, expensive and an intolerable infringement of people's privacy. It is really a Socialist doctrine and not a Tory one.'[48] Of course, any shift from selectivity would be very costly, and Labour proposed that it should be financed by reducing tax allowances for children – a proposal which

[45] CPA, CRD 3/7/26/41, J. Douglas to E. Heath, 20 May 1968, cited in Lowe, 'Social policy', p. 196. For the computer estimates, see CRD 3/7/6/3, EPG/66/107 and 109; the results were discussed in EPG/66/108, Economic Policy Group, minutes of 28th meeting, 26 July 1968.

[46] CPA, CRD 3/7/6/4, EPG/66/115, Economic Policy Group, minutes of 31st meeting, 3 Dec. 1968; EPG/66/119, minutes of 33rd meeting, 6 Jan. 1969; EPG/66/121, 34th meeting, 30 Jan. 1969; CRD 3/7/6/7, R. Maudling to J. Douglas, 3 July 1968; CRD 3/7/6/8, E. Heath to B. Reading, 7 Feb. 1969; R. Maudling to I. Macleod, 13 Mar. 1970; CRD 3/7/26/37, 'Tax package: the development of our thoughts in opposition', 27 July 1970; 'Tax package: the main proposals and our commitments', 29 July 1970.

[47] CPA, CRD 3/7/6/11, PG/8/B/65/9, K. Joseph to E. Heath, 1 Apr. 1965; PG/8/B/65/11, 'Note for Mrs Thatcher and Mr Geoffrey Howe: Sub-Group B's discussion of the economic effects of the present method of financing the social security services', J. Douglas, 15 Apr. 1965; PG/8/B/65/12, notes for 4th meeting held 14 Apr. 1965; PG/8/B/65/17, notes of the 6th meeting of Sub-Group B, 12 May 1965.

[48] CPA, CRD 3/7/26/14, John Nott to Anthony Barber, 9 Sept. 1968.

* John William Frederic Nott (b. 1932) was educated at Bradfield College and Trinity College, Cambridge. He was called to the bar in 1959 and worked for S. G. Warburg 1959–66. He was a Conservative MP from 1966 to 1983, serving as minister of state at the Treasury 1972–4, secretary of state for trade 1979–81 and defence 1981–3. He then moved into business as director of Lazards Brothers (and later chairman and chief executive) 1983–90, director and deputy chairman of Royal Insurance 1985–91, and other firms. (*Who's Who 2001*, p. 1544.)

would not appeal to Conservatives. Another possibility was a 'negative income tax', which was now advocated by Lady Rhys Williams's son, the Conservative MP Brandon Rhys Williams.*[49] 'The advantage of a negative income tax', remarked Brendon Sewill, 'is that it would produce a smooth decline in benefit as income increases, and thus ensure that there was always some incentive.'[50] The proposal was not simply a means of creating a single gradient of taxation and benefits; it was also a means of constraining spending on welfare. Rhys Williams suggested that part of the income tax should be hypothecated to the National Insurance Fund, with an identifiable income and proper targets for expenditure. At least one Conservative politician, John Nott, was enthusiastic:

I believe that the impact on the country would be tremendous and highly favourable if Ted Heath was able to make the question of negative income tax one of his main themes to the conference ... My own concern is that the Socialists are working hard on a precisely similar idea, which they will bring out as a counter to our proposals on 'selectivity'. Why can't we come out first with a system of this sort and fix it in the public's mind as a Tory proposal.[51]

Was it *really* a Tory proposal?

The problem with the negative income tax was that it ran counter to the encouragement of private welfare and would increase taxation. Mrs Thatcher was concerned about the implications for self-reliance, for the scheme assumed that social security was always provided by the state rather than by tax relief to private pensions or health insurance. Although Rhys Williams argued that 'any form of allowance against tax was a slanting of the tax system in favour of the recipient, and therefore just as destructive of self reliance as a grant', others were willing to condone government encouragement of certain activities. Barney Hayhoe[†] remarked that

there was a fundamental philosophical difference on this point. He felt that the income of the people in this country does not belong to the State, and that

---

[49] The proposal is in CPA, CRD 3/7/6/4, EPG/66/116, Economic Policy Group: the redistribution of income by the state: paper by Sir Brandon Rhys Williams, 11 Dec. 1968.

[50] CPA, CRD 3/7/26/10, B. Sewill to Bellars, Hayhoe, Patten and Marten, 6 Sept. 1968.

[51] CPA, CRD 3/7/26/14, Nott to Barber, 9 Sept. 1968.

[*] Brandon Meredith Rhys Williams (1927–88) was educated at Eton and worked for ICI, as assistant director of the Spastics Society and a consultant in recruitment; he was a Conservative MP from 1968 to 1988 and member of the European parliament 1973–84. (*Who Was Who, 1981–90*, vol. VIII, p. 636.)

[†] Bernard John (Barney) Hayhoe (b. 1925) was educated at Borough Polytechnic and as a tool room apprentice; he worked for the Armaments Design Department of the ministry of supply and the inspectorate of armaments from 1944 to 1963, and in the CRD 1965–70. He was an MP from 1970 to 1992, serving as parliamentary private secretary to the leader of the House and lord president of the Council 1972–4, parliamentary under-secretary of state for defence 1979–81, minister of state, civil service department, 1981, at the Treasury 1981–5, and minister of health 1985–6. (*Who's Who 2001*, p. 933.)

therefore the use of fiscal policy to encourage activities is quite different from State help for the needy. This is because on the one hand one is merely not taking away someone's money in certain circumstances, whereas on the other hand, where there is a grant, the money is being taken from someone else and given to those who are in these circumstances.

On this view, it was acceptable to give tax relief to private pensions which left an individual with his own money; to make a grant was another matter, particularly since the cost would fall on middle incomes, and transfer resources to low and high incomes.[52] Principle and electoral self-interest combined to block change, so leaving the problem of the 'poverty surtax' unresolved.

When considering tax revisions, there was a natural tendency to draw up a balance sheet of gains and losses for particular sections of society. In Maudling's opinion, the package was far too theoretical and did not pay sufficient attention to the effects on particular classes of taxpayers.[53] Such an approach seriously limited the room for change, for the only result of ensuring that no one was much worse- or better-off would be to return to the present structure of taxation.[54] The more radical (and less politically accountable) members of the CRD argued for a more adventurous approach, a fundamental revision of the fiscal constitution designed to affect attitudes to work and to raise labour productivity. 'This reform of taxation was only worthwhile', remarked Arthur Cockfield, 'on the basis that the whole economy would change. If attitudes remained the same, then the reform would have failed.'[55] It was precisely the psychological impact of tax reforms which Heath doubted. Why not, he wondered, achieve the same results by cutting public expenditure, introducing savings schemes and increasing wages?[56]

By 1970, policy on the future shape of taxation and the welfare state was shifting. The tax package promised economic growth from which everyone would benefit in the long run, with immediate losers recompensed by selective benefits. The accumulation of capital by the moderately prosperous was linked to the creation of efficiency through changes in the financing of social services. After 1970, the connection between

---

[52] CPA, CRD 3/7/26/11, Reading to Hayhoe, 'Family allowances', n.d.; Hayhoe to Heath, 11 Nov. 1968; EPG 66/116, 'The redistribution of income by the state', B. Rhys Williams, 11 Dec. 1968; group on negative income tax: negative income tax, paper by Research Department, July 1969; group on negative income tax: comments on Sir Brandon Rhys Williams's paper by Barney Hayhoe, 11 July 1969; minutes of a meeting to study the possibility of adoption of a scheme along the lines of that of Sir Brandon Rhys Williams.

[53] CPA, CRD 3/7/6/7, R. Maudling to J. Douglas, 3 July 1968.

[54] CPA, CRD 3/7/6/7, B. Sewill to I. Macleod, 8 July 1968.

[55] CPA, CRD 3/7/6/4, EPG/66/121, Economic Policy Group, minutes of 34th meeting, 30 Jan. 1969.

[56] CPA, CRD 3/7/6/4, EPG/66/121, Economic Policy Group, minutes of 34th meeting, 30 Jan. 1969, and CRD 3/7/6/8, E. Heath to B. Reading, 7 Feb. 1969.

efficiency and growth on the one hand and encouragement of property ownership on the other hand was redefined. Attention turned to the encouragement of home ownership with an extension of mortgage tax relief; and to the development of pensions and savings schemes with tax breaks. By such means, small accumulations of property were encouraged. Denationalisation was also added to the tax package. The party's commitment to privatisation had been hampered by the problem of finding buyers: the answer was to offer shares to a large number of small investors. By such means, argued Sewill, a policy of savings and ownership would provide the basis for a new electoral strategy:

In electoral terms, one of the Conservative party's biggest handicaps is that we are considered to be a party of the rich while Labour always rates best as 'the party most likely to look after all classes'. The theme of saving and ownership helps to fulfil the suggestion ... that we should turn this weakness to our advantage by showing that our escape mechanism – home ownership, occupational pensions, the security of savings – can be brought within the reach of all.[57]

Privatisation and 'popular capitalism' therefore gained a new significance in Conservative rhetoric. Unlike the proposals of the tax package, the strategy was a blatant appeal to the self-interest of the middling groups with scant regard either for the creation of efficiency or for the well-being of the poor. Or, to put it more positively, there was a growing realisation that the only way to escape from the existing constraints on growth was to appeal to self-interest, to offer incentives to enterprise.

The Conservatives returned to power in 1970, and Edward Heath's government was faced with the task of reversing some of Labour's innovations and implementing some of the proposals developed in opposition. Heath was pledged to abolish the SET. The proposal to make good the loss of revenue by an increase in employers' national insurance contributions was open to the criticism that it merely replaced one employment tax with another. The alternative was to introduce VAT in place of both SET and the purchase tax – and VAT was introduced in 1973. The caution of the policy group was abandoned and VAT was now justified as a fair tax, even in the absence of compensation to the poor. The purchase tax fell on goods and not services; the SET was a clumsy and unpopular attempt to extend taxation to services. VAT would cover goods *and* services, and exempt essential goods such as food, fuel, lighting and housing. It could therefore be argued that VAT was not a regressive tax. Further, it taxed goods on an equal basis, unlike the wide variation of the purchase tax, so extending the freedom of consumers.[58] Such arguments did not

[57] CPA, CRD 3/7/26/38, 'Saving and ownership', B. Sewill, 3 Jan. 1969.
[58] S. Sherborne, *VAT: Fair for All* (Conservative Political Centre, London, 1972).

convince everyone, for the purchase tax exempted the same goods and imposed higher rates on luxuries. It could be interpreted as a socially divisive policy, increasing indirect taxes in order to make concessions to the better-off. The standard rate of tax was reduced, earned income relief was raised for higher incomes, the estate duty was cut – and nothing was done to increase personal allowances to remove the poverty surtax.

Not surprisingly, the Labour party complained that the rich were receiving hand-outs from the Conservatives and the poor were paying the penalty. The attempt to create incentives and economic growth, to foster social cohesion and integration, was mired in social conflict and economic collapse. The ambitions of the 'balanced' tax package were not achieved: the hopes of an inclusive policy, in which everyone would gain from higher growth and resources would be available for a high standard of social services, were disappointed.[59] The package also placed a great deal of stress upon improved utilisation of labour and increased productivity, which would require a reform of trade union law, eased by improved productivity and higher wages. In the event, reform of trade union law was disassociated from a strategy of raising productivity by reallocating welfare costs; reform of trade union law was more easily portrayed as an attack on workers' rights. At the same time, Labour's corporation tax was amended in 1973 by introducing 'imputation': the corporation tax on business profits was set against the tax liability of the shareholder so that distributions no longer paid a higher rate. The integrative ambitions of the tax package were abandoned, and Heath left office at a time of unprecedented social tension.[60]

The demise of the 'balanced' tax package led to a harsher fiscal policy, a willingness to encourage savings and incentives with less concern for poorer members of society. Despite their later hostility, Heath established the groundwork for Thatcher by rejecting an obsession (as they saw it) with balance. There was a new assertiveness, a release from the attempt to ensure that no one lost from any change in the tax system. After all, the result might simply be that *all* lost from the collapse of growth and destruction of incentives. Social equity and fiscal balance were replaced by a concern for incentives – a change apparent in the arguments of Lawson. He dismissed the importance of a 'poverty trap' for low incomes as they crossed the threshold for paying income tax: the answer was to work harder and obtain higher incomes, so that the marginal rate would fall. By contrast, there was no escape at the top of the income distribution,

[59] Lowe, 'Social policy', pp. 194–200.
[60] The reform of the corporation tax was announced in PP 1970–1 L, *Green Paper on Reform of Corporation Tax*, and considered in PP 1970–1 L, *Report from the Select Committee on Corporation Tax*, which recommended the system of imputation.

where working hard and earning more led to extremely high marginal rates.[61] By 1979, many Conservative politicians realised that a different approach was possible. Perhaps integration was simply not feasible, for it was difficult to fund additional welfare without imposing an unpopular tax. Perhaps the 'selfish' behaviour of organised workers and the grave problems of the British economy in the 1970s indicated that integration had already collapsed and that radical steps were needed. The pursuit of incentives at the cost of social integration became possible.

Labour in opposition and power, 1970–1979

Labour did not accept this approach when it regained power in 1974, and Wilson's second government turned to the unfinished business of implementing its own project of fiscal reform. By the time Wilson took office, the SET had been swept aside and the corporation tax revised; membership of the EEC meant that VAT had to be retained. Attention turned to the wealth tax (allied to a cumulative tax on transfers of wealth) as a means of re-establishing an equitable fiscal system and pursuing equality in the distribution of income and wealth. As Douglas Jay argued in 1970,

further progress must come mainly through capital taxes than through taxes on income. This is first because less progress has been made, and inequality is still much greater, in the distribution of property than of incomes; and because any further pressure for still more progressive taxation on earned incomes would meet with strong popular resistance. It is a crucial new fact, not fully understood, that in a world of gradually falling money values, direct taxation, if rates are left where they are, takes a steadily increasing proportion of all but the lowest income.[62]

The wealth tax was justified as a means of restoring the balance of the fiscal system, on the grounds that taxation of income from employment had risen more than taxation of income from capital since the war. Labour's working party on capital taxation commented in 1973 that wealth taxation was justified by considerations of equity, but even more as

a further expression of the egalitarian philosophy particular to the Labour Movement . . . an egalitarian taxation system is not one which merely distributes the burden of taxation in accordance with an individual's taxable capacity. Rather it is one which uses the taxation instrument to achieve greater social equality. Successive governments have recognised the principle of using direct taxation to reduce disparities in the distribution of personal income. This contrasts with relative neglect accorded in the past to much greater inequalities in the distribution of personal wealth.[63]

[61] Lawson, 'Taxation or government expenditure?', pp. 29–30.
[62] LPA, Finance, Box IV, Study Group on Taxation, Re571/Jan. 1970, 'Tax policy in the 1970's', D. Jay.
[63] LPA, RD732/Apr. 1973, capital taxation: the reform of capital taxation.

At the same time, Labour proposed to *increase* the highest rates of income tax, in marked contrast to the Conservative case for the wealth tax.

Labour was concerned at the poverty trap as low earners crossed the tax threshold and paid a high marginal rate; the rates then fell as earnings rose and progression did not start until incomes were at a much higher level. How could Labour help small incomes without benefiting higher earners? Tax credits or negative income tax did not secure much support from Labour's working party, which feared that it would reduce the high marginal rates of tax on the poor without redistributing income. Of course, Conservative interest in the negative income tax rested on the removal of the 'poverty trap' rather than any wish to increase progression on higher incomes. Labour's working party had different ideas, preferring to create a more progressive scale on high incomes, with a removal of tax breaks on life insurance and mortgages, and higher taxation of unearned incomes and distributed profits. 'We reject the argument that higher tax rates on high incomes would act as a serious disincentive to effort. The real disincentives arise much lower down the income scale where the accumulated loss of means tested benefits combines with income tax to produce excessively high marginal tax rates.' The strategy would help incomes below £1,000, accounting for 40 per cent of electors of whom 57 per cent voted Labour. It would hit incomes above £2,000 accounting for 12 per cent of the electorate, of whom only 10 per cent voted Labour. Egalitarian principle and electoral calculation combined to support a shift to a more progressive income tax and the introduction of a wealth tax.[64] In 1973, *Labour's Programme for Britain* proposed an increase in the highest rates of income tax, with an investment income surcharge on lower incomes. At the same time, a progressive wealth tax would be an 'annual levy on the largest concentrations of private wealth', a form of capital levy to undermine capitalism rather than to stimulate a dynamic free enterprise society. Labour's case for a wealth tax therefore rested on a very different ideological basis from the Conservative party's

---

[64] LPA, Finance and Economic Affairs Sub-Committee minutes, 13 Mar. 1972, 24 Apr. 1972, 28 June 1972, 13 June 1973, 20 June 1973; RD302/Mar. 1972, negative income tax, D. Taverne; RD338/Apr. 1972, 1972 policy document: financial and economic section; RD357/May 1972, negative income tax and the tax credit system: proposals for a joint working party; RD486/Nov. 1972, programme of work, 1972/3; RD738/Apr. 1973, draft contribution to the policy statement: taxation; RD741/Apr. 1973, personal taxation: progressive and higher revenue, J. Sieve; RD772/May 1973, the poverty trap, income tax thresholds and reduced rate relief; RD806/May 1973, tax credit working party: interim report; RD822/June 1973, reduced rates of income tax; RD884/Sept. 1973, increased revenue from income tax; RD922/Nov. 1973, closing the tax loopholes: suggested lines of approach; joint working party on tax credits, minutes, 18 Oct. 1972, 30 Jan. 1973, 17 May 1973; the case for tax credits, J. Sieve; RD835/June 1973, interim statement; Re498/Feb. 1976, income taxation: high marginal low income rates and erosion of the tax base; Re605/Apr. 1976, increasing tax revenue.

and the NEDC's desire to stimulate efficiency and incentives by breaking down passive accumulations of capital and encouraging active creation.[65]

The marginal rate of wealth and income tax would be in excess of 100 per cent and it would, as Conservative critics of the wealth tax feared, be 'a further case of "soaking the rich"'.[66] The concerns were not confined to the Conservative party, for the Institute for Fiscal Studies – a think-tank created by Dick Taverne,* a former Labour MP – warned of the dire consequences of reducing inequality. The wealth tax 'could undermine the private enterprise sector of the mixed economy', and in the opinion of one Institute for Fiscal Studies publication, 'inequalities which result from hard work and enterprise combined with saving are not unfair and are not resented as unfair by the majority of the community; what seems unfair to most people is fortuitous capital gains and large inheritances'. The mistake, it seemed to the Institute for Fiscal Studies, was to assume that justice and equality were synonymous. The tax system might also 'be counter-productive in the promotion of the social cohesion which is one of its underlying objectives'. The wealth tax might lead to dissaving and increased consumption by the rich. On this view, a serious shortcoming of the wealth tax was that it attacked inequality at the top end by reducing the wealth of the rich without increasing the wealth of the poor. 'The wealth taken from the rich is not transferred to the poor but in the main increases the total wealth of the public sector of the economy and reduces that of the private sector.'[67] Here was a major ideological divide, which reopened the split found in the working group on equality of 1955/6. On the one side were those who felt that a simple distribution of wealth from

---

[65] On the wealth tax, see N. Kaldor, *Indian Tax Reform: Report of a Survey* (New Delhi, 1956); NEDC, *Conditions Favourable to Faster Growth*; J. S. Flemming and I. M. D. Little, *Why We Need a Wealth Tax* (London, 1974); Peacock, 'Economics of a net wealth tax'; Tress, 'A wealth tax is a wealth tax'; J. F. Due, 'Net worth taxation', *Public Finance* 15 (1960), 313–7; Labour party, *Labour's Programme for Britain: Papers Presented at the Annual Conference* (London, 1973); Millan, *Taxes for a Prosperous Society*; PP 1974 XVII, *Green Paper on Wealth Tax*.

[66] CPA, CRD 3/7/26/16, Conservatives and capital tax, T. E. B., 8 Aug. 1968; also CRD 3/7/26/9, the case against wealth tax.

[67] C. T. Sandford, J. R. M. Willis and D. J. Ironside, *An Annual Wealth Tax* (London, 1975), pp. 279–81; they preferred an accessions tax as a means of reducing inequality, which would tax wealth acquired fortuitously through inheritances and capital appreciation; unlike a death duty, it would tax the beneficiary. See Sandford, Willis and Ironside, *Annual Wealth Tax*, pp. 281–2, and their *An Accessions Tax* (London, 1973).

* Dick Taverne (b. 1928) was educated at Charterhouse and Balliol College, Oxford; he was called to the bar in 1954 and became a QC in 1965. He was a Labour MP from 1962 to 1972, when he resigned and was re-elected as a Democratic Labour MP for 1973–4. He served as parliamentary under-secretary of state at the Home Office 1966–8, minister of state at the Treasury 1968–9 and financial secretary 1969–70. He was director of the Institute for Fiscal Studies from 1970, director-general 1979–80 and chairman 1981–2. He was a member of the national committee of the Social Democratic party 1981–7, and stood as a candidate on two occasions. (*Who's Who 2001*, p. 2032.)

the rich to the poor was inadequate, merely spreading the assets of the rich in a thin layer over a large number of people without transforming their lives. As Tawney argued, it was better to divert as much wealth as possible from the rich to an active state which could direct welfare where it was needed.[68] On the other side were those like Taverne and refugees from Labour in the new Social Democratic party who felt that the emphasis on a larger state was out of touch with the desire of many electors to share in the wider diffusion of property. The split helps to explain why, in Gareth Stedman Jones's phrase, the Labour party was in a mess. In the past, the Labour party was able to rely on an identity between trade unionism, loyalty to various labour movements and voting for the party. Working-class culture was very self-contained from the late nineteenth century, forming what Stedman Jones terms 'the consciousness of the separateness of a caste', with a perception that employers and profits were antithetical to the interests of workers. This perception was starting to change, as trade unionism altered its character, moving into white-collar occupations and weakening in the affluent industrial districts; and the somewhat rigid and self-contained cultures of working and middle class became more permeable. Although Labour was able to attract sufficient middle-class support to form a government after the war, there were serious difficulties in the 1970s and 1980s. Policies of redistribution, of higher levels of income tax, were less likely to appeal to more prosperous workers, who were abandoning their old cultural loyalties; and middle-class progressives were increasingly aware that poverty was less an issue of low wages to be tackled by unions than a problem of the unorganised – of immigrants, children, single parents, the elderly. The identity with unions made it difficult for the party to adapt, and many of its policies seemed outmoded.[69]

In 1974, the new Labour chancellor, Denis Healey,* announced his intention of introducing 'an annual wealth tax on the rich'.[70] In fact, the wealth tax, like the capital levy before it, foundered on the rocks of political expediency. Rather than implementing the proposal, Healey referred

[68] See Whiting, 'Boundaries', pp. 161–2.

[69] G. Stedman Jones, 'Why is the Labour party in a mess?', in his *The Languages of Class: Studies in English Working-Class History, 1832–1982* (Cambridge, 1983), pp. 239–56; McKibbin, *Classes and Cultures*.

[70] *Parliamentary Debates*, 5th ser. 871, 26 Mar. 1974, cols. 312–13. The White Paper is at PP 1974 XVII, *Wealth Tax*, pp. 525–62.

* Denis Winston Healey (b. 1917) was born in Keighley and educated at Bradford Grammar School and Balliol College, Oxford, where he was briefly a communist. In 1945 he argued for an international socialist revolution before turning to attack fellow travellers. He ran Labour's international department from 1945 to 1952 and was an MP from 1952 to 1992. He served as defence secretary 1964–70 and chancellor of the Exchequer 1974–9, a period marked by the 1976 International Monetary Fund crisis and the beginnings of monetarism, and the attempt to impose pay restraint which broke in 1978/9. He was deputy leader 1980–3. (*Who's Who 2001*, p. 937; Robbins (ed.), *Biographical Dictionary*, pp. 193–4.)

it to a Select Committee which failed to reach agreement. There was a basic division over the nature of the tax. In Europe, the wealth tax was 'substitutive', a means of balancing the tax system between earned and unearned income, and reducing the income tax. Douglas Jay, the chair of the Select Committee, was more inclined to an 'additive' wealth tax in order to impose *further* burdens on capital and to promote equality. Jay's draft report was not accepted by the Select Committee, and the Conservative members produced their own report complaining that the government's proposal confused equity and equality. They feared that an additive tax would be paid from capital, so destroying the mixed economy, leading to dissaving, a flight of capital and a concentration of wealth in the hands of the state. The Conservatives argued for a different approach. Instead of increasing taxation on savings, incentives should be provided by a lower rate of tax on high incomes and the abolition of the income surcharge and taxation of long-term capital gains. Labour was also divided. The left wished to increase the power of the state and to shift the balance of the mixed economy. One member of the committee, Jeremy Bray,* argued that a redistribution of wealth from the rich to the poor would help investment, for most savings from small incomes were contractual unlike discretionary savings from large incomes. He felt that a more equal distribution of wealth and savings could be linked with a reform of the City and the creation of a new form of industrial democracy through a worker-managed society. Not surprisingly, many members of the party feared that these visions of public ownership and workers' democracy marked the triumph of utopianism and ideology over electoral and economic reality.[71]

The failure of the Select Committee to agree meant that Healey could drop the proposal as a result of 'administrative cost and political hassle'.[72] There were real problems of collection and valuation. As Kay and King pointed out, it could only be levied on quoted securities and bank accounts, which were a small proportion of assets: it could not be levied on houses and durable goods, pension rights, life insurance policies, works of art. It would, they concluded, fail to raise significant revenue or

---

[71] PP 1974–5 XXXVI, *Select Committee on a Wealth Tax, 1974/5, Vol. 1, Report and Proceedings of the Committee*, draft report proposed by the chairman, pp. 573–612; draft report proposed by Maurice Macmillan and others, pp. 650–99; draft report proposed by Jeremy Bray, pp. 636–47.

[72] D. Healey, *The Time of My Life* (London, 1989), 404; Whiting, 'Boundaries', p. 156.

* Jeremy William Bray (1930–2002) was educated at Aberystwyth Grammar School, Kingswood School and Jesus College, Cambridge. He researched in pure mathematics before joining ICI as a technical officer from 1956 to 1962. He was a Labour MP from 1962 to 1970 and 1974 to 1997, serving as parliamentary secretary at the ministry of power 1966–7, joint parliamentary secretary at the ministry of technology 1967–9. (*Who's Who 2001*, p. 243.)

produce any significant redistribution of wealth.[73] What was agreed by both Labour and Conservatives was the need to reform death duties, which had almost become a voluntary tax. A. B. Atkinson commented in 1972 that 'where those with good tax advisers – and perhaps few scruples – can pay little tax while others pay tax at rates up to 80 per cent, there can be little respect for the equity of taxation'.[74] An attempt was made to close one loophole by taxing gifts made prior to death, in a period gradually extended from one month to seven years. Even so, the amount of tax avoided in 1968 was put at £177m or about 10 per cent of the net capital value of all property assessed for estate duty.[75] In 1974, the estate duty was revised with a capital transfer tax on any gift above an annual exemption limit of £2,000 or a lifetime limit of £25,000. The rate of tax on gifts was lower than on transfers at death, and most people could ensure that they reduced their liability by making annual gifts up to the exemption limit or by setting up trusts. The tax produced little revenue and had no appreciable impact on the distribution of wealth. The government's continued concern for equality merely led to the appointment of a Royal Commission on the Distribution of Income and Wealth, whose impressively researched reports received scant attention from the new Conservative government with a different ideology.[76]

Of course, the Labour government was overwhelmed by more pressing economic problems with the International Monetary Fund crisis of 1976. In the late 1970s, the most detailed proposals for reform of the fiscal system came from economists associated with the Institute for Fiscal Studies, and particularly from an enquiry into direct taxation chaired by James Meade, and the study of the tax system by two young economists, John Kay* and Mervyn King.[†] Their main proposal was a form of

[73] Kay and King, *British Tax System*, p. 169; see also G. S. A. Wheatcroft, 'Administrative problems of a wealth tax', *British Tax Review* (1963), 410–22, and A. R. Prest, 'The Select Committee on a wealth tax', *British Tax Review* (1976), 7–15.

[74] A. B. Atkinson, *Unequal Shares: Wealth in Britain* (London, 1972), p. 129.

[75] E. G. Horsman, 'The avoidance of death duty by gifts *inter vivos*: some qualitative evidence', *Economic Journal* 85 (1975), 521.

[76] Kay and King, *British Tax System*, pp. 157–62; the reports of the Royal Commission on the Distribution of Income and Wealth appeared in eight volumes between 1974–5 and 1979–80.

* John Anderson Kay (b. 1948) was educated at the Royal High School, Edinburgh, University of Edinburgh and Nuffield College, Oxford. He was a fellow of St John's College, Oxford, from 1970 and lecturer in economics 1971–9. He moved to the Institute for Fiscal Studies as research director 1979–81 and director 1981–6; he was a professor at the London Business School 1986–96 and director of the Said Business School, Oxford, 1997–9. (*Who's Who 2001*, p. 1130.)

† Mervyn Allister King (b. 1948) was educated at Wolverhampton Grammar School and King's College, Cambridge. He was a research officer in applied economics at Cambridge 1969–76, and lecturer in economics 1976–7. He moved to Birmingham as professor of

expenditure tax, on the lines proposed by Kaldor in 1956. At that time, the CRD realised that it provided a solution to the socialists' dilemma of reconciling a search for equality with the harmful effects of high rates of tax on savings. By imposing taxes on income *spent*, savings could be helped without sacrificing the pursuit of equality.[77] In practice, Labour's tax policies largely ignored the encouragement of savings, and focussed on the creation of equality through attacks on large income and fortunes. After 1979, Conservative encouragement of savings was linked with *inequality*; the Institute for Fiscal Studies was offering a way of forging a link between equality, justice and growth. Kay and King advocated a 'lifetime expenditure tax', a measure of an individual's total use of resources over life which was the sum of consumption, gifts and bequests. The existing, separate taxes on income and capital were levied at different rates: capital gains paid 30 per cent, compared with the highest rate on investment income of 98 per cent. Owner-occupied housing, pensions and life insurance had tax advantages, and accounted for 88.9 per cent of personal saving in the UK in 1972–6 – a marked contrast with the US where they accounted for 56.0 per cent in 1972. By contrast, there was little personal saving in companies and unit trusts. These anomalies in the tax position of different forms of income and savings could be swept away by a single expenditure tax.[78] Meade's committee linked the expenditure tax with a 'new Beveridge scheme' to resolve the poverty trap and to set an acceptable standard of living for all citizens. Tax thresholds should be raised to avoid the overlap between supplementary benefit and income tax, and benefits should be set at a level sufficient to provide a minimum standard of living. The scheme would be costly, and tax rates would have to rise as a result, but the committee hoped to combine a minimum standard of life with the encouragement of enterprise and taxation of high levels of personal consumption.[79]

These schemes were portrayed by their authors as neutral and technical, an attempt to sweep away the confusion and anomalies of the existing fiscal system. However, it was one thing to claim that reform was logical and administratively practical; it was quite another to get any politician to introduce such a sweeping change. Both Labour and the Conservatives

investment from 1977 to 1984 and to the LSE 1984–95. He served on the Meade committee in 1978, and was president of the Institute for Fiscal Studies from 1999. He became a director of the Bank of England in 1990, and deputy governor in 1998. (*Who's Who 2001*, p. 1160.)

[77] CPA, CRD 2/10/8, proposals for a tax on expenditure, 9 July 1956.

[78] Kay and King, *British Tax System*, pp. 59–68, 87–104, 170–2.

[79] Institute for Fiscal Studies, *Structure and Reform of Direct Taxation*. For Meade's ideas, see also his *The Intelligent Radical's Guide to Economic Policy* (London, 1974).

took different approaches, with widely divergent assumptions – and the proposals of the Institute for Fiscal Studies had their own ideological motivation. The aim was to stimulate enterprise and to maintain free enterprise, unlike many members of the Labour party. In contrast with many members of the Conservative party, the proposals stressed the provision of a guaranteed minimum standard of life for all citizens. Existing inequalities were not justified by the need for incentives, and more equality was possible and desirable. Nevertheless, the Institute for Fiscal Studies felt that some inequality could be justified, on condition that wealth was held by a changing group of people who earned it. 'There is justice both in the left-wing criticism of the tax-structure for its failure to shake concentrations of wealth and privilege', remarked Kay and King, 'and in the right-wing criticism that it deprives people of the returns of effort and initiative. The present system gives us the worst of both worlds with maximal disincentive effect for minimal redistributive impact.'[80] Their arguments had little effect, as Labour headed for the political wilderness in pursuit of equality and state ownership, and the Conservatives embarked on the pursuit of incentive and inequality at the expense of social justice and social cohesion. The Social Democratic proposals of the late 1970s were scarcely practical politics at the time, and such large-scale reform of the tax system was somewhat unrealistic. Labour failed to rise to the challenge of Kay and King, to articulate a fiscal strategy of equality, social cohesion, justice and economic growth. Politicians who might have pursued this approach – such as Roy Jenkins – were marginalised within the Social Democratic party and the middle ground was abandoned by Labour and the Conservatives.

By 1979, electoral support for Labour's fiscal policies had weakened. Many former Labour voters were more interested in acquiring their own property and sharing in consumption than in the transfer of resources to an active state which seemed inefficient and unreliable. It was increasingly difficult to use the tax system as a means of extracting revenue from the rich in order to benefit the working class. The income tax was central to Labour's strategy of reducing the burden of taxation on the working class and passing it to those with a greater ability to pay. This strategy started to encounter serious electoral problems as a result of changes in the relationship between income tax and the social structure. Before the Second World War, taxes on income, property and profits hit the middle class, *rentiers* and landowners, and relieved the working class. The reduction in thresholds during the war, the increase in wages and the

[80] Kay and King, *British Tax System*, pp. 70–1.

introduction of PAYE brought many more workers into the reach of income tax – a process that continued throughout the 1950s and 1960s. Between 1945 and 1975, the number of income taxpayers rose from 17.5 to 20.5m – and a higher proportion of revenue was obtained from lower incomes. In 1949, a married man with two children needed to earn 187 per cent of average earnings before becoming liable to the standard rate of income tax; by 1975, the figure was a mere 44.6 per cent. In 1976, liability for income tax started with an earned income of £31.40 a week – yet the poverty line for a married man with two children was £43.50 in work (for the payment of family income supplement) or £35.05 out of work (for the payment of supplementary benefit). Incomes above £5,000 contributed only 10 per cent of government revenue, despite the high marginal rates of taxation. Raising further large sums from the income tax would hit 'moderately affluent' middle incomes, with serious electoral consequences for Labour. One solution was to attack wealth and capital. In the past, the capital levy identified a particular social group of *rentiers*, and Labour could claim to represent the propertyless and the enterprising against idle, functionless wealth. In the 1950s, 1960s and 1970s, *rentiers* were no longer such obvious figures to attack. The major holders of debt and shares were institutions such as insurance companies and pension funds rather than parasitical plutocrats; and the main reason for government borrowing was welfare rather than warfare. As Whiting has remarked, these changes were bound to compromise the egalitarian ambitions of the tax system, and make it difficult to broaden the tax base to capital and wealth.[81] At the same time, resistance to a highly progressive income tax was emerging from many members of the salaried middle class and the self-employed who felt, as the Conservative Central Office pointed out in 1977, that they were the victims of an inequitable tax system at a time of rapid inflation and high mortgage interest rates.[82] The relationship between taxation and income distribution was changing. At the beginning of the period covered by this book, the median voter had a modest income and did not pay income tax; there was strong electoral support for redistributive taxation. By the end of the period, the median voter paid income tax and was less inclined to support redistribution. Of course, there were also concerns about the impact of taxation on economic growth and incentives:

[81] Lowe, *Welfare State*, pp. 287–8; Whiting, 'Boundaries', pp. 149, 155; J. C. Odling-Smee and C. Riley, 'Approaches to the PSBR', *National Institute of Economic Research* 113 (1985), 65–80; B. Eichengreen, *The Capital Levy in Theory and Practice* (Centre for Economic Policy, London, 1989).
[82] CPA, CCO 4/10/293, 'Personal taxation', 23 Feb. 1977.

Table 10.3 *Structure of income tax, United Kingdom, France, Germany and USA, c. 1976*

	Threshold (£)	Initial rate (%)	Maximum rate (%)	Income for maximum rate (£)
UK	1,685	35	83	21,685
France	3,550	3.6	54	46,800
Germany	2,200	22	56	65,700
USA	4,000	25	50 (55.5 incl. local)	29,600

Source: Parliamentary Debates, 5th ser. 924, Written Answers to Questions, cols. 407–8.

redistribution seemed somewhat irrelevant if the result were to frustrate economic growth.

As Kay and King remarked, the tax system was highly progressive only in appearance; in reality, it was a sham, creating hypocrisy for all concerned. Mrs Thatcher exposed the sham and produced a tax regime in which appearances matched reality. The top rates of income tax were reduced from 98 per cent to 40 per cent, and the bottom rate from 33 to 25 per cent with the abolition of the reduced rate band for lower incomes. The investment surcharge was abolished, the capital gains tax indexed for inflation and the rate of capital transfer tax cut. Corporation tax was reduced, and the national insurance surcharge on employers abolished. The exemption of life insurance premiums was ended and tax breaks introduced for other forms of savings, especially in equities and unit trusts through Personal Equity Plans. Little was done to remove the poverty trap on low incomes, and indirect taxes rose as a proportion of total revenue. The shift may be seen as regressive, yet it also made administrative sense and might well have contributed to *maintaining* public spending. Kay and King pointed out that the basic rate of VAT in 1978 was 8 per cent and the standard rate of income tax 34 per cent. Consequently, there were greater problems of compliance with the income tax than VAT, and they recommended that rates should converge. This has happened, with VAT rising to 17.5 per cent. The shift from direct to indirect taxes offered a means of finding more revenue in the face of public resistance to taxes, of maximising revenues and minimising political costs – at least until the fuel tax protests of 2000. In 1978/9, the income tax provided 32 per cent of all government revenue; by 1988/9, it was down to 24 per cent. Income tax rates have been cut, especially for the rich; consumption taxes have risen; and capital taxation has been liberalised. The tax system changed

Table 10.4 *Structure of central government revenue: net receipts due to the Exchequer, 1969/70, 1978/9 and 1988/9 (percentage)*

	1969/70	1978/9	1988/9
Income tax and super-tax	38.6	45.9	35.7
Profits	12.8	9.7	15.2
Death duties	2.7	0.1	0.9
Stamps	0.9	1.1	1.9
Motor vehicle duty	3.1	2.7	2.3
Petroleum revenue tax	–	0.5	1.1
Customs and excise	37.0	33.7	40.9
Capital gains tax	1.0	0.9	1.9
Capital transfer tax	–	0.8	–
SET	3.9	–	–
National insurance surcharge	–	4.7	–
Total	100.0	100.0	100.0

Source: PP 1970–1 L, *113th Report of the Commissioners of Inland Revenue for the year 1969–70,* pp. 660–1; PP 1979–80 LXVIII, *112nd Report of the Commissioners of Inland Revenue for the year ended 31 March 1979,* pp. 26–7; *Board of Inland Revenue, 131st Report for the year ending 31 March 1989,* p. 54.

its structure, but government expenditure did not fall as a percentage of GDP. It was 42.2 per cent of GDP when Mrs Thatcher came to power, and 42.3 per cent in 1995/6.[83] For all her rhetoric, Mrs Thatcher did not roll back the state.

[83] Kay and King, *British Tax System,* p. 145; Steinmo, *Taxation and Democracy,* pp. 21, 171, 173; Hills, *Changing Tax,* pp. 11–13.

11 'Highly defensible ramparts': the politics of local taxation

By the turn of the nineteenth and twentieth centuries, the increasing cost of local government was placing immense strain on the local tax base which relied almost entirely on a rate on property – on housing, shops, factories, railways. This narrow tax base was causing serious political problems, for lower-middle-class house owners and shopkeepers were aggrieved that their profits were eroded by the costs of local government, and that other forms of income were not paying an adequate contribution. Further, the incidence of rates was regressive, for poor families spent a higher proportion of their income on housing. Reform of the local tax base proved highly contentious, not least because the Liberal government turned to the taxation of land values – an ideological assault on the unearned income of landowners that was productive of political controversy rather than revenue.

Rates continued to provide the basis of local taxation, which left two other solutions. One approach was to pass the cost of welfare from the local poor law to the central state, through old age pensions or insurance schemes: the successful reform of central taxation contributed to a change in the balance between the central and local state.[1] Another was for the central government to offer grants-in-aid to local government, either as fixed sums or in proportion to spending. The danger of proportionate or percentage grants was that local authorities might subvert control over the national budget – and the Treasury's concern that money might be spent irresponsibly was exacerbated by Labour's capture of Boards of Guardians and local authorities.[2] The structure of local taxation, and the contribution of the central state, became major issues in the Conservative government of 1924–9, with Churchill and Chamberlain taking different views. To Churchill, reform of local finance offered another way of assisting productive industry by reducing the burden of local rates and showing that the government was not merely assisting *rentiers*

[1] Daunton, 'Payment and participation'.
[2] See P. A. Ryan, '"Poplarism", 1894–1930', in P. Thane (ed.), *The Origins of British Social Policy* (London, 1978), pp. 58–83.

and financiers. To Chamberlain, the result of reducing the burden of local rates on industry might be to remove the incentive of responsible businessmen to serve as councillors. These debates were resolved in 1929, and laid the basis of local government finance for the next fifty years, up to the fiasco of the 'poll tax'.

Pressures on the national budget in the 1920s meant that the Conservative government was anxious to control local authority spending, and to ensure that grants from the central government did not undermine attempts to balance the budget. The Cabinet's committee on expenditure recognised the problem in 1926, noting with concern 'the extent to which State expenditure is linked with that of local authorities by the percentage system of grants'. Under this system, the central government was obliged to cover a defined percentage of any spending by the locality on a particular service, which meant that municipalities could adopt more expensive policies and extend their services at the (partial) cost of the central government. The committee on expenditure complained that

This system not only hampers Treasury control of the national finances, but inevitably weakens local responsibility and leads to uneconomical administration, which, even with the aid of large staffs, Government departments are unable to check. They regard it as a matter of great urgency to terminate this system at the earliest possible date and to substitute for it a basis of Exchequer aid independent as far as possible of the expenditure of individual authorities.[3]

On this view, percentage grants needed minute control of spending to protect the national taxpayer, and fixed grants would give more autonomy to the localities. However, there was always a suspicion that the motivation was economy rather than autonomy. Much would depend on the precise form of block grants and the extent to which they transferred resources to the poorer areas of the country.

Another technical issue, with major implications, was the question of valuation of property for the rates: what exactly should be valued, and on what basis? In 1896, at the end of a long period of agricultural depression, farmers were granted a rebate of half the rate on the grounds that they needed a larger amount of rateable property to earn their income than other traders. Industrial ratepayers could claim similar relief at a time of trade depression, which connected with the question of how to treat industrial plant and machinery. Should they be partially or entirely exempt from rates? In Scotland, the full rate was charged on plant providing motive power, heat and light, with process plant exempted. In England, the situation was not clear: some poor law unions imposed the full rate on all plant; others levied a reduced rate on process plant. In

[3] PRO, CAB27/305, CP54(26), Standing Committee on Expenditure, report, 9 Feb. 1926.

1925, a standardised procedure for rating machinery was proposed, and the point was seized upon by Churchill to make a major political point – to the alarm of Neville Chamberlain, the minister responsible for local government, who wished to concentrate on the reform of grants. Churchill had larger ambitions, aiming to convert Chamberlain's narrower technical concern for local government finance into a sweeping gesture, a rhetorical statement of the government's vision of economic recovery.[4] Reform of local government finance was to become a major theme of the Conservative administration of 1924 to 1929, leading to a new system of central–local government relations.

In Churchill's dismissive remark, Neville Chamberlain would make a good lord mayor of Birmingham in a bad year. The comment was not entirely fair, for he was a successful local politician with a firm grasp of the intricacies of local government finance, and a commitment to efficient municipal authorities. Indeed, in 1924 he refused the offer of the chancellorship for the less glamorous ministry of health, where he turned his mind to poor law reform and the introduction of a consolidated 'block grant' for poor law and health, fixed for five years according to the population and resources of each authority. Chamberlain argued that the result would be greater freedom for the localities, for the ministry would no longer need to investigate every proposal for expenditure in order to ensure that money was not being wasted. Instead, it could prescribe a minimum standard above which local authorities should have fairly wide discretion. The grants would also provide assistance to necessitous areas with decaying staple industries, so that poor areas could now come up to a basic minimum standard.[5] On the other hand, progressive or prosperous areas could no longer adopt a new, expensive policy at the partial cost of central government. Chamberlain felt that the change was desirable, for fixed grants would create fiscal responsibility, so preventing local councillors from passing the costs of their policies to national taxpayers and subverting the national budget. A large measure of decentralisation would be possible, for the local authority would be responsible for its own actions and so create an active political life on the basis of prudent finances. As a result, Chamberlain believed that 'large and responsible local health authorities may enjoy a wide measure of freedom, not only in their day-to-day administration, but also in the initiation of experiments

[4] PRO, CAB27/207, CP27 (23), interim report of Rating Reform Committee, 19 Jan. 1923; CP230 (23), second interim report, 10 May 1923; RTG 3, memorandum by the minister of health, 12 Jan. 1923.
[5] PRO, CAB27/263, UPC, rating of machinery, 25 Feb. 1925; meeting of committee, 16 June 1925; scheme for financial reform, memorandum by the minister of health, 29 May 1925.

adapted to their special local conditions'. He suggested that local authority areas should be widened from the poor law union to the county, so that richer areas would support poorer districts and at the same time 'extravagant' unions would be controlled by their more cautious neighbours. It meant freedom with responsibility, offering more discretion and reducing 'minute scrutiny' of spending.[6]

The Treasury was eager to adopt block grants for other services as well, in a single consolidated grant based on statistical measures and 'wholly independent of expenditure'.[7] Churchill justified the replacement of percentage by block grants

mainly as an escape from the present unsatisfactory position under which year after year the Exchequer was forced to find large sums of money for the activities of local authorities, whose policy could not be effectively controlled by the Government. The Government got no credit for their large grants. The pound for pound principle was a great incentive to expenditure, and easily lent itself to extravagance and waste.

In future, new initiatives would not be funded automatically and would involve a conscious decision by the government. The Treasury and Churchill emphasised control – sweetened by the offer of a generous grant.[8] Chamberlain was concerned that Churchill's characteristic preference for a wider scheme would 'overload the ship and wreck her but I suppose he will have to splash about a bit till he gets some water in his mouth'.[9] Above all, negotiation of a new system of block grants would involved a battle between the Treasury and spending departments which feared (with justice) that the proposals were a means of tightening control as well as offering responsibility. Churchill's patience was tried by the opposition of smaller units of local government which would lose functions to larger authorities, and by the self-interest of government departments in protecting their spending plans. In 1927, he announced that the Treasury would not provide the finance for a generous new block grant

if the political recruiting powers of the small local bodies are too strong, if the particularism of the Government Departments is too pronounced, if the love of Whitehall for Whitehall control is too deep-seated, if at every stage we have to buy

---

[6] PRO, CAB27/339, Cabinet Committee on Block Grants 1927, GC(27) 1st meeting, 23 Feb. 1927; CAB27/263, scheme for financial reform, memorandum by minister of health, 29 May 1925.

[7] PRO, CAB27/305, NE4, Board of Education estimates, note by Treasury, 26 Oct. 1925; CP54(26), Standing Committee on Expenditure, report, 9 Feb. 1926.

[8] PRO, CAB27/305, NE40, report of Colwyn Committee on education estimates, 16 Feb. 1926.

[9] Birmingham University Library, NC18/1/505, Neville to Hilda Chamberlain, 17 Oct. 1925.

off opposition with public money and with unsymmetrical compromise... Bad as is our present system, it works; and if the Cabinet make a firm resistance to departmental pressures for increases in Police, in Education, in Health Services, etc, it may be made to work without immediate heavy new expense. It would certainly not be in the interest of the Exchequer to quit these highly defensible ramparts for the purpose not of facilitating a great reform, but merely of substituting a new unpopular and more costly muddle for an old muddle.[10]

Churchill's frustration with the problems of reforming block grants was soon forgotten in the excitement of a new policy with potentially greater electoral appeal than the technicalities of central–local government financial relations: the derating of industry.[11]

The attraction of derating industry was that local property rates could be seen as hitting productive interests. Rates were paid regardless of profitability and therefore did not reflect ability to pay.[12] In the depressed areas, rates were high to support the unemployed, so that industry was less competitive and unemployment rose still further. In the opinion of an official at the Inland Revenue, local authorities were tempted to treat large industries 'as a sort of milch cow to provide revenue for extravagant local schemes. To all intents and purposes productive industry suffers taxation for local purposes without representation and the areas in which it pays the highest proportion of rates are apt to fall into the charge of the most wasteful administrators.' Churchill seized on derating as a device 'to help productive industry and agriculture by an immense reduction in the burden of Local Rates', and to provide a popular programme for the next election.[13] In Churchill's view, it was 'economically unsound to tax instruments of production':

The imposition of rates upon productive plants is double taxation. It is an invidious impost which falls with increasing weight as the instruments become more bulky and afford employment to large numbers of manual workers and is a contributory factor to the disastrous unemployment which has now become chronic. The task set to a British employer of labour on a large scale is exceptionally difficult. Compared to the profits yielded to bankers and merchants or producers who do not require to use large plants or employ many work people, the rewards of industry have seriously and rapidly diminished. An employer paying wages to a large number of work people must at the present time in this country be regarded as rendering a service to the community rather than obtaining a privilege at their hands. In strict equity individuals should be taxed according to what they have to spend and enjoy and not according to the class of gainful occupation they pursue.

[10] PRO, CAB27/339, memorandum by the chancellor of the Exchequer, 21 Mar. 1927.
[11] PRO, CAB27/365, P(28)22, annex IV. The complete derating of industry, note by the president of the Board of Trade, 27 Mar. 1928.
[12] PRO, CAB27/339, GC(27) 1st meeting, 23 Feb. 1927.
[13] PRO, IR75/116, Churchill to A. W. Hurst, 4 June 1927.

If the balance is to be loaded at all, it should certainly not be against those who are discharging a pressing and vital function to the community and who are flagging under the load they bear.[14]

Above all, Churchill justified derating on grounds of high principle, as a way of offsetting the political dangers that other policies (especially the payment of interest on the debt and the decision to return to the gold standard) seemed hostile to productive industry. It would complete the task of the budget of 1925 of recreating balance in the fiscal system:

By resuming the gold standard we have helped the merchant, the banker and above all the consumer; by remitting sixpence upon the income tax we have benefited the general taxpayer and especially the rentier; by the Widows' and Old Age Pensions Acts we have given a new and most important security to the wage-earner. But so far we have done nothing for the producer on whose continued vitality the heart-beat of the nation depends ... the final effort of our finance in the present Parliament should be devoted to aiding the hard-pressed producer, manufacturing and agricultural, and especially the basic producer, who is the most hard-pressed. The advocacy of a general system of protection for home manufactures and home-produced food would divide the country upon lines much less advantageous to the Conservative Party than the present cleavage between Socialism and anti-Socialism ... The vast additions to the consuming vote contemplated in the female franchise seem in themselves conclusive against the policy of protective taxation of food ...
There is a profound difference between conferring favours upon producers at the expense or alleged expense of the consuming population and relieving producers from undue, exceptional and invidious burdens. The long successes of Liberalism in the nineteenth century in the political and economic sphere were due to the fact that their policy consisted mainly in striking off out-worn fetters on the enterprise and growing manhood of the nation. The relieving of the producers from their present oppression by antiquated laws constitutes almost the only remaining large task of liberation within the reach of governments in these days.[15]

Here was a policy designed to unite consumers and producers in a new alliance of efficiency and incentives – and an alternative to the introduction of tariffs to which Churchill was so firmly opposed.[16]

Churchill felt that Chamberlain's more limited and cautious poor law scheme did not go far enough. As ever, Churchill wanted a 'large new

---

[14] PRO, CAB27/365, P(28)21, 2nd report of Policy Committee CP105(28), annex III, 'Is it equitable and wise that industry should make no contribution to local rates?', W. S. C., 28 Mar. 1928.

[15] PRO, CAB27/365, CP8(28), memorandum by the chancellor of the Exchequer, 20 Jan. 1928.

[16] On the issue of protection, see PRO, CAB27/365, CP72(28), the chancellor of the Exchequer's plan: memorandum by the secretary of state for dominion affairs, 8 Mar. 1928.

constructive measure' at a cost of £30m, a sum available both from cuts in expenditure and from the new petrol tax which would provide a 'mass of manoeuvre . . . a lever . . . big enough to shift things with'. As Churchill argued, rating was a 'mass of compromises, makeshifts and anomalies', and could only be reformed 'on the flood tide . . . of some big financial scheme . . . which conciliates farmers and manufacturers by a substantial boon, and which at the same time provides a *douceur* to the local authorities'.[17] By linking derating of industry with Chamberlain's reform, he offered Baldwin 'a steam roller flattening out all the petty interests which have obstructed Block Grants and rating reform'.[18] Of course, Chamberlain was horrified, fearing that he had 'gone off the deep end and is in full cry after a new and I fear fantastic scheme'.[19]

The initial idea submitted by the Inland Revenue was to abolish the local rate on railways, docks, factories, gas works and mines at a cost of £60m, to be covered by £30m from a rate on net profits which would reflect ability to pay, and a further £30m from Churchill's 'mass of manoeuvre'. The new rate on profits would be removed from local control, so that industry could locate in the most suitable areas 'without reference to such accidental considerations as the proportion of rich people resident in the area or the success of a "progressive" party at the polls'. Churchill was attracted by the scheme – as Chamberlain commented, it was 'characteristic of Winston in its originality, audacity and vagueness'. It met resistance within the Treasury, for Hopkins pointed out that it did nothing to solve the anomalies of grants to local authorities, and it would not 'offer any handle to enable the Government to compel a campaign of economy among local authorities'. Hopkins was sceptical whether a shift from rates to a profit tax would help industry. The problem, as he saw it, was the incidence of taxes. He argued that rates were passed to the consumer or the landlord; by contrast, a tax on profits fell on the producer and would be paid by efficient firms making a profit. A shift from rates to a profits tax would therefore help struggling firms who would pay less in future, at the expense of prosperous firms who would pay more.[20]

[17] Cambridge University Library, Baldwin vol. 5, ff. 169–70, Churchill to Baldwin, 7 Jan. 1928.
[18] Cambridge University Library, Baldwin vol. 5, D2.2, ff. 116–19, Churchill to Baldwin, 18 Feb. 1927; ff. 121–4, Chamberlain to Churchill, 28 Mar. 1927; ff. 125–35, Churchill to Baldwin, 6 June 1927; Churchill to Chamberlain, 7 June 1927, Gilbert, *Churchill, V, Companion I,* pp. 1010–11.
[19] Birmingham University Library, NC2/22, 16 June 1927; see also his report of the views of Grigg and Fisher, 9 and 17 Dec. 1927.
[20] PRO, T170/10, 'Local taxation: a scheme of reform', A. W. Hurst, 9 Mar. 1912; IR75/116, 'The reform of the rating system', A. W. Hurst, 8 June 1927; 'RVNH's draft reply, ?21 June 1927' and 'Rating reform', R. V. N. H., 21 Oct. 1927.

Above all, Hopkins feared a partial solution, and was concerned that Chamberlain's reform of health might placate local authorities and so lead to difficulties in creating larger authorities and introducing a general block grant. Consequently, Hopkins and Churchill felt that Chamberlain's co-operation was essential to create a wider reform of local government finance.[21] Churchill felt that the technical reform of local government finance could only be carried on the back of a scheme with greater electoral appeal than block grants:

the general public... will not understand it at all or trouble themselves on the matter. No doubt they would be glad to know that sounder relations were being established between public and local finance. But the movement of public opinion does not depend on this. It depends on the relief accorded to the producers and the consequent stimulus to industry and employment. On that and that alone the driving power of the whole scheme depends. But do not underrate the immense force of that drive.[22]

Negotiations between Churchill and Chamberlain proved tense and complicated, with mutual suspicion and dislike.[23]

Churchill reluctantly dropped the proposed rate on profits and instead accepted an alternative proposed by Harold Macmillan – a uniform national rate for producers in place of two-thirds of the existing rates, so lightening the burden on basic industries and allowing firms to settle anywhere in the country. As Macmillan pointed out, there was always the hope that the remaining third would be removed, unlike the profits tax which was a new imposition and a possible 'horrid engine of fiscal extortion'.[24] Chamberlain was not convinced, for he was anxious to retain some 'direct connection between the industry of a locality and the machinery of its local government' which would disappear with a flat national rate.[25] He was concerned that 'in many of the large areas the bulk of the money spent by the local authorities would come from the Treasury and central control would at the same time be loosened. It seems to me that such a position would involve serious dangers to local government.' In the event, industry paid part of the *local* rate, so retaining some interest in

[21] PRO, IR75/116, 'Rating reform', R. V. N. H., 21 Oct. 1927; Churchill to Chamberlain, 18 Oct. 1927, Gilbert, *Churchill, V, Companion I*, p. 1062.

[22] PRO, IR75/116, W. S. Churchill to Hurst and Hopkins, 18 Nov. 1927.

[23] Cambridge University Library, Baldwin vol. 5, ff. 141–5, memorandum on the chancellor's scheme; memorandum by Neville Chamberlain, Christmas 1927; Birmingham University Library, NC18/1/600, N. C. to Hilda, 11 Dec. 1927; see, for example, Chamberlain to Churchill, 14 Oct. 1927 and 20 Dec. 1927, Gilbert, *Churchill, V, Companion I*, pp. 1061, 1148–9.

[24] Cambridge University Library, Baldwin vol. 5, ff. 146–56, Churchill to Baldwin, 4 Jan. 1928; ff. 160–5, H. Macmillan, 1 Jan. 1928.

[25] PRO, CAB27/365, CP105(28), Cabinet Policy Committee, second report, 29 Mar. 1928; Birmingham University Library, NC2/22, 21 Mar. 1928.

local administration. As Chamberlain admitted, the logic of Churchill's scheme was impaired, for depressed industries still paid higher rates in the necessitous areas, with harmful consequences for competitiveness. However, he felt that the benefits of industrial involvement in local government outweighed the disadvantages.[26]

Churchill's scheme reduced the revenue of local authorities, and was combined with Chamberlain's block grants in order to provide additional finance for the poor law and health. Churchill was willing to spend £3m as the 'indispensable driving power' to secure local authority agreement to larger local authority areas and to extend block grants to other services. This revenue came from the new duty on imported oil.[27] Here was the basis for the programme of 1929. In the event, it did not provide the Conservatives with a programme to secure victory in the general election, for Labour returned for a second minority government. It did mark a fundamental change in the finance of local government. No new source of local taxation was created – and instead the existing tax base was narrowed, and the trend to central taxation confirmed.

The Exchequer's contribution was fixed for five years in 1929, and the Treasury was anxious that the grant should not be increased and even hoped that it might be reduced. In fact, local authority expenditure had risen since 1929, implying an *increase* of £500,000 in the grant in 1934. The ministry of health warned against any attempt to force the local authorities to accept the existing level of grant, on the grounds that the measure had been implemented with 'surprising smoothness considering their complications and the revolutionary nature of them'. At most, the local authorities should be told that an increase would be postponed. Rather surprisingly, the general view within Whitehall was that the increase should be awarded: the Exchequer had benefited from a cut in teachers' salaries, and it did not seem worth damaging the new principle of the block grant for the sake of a modest saving. Hopkins acceded, merely reserving his position in the event of a further round of economy cuts.[28] In other words, the shift to block grants had not eroded

[26] Birmingham University Library, NC2/22, 21 Mar. 1928, 28 Mar. 1928, 4 Apr. 1928, 18 Apr. 1928, 20 Apr. 1928.
[27] PRO, CAB27/365 P(28)4, Cabinet Policy Committee, memorandum by president of Board of Education, 30 Jan. 1928; CAB27/365, P(28)6, Cabinet Policy Committee, 'Fixed rate to be levied by local authorities and proceeds to go to them', memorandum by minister of health, 27 Feb. 1928; CAB27/365, P(28)12, Cabinet, 2nd report of Policy Committee, annex 1, first report of Policy Procedure Committee, appendix VI, memorandum by secretary of state for war, 11 Mar. 1928; CAB27/365, CP8(28), memorandum by the chancellor of the Exchequer, W. S. C., 20 Jan. 1928; P28(9), Cabinet Policy Committee, memorandum by chancellor of the Exchequer, 9 Mar. 1928.
[28] PRO, T161/590/S37869/1, E. S. Strohmenger to Gilbert, 23 Mar. 1932; Gilbert to Fisher, 7 Apr. 1932; note by R. V. N. Hopkins, 19 Apr. 1932.

the finances of local authorities to anything like the extent that seemed likely in 1929.

Although the immediate political danger of a local fiscal crisis had receded since the Edwardian period, the basic problem of the rates was not solved. Local authorities remained dependent on a single local tax, which had now been further narrowed. In the medium term, the payment of block grants masked the potential danger, for rates formed a smaller share of disposable income. Further, the decline in private rented housing and the partial derating of industry reduced the potential support for a strong ratepayers' movement. For its part, the Labour party was critical of the Conservative response to local taxation. In its view, reliance on the rates relieved the (progressive) taxpayer at the expense of the (regressive) ratepayer; and reduction in rates on industry relieved wealthy ratepayers who were protected by tariffs and did nothing for householders, shopkeepers and utilities which continued to pay the rate in full. In the opinion of Labour, 'most sinister of all' was the changed relation between local and central finance. This was

obviously designed to restrict the expenditure of the State at the cost of crippling the expansion of social services of vital importance. The consolidation of the health grants, while offering a measure of relief to certain districts at the expense of others, will take money from authorities that have been active in their care for public health in order to assist those that have hitherto neglected their duties. The stabilisation of Exchequer grants for a period of five years will prove, it is to be feared, peculiarly disastrous, for it will supply reactionary Local Authorities with a weapon which they will use to check the growth of education and other social services, while progressive authorities will find in it a grave obstacle to beneficial developments that are long overdue.[29]

The policy favoured by Labour was to transfer the costs of the unemployed to central taxation and to increase local revenue by taxation of land values and an extension of municipal trading.[30]

Labour thinking on the finance of local government tended to refer back to the Liberal land campaign and the attack on the unearned increment. In 1920, the party's conference protested at the 'unjust and oppressive' cost of national services on the localities, and proposed that the burden should be shifted to holders of property who would pay the economic rent of their land or minerals to a common fund, which would then be returned to the localities in proportion to their needs.[31] In 1923 and 1925, conference proposed a more modest reform of the rates, based on grants to help poor local authorities and rebates to poor ratepayers,

[29] Labour party, *Labour and the Nation*, pp. 9–10.
[30] A. Greenwood, *The Tory Government's Higher Rates Scheme Exposed!* (London, 1929).
[31] *Labour Party: Report of the Twentieth Annual Conference* (London, 1920), pp. 184–5.

with an increase in the rate on unoccupied houses and vacant building land, or on land values created by the community.[32] However, little progress was made in devising a programme for local government, for there was disagreement over its future structure. In the early 1930s, Attlee argued that a socialist government should appoint commissioners to direct local authorities; there was a case for more national control and finance, to ensure that minimum standards were reached throughout the country, supported by progressive national taxation. Others argued for a reorganisation of local government on the basis of regions, which would create more effective local initiative and democratic control, with a new source of finance.[33] Once again, attention turned to land taxation. Snowden introduced a land tax in 1931, but it was repealed in 1934. In the 1930s, Labour-controlled local authorities took up the issue, and pressed for powers to impose a rate on site values. Indeed, in 1938 the London County Council drafted a bill to allow it to rate site values.[34] A Conservative parliament would not pass such a measure – and there was also some scepticism within the Labour party. Should land be taxed or nationalised? The party was committed to nationalisation as its long-term ambition, so that taxation was either a means to that end, or a short-term expedient.[35]

These debates over the form of local government were apparent in the plans to reform the health service: should it be run by local authorities such as the LCC which started to co-ordinate community health care in the 1930s; or should a new, centrally financed and non-democratic system of health authorities be created? Similarly, should municipal ventures in gas and electricity be replaced by nationalised industries, with appointed boards and national control? The outcome was largely nationally financed and controlled services. Rather than extending municipal ownership as a way of increasing local financial resources, the utilities were transferred to national bodies. Policy debates within the party did not provide any easy answer to the vexed issue of the rates. In 1942, a party paper on the financial structure of local government argued for a new regional system of government, of sufficient size and financial resources to provide the same level of service at much the same cost throughout the country.[36] The aim

---

[32] *Labour Party Annual Conference, 1923*, pp. 242–3, 246–7, and *Labour Party: Report of the Twenty-Fifth Annual Conference* (London, 1925), pp. 271–5.

[33] *Labour Party Annual Conference, 1933*, pp. 215–16, 236.

[34] For example, see the debates in LCC, *Minutes of Proceedings, 1934 (1)*, 15–16 May 1934, p. 812; *1934 (2)*, 16 Oct. 1934, p. 378; *1936 (2)*, 14 July 1936, pp. 37–57; *1937 (1)*, 9 Feb. 1937, p. 65; *1938 (2)*, 26 July 1938, pp. 218–23; 15 Nov. 1938, pp. 388–91.

[35] See LPA, Home Policy Committee, Box I, minutes, Nov. 1937 to Sept. 1953, 18 Oct. 1938 and 21 Feb. 1939.

[36] LPA, RDR118/July 1942, Machinery of Local Government Sub-Committee, the financial structure of a reorganised system of local government: provision proposals.

was to ensure that rates were more or less even over the country – but the party's report on local finance of 1943 rejected rates as a regressive tax on a necessity of life, a situation made worse by the derating of agriculture and industry. 'Why do we support a method of raising money for local purposes in inverse ratio to ability to pay', wondered the report, 'whereas this principle has long been adopted when money is needed for national purposes?' The income tax was the fairest form of taxation – and the obvious solution was a local income tax.[37] In fact, it proved easier to shift the cost of social services from local to central government. Reform of local government finance was not high on the agenda of the Labour party.

By contrast with the endless discussion of the structure of central government taxation, remarkably little attention was paid to the form of local government after the Second World War. A narrow local rate on property survived, and to the extent that there was a debate on local taxation, it was connected with the highly contentious and divisive issue of land taxation which was linked with the ambition to improve regional and urban planning. In 1942, the Expert Committee on Compensation and Betterment, chaired by Lord Justice Uthwatt, dealt with two connected issues: the terms of compensation to be paid for compulsory purchase of land for public use; and the imposition of a betterment levy for those who gained from public action or expenditure. The committee's answer was radical and ambitious: all undeveloped land should be nationalised and owners compensated at the recent price for agricultural land. Until the land was needed for development, the owner could remain on the property. When the land was needed for development, the owner would be evicted and offered a further sum in compensation. The state would be the sole buyer, and would take the increment in the site value when it was sold or leased to a developer. Further, all property owners should pay a betterment levy of 75 per cent of any increase in the value of the site.

The proposal was not welcomed by Conservative members of the coalition; it was partially implemented by Labour in the Town and Country Planning Act, 1947. It nationalised the right to develop land, but did not give the state a monopoly of land purchases: private owners could still sell to private developers, with the state controlling the right to develop the site by the power of granting planning permission. Of course, many owners of land would lose any chance to make a profit from development; and others would gain from greatly increased values. In order to deal with this problem of equity, the act made two proposals: first, to pay

---

[37] LPA, RDR215/May 1943, Labour party, Machinery of Local Government Sub-Committee, rates.

compensation for the loss of development rights; and secondly, to impose a 'development charge' of 100 per cent of the increase in site value. The system was immensely complex – and deeply impracticable. The payment of £300m of compensation was due in 1954; in 1953, the Conservative government decided to abolish it. The development charge prevented the land market from functioning, and was also abolished. Hence a landowner who secured planning permission now received a large speculative profit, and the state did not remove the 'unearned increment' it created. On the other hand, if land was compulsorily purchased for a new road or school, the owner only received the existing use value rather than the development value of the site. The grievance was removed in 1959, when the full market value was paid.[38]

Labour's approach to the land question therefore came to little, and did not resolve the problem of local government finance. After the Second World War, the Labour government merely adjusted the block grant system in 1948, when it introduced an 'Exchequer equalisation grant' which ensured that all local authorities were provided with resources equivalent to the national average rateable value per head of population, adjusted according to the population profile of the area. The aim was to ensure a much greater equality of resources across the country, and it worked reasonably well until the late 1950s. In 1958, the Conservatives again modified the scheme with the introduction of a 'rate deficiency grant', and the replacement of remaining percentage grants with a general grant based on per capita needs. Unfortunately for the government, Conservative areas lost out, especially when rateable values were reassessed in 1963. Indeed, the periodic national revaluation of rateable values became a point of potential conflict.[39]

Keith Joseph promised to relieve domestic ratepayers, and shortly before the Conservatives lost power he appointed a committee to consider the impact of rates, and to advise on possible alternatives such as taxes on site values, payrolls, sales, fuel or a poll tax. Not surprisingly, the committee found that rates were regressive and inequitable. The incidence of rates rose from 2 per cent on high incomes to 8 per cent on low incomes;

[38] PP 1941–2 IV, *Final Report of the Expert Committee on Compensation and Betterment*; for the Uthwatt report and the 1947 act, see P. Hall, *Urban and Regional Planning* (Harmondsworth, 1974), pp. 100–3, 114–17.

[39] For the details of these schemes, see J. H. Warren, *The English Local Government System* (6th edn, London, 1961); A. McConnell, 'The recurring crisis of local taxation in post-war Britain', *Contemporary British History* 11, no. 3 (1997), 43–6; T. Travers, *The Politics of Local Government Finance* (London, 1986), pp. 5–6, 10–13. The regressive impact of the rates was shown in PP 1964–5 XXII, *Committee of Enquiry into the Impact of Rates on Households*. See also S. J. Bailey and R. Paddison (eds.), *The Reform of Local Government Finance in Britain* (London, 1988); A. McConnell, *State Policy Formation and the Origins of the Poll Tax* (Aldershot, 1995).

and it was also a greater burden on one and two person households. The committee did not offer any immediate solution when it reported to the new Labour government. A poll tax on members of the household who did not pay rates was rejected as crude, regressive and difficult to collect; a tax on consumption of gas and electricity was also regressive and hit industry; a local duty on vehicles would entail a loss of revenue for the Exchequer and complicate regional policy. Three possibilities were left: a local sales, income or payroll tax. All had serious problems. How could a local income tax be collected by place of residence rather than employment? How could a sales tax with local variations operate when shoppers would simply drive to the districts with the lowest level? A payroll tax would increase costs, confuse regional policy and apply to places of work rather than residence. Indeed, D. J. S. Hancock was reluctant to give *any* new tax to the local authorities. As he pointed out, there were very few good taxes, and it was a waste to give them to the localities to use or not as they wished. Was there any point in giving local authorities more taxing powers in a small country such as Britain, which would merely restrict the government's own tax policy? In other words, rates should remain the only local tax, and any reform should simply focus on the method of distributing grants from the centre.[40]

In 1966, the Labour government announced that 'there is an urgent need to bring relief to those who are already hard-pressed and to prevent rates continuing to grow at a rate which will make them a burden to an increasing section of the community'. The government's policy was to shift the burden from rates to general taxation, an ambition supported within Whitehall. At the same time, the land question reappeared with the Land Commission Act, 1967. The ambition of some members of the government was to implement the Uthwatt proposals in full, by setting up a Land Commission to buy all land needed for development. In the event, a more modest proposal was implemented: the commission would gradually build up a 'land bank' for development; and a betterment levy of 45 to 50 per cent would be paid by the seller when the gain was realised. The aim was to give the owner some incentive to develop land, which was completely removed in 1947, while taking some betterment for the community. Once again, the scheme came to an end with its repeal in 1970.[41]

---

[40] PRO, T230/389, review of central and local government finance and of the rating system; tax aspects; T320/390, TWP(65)1 (final), Treasury examination of local government finance: report of working party on local taxation, 1 Jan. 1965; D. J. S. Hancock, 15 Jan. 1965; T320/462, PSI committee, local government taxation, report, 8 Apr. 1965; local government finance, Apr. 1965.

[41] For details, see Hall, *Urban and Regional Planning*, p. 118; for the scepticism of Crossman, see *Diaries of a Cabinet Minister*, vol. I, pp. 78, 101–2, 239, 260.

Although Richard Crossman,* the minister of housing and local government, was sceptical about the Land Commission and the new ministry of land and natural resources, he was no more successful in his plans of reform of local government finance. He abandoned his initial idea of a more progressive local income tax, and in 1966 turned instead to rate rebates to reduce the burden on the poorer ratepayers, largely funded from central taxation. This was seen as a preliminary step towards a larger scheme of rate reform linked with a restructuring of the existing system of central government grants. The 'tortuous administrative monstrosities' of the rate deficiency grants and the general needs grants were combined into a single rate-support grant.[42]

The solution was admittedly a stop gap, and the Labour government appointed a Royal Commission on Local Government. It reported in 1969, and seemed to offer an opportunity to break through the constraints on both Conservative and Labour governments. The commission argued for a reduction in the number of units of local government, and the Heath administration reduced them to a third of their previous level. The report then argued that these large, effective authorities should have their own resources to become 'self-governing institutions'. As the Royal Commission remarked, all the 'productive, progressive and elastic taxes' went to the central government, leaving local government only with the rates so that British local authorities were among the least autonomous in Europe. The report argued that if local self-government were desirable, an adequate local taxation system should be provided. However, local finance was not within the terms of reference of the commission, and the consideration of the issue was simply overwhelmed by the more pressing problems of the oil crisis. In reality, it was easier to make more grants from central taxation with a consequent demand by the Treasury for greater control. The outcome was unfortunate: the structure of local government was fundamentally changed with the creation of new, and

---

[42] PP 1965–6 XIII, *Local Government Finance, England and Wales*, p. 4; Crossman, *Diaries of a Cabinet Minister*, vol. I, pp. 72, 76, 303, 327–8, 349, 402, 419, 620; Travers, *Politics of Local Government Finance*, chapter 3; PP 1968–9 XXXVIII, *Royal Commission on Local Government in England, Volume I: Report and Maps*.

* Richard Howard Stafford Crossman (1907–74) was educated at Winchester and New College, Oxford, where he taught philosophy and developed the proposition that democracy was fraudulent while the ordinary citizen was deluded by authority. He was concerned to show how decisions were made in the name of the electorate. He left Oxford University for the Workers' Educational Association and the *New Statesman*, and was Labour leader of the Oxford City Council 1936–40. He was a Labour MP from 1945 to his death; in 1964, he became minister of housing and local government, in 1966 leader of the Commons and in 1968 secretary of state at the new Department of Health and Social Security. In 1970, he returned to the *New Statesman* as editor, but was removed within two years; he then edited his diaries. (Robbins (ed.), *Biographical Dictionary*, pp. 112–14.)

largely unloved, authorities, without reforming their finances. Although the Conservative manifesto for 1974 promised to abolish domestic rates and 'replace it by taxes more broadly based and related to people's ability to pay', no precise proposal was forthcoming.[43]

When Labour won the election in 1974, the immediate response was to increase government grants to cover inflationary pressures on local authorities. The government also appointed a further committee to propose a long-term solution, which recommended that the government should make a clear decision whether responsibility should be placed on the centre or the localities. As the committee pointed out, the government 'must be accountable to the electorate at large through Parliament for the amount of taxes it raises. It cannot provide local authorities with a preponderant share of their income . . . without sooner or later taking responsibility for their expenditure.' The majority report argued that a 'vital local democracy' required an increase in the role of local taxation, and specifically a local income tax. The government took a more cautious line, rejecting both centralist and local approaches and arguing for the *status quo*. Abolition of the rates was opposed, on the grounds that a transfer to national taxes would erode local democracy; no thought was given to a new form of local taxation which might *sustain* local democracy. Of course, the government was more concerned with the need to restrict expenditure as a result of the International Monetary Fund crisis of 1976.[44]

These schemes were extremely technical and made little impact outside the finance offices of local authorities. Local taxation was not an issue for most people. The limited local tax base was masked and the regressive nature of rates moderated, so that most people were not sensitive to the level of rates. In the mid-1970s, rates were only a little over 2 per cent of personal disposable income, and most voters were unconcerned. Nevertheless, the system was riddled with problems which were exposed in the 1980s. The lack of a buoyant local tax meant that more funds came from the centre – with a greater desire for control over the 'extravagance' of the localities. In the 1980s, the Thatcher administration aimed to reduce public expenditure, especially by local authorities that were still in many cases Labour (or even Militant) controlled. In 1980, block grants were swept away and replaced by expenditure targets for each local authority; more emphasis was placed on the unit cost of providing a service than on

---

[43] PP 1968–9 xxxviii, *Royal Commission on Local Government*, p. 173; PP 1969–70 xviii, *Reform of Local Government in England*; PP 1970–1 xxxii, *The Future Shape of Local Government Finance*; Butler, Adonis and Travers, *Failure*, pp. 19–22; McConnell, 'Recurring crisis', 47–9; Travers, *Politics of Local Government Finance*, chapter 4.

[44] McConnell, 'Recurring crisis', 49–50; PP 1975–6 xxi, *Report of the Committee of Enquiry into Local Government Finance*; Butler, Adonis and Travers, *Failure*, pp. 23–4.

formulae to calculate need. In 1982, the government took further powers to withhold grants when authorities exceeded their spending limits, and in 1984 'rate capping' was introduced. Not only was the government controlling the amount of central aid; it now removed the right of local authorities to set their own rates.[45]

Furthermore, local authorities were deprived of still more functions. Up to 1931, larger local authorities gained at the expense of smaller bodies as more responsible and efficient. Thereafter, functions were taken away from the localities, with the creation of the Unemployment Assistance Board in 1934, the transfer of main or 'trunk' roads to the ministry in 1936, the creation of the NHS in 1948, the nationalisation of local utilities and the transfer of water, sewerage, drainage to regional water authorities. Nevertheless, local authorities still had major functions in housing, education and personal social services in the 1950s and 1960s. These were challenged after 1979 with a drastic curtailment of council house building and the sale of existing stock to tenants. Councils obtained large sums of money from these sales, but could not spend them. The power of local authorities over schools was reduced, for they could now 'opt out' of local control and become 'fund holders'. The autonomy of local government declined still further.

The difficulties of local government finance arose in part from the timing of property valuation and the tensions it created. The periodic revaluation of property for rates was disrupted by the outbreak of war. In 1948, responsibility for revaluation was passed to the Inland Revenue and the details were finalised in 1956. However, the government feared the political consequences of a sudden increase from existing prewar valuations. It therefore decided, for understandable political reasons, to revalue domestic property at 1939 values, shops and offices at 80 per cent of their value in 1955 and industry at 50 per cent. The problem merely returned at the next valuation in 1963. Revaluation in England and Wales led to considerable political difficulties, for values were reduced in some areas and increased in others – particularly prosperous Conservative areas which did not benefit from the rate deficiency grant. The problem again came to a head with the delayed revaluation of 1974, at a time of growing local authority expenditure and the onset of rapid inflation. Ratepayers were increasingly sensitive to the level of rates and the lack of a connection with ability to pay – and in some cases to the perception that services were poorly run and inefficient. These tensions were tackled by increased central government grants and rebates rather than a controversial reform of local government finance, at a time when the

---

[45] G. C. Baugh, 'Government grants-in-aid of the rates in England and Wales, 1889–1990', *Historical Research* 65 (1992), 235–7; Butler, Adonis and Travers, *Failure*, pp. 22–45.

government had more pressing concerns of wage restraint and balance of payments crises. Despite the general realisation that local government needed reform, nothing was done.[46]

Initially, Mrs Thatcher's government took a similar line of inaction and announced in 1983 that there was no feasible alternative to the rates. The system finally crumbled in 1985. Property revaluation in Scotland coincided with a decline in manufacturing, rising house prices and a cut of 16 per cent in central government grants between 1980/1 and 1985/6. The result was an increase of domestic rate bills by 21 per cent in 1985, and a struggle between the Conservative government and Labour-controlled councils in Scotland over cuts in public spending. Consequently, there was a serious crisis in Scotland where the Conservative party was electorally weak and local finance was a convenient weapon for the opposition. Similar difficulties were likely to arise when revaluation was implemented in England and Wales. Already, the system of rate capping was under challenge by Labour-dominated councils, both in the courts and by refusing to set rates. Mrs Thatcher was fighting a battle on two fronts, against the miners and against the Labour bosses of the large metropolitan authorities, and the technicalities of local government finance took on a new moral fervour.[47] The local finance system was descending into chaos, and inaction now seemed indefensible. The case for change seemed compelling, and the solution was the community charge or poll tax – a flat tax on earning non-householders.

Schemes on the lines of the poll tax had been rejected on several occasions as regressive and difficult to administer, and the idea was again rejected by various party, government and parliamentary bodies in the early 1980s. Indeed, the White Paper of 1983 even recommended that rates should remain the major source of local finance for the 'foreseeable future'. However, the notion of a poll tax started to take on its own life within Conservative think-tanks.[48] The case for the poll tax should be understood as part of a desire to create responsible and prudent electors. The government wished to roll back the state and to isolate left-wing opponents, and this meant reforming or abolishing the rates which were now a tool used by local authorities against the centre and the government's attempts to manage the economy. Nevertheless, Mrs Thatcher was not simply a centraliser who wished to curtail local government. She wished to reform local government finance in order to recreate responsible and dependable local government, with cost-conscious electors. The problem, as she saw it, was that the majority of local electors did not pay local

---

[46] McConnell, 'Recurring crisis'.
[47] Butler, Adonis and Travers, *Failure*, pp. 41–6; McConnell, 'Recurring crisis', 50–4.
[48] Butler, Adonis and Travers, *Failure*, pp. 23, 25, 32–9.

taxes which were the responsibility of the head of household, and even they might have a rebate. As Kenneth Baker* pointed out, there were about 40 million electors in Britain, of whom 18 million received rate demands; about 4 million were granted rebates, so only 14 million actually paid local taxes. In inner city areas – usually controlled by Labour – even fewer electors paid local taxes, for the bulk of the rates were paid by businesses and perhaps half the households received rebates. The result was seen to be 'growing anarchy' with 'minimal incentive in many local authorities voluntarily to keep down spending or rates because someone else would pick up most of the tab'.[49] The analysis could descend into a somewhat paranoid fear of ideologues in the town halls, overlooking the real social problems of the inner city and the need for expenditure. It did suggest a solution: to make every elector a taxpayer, so that financial prudence would be reasserted, and local government could be freed of central control. In the words of Nicholas Ridley,[†] the new tax was 'a logical step towards greater local authority freedom: it should allow us to stand much further back from local government because the electors will stand much closer'.[50]

Although the case for the poll tax was strongly articulated, the potential shortcomings were simply ignored. Caution was abandoned, and the review took on its own momentum in an atmosphere of radical innovation and defiance of established views. The Cabinet did not really consider the issue. Although Cabinet committees were involved in the discussions, the pace was set by parallel, informal meetings dominated by a small group of enthusiasts. Ministers came and went, and the Treasury and chancellor were more concerned with the exchange rate than the technicalities of local government finance. Crucially, the Department of the Environment took a hostile view of local government. In the past, the department and

---

[49] Butler, Adonis and Travis, *Failure*, p. 52.

[50] Butler, Adonis and Travers, *Failure*, p. 266.

* Kenneth Wilfred Baker (b. 1934) was educated at St Paul's School and Magdalen College, Oxford. He was a Conservative MP from 1968 to 1997, serving as parliamentary private secretary to the leader of the opposition 1974–5; minister of state and for information technology at the Department of Trade and Industry 1981–4; minister for local government 1984–5; secretary of state for the environment 1985–6 and for education and science 1986–9; chancellor of the Duchy of Lancaster 1985–90; chairman of the Conservative party 1989–90 and Home Secretary 1990–2. (*Who's Who 2001*, p. 89.)

† Nicholas Ridley (1929–93) was educated at Eton and Balliol College, Oxford; he worked for civil engineering contractors, and served as a Conservative MP from 1959 to 1992. He was parliamentary private secretary to the minister of education 1962–4; parliamentary secretary to the minister of technology 1970; parliamentary under-secretary of state at the Department of Trade and Industry 1970–2; minister of state at the Foreign and Commonwealth Office 1979–81; financial secretary to the Treasury 1981–3; secretary of state for transport, 1983–6; secretary of state for the environment 1986–9; secretary of state for trade and industry, 1989–90. (*Who Was Who 1991–5*, vol. IX, pp. 467–8.)

its predecessors acted as the supporter of the local authorities against the desire of the Treasury to impose controls. In the 1980s, the Department of the Environment itself was alarmed by the actions of local authorities, and was eager to devise a fiscal system to reassert what it saw as responsibility. The advice of civil servants was poor, and there was a woeful ignorance of the system of local taxation in other countries. No other country in the Organisation for Economic Co-operation and Development had a flat-rate tax; all but four had a local property tax, and over half had a local income or profits tax. There was also a failure to consult local financial officers, in contrast to the care of the Treasury in consulting the Inland Revenue or Customs and Excise before any new tax was introduced. The Department of the Environment moved from the premise that the existing system of grants was not working to the conclusion that the poll tax was the solution. Parliamentary control was no more effective and had virtually no impact, whether in terms of backbench pressure, review by a Select Committee, or warning from the Lords. The Labour opposition in parliament was anxious to distance itself from the policies of the Militant local councils, and was therefore reluctant to make an issue of the poll tax. Although there was some opposition from Conservative MPs and from the chancellor of the Exchequer, the poll tax went ahead.[51]

The new tax came into effect in Scotland in 1989 and England and Wales in 1990.[52] It was to have a short and unhappy life, creating the most serious threat to Mrs Thatcher's government. The shortcomings of the tax soon became apparent. As far as the government was concerned, the poll tax was fairer. Why should widows on small pensions pay the same rates as a family with several wage-earners in an identical house? Undoubtedly, the widow did have a grievance – but it was easily resolved by rebates to low incomes. A flat-rate poll tax threw up another image of a hugely rich City banker in a massive house, paying the same local tax as a poorly paid manual worker in a small terraced house. The tax was regressive, and meant a considerable increase in the tax bills of lower-income families at a time of rising inequality and unemployment. It stood as a powerful symbol of other changes introduced by the government, such as the attack on trade unions and the challenge to public sector employees.

The poll tax was replaced by a new council tax that placed houses in bands according to their value; the local authority then set a charge for each band, with some account of the size of the household. The rates had finally disappeared, but it was not clear that local autonomy would

[51] Butler, Adonis and Travers, *Failure*.
[52] Butler, Adonis and Travers, *Failure, passim*; McConnell, 'Recurring crisis', 55–7.

reappear. The claim that the poll tax would release local government from central control was always treated with scepticism, given the government's record in imposing strict limits on spending, the abolition of the Greater London Council and the creation of non-elected agencies. Arguments about the need for a close link between paying taxes and voting were abandoned, and a new rhetoric was substituted: the local resident as the consumer of services. Accountability was best achieved by the use of audits and internal markets, by contracting out or privatising services, with standards set by citizens' charters and regulators. The demise of the poll tax meant a further drop in local autonomy with a still greater reliance on central grants, and the level of expenditure of every local authority set from Whitehall.

The problems with reform of local government finance exposed the same difficulties as the reform of central government finance in the 1960s and 1970s: the failure of the machinery of government to permit a rational, careful discussion of the fiscal system. Officials were highly competent in explaining what could *not* be done, defending the *status quo* and frustrating change. Their approach found faults with any new scheme, without considering in depth the shortcomings of the present system. The result might be frustration and the appearance of bold ideas from politicians that were not tested against the accumulated experience of civil servants. Indeed, even civil servants lost patience with the existing system and supported sweeping change. These proposals were considered in conditions of secrecy, so that parliament did not act as check – and in the case of the poll tax, Labour's leadership was anxious to distance itself from local councils in the hands of militants. As a result, a major change in the fiscal system was introduced with inadequate discussion; a bold and imaginative political measure was taken, without sufficient attention to the need for compliance which the revenue departments had stressed so much in the past. The introduction of the poll tax expresses, in extreme form, the wider failure of British government in reforming the fiscal system after the Second World War.

12   Conclusion

By 1979, there were few defenders of the British fiscal system as scientific, equitable and fair. On the contrary, it was widely seen as confused and even harmful. Economists were highly critical of the British tax system, complaining that its complexity, anomalies and loopholes imposed high compliance costs and distorted economic behaviour. New taxes were introduced and existing taxes modified for short-term reasons, without adequate discussion, and with sudden, incompatible changes. In 1978, John Kay and Mervyn King argued that the level of extraction had less impact on the economy than the 'muddle and complexity' of the tax system. In their opinion, taxes did not affect *aggregate* savings, but the *way* people saved was highly sensitive to the tax position of different forms of savings, and decisions might be guided by fiscal rather than economic efficiency. Indeed, Kay and King felt that the only rational response to the British tax system in the late 1970s was incredulity. 'No one would design such a system on purpose and nobody did. Only a historical explanation of how it came about can be offered as a justification. That is not a justification, but a demonstration of how seemingly individually rational decisions can have absurd effects in aggregate.'[1]

This book has provided a detailed historical explanation of how the British tax system came about, showing how individual decisions, each with a clear logic and rationale, produced confusion and growing dissatisfaction by 1979. As Kay and King argued, the British tax system was not designed as a system, and their ambition was to create coherence and order, to sweep away the confusion of the existing historical accumulation of measures and policies. A historian might be somewhat sceptical about their heroic proposals of reform and simplification. After all, other economists had proposed reform in the past, not least Nicholas Kaldor – and what might appear logical and consistent to one person might seem ideologically loaded to another. The important point is whether economic ideas and knowledge penetrate the machinery of government – as

[1] Kay and King, *British Tax System*, pp. 1, 238–41, 246.

Kaldor's did, in part, through his role as the adviser to James Callaghan. The proposals of Kay and King were associated with the Institute for Fiscal Studies, and had most political purchase with the Liberals and Social Democratic party. The prospect of any immediate political success was therefore remote – and Mrs Thatcher's election victory in 1979 meant that reform of the fiscal system moved in a different direction. At this point, economic ideas were more likely to come from the Institute of Economic Affairs than the Institute for Fiscal Studies, whose influence was felt in the longer term as a highly regarded academic research unit.

It is one thing to have ideas and knowledge; it is another thing to insert them into policy debates. The approach adopted in this book rests on the belief that both ideas and material interests must be located in the institutional context of policy-making. Different state structures and institutions are more or less accessible to new knowledge and ideas, with a greater or lesser degree of diversity and continuity in official opinion. In Britain, the powerful ethos of the Treasury and the administrative continuity of the civil service recruited from the elite universities meant that there was resistance to change, a defence of the *status quo* against politicians and economists who proposed reform, and a stress on discretion or secrecy. Much of the official tradition was created in the later nineteenth century, when it solidified into the Gladstonian orthodoxy analysed in *Trusting Leviathan*. This official position was more homogeneous than in the United States, where many civil servants changed with the administration and the institutional structure was more fragmented, with competing centres of power between different branches of government and within the executive.[2]

The massive authority of official traditions did not simply create hostility to change and impose a dead-weight on reform. A simple stress on confusion misses the point that the Treasury and the revenue boards developed a positive, articulate culture of compliance and equity which was most apparent in the restabilisation of taxation after the First World War. The Treasury and revenue departments were very concerned that the fiscal system should not be used in the interests of one class or group against another, in a way that would threaten consent and trust in the state. At the end of the war, with an immense burden of debt and conflict over the best way of escaping from the costs of debt service, the concern for balance and fairness was crucial in restabilising British society and

---

[2] Furner and Supple, 'Ideas, institutions and state', pp. 7, 35; M. Weir, 'Ideas and the politics of bounded innovation', in S. Steinmo, K. Thelen and F. Longstreth (eds.), *Structuring Politics: Historical Institutionalism in Comparative Analysis* (Cambridge, 1992), pp. 188–216; see also M. J. Smith, *Pressure, Power and Policy: State Autonomy and Policy Networks in Britain and the United States* (Hemel Hempstead, 1993), pp. 6–11.

politics. The state should not be seen as the prisoner of any particular interest, whether of the City of London concerned for financial stability, of industrialists anxious about their competitive position, of Labour and unions pressing for a capital levy or of income taxpayers demanding an end to 'waste'. Officials had their own highly developed commitment to the financial standing of the state in the money markets and its relations with the taxpaying public. As a result, the credit of the British state survived and relations with the taxpaying public were re-established with greater success than in most other countries.

Priority was given to compliance and balance – to the need to ensure that taxpayers paid with a minimum of resentment, and that taxes were not seen as offering selfish advantages to one group over another. Officials were less concerned about certain other features of the tax system at the end of the First World War. The prime concern of officials was with the use of taxes to extract revenue for the state rather than to shape the economy and society, or the desire to stimulate growth or create justice. Of course, politicians *did* wish to use the tax system in pursuit of different normative assumptions about the desirable shape of society, as well as with an eye to more immediate electoral advantage. On the whole, officials condoned the politicians' programmes, always provided that they did not threaten the apparent equity of the fiscal system and did not undermine consent. Indeed, the political programmes might even sustain consent and protect the revenue by adjusting the tax system to changing electoral and political circumstances. Thus general tax breaks to family men were accepted by the Treasury and Inland Revenue; any scheme which offered more specific tax breaks and loopholes was firmly opposed as a threat to the revenue and to the fairness of the fiscal regime.

In defending their assumptions, the Treasury and revenue boards were much less concerned about the impact of taxes on the rest of the economy, with the exception of the financial system on which the state depended for loans. At the end of the First World War, the Treasury was much more alarmed about the threat posed by the floating debt to financial stability than the potential impact of high levels of taxation on industrial competitiveness. Here some historians would claim that the Treasury and economic policy were dominated by the City of London over the Treasury.[3] However, the situation was considerably more complex. The Treasury had a shrewd awareness of the dangers of the floating debt to monetary stability, and hence to the 'real' economy. Industry, on their account, had more to fear from financial chaos than from higher taxes needed to service the debt and convert 'floating' short-term into

---

[3] For example, Cain and Hopkins, *British Imperialism*.

long-term debt. Their argument was not simply special pleading in favour of the City, for the Bank of England and leading bankers wanted *higher* taxation to pay off the debt – an approach rejected by politicians and officials with a clearer sense of the political constraints on their action. Politicians and officials had their own reasons for seeking financial stability, quite apart from the specific interests of the City; and Churchill was very anxious to remove the impression that policies were biased towards the City. The concern for the stability of the state and the financial system meant that the complaints of industry over the definition of profit and income, capital and depreciation, were largely ignored at the end of the war, when the Treasury argued that only industry had the ability to bear taxation. Nevertheless, taxation of profits was abolished in 1924 and the burden of rates was reduced in 1929.

What does stand out between the wars is the lack of a conscious attempt to use the tax system to encourage growth or to manage the economy. Debates over the fiscal system were more concerned with issues of equality and justice, focussing on normative assumptions about the social purposes of the economy, and in particular the role of the market and competition, and the distribution of income and wealth. These debates were not explicitly or primarily about securing an immediate increase in the rate of economic growth; rather, the concern was with a broader definition of the underlying moral and social purposes of the economy. Of course, these normative assumptions about the desirable form of economic life did also have implications for the nature and motivation of growth, why it took place and for what ends. Churchill's budget of 1925 and Baldwin's rhetoric reflected their desire to preserve a dynamic free market economy, based on incentives to middle-class families – an approach which rested on offering welfare benefits as a safety net, and removing the worst excesses of large, accumulated fortunes. They sought a wide diffusion of property within a capitalist economy, from which all could benefit.

By contrast, Labour politicians and economists argued that large fortunes and incomes had a large 'social' element of Rent that could be taken by the state without harming the economy. Indeed, a more egalitarian society would remove the horrors of poverty and social injustice – and would lead to growth by increasing domestic consumption. There was less agreement within the Labour party about the role of the market and incentives in the operation of the economy. Were 'active' profits morally justifiable or economically desirable? Should the market be replaced by planning and nationalisation, or would equality create a fairer society of discriminating consumers and craft producers? On the whole, Labour was suspicious of the capital market as the source of socially created wealth, and after the Second World War moved towards retentions of profits within large firms as its preferred policy. Growth would not come from individual incentives, with high incomes and profits encouraging enterprise and initiative. Rather, a high level of equality would create a strong market and foster a sense of organic solidarity. The external capital market was rejected as a source of speculation and waste; retained profits were in the hands of efficient managers and technicians concerned for long-term growth. By the end of the Labour government of 1945–51, some leading officials – and even some Labour advisers – were concerned about the consequences of such an approach for flexibility and dynamism.

The limitations of the Treasury's and revenue boards' perception of the tax system became more apparent from the 1950s. Their approach created a high level of legitimacy and trust in the state in the second half of the nineteenth century and into the twentieth century, and helped to negotiate the crises of the First World War and postwar stabilisation. At some point, there was a danger that stability could be at the cost of economic efficiency, and could lead to stasis. The fiscal system was part of a wider set of institutional rigidities dating from the later nineteenth century that locked the economy into an equilibrium of low effort and low productivity. Profits were kept down so that wages demands were modest. At the same time, firms were sheltered from competition by protection and import controls.[4] This outcome rested on an institutional structure dating to the second half of the nineteenth century. Trade unions were widely accepted, incorporated into the institutional structure of wage-bargaining with the creation of boards of conciliation in the later nineteenth century, and given considerable power both on the shop-floor and through the absence of legal constraint on their power to strike in the Trade Disputes Act of 1906. Acceptance was allied with an adversarial attitude by unions and the Labour party that profits were at the expense of labour, in a zero-sum game. There was a widespread assumption that working with unions created order and efficiency in industry, and that unions created a responsible, respectable workforce. Despite concern in some industries, such as engineering, that the result might be to prevent the adoption of new, high-productivity machinery, the system of labour relations proved difficult to challenge. It was widely accepted by public opinion and by politicians aware of the power of organised labour. The Labour party was funded by the unions – and the Conservatives were reluctant to support an outright attack on their power which would simply confirm the worst

[4] See Broadberry and Crafts, 'British economic policy'; Crafts, 'Economic growth' N. F. R. Crafts, 'Institutions and economic growth: recent British experience in an international context', *West European Politics* 15 (1992), 16–38. On import controls, see A. S. Milward and G. Brennan, *Britain's Place in the World: An Historical Inquiry into Import Controls, 1945–1960* (London, 1996).

assumptions of their opponents. Even after the general strike, Baldwin was concerned that the government should not seriously challenge the existing pattern of labour relations; and during the Second World War unions were an important part of the management of the war economy. Obviously, the postwar Labour government continued to be aware of the power of unions, not simply because of their close institutional links but also because of the need to secure wage restraint. The result was not so much corporatism, with the economy run by the government and various organised interests. Rather, the government tried to secure the acceptance of both sides of industry to a deal to control inflation: unions would restrain wages, if profits were controlled. Arguably, the result benefited neither side and harmed the performance of the economy. Hard decisions were avoided. The deal operated with acceptable results so long as the British market was insulated from both foreign and domestic competition. Until the late 1950s, there was a low level of internal competition, with many prices controlled by the government, by cartels and by retail price maintenance. At the same time, import controls and protection kept out cheaper (and often higher-quality) foreign goods. As a result, the low-effort–low-productivity system offered reasonable profits and wages, at the expense of lower growth than in other major industrial economies.[5] Politicians in the 1950s and 1960s continued to operate within the institutional framework created in the late nineteenth century, and the fiscal system was constrained. Was it safe to offer incentives to higher incomes and profits if the result were simply to inspire demands for higher wages, which would outstrip productivity growth? Labour politicians were ideologically hostile to such a solution, and Conservative politicians were constrained by the institutional system – and might even accept its virtues. A fundamental change of fiscal policy would depend upon a much wider shift in assumptions to break out of the low-effort equilibrium: an attack on the power of the unions, the creation of a more competitive environment both in the private and public sector with privatisation and the creation of internal markets.

There was a growing realisation by 1960 that the British economy faced serious difficulties and needed to undergo a process of 'modernisation'. There was no single consensual view of what policies should be pursued – and the machinery of government was not well equipped to formulating a clear view of the fiscal policies needed to deal with the problems of the British economy, or making a thorough assessment of the overall impact of taxation on the economy. The view now emerging among historians

[5] See, for example, W. Lazonick, *Competitive Advantage on the Shop Floor* (Cambridge, Mass., 1990), and E. H. Phelps Brown, *The Origins of Trade Union Power* (Oxford, 1983).

of the British state in the 1950s and 1960s is that the process of policy formation was extremely complex, with a lack of co-ordination and cohesion. Individual departments were often inflexible in their adherence to existing practices and assumptions, even when the context had changed. The concerns of the revenue boards for administrative convenience and ease of collection, their hostility to proposals for fiscal reform in pursuit of economic growth rather than revenue, tended to block more substantial change, leading to tinkering which avoided major questions of the overall shape of the fiscal system. Part of the problem was the nature of expertise within the revenue boards, and the endemic secrecy of the civil service. Rather than offering protection from self-interest and a guarantee of discretion, it was now becoming a curse of limited knowledge and lack of context.[6] The revenue departments and Treasury failed to move from a concern for balance, equity and compliance to a wider approach. Officials had an extremely detailed grasp of procedure and could show the impracticability of proposals; they were less competent at assessing the economic impact of the existing tax system or of proposals for reform. At most, they concentrated on the economic impact of individual taxes, and lacked the technical skills to consider the tax system as a whole. Although the Board of Trade argued for a wider sales tax, on the grounds that it would be less disruptive to the economy, officials from Customs and Excise opposed radical change to the purchase tax on grounds of administrative convenience. Debates within the Budget Committee concentrated on the immediate needs of the next budget at the expense of the longer-term shape of the tax system – and when major changes were considered, they usually fell back on administrative detail. The few officials who did attempt to develop a systematic and coherent policy of reform of the tax system were themselves the victims of bureaucratic obstructions as much as their ministerial masters. The state was not a single monolithic body, and it was not in the grip of one interest group. Rather, it was fragmented and its relations with the rest of society depended on a preference for neutrality and what has been called a 'centreless society'. The aim of officials was to work with the existing structures in order to preserve the legitimacy of the state.[7]

---

[6] For a discussion of secrecy in government, see D. Vincent, *The Culture of Secrecy: Britain, 1832–1998* (Oxford, 1998), and Daunton, *Trusting Leviathan*, p. 382.

[7] See for example, P. Brigden, 'The state, redundancy pay, and economic policy making in the early 1960s', *Twentieth Century British History* 11 (2000), 256–8; R. Lowe and N. Rollings, 'Modernising Britain: a classic case of centralisation and fragmentation', in R. Rhodes (ed.), *Transforming British Government*, vol. I: *Changing Institutions* (Basingstoke, 2000), pp. 99–118; and Ringe and Rollings, 'Responding to relative decline'.

Although official fear of politicians' short-sighted reactions to immediate pressures was often justified, the result of their narrow, technical
advice was simply to make policy more incoherent when ministers side-
stepped officials in order to follow their own nostrums. By the early 1960s,
the emergence of competition within Britain and from overseas started
to threaten the existing low-effort, low-productivity bargain and its institutional basis. Some Conservative politicians, officials and economists
wished to encourage competition as a shock to break out of the existing
pattern of low growth; what they did not anticipate was the scale of the
shock and the inadequacy of the response by industry. The tax system
now became a central element in debates over growth – and it may be
argued that confusion was confounded in the 1960s and 1970s, as a result
of mutually inconsistent reforms designed to resolve the problems both
of the tax system and the British economy as a whole. The failure of the
Conservative government to introduce major structural reforms to the
tax system by 1964, and the weaknesses in the machinery of government
in taking a more active role in reform, meant that the Labour government introduced radical changes in 1965. In the 1950s, there had been a
somewhat spurious sense of consensus as a result of inertia; in the 1960s
and 1970s, both Labour and Conservative politicians were thinking along
similar lines about the need for a wider sales tax and a tax on wealth or
payrolls. However, any chance of an agreed programme was lost, for officials did not create a technical, neutral or balanced case for reform. On
the whole, they were negative and ill-informed about the economic consequences of the existing system. The result was that politicians tended
to act in the absence of official advice, shaping their policies in opposition
with little official advice or consultation. The machinery of government
failed to produce coherence and co-ordination which was critically important in the case of taxation where technical expertise and consistency
over time are crucial. Instead, politicians drew ideas from outside the official world, and a chancellor could then push through his proposals with
minimal scrutiny by other ministers or by the Commons. Policy in the
1960s and 1970s started to lurch from one approach to another, without resolving fundamental issues such as the 'poverty surcharge' or the
relationship between taxes and benefits. The result of the inconsistency
of policies, and the neglect of serious problems, was a growing threat to
the legitimacy of taxation precisely in the way the Treasury feared after
the First World War.

Of course, there were wider international difficulties in the 1970s with
the oil crisis and recession, but Britain faced its own particular problems. Although internal and international competition was now at a

much higher level than in the previous quarter of a century, many other elements of the low-effort equilibrium remained in place. The failure of the Labour government to implement reform in labour relations in the late 1960s threatened to leave the unions to the less tender ministrations of the Conservatives. For all his ambitions of tackling union power, Edward Heath faced defeat at the hand of the miners in 1974, and it was left to the Thatcher administration to make major reforms in trade union law. After the International Monetary Fund crisis of 1976, control of inflation started to shift from reliance on an incomes policy to monetarism and to the previously unspeakable thought that unemployment was an acceptable way of limiting wage-push inflation. The institutional patterns of the previous century were fractured in an attempt to escape from the low-effort, low-productivity bargain, with high social and economic costs in terms of lost jobs. Meanwhile, the fiscal system was reformed to offer incentives to high income-earners and for savings, without countervailing welfare benefits for low incomes which had been proposed in the 1960s.

Perceptions of the tax system changed not only as a result of concerns over economic growth, but also as a reaction to shifts in the social and electoral structures. At the beginning of the period, many voters did not pay income tax, for the income of the median voter was below the tax threshold. Labour could easily appeal to progressive taxation of income or profits in order to redistribute income and wealth; the task of the Conservatives was to contain this challenge as far as possible. Indeed, it is not clear that it could contain the challenge, and some of its success was in devising a strategy which allowed progressive taxation without alienating its core supporters among modest middle-class family men. Indeed, many of these middle-class electors supported public spending after the Second World War as desirable, offering them better education and health than was previously available from the private market between the wars. By the 1970s, the situation was changing. The decline of employment in traditional heavy industries, the growth of more service and white-collar employment, and the emergence of a more affluent consumer society, meant that attitudes started to change. Public consumption started to appear inefficient and expensive, and many more prosperous voters wished to have more discretion over their patterns of consumption. Meanwhile, the increase of wages and salaries, and a more equal distribution of income, meant that more voters moved into the payment of income tax. The median voter was now likely to pay income tax – and at a high marginal rate. The politics of taxation started to change, and Labour's appeal to progressive taxation of income and profits was much less appealing than in the past.

The fundamental question posed by John Rawls in his theory of justice in 1972 was the extent to which the pursuit of social justice and equality may be at the expense of incentive and growth.[8] In his view, we need to ask whether the attempt to create a just society harms incentives to such an extent that the poorest members of society are worse off. Arguably, the fiscal policies pursued after the Second World War did have this effect, when the encouragement of retentions and hostility to distributions, whether from ideological animosity or the practical need to impose wage restraint, sustained the low-effort equilibrium. The question was how to escape. The tax package devised by the Conservatives in opposition between 1964 and 1970 offered one solution, a combination of incentives and social inclusion in an opportunity state. The opportunity was missed. Labour's policy was somewhat ambivalent, with a fear of private profit and higher incomes. The proposal of some senior Labour politicians and advisers to create a free market based on justice and equality with a wide diffusion of wealth, was not pursued. By 1979, mounting hostility to the 'abuses' of the unions, the sense of crisis in the public sector, and the weakness of Britain's international economic situation, created the way for a shift towards growth and personal incentives. Defenders of the shift in policy argue that the pursuit of individual self-interest has benefited everyone in increasing growth. Critics fear that the pursuit of growth has been at the expense of social justice and inclusion, but their views have not been popular with the electorate. It remains to be seen if the balance between growth and justice, between incentives and equality, will shift again in the future. Will tax harmonisation within the European Union lead to a fundamental change in the fiscal system, and change the institutional processes for shaping policy? The task of creating a just system of taxation continues to be at the heart of politics.

[8] J. Rawls, *A Theory of Justice* (Oxford, 1972).

Appendix: chancellors of the Exchequer and prime ministers, 1908–1983

	Chancellor		Prime minister
Liberal			
16 Apr. 1908	David Lloyd George	7 Apr. 1908	Herbert Asquith
27 May 1915	Reginald McKenna		
Coalition			
11 Dec. 1916	Andrew Bonar Law	7 Dec. 1916	David Lloyd George
14 Jan. 1919	Austen Chamberlain		
5 Apr. 1921	Robert Horne		
Conservative			
25 Oct. 1922	Stanley Baldwin	23 Oct. 1922	Andrew Bonar Law
11 Oct. 1923	Neville Chamberlain	23 May 1923	Stanley Baldwin
Labour			
23 Jan. 1924	Philip Snowden	22 Jan. 1924	Ramsay MacDonald
Conservative			
7 Nov. 1924	Winston Churchill	4 Nov. 1924	Stanley Baldwin
Labour			
8 June 1929	Philip Snowden	5 June 1929	Ramsay MacDonald
National/coalition			
9 Nov. 1931	Neville Chamberlain		
		7 June 1935	Stanley Baldwin

28 May 1937	John Simon	28 May 1937	Neville Chamberlain
13 May 1940	Kingsley Wood	10 May 1940	Winston Churchill
28 Sept. 1943	John Anderson		

Labour

28 July 1945	Hugh Dalton	26 July 1945	Clement Attlee
17 Nov. 1947	Stafford Cripps		
25 Oct. 1950	Hugh Gaitskell		

Conservative

27 Oct. 1951	Richard Butler	26 Oct. 1951	Winston Churchill
		6 Apr. 1955	Anthony Eden
22 Dec. 1955	Harold Macmillan		
14 Jan. 1957	Peter Thorneycroft	10 Jan. 1957	Harold Macmillan
7 Jan. 1958	Derick Heathcoat Amory		
27 July 1960	Selwyn Lloyd		
13 July 1962	Reginald Maudling		
		16 Oct. 1963	Alec Douglas-Home

Labour

16 Oct. 1964	James Callaghan	16 Oct. 1964	Harold Wilson
30 Nov. 1967	Roy Jenkins		

Conservative

20 June 1970	Iain Macleod	19 June 1970	Edward Heath
25 July 1970	Anthony Barber		

Labour

5 Mar. 1974	Denis Healey	4 Mar. 1974	Harold Wilson
		5 Apr. 1976	James Callaghan

Conservative

5 May 1979	Geoffrey Howe	4 May 1979	Margaret Thatcher
11 June 1983	Nigel Lawson		

Bibliography

ARCHIVES

BIRMINGHAM UNIVERSITY LIBRARY

Austen Chamberlain Papers
Neville Chamberlain Papers

BODLEIAN LIBRARY, OXFORD

Conservative Party Archive

BRITISH LIBRARY OF ECONOMIC AND POLITICAL SCIENCE

Dalton Papers

CAMBRIDGE UNIVERSITY LIBRARY

Baldwin Papers

CHURCHILL COLLEGE ARCHIVES

McKenna Papers

HOUSE OF LORDS RECORD OFFICE

Bonar Law Papers
Lloyd George Papers

PEOPLE'S HISTORY MUSEUM, MANCHESTER

Labour Party Archive

MODERN RECORDS CENTRE, UNIVERSITY OF WARWICK

FBI Papers
TUC Papers

NUFFIELD COLLEGE, OXFORD

Fabian Society Papers

PUBLIC RECORD OFFICE, KEW

Boards of Stamps, Taxes, Excise, Stamps and Taxes, and Inland Revenue
  IR63 Board of Inland Revenue: Budget and Finance Bill Papers, 1869–1967
  IR64 Board of Inland Revenue: Statistics and Intelligence Division: Correspondence and Papers, 1858–1977
  IR74 Board of Inland Revenue: Private Office Papers: Memoranda, 1700–1967
  IR75 Board of Inland Revenue: Private Office Papers: Committee Papers, 1894–1972
  IR113 Board of Inland Revenue: Directors of Statistics: Budget Papers, 1919–34
Cabinet Office
  CAB23 War Cabinet and Cabinet: Minutes, 1916–39
  CAB24 War Cabinet and Cabinet: Memoranda, 1915–39
  CAB27 War Cabinet and Cabinet: Miscellaneous Committees, 1915–39
  CAB37 Cabinet Office: Cabinet Papers, 1880–1916
  CAB129 Cabinet Memoranda, 1945–70
Prime Minister's Office
  PREM11: Prime Minister's Office: Correspondence and Papers, 1951–64
Treasury
  T161 Supply Department: Registered Files, 1905–61
  T170 Papers of Sir John Bradbury, 1870–1922
  T171 Chancellor of the Exchequer's Office: Budget and Finance Bill Papers, 1859–1979
  T172 Chancellor of the Exchequer's Office: Miscellaneous Papers, 1792–1962
  T176 Papers of Sir Otto Niemeyer, 1906–30
  T227 Social Services Division: Registered Files, 1913–69
  T230 Cabinet Office, Economic Section and Treasury, Treasury Economic Advisory Section: Registered Files, 1939–70
  T320 Treasury: Public Income/Outlay Division: Registered Files, 1960–9

PARLIAMENTARY PAPERS

PP 1914 L, *Finance Accounts of the UK for 1913–14.*
PP 1919 XXIII pt I, *Royal Commission on Income Tax, First and Third Instalment of Minutes of Evidence.*
PP 1919 XXIII pt II, *Royal Commission on Income Tax, Fifth Instalment of Minutes of Evidence.*
PP 1919 XXXII, *Finance Accounts of the UK for 1918–19.*
PP 1920 VII, *Report from the Select Committee on Increases of Wealth (War).*
PP 1920 XVIII, *Report of the Royal Commission on the Income Tax.*
PP 1920 XIX, *Report from the Select Committee on Land Values.*
PP 1920 XXVII, *Finance Accounts of the UK for the year ended 31 March 1920.*
PP 1921 XIV, *64th Report of the Commissioners of Inland Revenue for the year ended 31 March 1921.*
PP 1927 XI, *Report of the Committee on National Debt and Taxation.*
PP 1929–30 XV, *72nd Report of the Commissioners of Inland Revenue for the year 1928/29.*

PP 1929–30 xviii, *Finance Accounts of the United Kingdom for the year ended 31 March 1929.*

PP 1938–9 xii, *82nd Report of the Commissioners of Inland Revenue for the year ended 31 March 1939.*

PP 1938–9 xvi, *Finance Accounts of the UK for the year ended 31 March 1939.*

PP 1941–2 iv, *Final Report of the Expert Committee on Compensation and Betterment.*

PP 1945–6 xv, *Finance Accounts of the UK for the year ended 31 March 1946.*

PP 1948–9 xvii, *91st Report of the Commissioners of Inland Revenue for the year ended 31 March 1948.*

PP 1950–1 xvi, *Report of the Commissioners of Inland Revenue.*

PP 1950–1 xx, *Report of the Committee on the Taxation of Trading Profits.*

PP 1950–1 xxi, *Finance Accounts of the UK for the Financial Year 1950–1.*

PP 1952–3 xvii, *Royal Commission on the Taxation of Profits and Income, First Report.*

PP 1953–4 xix, *Royal Commission on the Taxation of Profits and Income, Second Report.*

PP 1955–6 xxvii, *Royal Commission on the Taxation of Profits and Income, Final Report.*

PP 1962–3 xxvi, *Finance Accounts of the UK for the Financial Year 1962–3.*

PP 1963–4 xix, *Report of the Committee on Turnover Taxation.*

PP 1964–5 xxii, *Committee of Enquiry into the Impact of Rates on Households.*

PP 1965–6 xiii, *Local Government Finance, England and Wales.*

PP 1968–9 xxxviii, *Royal Commission on Local Government in England, Volume I: Report and Maps.*

PP 1969–70 xviii, *Reform of Local Government in England.*

PP 1970–1 xxxii, *The Future Shape of Local Government Finance.*

PP 1970–1 l, *Green Paper on Reform of Corporation Tax.*

PP 1970–1 l, *Report from the Select Committee on Corporation Tax.*

PP 1970–1 l, *113th Report of the Commissioners of Inland Revenue for the year 1969–70.*

PP 1974 xvii, *Green Paper on Wealth Tax.*

PP 1974–5 xxvi, *Report of the Commissioners of Inland Revenue for the year ended 31 March 1974.*

PP 1974–5 xxxvi, *Select Committee on a Wealth Tax, 1974/5, Vol. 1, Report and Proceedings of the Committee.*

PP 1975–6 xxi, *Report of the Committee of Enquiry into Local Government Finance.*

PP 1979–80 lxviii, *122nd Report of the Commissioners of Inland Revenue for the year ended 31 March 1979.*

OTHER OFFICIAL PAPERS

Appendices to the Report of the Committee on National Debt and Taxation (London, 1927).

Chancellor of the Exchequer and secretary of state for social services, *Proposals for a Tax Credit System* (London, 1972).

The EEC Reports on Tax Harmonisation: Report of the Fiscal and Financial Committee (Amsterdam, 1963).

Minutes of Evidence Taken Before the Committee on National Debt and Taxation (2 vols., London, 1927).
NEDC, *Conditions Favourable to Faster Growth* (London, 1963).

OTHER SERIALS

American National Biography.
Annual Conferences, Labour Party.
Dictionary of National Biography.
LCC, *Minutes of Proceedings.*
Parliamentary Debates.
Who's Who.
Who Was Who.

PRIMARY PRINTED SOURCES

Arnold, S., 'A capital levy: the problems of realisation and valuation', *Economic Journal* 28 (1918).
Atkinson, A. B., *Poverty in Britain and the Reform of Social Security* (Cambridge, 1969).
    Unequal Shares: Wealth in Britain (London, 1972).
Balogh, T., 'Differential profits tax', *Economic Journal* 68 (1958).
Barna, T., 'Those "frightfully high profits"', *Oxford Bulletin of Statistics* 11 (1949).
Bentham, J., *Constitutional Code for the Use of All Nations and All Governments Professing Liberal Opinions* (London, 1830).
Bower, F., 'Some reflections on the budget', *Lloyds Bank Review* n.s. 65 (1962).
Brailsford, H. N., Hobson, J. A., Creech Jones, A. and Wise, E. F., *The Living Wage* (ILP, London, 1926).
Bruce, D., 'A review of socialist financial policy, 1945–49', *Political Quarterly* 20 (1949).
Cairncross, A. (ed.), *The Robert Hall Diaries, 1947–1953* (London, 1989).
    The Robert Hall Diaries, 1954–1961 (London, 1991).
Caradog Jones, D., 'Prewar and postwar taxation', *Journal of the Royal Statistical Society* 90 (1927).
Carter, G. R. and Houghton, H. W., 'The income tax on wages by quarterly assessment', *Economic Journal* 28 (1918).
Chambers, S. P., 'Taxation and incentives', *Lloyds Bank Review* n.s. 8 (1948).
    'Taxation of the supply of capital for industry', *Lloyds Bank Review* n.s. 11 (1949).
Churchill, W. S., *Liberalism and the Social Problem* (London, 1909).
Clark, C., *A Socialist Budget* (London, 1935).
Conservative party, *The Campaign Guide 1959: The Unique Political Reference Book* (London, 1959).
    The Campaign Guide 1964: The Unique Political Reference Book (London, 1964).
Cox, H., *The Capital Levy: Its Real Purpose* (National Unionist Association, n.d.).
Crosland, C. A. R., *The Future of Socialism* (London, 1956).
    Socialism Now, and Other Essays (London, 1974).

Crossman, R., *Diaries of a Cabinet Minister*, vol. I: *Minister of Housing, 1964–66* (London, 1975).

Dalton, H., *Some Aspects of the Inequality of Incomes in Modern Communities* (London, 1920).

'The measurement of the inequality of incomes', *Economic Journal* 30 (1920).

Capital Levy Explained (London, 1923).

Principles of Public Finance (6th edn, London, 1930).

Practical Socialism for Britain (London, 1935).

Financing Labour's Plan (London, 1946).

'Our financial plan', in H. Morrison *et al.*, *Forward from Victory! Labour's Plan* (London, 1946).

Davenport, N., *Memoirs of a City Radical* (London, 1974).

Dilnot, A. W., Kay, J. A. and Morris, C. N., *The Reform of Social Security* (Oxford, 1984).

Due, J. F., 'Sales taxes in western Europe, II: the multiple-stage sales taxes', *National Tax Journal* 8 (1955).

'Net worth taxation', *Public Finance* 15 (1960).

Durbin, E. F. M., *How to Pay for the War: An Essay on the Financing of War* (London, 1939).

Problems of Economic Planning: Papers on Planning and Economics (London, 1949).

Edgeworth, F. Y., *Papers Relating to Political Economy*, vol. II (London, 1925).

Elkan, W., 'A public sector without bounds', in Institute of Economic Affairs, *The State of Taxation* (London, 1977).

Fabian Society, *Capital and Land* (Fabian Tract 7, London, 1888).

English Progress Towards Social Democracy (Fabian Tract 15, London, 1890).

The Unearned Increment (Fabian Tract 30, London, 1891).

The Difficulties of Individualism (Fabian Tract 69, London, 1896).

Socialism and Superior Brains (Fabian Tract 146, London, 1909).

Field, F., Meacher, M. and Pond, C., *To Him Who Hath: A Study of Poverty and Taxation* (Harmondsworth, 1977).

Flemming, J. S. and Little, I. M. D., *Why We Need a Wealth Tax* (London, 1974).

Galbraith, J. K., *The Affluent Society* (London, 1958).

The New Industrial State (London, 1967).

Gilbert, M., *Winston S. Churchill, Volume V, Companion Part I, Documents: The Exchequer Years, 1922–29* (London, 1980).

Greenwood, A., *The Tory Government's Higher Rates Scheme Exposed!* (London, 1929).

Grigg, P. J., *Prejudice and Judgment* (London, 1948).

Hall, R. L., *The Economic System in a Socialist State* (London, 1937).

Hayek, F. A., *Road to Serfdom* (London, 1944).

Healey, D., *The Time of My Life* (London, 1989).

Henderson, H. D., *Inheritance and Inequality: A Practical Proposal* (London, 1926).

[Henderson, H. D.], 'The limits of insular socialism', *The Nation* 46 (30 Nov. 1929).

Hicks, J. R., 'The empty economy', *Lloyds Bank Review* n.s. 5 (1947).

Hicks, U. K., *The Finance of British Government, 1920–36* (London, 1938).

Hirst, F. W., *The Political Economy of War* (London and Toronto, 1915).

Hobson, J. A., *Taxation* (London, Labour party, n.d.).
The Evolution of Modern Capitalism (London, 1894).
Imperialism: A Study (London, 1902).
The Economics of Distribution (London, 1906).
The Industrial System: An Enquiry into Earned and Unearned Income (London, 1909).
Taxation in the New State (London, 1919).
The Economics of Unemployment (London, 1922).
Hook, A., 'A tax on capital and redemption of debt', *Economic Journal* 28 (1918).
Horsman, E. G., 'The avoidance of death duty by gifts *inter vivos*: some qualitative evidence', *Economic Journal* 85 (1975).
Ilersic, A. R., 'Taxes, 1964–66: an interim appraisal', *British Tax Review* (1966).
Institute for Fiscal Studies, *The Structure and Reform of Direct Taxation: Report of a Committee Chaired by Professor J. E. Meade* (London, 1978).
Jay, D., *The Nation's Wealth at the Nation's Service* (London, 1938).
Paying for the War (London, Labour party, 1940).
Jenkins, R., 'The investment programme', *Socialist Commentary* 13 (1949).
Fair Shares for the Rich (Tribune pamphlet, London, 1951).
Jones, T., *Whitehall Diary*, vol. I: *1916–1925*, vol. II: *1926–1930*, ed. K. Middlemass (London, 1969).
Kaldor, N., *An Expenditure Tax* (London, 1955).
Indian Tax Reform: Report of a Survey (New Delhi, 1956).
'A positive policy for wages and dividends', in N. Kaldor, *Essays in Economic Policy*, vol. I (London, 1964).
Causes of the Slow Rate of Economic Growth of the United Kingdom: An Inaugural Lecture (Cambridge, 1966).
The Economic Consequences of Mrs Thatcher (London, 1983).
Kay, J. A. and King, M. A., *The British Tax System* (Oxford, 1978).
Kennan, K. K., *Income Taxation: Methods and Results in Various Countries* (Milwaukee, 1910).
Kennedy, C. M., 'Monetary policy', in G. D. N. Worswick and P. H. Ady (eds.), *The British Economy, 1945–1950* (London, 1952).
Keynes, J. M., 'The end of laissez-faire', reprinted in his *Essays in Persuasion* (London, 1931).
General Theory of Employment, Interest and Money (London, 1936).
How to Pay for the War (London, 1940).
The Collected Writings of John Maynard Keynes, vol. XVI: *Activities 1914–1919: The Treaty and Versailles*, ed. E. Johnson (London, 1971).
A Tract on Monetary Reform (London, 1923), in *Collected Writings of John Maynard Keynes*, vol. IV (London, 1971).
The Collected Writings of John Maynard Keynes, vol. XVII: *Activities, 1920–22: Treaty Revision and Reconstruction*, ed. E. Johnson (London, 1977).
The Collected Writings of John Maynard Keynes, vol. XXII: *Activities, 1939–45: Internal War Finance*, ed. D. Moggridge (London, 1978).
The Collected Writings of John Maynard Keynes, vol. XXVII: *Activities, 1940–46: Shaping the Post-War World: Employment and Commodities* (London, 1980).

Keynes, J. M. and Henderson, H. D., *Can Lloyd George Do It? An Examination of the Liberal Pledge* (London, 1929).

Knauss, R., *Die deutsche, englische und französische Kriegsfinanzierung* (Berlin and Leipzig, 1923).

Kolthammer, F. W., *Memorandum on Problems of Poverty No. 1: Some Notes on the Incidence of Taxation on the Working-Class Family* (Ratan Tata Foundation, London, 1913?).

Labour party, *Labour and the War Debt: A Statement of Policy for the Redemption of War Debt by a Levy on Accumulated Wealth* (London, n.d.).

Labour and the New Social Order (London, 1918).

National Joint Council of the General Council of the TUC, Executive Committee of the Labour Party and Parliamentary Labour Party, *Labour and National 'Economy'* (London, 1922).

Labour and the Nation: Statement of the Labour Policy and Programme (London, 1928).

Currency, Banking and Finance (London, 1932).

Labour Believes in Britain: A Statement of Policy for Discussion at the Labour Party Conference (London, 1949).

Your Personal Guide to the Future Labour Offers You (London, 1958).

Labour's Programme for Britain: Papers Presented at the Annual Conference (London, 1973).

Lawson, N., 'Taxation or government expenditure?', in Institute of Economic Affairs, *The State of Taxation* (London, 1977).

Lees, D., 'Poor families and fiscal reform', *Lloyds Bank Review* n.s. 86 (1967).

Lees-Smith, H. B., *The Surtax* (London, 1928).

Liberal party, *Britain's Industrial Future: Being the Report of the Liberal Industrial Inquiry* (London, 1928).

Little, I. M. D., 'Higgledy piggledy growth', *Bulletin of the Oxford Institute of Statistics* 24 (1962).

McKenna, R., *Post-War Banking Policy: A Series of Addresses* (London, 1928).

Mallet, B. O. and George, C. O., *British Budgets, Second Series, 1913/14 to 1920/1* (London, 1929).

Marshall, A., *Principles of Political Economy* (London, 1893).

Meade, J. E., *Planning and the Price Mechanism* (London, 1948).

Efficiency, Equality and the Ownership of Property (London, 1964).

The Intelligent Radical's Guide to Economic Policy (London, 1974).

Mill, J. S., *Principles of Political Economy* (London, 1948).

Millan, B., *Taxes for a Prosperous Society* (Fabian Research Series, London, 1963).

Mitchell, A. A., 'A levy on capital', *Economic Journal* 28 (1918).

Paish, F. W., 'The real incidence of personal taxation', *Lloyds Bank Review* n.s. 43 (1957).

Parker, H., *Instead of the Dole: An Enquiry into the Integration of the Tax and Benefit System* (London, 1989).

Peacock, A., 'Economics of a net wealth tax for Britain', *British Tax Review* (1963).

Pethick-Lawrence, F. W., *A Levy on Capital* (London, 1918).

The National Debt (London, 1924).

National Finance (Fabian Tract 229, London, 1929).

An Emergency Tax on Wealth (London, 1939).

Pigou, A. C., *Wealth and Welfare* (London, 1912).
'A special levy to discharge war debt', *Economic Journal* 28 (1918).
A Capital Levy and a Levy on War Wealth (London, 1920).
Pigou, A. C. (ed.), *Memorials of Alfred Marshall* (London, 1925).
Prest, A. R., 'A tax on expenditure?', *Lloyds Bank Review* n.s. 42 (1956).
'A value added tax coupled with a reduction in taxes on business profits', *British Tax Review* (1963).
'The negative income tax: concepts and problems', *British Tax Review* (1970).
'The Select Committee on a Wealth Tax', *British Tax Review* (1976).
'What is wrong with the UK tax system?', in Institute of Economic Affairs, *The State of Taxation* (London, 1977).
Reddaway, B., *First Report, on the Effects of Selective Employment Tax: The Distributive Trades* (London, 1970).
Revell, J. R. S., 'Assets and age', *Bulletin of the Oxford Institute of Statistics* 24 (1962).
Rhys Williams, J., *Something to Look Forward To: A Suggestion for a New Social Contract* (London, 1943).
Ricardo, D., *On the Principles of Political Economy and Taxation* (1817), ed. P. Sraffa (Cambridge, 1951).
Rickards, G. K., *The Financial Policy of War: Two Lectures on the Funding System and on the Different Modes of Raising Supplies* (London, 1855).
Rignano, E., *Di un socialismo in accordo colla dottrina economica liberale* (Turin, 1901).
Per una riforma socialista del dritto successario (Bologna, 1920).
The Social Significance of Death Duties, Adapted from Dr Shulz's Translation from the Italian by J. Stamp (London, 1925).
Robertson, D. H., 'The Colwyn Committee, the income tax and the price level', *Economic Journal* 37 (1927).
Ruskin, J., *Unto This Last* (London, 1860).
Samuel, H., 'The taxation of various classes of the people', *Journal of the Royal Statistical Society* 82 (1919).
Sandford, C. T., Willis, J. R. M. and Ironside, D. J., *An Accessions Tax* (London, 1973).
An Annual Wealth Tax (London, 1975).
Schumpeter, J., 'The crisis of the tax state', in A. Peacock, R. Turvey, W. F. Stolper and E. Henderson (eds.), *International Economic Papers*, vol. IV (London and New York, 1954).
Seers, D., 'Undistributed profits', *Socialist Commentary* 15 July 1951.
Self, R. C. (ed.), *The Austen Chamberlain Diary Letters: The Correspondence of Sir Austen Chamberlain with his Sisters Hilda and Ida, 1916–37* (Royal Historical Society, London: Camden 5th ser. 5, 1995).
Sherborne, S., *VAT: Fair for All* (Conservative Political Centre, London, 1972).
Shirras, G. F. and Rostas, L., *The Burden of British Taxation* (Cambridge, 1942).
Shoup, C. S., *The Sales Tax in France* (New York, 1930).
Sidgwick, H., *Principles of Political Economy* (2nd edn, London, 1887).
Snowden, P., *Wealth or Commonwealth: Labour's Financial Policy* (London, n.d.).
Labour and National Finance (London, 1920).

Labour and the New World (London, 1921).

An Autobiography, vol. II: *1919–1934* (London, 1934).

Stamp, J. C., *British Incomes and Property* (London, 1916).

'The special taxation of business profits in relation to the present position of national finance', *Economic Journal* 29 (1919).

'Taxation of capital and "ability to pay"', *Edinburgh Review* 20 (1919).

Fundamental Principles of Taxation in the Light of Modern Developments (London, 1921).

Wealth and Taxable Capacity (London, 1922).

Studies in Current Problems in Finance and Government (London, 1924).

The Christian Ethic as an Economic Factor: The Social Service Lecture (London, 1926).

Taxation during the War (London, 1932).

Streeten, P., 'Report of the Royal Commission on the Taxation of Profits and Income', *Bulletin of the Oxford University Institute of Statistics* 17 (1955).

Streeten, P. and Balogh, T., 'A reconsideration of monetary policy', *Bulletin of the Oxford University Institute of Statistics* 19 (1957).

Tawney, R. H., *The Acquisitive Society* (London, 1921).

Equality (London, 1952 edn).

Titmuss, R. M., *Poverty and Population* (London, 1938).

Problems of Social Policy (London, 1950).

Essays on the Welfare State (London, 1958).

Tress, R. C., 'A wealth tax is a wealth tax', *British Tax Review* (1963).

Walker, F. A., 'The source of business profits', *Quarterly Journal of Economics* 1 (1886–7).

Webb, S., 'The rate of interest', *Quarterly Journal of Economics* 2 (1887–8).

'The rate of interest and the laws of distribution', *Quarterly Journal of Economics* 2 (1887–8).

National Finance and a Levy on Capital: What the Labour Party Intends (Fabian Tract 188, London, 1919).

Webb, S. and B., *Problems of Modern Industry* (London, 1898).

A Constitution for the Socialist Commonwealth of Great Britain (London, 1920).

Wedgwood, J., *The Land Question: Taxation and Rating of Land Values* (London, TUC and Labour party, 1925).

The Economics of Inheritance (London, 1929).

'How far can a Labour budget go?', *Political Quarterly* 1 (1930).

Wheatcroft, G. S. A., 'Administrative problems of a wealth tax', *British Tax Review* (1963).

Whitaker, J. K. (ed.), *The Correspondence of Alfred Marshall, Economist*, vol. III: *Towards the Close, 1903–1924* (Cambridge, 1996).

Whitley, J. D. and Worswick, G. D. N., 'The productivity effects of select employment tax', *National Institute Economic Review* 56 (1971).

Wootton, B., *In a World I Never Made: Autobiographical Reflections* (London, 1967).

Young, M., *Small Man: Big World. A Discussion of Socialist Democracy* (London, 1949).

SECONDARY SOURCES

Anderson, O., *A Liberal State at War: English Politics and Economics during the Crimean War* (London, 1967).

Arnold, A. J., 'Profitability and capital accumulation in British industry during the transwar period, 1913–24', *Economic History Review* 52 (1999).

Arrow, K., *The Limits of Organization* (New York, 1974).

Bailey, S. J. and Paddison, R. (eds.), *The Reform of Local Government Finance in Britain* (London, 1988).

Balderston, T., 'War finance and inflation in Britain and Germany, 1914–18', *Economic History Review* 2nd ser. 42 (1989).

Baldwin, P., *The Politics of Social Solidarity: Class Bases of the European Welfare States, 1875–1975* (Cambridge, 1990).

'Beveridge in the *longue durée*', in Hills, Ditch and Glennester (eds.), *Beveridge*.

Baugh, G. C., 'Government grants-in-aid of the rates in England and Wales, 1889–1990', *Historical Research* 65 (1992).

Beer, S., *Britain Against Itself: The Political Contradictions of Collectivism* (London, 1982).

Modern British Politics: Parties and Pressure Groups in the Collectivist Age (London, 1982).

Bellamy, C., *Administering Central–Local Relations, 1871–1919: The Local Government Board in its Fiscal and Cultural Context* (Manchester, 1988).

Booth, A., 'Inflation, expectations, and the political economy of Conservative Britain, 1951–64', *Historical Journal* 43 (2000).

Bresciani-Turroni, C., *The Economics of Inflation: A Study of Currency Depreciation in Post-War Germany*, trans. M. E. Sayers (London, 1937).

Brigden, P., 'The state, redundancy pay, and economic policy making in the early 1960s', *Twentieth Century British History* 11 (2000).

Brittain, J. A., *The Payroll Tax for Social Security* (Brookings Institute, Washington DC, 1972).

Broadberry, S. N., 'The impact of the world wars on the long-run performance of the British economy', *Oxford Review of Economic Policy* 4 (1988).

Broadberry, S. N. and Crafts, N. F. R., 'British economic policy and industrial performance in the early post-war period', *Business History* 38 (1996).

'The post-war settlement: not such a good bargain after all', *Business History* 40 (1998).

Brooke, S., 'Problems of "socialist planning": Evan Durbin and the Labour government of 1945', *Historical Journal* 34 (1991).

Brownlee, W. E., 'Economists and the formation of the modern tax system in the US: the World War I crisis', in Furner and Supple (eds.), *The State and Economic Knowledge*.

Federal Taxation in America: A Short History (Cambridge, 1996).

'Reflections on the history of taxation', in W. E. Brownlee (ed.), *Funding the Modern American State, 1941–1995: The Rise and Fall of the Era of Easy Finance* (Cambridge, 1996).

'Tax regimes, national crisis, and state building in America', in W. E. Brownlee (ed.), *Funding the Modern American State, 1941–1995: The Rise and Fall of the Era of Easy Finance* (Cambridge, 1996).

Brudno, W. W. and Hollma, L. D., 'The taxation of capital gains in the United States and the United Kingdom', *British Tax Review* (1958).

Bulpitt, J., *Territory and Power in the United Kingdom: An Interpretation* (Manchester, 1983).

Butler, D. and Kavanagh, D., *The British General Election of 1992* (Basingstoke, 1999).

Butler, D., Adonis, A. and Travers, T., *Failure in British Government: The Politics of the Poll Tax* (Oxford, 1994).

Cain, P. J. and Hopkins, A. G., *British Imperialism: Innovation and Expansion, 1688–1914* (London, 1993).

Cairncross, A. and Watts, N., *The Economic Section, 1939–1961: A Study in Economic Advising* (London, 1989).

Cannadine, D., *Class in Britain* (London and New Haven, 1998).

Cawson, A., *Corporatism and Welfare* (London, 1982).

Clarke, P. F., *Liberals and Social Democrats* (Cambridge, 1978).

'The Treasury's analytical model of the British economy between the wars', in Furner and Supple (eds.), *The State and Economic Knowledge*.

Collini, S., *Liberalism and Sociology: L. T. Hobhouse and Political Argument in England, 1880–1914* (Cambridge, 1979).

English Pasts: Essays in Culture and History (Oxford, 1999).

Corry, B. (ed.), *Unemployment and the Economists* (Cheltenham, 1996).

Cowling, M., *The Impact of Labour, 1920–24: The Beginning of Modern British Politics* (Cambridge, 1971).

Crafts, N. F. R., 'Economic growth', in N. F. R. Crafts and N. Woodward (eds.), *The British Economy since 1945* (Oxford, 1991).

'Institutions and economic growth: recent British experience in an international context', *West European Politics* 15 (1992).

Crewe, I. and Grosschalk, B. (eds.), *Political Communications: The General Election Campaign of 1992* (Cambridge, 1994).

Cronin, J. E., *The Politics of State Expansion: War, State and Society in Twentieth-Century Britain* (London, 1991).

Cross, C., *Philip Snowden* (London, 1966).

Crystal, D. (ed.), *The Cambridge Biographical Encyclopaedia* (2nd edn, Cambridge, 1998).

Daunton, M. J., 'Introduction', in M. J. Daunton (ed.), *Councillors and Tenants: Local Authority Housing in English Cities, 1919–39* (Leicester, 1984).

'How to pay for the war: state, society and taxation in Britain, 1917–24', *English Historical Review* 111 (1996).

'Payment and participation: welfare and state formation in Britain, 1900–51', *Past and Present* 150 (1996).

Trusting Leviathan: The Politics of Taxation in Britain, 1799–1914 (Cambridge, 2001).

Daunton, M. J. (ed.), *Cambridge Urban History of Britain*, vol. III: *1840–1950* (Cambridge, 2000).

Davenport-Hines, R. P. T., *Dudley Docker: The Life and Times of a Trade Warrior* (Cambridge, 1984).

Davis, J., 'Central government and the towns', in Daunton (ed.), *Cambridge Urban History of Britain*, vol. III.

Dewey, C., 'The end of the imperialism of free trade: the eclipse of the Lancashire lobby and the concession of fiscal autonomy to India', in C. Dewey and A. G. Hopkins (eds.), *The Imperial Impact: Studies in the Economic History of Africa and India* (London, 1978).

Doyle, B. M., 'The changing functions of urban government: councillors, officials and pressure groups', in Daunton (ed.), *Cambridge Urban History of Britain*, vol. III.

Duffy, A. E. P., 'New unionism in Britain, 1889–90: a reappraisal', *Economic History Review* 2nd ser. 14 (1961).

Durbin, E., *New Jerusalems: The Labour Party and the Economics of Democratic Socialism* (London, 1985).

Eckstein, H., *Pressure Group Politics: The Case of the British Medical Association* (London, 1960).

Edgerton, D., *England and the Aeroplane: An Essay on a Militant and Technological Nation* (Basingstoke, 1991).

Eichengreen, B., *The Capital Levy in Theory and Practice* (Centre for Economic Policy, London, 1989).

Ellison, N., *Egalitarian Thought and Labour Politics: Retreating Visions* (London, 1994).

Feinstein, C., *Statistical Tables of National Income, Expenditure and Output of the UK, 1855–1965* (Cambridge, 1972).

Ferguson, N., 'Public finance and national security: the domestic origins of the First World War revisited', *Past and Present* 142 (1994).

Paper and Iron: Hamburg Business and German Politics in the Era of Inflation, 1897–1927 (Cambridge, 1995).

The Pity of War (London, 1998).

The Cash Nexus: Money and Power in the Modern World, 1700–2000 (London, 2001).

Fforde, M., *Conservatism and Collectivism, 1886–1914* (Edinburgh, 1990).

Finer, S. E., 'Adversary politics and electoral reform', in S. E. Finer (ed.), *Adversary Politics and Electoral Reform* (London, 1975).

Flemming, J. S., 'Debt and taxes in war and peace: the case of a small open economy', in M. J. Boskin, J. S. Flemming and S. Gorini (eds.), *Private Savings and Public Debt* (Oxford, 1987).

Forsyth, D. J., *The Crisis of Liberal Italy: Monetary and Financial Policy, 1914–22* (Cambridge, 1993).

Francis, M., 'Economics and ethics: the nature of Labour's socialism, 1945–51', *Twentieth Century British History* 6 (1995).

French, D. W., *British Economic and Strategic Planning, 1905–15* (London, 1982).

British Strategy and War Aims, 1914–16 (London, 1986).

The Strategy of the Lloyd George Coalition (Oxford, 1995).

Furner, M. O. and Supple, B., 'Ideas, institutions, and state in the United States and Britain: an introduction', in Furner and Supple (eds.), *The State and Economic Knowledge*.

Furner, M. O. and Supple, B. (eds.), *The State and Economic Knowledge: The American and British Experience* (Cambridge, 1990).

Gamble, A. M. and Walkland, S. A., *The British Party System and Economic Policy, 1945–83: Studies in Adversary Politics* (Oxford, 1984).

Gilbert, B. B., 'David Lloyd George: the reform of British land-holding and the budget of 1914', *Historical Journal* 21 (1978).

Gilbert, M., *Churchill's Political Philosophy* (Oxford, 1981).

Glennester, H. and Evans, M., 'Beveridge and his assumptive worlds: the incompatibilities of a flawed design', in Hills, Ditch and Glennester (eds.), *Beveridge.*

Gospel, H. F., *Markets, Firms and the Management of Labour in Modern Britain* (Cambridge, 1992).

Green, E. H. H., 'Radical conservatism: the electoral genesis of tariff reform', *Historical Journal* 28 (1985).

   The Crisis of Conservatism: The Politics, Economics and Ideology of the British Conservative Party, 1880–1914 (London, 1995).

   'The Conservative party, the state and the electorate', in M. Taylor and J. Lawrence (eds.), *Party, State and the Electorate in Modern Britain* (Aldershot, 1996).

   'The Treasury resignations of 1958: a reconsideration', *Twentieth Century British History* 11 (2000).

Green, S. and Winter, D., *Agency Costs and Tax Compliance – Should We Care About Accountants?* (Administration, Compliance and Governability Program Working Paper 15, Australian National University, Canberra, 1993).

Hall, P., *Urban and Regional Planning* (Harmondsworth, 1974).

Harling, P. and Mandler, P., 'From "fiscal-military" state to laissez-faire state, 1760–1850', *Journal of British Studies* 32 (1993).

Harris, J., 'The transition to high politics in English social policy, 1889–1914', in M. Bentley and J. Stevenson (eds.), *High and Low Politics in Modern Britain* (Oxford, 1983).

   'Enterprise and the welfare states: a comparative perspective', *Transactions of the Royal Historical Society* 5th ser. 40 (1990).

   'Political thought and the welfare state, 1870–1940: an intellectual framework for British social policy', *Past and Present* 135 (1992).

Harrison, R., 'The War Emergency Workers' National Committee, 1914–20', in A. Briggs and J. Saville, (eds.), *Essays in Labour History, 1886–1923* (London, 1971).

Hay, R., 'Employers and social policy in Britain: the evolution of welfare legislation, 1905–14', *Social History* 4 (1977).

Hennock, E. P., *British Social Reform and German Precedents: The Case of Social Insurance, 1880–1914* (Oxford, 1987).

Hills, J., *Changing Tax: How the Tax System Works and How to Change It* (Child Poverty Action Group, London, 1988).

Hills, J., Ditch, J. and Glennester, H. (eds.), *Beveridge and Social Security: An International Perspective* (Oxford, 1994).

Hobson, J. M., 'The military-extraction gap and the wary Titan: the fiscal-sociology of British defence policy, 1870–1913', *Journal of European Economic History* 22 (1993).

Houghton, D., 'The futility of taxation by menaces', in A. Seldon (ed.), *Tax Avoison: The Economic, Legal and Moral Inter-relationships between Avoidance and Evasion* (Institute of Economic Affairs, London, 1979).

Howson, S., 'The origins of cheaper money, 1945–7', *Economic History Review* 40 (1987).

Hutchison, T. W., *Economics and Economic Policy in Britain, 1946–66* (London, 1968).

Jacobs, M., 'The politics of plenty: consumerism in the twentieth-century United States', in M. Daunton and M. Hilton (eds.), *The Politics of Consumption: Material Culture and Citizenship in Europe and America* (Oxford, 2001).

James, H., 'The causes of the German banking crisis of 1931', *Economic History Review* 2nd ser. 37 (1984).

The German Slump: Politics and Economics, 1924–36 (Oxford, 1986).

Jarvis, D., 'Mrs Maggs and Betty: the Conservative appeal to women voters in the 1920s', *Twentieth Century British History* 5 (1994).

'British Conservatism and class politics in the 1920s', *English Historical Review*, 111 (1996).

Johnson, P., 'Risk, redistribution and social welfare in Britain from the poor law to Beveridge', in M. J. Daunton (ed.), *Charity, Self Interest and Welfare in the English Past* (London, 1996).

Kavanagh, D., *Thatcherism and British Politics: The End of Consensus?* (Oxford, 1987).

'The postwar consensus', *Twentieth Century British History* 3 (1992).

Kavanagh, D. and Morris, P., *Consensus Politics from Attlee to Thatcher* (Oxford, 1989).

King, M. A., *Public Policy and the Corporation* (London, 1977).

Kruedener, J. von, 'The Franckenstein paradox in the intergovernmental relations of imperial Germany', in P.-C. Witt (ed.), *Wealth and Taxation in Central Europe: The History and Sociology of Public Finance* (Leamington Spa, 1987).

Krugman, P., *Peddling Prosperity: Economic Sense and Nonsense in the Age of Diminished Expectations* (New York, 1994).

Lacey, M. J. and Furner, M. O. (eds.), *The State and Social Investigation in Britain and the United States* (Cambridge, 1993).

Langford, P., 'Politics and manners from Sir Robert Walpole to Sir Robert Peel', *Proceedings of the British Academy* 94, *1996 Lectures and Memoirs* (Oxford, 1997).

Laursen, K. and Pedersen, J., *The German Inflation, 1918–23* (Amsterdam, 1964).

Lawrence, J., 'Class and gender and the making of urban Toryism, 1880–1914', *English Historical Review* 108 (1993).

Lazonick, W., *Competitive Advantage on the Shop Floor* (Cambridge, Mass., 1990).

Lindert, P. H., 'The rise of social spending, 1880–1930', *Explorations in Economic History* 31 (1994).

'What limits social spending?', *Explorations in Economic History* 33 (1996).

London and Cambridge Economic Service, *The British Economy: Key Statistics, 1900–70* (London, 1971).

Lowe, R., 'Resignation at the Treasury: the Social Services Committee and the failure to reform the welfare state', *Journal of Social Policy* 18 (1989).

'Taxing problems', *Labour History Review* 57 (1992).

'Social policy', in S. Ball and A. Seldon (eds.), *The Heath Government: A Reappraisal* (London, 1996).

The Welfare State in Britain since 1945 (2nd edn, Basingstoke and London, 1999).

Lowe, R. and Rollings, N., 'Modernising Britain: a classic case of centralisation and fragmentation', in R. Rhodes (ed.), *Transforming British Government*, vol. I: *Changing Institutions* (Basingstoke, 2000).

Lynch, F. M. B., 'A tax for Europe: the introduction of value added tax in France', *Journal of European Integration History* 4 (1998).

McConnell, A., 'The recurring crisis of local taxation in post-war Britain', *Contemporary British History* 11, no. 3 (1997).

State Policy Formation and the Origins of the Poll Tax (Aldershot, 1995).

McDonald, A., 'The Geddes Committee and the formulation of public expenditure policy, 1921–22', *Historical Journal* 32 (1989).

Mackenzie, R. T., *British Political Parties* (London, 1965).

McKibbin, R., 'The economic policy of the second Labour government, 1929–31', *Past and Present* 68 (1975).

'Class and conventional wisdom: the Conservative party and the "public" in interwar Britain', in his *Ideologies of Class*.

The Ideologies of Class: Social Relations in Britain, 1880–1950 (Oxford, 1990).

Classes and Cultures: England, 1918–51 (Oxford, 1998).

Macnicol, J., 'Beveridge and old age', in Hills, Ditch and Glennester (eds.), *Beveridge*.

The Politics of Retirement in Britain, 1878–1948 (Cambridge, 1998).

Maier, C., *Recasting Bourgeois Europe: Stabilization in France, Germany and Italy after World War I* (Princeton, 1975).

Mann, M., *The Sources of Social Power*, vol. II: *The Rise of Classes and Nation States, 1750–1914* (Cambridge, 1993).

Manzer, R. A., *Teachers and Politics: The Role of the National Union of Teachers in the Making of National Educational Policy in England and Wales since 1944* (Manchester, 1970).

Marquand, D., *Ramsay MacDonald* (London, 1977).

Marsh, D. and Grant, W., 'Tripartism: reality or myth?', *Government and Opposition* 12 (1977).

Marsh, D. and Rhodes, R. (eds.), *Policy Networks in British Government* (Oxford, 1992).

Matthew, H. C. G., *The Liberal Imperialists: The Ideas and Politics of a Post-Gladstonian Elite* (Oxford, 1973).

Matthew, H. C. G., McKibbin, R. I. and Kay, J. A., 'The franchise factor in the rise of Labour', *English Historical Review* 91 (1976).

Melling, J., 'Welfare capitalism and the origins of the welfare states c.1870–1914', *Social History* 17 (1992).

Middlemass, K., *Politics in Industrial Society: The British Experience since 1911* (London, 1979).

Power, Competition and the State, vol. I: *Britain in Search of Balance, 1940–61* (Basingstoke, 1986).

Middleton, R., *Towards the Managed Economy: Keynes, the Treasury and the Fiscal Policy Debate of the 1930s* (London, 1985).

Government versus the Market: The Growth of the Pubic Sector, Economic Management and British Economic Performance, c1890–1979 (Cheltenham, 1996).

The British Economy since 1945: Engaging with the Debate (Basingstoke, 2000).
Milward, A. S. and Brennan, G., *Britain's Place in the World: An Historical Inquiry into Import Controls, 1945–1960* (London, 1996).
Mitchell, B. R., *British Historical Statistics* (Cambridge, 1988).
Mitchell, B. R. and Deane, P., *Abstract of British Historical Statistics* (Cambridge, 1962).
Morgan, E. V., *Studies in British Financial Policy, 1914–25* (London, 1952).
Murray, B. K., *The People's Budget, 1909/10: Lloyd George and Liberal Politics* (Oxford, 1980).
Nottingham, C. J., 'Recasting bourgeois Britain? The British state in the years which followed the First World War', *International Review of Social History* 31 (1976).
Odling-Smee, J. C. and Riley, C., 'Approaches to the PSBR', *National Institute of Economic Research* 113 (1985).
Offer, A., *Property and Politics, 1870–1914: Landownership, Law, Ideology and Urban Development in England* (Cambridge, 1981).
Olson, M., *The Logic of Collective Action: Public Goods and the Theory of Groups* (Cambridge, Mass., 1965).
The Rise and Decline of Nations: Economic Growth, Stagflation and Social Rigidities (New Haven and London, 1982).
Peden, G. C., *British Rearmament and the Treasury, 1932–39* (Edinburgh, 1979).
'The "Treasury view" on public works and employment in the interwar period', *Economic History Review* 2nd ser. 37 (1984).
'The Treasury view in the interwar period: an example of political economy?', in Corry (ed.), *Unemployment and the Economists.*
The Treasury and Public Policy, 1906–1959 (Oxford, 2000).
Pedersen, S., *Family, Dependence, and the Origins of the Welfare State: Britain and France, 1914–45* (Cambridge, 1993).
'From national crisis to "national crisis": British politics, 1914–31', *Journal of British Studies* 33 (1994).
Phelps Brown, E. H., *The Origins of Trade Union Power* (Oxford, 1983).
Piachaud, D., 'Taxation and social security', in C. Sandford, C. Pond and R. Walker (eds.), *Taxation and Social Policy* (London, 1980).
Pimlott, B., 'The myth of consensus', in L. M. Smith (ed.), *The Making of Britain: Echoes of Greatness* (London, 1988).
Pond, C., 'Tax expenditure and fiscal welfare', in C. Sandford, C. Pond and R. Walker (eds.), *Taxation and Social Policy* (London, 1980).
Ramsden, J., *The Making of Conservative Party Policy: The Conservative Research Department since 1929* (London, 1980).
Rawls, J., *A Theory of Justice* (Oxford, 1972).
Rhodes, R., *Understanding Governance* (Buckingham, 1997).
Rhodes, R. and Dunleavy, P. (eds.), *Prime Minister, Cabinet and Core Executive* (Basingstoke, 1995).
Ricci, D. M., 'Fabian socialism: a theory of rent as exploitation', *Journal of British Studies* 9 (1969–70).
Ringe, A. and Rollings, N., 'Responding to relative decline: the creation of the National Economic Development Council', *Economic History Review* 52 (2000).

Ritschel, D., *The Politics of Planning: The Debate on Economic Planning in Britain in the 1930s* (Oxford, 1997).

Robbins, K. M. (ed.), *The Blackwell Biographical Dictionary of British Political Life in the Twentieth Century* (Oxford, 1990).

Roberts, R. O., 'Ricardo's theory of public debts', *Economica* n.s. 9 (1942).

Rogow, A. and Shore, P., *The Labour Government and British Industry* (Oxford, 1955).

Ryan, P. A., '"Poplarism", 1894–1930', in P. Thane (ed.), *The Origins of British Social Policy* (London, 1978).

Sabine, B. E. V., *A History of Income Tax* (London, 1966).

Semmel, B., *Imperialism and Social Reform: English Social-Imperial Thought, 1895–1914* (London, 1960).

Skidelsky, R., *Politicians and the Slump: The Labour Government of 1929–31* (London, 1967).

Oswald Mosley (London, 1975).

John Maynard Keynes, vol. I: *Hopes Betrayed, 1883–1920* (London, 1983).

John Maynard Keynes, vol. III: *Fighting for Britain, 1937–46* (London, 2000).

Skocpol, T., 'Bringing the state back in: strategies of analysis in current research', in P. B. Evans, D. Rueschmeyer and T. Skocpol (eds.), *Bringing the State Back In* (Cambridge, 1985).

Protecting Soldiers and Mothers: The Political Origins of Social Policy in the United States (Cambridge, Mass., 1992).

Smith, M. J., *Pressure, Power and Policy: State Autonomy and Policy Networks in Britain and the United States* (Hemel Hempstead, 1993).

The Core Executive in Britain (Basingstoke, 1999).

Smith, T., *The Politics of the Corporate Economy* (Oxford, 1979).

Solomou, S., *Themes in Macroeconomic History: The UK Economy, 1919–1939* (Cambridge, 1996).

Spaulding, H. B., *The Income Tax in Great Britain and the United States* (London, 1927).

Stebbings, C., '"A natural safeguard": the General Commissioners of income tax', *British Tax Review* (1992).

Stedman Jones, G., 'Why is the Labour party in a mess?', in his *The Languages of Class: Studies in English Working-Class History, 1832–1982* (Cambridge, 1983).

Steinmo, S., 'Political institutions and tax policy in the United States, Sweden and Britain', *World Politics* 41 (1988–9).

Taxation and Democracy: Swedish, British, and American Approaches to Financing the Modern State (New Haven, 1993).

Steinmo, S., Thelen, K. and Longstreth, F. (eds.), *Structuring Politics: Historical Institutionalism in Comparative Analysis* (Cambridge, 1992).

Stopforth, D., 'Sowing some of the seeds of the present anti-evasion system – the 1920s', *British Tax Review* (1985).

'Charitable convenants by individuals – a history of the background to their tax treatment and their cost to the Exchequer', *British Tax Review* (1986).

'Settlements and the avoidance of tax on income – the period to 1920', *British Tax Review* (1990).

'1922–36: halcyon days for the tax avoider', *British Tax Review* (1992).

Stout, D. K., 'Incomes policy and the costs of the adversarial system', in S. E. Finer (ed.), *Adversary Politics and Electoral Reform* (London, 1975).

Supple, B. E., *The History of the British Coal Industry*, vol. IV: *1913–1946: The Political Economy of Decline* (Oxford, 1987).

Surridge, K. T., *Managing the South African War, 1899–1902: Politicians v Generals* (Woodbridge, 1998).

Tanner, D., *Political Change and the Labour Party, 1900–18* (Cambridge, 1990).

Taylor-Gooby, P., *Public Opinion, Ideology and State Welfare* (London, 1985).

Thane, P., 'The working class and state "welfare" in Britain, 1880–1914', *Historical Journal* 27 (1984).

Thompson, N., 'Hobson and the Fabians: two roads to socialism in the 1920s', *History of Political Economy* 26 (1994).

Tomlinson, B. R., *The Political Economy of the Raj, 1914–47: The Economics of Decolonisation in India* (London, 1979).

Tomlinson, J., 'Planning: debate and policy in the 1940s', *Twentieth Century British History* 3 (1992).

'Mr Attlee's supply-side socialism', *Economic History Review* 47 (1993).

'Attlee's inheritance and the financial system: whatever happened to the National Investment Board?', *Financial History Review* 1 (1994).

'Welfare and economy: the economic impact of the welfare state, 1945–51', *Twentieth Century British History* 6 (1995).

Democratic Socialism and Economic Policy: The Attlee Years, 1945–51 (Cambridge, 1997).

Tomlinson, J. and Tiratsoo, N., '"An old story, freshly told?" A comment on Broadberry and Crafts' approach to Britain's early post-war economic performance', *Business History* 40 (1998).

Toye, R., 'Keynes, the Labour movement and how to pay for the war', *Twentieth Century British History* 10 (1999).

Travers, T., *The Politics of Local Government Finance* (London, 1986).

Trentmann, F., 'Wealth versus welfare: the British left between free trade and national political economy before the First World War', *Historical Research* 70 (1997).

'Political culture and political economy: interest, ideology and free trade', *Review of International Political Economy* 5 (1998).

Turner, F., *Contesting Cultural Authority: Essays in Victorian Intellectual Life* (Cambridge, 1993).

Turner, J., 'The politics of "organised business" in the First World War', in J. Turner (ed.), *Businessmen and Politics: Studies of Business Activity in British Politics, 1900–45* (London, 1984).

British Politics and the Great War: Coalition and Conflict, 1915–18 (New Haven and London, 1992).

Vincent, D., *The Culture of Secrecy: Britain, 1832–1998* (Oxford, 1998).

Ward, P., *Red Flag and Union Jack: Englishness, Patriotism and the British Left, 1881–1924* (Woodbridge, 1998).

Warren, J. H., *The English Local Government System* (6th edn, London, 1961).

Webster, C., *The National Health Service: A Political History* (Oxford, 1998).

Weir, M., 'Ideas and the politics of bounded innovation', in Steinmo, Thelen and Longstreth (eds.), *Structuring Politics*.

Wheatcroft, G. S. A., 'The tax treatment of corporations and shareholders in the United States and Great Britain', *British Tax Review* (1961).

Whiting, R. C., 'The Labour party, capitalism and the national debt, 1918–24', in P. J. Waller (ed.), *Politics and Social Change in Modern Britain: Essays Presented to A. F. Thompson* (Brighton, 1987).

'Taxation and the working class, 1915–24', *Historical Journal* 33 (1990).

'Taxation policy', in H. Mercer, N. Rollings and J. Tomlinson (eds.), *Labour Governments and Private Industry: The Experience of 1945–51* (Edinburgh, 1992).

'The boundaries of taxation', in S. J. D. Green and R. C. Whiting (eds.), *The Boundaries of the State in Modern Britain* (Cambridge, 1996).

'Ideology and reform in Labour's tax strategy, 1964–70', *Historical Journal* 41 (1998).

The Labour Party and Taxation: Party Identity and Political Purpose in Twentieth-Century Britain (Cambridge, 2000).

Williamson, P., *Stanley Baldwin: Conservative Leadership and National Values* (Cambridge, 1999).

Wilson, T. and Hopkin, B., 'Alexander Kirkland Cairncross, 1911–1998', *Proceedings of the British Academy* 105, *1999 Lectures and Memoirs* (Oxford, 2000).

Winkler, J. T., 'The corporate economy: theory and administration', in R. Scase (ed.), *Industrial Society: Class, Cleavage and Control* (London, 1977).

Winter, J. M., *Socialism and the Challenge of War: Ideas and Politics in Britain, 1912–18* (London, 1974).

Wolfe, W., *From Radicalism to Socialism: Men and Ideas in the Formation of Fabian Socialist Doctrine, 1881–9* (New Haven, 1975).

Woodward, N., 'Labour's economic performance, 1964–70', in R. Coopey, S. Fielding and N. Tiratsoo (eds.), *The Wilson Governments, 1964–70* (London, 1993).

Wrigley, C. J., *Lloyd George and the Challenge of Labour: The Post-War Coalition, 1918–22* (Hemel Hempstead, 1990).

THESES

Francis, M., 'Labour policies and socialist ideas: the example of the Attlee government, 1945–51', DPhil thesis, University of Oxford, 1993.

Pemberton, H., 'The 1961 budget', MA dissertation, University of Bristol, 1991.

Short, M. E., 'The politics of personal taxation: budget-making in Britain, 1917–31', PhD thesis, Cambridge, 1985.

Thompson, J., 'The idea of "public opinion" in Britain, 1870–1914', PhD thesis, University of Cambridge, 1999.

Toye, R. J., 'The Labour party and the planned economy, 1931–51', PhD thesis, University of Cambridge, 1999.

Index

Note: page numbers in bold refer to tables and figures

abatement, to reduce tax burden, 47
ability to pay: definition, xiv, 11, 52; as
  doctrine, 103, 208; political assessment
  of, 42–3; purchase tax and, 240; see also
  assessment
Accepting Houses Committee, 77
accountability: local, 359; of regulatory
  bodies, 112–13
accountants, professional, 6–7, 110
administration of taxes, 366; capital gains
  tax, 215, 261; centralisation of, 113; and
  co-operation of taxpayers, 6, 215; costs
  of VAT, 294; income tax, 108–9;
  PAYE for income tax, 180; problems
  of compliance, 48, 193, 337;
  retail turnover tax, 239–40, 313;
  see also collection of tax
agriculture: and concept of Rent, 50; rates
  relief for, 340; taxation of profits, 91
alcohol, duties on, 117, 118, 119
Amery, Leo, 94n
Anti-Waste League, 76
army: First World War, 40–1; conscription,
  50, 57
Asquith, H. H., 57
assessment: by Inland Revenue, 109–10,
  113; of liability on wages, 178–9; by
  local lay commissioners, 6, 109–10;
  self-assessment, 215; of super-tax, 109,
  111–12; tax codes for PAYE, 179;
  variations in periods of, 109, 113
assessors, taxpayers as, 6
Association of British Chambers of
  Commerce, 22, 266
Atkinson, A. B., 333
Attlee, Clement, 187n, 279, 349; and
  National Debt Enquiry (1944), 187–8;
  on taxation of capital, 214
Australia, 159

Baker, Kenneth, 357 and n
balance of payments, 194, 356; deficit,
  293; and devaluation, 293; Treasury
  concern for, 169, 170
Baldwin, Stanley, 93, 93n, 125, 127, 363
Balogh, Thomas, 287n, 296; tax proposals,
  287–8, 290–1, 293
Bank of England, 76, 77, 363;
  nationalisation of, 163
Bevan, Aneurin, 225, 225n, 264
Beveridge, William, 309
Bevin, Ernest, 178–9, 178n, 184, 200, 220
Biffen, John, 318 and n
Birch, Nigel, 234 and n
Blackett, Basil, 88, 88–9n
Board of Trade: and Budget Committee,
  232; and depreciation allowances, 207;
  and export incentives, 243; and
  investment allowances, 255; and
  purchase tax, 219; support for turnover
  tax, 239, 366
Boards of Guardians, 339
Boer war, 11, 36
Bonar Law, Andrew, 39, 39–40n
Bower, Frank, 209 and n, 237–8
Boyd-Carpenter, John, 230, 230n
Boyle, Edward, 267 and n, 303–4
Bradbury, John, 43n, 69; war finance
  policy, 43–4, 45
Bray, Jeremy, 332 and n
bread, price of (First World War), 56
Bridges, Edward, 226 and n, 248–9, 250
British Medical Association, 20
Broadberry, S. N. and Crafts, N. F. R., 228
Brook, Norman, MP, 231–2
Budget Committee: opposition to
  turnover tax, 241, 244; restructured
  (1965), 272; work of, 232–3, 270–2,
  273, 366

budget surpluses, to repay national debt,
    62, 88, 99, 127
budgets: 1925 (Churchill's), 124–6, 132–6,
    139–40, 344, 363; 1929 (Churchill's),
    29; 1930–1 (Snowden's), 155–7,
    158–9; 1945–6 (Dalton's), 199; 1949
    (Cripps's), 210; 1956 (Macmillan's),
    251–2; 1961 (Selwyn Lloyd's), 259–60,
    261, 268, 269; 1965 (Callaghan's), 275,
    290; annual, 18–19, 20; principle of
    balance, 62, 88, 157, 259, 327
business corporations, 32–3, 224; control
    of investment, 151, 319–20; favoured
    by Dalton, 204–5, 254, 292; role in
    economic management, 201–2, 223–4,
    226–7, 248; taxation of, 89, 90–1, 93,
    252; see also corporation tax; industry;
    retained profits
Butler, R. A.: as chancellor, 230, 230n,
    231–2, 234, 250; policy of 'long, slow
    grind', 232, 235

Cabinet, 20, 298; committee on
    expenditure (1926), 128
Cairncross, Alec, 244–5 and n, 294; on
    reform of tax system, 244–6, 247, 274
Callaghan, James, 25n, 285; as chancellor,
    275, 290–9, 300–1; and Kaldor, 25,
    290, 291–2, 296–8, 299, 361
Canada, taxation of profits, 90
Cannadine, David, 26
capital: as incentive, 307–8; and income
    flow, 212, 213; Liberal support for, 67;
    return on (industry 1910–20), 84–5;
    spending from, 214; taxation of, 210,
    212–17, 283, 307–8, 316–18; valuation
    of, 212, 332; see also capital gains tax;
    capital levy; death duties; profits;
    wealth tax
capital assets: depreciation of, 196,
    209–10; tax allowances on, 167, 196,
    206–7
capital flight, risk of, 150, 332
capital gains, 94n, 260
capital gains tax, 212–13, 214–15, 252,
    286; Callaghan's long-term, 292–3,
    318–19; indexed for inflation, 337;
    introduced, 259, 260–1
capital levy, 213; arguments against, 71–3,
    188–9; debate renewed (1945–51),
    215–16; Labour party's policy of, 49,
    50, 54, 66–74, 94, 98, 284; proposals for
    assets surrendered, 66, 70–1; rejected in
    war-time, 69; to remove suppressed
    inflation, 216; to repay national debt, 64;

Ricardo's proposal, 62; Second World
    War debate on, 183, 187–9
capital markets, 31; effect of capital levy
    on, 72, 73, 188; for growth and
    efficiency, 248; Labour hostility to, 146,
    164, 204, 248, 291, 363–4; rejected by
    gosplanners, 192
capital transfer tax, 337
capitalism, 52, 160; as basis of economic
    prosperity, 124, 248; benefits of, 125,
    135; Labour intention to undermine,
    329–30; popular, 326
central government: size of public sector
    (1979), 1, 335; welfare spending by, 9,
    10, 13, 29
Chamberlain, Austen, 76 and n; and levy
    on war wealth, 78–80
Chamberlain, Neville, 139n; as chancellor
    (1931–7), 167; on Churchill, 139, 141;
    and local government, 340, 341–2,
    344–5, 346–7; and national defence
    contribution (NDC), 172–3; reduction
    of taxes, 167; restoration of welfare
    benefits, 167
Chambers, Paul, 223 and n, 263
chancellors of the Exchequer, 2, 18–19;
    caution of (1951–64), 233; constraints
    on, 106–7, 232
charities, covenants to, 111
cheap money: to reduce debt service costs,
    188; to weaken rentiers, 199
children's allowances, 7, 12, 103, 106,
    114; increases, 41, 75, 167; see also
    family allowances
Churchill, Winston, 19n; 1925 budget,
    124–6, 132–6, 139–40, 344, 363; appeal
    to middle classes, 136–7, 140–1; as
    chancellor (1924–9), 19, 65–6, 77,
    122–41; changes to super-tax, 111–12,
    119, 132–4; concessions to working
    class, 134–6, 137, 141; creative
    accounting of, 128–32; on economic
    policy, 123–5, 128; further schemes,
    140–1; and hypothecation of Road
    Fund, 130–1; income tax reforms,
    122, 136–7; Liberal policies on
    wealth, 122–3, 135, 137; and local
    goverment finance, 154, 339–40,
    341–7; and national debt, 123, 125–7;
    as prime minister (1951–5), 230,
    231; return to gold standard, 63, 122,
    124, 344; support for corporation
    tax, 92; support for levy on war
    wealth, 80; view of social policy, 34,
    102, 107, 124, 134–6

City of London, 24, 362; and floating debt
(1920s), 77–8; influence on fiscal policy,
21, 78, 165–6; and levy on war wealth,
79–80
civil service: caution of, 24, 25–6, 106–7,
366–7; continuity of, 361; criticism of
Labour policies, 222–3; narrow
concerns of, 263, 273, 366–7; relations
with interest groups, 99–100, 362;
relations with politicians, 25–6, 233,
254; role in fiscal policy-making, 18, 22,
270–2, 273–4; support for reform of
fiscal system, 359; see also Board of
Trade; Customs and Excise; Inland
Revenue; Treasury
class: and balance of tax system, 5;
war, 53
Cockfield, Arthur v, 228 and n, 312, 325
collection of tax, 6, 366; payment by
stamps, 178; and period of assessment,
113; on retail turnover, 95, 96, 313; on
small incomes, 48, 113–14, 177–80; at
source, 6, 108, 113; VAT, 246, 294; of
wealth tax, 332; see also administration
of taxes; Pay As You Earn
Colwyn, Lord, Committee on National
Debt and Taxation (1927), 73,
151, 165, 227
commissioners: local, as adjudicators, 110,
112; tax assessment by, 109–10;
taxpayers as, 6, 48
Committee on National Debt and
Taxation, report (1927), 73, 151, 165
Committee on the Review of Taxation
Policy (1962), 245
community charge, 3, 298, 340, 356–9;
rejected (1964), 352, 356; shortcomings
of, 357–8
compensation: for indirect taxes, 243; land
development, 350; for nationalised
property, 162, 163
competition: Conservative encouragement
of, 254, 321; and economic growth, 363;
on exports, 237, 245–6, 293; limited,
206, 365, 367–8; private business and,
204
competition policy, 228
compliance, 193, 359, 361, 362; capital
levy and, 72; costs of, 360; and PAYE,
180; poll tax and, 3; problems of, 48,
193, 337; see also consent to taxation
Confederation of British Industry see
Federation of British Industries (FBI)
confiscation, as means to nationalisation,
161–2

conscription: First World War, 50, 57; of
labour (Second World War), 186
consensus on fiscal policy, 17 and n, 30
consent to taxation, 12, 13, 106, 270; and
capital levy, 72; and high rates, 108; and
increased expenditure, 174; maintained
after First World War, 65, 101, 103,
107; middle classes, 119, 122; see also
compliance
Conservative governments: 1924–9,
Baldwin, 122–4, 142, Churchill as
chancellor, 124–41; 1951–64, failure to
reform tax system, 247, 249–50, 274–5,
277–8, 280, 367, fiscal policy, 227–8,
229, 233–7, 243–4, 'savings and
incentives' policy, 251–2; 1970–4,
Heath, 303, 304, 326–7, introduction of
VAT, 299, 301; 1979–90, Thatcher, 1,
337–8, 354–5, 356–9, 361
Conservative party, 1, 61, 274–5, 284;
attitude to property, 65, 67, 315; and
class politics, 65–6, 236; electoral
identity, 125, 128, 137–8, 140–1; fiscal
policy debate (in opposition from 1964),
280–1, 305–6; and goal of social
integration, 124–5, 275, 301, 303, 327;
'opportunity' policy, 236, 308, 315–16,
369; in opposition (1964–70), 213, 278,
300–1, 302–26; opposition to capital
levy, 71–2; Policy Committee on
Economic Growth (1962), 263; Policy
Group on Future Economic Policy
(1965), 306; reluctance to oppose trade
unions, 364–5; and tariff reform, 37;
Taxation Policy Committee, 305–6; view
of incentives, 30, 34, 236, 251–2, 257–9
Conservative Research Department
(CRD): on labour costs, 312; and social
services funding, 266; and tax structure,
274, 325; on taxation of middle class,
235–6, 257–8
consumption: changing attitudes to, 368;
and deferred tax credits, 184–5; moral
assumptions about, 6, 283, 287–8;
reduced by inflation, 43–4, 64; taxation
to control, 195, 196, 211, 218–19; of
taxed commodities, 117, 119; war-time
controls over, 183, 184–5; working-class,
59; see also indirect taxes; purchase tax
corporation tax (1920–4), 91, 92–4, 154,
155, 199; Callaghan's (1965), 290–3,
318–19, 327; German system, 319–20;
'imputation', 327; proposed by
Conservatives (1958–62), 252–3;
reduced, 337; see also profits

corporations, state (favoured by Labour), 248; *see also* business corporations
corporatism, 20–1, 99, 100
council housing, sale of, 1, 355
council tax, to replace poll tax, 358–9
covenants, to charities, 111
Crimean war, 8, 38
Cripps, Stafford, 116n, 216, 220–1; 1949 budget, 210; on nationalisation, 161–2
Crosland, Anthony, 205, 205–6n
Crossman, Richard, 290, 298, 353 and n
currency: depreciation, 64; devaluation, 293, 294, 299
customs duties, 7, 260; on imports (1915), 45, 155; percentage contribution of, 174
Customs and Excise: and Budget Committee, 232, 233; hostility to VAT, 246, 296; resistance to change, 270; resistance to sales tax, 239–40, 366

Dalton, Hugh, 19n, 30, 123, 254; as chancellor, 19, 199, 200–3, 217; commitment to equality, 149–52; and company taxation, 94, 199; differential profits tax (1947), 154, 164, 200–1, 202–5; and NIB, 162–4; on pension funding, 143; postwar budgets, 199; and Rignano scheme, 74n, 147–8, 199; taxation of retained profits, 154, 164, 200–1
Davenport, Nicholas, 199–200
death duties, 8, 117, 212; after First World War, 59, 124; avoidance of, 213, 333; Churchill's changes to, 132–3, 135; favoured by Dalton, 126, 213; graduation of, 136; high rates (1951), 229; increased on large estates, 199, 213; Labour support for, 144, 149–50, 190, 198; need to reform, 333; Rignano scheme, 147–8
debt *see* national debt
defence expenditure, 8, 10–11, 55–6; and national defence contribution (NDC), 172–3; as percentage of GDP, 2, 3; rearmament (1930s), 169–74; reduced, 277, 303
deferred pay, 182, 184–5
deficit finance: as counter-productive, 170; Keynes's policy on, 163, 164, 169–70; for rearmament, 172
deflation, 39; postwar policy of, 63, 77, 102, 159
degression of income tax, 107

demand, inflationary, 194, 217
demand management, 217; Keynes's theory of, 164, 192
demography, and attitude to taxation, 27–8
denationalisation, 326
Department of Economic Affairs, 294
Department of Environment, hostility to local government, 357–8
devaluation *see* currency
differentiation, 12, 73, 263; and business profits, 198, 200–5, 208–9, 248–50; Conservative view of, 315–16; of forms of income, 103, 107, 115–17, 167; Labour support for, 190, 290–1
direct taxes (1913–30), 46; Conservative changes (1951–64), 247–56; increased proportion, 8, 57, 99, 174; limits of, 156, 158; Meade enquiry (1978), 333; as percentage of revenue, 15, 304; shift from, 1, 185–6, 238–43, 294; *see also* death duties; income tax; profits; super-tax
distributed profits: German system of corporation tax, 319–20; Labour hostility towards, 248, 319; taxation of, 91, 154–5, 200–1, 202, 211, 251; *see also* dividends; retained profits
distributive justice, 59, 101; definitions of, 29–30; Labour view of, 52; *see also* redistribution
dividends: limitation, 210–12, 216, 248, 250; as reward for initiative, 249, 319; taxation of, 154–5, 204, 291; voluntary restraint, 200, 210; *see also* shares
Durbin, Evan, 162 and n, 176, 186–7, 192

earned income: and differentiation, 6, 115–17, 315; incidence of taxation, 121, 168, 169; tax on (1918–20), 117
Eccles, David, 251–2, 251n
economic crisis: (1931), 158–60; (1970s), 327, 328, 353, 367; IMF crisis (1976), 333, 354, 368
economic depression: (1930s), 13, 64; risk of, 62
economic growth, 8, 101, 124–5, 363; to 1964, 277; and commitment to equality, 150–1, 211–12, 287–9; Conservative assumptions about, 302–3, 319–22, 325–6; to finance Second World War, 169; and forms of direct taxation, 247–8; and free market, 223, 363; recovery after Second World War, 194–6, 364; role of services, 300; supply-side approach, 201, 217;

taxation and, 29, 270–1, 272–3, 287,
304–5, 336–7; *see also* incentives
economic planning, 31, 32, 147, 248, 291;
role of business corporations, 201–2,
223–4, 226–7, 248; taxation as device
for, 190–3
economic policy, 21, 233, 254, 255–6,
268–9; 1930s, 164–9; Churchill's view
of 123–5, 128; ideological differences
on, 247–52, 335–7; postwar, 62–3,
123–4; of second Labour administration,
142–3; *see also* incentives
economic regulators, 267–8; surcharges,
268–9
Economic Section *see* Treasury
economic structure: changes in, 27–8,
368–9; problems of, 159, 293; use of
taxation to shape, 191, 362
economies of scale, 31
Economist Intelligence Unit, 304
economists: in government departments,
233; influence on politicians, 25, 26–7,
68–9; studies of fiscal system, 4–5, 30,
333–5, 360–1
economy, 31, 240; effects of redistribution
on, 211–12, 336–7; importance of
stability, 102, 132, 165–6, 363; income
tax reductions to stimulate, 62, 128,
133, 219–20, 307–8; inflexibility of,
196, 222; loss of competitiveness, 237,
245–6, 293, 294–5; low effort, low
productivity, 196, 228, 250, 269, 292,
364, 368–9; monetary controls over,
293; need to modernise, 311, 365–6;
relationship with welfare state, 225, 265;
and social justice, 246, 247; statistical
analysis (Inland Revenue), 153; taxation
to balance, 191, 192, 362; Treasury view
of, 169–71, 272–3, 362; world, 164,
170; *see also* industry; productivity
Eden, Anthony, 250 and n, 257, 260
education, 76, 282, 355
efficiency: competition and, 206, 321;
economic, 191, 192, 195; effect of
taxation of profits on, 204–5; and social
justice, 281; and welfare state, 34, 225
elderly, interests of, 21–2, 27–8; *see also*
pensions
electoral advantage, 24, 106
empire, fiscal burden shifted to, 8, 11
employers: and administration of tax, 48;
labour costs, 169, 265, 294–5, 311–12;
welfare provision by, 9–10, 34
employment, salaried, 109
employment (payroll) tax, 265–6, 267

enterprise, and risk, 222, 224, 231, 248–9,
302–3
enterprise state, 34–5
equality, 282; balanced against incentives,
29, 149, 151, 192–3, 211–12, 248;
capital taxation to produce, 215–16,
328–9; as desirable, 17, 31, 52; and
economic growth, 364; and justice,
330–1, 334, 369; Labour party
commitment to, 1, 149–52, 192, 194,
211–12; Labour party study group on,
283 and n, 288–9; of opportunity, 282,
283; of outcome, 282; and property
ownership, 288–9, 315; for social justice,
281–3, 369
equity: concern for, 81, 185, 193, 256;
pragmatic and principled distinction,
101; principle of, 5–6, 52, 74, 191, 361
Eugenics Society, 181
European Economic Community (EEC),
237, 273; adoption of VAT, 97, 241–2,
246–7, 314; Balogh's opposition to, 288;
corporation taxation, 319; welfare
funding, 264, 304; *see also* France;
Germany
European Union, tax harmonisation, 35,
97, 369
excess profits duty (EPD): continuation of,
79, 81, 83–4, 91–2; introduced (1915),
41, 55–7; preferred to levy, 92; reduced
(1919), 90
excess profits tax (Second World War),
177, 190, **195**; abolished, 200
excise duties, 7, 260; declining proportion
of, 174, **175**
exemption limits *see* threshold
(for taxation)
expenditure (central government):
Churchill's policy on, 128–9, 138–9;
debt charge as percentage of, **58**;
elasticity of, 103, 105; Geddes
Committee on (1921/2), 82–3; Keynes's
view on, 164; Labour levels of, 207,
225–7; limits on, 8, 174; net accounting,
129; as percentage of GDP, **2**, **3**, 8, 338;
postwar control of (1920s), 65; public
support for, 4, 35; reduction of, 225,
231, 264, 323; under Thatcher, 338;
see also defence expenditure; social
expenditure; welfare
expenditure tax: Kaldor's proposals, 286;
Kay and King's proposals, 334;
personal, 286
Expert Committee on Compensation and
Betterment, 350

exports: competitiveness on, 237, 245–6, 293; effect of turnover tax on, 96, 241; measures to assist, 296

Fabian Society, 147
fairness, concept of, 13, 81, 185, 193, 361
families (married couples with children): Churchill's appeal to, 137, 140–1; incidence of taxation on earned income, **121**, 167, **168**, 169, 336; income tax adjustments, 128; middle-class, 102, 231; patriarchal definition of, 114; political identity of, 105–6; rate of income tax, **104, 138, 276, 278**, 336; tax allowances, 7, 75, 106, 167, 362; tax benefits removed (Second World War), 180–1; taxation of, 114–15; use of trusts, 110, 111
family allowances, in cash, 181–2
Federation of British Industries (FBI), 22, 154; call for income tax cut, 86–7, 92; on economic inflexibility, 222; on German corporation tax, 320; hostility to postwar taxation, 82, 83–6; influence on fiscal policy, 19–20; and need for incentives, 208–9; support for shift to indirect taxes, 238–9; and taxation of industry (1945–51), 196–7, 206–9; view of German postwar economy (1920s), 63
Ferguson, Niall, 64, 65
Finance Act (1920), 103, 117
First World War, 5, 40–1, 50, 57; effects on tax system, 12–13, 57, 59, 176; postwar problems, 36; and re-establishment of fiscal constitution, 98–102, 107, 176, 361; taxes on lower incomes, 114, 119; see also 'floating debt'; national debt; war finance
fiscal constitution: in 1914, 5–6, 8, 11, 36–8; debates on, 227–8, 232, 303; inflexibility of, 17–18, 277–8, 359, 361; and net accounting of government expenditure, 129; principle of balance in, 5–6, 8, 62, 256, 361, 362; re-established after First World War, 98–102, 107, 176, 361; stability of, 13, 64, 65–6, 74, 88, 101
fiscal policy, 18–19, 366–7; Churchill's changes (1925), 124–6; consensus on, 17 and n, 30; Conservative debate on, 280–1, 305–6; for economic growth, xiv, 1, 124–5, 244–6; lack of perspective in, 270–2; limits of, 221–8; options (1960s), 275; see also civil service;

Conservative governments; Labour governments; Treasury
fiscal system: balance in, xiv, 5, 8, 25, 256, 327; Conservative failure to reform, 247, 249–50, 274–5, 277–8, 367; economic studies of, 4–5, 30, 333–5, 360–1; FBI working party on, 242–3; imbalance in, 304; incoherence of, 5, 25, 270–1, 273–4, 359, 360; Labour reforms (from 1964), 196, 275, 279–80, 299–300; Liberal reforms (1906–11), 11–12; need for reform (1950), 222, 227–8, 235–7, 280; politics of, 5, 242; radical schemes for reform (1970s), 333–5; schemes to integrate with welfare, 310–11; social contract of, 119; social purpose of, xiv, 52, 246, 362; see also civil service; legitimacy
Fisher, Warren, 139n; on Churchill as chancellor, 139–40; and need for rearmament (1930s), 171–2, 173–4
'floating debt' (after First World War), 13, 59, 76–9, 82–3, 99, 362
foreign holdings, for tax avoidance, 111
France: capital tax proposed, 72; fiscal system, 37, 242; income tax rates (1976), **337**; indirect taxes, 96–7, 237; national debt, 36, 64; national income tax (1914), 12; social service funding, 264, 295, 304; taxation as percentage of GNP, **305**; *taxe sur la valeur ajoute* (TVA), 97, 241–2, 313
franchise: extensions of, 8, 74, 119; link with taxation, 7, 27, 119; universal manhood suffrage (1918), 59, 76, 119; for women, 105–6
free market economy, 191, 223, 302, 363
free trade, 7–8, 11, 59, 122
friendly societies, 9, 10

Gaitskell, Hugh, 162 and n, 205, 211
Galbraith, J. K., 32
Geddes, Sir Eric, 82n; committee on government expenditure, 82–3
General Agreement on Tariffs and Trade (GATT), 237, 243
General Medical Council, 113
general strike (1926), 99, 124, 142
Germany, 40, 44; capital market, 291; hyperinflation, 63, 64, 77, 99; income tax rates (1976), **337**; indirect taxes, 96, 237; local taxation, 10; national debt, 36, 64, 77; Nazi, 169, 170–1; postwar, 63–5, 85; reparations, 36, 64; social service funding, 10, 295, 304, 311–12;

taxation as percentage of GNP, **305**;
turnover tax (*Umsatzsteuer*), 96, 241;
weakness of tax system, 12, 37, 65;
Wehrbeitrag (defence levy) (1913), 72
gift tax, 286
Gladstone, W. E., 148; *see also* fiscal
constitution
gold standard, 39; return to (1925), 62,
122, 124, 142, 344
'gosplanners', 31, 191–2
government, machinery of, 254, 269–75,
277–8; and failure to allow fiscal reform,
359, 365–6; permeability to ideas,
18–21, 26–7, 279–80, 360–1; *see also*
Budget Committee; civil service; Inland
Revenue; Treasury
government departments, 20; and Budget
Committee, 232–3
government stock and bonds, 36, 126, 156
graduation of tax, 8, 11; income tax, 103,
107–8, 190, 220; on industrial profits,
89, 90–1
Great Britain, 40–1, 170–1; and economic
depression (1930s), 65; fiscal system
compared, 242, 304; international
trading position, 194, 369
Greater London Council, abolished, 359
Gregg, Cornelius, 156 and n, 177, 183–4
Grigg, James, 112 and n, 122, 137, 166

Hall, Robert, v, 161 and n, 226–7; on
employment tax, 265–6; in favour of
private enterprise, 248–9; on investment
allowances, 255; and need to restructure
taxation, 232, 234; on taxation of
profits, 203; view of high marginal rates,
257; on wage restraint, 241n
Hancock, D. J. S., 233 and n, 272–3, 352
Harcourt, William, graduated death
duties, 136
Hawtrey, R. G., 38 and n, 87–8
Hayek, Friedrich von, 30 and n, 32,
191–2
Hayhoe, Barney, 324–5, 324n
Healey, Denis, 331–2, 331n
health insurance, 129–30, 264
health services: local provision, 34, 346,
347; *see also* National Health Service
Heath, Edward, 32–3 and n, 319, 325,
368; and local government
reorganisation, 353–4
Heathcoat Amory, Derick, 266–7, 266n
Henderson, H. D., 181 and n, 214
Hicks, J. R., 187 and n, 189, 214, 216
Hirst, F. W., 36

Hobson, J. A., 89–90, 89n; theory of Rent,
147
Hopkins, Richard, 108 and n, 132, 134,
156; on indirect taxes, 186; and limits of
taxation, 171, 173; on local government
taxation, 345–6, 347–8; and principle of
income tax, 167
Horne, Robert, chancellor (1921–2), 92
and n, 93
Houghton, Douglas, 180 and n, 279, 285,
289
house-building programme, 76
housing: council, 1, 355; owner-occupied,
307, 326, 334
hyperinflation: effects on savings, 64;
Germany, 63, 64, 77, 99
hypothecation, 6, 35, 312; for national
insurance, 324; of NHS tax, 267; of
Road Fund tax, 130

identities, political construction of, 23, 61,
67–8, 134–5, 275; and social affinity,
27, 102; *see also* class; *rentiers*
imperial preference, 7–8, 11
imperialism, 11
import duties, 45; fuel, 131, 347
imports, effect of turnover tax on, 96
incentives, 17, 29, 123; balance with
equality, 29, 149, 151, 192–3, 211–12,
248, 369; balanced with inflation
control, 216; Churchill's concern for,
124–5, 128, 133–4; Conservative view
of, 30, 34, 251–2, 257–9, 315–22; effect
of high taxation on, 17, 29, 165, 176,
195–6, 211; effect of state welfare on,
34; for enterprise state, 34–5, 224, 308,
368; for exporters, 243–4; FBI demand
for, 208–9; and function of profits, 205;
ideological differences on 257, 327,
329–31; and income tax, 219–20;
Labour view of, 192–3; and 'risk
money', 222, 224, 231; for savings,
251–2, 262–3, 275, 337; and social
integration, 124–5, 275, 301, 303,
306–8, 327–8
income: definitions of, 209, 214;
differentials, 100, 220, 282; inequalities
of, 283; percentage taxation of, **120**;
sources of, 113, 214
income tax, 74, 105, 108; Colwyn
committee recommendations, 73, 151;
on companies, 252, 253; on earned
income, **117**; exemptions from, 46–7,
47, 75; incidence of, **42**, 74, **121**, **168**,
224, 335–7, **337**; increased (1915), 41;

income tax (*cont.*)
   increased (1938), 173; Labour policy on
      (1945–51), 219–21; Liberal reforms
      (1909–14), 37; on lower incomes, 46–7,
      309–10, 336–7; need for reform, 8, 103;
      negative, 323, 324–5; as percentage of
      revenue, **15**, 57, 304, 337; progressive,
      11–12, 132, 329, 337; rates, 47, **47**, 74,
      195; reduction to stimulate economy,
      128, 133, 219–20, 307–8; reduction to
      stimulate industry, 86–7, 92; reductions
      (from 1979), 1, 337–8; Royal
      Commission (1920), 103, 105–6,
      107–22; Snowden's changes (1930),
      155; standard rate, **14**, 220, 224, 257–8,
      327; structure, **138**, **337**; *see also*
      Pay As You Earn; threshold
income tax schedules: schedule A, 108,
   109, 262; schedule C, 108; schedule D,
   109; schedule E, 109
Income Taxpayers Society, 112
Independent Labour Party (ILP), 7, 31;
   and Hobson's theory of Rent, 147;
   motion on public ownership, 52–3
India, 11
indirect taxes, 7, 35, **46**, 185; 'cascading'
   turnover tax, 95–6, 237, 241, 313;
   Conservative consideration of
   (1951–64), 237–43; to control inflation,
   217–19; to encourage savings, 307; and
   free trade, 7–8; incidence of, 117, 174;
   move towards, 1, 185–6, 238–43, 300–1;
   narrow range of, 119, 294, 304; for
   opportunity state, 11–12, 307; as
   percentage of revenue, **15**, 94, 218,
   237, 337; in postwar policies, 94–8,
   174; regressive on poor, 96, 118,
   237–8, 245; on retail turnover, 95,
   96–7, 239–40, 313; stamp duties, 96;
   see also consumption; customs duties;
   excise duties; purchase tax; sales tax;
   value added tax
industry, 9, 199; corporation tax (1920),
   91, 92–4; and EPD, 41, 55–7, 83–4;
   hostility to levy on war wealth and EPD,
   80–1; identified as war profiteers, 23,
   84–5; Inland Revenue view of, 87, 97–8,
   153, 203, 207; interests of, 22, 154,
   362–3; links with local government, 341,
   346–7; local rates relief, 154, 339, 340,
   343–4, 345–7; need to raise productivity,
   83–4; postwar recovery, 101, 102; return
   on capital, 84–5; taxable capacity, 83–6;
   and taxation of business profits, 82,
   83–94, 166; and taxation of profits

(1945–51), 196–212; Treasury view of,
   198, 203, 210–11, 224–5; *see also*
   business corporations; Federation of
   British Industries; investment;
   nationalisation; retained profits
inequality, justification for, 330–1, 334,
   335
inflation: 1970s, 336; after Second World
   War, 194; control of, 194–5, 206, 208,
   216–17, 222, 365; cost-push, 34; effect
   on debt repayments, 62–3, 77; First
   World War, 50, 176; and gold standard,
   39; monetary controls over, 35, 293,
   368; and reduced consumption, 43–4,
   250; and taxation of profits, 249; and
   wage restraint, 241n, 264; wage-push,
   368
initial allowances, for corporate
   investment, 253, 254, 255
Inland Revenue: and Budget Committee,
   232–3; and business taxation, 203, 207;
   on capital gains tax, 215, 261; and
   collection of indirect tax, 95, 96; and
   concessions to industry, 197–8, 210,
   343, 345; and EPD, 89–90; hostility to
   revised corporation tax, 252–3, 254,
   292; and income tax, 108–9, 111–12,
   219–20; and introduction of PAYE,
   177–80; and limits of direct taxation,
   156, 158; measures against tax
   avoidance, 110–11; narrow concerns of,
   263, 273; and purpose of taxation,
   152–3, 184–5; rates valuation by, 355;
   resistance to change, 269–70, 359; and
   use of tax incentives, 263; view of capital
   levy, 69; view of investment allowances,
   255–6; view of surtax, 153; view of
   taxation of industry, 87, 97–8, 153, 203,
   207; *see also* collection of tax
Institute of Economic Affairs, 281, 361
Institute for Fiscal Studies, 330, 333–4,
   361
insurance: contributory schemes, 10, 226,
   265, 309; national health, 129–30, 264,
   324; surcharges on contributions, 268;
   see also national insurance contributions
interest groups, 20–2, 24, 362; and policy
   formation, 99–100
interest rates, 126, 188–9, 223; and cheap
   money, 188, 199
International Monetary Fund (IMF), crisis
   (1976), 333, 354, 368
investment: bureaucratic control of, 151,
   202, 319–20; corporate, 254–6; effect of
   capital levy on, 71; fiscal control over,

202–4; and industrial growth, 153–4, 188–9, 224, 248; National Investment Board proposed, 162–4, 202; *see also* capital; retained profits; savings
investment allowances, 254–6
investment income, higher taxation of, 23
Italy, 64, 264

Japan, 169
Jay, Douglas, 162 and n, 192, 223; and wealth tax, 328, 332
Jenkins, Roy, 201n, 299, 335; on fairness in taxation, 284–5; on taxation of capital, 212, 214–16; on taxation of profits, 201, 205
Joseph, Keith, 322 and n, 323, 351
justice, equality and, 330–1, 369; *see also* distributive justice; social justice

Kaldor, Nicholas, 25n, 210, 247, 281, 334; on capital gains tax, 292–3; on economic stagnation, 222; expenditure tax, 286; influence on Callaghan, 25, 290, 291–2, 296–8, 299, 361; 'integrated' tax system, 286–7, 360; minority report to Royal Commission, 253, 279; and proposed corporation tax, 253; and SET, 297–8; and VAT, 294–7, 298–9
Kay, John, 333n; study of tax system (1978) (with Mervyn King), 5, 333–5, 337, 360–1
Keynes, John Maynard, 44n, 188; criticism of war finance policy, 44–5, 55; deficit finance policy, 163, 164, 169–70; economic policy for, 1930s, 164–9; and family allowances, 181–2; and large-scale business, 32; on possibility of capital levy (1942–3), 187, 188, 189; and taxation of business profits, 198, 203–4; taxation on capital, 64, 213; use of taxation to balance economy, 191, 192; war finance measures, 177, 182–3, 185, 186
King, Mervyn, 333–4n; study of tax system (1978) (with John Kay), 5, 333–5, 337, 360–1
Knauss, Robert, 38
Knowles, Lillian, 106 and n, 115
Korean war, 210

labour, costs, 169, 265, 294–5, 311–12; inefficient use of, 312–13, 327; organised, 23, 28, 97, 328, 364–5; TUC definition of, 21–2; *see also* trade unions

Labour governments, 1924 minority, 146; 1929 minority, 142–3, 152, 160, fiscal policy, 143–64, *see also* Dalton, Hugh; Snowden, Philip; 1945–51 Attlee, 194, 365, limits of fiscal policy, 221–8; 1964–70 Wilson, fiscal policy, 275, 278, 290–301, tax reforms, 275, 279–80, 290–3, 299–300; 1974–9 Wilson/ Callaghan, 328, 331–5, Blair (from 1997), 4, 35
Labour party, 11, 52, 61, 331; and 1931 financial crisis, 160; attack on *rentiers*, 28, 50, 60, 68, 74, 144; attitude to business profits, 204–5; and the capital levy policy, 66–74, 94, 98; and Churchill's, 1925 budget, 133, 135, 139–40, 143–4; clause IV debate (1959), 205; control of local authorities, 339, 354, 356; electoral support for, 67, 221, 335–7; emphasis on nationalisation (after 1931), 160–4; Home Policy Committee statement (1940) 190; and Liberal policies, 66–7, 348; on local government finance, 348–51, 353–6; and middle-class support, 155, 221, 331, 336–7; in opposition (1951–64), 281–90; in opposition (1979–97), 3–4, 358; opposition to corporation tax (1920–3), 93–4; opposition to indirect taxes, 186, 218; pursuit of equality, 31, 144, 176–7, 275, 279, 281–4, 363–4; rise of, 60, 74; surtax policy (1928), 73, 151–2; and taxation of capital, 189–90, 213, 336; taxation policy, 53–4, debate (1951–64), 281–90, at end of Second World War, 190–3, 194–6, (to 1931), 143–60; tensions between radical and pragmatic politics, 146, 192–3, war finance policy, 49–50, 55; *see also* Independent Labour Party (ILP); Labour Representation Committee (LRC)
labour relations: reform, 368; structure of, 206, 364–5
Labour Representation Committee (LRC), 1901 conference, 52–3
labour theory of value, 53
land: compulsory purchase, 350; right to develop, 350–1, 352
Land Commission Act (1967), 352
land values: Snowden's tax on, 157, 349; taxation of, 37, 152; *see also* rates
Law Society, 113
Lawson, Nigel, 281 and n, 317, 327–8

Lee, Frank, 238n, 267–8, 270–1; and reform of purchase tax, 238, 246
Lees-Smith, H. B., 143 and n, 144, 152
legitimacy (of tax system), 8, 12, 103, 107; Churchill's perception of, 132; threatened (1960s and 1970s), 280, 281, 300, 303, 367
Leith-Ross, F. W., 129 and n
Lewis, W. Arthur, 288–9, 288n
Liberal party: decline of, 60, 66; government (1906–15), 9, 115; and Kay and King's proposals, 361; and land taxation, 37, 67; and middle-class support, 105
Liberals, independent, support for capital levy, 54
life insurance premiums, tax relief on, 7, 262, 334, 337
Lindert, Peter, 27
Lloyd, Selwyn, 259n; 1961 budget, 259–60, 261, 268, 269
Lloyd George, David, 3–4n, 57, 135, 142; and land tax, 3, 39, 116; postwar coalition government, 76, 78, 81; support for middle-class voters, 136–7; war finance, 38, 39–41
local government: assigned revenues, 130; block grants, 341–3, 346, 347–8, 351, 354; central government funding, 347–9, 350, 354–5; grants-in-aid to, 339, 340; incidence of taxation, 117–18; involvement of industry in, 341, 346–7; limits on expenditure, 354–5, 359; local income tax considered, 350, 352, 354; percentage grants, 340; and planning, 350–1; rate-support grant, 353; rates relief for industry, 154, 339, 343–4, 345–7; reduced responsibilities, 355; regional system proposed, 349–50; structural reorganisation (1974), 353–4; Thatcher government reforms, 3, 354–5, 356–9; welfare spending, 8, 10, 347; see also poll tax; rates
London Chamber of Commerce, 77
London County Council, 349
Lowe, Rodney, 17, 322

MacDonald, Ramsay, 49 and n, 54
McKenna, Reginald: as chancellor, 41–5, 57; and principle of 'normal year', 41–2, 43, 55, 57; on taxable capacity of industry, 84, 85, 86n
McKibbin, Ross, 76, 98, 141; on second Labour administration, 142, 159
Macleod, Iain, 300 and n, 318, 322

Macmillan, Harold, 235–6n, 250; as chancellor, 251, 263, 269; on incentives, 257, 300; local taxation of industry, 346; as prime minister, 235–6, 261, 263–4, 266; on savings, 261–2
Macnicol, J., 100, 309
Mallet, Bernard, 117–18, 117n
Mann, Michael, 8
Manzer, R. A., 20
market, and allocation of resources, 191–2, 319
married couples see families
married men's allowance, increased, 106, 114, 167
Mass-Observation, 183
Maudling, Reginald, 243n, 261, 319, 325; and turnover tax, 243–4
Meade, James, 4–5n, 32, 192, 217; and annual tax on capital, 213; and differential taxation of profits, 202–3; enquiry into direct taxation, 4–54, 333; on possibility of capital levy (1942–3), 187–8, 189
means testing, 296, 309, 323–4
median voter, and support for redistributive taxation, 27, 33, 336, 368
Mellon, Andrew, 101
middle class, 23, 119, 122; and anti-waste campaign, 75, 76, 98; burden of income tax reduced, 99, 124, 134–7, 140–1, 220–1; Conservative concessions to, 236–7, 251, 257–60, 263, 327, 363; effect of Snowden's, 1931 budget on, 158–9; fear/resentment of working class, 76, 98; high tax levels, 75, 231; importance of electoral support of, 136–7, 181, 221, 322–3, 335–7, 368; and Labour party, 155, 221, 331, 336–7; and Liberal party, 105; and social affinity, 27; support for social welfare, 27, 122, 174; use of welfare state, 225, 282, 368; see also median voter
Mill, J. S., 148
Millan, Bruce, MP, 317 and n
Mond, Alfred, 81 and n, 92
monetarism, 368; and control over inflation, 35, 293, 368
Montagu, E. S., 92 and n
morality, and assumptions about consumption, 6, 283, 287–8; and balance of tax system, 5–6; of capitalism, 52
Morgan, E. V., 42
Morrison, Herbert, 221
mortgage interest, tax relief on, 262, 334

Napoleonic wars, 12, 13, 60
national debt, 36; after First World War,
   36, 59, 176, 194; after Second World
   War, 187–9, 194; capital levy to reduce,
   68–74; Churchill's approach to, 123,
   125–7; forced loan for, 126; held by
   rentiers, 23, 59, 63; increases, 124, 126;
   obligation to reduce, 6, 67, 70, 102,
   123; as percentage of government
   expenditure, **58**; as percentage of
   government income, **62**; repayment from
   budget surplus, 62, 88, 99, 127; seen as
   guarantee of credit and security, 6, 60;
   and social tensions, 63–4; *see also*
   'floating debt'
National Debt Enquiry (1944), 187–9
national defence contribution (NDC),
   172–3, 190, 196–7; converted to profits
   tax, 173, 200
National Economic Development Council
   (NEDC), 20, 263, 272; report on
   economic growth, 266, 289; and wealth
   tax, 316, 330
'National' government (MacDonald
   1931–5), 158–60
National Health Service (NHS), 33, 225,
   226, 282; funding, 264, **265**, 267
national insurance contributions, 243, 259,
   294; employers', 265, 268, 295, 337;
   flat-rate, 118, 143, 265, 295, 309
National Investment Board (NIB),
   proposed, 162–4, 202, 223
National Union of Teachers, 20
nationalisation, 71, 248, 287–8; combined
   with private ownership, 162–3; and
   economic planning, 192; Labour
   measures, 199; of right to develop land,
   350–1; Snowden's vision of, 146;
   see also public ownership
negative income tax, 329; Conservative
   consideration of, 323, 324–5
Neild, Robert, 298 and n
neutrality: of state, 13; of tax, 13, 107, 314
Niemeyer, Otto, 87 and n, 88, 126–7; on
   Rignano scheme, 148–9
'normal year': concept of, 41–2, 43, 55,
   57, 169; and justification for expenditure
   cuts, 82–3
Norman, Montagu, 131 and n
Northcliffe, Alfred Harmsworth, Lord,
   75 and n
Nott, John, 323–4, 323n

Old Age Pensions Act, 344
Olson, Mancur, 20

opportunity state, 34, 236, 308, 315–16,
   369; indirect taxes for, 11–12, 307;
   see also incentives
Organisation for Economic Co-operation
   and Development (OECD), 258, 304

Padmore, Thomas, 274 and n
Paish, George, 44 and n, 55
parliament: confidence in, 6; and
   introduction of SET, 298; negotiating
   role of, 22, 99–100; *see also* Cabinet
partnerships, private, taxation of profits, 91
Pay As You Earn (PAYE), 113, 114,
   179–80, 336
payroll subsidies, regional, 294–5
payroll taxes, consideration of, 311–13,
   312n; *see also* employment tax; selective
   employment tax
pensions: contributory, 122, 143, 309;
   extension of, 124, 136, 143; private 309;
   state (tax-funded), 33, 309; tax
   allowances on, 334; war, 36; widows',
   102, 128, 344
Personal Equity Plans, 337
personal savings, 248, 256, 261–2; effect
   of hyperinflation on, 64; tax breaks for,
   1, 337
personal taxation *see* families; income tax;
   indirect taxes; personal savings; savings;
   small incomes; unearned income
Pethick-Lawrence, F. W., 61–2 and n,
   144, 186
petrol duty, 119, 130, 131, 157, 345
Pigou, A. C., 30 and n, 69
planning (regional and urban), 350; Town
   and Country Planning Act (1947),
   350–1
plant and machinery: allowances on
   depreciation, 167, 196, 206–7, 210;
   local rates on, 340–1
Plowden, Edwin, 234 and n, 254
political parties: discipline of, 20, 25; and
   identity of supporters, 61; realignment,
   60, 107
political system, adversarial, 17 and n, 25,
   281
politicians: and construction of identities,
   23, 134–5, 275; image of probity 6;
   relations with civil service, 25–6, 233,
   254; role in fiscal policy-making, 18,
   272, 362–3, 367; visions of society,
   26, 280–1
politics, and role of taxation, xiii, 106,
   362–3
poll tax *see* community charge

poor law, 28; reform (1929), 341, 344–5
popular capitalism, 326
poverty, structure of, 331
poverty trap, 258, 299–301, 309–10,
    327–8; and incidence of income tax,
    336; political concern about, 329, 334
Powell, J. Enoch, 233 and n, 267
press, and anti-waste campaign, 75, 76
Prest, A. R., 315n
prices, 32, 85, 209; absence of information
    on, 191–2; controls on, 206, 216, 222;
    effect of income tax on, 165; and labour
    costs, 312; and trading profits, 196
Prices and Incomes Board, 20
private enterprise, 32, 204, 222, 248–9;
    restricted, 224
private ownership: combined with
    nationalisation, 162–3; Conservative
    commitment to, 262, 307, 326; socialist
    views of, 52, 161, 192, 282, 283, 288–9
private property, 64; and nationalisation
    policy, 161, 162, 163
privatisation, 1, 326; of local services, 359
producers and parasites distinction: and
    attack on *rentiers*, 60–4, 71; and
    distributive justice, 102; Labour party
    tax policies, 53–4
productivity: and equality, 281–2; low,
    83–4, 169, 196, 224–5; need to improve,
    311, 321, 327; taxation to increase,
    194–5, 210
professions, taxation of profits, 91
profit motive, 281, 288
profits: balanced against productivity, 281;
    Conservative view of, 318–19;
    corporation tax proposed, 252–3;
    definition of industrial, 197; differential
    tax on (1947), 200–1, 204–5, 229;
    graduated tax on, 89, 90–1; for
    investment, 166; Labour party policy on,
    200, 204–5, 223, 284–5; NDC as tax
    on, 173; reform of taxation of, 252–6;
    tax raised (1949), **195**, 208, 210;
    taxation of, 196–212, 222, 247, 345,
    363; trading, 196; *see also* capital gains
    tax; corporation tax; distributed profits;
    excess profits duty (EPD); industry;
    retained profits
property: forms of, 23; local taxes *see* rates;
    political divisions over, 65, 67, 288–9,
    315; private, 64, 161; valuations,
    262, 340
property speculation, 261
proportionality, principle of, 8, 11
protection *see* tariffs

public opinion: and 1979 election, 1, 4;
    as interpreted by politicians and civil
    servants, 26; support for taxation of
    profits, 90–1; *see also* tax revolts
public ownership, 31–2, 53; of assets sold
    to pay capital levy, 66, 70–1; Labour
    party commitment to, 205, 283–4, 332;
    see also nationalisation
purchase tax, 96, 218–19, 229, 238;
    Conservative debate about, 313–14;
    differentials, 238; effect on
    manufacturing, 219; introduced (1942),
    185–6; reforms considered, 237–41,
    243–7, 313–14; superseded by VAT,
    326–7

rates (local property), 28, 262; alternatives
    to, 351–2; capped (1984), 355, 356;
    collapse of system (1985), 356–7;
    Conservative committee on (1964), 351;
    narrow base, 339, 347, 348; rebated,
    353, 357; regressive incidence of, 339,
    348, 350; relief for industry, 154, 343–4,
    345–7, 363; on site values, 349; strain
    on (1900s), 339; valuation for, 340, 351,
    355; *see also* council tax; poll tax
rationing, 185, 217
Rawls, John, 30, 369
rearmament: for Korean war, 210;
    national defence contribution (NDC)
    for, 172–3; for Second World War,
    169–74
redistribution: economic effects of,
    211–12, 336–7; FBI opposition to,
    207–8; Labour policy on, 146, 150, 163,
    176–7, 196, 281, 330–2; popular
    support for, 27, 33, 336; TUC demands
    for, 7, 9; of wealth, 11–12, 317; and
    welfare state, 225, 282
Rees-Mogg, William, 307 and n, 317–18
Reform Act (Representation of the People
    Act) (1918), 7, 60
regional water authorities, 355
regions, subsidies to, 294–5, 296
regression: in fiscal-welfare system, 246; in
    flat-rate insurance contributions, 265,
    309; indirect taxes, 96, 118, 237–8, 245;
    in local rates system, 339, 348, 350,
    351–2; of poll tax, 358; of SET, 314; of
    VAT, 326
Rent: concept of, 31, 50–1, 363; Hobson's
    theory of, 147; Liberal opposition to, 67;
    Snowden's attack on, 145
rentiers, 23; definitions of, 156–7;
    institutions as, 336; Labour party attack

on, 28, 50, 60, 68, 74, 144; and national debt, 23, 59, 63; postwar radical attacks on, 60–4, 116
reparations, Germany, 36, 64
resources, allocation of, 191–2, 223, 319
retained profits: assumptions about, 24, 223–4, 291–2, 319, 363–4; for investment, 164, 166, 194–5, 205, 208–9, 222; tax relief for, 198, 200–1, 206–7; taxation of, 91, 153–4, 249, 253, 319–20; *see also* distributed profits
Revenue Bill (1920), 110
revenue (central government), 73; and capacity of state, 28; income (1914–19), **40**; structure of, **16**, 46, **140**, **187**, **195**, **278**, **338**; taxes as percentage of, **15**, 336
Review of Taxation Policy Committee, 271
Rhys Williams, Brandon, 324 and n
Rhys Williams, Juliet, Lady, 310
Ricardo, David, 50–1, 62
Ridley, Nicholas, 357 and n
Rignano, Eugenio, death duties scheme, 74n, 147–8, 199
risk: discouraged by differentiation, 316; and enterprise, 222, 224, 231, 248–9, 302–3
Road Fund tax, 130
roads, central responsibility for, 355
Rothermere, Harold Harmsworth, Lord, 75 and n
Royal Commissions: on the Distribution of Income and Wealth (1974–80), 333; on the Income Tax (1920), 103, 105–6, 107–22; on Local Government (1974), 353–4; on the Taxation of Incomes and Profits (1951), 221, 249–50, 279, 291, 310; minority report (Kaldor), 253, 279, 291
Russia, revolution (1917), 36

St John-Stevas, Norman, 300 and n
sales tax, 45, 97, 174; proposed, 91, 239
Samuel, Herbert, 78–9, 78–9n, 166; analysis of tax system, 118
Sankey Commission, on coal mines, 71
savings, 165, 200, 307; compulsory (war-time), 183–4; corporate, 146; as incentive, 251–2; Labour attitude to, 223–4, 288–9, 334; tax incentives for 200, 262–3, 334; as unearned income, 116, 223, 337; *see also* personal savings
Schumpeter, Joseph, 12–13
Scotland: local rates, 340; property revaluation (1985), 356

Second World War, 13; and consensus, 17 and n; rearmament for, 169–74; *see also* war finance
secrecy, in fiscal policy-making, 18–19, 359, 361, 366
Select Committee on Increases of Wealth (War), 79, 81
selective employment tax (SET): abolition, 326; Conservative attacks on, 300, 314; introduced (1966), 25, 293, 297–8, 313
self-interest, 302, 326, 369
self-reliance, 116, 136, 141, 324–5
services: largely untaxed, 245–6, 294; role in economic growth, 300; selective employment tax on, 297–8
settlements, use of, 110, 111
Sewill, Brendon, 324
shares: popular ownership of, 248, 326; value of, 214; *see also* dividends
Short, M. E., 83, 119
Simon, John, as chancellor (1937–40), 170–1, 177
sinking fund, 62, 88, 93, 188; Churchill's policy on, 126–7, 129–30; suspension suggested, 86, 87
small incomes: collection of tax on, 48, 113–14, 177–80; compensation for indirect taxes, 243; concessions on unearned income, 116–17, 167; high marginal rates on, 329; Snowden's increased taxation of, 158–9; tax allowances to benefit, 219; *see also* wages; welfare
Snowden, Philip, 53n, 145–6; abolition of corporation tax (1924), 93, 199; as chancellor (1929–31), 145, 155–9; land tax, 157, 349; relations with Treasury, 145, 156, 159; on social reform, 53, 107, 123, 146
'social affinity', 27, 102
Social Democratic Party, 331, 335, 361
social expenditure: as percentage of GDP, **2**, **3**; postwar reconstruction (1920s), 76, 83, 99
social integration, and incentives, 124–5, 275, 301, 303, 306–8, 327–8
social justice: Labour policy of equality for, 281–3; tax system and, xiv, 52, 246, 369
social reform, Labour party policy, 53–4, 190
social structure: changes in, 27, 275, 368–9; taxation to alter, 52, 106
social tension, 62, 63–4; 1970s, 327
socialism, objectives of, 160, 161–2

Socialist Democratic Federation (Marxist), 53
socially created wealth, 11, 31, 50–1; appropriation of, 123, 146, 199; Labour policy on, 198, 248, 284, 363–4; and nationalisation, 201; *see also* land; unearned income
South Africa, Boer war, 11
South Wales Miners' Federation, 48
'spontaneous' income *see* unearned income
Stamp, J. C., 89n, 110, 150; on taxable capacity of industry, 85n, 86n, 89–90
stamp duties, France, 96
state: autonomous needs of, 22–3, 100, 362; capacity of, 28; importance of currency stability, 64; importance of economic stability, 102, 132, 165–6, 363; legitimacy of, 6, 65; as neutral, 13, 362; *see also* central government; expenditure (central government); public ownership
'stealth taxes', 4
Stedman Jones, Gareth, 331
Stock Exchange, 77
subsidies: for essential goods, 177, 217; on food, 240, 250, 277, 303; on housing, 250, 303
sugar duty, 118, 119, 155
super-tax: assessment of, 109, 111–12; Churchill's changes to, 119, 132–4; combined with income tax, 111–12, 134; as proportion of revenue, 57; threshold unchanged (1925), 132
surcharges: on employers' insurance contributions, 268; on excise duties, 268; investment, 337; on purchase tax, 268
surtax: additional graduated, 151–2, 198, 220; additional (levy on war wealth), 73, 74, 78–81; Conservative concessions on, 258, 259; on large incomes, 199, 220; limits unchanged (1918–51), 230–1; Snowden's increases, 155, 159
Sweden, 159, 203

take-over speculation, 261
tariff reform, 11, 37, 67
tariffs: to balance turnover taxes, 96; protective, 119
Taverne, Dick, 330 and n, 331
Tawney, R. H., 118 and n, 214, 331
tax allowances: on capital assets, 167, 196, 206–7; for capital expenditure, 197; for corporate investment, 254–6; on depreciation of plant and machinery,

167, 196, 206–7, 210; to encourage savings, 257, 337; for families, 7, 75, 106, 114, 167, 362; First World War, 47, 47, 75; and graduation of income tax, 107; on pensions, 334; personal, 114, 220; reduced (Second World War), 177; for reinvested company profits, 166, 205; *see also* children's allowances; threshold
tax avoidance, 110–11; of death duties, 213, 333
tax credits, 323, 329; deferred pay as, 184
tax evasion, 110
tax harmonisation (EU), 35, 97, 369
tax law, fragmented nature of case law, 6–7
tax reliefs, 7; on life insurance premiums, 7, 262, 334, 337; on mortgage interest, 262, 334; on retained profits, 198, 200–1, 206–7
tax revolts: against fuel price (2000), 4, 35, 337; against poll tax, 3; South Wales Miners' Federation (1919), 48
taxable capacity: of industry, 83–6; and married women's income, 114–15; *see also* ability to pay
taxation: calculation of incidence, 117–19; effect on incentives, 17, 29, 165, 176, 195–6, 211; to extend public ownership, 283–4; to extract revenue, 184–5, 362; to finance war, 36, 38, 169, 176; link with franchise, 7, 27, 119; link with social benefits, 182; as percentage of GDP/GNP, 1, 8, 229, **305**; progressive, 69, 193, 337; to shape economic behaviour, 32, 190–3, 211–12, 228, 362; to shape economic structure, 191, 362; structure of, 1, 277–8, 303–7; and welfare, 119, 308–11; *see also* fiscal constitution; fiscal system
taxation levels, 304; at end of First World War, 57; FBI concern over, 242–3; high marginal rates, 223, 226, 229, 257, 304, 310, 368; on low incomes, 329
taxpayers: acceptance of need for rearmament, 173–4; co-operation with tax administration, 6
tea, duties on, 119, 155
Thatcher, Margaret, 1 and n, 30, 289, 323; incentives without social integration, 275, 328; and local government, 354–5, 356–9; revision of tax regime, 337–8, 361; on self-reliance, 324; trade union law reform, 368
Thorneycroft, Peter: as chancellor, 233–4, 233n, 236–7, 263, 266; on purchase tax reform, 238, 241; resignation, 241n, 274

threshold (for taxation), 100, 157, **311**, 368; and poverty trap, 258, 299–301, 309–10, 334; reduced (First World War), 114, 119; for surtax raised (1961), 259
thrift, 116; *see also* personal savings; savings
Tillett, Ben, 49–50, 49n
Titmuss, Richard, 246, 246–7n, 282
tobacco, duties on, 117, 119, 155
Tomlinson, J., 225–6
Town and Country Planning Act (1947), 350–1
trade: balance of payments, 169, 170, 194; international, 62, 85, 194, 237, 369
Trade Disputes Act (1906), 364
trade union law reform, 327, 368
trade unions, 9, 10, 75, 186; and control of inflation, 206, 311; decline of, 28, 275; and Labour party identity, 331; and male wage, 183; power of, 364–5; on profits, 205; and wage restraint, 21, 200, 260, 264, 274–5
Trades Union Congress (TUC), 7, 9, 21, 74; and 1931 financial crisis, 160; Economic Committee, 183; and income tax, 220; influence on fiscal policy, 20, 362; and investment allowances, 255; opposition to indirect taxes, 240–1
Treasury, 20; basic assumptions of, 101, 132, 140, 280; and Budget Committee, 232; and Colwyn Committee, 165, 227; concern for international reputation, 170–1; criticism of Labour policies (1948–51), 224–5, 226–7, 248–9, 279; and dangers of floating debt, 77–8, 82–3; and economic policy in, 1930s, 164–9, 170–1; Economic Section, 184, 187–8, 232, 245, 255, 272; ethos of, 24, 270, 359, 361, 362; hostility to revised corporation tax, 252–3, 254; impatience with Conservative chancellors, 232–3, 234; on indirect taxes, 97; and local government finance, 342–3, 345; and need for fiscal reform, 24–5, 232, 274, 280; and needs of defence expenditure (1930s), 171–2; policy on national debt, 88, 125–7, 132; and principles of income tax, 166–7; Public Income and Outlay Division, 272; Public Sector Income Committee, 295, 296; and re-establishment of fiscal constitution, 98–102; rejection of Keynes's policy, 169–71; resistance to tax cuts, 87; restructured (1962), 272–3; support for industry, 198, 203, 210–11, 224–5; view of capital levy, 69–70; view of economy,

169–71, 249, 272–3, 362; view of welfare state, 225–7, 309; and war finance, 55, 56
Treasury bills, 128
trust, creation of, xiii–xiv, 8, 280
trusts, use of, 110, 111, 316

unearned income, concessions to small incomes, 116–17; contrasted with earned, 6, 23; and differential taxation, 115–17, 315; Fabian view of, 51–2; Labour assumptions about, 198, 283, 284; as Rent, 51; *see also* investment income; savings
unemployment, 21, 35, 142, 174–5; to limit inflation, 368; and need to maintain welfare spending, 132; reduction of, 122
Unemployment Assistance Board (1934), 355
unemployment relief, deficit (1931), 157, 158
United States, capital gains tax, 214; civil service structure, 361; concessions to business, 101, 207; Economic Co-operation Administration, 242; fiscal policy, 18; income tax rates (1976), **337**; payroll tax, 312n; tax system 18, 215; taxation of corporate profits, 89, 90, 204; welfare spending, 9
Uthwatt, Lord Justice, Compensation and Betterment Committee, 350
utilities, local control of, 349; nationalised, 355
utility goods, exempt from purchase tax, 186, 218

value added tax (VAT), 97, 242–3; adopted in EEC/EU, 97, 241–2, 246–7, 314; Conservative consideration of, 314–15, 320, 323; debate on, 243–7, 289; to fund social security (Kaldor's scheme), 294–6; introduction of, 246–7, 299, 301, 326–7; Labour debate on, 293–7; political dangers of, 298, 326; to raise revenue, 298–9; rate raised, 337
Vinter, F. R. P., 270 and n, 271
virement of funds rejected, 6

wage restraint, 195, 200, 208, 222, 241n, 356; and control of inflation, 241n, 264; need for TUC consent, 21, 200, 260, 274–5; and taxation of profits, 253, 254; threatened by indirect taxes, 240–1
wage-bargaining, 364

wages, 63, 97, 99; collection of tax on, 113–14, 177–80; narrowing differentials, 100

Wages Board, 210

War Emergency Workers' National Committee (WEWNC), 49, 50, 74

war finance, First World War, EPD (excess profits duty), 41, 55–7; from loans, 36, 38, 42, 59, 169, 176; and 'normal year' concept, 41–2, 43, 55, 57, 59

war finance, Second World War, 176–7; deferred pay, 182, 184; excess profits tax, 177, 184; Keynes's proposals, 182–3; postwar credits, 183–4

war finance, from taxation, 36, 38, 169, 176

War Loan Act (1919), 128

war profiteering, illusionary, 84–5

war profiteers, 23, 50, 188; and EPD, 41, 49, 55–7; and levy on war wealth, 73, 74, 78–81

'waste': and Geddes committee on expenditure, 82–3; popular campaign against, 75, 76, 81, 362

Watkinson, Harold, 235–6, 235n

wealth: active, 123, 124; distribution skewed, 308, 315; inequality of, 282, 283; inherited, 116, 124, 145, 149–50, 152; redistribution of, 11–12, 317; transfer to active state, 330–1; see also capital; death duties; socially created wealth

wealth tax, 213, 286, 299; annual, 189–90; Conservative consideration of, 316–18; Labour proposals for, 328–33; Select Committee on, 332

Webb, Sidney, 51n, 115; and capital levy, 71–2; and concept of Rent, 51–2, 147; Labour and the Nation manifesto, 147; and nationalisation, 71

Wedgwood, Josiah, 150–1 and n

welfare: changing attitudes to, 7, 139, 175, 368; contributory, 10, 226, 266, 289, 294, 309; during depression, 100; effect on efficiency, 34; employers' provision, 9–10, 34; expenditure cuts considered, 264–7; local authority provision, 8, 10, 339; middle-class support for, 27, 122, 174–5; private provision, 1, 9; relation to defence spending, 11; selective benefits, 307, 321, 323, 325; state provision, 9, 10, 339, 350; tax-funded, 10, 13, 17, 225, 264–7, 304

welfare state: construction of, 194, 308–9; redistributive consequences of, 225, 282; strain on fiscal system, 303, 304, 308–11

Wider Share Ownership Group, 263

widows, pensions for, 102, 344

Widows' Pensions Act, 344

Williamson, Philip, 125

Wilson, Harold, 200, 259 and n, 296; and devaluation, 293

wives' allowances, introduced (1918/19), 75

women: family allowances for, 21, 75; franchise, 105–6; incomes aggregated with husbands', 114–15; widows' pensions, 102

Woodcock, George, 279

Woolton, earl of, 231 and n

Wootton, Barbara, 74n

working class: and capital levy, 70; changing identity of, 27, 28, 331, 368; and Churchill's income tax reductions, 133, 137, 141; incidence of taxation on, 117–19, 138n; need for political support of, 78–9, 80–1, 136–7; organised, 8–9; patriotism of, 54–5; and taxes on consumption, 59, 100; transfer payments to, 174–5

2676736R00213

Printed in Great Britain
by Amazon.co.uk, Ltd.,
Marston Gate.